Along the tracks of Cobb and Co.

Back to the Beginning

History speaking for itself ...

Research and compilation by Hazel Johnson

For my grandchildren ... to help them appreciate the value of
'unyielding courage, determination and resilience', from those who have come before us.

Author's Note

In 2024, I attended an ANZAC Service in Clifton, Queensland, where a heartfelt poem was read by an old Digger. The service was deeply moving—just one of many commemorations held across our great country of Australia. The sense of gratitude and respect for our servicemen and women was tangible. It's a feeling I know well, having had many family members who have fought for Australia's freedom and future.

Indeed, all those who have fought for, or helped build, our great nation—regardless of cultural heritage—have my utmost admiration and respect. As the song written in 1987 by Bruce Woodley (The Seekers) and Dobe Newton (The Bushwackers) so powerfully expresses:

> *"We are one, but we are many ...*
> *I am, you are, we are Australian"*
> (Lyrics.com)

Courtesy of John Elliott, writer/photographer

My hope is that the 'Along the tracks of Cobb and Co.' Book Series, is not only an engaging read but pays homage to the pioneers of Australia—including the firm of Cobb and Co., 1854-1929.

'Along the tracks of Cobb and Co.'—Back to the Beginning' (Victoria & the Goldfields) explores the commencement of Cobb and Co. in 1854, by the Americans. Travel through Melbourne, and beyond, as you revisit Victoria during the gold rush years.

"Place, the front of Adams and Co.'s express office ... Four unmistakably well-bred quadrupeds paw Collins street eager for action ... [Passengers] take their places upon seats ranged very conveniently in three rows on the inside, and the body of the vehicle is very comfortably hooped and canvassed over as a protection from the weather. There are also other seats on the outside, almost all of which are soon occupied ... 'the hour is come' ... [The driver] very deliberately mounts the box ... gathered the ribbons in his hands, when one—two—goes the Post Office clock. Before the third stroke, off bounds our nags ... we rattle away through the yet clear Elizabeth-street at the satisfactory rate of some eleven or twelve miles an hour ... what a terrible noise the coach makes, I hope we shall have no accident ... they dash through a deep mud hole. Bump goes every head nearly to the ceiling of the coach, and down comes every one upon his seat ... then the new passenger, a lucky digger, jumps in and takes his seat. Away go the prads as before at a rattling pace. The bumps are occasionally almost dislocative of the anatomy of the passengers ..." Clearly, the grand old days of Cobb and Co. were not all romance and high adventure!

Now you may ask, What makes this book series different? While many works on Cobb and Co. revisit well-worn narratives, my aim is to retell the story with authenticity—drawing primarily on excerpts written between the mid-1800s and early 1900s, and in doing so, allowing history to speak for itself. Historical accuracy has been carefully maintained, with original spelling, punctuation, and grammar preserved throughout. The evolution of photography—evident in both the availability and quality of surviving images—further enriches this story of change.

I acknowledge that the accounts in this series only briefly touch on the rich cultural history of Australia's First Peoples and their interactions with others during this period of colonisation.

> *"ANZAC was their official name, but 'Digger' is what the soldiers called themselves. Where do you think the name came from? Some people think it was used because many soldiers had worked in the goldfields of Ballarat and Bendigo before the war. Others think is was used because of all of the digging in the trenches. For whatever reason, it is the name the soldiers preferred. Today, if you call someone a Digger it means they are your mate."*
> (ANZAC Day Commemoration Committee [Queensland] Incorporated, 2024)

Acknowledgement of Country

We acknowledge the Traditional Custodians of the land
on which the Cobb and Co. stage coaches travelled.
We pay our respect to Elders past, present and emerging,
and extend our deep respect to all Aboriginal and Torres Strait Islander Peoples.

TITLES

Book 1
Along the tracks of Cobb and Co. —The Great Northern Road
(Tenterfield to Warwick)

Book 2
Along the tracks of Cobb and Co. —The Western Run
(Brisbane, Toowoomba, Roma & Charleville)

Book 3
Along the tracks of Cobb and Co. —The New South Wales Headquarters
(In & Around Bathurst)

Book 4
Along the tracks of Cobb and Co. —Back to the Beginning
(Victoria & the Goldfields)

Book 5
Along the tracks of Cobb and Co. —Cobb's Coach Drivers

Book 6
Along the tracks of Cobb and Co. —The Roaring Days !
(Amusing Anecdotes & Tales of Grit and Graft)

Book 7
Along the tracks of Cobb and Co. —Queensland
(Brisbane & Beyond) (Release date … late 2025)

Print | Audiobooks | eBooks
Copyright by Hazel T. Johnson

First Edition June 2024, Reprinted February 2025, Reprinted July 2025

Content mainly courtesy of Trove (The National Library of Australia) and its many partners including State Library of Victoria, State Library of New South Wales, State Library of Queensland, State Library of Western Australia, and State Library of South Australia. Photographs taken before 1955 and maps created before 1955 are out of copyright (Australian Copyright Council). Thanks to the other contributors of photos and/or information, to assist in the telling the story of Cobb and Co. in Australia. Spelling, punctuation and grammar as per historical sources. Every attempt has been made to ensure the correct use and acknowledgement of all sources. The information in this book is by no means exhaustive. Corrections and/or contributions welcome for the next edition. Cover image: ca. 1900-1940 Horse drawn vehicle (State Rivers and Water Supply Commission, photographer) — Courtesy State Library Victoria.

Available from www.cobbandcotracks.au or local outlets

Further contact: email dvhtjohnson@gmail.com; Mobile phone +61 417984455

ISBN 978-0-6459759-1-8

This book was printed by: IngramSpark

Typeset in Garamond

Contents

4	**Author's Note**
8	**Chapter One:** First came gold, then Cobb and Co.
24	**Chapter Two:** Life in Melbourne and beyond
52	**Chapter Three:** Cobb and Co. proprietors
80	**Chapter Four:** Coaching Victoria 1850s
92	**Chapter Five:** Coaching Victoria 1860s
110	**Chapter Six:** Coaching Victoria 1870s & 1880s
128	**Chapter Seven:** Coaching Victoria 1890s & 1900s
140	**Chapter Eight:** Coaching Victoria 1910 onwards
154	**Chapter Nine:** Livery and bait stables
164	**Chapter Ten:** Cobb and Co. faded into the shadows
174	**Appendices**
196	**Reference List**

15

86

87

Chapter One

First came gold, then Cobb and Co.

A Ballad for Cobb and Co.

To the axle in ruts, and a heave o'er the stumps,
In the days that had few compeers ;
O'er the 'corduroy' road, with its rollicking bumps,
And a cargo of pioneers.
Aye, the brave pioneers—rugged battlers of old,
Whose pulses were stirred with the dream of gold,
In the Cobb and Co; dashing years ! ...

There are many yet living to tell the tale
Of the swaggering coaching days,
When the nuggets flew round like a shower o hail,
And the fun of the bullock drays ;
Of the roar of the camps, and many a spree,
And the hardships that prefaced a digger's glee—
When he struck on the 'patch that pays' !

By Walter Robb.
(A Ballad for Cobb and Co., Verses 3 & 5, 15 May 1902, p.15)

ca. 1894-1909 Walhalla Road (Thomas Henry Armstrong, 1857-1930) - Courtesy State Library Victoria

> **9 OCT 1869, EMERALD-HILL, THE FLOODS.**
> "A great disaster has been spared, and the floods, we are happy to say, are in course of subsidence. Of course much harm has been done, but it is far less than that effected by the inundation of October, 1866, and inconsiderable in comparison with the wide-spread ruin caused by the rising of the waters in December, 1863. On the latter occasion the area covered by water was immense, and in, some cases the Yarra, as it ran past the Melbourne wharves, made a clean sweep to the sea. Where the extent of covered surface is so extensive, the difference even of a foot is of vast consequence, and we find that the highest point attained on the present occasion was 6ft. 4in. below the highest level in 1863, and 3ft., 2in below the highest level in 1866 ... The planked way from Emerald-hill to the river bank was well above the flood level, and there was considerable traffic upon it all day long." (The Floods, 19 Oct 1869, p.5)

Victoria—Back to the beginning

"In 1851, Victoria was separated from the government of New South Wales, and started as an independent Colony ... Melbourne, the capital of Victoria ... Geelong, the second town in Victoria ... The chief inland towns are—Ballarat, Sandhurst, Castlemaine, Maldon, Maryborough, Beechworth, Clunes, Ararat, Buninyong, Carisbrook ... The principal agricultural inland towns are—Kyneton, Kilmore, Hamilton, Gisborne ... The principal seaport towns are—Portland, Belfast, Warrnambool .... There are 600 miles of main roads formed and metalled, and 500 miles cleared ... The Post-Office revenues for the past year (1861) amounted to 127,869*l*. In the conveyance of inland mails the number of miles travelled was 1,511,381. The number of post-offices in Victoria is 365 ; 5,166,149 letters, and 2,818761 newspapers were posted in the course of the year.

The climate of Victoria is most genial, closely resembling that of Italy ... beautiful clearness of the sky ... the purity of the air exercises a strong influence on the habits and temperaments of the inhabitants, who certainly appear more cheerful, buoyant, and happy, than those who dwell in colder latitudes ... the most delicate flowers ... grow luxuriantly in the open air in Victoria ... Mineral Products—Gold ... Silver (St. Arnaud's) ... Tin Ore (Oven's District, Taradale, Strathbogle) ... Antimony (Heathcote) ... Iron (Sandhurst) ... Kaolin (various parts of the colony)" (A few particulars supplementary to the catalogue of the products of the Colony of Victoria, Australia, compiled by J. G. Knight, 1862)

By 1885, Victoria had evolved into a land of promise and progress. "There is probably no country in the world that offers such attractions to the working man as Victoria. There, it is not unusual for the agricultural labourer, the artisan, and the mechanic ... What is called the eight hours system, founded upon the division of the day into three parts of eight hours each—one to be devoted to labour, one to recreation, and one to rest—has been in existence for the last 28 years ... To professional men, clerks, shopmen, and shopwomen, the certainty of remunerative employment is not so absolute ... Many succeed beyond their warmest aspirations, whilst others fail utterly. Industry, perseverance, and, it may be added, versatility, will in time conquer many difficulties ... Those desirous of entering into farming pursuits can either get land in fee-simple direct from the Crown at a cost of £1 per acre, payment of which may extend over twenty years, without interest ...

Safe and profitable investments are plentiful ... Remember that even in the most palmy days of gold getting, the precious metal was not to be picked up in the streets, but had to be wrung from the soil by hard and persevering toil.

'Work, honest work!'

must still be the watchword of him who desires success." (Handbook to the Colony of Victoria, 1885, pp.7&8)

By 1889 Melbourne had been completely transformed. "Marvellous Melbourne, the Queen City of the South ... The discovery of gold gave the colony a wonderful impetus at the time ... they sought for gold and found it ... which fanned the excitement to a frenzy ... Victoria was crowded with searchers for fortune ... Who would recognise the 'bush town' of only thirty or forty years ago? The streets were full of gum-tree stumps and deep ruts and the principal thoroughfare, Elizabeth Street, was for months a year a flooded quagmire, in which bullock drays are daily bogged, and on one occasion a waggon and sum of horses were absolutely swallowed up. Iron buildings and bark 'humpies' were seen and what is now the important municipality of South Melbourne was a field of tents known as Canvas Town. Melbourne is now one of the most beautiful capitals of the world ... Mr. Anthony Trollopoli described it as 'one of the most successful cities on the face of the earth' ... wide streets ... broad side-walks ... tree planting ... buildings of great architectural merit ... wharves on the banks of the Yarra now give accommodation to large ocean-going steamers ... Everything to make life content and easy can be procured in Melbourne." (The Palace Hotel, 1889, p.79)

The goldfields

To understand the origins of Australia's gold fever, we return to September 1850. At the time, reports noted: "This colony (New South Wales) is becoming a mining country as well as South Australia. Copper, lead, and gold, are in considerable abundance in the schists and quartzites of the Cordillera." (The Golden Dream, 16 Sep 1850, p.4) By 1851, excitement had spread further into Victoria: "Gold has been found in quantities at Mount Alexander, Clunes, and Buninyong, throughout an extent of country 30 miles in length. It has been found in smaller portions at the Anakie Hills and Batesford, in a line of country 40 miles south-east from Ballarat. It has been washed in small quantities from the alluvium of Anderson's Creek, south bank of the Yarra, ninety miles east from Ballarat. Anderson's Creek probably belongs to a separate auriferous range, which has yet to be explored. The Wardiyallock ranges, the upper branches of Mount Emu Creek, Fiery Creek, and the Hopkins are everywhere intersected and strewn with quartz, evidently a continuation of the same system of rocks as those around Buninyong. The whole of these watercourses, with the Moorabool and Leigh, if not also the Avoca and other rivers on the northern slope of the dividing ranges, will, there is every likelihood, prove auriferous. Taking these considerations in conjunction with our knowledge of the gold fields several hundreds of miles to the northward, in the territory of New South Wales, we think we are justified in supposing that the Australian Gold Fields will rival, if they will not speedily excel, the world famous fields of California." (News from the Diggings, 29 Sep 1851, p.2)

Conveyance to the goldfields

"When gold was discovered in Victoria, in 1851, and up to the middle of 1853, the only means of conveyance to the then existing gold fields, Mount Alexander, Bendigo, and Ballarat, was by paying a carrier so much for head for the carrying of the passengers' swags and tools, the men walking, and, of course, camping out at night.

The average daily distance was 25 or 30 miles, and for this each man was charged £3, finding himself in food on the road." (The Contributor, 25 Nov 1908, p.1405)

"Back forty years in my life, and in my mind's eye I saw again the first conveyance leaving Melbourne for Forest Creek. This now historical first coach was owned by Emanuel King, who, at that time, February 1852, was conducting a barber's business in Bourke-street, about three doors east of the post-office. The conveyance was a two-wheeled van, drawn by three horses ... The fare to Forest Creek [Mount Alexander] was £3, the journey, 75 miles, occupying two days, the passengers camping out one night en route. This style of conveyance continued until the beginning of 1853, when Foster and Vinge, who had been for some years running the overland mail from Melbourne to Sydney, came upon the scene. They introduced four-horse coaches, and fares were still £3. 'King's' line was taken off, probably purchased by Foster and Co., in November, 1852." (Reminiscences of Cobb and Co., 14 Jan 1898, p.2)

"About the middle of 1853 a change came over this mode of transit." (The Contributor, 25 Nov 1908, p.1405) In that same year, "Freeman Cobb came to Melbourne ... with George Mowton, to form a branch of Adam and Co, famed in the United States as express carriers." (Death of the Founder of Cobb and Co., 28 Sep 1878, p.3) By "the end of 1853 was to be seen any day in Collins-street, at, and about Adams' Express Office, which stood then just about where the Bank of N.S.W. now stands, a small, thin, wiry little man, slightly lame ... This was Freeman Cobb." (Reminiscences of Cobb and Co, 14 Jan 1898, p.2) Initially, he was "carrying from Liardet's (Port Melbourne) to the City of Melbourne for a start but 'no road' across the swamp between Emerald Hill, now South Melbourne, and the river was such a quagmire that their waggons sank to the hubs." (a [?] Drive, 31 July 1937, p.4) "Hauling their waggons through the mud ... they gave it up." (Old Coaching Days, 10 Jun 1922, p.7) "They advised their principals in the United States [Adams and Co.] against the carrying business, but told them that there was a good opening for a real up-to-date line of coaches to the diggings ... the United States companies turned down the coaching proposition." (a [?] Drive, 31 July 1937, p.4)

Following this, "George Francis Train ... says: *I told Freeman Cobb, who was then with Adams and Co, that I wanted him to start a line of coaches between Melbourne and the gold-mines, a distance of about sixty miles. I advanced the money for the enterprise, and a line was established, the first in Australia ... These were the first coaches seen in that continent.*" (My Life of Many States and Foreign Lands, 1902, pp133-134) "Many of us witnessed the first efforts of Freeman Cobb to establish communication between the metropolis and the interior, and know how pluckily he in his two horse conveyance conveyed half a dozen passengers from Melbourne to Sandhurst in three days, through difficulties that were deemed at the time almost insurmountable." (Kyneton, 16 Sep 1859, p.3)

Freeman Cobb "was a young American destined to impress his personality so deeply upon the coaching business during his brief career in Victoria that his name has survived as a synonym of the 'coaching days' while those of most of his associates and successors have been forgotten." (Cobb and Co., 20 May 1922, p.5)

It has also been stated that it was Freeman Cobb's brother, E. Winslow Cobb (Elisha Winslow Cobb), who started the coaching business. "Winslow Cobb, a pleasant American, founded the coaching system of Victoria. George Mowton, another American (of Adams and Co.), introduced the first buggy." (Under the Verandah, 27 Mar 1869, p.17) Another source adds: "The name 'Cobb and Co.' is about all there ever was to associate Winslow and Freeman Cobb with the great system of passenger transport in Australia." (Stories of the Cobb & Co Coaching Days, 19 Dec 1920, p.18)

Evidence shows E. Winslow Cobb, Freeman Cobb, George Mowton and Geo. F. Train were all active business men in Melbourne during that time. See *Appendix 1: The Americans*

Cobb and Co. commenced

Nevertheless, "we get to solid ground of documentary evidence with the following advertisement in 'The Argus,' Melbourne, of January 30, 1854:—AMERICAN TELEGRAPH LINE OF COACHES. Daily communication between Melbourne, Forest Creek and Bendigo. Cobb and Company beg to announce that they have determined to run a line of well-appointed coaches between the above places, starting from the Criterion Hotel, every morning (Sunday excepted), at 6 o'clock, and from Forest Creek, daily, at the same hour. The vehicles intended to run are the new American coaches, recently imported, and acknowledged to be the easiest conveyances in the colony. The first coach will start from the Criterion on Monday, January 30, and every attention will be given to ensure punctuality. Cobb and Co. Proprietors ...

Mr. Lovell Smith, who has made a study of the early history of Cobb and Co., says that the vehicles thus advertised were light Concord coaches, round-bodied, and handsomely upholstered. That they were not suitable for winter traffic is evident from the fact that as the year wore on the service was suspended, and was not resumed until spring was well advanced. Travellers to and from Castlemaine, says 'The Argus' of October 12, 1854, will be glad to find by the advertisement which appears in another column that Messrs. Cobb and Co., who last season won golden opinions from all sorts of people for the punctuality and speed which characterised their mode of conducting their business as proprietors of passenger conveyances between Melbourne and the diggings, have reappeared on the field of action. Traditions vary slightly as to the names of Cobb's three partners." (Cobb and Co., 20 May 1922, p.5)

However, "Cobb's three original partners ... a very simple fact ... were John Lamber, James Swanton, and John Murray Peck (my father) ... within 12 months Lamber retired and Arthur Blake came into the partnership ... the famous 'Jack' or 40 passenger and six-horse coaches brought to Australia ... did so much to enhance and spread the fame of Cobb and Co. They were all thorough-brace swung, and turned out to be the most suitable and popular for the purposes of the goldfields traffic on the main roads ... Thanks to the activities of the Central Road Board, conditions of travel were rapidly improving." (Old Coaching Says, 10 Jun 1922, p.7)

"The coaches of this line [Cobb and Co.] spread from the Great centre like a network over the colony—going direct to Swan Hill, communicating with Deniliquin and Moama, and performing daily journeys to Melbourne, Ballarat, Ararat, and the intermediate places. Twenty-six coaches belonging to this firm arrive at and depart from Castlemaine daily ; and the horses they possess number over 600. To these great dimensions has Freeman Cobb's 'speculation' expanded in the course of a few years.—M. A. Mail." (Title Deeds, 16 Sep 1859, p.3)

"To the present generation of Australians the name of Cobb and Co. is only a memory. They have heard, of Cobb's being connected with the early back country passenger traffic before the advent of railways, and have no idea of the important part this great and enterprising firm took as pioneers in developing the Australian continent." (The Contributor, 25 Nov 1908, p.1405)

1886 Off to Bendigo (The Picturesque Atlas of Australasia) - Courtesy The University of Queensland

ca. 1900-1920 Stage coach laden with luggage and many Chinese people en route to the gold fields - Courtesy State Library Victoria

ca. 1914-1941 Selector's Home, Fumina - Courtesy State Library Victoria

ca. 1892 Miner's hut in the bush at Mount Victoria (Arthur Colin Mackenzie, 1860-1919, photographer) - Courtesy State Library Queensland

1895 Water Sold Here, On the track (Archibald Sanderson, 1870-1937, photographer) - Courtesy State Library Western Australia

ca. 1900 Miners on Bullock Cart at Settlement, Gippsland, Victoria - Courtesy Museums Victoria

ca. 1886 A Selector's hut in Gippsland (N. J. Caire, 1837-1918, photographer) - Courtesy State Library Victoria

ca. 1905 General Store on a New Goldfield - Courtesy State Library Victoria

1895 Stone House (Archibald Sanderson, 1870-1937, photographer) - Courtesy State Library Western Australia

1861 Henry Jackson's Store, View Point, Sandhurst [Bendigo]
(Benjamin Pierce Batchelder, 1826-1891, photographer) - Courtesy State Library Victoria

ca. 1900-1018 Diggers' hut at the Springs, Victoria
(N. J. Caire, 1837-1918, photographer) - Courtesy State Library Victoria

ca. 1895 -1917 Cobb & Co. coach and horses outside Harcourt, Warburton,
(Gustav Damman, Melbourne, 1871-1975, photographer) - Courtesy State Library Victoria

1905 Mud-brick houses on the Eastern Goldfields - Courtesy State Library Western Australia

1910-1930 Cobb and Co. Clifton Coach (Ruth Hollick, 1883-1977, photographer) - Courtesy State Library Victoria

ca. 1855-1895 Family Group Outside House With Morewood & Rogers
Iron Roof, Geelong - Courtesy State Library Victoria

ca. 1861 Great Eastern Tunnel, 1500 feet long, Jim Crow diggings, Daylesford
(Richard Daintree, 1832-1878, photographer) - Courtesy State Library Victoria

ca. 1861 Gold Mining Scene (Richard Daintree, 1832-1878, photographer) - Courtesy State Library of Victoria

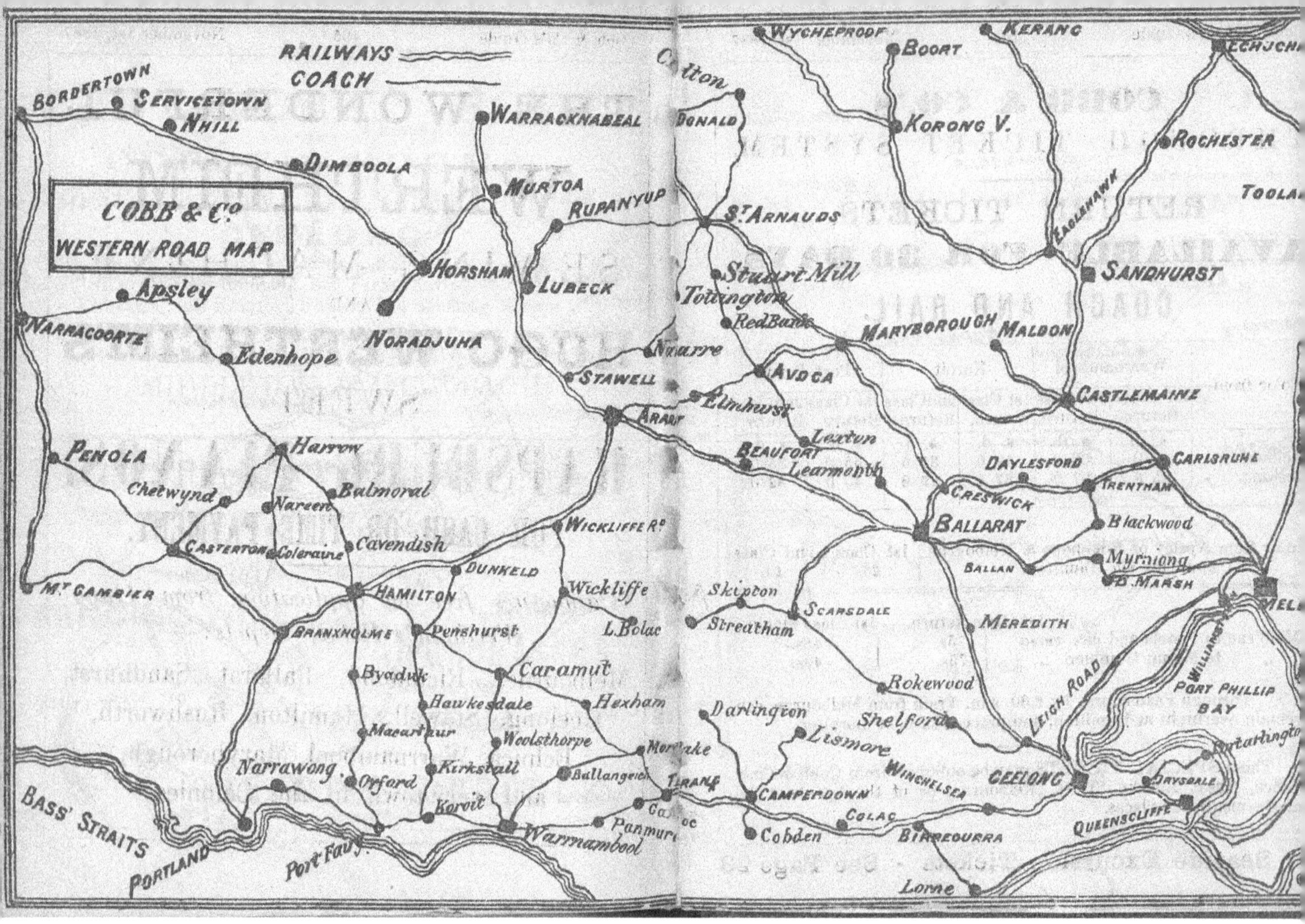

1880-1887 Cobb & Co's traveller's guide, Geelong : Cobb and Company - Courtesy State Library Victoria

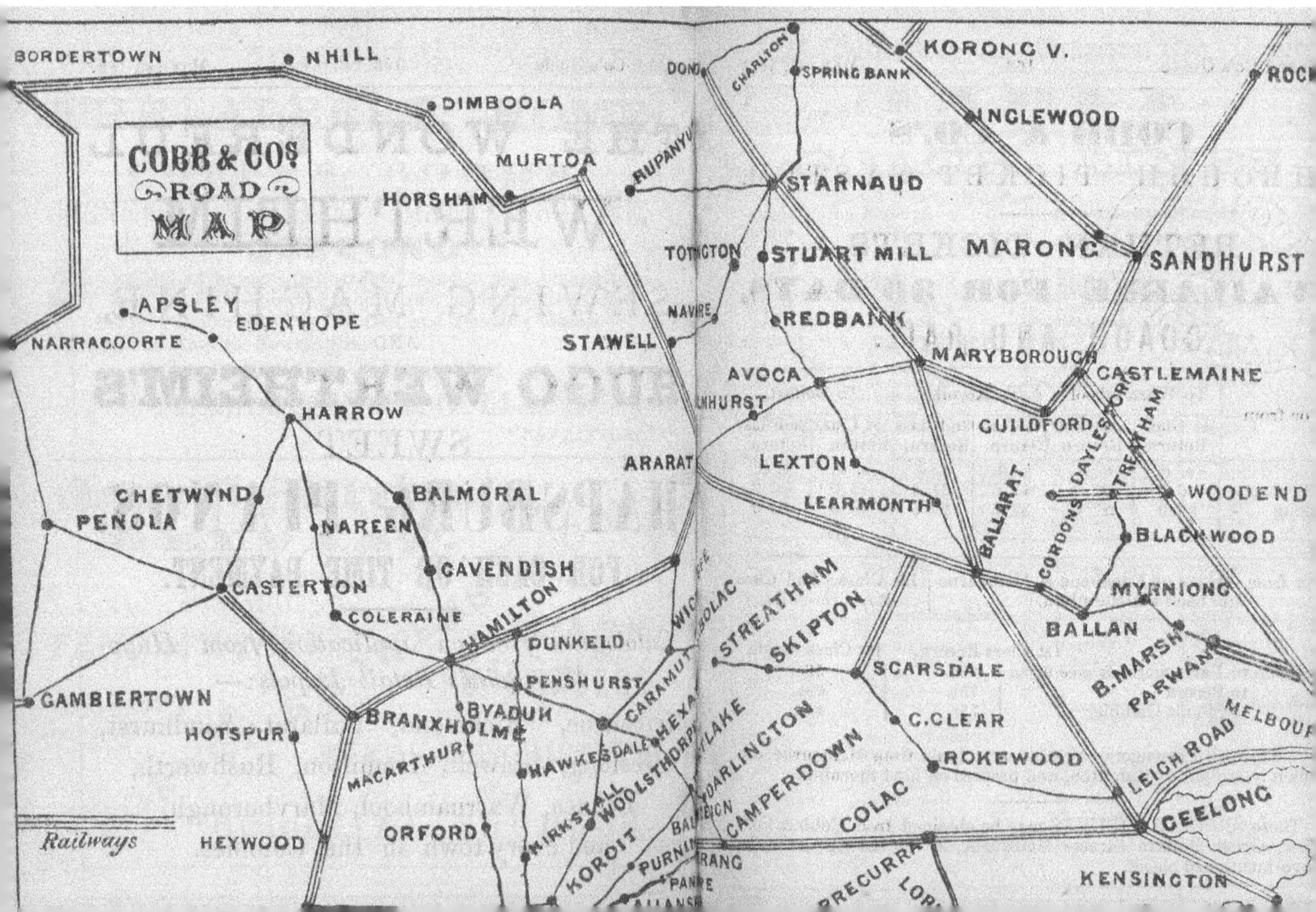

More coaching routes can be viewed on map *Commercial map of Victoria and Riverina showing pastoral districts, railways, counties, towns, coach routes &* - Courtesy National Library Australia

ca. 1854-1862 Mining Scene, possibly Clunes - Courtesy State Library Victoria

ca. 1860-1870 Double-storey bluestone residence with return verandah
(Charles Nettleton, 1826-1902, photographer) - Courtesy State Library Victoria

Chapter Two

Life in Melbourne and beyond

The Dream of Gold
THE SQUATTING ERA.

... Oh when if ever shall be found,
A nugget on Victorian's soil ?
And who can say aurif'rous ground
Will here repay the digger's toil.
Yet all things must as now remain
Until the fated gold appears,
Come then prospectors mad and sane
And cause at once the change of years.

* * *

THE DISCOVERY.
The gold was found—the charm was snapt ;
There rose at once a sudden trade,
And bankers laughed, and merchants clapped
On cent. per cent., and fortunes made.
The golden find enriched them all ;
And Miller wept for joy aloud.
A hubbub shook the Civic hall ;
And shouts and cheering shook the crowd.

The panic ceased, the prices rose,
The tide that ebbed began to flow,
For swift the news to Sydney goes
Of Ballaarat and Bendigo.
And all along the northern road,
With picks and shovels, carts and drays,
Men after men, and load by load,
Prospective diggers fill the ways.

Here lawyers quit their briefs and pleas,
Or hopes of briefs— 'tis all the same.
There doctors cast aside their fees,
All bent upon a single game.
Merchants and scholars, rogues and fools,
Old, young, strong, weak, halt, lame, sick, well,
Pour forth with swags and diggers' tools,
To meet a fate that time shall tell.

By Alfred Pennyson.
(The Dream of Gold, Verses 5, 6, 7 & 8, 25 Jun 1856, p.3)
1873 Mining Exchange, Shamrock Hotel, Sandhurst (Oswald Rose Campbell, 1820-1887)
- Courtesy National Library Australia

Victoria—Fire, flood, mud & snow

1855, "Melbourne ... The weather continues dreadfully warm, and there is but little sign of change. Sunday was one of the warmest days I felt during several years of colonial experience, not even excepting the memorable Black Thursday. The 'ometer' stood at 132 in the sun, and 118 in the shade, and there is no perceptible diminution of heat to-day." (Melbourne, 31 Jan 1855, p.2)

Only a few years earlier, in 1851, came one of the most harrowing bush fires in the state's history: "Mount Macedon. To the Editor of the Argus. Sir,—I write in the midst of desolation, Thursday morning was ushered in with a fierce hot wind, which, as the day advanced, grew stronger and stronger. For three weeks bush fires have been raging to the westward and northward of the Bush Inn. About mid-day, the whole of Mount Macedon and the ranges were one sheet of flame, careering on at the speed of a race horse, carrying all before it as clean as a chimney newly swept. The destruction in the vicinity of the Bush Inn is appalling. On Messrs Riddle and Hamilton's cattle station, the cottage, huts, hay, wheat, oats, stock yard, paddock fences, all are in ruins. Peter and David Murray, who rented the dairy, have lost all they possessed, barely escaping with their lives. The same gentlemen have also lost three out station huts ; their loss, not taking the loss of fences into account, must be many hundreds of pounds.

At the police station, Mr Powlett has lost two large hay stacks, his cottage and other buildings nearby barely escaping. But for a number of men being at the Bush Inn, it, along with up-wards of seventy tons of hay and grain, must have been burned to the ground, the fire being within the fence surrounding the hay and grain, as well as burning the dry straw at the stable doors. The blacksmith's and farm servants' huts were burned with all belonging to the poor men. Mr Roberton has his bridges, drays, fences and garden destroyed ; his house, huts, and grain have escaped in a most wonderful manner, as well as one of his shepherds along with his flock, being completely surrounded with the flames ; the noise the shepherd was making brought a man who was running for his life, seeking a place to get through ; seeing there was no hope, except they got through the flames, they drove the sheep back to a bare piece of ground meeting the fire ; the two men set to, as a matter of life, with green boughs, and beat out as much as barely allowed the sheep to get through, thus getting to the wind-ward and behind the fire and saving both themselves and the sheep.

On the mountain where a number of splitters and sawyers are employed they have lost all. One man named Jones who is employed carting timber has lost two valuable draught horses and a bullock dray, one of the splitters has also a fine mare burnt to death. Taylor's wife is severely burnt about the breast and arms, the wife of Dooling another splitter was in flames but providently saved by a man wrapping her in a wet blanket. Edward Morris, another splitter who has a wife and a large family of children have all escaped as well as their hut. Being a man of nerve and near the water, he and his wife managed admirably, he however as well as all the people employed in sawing and splitting have lost their tools and stuff, which taken in the aggregate will amount to more than £150 ; some of them, especially the women Taylor and Dooling have not a rag left to cover them. A bullock driver named Bill fetching a load of timber from the mountain not enclosed by the fire, he unyoked his bullocks to give them a chance of escape, seeing all hope cut off for himself, he laid hold of the tail of one and giving a shout, which along with the instinct of the animal cleared him of all danger.

Cattle are found in every direction, dead and dying many of them with their entrails protruding. Surely, Sir, inquiry ought to be made as to the cause of these fires being lighted, it will not do for every man who has more grass on his run than he has stock to eat it, to put a fire stick in, merely because he may wish for something green for a lambing flock. As the writer of this is in possession of facts that such was the case, and is ready to come forward with evidence that part of the destruction in this neighbourhood was occasioned by a person doing as described, he calls on those, whose duty it may be, to cause a searching enquiry into the matter. Your most obedient servant, A. Macedonian P.S.—I enclose my name, that the public Prosecutor, or any other public officer may know where to find me." (Bush Fires—Mount Macedon, 12 Feb 1851, p.2)

Decades later, the legacy of this devastation was still remembered: "The 91st Anniversary ... of the most disastrous bush fires ... The fires were believed to have been caused by two careless bullock drivers, who left their camp fire near Diamond Creek smouldering, though this would not account for the simultaneous conflagrations in other parts of the colony. A settler named McLellan, who lived near Diamond Creek, went out to fight the flames. In his absence the fire swept round and consumed his dwelling, his wife and five children. Several shepherds were caught unprepared and burnt to death or died later. In the Geelong district it is estimated that 2000 tons of hay and 5000 bundles of wheat were destroyed. Two squatters each lost 4000 sheep, the total loss of one of them (including crops and wool) being £4000 ... The stable doors of one homestead were opened for the terrified animals to escape, but they ran back to the stable and perished ... The sun resembled a ball of fire, even ships twenty miles out in the Bay had the unique experience of embers falling on the decks ... Other bushfires have, of course, swept this State, the most notable being those in 1926 and 1939. In the former, 31 lives were lost, more than 150 homes were destroyed, and over 700 timber workers deprived of employment. Hundreds were homeless and destitute." (Black Thursday, 5 Feb 1942, p.3)

Similarly, a retrospective from 1952 recounted the widespread destruction that occurred on 'Black Thursday': "The fires of '51 saw Victoria swept by one of the most disastrous bushfires Australia has ever known ... The summer, had been exceptionally hot and dry. The whole country was covered with, a whitish brown, dry and combustible grass. With the exception of Gippsland, where the grass was green and the rivers full, the stage was set for a major blaze. To add to the setting, the recent winter floods had caused, an excessively dense growth of vegetation ... Fires broke out simultaneously in the country around Western Port, the Dandenong Forest and the Ranges, thence to Mount Macedon and the Barrabool Hills. Spreading quickly from the Black Forest across the Loddon district, they crossed the Pyrenees, and finished up by attacking Mount Gambier on the South Australian border ... dense smoke which stretched right across Bass Strait and even darkened the sky over Tasmania ... For weeks, Victoria was a scene of desolation." (Black Thursday, 31 Dec 1952, p.2)

In contrast, "the great flood (1863) was a sight ! The waters reached into Flinders-lane, and tore across St Kilda-road between Princes Bridge and the Immigrants' Home, and down the flats to Sandridge, where it broke a hole in the shore, which is the little harbor for fishing boats now. The railway was flooded over the embankment and rail, and it looked as if the train was running on the water. This flood showed where a canal should have been excavated—a second river to the Yarra—to give more shipping accommodation to the ships in the harbor of Melbourne." (Melbourne in 1854, 18 Dec 1924, p.8)

This event was later analysed in detail: "In the month of December, 1863, a storm burst over the valley of the River Yarra, which led to the drowning, by floods, of the low-lying lands in the districts of Hawthorne, Heidelberg, Richmond, South Yarra, Emerald Hill, and Sandridge, as well as the depressed levels immediately around Melbourne. Although human foresight could not possibly have foretold this particular occurrence, we must not forget that the several floods by which the same districts had been previously visited ... ought to have prepared us for the advent of such a disaster ... However, the danger was apparently so distant that we took no precautions whatever to provide against it." (1864 The Report of the Yarra Flood Commission, Robert Adams, p.2)

Unpredictable weather didn't end there. In 1905, snow fell in Melbourne: "Extraordinary weather has prevailed in Melbourne for the past few days. Rain commenced early on Saturday evening, bringing with it bitterly cold winds. Showery weather continued all day Sunday, and early this morning a fall of snow took place in the metropolis. This was particularly noticeable in the Northern suburbs. Mr Baracchi on being interviewed said that the extremely cold weather was due to a cyclonic depression, which he thought would soon pass away. On being asked if he could recollect when snow had fallen in Melbourne before he said he could not. As far as his reports were concerned the fall was not heavy in any part of the metropolis. The thermometer recorded a temperature of 35.5 last evening. No great quantity of rain has fallen, the gauge at the Observatory at 10 o'clock to-day only recorded a rainfall of 48 points." (Snow in Melbourne, 26 Sep 1905, p.3)

Back to the 1850s, during the early days of the colony: "*The conditions which exist in Melbourne at the present time are chaotic. There are only two wharves, which are congested with articles of every description. With my baggage, I was landed on the banks of the river which flows through the centre of the town. It is the middle of winter and everything here is a sea of mud. There are, of course, no macadamised roads.* So wrote John Walker, who arrived in Melbourne in 1850 by the ship Lord Metcalfe ... other letters told of the romantic gold-digging days and life in Melbourne in the 'forties' and 'fifties' ... *Gold has been found at a place called Ballarat, and every person in Melbourne seems to have gone mad with excitement. The town is full of people, and conveyances of all kinds are being commandeered to carry merchandise and mining tools to the goldfields ... such another wonderful discovery of gold can never be made.*" (Early Melbourne, 7 Dec 1925, p.6)

Ramblings about early Melbourne

In the bustling heart of the 1850s, amid gold fever and rapid colonial growth, the following observations were recorded by a gold-seeker. "There are many pleasant spots in its vicinity where one given to rambling may spend a quiet afternoon ... I do not remember who it was that said a London shopkeeper was only to be properly known when he got rid of the smoke on a Sunday ; and verily I believe the remark applies with great truthfulness to the shopocracy of Melbourne, as well as to those of the insignificant village on the banks of the Thames ...

Sabbath recreation, are St. Kilda and Lairdet's Beach, both situated on the margin of the noble bay, nearly opposite Williams Town. Although Melbourne possesses a tolerably fair steam fleet, in the shape of various tug boats, belonging chiefly to Captain Cole, not one of these vessels are allowed to ply on Sunday ; and hence, as may be supposed, there is upon one day in the week at least a very great demand for horseflesh. In fact, the horse market, I mean the bazaars and livery stables, upon a Sunday morning present quite an animated spectacle, for here almost every masculine biped of the genus homo considers it his peculiar privilege to mount a horse on Sunday, without, be it remembered, the smallest reference to the fact as to whether he can ride or not ; and permit me to say that sundry jokes have been cracked at sailors on horseback, but were the perpetrators of these puns to see a lot of diggers and shopmen in Melbourne mounted on their Sunday Rozinantes, henceforth and for ever they would hold their peace. Scenes the most laughable occur, and yet all seems to be in good part. The fellows have come out to enjoy themselves, and are not to be put out of humour by trifles.

St. Kilda lies about three miles from Melbourne, on the south side of the Yarra, and as there is no highway, except the usual bush ruts, after the Prince's Bridge is crossed, the walk or ride, which you please, is very pleasant. Arrived at the village, you are somewhat surprised at the appearance of rapid growth which everything indicates. Houses (wooden, of course) are in course of construction, some nearly finished, others but commenced ; and yet so eager are the people for house accommodation, that the shingles are scarcely on the roofs before they are tenanted. At St. Kilda there is a very fine hotel, at which I can assure you they charge very fine prices; but then, Lord bless you, in the go-a-head city, as Melbourne is now called, who cares for a handful of silver. I was much pleased to observe here a taste more generally diffused for the cultivation of flowers than is to be found generally about Melbourne. I like to see those pretty little plots of ground in front of dwelling-houses neatly and carefully cultivated ... The ramble from St. Kilda to Liardet's Beach, by the margin of the wide and noble bay, a distance of about two miles, is both healthful and agreeable—not that the scenery of the bay is of such a description ... there is nothing to relieve the dull monotony of the place.

At Lairdet's, however, the scene changes, and from the solitude of the shore and your own reflections ... you are once more aroused by the din of human voices. Here they are again—shopkeepers, shopmen, diggers, ladies, diggers' wives ; horses, hackney carriages, shandys, gigs, and almost every possible and sometimes very questionable modes of conveyance, all congregated on the sand. Pedestrians wandering, promenading, flirting, drinking, laughing, talking on the pier and in the shade of the cool verandahs, pic-nics in the scrub, mirth and merriment everywhere ; boatmen lustily bawling for passengers, and waiters for more drink at the bar of the hotel. Tents are pitched upon all the ground surrounding this house of entertainment, wherein many a new chum for the first time indulges in a glass of ale, and when he has paid six-pence ... A good deal of novelty is added to this scene by the constant transit to and from a large ship, the Duke of Bedford, which is here moored off the pier, and turned into a model lodging-house. *Bed and board, sir,* said our conductors on board the other day, *for two pounds a week* ; *delightful marine residence and boatage found into the bargain.* Decidedly the accommodations are excellent, and the worthy proprietor, I was informed, keeps a good table. I need scarcely say that his apartments are full ; and it would be well if a few more of the dozens upon dozens of idle ships now lying in harbour were turned to an equally useful and profitable account to their owners.

I was a good deal surprised to find amidst all the recreations of all classes and all kinds who visit the beach upon Sunday so little riot or intoxication. That an immense amount of liquor is drink there is no doubt ; but still, except upon the arrival of a lot of 'new chums,' with more money than sense, you will hardly observe any riot or drunkenness ...

The road from the beach to town lies through a low marshy scrub, which presents not one single pleasing feature, except indeed we were to diverge at the Emerald Hill and take a look in at the encampment. This encampment, it will be observed at a glance, consists but of the tents of old diggers in *transitu* to the Mount or elsewhere. You are scarcely on the hill till that fact becomes painfully apparent. There are the coverings erected by poor new-comers to shelter them from the heavens and to make a temporary but safe refuge for themselves, their luggage, and their families. And, oh such squalor, such misery, and such a ground for imbibing the seeds of diseases, which may never again be eradicated from the system! ...

The Botanic Garden is another favourite resort for the Melbournite upon Sunday; but its visitors are of a different class. This is the ground where half the 'matches' which grace our churches daily are contracted; and here it is that newly married husbands display to wandering swains their lovely and loving brides, at least during the honey moon it is so. The collection of flowers is not of the best description, being rather too gaudy and too common for such a place; but if they be gaudy there is some excuse to be found for the curator, in the circumstance that he is naturally driven to compete with gardeners of the human flowers who perambulate his walks. Such a blaze of silk and satin, such bonnets, such feathers, flowers (artificial, of course), and such ribbons—such finery of all kinds as is displayed on that little piece of ground on one single Sunday would set your brains a wool-gathering as to how on earth Melbourne produced as many dress and bonnet makers as could rig out this mart of fashion. I was particularly struck with the freshness and beauty of many of the charming belles who frequent the gardens, regular Baby Blakes in their way, contrasting strongly with the general sallow and somewhat acclimatized style of female beauty prevalent about Sydney. They are generally handsome, and fresh in colour; but then, if they should chance to open their lips, the delusion is at once dispelled, and the dimpled cheeks and laughing eyes which but a moment before you had been ardently admiring, is transformed into the most unsophisticated lumps of barbarous ignorance that has ever been pitchforked into the world ...

Far different, however, are the scenes to be witnessed here sometimes; and amongst the many strange vicissitudes of fortune which I daily witness, none strikes me so painfully during my stay here, as the forlorn condition of the newly arrived passengers from Europe. The convict is cared for, tended, fed, housed, clothed, and respectably treated ... Thousands, tens of thousands of sturdy artizans and labourers are poured upon her shores weekly—her gold revenue produces nearly £900,000 a year, independently of all other sources of income, and yet not a hovel, not a shed, not a free tent, has been appropriated for the use even for a night of those hardy adventurers, who have been wiled to her shores ...

Men will begin to speculate upon the expediency of retaining a Government which does nothing but batten on the vitals of the public, whose every act either betokens gross carelessness, gross ignorance, or what is still worse, gross favouritism, almost amounting to misappropriation of the public money. Men will ask, and the question must be answered, what has become of the revenues of the colony? ... It is melancholy to reflect on the increased amount of human suffering, which is patiently endured by new-comers here ...

The public buildings of Melbourne are of a most inferior description, both in point of architectural style and internal accommodation. The only building of note at all adequate to its requirements is the Mechanics' Institution; and it has now to do the treble duty of Concert Hall, Assembly Room, and Town Hall, including offices, etc, for the Town Clerk. The library attached to the Institution is very good indeed, and the rooms spacious and commodious, much better than your School of Arts ...

The state of the weather has improved considerably of late, and business is very brisk with us, as commercial men say, has an upward tendency. Markets are decidedly getting much higher, whilst I question if wages are rising in proportion, notwithstanding that the exodus to the diggings continues unabated." (Jottings from the Note-book of a Gold-Seeker, 13 Oct 1852, p.2)

Business news

The American business presence in Melbourne was already active by 1853. "The Fourth of July ... a meeting of the American residents ... take into consideration the best method of celebrating the coming Anniversary of American Independence ... The following committee were then appointed by the Chair ... George Francis Train, Massachusetts ... George Mowton, Pennsylvania, E. Winslow Cobb, Delaware." (The Fourth of July, 21 Jun 1853, p.7) Just weeks later the "Anniversary of the Declaration of American Independence ... was celebrated on Monday evening ... An excellent band lent its enlivening strains to enhance the gaiety of the evening ... George Mowton, Esq., Penn. vice-president ... members of the Committee ... Messrs. George F. Train, Mass., second vice-president ... E. W. Cobb ... Mr. Mowton, at the request of the chairman, read slowly and with good emphasis the Declaration of Independence ... Mr. Geo. F. Train next read the following address, from the pen of Mr. Peck ... who was unable to deliver in person ... *We who are present will always be able to recollect with pride, at this time, in this most remarkable vicinity, where all bustle and resort, and a populous and beautiful city [Melbourne] is rising around us like an exhalation, we did not forget the far land of our birth ... though now Australians ... We are in the van of a great immigrant expedition which is concentrating in this colony from all parts of the globe; and which has already thronged these streets with such a crowd of busy men as can hardly be found anywhere but in the oldest commercial cities ... We have not reached the lawless neighborhood we read of ... we are in a quietly disposed town, under an efficient police ... considering the numbers and adventurous disposition of the population that is pouring through it, far exceeds all reasonable expectation.*" (Geelong, 6 Jul 1853, p.3)

Meanwhile Melbourne was showing "general improvement in business ... Wheat and Barley are nominal, but Oats meet an improving demand at our quotations, as also Maize, which recent high prices seem to have permanently established in our market as a substitute for Oats. Bran is worth 2s., and Potatoes £20 to £30, where of good quality. Fruit comes in slowly as yet, and yields high rates, Apples being worth 16s. to 18s. per bushel. Jams and Jellies are also inquired after, and would bring 1s. 2d. to 1s. 6d. per lb., Bacon, Ham, Cheese, and Butter are all in good consumptive demand ... Colonial Butter has of late been undersold ... Wines and Spirits have been in good supply ... Sugar has come to hand in very large quantities, and the market is dull, and sales difficult. Tea has also been largely imported, but the consumption is very great, and prices are maintained. Building materials of all kinds are in very great demand ... Wooden houses also find ready sale.

Gold has risen from 70s. 3d. to 73s. 3d. this day. The escorts have brought 233,905 ozs., and the accounts from the diggings are much more favourable. A nugget of 120 lbs. weight has been found at Ballarat. Wool is firm at late rates, and large quantities have come to town and been exported to England, a considerable portion unwashed." (Circular, 12 Feb 1853, p.5)

By 1855, Victoria's population approached 200,000. "Approximate Population ... Colony of Victoria ... 198,496 ... Estimate of 2500 [First Nations Peoples] Imports: Carriages imported from United States of America 9,384 (Total 103,827) ... Horses (Total 14,600) ... Saddlery (Total 86,088) Exports: Gold 8,644,529 ounces." (Statistics of The Colony of Victoria, 30 Jan 1855)

Across the shipping sector, prominent Americans were active. "Royal Mail. White Star Line of Liverpool and Australian Clipper Packet Ships ... semi-monthly mails ... The reputation of this line for punctuality, speed, and prompt delivery of freight, is well known to the importer ... Geo. F. Train and Co." (Advertising, 28 Sep 1855, p.4)

Even amid commerce, personal notices appeared in the newspapers. "LOST, Wednesday, a small, low, and long bodied Brown Shaggy SKYE TERRIER DOG, clipped ears, and long tail. Whoever will bring the same to E. W. Cobb and Co., 122 Collins-street west, will receive a Guinea Reward." (Advertising, 29 Aug 1856, p.8)

Years later, a candid assessment of merchant character emerged: "I have never seen any men so easily elated or depressed as the citizens of Melbourne. As for the merchants, should any article rise in price, they rub their hands and chuckle at the fortune by which they are to be rewarded, but let prices fall, and a gloom overshadows them like a moonless night. Hence it is that because wool has fallen a penny a pound, those who have advanced on that staple think that wool is about to be worthless, while it must at least for this generation, be one of the most indispensable of the world's wants." (Melbourne Business Men, 15 May 1869, p.2)

By 1885, "a very efficient postal system exists in Victoria, and post-offices are established throughout the length and breadth of the colony; 1,295 of such institutions now exist, as against 1,007 five years since. In the same quinquennial period, the letters and newspapers despatched and received in a year increased from 33,000,000 to 45,000,000. The postage on letters to places in any of the Australasian colonies is twopence per ounce, and on news-papers one halfpenny each. The postage on letters to the United Kingdom is sixpence, and on newspapers one penny ... Railways in Victoria ... At the end of 1883, 1,562 miles were open for traffic, 205 miles of which were laid with double lines. The cost of construction, inclusive of rolling-stock, and building a bridge over the Murray to connect with the New South Wales lines, was over £21,100,000, or an average of about £13,500 per mile; of this amount about £18,544,000 was raised by means of debentures, and the remainder—being about 12 per cent— was paid from the general revenue. About 5,700,000 miles were travelled during the year ...

Telegraphs in Victoria are Government property, and are worked in connexion with the Post-office. Telegraphic communication exists between 365 stations within the colony, and the Victorian lines are connected besides with the lines of New South Wales, and by means of them with Queensland and New Zealand. They are also connected with the lines of South Australia, and by their means with Western Australia and with the Eastern Archipelago, Asia, Europe, and America. They are likewise united with a submarine cable to Tasmania." (Handbook to the colony of Victoria/prepared under the direction of the Victorian Government by Henry Heylyn Hayter, Published Melbourne : John Ferres, Govt. Printer, 1885)

As time passed, small business success stories continued to flourish in Melbourne. "We have now pleasure in reverting to the subject in connection with the recent alteration and enlargement of the Mr. E. Comber's Merchant Tailoring Establishment, Clarendon-street. The energy and tact shown by the head of this firm has enabled him to double the business of his establishment during the past twelve months. To meet the requirements of this public favour, he has not only taken in the whole of the upper living rooms for workrooms, but has removed the wall that formerly divided the dining room from the front shop, thus throwing the whole of the ground floor into one spacious shop. This has been neatly fitted with mirrors and shelving the whole being beautifully lit at night with the best Argand burners, as used in first-class shops in England. A very extensive stock of the latest and best cloths and gentlemen's out fittings has just been opened, making a showy and tempting display. Mr. Comber imports directly for the English and Continental markets. Some idea of the extensive business done by this enterprising South Melbourne tailoring establishment may be gathered when we say that two first class cutters and fifty workmen are kept constantly employed." (South Melbourne Business Enterprise, 13 Dec 1886, p.3)

In 1894, "an old, resident of Albury who 50 years ago was living in Victoria, informs me that the period of depression through which Australia is passing is no more disastrous than that experienced in 1843 ... In 1840 or 1841 there had been a land boom in Melbourne, in which people went mad in the frantic desire to traffic in real estate. Then, as a few years ago, land sales were the main excitement of the day, and the traffic was accompanied by the wholesale consumption of champagne. Everybody was going

to be rich 'beyond the dreams of averice,'

and everyone squandered money right royally. By and by came the reaction. Mercantile houses came down with a crash, station property was a mere drug in the market, and real estate could hardly be given away. There was no employment for artisans, and skilled tradesmen were glad to shoulder their swags, march away into the bush, and hire out—when they got a chance—on a station for £13 a year and rations. And such rations—10lb. of meat, 2lb. of black sugar, ¼ lb. of alleged tea, and a peck of wheat which had to be ground in a handmill before it could be turned to account for food ... To make matters worse, in the face of this terrible condition of affairs, there was a large influx of immigrants from Ireland. There was no work for these people ... The Government of the day could not well see those men starve, and the immigrants were set to work to make a corduroy road from the punt to Lairdet's Beach.

But Victoria revived, and Melbourne rose to a height of glory which at that time not even the most sanguine would have dared to anticipate. The moral of all this, is obvious. Victoria, New South Wales, and Australia generally will again recover, and five years hence the hard times we are passing through will be absolutely forgotten, or remembered only as an uncomfortable dream of the nightmare order." (Miscellaneous Items, 16 Mar 1894, p.4)

In lighter news, by 1913 community spirit remained alive and well. "Post Office Picnic. Two Post-office employes' picnic takes place on Saturday and on that day no business will be transacted after.—10 a.m. at the following brunch post and telegraph offices: —Bourke street east, City road, Elizabeth street north, Hotham Hill receiving house, [?] , Market Street, Public Offices, William street (Menzies' Hotel). The suburban post and telegraph offices will be closed at 10 a.m."

Entertainment

In 1856, the social calendar featured events like the Easter Monday Select Ball and Supper at the Porcupine Inn on the Bendigo Road. "The Undersigned begs to inform his Friends and the Public generally that a Select Ball and Supper will take place at the Porcupine Inn, on the Bendigo-road, on the evening of Easter Monday (St. Patrick's Day), 17th March, when he hopes to have the pleasure of meeting as many as can make it convenient to attend. A first-rate band has been engaged and every preparation and convenience made for the accommodation of ladies, gentlemen, their horses. &c. The wines and, in short everything, will be first class. Tickets may be had at the Porcupine Inn, and of the following gentlemen, who have kindly consented to act as stewards: Mr. G. Lambert, Cobb and Co.'s office, Melbourne ; Mr J. Gardiner, Cobb and Co.'s office, Castlemaine ; Mr. G. Millbanks, Castlemaine ; Mr. G. W. Haycock, Cobb and Co.'s office, Bendigo ; Mr. Harvey, Bendigo Hotel, Bendigo ; Mr. Gregson, Golden Gully, Bendigo. Tickets, not transferable, to admit lady and gentleman, exclusive of wines, £1 1s. JAMES M'LAREN. N.B.—The famous pack of Kangaroo dogs will meet on Tuesday, the following morning, to hunt the kangaroo. Excellent sport is certain." (Advertising, 13 Mar 1856, p.3)

In 1873, the "Opening of the Opera Season included "Lucrezia Borgia. The commencement of a new season of opera is looked upon in Melbourne as an event of considerable social importance. For so many months in the year it is the familiar lounge of the wealthy and those who affect fashion, and the number of people in this city who prefer the lyric drama to all other kinds of amusement is so great, that whenever the season returns there is a large audience always ready to fill the house as soon as the doors are opened.

For this season the directors, Messrs Lyster and Cagli, have secured the new house in Bourke street formerly known as the Prince of Wales Theatre and having re-christened it the Opera house, have also made some interior alterations in order to adapt it to the work to which it is now specially. In the stalls and upper circle all the side boxes have been done away with. New and improved entrances have been made to the pit and stalls. The approach leading from Bourke street to the dress-circle has been redecorated, and now presents a very handsome appearance. It is in the dress circle itself that most alteration is apparent and there such a complete transformation is visible that no vestige of its former shabby condition remains. The boarded ceiling has been canvassed over and coloured with blue panels upon a creamy ground, lined off with gilt mouldings. A highly ornamental border runs round the wall at its junction with the ceiling, and forms part of one long continuous ventilator. The walls are coloured with blue panels upon a light ground, each panel being adorned with gold stars and lined with gilt moulding. Two ventilating windows have also been opened at this level in the side walls The dress circle, fitted with cushions of a light and pleasing colour, is entirely free from partitions of any kind, except where the Governors box has been railed off in the centre by means of massive brass rails supporting blue curtains. The whole space is richly carpeted, and chairs and sofas occupy the space at the back. The old gas-fittings have been all removed, and are now replaced by a number of gas burners of elegant design.

Nothing that has hitherto been done in Melbourne in the way of theatrical decoration equals this part of the new Opera house, and it is only fair therefore to mention the names of the tradesmen who deserve the credit of it. These are Mr. W. Dean, of Elizabeth street, decorator, Mr. Tubbs of Messrs. Buckley and Nunn's, upholsterer, and Mr. Dempster, of Russell street, gasfitter.

The house filled shortly after the doors were opened, and at 8 o'clock Signor Zelman, who had been loudly applauded on entering the orchestra, gave the signal, and the band played the National Anthem, the whole company upstanding and applauding heartily on the conclusion of it. The appearance of so large an assemblage at this time was very handsome indeed, and particularly so in the first tree, which was all ablaze with bright lights, bright looks, and the varied tints belonging to the adornments of the ladies. With such surroundings there is every inducement for ladies this season to appear at their very best—not that they need any hint concerning such a generally instinctive and spontaneous effort—but it will be satisfactory for them to know that what their good taste prompts them to do, can scarcely be otherwise than in thorough keeping with the style of the new Opera house. The orchestra, which is a most important item in the general strength of the company." (Opening of the Opera Season, 10 Mar 1873, p.7)

The next week, the newspaper noted "lost, near Opera-house, gold bracelet, diamond setting. Finder rewarded. A. W. Robertson, Cobb and Co." (Advertising, 19 Mar 1873, p.8)

By 1890 there was "phonograph entertainment. The first public phonograph entertainment in Melbourne was given on Monday evening at the Atheneum Hall, before a large audience. In an introductory lecture Professor Archibald described how the idea of the invention was first suggested and subsequently perfected. By means of a magic lantern pictures of the early repeating machines were projected on a white sheet, and their mechanism was carefully explained. Diagrams were also shown of the incidents of sound waves as indicated in the varying forces of the voice in pronouncing different sentences. Finally it was demonstrated how the beating of the voice upon a sensitive diaphragm set a needle in motion, which registered vibration upon wax, and how on the needle being subsequently redrawn over the same track thus made the diaphragm emitted the same sounds as those first breathed into it ... A phonograph on the stage was set in motion. All sorts of exercises were reproduced from it quite automatically, including cornet solos by Arthur Smith, of Covent Garden Opera, coach horn calls by the same performer, cornet solos from New York, banjo solos by Mr. W. H. Vane, of Liverpool," (The Phonograph Entertainment, 12 Jul 1890, p.4) while by 1929 "talkie entertainment sound and talking pictures which will soon form part of the entertainment of Melbourne have aroused high expectations. There have been many and ingenious attempts to synchronise sound and movement in pictures, but only recently have results given indications of the achievement of complete success. The Fox Movietone and the Vitaphone of Warner Brothers are linked up in the Western Electric system which will be common to all Australian places of entertainment which Hoyts Theatres Ltd. and Union Theatres have set apart as 'talkie' houses. There rc certainly many persons who do not think that 'talkies' will last." (Talkie Entertainment, 12 Jan 1929, p.28)

Not every social event went smoothly. "The Entertainment in aid of the Street Tree Planting Fund last Friday evening was somewhat of a failure. The attendance was not half as large as usual at local concerts, and a portion of the audience was in a very disagreeable humour. The idea of holding the entertainment on the night of the Coursing Match resulted in bringing some into the Hall in a very elevated condition, which altogether prevented anyone from enjoying the finer portions of the programme." (Entertainment, 28 Aug 1891, p.2)

"But theatre and concert-loving as are Victorians generally, it is in the out-door sports that they chiefly relax. Cricket, lawn tennis, football, rowing, yachting, and bicycle riding being the most popular amusements. There are no more perfect arrangements of the kind in the world than those of the Melbourne Cricket Ground, where the members' pavilion is not only a 'grand stand,' but possesses dining, billard, and bathrooms ... horse-riding absorbs the affections of the Victorian people ...

At Flemington, only three and a half miles from the centre of the city, the greatest race in Australia, the 'Melbourne Cup,' run early in November (our Spring) ... 'Cup Week' ... the city is given over to gaiety and pleasure ... Derby ... 'Cup Day' ... balls, dinner and garden parties ... Steeplechase ... not less than 100,000 people ... policemen are conspicuous by their rarity, there is scarcely a trace of drunkenness ... nothing but good-humoured order prevails." (The Palace Hotel [Bourke Street] guide to Melbourne, 1889)

By 1884, the Melbourne Cup had already become a celebrated tradition. "24 Melbourne Cups that have been run ... winners were ... Archer (twice), The Barb, Tim Whiffier, Glencoe, Pearl, Quack, Chester, Calamia Grand Flaneur, Zulu,, Martini-Henry, Banter (? Banker), Lantern, Toryboy, Warrior, Nimblefoot, Don Juan, Haricot, Wollomai, Briseis, Darriwell, and Malua, The Assyrian." (Melbourne Cup Winners, 6 Dec 1884, p.6)

Now for a "A FUNNY STORY ... suspicion arose ... jockey ... The suggestion was that he had an electric battery inside his jacket when he rode ... This is perhaps the first time in the history of racing in this State that anyone suggested that a rider used an electric battery when riding. There was, however, a case in Western Australia. One day a boy was riding in a race, and in pulling his horse up the animal fell and the boy was killed. When carried in to the hospital his jacket was removed, and a small electric battery was discovered. How this is employed may be pointed out. The battery is fastened to the waist, and a wire is run down the leg of the jockey and connected with his spur. Then there is another wire passed from the jockey's waist and along the arm to about the elbow. To this is attached a piece of elastic, and the latter has a loop at the end of it. The rider takes this loop into his hand, end as he strains on it the battery is set in motion and connects with the spur. Well, towards the end of the race, when the horse is running home from the distance, the jockey pricks his mount with his heel, and of course gives the horse an electric shock. This is supposed to be an aid to making the horse put in a fast run to wind up with ... Some little time ago an old Melbourne trainer gave it as his opinion that a battery had never been used in a race at Flemington." (A Funny Story, 8 Jun 1912, p.21)

Cobb and Co.'s coaching, Melbourne

1854 – "American Telegraph Line of Coaches.—Daily Communication between Melbourne, Forest Creek and Bendigo—Cobb and Co. beg to announce to the public that they have determined to run a line of well-appointed Coaches between the above places, starting from the Criterion Hotel every morning, (Sunday excepted) at 6 o'clock, and from Forest Creek, daily, at the same hour. The vehicles intended to run are the new American coaches, recently imported, and acknowledged to be the easiest conveyances in the colony. The first coach will start from the Criterion, on Monday, January 30th, and every attention will be given to ensure punctuality Cobb and Co., Proprietors." (Advertising, 31 Jan 1854, p.3)

1854 – "Telegraph Stage Line, from Melbourne to Castlemaine, Bendigo, and Maryborough, via Essendon, Keilor, Gap, Gisborne, Woodend, Carlsruhe, Kyneton, Malmesbury, and Elphinstone, carrying Adams and Co.'s Inland Express daily. Cobb and Co." (Advertising, 25 Nov 1854, p.8)

1855 – Cobb and Co.'s Booking Offices "Melbourne ... Adams and Co.'s Office, No 69 Collins-street,—T. K. Newton, agent. Telegraph Stage office, No. 23 Bourke-street,—F. J. Rogers, agent. Castlemaine ... Prince of Wales Hotel,—I. B. Lamber, agent. Bendigo ... Haycock's Office,—G. W. Haycock, agent. Maryborough. Telegraph Store,—Hewitt and Co., agents. Cobb and Co., Proprietors, Melbourne." (Advertising, 2 Jun 1855, p.1)

1855 – "Telegraph Stage Office and General Agency Depot, No. 23, Great Bourke-street East, Melbourne. The proprietors beg to inform the public, that they have opened the above concern for the forwarding of merchandise, luggage, and swags, to the several diggings, and all the Australasian colonies ; the delivery of parcels throughout Melbourne and suburbs; the receiving and delivery of letters and packages from and to all parts of the colony, America, and Europe ; the procuring of situations for male and female servants, of every description ; the negotiation of partnership ; the sale and letting of land and houses ; the despatching of stage coaches to the various diggings, including Cobb & Co.'s celebrated Telegraph Line of American coaches ; in a word, all that can be expected from an establishment of this kind, is to be procured at this house. F. J. Rogers & Co. Agent for Bendigo. G. W. Haycock." (Advertising, 6 Oct 1855, p.1)

1855 – "Contracts Messrs. J. W. Cobb and Co. tender for the conveyance of the mail daily between Melbourne and Mount Blackwood ... been accepted." (Local Intelligence, 13 Oct 1855, p.5)

1855 – "Reduced Fares. Cobb And Co.'s Coaches To Castlemaine. Fare, £2 10s. Booking Offices—Telegraph Stage Offices, 23 Bourke street. Victoria Booking Office, Bull and Mouth. Cobb And Co., Proprietors." (Advertising, 21 Nov 1855, p.8)

1855 – "Telegraph Stage Office, and General Agency Depot, No. 23, Great Bourke-street East ... having purchased the above concern ... Merchandise, Luggage, Swags, and Parcels forwarded at the shortest notice and lowest rates. Cobb and Co.'s Coaches start every day for Castlemaine, Bendigo, Maryborough, &c ... T. K. Newton, Proprietor." While written on the same page "Romantic Township of Broadmeadows—Two Acres for Sale, overlooking the old church ruins and the valley of the Moonee Ponds. W. F. Westall, 49 Queen-street. Title—Crown grant." (Advertising, 26 Nov 1855, p.8)

Off for the goldfields

"OFF FOR THE GOLDFIELDS. (From The Melbourne Morning Herald, June 18. 1855) Time, a quarter to six on a very dark, and cloudy Melbourne May morning; place, the front of Adams and Co.'s express office, near the corner of Collins and Queen streets ; present, the principal object, Cobb's coach, ready horsed and coachmanned. Four unmistakably well-bred quadrupeds paw Collins street eager for action, and the driver is a tall, thin, athletic Jonathan, cool and polite, with a sharp nose, which serves as index to as thoroughly acute a collection of features as ever were seen together upon one countenance. He strides round his charge in his long boots, his nose and eyes intensely investigative you feel sure, though you cannot in the yet dark morning distinctly see either. He adjusts a strap here, and a buckle there. He pats this horse, and exchanges a confidential communication that the passengers now come up pretty briskly, as if afraid of being too late. Most of them have comforters round their necks, and all of them are evidently dressed in a hurry. They take their places upon seats ranged very conveniently in three rows on the inside, and the body of the vehicle is very comfortably hooped and canvassed over as a protection from the weather. There are also other seats on the outside, almost all of which are soon occupied.

Cobb is evidently prospering, and deserves it. A hasty glance through the gloom of the inside reveals a mixture of commercial faces squatter faces ; and professional faces. There are also two ladies; One is a young wife just arrived from England, and going to join her husband at Bendigo—this fact we cannot help overhearing as conveyed in the communicativeness of female talk—the other is a very young girl, pretty and intelligent, going back to her family at Sandhurst from a sometime stay in Melbourne. The latter is evidently under the protection of one who somehow does not seem to be either her cousin, or uncle, or father, or husband ; but he presides over her with a chancery severity of guardianship, as of one having responsibility combined with authority ... There are few of the observation we are enabled to make upon our travelling companions after everybody is settled down into his or her place, and whilst waiting now impatiently to be off.

Half a dozen loungers are collected even this early to see us depart ; for the last few minutes before the start of a public coach seems to be everywhere a matter of interest to chance wayfarers. Two small boys now rush up with the morning's 'Herald' and 'Argus,' just wet from the machines. *Come*, cries an impatient voice from the inside, *we're all ready now, what are we waiting for? Six o'clock*, pithily responds the sharp-faced Jonathan. *Why, it is six*, replies the other. *Not by the Post-office*, rejoins the driver. He calmly exchanges a few sentences with one or two of the attendants, and then, with an apparently satisfied feeling that 'the hour is come' ... he very deliberately mounts the box. He has no sooner gathered the ribbons in his hands, when one—two—goes the Post Office clock. Before the third stroke, off bounds our nags to the *Hi!* of Razorface as we dash down Collins street. Murmurs of *Wonderful fellow, Jonathon*, and *Punctual devils they are, to be sure*, are exchanged amongst our insides as we round the corner, cleverly clearing a Corporation cut, and we rattle away through the yet clear Elizabeth-street at the satisfactory rate of some eleven or twelve miles an hour.

What a terrible noise, says little Cestui-quo trust, to the Trustee, *what a terrible noise the coach makes, I hope we shall have no accident, I'm a terrible coward. It's all right*, returns the Trustee, *I believe in Cobb and in all his coaches. They are as strong as iron, wood and leather can make them, and I've immense confidence in the fine passenger-assuring composure of that sharp-faced charioteer. He is master of his business. Hi*, shouts the driver at this very point, to his horses, as they dash through a deep mud hole. Bump goes every head nearly to the ceiling of the coach, and down comes every one upon his seat, as if concussion of the brain were not known in Victoria. *Oh ! gracious! cry the ladies. D—a*, grinds the squatter from between his hard set teeth. *Did you say something about compensation, sir ?* asks another of the squatters, as if having merely caught the latter syllabics of Corydon's exclamation. *All right*, cries a hopeful passenger, and away we continue to rattle at the old rate, and you feel, for you cannot see, that our driver's eyes and mouth are still looking keen and composed as ever.

And so we come to Flemington. A man here shouts to us from the roadside. *Is that the coach to Castlemaine ?* We pull up. Two men come forward, each with two bundles. One only be accommodated, so he screws his bundles in amongst a labyrinth of legs, under seats, and then the new passenger, a lucky digger, jumps in and takes his seat. Away go the prads as before at a rattling pace. The bumps are occasionally almost dislocative of the anatomy of the passengers, but by degrees we learn to guard against them, and they seem to be tolerated in consideration of the pace.

In something like an hour and a quarter we reach Keilor, the road to this place being greatly improved in the last two years. Here we change horses for the first time, an operation which on this journey takes place about every ten or eleven miles. Having taken no contemporary note of the fact, I really forgot whether we breakfasted here, or ten miles onwards. All I know is—my brain being shaken into a sort of mere semi-conscious batter—that we did breakfast somewhere and that it was not good ... This business takes about twenty minutes. It is now broad daylight, and we are gratified to find that on all sides of us (as we travel) land is being extensively, enclosed and cultivated and every now and then we see a plough at work." (Glances at the Gold-fields of Victoria, 26 Jun 1855, p.3)

Freeman Cobb leaves Australia—Cobb and Co. continues

1856 – DINNER "Freeman Cobb, Esq.—We have much pleasure in learning that a complimentary dinner is to be given to this gentleman on his departure from the colony by the Royal Charter. Mr. Cobb has conferred great benefits on the country by his energetic and successful efforts to establish communication with the interior, and we sincerely trust that a large party of good colonists will meet him, and show that they appreciate his services. We are authorised to state that the dinner will take place at the Criterion Hotel, on Friday, the 23rd inst., and that tickets can be had on application to the following parties:—Messrs. Rogers, Warfield, Lord, and Co.; Messrs. Fisher, Ricards, and Co.; H. Flint, Esq., Bourke-street; and Lachlan Mackinnon, Esq., Argus office.— Argus." (Advertising, 23 May 1856, p.3)

1857 – "COACHING.—We observe that Messrs. Cobb and Co. have found it necessary, in order to meet the increasing passenger traffic between the city and the Mount Alexander gold-fields, to run a line of stages, leaving Melbourne at half-past seven a.m., in addition to their six and eight o'clock lines.

The high repute in which Cobb and Co. stand as coach proprietors, and the excellence of their arrangements for the despatch and accommodation of passengers, is a guarantee to the public that the extension of their operations will be marked by those characteristics which have won for them so large a share of public support." (Domestic Intelligence, 15 Oct 1856, p.5)

1857 – "TENDERS ... for alterations and additions to Messrs. Cobb and Co.'s Offices, Bourke-street." (Advertising, 10 Nov 1857, p.3)

1859 – "NOTICE. The proprietors of Cobb and Co.'s Telegraph line of coaches, beg to intimate to the public that they are in no way connected with a certain two-horse line, styled Cobb's Washington Express, or the Little Go. They are induced to give this notice in consequence of numerous enquiries having been made at their offices concerning their connection with the said line, an erroneous impression which the very close approximation to the title of Cobb and Co. seems to have given rise to. (Signed) Cobb & Co., Per E. T. Foley, Agent." (Advertising, 8 Mar 1859, p.1)

1860 – "NOTICE.—On and after Wednesday, 29th August, Cobb and Co.'s Booking Office will be at No. 35 Bourke street, next door to the Albion Hotel." (Advertising, 14 Sep 1860, p.3)

1861 – "COBB AND CO.'S AUSTRALIAN EXPRESS PARCELS DELIVERY. Principal Offices : No. 90 Bourke street east. No. 81 Collins street west. Express Waggons leave the Company's Central Depot, No. 90 Bourke street east, to deliver parcels throughout Melbourne ... Parcels will be delivered at any of Cobb and Co.'s offices, at the various townships in the interior ... additional rates for inland carriage ... stamps may be purchased at any of the booking stations in Melbourne and the suburbs, at any Cobb and Co.'s offices in the interior, or at the following stations in the city, where order boxes will be found ... Messrs Sands and Kenny, 46 Collins street west; Mr S. Mullen, 25 Collins street east; Mr M. T. Gason, 139 Elizabeth street; Mr H. T. Dwight, 234 Bourke street east; Mr A. J. Smith, 30 Swanston street; Additional order-boxes at—Victorian Railway Station, Spencer street; Melbourne and Hobson's Bay Railway Station, Flinders street; Cole's Wharf, Flinders street; M'Combe's Auction Mart, 81 Collins street west; Criterion Hotel, Collins street; J. Scott, Gertrude street, Collingwood; W. Costerton, chemist, Simpson's Road, opposite Shelley's Hotel. Suburban Offices and Agents : Richmond — B. Griffiths, Post-office, Bridge road; St. Kilda — W. Arnott, Post-office, 93 High street; Prahran — T. Angior, Post-office, Chapel street, near Gardiner's Creek road; South Yarra — T. Evans, auctioneer, Punt road; Windsor   T. A. Ewing, Post-office, Medical Hall, Chapel street; North Melbourne — J. W. Hind, 66 Madeline street, corner of Queensberry street; Collingwood — T. Maconochie, 87 Smith street ... Australian Stage Co. C. Russell, Manager." (Advertising, 22 March 1861, p.8)

Farewell Melbourne

1885 – "THE TRAVELLER ... Melbourne To Adelaide. So farewell Melbourne the Marvellous, city of towering warehouses, Parliament Houses—the new one as yet unfinished—Law Courts, Free Libraries, a colossal Post-Office, a monumental Town Hall, Colleges, Institutes, Cathedrals, Churches and Chapels innumerable, stately Government Offices, multitudinous drinking-bars—of which the sprightly barmaids are threatened with extinction under the clauses of Mr. Berry's new Licensing Bill.

Farewell Melbourne, city of handsome, elegant, and well-patronised theatres. At the Opera-house just now that approved actor, Mr. George Rignold, is, with Miss Kate Bishop, delighting the lieges in 'Called Back.' At the Theatre Royal the ever-green and always fascinating Mr. Dion Boucicault is drawing crowded houses nightly to see, now 'The Jilt' ... To the Nugget Theatre another class of the pleasure-loving Melbournians rush to see 'Oliver Twist' and 'The Streets of New York' ...

Farewell, then, Melbourne, city of clubs that are solemn and clubs that are sprightly, but all overflowing with thoughtful courtesy and generous hospitality all ready to be extended—from the puissant Melbourne Club, the resort of the proudest merchants and bankers and the most patrician squatters, to the genial Yorick, the chosen haunt of the wits and scholars of Melbourne ... fare-well to all the doctors, and especially farewell to all the Brobdingnagian Banks in Collins-street.

I cannot help it. I have been mildly accused by friends in this country of having 'Bank on the brain,' and such, perhaps, may be the case. But, I repeat, I cannot help it. When you first visit Venice do not the palaces on the Grand Canal take your breath away ? At Pisa are you not continually haunted by the Leaning Tower ? At Moscow is not the image of the Kremlin ever before you ? In Australia generally, and in Melbourne in particular, it is the Banks that haunt you, and subdue your sense to one absorbing feeling of wonder and reverence ... now of marble, now of bluestone, now of Kangaroo Point stone ... they smell of riches ... farewell Melbourne—until, at least, I return to survey thy marvels again, including thy big butchers' shops, thy brilliant suburbs, thy crowded omnibuses, thy splendid Botanical Gardens, thy remarkable Waxworks, and Mr. Cole's book arcade in Bourke-street.

A big steamer awaits me at the wharf, and I am bound for Adelaide." (The Traveller, 12 Sep 1885, p.42)

PRINCES BRIDGE Melbourne ... Length 3 spans 100 feet each, Width 99 feet inside of parrapet, Cost £1,500,000. (1889 Reminiscence of a visit to Victoria, Australia, April 1889, Part 1)

1840 Melbourne taken from near the west end of Collins Street (Feby) - Courtesy State Library Victoria

ca. 1880 [?] Corner Elizabeth and Bourke Street, Melbourne - State Library Victoria

1895 View of Flinders Lane, Melbourne (Looking west from Swanston Street) - Courtesy State Library Victoria

August 1889 On the sands, St. Kilda (Reminiscence of a visit to Victoria, Australia, April 1889 Part II, John Steel Jnr.) - Courtesy State Library Victoria

ca. 1860-1869 Sandridge now Port Melbourne - Courtesy State Library Victoria

1887 The Lawn at Flemington on Melbourne Cup Day - Courtesy State Library Victoria

ca. 1885 Flemington Race Course - Courtesy State Library Victoria

ca. 1880 T. White Family Butcher Shop, South Melbourne, Victoria (T. Chuck, photographer)
- Courtesy of Museums Victoria Collections

1889 Centennial Exhibition, Column representing Australian Gold, Australia's contribution to the world's gold (Reminiscence of a visit to Victoria, Australia, April 1889 Part I) - Courtesy State Library Victoria

1863 Great Flood in the Yarra, view from Princes Bridge looking South along the causeway which was impassable from the 15 to the 22 December 1863, being covered with a raging torrent 5 feet deep - Courtesy Museums Victoria Collections

1891 Great flood of July (J. J. Blundell) - Courtesy State Library Victoria

16 Dec 1863 Flood, Railway Station Flinders St., Melbourne - Courtesy State Library Victoria

1900-1909 Mitchell River in flood, Bairnsdale (W. Stanley Vogt) -
Gippsland and Regional Studies Collection (GRSC), Courtesy Federation University Australia

GEELONG

"Geelong, the town is seen to be girt about on its landward side by a zone of bowery suburbs composed of pretty villa and cottage residences, each with its appurtenance of flower gardens, and many of them embosomed in shrubberies ... On the high ground surrounding the town are the Scotch College, the Roman Catholic Orphanage and Convent of St. Augustine, and numerous handsome mansions. The town itself is one of the prettiest in Victoria, having the river Barwon at its back, and the waters of the Bay, enclosed by a picturesquely-curving shore, running out into miniature capes at Point Henry and Point Lillias ... In the heart of the town, what was formerly the large open space known as 'Market Square' is now covered, so far as its central area is concerned, by the exhibition building, in which are a theatre, gymnasium, assembly hall, and all the structures necessary for market purposes. Geelong contains as many as five-and-twenty places of worship, nine or ten banks, most of them handsome edifices, a grammar school, several State schools, a free library, a mechanics' institute with a thousand members and possessing a library of twenty thousand volumes ; the public buildings include a town hall, court-house, gaol, hospital, benevolent asylum, and government and other offices. The place is lighted with gas, and is supplied with an abundance of pure water from four reservoirs fed by gravitation from Stony Creek and the river Moorabool. An esplanade planted with trees connects the town with the botanical gardens, which are among the oldest in the colony ...

The country abounds in rabbits, and a manufactory for the preparation of the flesh for export was established at Colac, but it is not now fully employed, the cost of the raw material being beyond the paying rate. At Stoneyford and Camperdown there are similar preserving works which do more business. The rabbits are caught in traps and are sent in baskets from several stations along this line to the Geelong and Melbourne markets, as well as to the manufactories. The trappers are a queer nondescript class, mostly old men, who bear about their persons traces of much hard work and exposure. One man will work about a hundred traps, setting them before dark in well selected places ; these traps, which are not baited but partially concealed with a little loose earth, are each tethered to an iron pin driven into the ground to prevent the trapped animal running away with it. Once during the course of the night the sportsman goes round and resets them, after taking out any animals that may have been caught, and at daylight he repeats the visit to reap a second harvest. All that the trappers get for the rabbits is two shillings a dozen, and from eightpence to tenpence a dozen for their skins ; hence trapping is not a lucrative business, since the rabbits, innocent as they look, are extremely cunning, and soon become a match for their enemies." (The Picturesque Atlas of Australasia, 1888, p.256)

1886
Rabbit Trapper,
Colac,
The Picturesque
Atlas of Australasia,
p. 315

BALLARAT

"A Garden City, bright and fair to view,
From out primeval forests quickly grew;
Founded on gold, her portals surely stand,
While truth and honor guide our favored land
With crystal lakes and mines of fairy growth,
The Golden Centre of the Sunny South.

... IRWIN'S PROVINCIAL Commercial & Family Hotel (Opposite the Railway Station,) Lydiard Street, Ballarat. This old-established House has been thoroughly renovated, and fitted with every modern luxury. Moderate charges. Depot for Cobb and Co.'s Coaches. Passengers called for early trains and coaches. WILLIAM IRWIN, Proprietor ... F. Smith ... Pastrycook and Confectioner, Ballarat Café ...

Scarcely any one would imagine that thirty years ago a dense forest of heavy timber covered the site now occupied by the good city of Ballarat—or Ballaarat—a name given by the [First Nations Peoples], signifying a resting place or camping ground. At that time, a clear and limpid stream of water, the Yarrowee Creek, fed by the perennial springs of Mount Warrenheip, found its devious way through the level grassy flat, dotted here and there with the picturesque lightwood tree and the fragrant wattle ... selected by the early settlers as a choice site for a squatting homestead, and might have so remained but for the discovery of gold in 1851, which at once attracted a large population of hardy pioneers, who speedily set about forming a township, at first of canvas tents, but which has long since developed into brick and stone, and ranks as the Second City of Victoria, having a population of about 40,000, divided into three municipalities ...

The visitor who may arrive at the Western Railway Station, in Lydiard Street, will find no difficulty in locating himself, as the various hotels have a world-wide reputation, both for comfort and economy. Amongst these may be mentioned Craig's Royal Hotel, Lydiard Street, patronised by Royalty in the person of the Governor—Mr. G. Thompson, Proprietor ; Lester's Hotel, Sturt Street ; The George Hotel, Lydiard Street ; Brophy's Hotel, Sturt Street ; Buck's Head Hotel, Bridge Street ; Royal George Hotel, Lydiard Street ; Stork Hotel, Armstrong Street ; Irwin's Commercial Hotel, opposite Railway Station; Sayle's Edinburgh Castle Hotel, Armstrong Street ; Adelphi Hotel, Sturt Street ; Kirk's Unicorn Hotel, Sturt Street ; Fussell's Hotel, Sturt and Albert Streets ; Antcliffe's Club Hotel, Lydiard Street ; Town Hall Hotel, Armstrong Street ; Earl of Zetland Hotel, Bridge Street, &c., &c ... Sturt Street is the main artery, running east and west, and is intersected at right angles by Lydiard Street, the Post Office being at the north-east corner ... Cab Stand, where comfortable carryalls and buses may be had to all parts of the town and suburbs, at very reasonable fares ... Sturt Street may be easily distinguished by its extra width of 198 feet, the centre being planted with oak and eucalyptus, together with hardy shrubs, judiciously interspersed with seats, the whole forming a refreshing shade, and a pleasant relief to the eye, and giving rise to the well-earned title of the 'Garden City of Victoria,' bestowed by a celebrated traveller who was by no means a green-horn ...

City Hall ... Clock Tower ... cleanliness of the city and the busy bustle of its streets ... Gibbings' Livery Stables ... St. Patrick's Cathedral ... Presbyterian Church ... Fire Brigade Station, with its castellated tower ... Ballarat District Hospital, founded in 1856, one of the most extensive and useful institutions in Victoria, giving accommodation, gratis, to 150 in-patients, and medical advice and medicine to 600 out-patients per week.

It is justly considered a model of cleanliness and good management, and is peculiarly beneficial in a district where, in addition to all the ills that flesh is heir to, mining accidents are of necessity so frequent … Ballarat stands A 1 as a healthy locality ; even seaside Geelong has a mortality of 18*50 per 1000; Melbourne, 18*74 per 1000; and Sandhurst, 22*85 per 1000; while Ballarat, with its hospital, its asylums, and its dangerous mines, is only 17*08 per 1000 … its invigorating climate, good drainage, and cheap living render it a most desirable place of permanent residence … it may be mentioned that hundreds of citizens who went home to the old country for the purpose of settling down, after roaming over England, America, and the Continent, have returned to take up their permanent abode here, where all the advantages and comforts of modern civilization are to be found—the universal verdict being that

'there is no place like Ballarat after all' …

A little distance north of Sturt Street may be distinguished the clear and glistening waters of Lake Wendouree, covering an area of about 600 acres, the margin being tastefully laid out and planted all round, a distance of nearly four miles. Here may be seen flour mills, distilleries, tanneries, &c. together with handsome villa residences … At the eastern end is a handsome Fountain and Jetty, together with a number of private Boat Houses, in which are kept a fleet of racing yachts, second to none in the colonies, regatta matches being sailed each Saturday afternoon during the season … The Lake contains an unlimited supply of trout, bream, carp, and perch, the latter sometimes reaching a length of 17 or 18 inches, and weighing four or five pounds ; a fine trout caught the other day measuring over two feet long, and weighing 10 lbs …

Entering one of the numerous and tastefully-fitted up steam boats the voyage across is soon made (the distance being a good mile) to the Botanic Gardens … The gardens also contain … an acacia walk or 'lover's avenue,' a mile long, the whole under the able supervision of Mr. Longley, the curator … Bridge Street, especially on Saturday night … crowds of people shopping … Grenville Street … large wooden structure, capable of seating 3500 people, called the Alfred Hall … Victoria Street or Melbourne Road, three chains wide, planted with a double row of trees on either side, lined by pleasant gardens and tasteful private residences (broken here and there by quartz mining companies in full work) …

A short distance east of this will be found a historical locality, the site of the Eureka Stockade, where, on the morning of the 3rd December, 1854, the insurgent diggers, in arms against the oppression of the Victorian Government of that day, were defeated by the Queen's troops and police, after a short but determined resistance, a full account of which and of many other interesting early reminiscences of the town may be obtained in Mr. Withers' 'History of Ballarat' …

Perhaps one of the most important and novel sights of the town is the 'Corner,' in Sturt Street, where mining shares are bought or sold, but seldom exchanged ; the Mining Exchange is hard by, and the brokers, to the number of several hundreds, push their business out into the street, so that if you deal there you can scarcely be said to be taken in. Vast sums of money change hands daily, 50,000 in 'a single line' being looked upon as an ordinary transaction …

And now to epitomise. This up-country town is less than thirty years old, and extends north and south about five miles in a direct line, east and west about four-and-a-half miles, being one continuous line of buildings, covering 9500 acres, containing 90 miles of made streets, 10,000 residences, 56 churches, 500 hotels, and 20 state schools, with from 300 to 1000 scholars in each, besides colleges and private educational establishments of a high order. Under-ground are 90 miles of water pipes and 60 miles of gas pipes, to say nothing of gold mines, where horses are kept who never see the light of day, and where the precious metal is still being obtained to increase the world's treasures and add to the well-established prosperity of Ballarat, the

'Golden Centre of the Sunny South.'

Cobb's Coach Office is in Lydiard Street next to the Royal George Hotel, and thence coaches run to : St. Arnaud Road—Miners' Rest, 1s. 6d. ; Blowhard, 2s. ; Lear-month, 2s. 6d. ; Mount Bolton, 3s. ; Springs, 4s. ; Lexton, 5s. ; Lamplough, 5s. ; Avoca, 5s. ; Percydale, 6s. 6d. ; Moonambel, 5s. ; Red Bank, 5s. ; Stuart Mill, 5s. ; St. Arnaud, 5s. ; Landsboro', 10s. ; Stawell, 20s. ; Donald, 12s. 6d. ; Morton Plains, 20s. ; East Charlton, 12s. 6d.

Skipton Road—Smythesdale, 1s. ; Scarsdale, 1s. ; Newtown, 1s. ; Piggoreet, 2s. ; Derwent Jacks, 4s. 6d. ; Cape Clear, 5s. ; Bull Dog, 6s. ; Rokewood, 7s. 6d. ; Staffordshire Reef, 3s. ; Kangaroo, 3s. 6d. ; Carngham, 4s. ; Chepstowe, 6s. ; Linton, 2s. 6d. ; Skipton, 5s. ; Streatham, 10s. ; Bolac, 14s. ; Wickliffe, 14s. ; Wickliffe Road Station, 14s.

Gordons Road—Millbrook 'Moorabool,' 1s. 6d. ; Gordon, 2s. ; Egerton, 2s. ; Ballan, 4s. ; Blackwood, 7s. 6d. ; Trentham, 12s. 6d. ; Myrniong, 7s. 6d. ; Bacchus Marsh, 7s. 6d. ; Melton, 7s. 6d. ; Keilor Road Station, 7s. 6d.

Livery Stables. R, Gibbings', Doveton Street ; Wellington's, Armstrong Street, also Omnibus Proprietor ; Craig's Hotel Livery Stables, Bath Street ; Bull's Livery Stables, Doveton Street ; Old Harry's Stables, Peel Street. PUBLIC BATHS. The City Baths, Armstrong Street, swimming, 3d. ; first-class hot, 1s. 6d. ; second-class hot, 1s. ; third-class hot, 6d. ; hydropathic, 2s., or 6 tickets for 9s, ; also Grimbley's Baths, in Grenville Street." (Niven's guide book and souvenir of Ballarat : the garden city of Victoria, 1880-1889)

SANDHURST/BENDIGO

"Our artist has presented us with two illustrations of Sandhurst, one of Sandhurst as it was in 1853, and the other of that city as it stands in 1878, after the lapse of a quarter of a century. The strange contrast suggested by the two scenes gives us a fair idea of the rapidity and permanence of colonial or at any rate Victorian progress, and it shows the magic influence of gold in concentrating population and laying the foundation and securing the prosperity of a large district. The canvas town has grown into a vast city, ornamented with beautiful buildings, streets and gardens; and what was once but a temporary camping ground for armies of eager gold seeking diggers has become the lasting home of thousands of families, and the head centre of extensive enterprises, and industries. In earlier and slower times it would have taken centuries to have produced the city of Sandhurst, but there is a great difference between the wealth of the world in the days when the capture of a Spanish galleon laden with a few thousand pounds of gold was considered a prize of which the genius of a Chatham might be proud, and the present time, when tons of gold are yearly sent to England from the colonies without exciting any surprise or comment.

The city of Sandhurst is situated in the Valley of Bendigo, 101 miles from Melbourne, and at an elevation of 750 feet above the level of the sea. It is built on the east and west banks of the Bendigo Creek, which rises in the northern outskirts of the Mount Alexander ranges.

Looking north-east from these ranges, the highest peaks being Mount Herbert and Big-hill, the district may be seen stretching away down the valley as far as the eye can reach, the prospect being here and there broken by a succession of hills, among which the city stands. The sight to be seen from Big-hill now is far different from that which greeted the eyes of the traveller in 1853. Then the gentle slopes were for miles dotted with the white clusters of diggers' tents. Now, on every hand as we approach the city are to be seen marks of settlement, industry and wealth, all of which attest the transformation of the past, and the prosperity and success of the present. Now, instead of reaching Sandhurst in a Yankee waggon or a coach, we are conveyed there along a line of railway, the best and most expensive in the world, and a few minutes after dashing through the Big-hill Tunnel we are landed safely at the Mitchell street station, which is one of the most substantial and elegant railway stations of which the colony can boast. It is from Quarry-hill, a ridge adjacent to the railway station, and overlooking the main street of the city, that our artist gives us a bird's-eye view of Sandhurst as it is.

The name of Bendigo is one of world-wide fame, and the city is to old identities still more familiarly known by that name than that of Sandhurst. It is famous for its rich yields of gold in the early days of alluvial diggings, and still more celebrated in later days for its wealthy quartz mines and splendid wines. In 1853-4 Bendigo was the great wonder of the day, and the extent and activity of the field of industrial operations which it presented in that early time has hardly since been parallelled in the history of the colony. In the middle of 1852 it is estimated there were 50,000 diggers working on the banks of the Bendigo Creek where the city now stands. Those were the jolly times when gold was thrown away ; when £1 per ton per mile was charged for the carriage of goods; and when flour was £200 per ton. The alluvial diggings, however, were worked out in ten years, and then attention began to be directed to the quartz reefs as more lasting sources of wealth.

Ballarat has eclipsed Sandhurst in the rich and extensive character of her alluvial deposit, but Sandhurst has been unequalled by any district in Victoria for the steady and payable yields of its quartz mines. There are three main lines of reefs running through the city north and south. Those are clearly indicated in the bird's-eye view, the Hustler's Reef, the Garden Gully Reef and the New Chum and Victoria Reef. The Victoria Reef was opened in 1853 by Theodore Ballerstedt, an old pioneer in Bendigo mining, who, according to tradition, took tons of gold out of his mine, but never sank very deep. Almost simultaneously with the discovery of gold on the Victoria Reef the Hustler's Reef was opened by two men named J. Hustler and J. Harris. Last of all the Garden Gully Reef, situated between the two just named, was discovered and worked, and it has proved the richest and the largest in the district.

In 1855 Sandhurst was erected into a municipality, having an area of 3961 acres. Since that Quarry-hill, Golden Gully and Long Gully were added, making its area amount to 7500 acres. In 1871 it was proclaimed a city under Act of Parliament, and its population and revenue have continued to increase until at present it contains 27,000 inhabitants, and has an annual revenue of £25,600.

There are altogether 7190 dwellings within the boundaries of the city, to say nothing of a large number of splendid public buildings. Among these are the Royal Princess's Theatre, admitted to be next to the Academy of Music in Melbourne, the model theatre of Victoria; the Masonic Hall, unequalled by any building belonging to the Masonic brotherhood in Australia; a magnificently built hospital, which cost about £20,000; an asylum, which cost £18,000; two grand State schools, one on Gravel hill, and the other on Camp-hill, both being conspicuous edifices in our illustration. The gardens which are seen in the centre of the city is the Rosalind Park; or more commonly known as the Camp Reserve, from the circumstance that it was the site of the old police camp, as shown in the picture of Bendigo in 1853. This sketch represents the north-eastern slope of Camp-hill with Commissioner's Gully, now the site of a pretty reservoir, a cricket ground and bowling green in the background, and the police barrack in the front. Here was built the Government Treasury of those palmy days, and many who were then young preserve a lively recollection of splendidly mounted troopers and red jackets, who used to do patrol duty on this identical spot ... That scene, however, is now a thing of the past, though at this distance of time it becomes interesting to contemplate, when we compare it with the beautiful reserve which now graces the centre of the city, with its acclimatised trees and flowers, its cooling fountain and shady bower, and all the appearances of civilisation and culture." (Sandhurst—Past and Present, 27 Dec 1878, p.218)

Castlemaine

"*My first visit to Castlemaine, says Mr. Joseph Parker, was in 1845, when I accompanied my father, who came to hold an inquest ... he had a stump for the magisterial chair, and a policeman's back for his desk ... in a casual way he drops the remark, I washed gold in the Jim Crow Creek, 20 miles from Castlemaine, in 1849. I and three brothers were looking for rubies, at least there were red stones in the stream we thought were rubies; and we washed a lot of fine flaky yellow metal. I know now that it was gold. We gave it to our father, who sent it down to Governor Latrobe, and that's the last we heard of it.*" I feel fascinated at having before me the earliest living gold digger in Australia, who had fortune within his grasp if he had pursued the quest, or if the discovery had not been ignored by the then governing powers ... *It was in the same year, '49, continues Mr. Parker, that a [First Nations person] found a nugget at Forest Creek. He picked it up from amongst the tussocks to throw at a parrot. Forest, the shepherd, got it, and just kept it as a curiosity. He went away to some other station, but in '51, when the diggings started, returned and washed out gold in the creek, near his old hut*' ...

The rush to Forest Creek took place in [18]'51, before gold was discovered at Bendigo. Castlemaine became the camp for a detachment of the 40th Regiment, with Colonel Bull as the first Gold Commissioner. A township was surveyed, and the first land sale took place in March, 1853 ... The whole country seems to be turned inside out, and presents only a broken and irregular surface of many colored earths. In various places horse puddling machines are at work breaking up and rewashing for the second or third time auriferous earth from which the earlier diggers had, as they thought, extracted all the gold, but which is still found to contain quite sufficient to repay their successors ... Past Forest Creek we find at Castlemaine, which joins it, a neatly laid out township, with streets and squares, stone, brick and iron stores and houses, a church and chapels, large, substantial inns and all the essentials of an old community ... Castlemaine, according to this, had made great progress in two years' time ... One of my best authorities on the early days here is Mr. Norval Edwards, who owns to 91years. He is from the West county, a native of Frome, Somersetshire. He landed in Melbourne in 1851, and came straight up to Forest Creek, now Chewton. The diggings had just broke out. For miles the country was pegged out. The scrub was being cleared away, and tents erected in the bush.

As we sit in Mrs. Murphy's hospitable hotel, I, listening to this aged veteran, recognise the wonderful vitality of the early pioneers. *All,* says he, *that has been written about the early digging days is not up to the reality. No matter how extravagant it might seem, the truth was more startling. I have seen a man penniless in the morning, with no credit at the store, and have given him a few nuggets to buy tucker. Two hours afterwards he has come to me with two pannikins filled with dust, telling me to help myself. There were all sorts here ... the police ... were pretty rough on the diggers. There was too much chasing and chaining to logs ... After the Eureka stockade things were made better for the diggers ...*

At the Castlemaine Hotel there is the legend 'Cobb and Co.'s Office,' one once well known throughout the land, but now rapidly disappearing. In a few years I expect Cobb will ... be only a tradition. I do not think it is fully recognised that the early coaching men in Victoria were amongst the unappreciated pioneers of civilisation here. A more useful, arduous, or honorable occupation could not be found than in tooling the Mount Alexander coach over the Dividing Range, through the Black Forest, and across the Keilor Plains. In the fifties the arrival of the Melbourne coach at night was a great event at Castlemaine. All the notables sat up at the hotel waiting to hear the news. If the walls could speak one would have quaint reminiscence of the jests of Mr. Nicholas Fitzgerald; of the hearty laugh of Sir Thomas M'Ilwraith, then engineer for Cornish and Bruce, contractors for the railway; and of the quieter humor of Mr. A. W. Robertson. The days when Cobb was a power at Castlemaine are still regretted. People speak to me of Mr. Sweeny with the respect due to an honored pioneer; and Johnston's, of the livery stables, proudest boast is that his father came out to this country under engagement to Cobb's, as overseer at Castlemaine ... I love the Pioneers." (Castlemaine, 30 Sep 1893, p.32)

Just a snippet—1880s

"ALLANFORD ... a postal township and money-order office ... It is reached by Cobb's coach from Geelong. There are three places of worship in the town, and a common school; also two hotels. Population, 370 ... The township, and, in fact, the entire district, is liable to be flooded by the overflow of the Hopkins. In 1854, these floods rose to the height of 22 feet.

ARARAT ... Besides the quartz and alluvial mines, for which the district is famed, the agricultural, pastoral, and wine-making interests are well established ... two large flour mills, a meat-preserving factory, and soap and candle works, as well as several large hotels the most important and commodious being the Bull and Mouth, Scotts, Commercial, and the Ararat ... Stawell ... Ararat ... Hamilton ... at present the connection with these places is by coach which runs daily.

AVOCA ... The population of the town alone is 900 ... The hotels are the Avoca, Union, Victoria, Commercial, Bull and Mouth, and Albion. Both alluvial and quartz mining are carried on in the district.

BACCHUS MARSH ... a small township and telegraph, savings' bank, and money-order office, of about 500 inhabitants ... Coaches run to Keilor road station twice daily, and connect with the train. A coach also goes to Ballaarat every day, Sundays included ... The Border Inn is the principal hotel ... A county court is held every six months, and a court of petty sessions fortnightly.

BAIRNSDALE ... The hotels are the Commercial, Main, Court House, Bridge Imperial, and Club ... there are valuable lead and silver mines at Buchan, about 50 miles from Bairnsdale. Hop growing is now being profitably carried on ... When the lakes are opened (about six months of the twelve) there is weekly communication with Melbourne by steamer; Cobb's coaches also run from Melbourne via Sale daily ... The townships in the Bairnsdale district are Lucknow (2 miles), Allanvale (12 miles), Sarsfield (12 miles) Bruthen (15 miles), Omeo (70 miles), Swift's Creek (64 miles), Bendoc (170 miles), Bonang (180 miles), Crooked River (90 miles), each of which are mining townships ... There is a tri-weekly coach and mail communication via Sale with the metropolis.

BALLAARAT ... has for some time been the leading gold-field town of Victoria, and is now the next city in importance to Melbourne. It owes its present position to being the centre of perhaps the richest gold-yielding district in the world ... two fire brigades ... 84 miles of made streets, 164 miles of footpath, over 10,000 dwellings, and 47,156 inhabitants ... The hotels and inns are numbered at about 300, with eight iron foundries, thirteen breweries and distilleries, four flour mills, a woollen mill, and other factories.

BEECHWORTH ... It is the principal town of the Murray district and of the celebrated Ovens gold-fields ... The hotels are the Star Alliance, Oriental, Imperial, Victoria, Albion, Commercial, Post Office, Corner, and others ... Population of the town is about 3,167 persons.

BELFAST/PORT FAIRY ... a seaport town ... Melbourne, to and from which four steamers ply weekly; there is also overland communication by coach daily from Geelong ... The population of the borough is estimated at about 2,484 persons ... There are two steam flour-mills in the town ... It is entirely surrounded by water, and is much frequented by sightseers.

BUNINYONG ... a mining and agricultural township ... The principal hotels are the Buninyong, Crown, Courthouse, Exchange, Robert Burns, Eagle and Princess Royal ... There are 13 distinct reefs and 16 squares miles of auriferous ground being worked ... the town has been principally famous for the gold-fields in the vicinity ... About 3 miles distant from Buninyong is the celebrated Hiscock's reef, named after Hiscock, who is said to have been the discoverer of gold in Victoria, and to have found it in this place. The population is over 1,814, of the entire shire, 16,000. The Buninyong Telegraph is the local newspaper, and is published three times a week." (The Australian handbook and almanac and shippers' and importers' directory, 1876) while in 1887 "Gold was found here in the very beginning of the goldfields era, but it does not seem to be fully known whether it was first discovered at Buninyong, at Clunes, or at Forest Creek ...

1851 Gold buyer, Forest Creek (S. T. Gill,
1818-1880, artist) - Courtesy State Library Victoria

The little town is thoroughly complete as to its roads and bridges, and it possesses valuable public institutions. But it is not so interesting from a pictorial point of view as it was in the 'fifties.' There was then a continual stream of passengers between Geelong and the golden land of the Caledonian lead and the 'jewellers' shops' of Ballarat East, and as there were no railways to carry them, and Messrs. Cobb and Co. had not yet systematised the passenger traffic by coach, most of the adventurers effected their journey on foot, while paying carriers and draymen for the conveyance of their luggage. A hundred horse and bullock teams would be timed to arrive at Buninyong at nightfall, and then brisk business ensued during the hours of the evening, the travellers purchasing their provisions and other necessaries at the stores, while the drivers attended to the wants of their cattle.

When the American coaching firm had got into fair working order, with their springless vehicles supported on leathern thorough-braces after the manner of 'out-west' stages, they rapidly came into a large business at high rates, and made money as rapidly. They began with four-horse teams, which soon gave place to teams of six and eight, and some of their drivers were eminent public characters. 'Cabbage-tree Ned' and 'Gin-and-Bitters' were as well-known as Mr. Latrobe or Sir Charles Hotham, and though they were rough men, given to 'cussing up grades,' they were exceedingly skilful whips, and could control a team of half-broken horses in a way that an English coachman, though perhaps more …

The surrounding district has both alluvial and gold-bearing quartz mines, but the latter are now the more productive. Three miles off lies Hiscock's Reef, named after its discoverer, who is one of two or three claimants to the honour of having been the first discoverer of gold in Victorian territory. Buninyong is now a very pretty and healthy little township, and should by no means be omitted by those who wish to study the district." (Picturesque atlas of Australasia/edited by Andrew Garran, p.269)

"CARISBROOK … a municipal town and money-order office, post-office savings' bank, and railway and telegraph stations, on Tullaroop, Mount Greenock, and Deep Creeks … The hotels are the Carisbrook, Kirk's, Railway, and Britannia. There is a mechanics' institute, with library in the town … four churches, common school … and racecourse. The local industries consist of a tannery and steam flour-mill. The population numbers 941 persons. The district is an agricultural one.

CASTLEMAINE … a place of great importance in the early days of the gold-fields … It is located at the junction of the Barker's and Forest creeks … The town is lighted with gas, and supplied with water from the Malmsbury and Expedition Pass reservoirs, and has a population of 7,308 persons. The district numbers 18,941 souls. The diggings in the neighbourhood were once very numerous, and were among the first discovered in Australia … The hotels are the Criterion, Castlemaine, Imperial, Cumberland, Royal, Corner, Bedford, Goldsmith's, and many others.

CLUNES … Gold was first discovered here on July 1 1851. The mining is principally quartz reefing … The Club, Bull and Mouth, and Nag's Head are the principal hotels … The town and mines are well supplied with water from the Bullarook forest. The waterworks, which are the most perfect of their kind in the colony, cost £75,000." (The Australian handbook and almanac and shippers' and importers' directory, 1876)

"Clunes is reached at a distance of twenty-three miles from Ballarat … Since 1857, the Port Phillip company, using the very best obtainable skill and the most highly improved mechanical appliances, has compelled the quartz to yield up gold to the value of about two million sterling, while the New North Clunes company has realised about half that amount in one-half the time … The town has had its trials by ordeal of fire and of water, and was at one time flooded out as regards its low-lying shops and houses, while those on a higher level were suffering a conflagration. Nevertheless it has triumphed over all its difficulties, and is now a flourishing and important settlement in the enjoyment of self-government and of all the appliances of civilisation." (Picturesque atlas of Australasia/edited by Andrew Garran, p.270)

"CRESSY … a post town and money-order … on the road between Geelong and Warrnambool, the coaches to and from which places pass through the town. Squatting is almost exclusively followed in the district.

CRESWICK … an important gold-fields township … on the Tullaroop creek … a good hospital, mechanics' institute with 1,000 volumes, post and telegraph office, court house, police barracks, railway station, and many well-built business premises; there are also branches of the Australasian, New South Wales, and Commercial Banks … The hotels are the British, American, Bull and Mouth, Bridge, Farmers' Arms, and others. There are a new and commodious State school (to seat 800 children), also grammar and private schools … The diggings in the neighbourhood are of great extent and richness. They were discovered early in 1852.

DAYLESFORD … a thriving township, money-order office, and telegraph station, in the county of Talbot, electoral district of Creswick, and police district of Castlemaine, on the Wombat creek, a few miles from the river Loddon, 78 miles NW. of Melbourne. The town, which is a comparatively large one, contains a mechanics' institute, with a library of 1,035 volumes, has a county court, court of general sessions, a hospital, branches of the Colonial, Victoria, and Union Banks, and many well-built stores, also a masonic hall, and the various orders of friendly societies are largely represented. There are agencies of the Queen, London and Lancashire, Imperial, London, Liverpool and Globe, National, Victoria, Alliance, and Mutual Provident Insurance Companies. The principal hotels are the Victoria, Volunteer, Royal, Royal Mail, and Commercial. The Church of England, Wesleyan, and Roman Catholic bodies have roomy and substantial buildings, while the Presbyterians, Bible Christians, and Primitive Methodists have smaller churches. A State school, to hold from 800 to 1,000 scholars, and a temperance hall, are about to be erected.

The population numbers, within the municipal precincts, about 5,000 persons, the entire district being 18,525. The newspaper is the Daylesford Mercury. The district has many farms, and the breadth of land under cultivation is rapidly increasing, but mining is the principal business of the people … The diggings were principally alluvial, and the leads comparatively shallow ; but the great body of miners are now employed in working the quartz lodes. There are numerous gold-mining companies, who pursue their operations in the most approved method, with expensive machinery. Several of these companies are reported to be doing well. Three coaches run daily to Malmsbury railway station, connecting with the trains for Melbourne ; coaches also leave daily for Castlemaine, and for Guildford, and Ballaarat via Creswick." (The Australian handbook and almanac and shippers' and importers' directory, 1876)

"Sweet Daylesford, loveliest village of the hills and valleys! A village only in the poetical sense, for it has been a borough longer than any country town in Victoria, and is a large and important centre.

But what strikes the visitor more than anything else as he walks from the railway station, is the manner in which the houses spread themselves over a wide area, so that each and all enjoy that degree of isolation which ensures freedom, the practice of horticulture, and the enjoyment of the fresh and bracing climate. And what a climate it is! In the middle of summer, when dwellers in cities are being slowly done to death by the devastating influence of hot winds, and intolerable atmosphere, Daylesford, in happy comparison, is cool, calm, and content ... Who would fardels bear to groan and sweat under a weary life in congested cities, when they may seek Daylesford and peace! There are folk who feel it requisite in the summer season to fly to adjoining colonies for rest and change, and our object in this holiday number is to show that such a course is unnecessary when we have so many charming resorts in Victoria ... Daylesford is the natural centre of a bewilderingly large number of beautiful places, and spots of interest.

So far back as 1852 an intrepid band of pioneers pushed their way into these mountainous regions, and the discovery of gold occasioned a great rush to the localities which became, and have continued, known as Wombat Flat, Connell's Creek, Doctor's Gully, Sailor's Gully, and the Racecourse. The original name bestowed upon what is now Daylesford was Jim Crow ... Among others who constituted the early settlers, were many Italians, numbers of whom still remain. Gold was, of course, the principal quest in the feverish excitement, and in the natural sequence of events the land was tested for its agricultural value. The result is evidenced to day, in the acres and acres of ground under cultivation, 'where health and plenty cheer the laboring swain'." (Daylesford, 1 Dec 1900, p.43)

"DIGGER'S REST ... a post town and railway station on the Victorian railways ... The Digger's Rest is the name of the hotel. The land in the district is best suited for sheep and cattle farming. A local resident describes it as 'dreary, monotonous plain, possessing few features of value.'

DRUMMOND ... a post town ... The communication is by means of Cobb's coach from Malmsbury. The Coliban river and the Back and Kangaroo creeks are the nearest streams. Agricultural district.

ELPHINSTONE ... a small township and station, on Sawpit Gully creek ... It is near the Coliban waterfalls where there is good fishing to be got, and the scenery is beautifully picturesque, while the locality is noted for its salubrious character. Mining was extensively followed in the district ... Hotels, Burns' and Lonsdale's. Population 250.

EMERALD HILL ... a municipal town suburban to Melbourne, on the Sandridge road about 13 miles south of the city, and very near what was once known as Canvas Town ... To those who enjoy yachting, the ornamental waters in the Albert park are a great attraction. The population is returned at 19,500.

GISBORNE ... a post town, money-order office ... on the Saltwater river and the Mount Alexander road ... The hotels are the Telegraph, Victoria, and Gaythorne. The surrounding land is principally of an agricultural character, in some parts heavily timbered. In March, 1875, 716 acres of wheat, 1,273 of oats, 281 of potatoes, and 16 of vines were under cultivation. Population of town, 600 ; town and shire 3,796. The local paper is the Gisborne Times, published every Saturday.

GRAYTOWN ... a municipal town ... The hotels are the Bendigo, Caledonian, Post Office, and London. Cobb and Co.'s booking office is at the Post Office Hotel.

HAMILTON ... the metropolis of the western interior, is situated on the Grange Burn creek, ... 219 miles W. of Melbourne. It contains a fine hospital and benevolent asylum, a shire office, a mechanics' institute, with a library of 1,760 volumes, town hall, and the usual Government buildings ... The Alexandra College for Ladies is now completed, having cost £3,500, and a new State school capable of accommodating 500 children is in course of erection. A large building on the site of the present post-office is soon to be erected to accommodate the Treasury Land Office, and Post and Telegraph offices. ... the Western Racing Club furnishes a grand meeting once a year, with occasional programmes of bye-races ... There are eight hotels, of which the Victoria and the Commercial are the principal, besides numerous stores and business establishments ... including the suburbs, the town may be said to contain about 4,000 people ... Hamilton is at present the coaching centre for the whole of the western district.

HASTINGS ... a post town ... It can be reached from Cobb's office, and occasionally by steamer. The hotels are the Bay View and Westernport ... is an extensive fishing station, and supplies the Melbourne market to a considerable extent. The neighbourhood is also noted for its orchards. Two new industries in the shape of salt-works have recently been projected, but are at present stopped.

HEXHAM ... a post town, telegraph station, and money-order office ... The hotel is the Woolshed. Population, about 300. The surrounding country is mostly of a pastoral character.

HIT OR MISS ... a postal town ... Population, said to be 80. There is mining all round at a short distance. It is supposed to be deep ground, and that the courses of deep leads will be discovered.

INGLEWOOD ... a mining town ... Coaches ply regularly to and from the railway, also from Dunolly ... The hotels are the Royal, George, Adelphi, Harp of Erin, Pelican, Empire State, and 'Forget-me-Not.' ... The gold is principally found in quartz reefs, and employs several crushing mills in its reduction.

KILMORE ... a municipal town ... It is situated on the creek of the same name on the Beechworth road ... the district is an agricultural one ... wheat ... oats ... barley ... potatoes ... hay ... The town contains a mechanics institute ... a hospital, and the usual official buildings. The Episcopalians, Presbyterians, Primitive Methodists, and Wesleyans, and Roman Catholics have places of worship, with schools attached to them. There is also a State school ... Victoria and Colonial Banks, and agencies of the Alliance, Victoria, Northern Imperial, Mutual Provident, National, and Liverpool and London and Globe Insurance Companies ... 78 miners are employed on the 27 miles of auriferous ground in the district. The plant in use is valued at £1,800, and consists of 1 steam-engine of 25 horse-power, 2 crushing machines and 16 head of stamps. The Kilmore, Royal Oak, All Nations, Railway, and Criterion are among the leading hotels. The Kilmore Free Press and Kilmore Advertiser are the local newspapers.

KYNETON ... is an important agricultural and mining town upon the river Campaspe, 52 miles NW. of Melbourne by road, and 57 by railway. The population is nearly 3,000, and the town has upwards of 10 miles of macadamised streets, and 16 miles of footpaths.

It is lighted with gas, and is well built and laid out. The principal buildings are the court-house, post-office, hospital, mechanics' institute ... halls ... Branch Banks ... six churches ... Insurance Companies ... and nineteen hotels ; among the leading are the Junction, Alexander's, Wedgwood's, the Newmarket, and Royal Oak. Its manufactures comprise three breweries, three flour-mills, two implement manufactories, and a coach factory ... wheat ... barley ... potatoes ... pease, beans, millet, and sorghun ... hay ... wine ... A weekly grain market is held, and a fair takes place every month in the shire yard for the interchange of horses, cattle, and farm stock of all kinds. There is an exhibition of stock and farm produce held annually in the yards of the Kyneton Agricultural Association ... There are about 30 mining companies engaged in the search for gold. Several of the quartz reefs are of proved richness, and in some instances expensive plants have been erected for their development. The mining plant is valued at £69,524 ; 549 horse-power being employed in driving 24 engines ... schools, including two superior boarding establishments for boys, and two for girls.

Outside the shops in the high street, the carts, buggies and drays of rural folk who have come in shopping are drawn up, and are receiving parcels and packages of divers shapes and sizes. The yards of agricultural implement makers are occupied with ploughs, carts and waggons in various stages of manufacture or repair, and inside the wayfarer may

> *See the flaming forge,*
> *And hear the billows roar,*
> *And catch the burning sparks that fly*
> *Like chaff from a threshing floor.*

LAMPLOUGH ... is a post town ... reached by rail to Maryborough or Ballaarat, and coach thence. There are two hotels ... The population of the township numbers about 100.

LATROBE BRIDGE (Longford) ... a post town ... situated at the junction of the Glengarry and Thompson rivers ... Population, about 60. The route is via Port Albert, by steamer, thence by coach 47 miles, or by Cobb's Gipps Land coach to Sale. Pastoral district." (The Australian handbook and almanac and shippers' and importers' directory, 1876)

"LEXTON From Clunes the railway trends north-west and crosses Stony Creek, upon which stands the hamlet of Caralulup ; a short distance to the south-west of this village is Mount Mitchell, and still farther in the same direction the little quartz-reefing settlement of Lexton, which, by a coach line, is in communication with the railway at Talbot Station." (Picturesque atlas of Australasia/edited by Andrew Garran, p.271)

1864 Sheep Shearing, (Frederick Grosse, 1828-1894, engraver) - Courtesy State Library Victoria

"LILYDALE ... a village and money-order office on the Olinda creek ... There is daily coach communication from the Albion Hotel, Bourke Street ... Lilydale has four hotels, a State school, and English, Presbyterian, United Free Methodist, and Roman Catholic places of worship. Population, 350.

LINTON ... Gold was first found here in the winter of 1855.

LISMORE ... a post town ... with which the communication is by Cobb's coach from Geelong twice a week. Nearest water Brown's Water Holes. The township numbers one hotel, two stores, a church, and a manse ; the district is of a pastoral and agricultural character.

LOCKWOOD ... county of Bendigo, a post town on Bullock creek ... Sandhurst, on the Melbourne and Echuca line, is the nearest railway station, and is distant about 9 miles in an easterly direction ; Cobb's coaches running daily. There are four hotels ... There are quartz reefs in the neighbourhood ... orchards and vineyards. Population, 120.

MANSFIELD a post town ... It is situated on Ford's creek ... Cobb's coaches daily from Sandhurst. The hotels are the Marong, East Lothian, Sims', and Bullock Creek ... There are also two quartz-crushing plants at work.

MATLOCK ... is the extreme eastern township in the county ... The main road to North Gipps Land turns off at this point, running through Jordan, the Red Jacket, and Aberfeldy to Walhalla and Sale. The surrounding ranges abound with quartz reefs ... The township is the business centre ... There is daily mail communication with Melbourne—three times a week via Jamieson and thrice by Marysville on the Yarra track, Cobb's coach reaching the latter place throughout the year, and thence by pack-horse to Matlock and Wood's Point. In December 1873, the whole of Matlock was destroyed by fire nor has it been re-built, except so far as one store. The township now consists of two stores, one hotel (the All Nations), a State school, a post-office, and a few houses. Population, 217.

MOONAMBEL ... a rising township and money-order office situated on the Mountain creek ... Three of Cobb and Co.'s coaches arrive and depart daily for Ballaarat, St. Arnaud, and Pleasant creek ... There are two hotels in the township, the Commercial (Glover's), and the Shire (Gilchrist's). There is also one flour-mill and a large soap manufactory in the township. Mining and farming are the chief industries of the inhabitants, who number about 280.

PENSHURST ... a township, telegraph, and money-order office ... The traveller can take the rail to Geelong, and thence the coach ... a steam flour-mill and two tanneries ... stone churches ... a State school, four hotels—Penshurst, Prince of Wales, Cricketers' Arms and Victoria, a shire hall, temperance hall and a mechanics' institute. The banks are the Victoria and National, and the insurance agencies the Alliance, Queen, and National. Mount Rouse was formerly an extinct volcano ; it belongs to the town, and is used as a place of recreation for the inhabitants. Population, about 600. There is a Moravian mission at Herrubut, near Penshurst.

PIGGOREET ... a postal, telegraphic, mining town ... Ballaarat is the nearest railway station, 21 miles distant, and is reached by coach daily. Coaches also run to Smythesdale 9 miles distant ... There are several sheep stations in the district. Population, 416 ... three hotels—the Court Royal, Royal Mail, and Try Again. The mining villages in the vicinity are Golden Lake, The Exchequer and Derwent Jacks. Each has but a small population.

PORTARLINGTON ... a postal town ... is reached by rail to Geelong, and thence either by coach, sailing craft, or occasional steamer in the summer months. There are two hotels, the Family and the Bay View ...

The district is an agricultural one, and has achieved some celebrity for the fine onions it produces. The population numbers 270 persons ; but in the summer many persons from Geelong and Melbourne reside here, it being an excellent seaside watering place.

QUEENSCLIFF ... at the entrance of Port Phillip Bay ... on a small peninsula, which is connected with the mainland by a narrow neck of land, about 400 yards in width. Two lighthouses mark the entrance ... Coaches run daily to and from Geelong, 20 miles distant, in winter, and twice daily during the summer months, when a steamer also plies three times a week to and from Melbourne ... the new baths recently erected by the Borough Council being both safe and commodious. Among the hotels are the Royal, the Australasian (better known as Adman's Hotel), Commercial, Victoria, and Barkly Arms.

RAGLAN a township on Fiery creek, 122 miles WNW. of Melbourne, on the railway line between Ararat and Ballaarat. A coach runs to Beaufort railway station, 7 miles, daily. The Fiery Creek Diggings, at one time about the richest in the colony, are in the vicinity.

ROKEWOOD ... a post town ... The principal hotel is called the Rokewood ... In the neighbourhood are some diggings of a not very prolific character ... The nearest railway station is Leigh Road ; to this a coach runs regularly. Population, 276.

SALE ... is the principal town in the Gipps Land district. It is situated on the Thomson river, 140 miles ESE. of Melbourne, the communication with which is overland by daily coach, a journey of 24 hours, or by steamer, via the Lakes, passengers embarking at the Latrobe Wharf, a distance of 3 miles from Sale, thence by steamer. A line of railway from Melbourne to Sale is now in course of construction ... The hotels are the Club, Royal Exchange, Albion, Prince of Wales, Criterion, Cricket Club, Star, and some others. Three breweries, a flour-mill, and a tannery are in operation. It is a money-order office, savings' bank, and post-office, and also a telegraph station. The population is about 3,200 ... The police have their head-quarters here.

SANDHURST more familiarly known under its old name of Bendigo, which is, however, the native name applied to the whole district, is a postal, telegraphic, money-order and savings' bank borough township ... The electoral district comprises Sandhurst proper and its suburbs, Lockwood, Long Gully, and Spring creek, and is represented in Parliament by two members, the present ones being Messrs. Angus Mackay and R. Burrowes ... on the Bendigo creek, and on the main line of railway between Melbourne and Echuca ... considered by some to be second only in the colony to Melbourne, the metropolis ... This may fairly be considered to be the metropolitan gold-field ... The discovery of rich alluvial deposits of gold in 1851 ... At present there are about 800 quartz mining leases in the district, covering an area, speaking approximately, of 18,000 acres ...

The main street, named Pall Mall, abounds on one side with fine handsome and imposing brick and stone shops and stores, the opposite side being a reserve known as Rosalind Park ... the Lyceum and Royal theatres, and St. James's Hall ... The city is well lighted with gas, and supplied with water from the Bendigo Waterworks ... The industries of Sandhurst, beside that of gold mining, are numerous, the most important being large iron-founding, coach-building, pottery, stone-cutting tanning, brick and tile-making, cordial manufacture, farming and wine growing dimensions ... Hotels are very numerous : the leading ones are the Metropolitan, Freemasons', Shamrock, Temple Court City Family, Lyceum, Commercial, Exchange and Victoria. Population, 25,000. Mining operations in the entire Sandhurst district give employment to 7,263 miners ... There are 148 horse puddling-machines, 1,420 stamp-heads, and numerous smaller appliances, the value of the whole being estimated at £505,580.

SANDRIDGE ... the port of Melbourne, is situated on Hobson's Bay ... There is also a good road communication. The business of the town is almost entirely dependent on the shipping. There are two piers, the Railway and the Town Pier, jutting a long way into the bay, alongside which ships of almost any tonnage can lie and be rapidly loaded or discharged, there being numerous steam cranes for that purpose. The population is about 7,200. Royal, Brunswick Pier, and London are the principal hotels. The record (published weekly) is the local paper. Sandridge has a sugar works (lately burned down) and a biscuit factory (Swallow and Ariell's).

SERPENTINE CREEK ... is a post town and telegraph station ... is reached thence by Cobb's coach from Sandhurst ; fare, 20s. The hotels are the Serpentine, Commercial, and Telegraph ... The district is agricultural and pastoral, and although the soil is clayey, there is fair loamy land on the alluvial flats bordering the creek, well adapted for the growth of wheat.

STRATFORD ... a township, telegraph, and money-order office, and post-office ... Access from the metropolis is by Cobb's coach to Sale daily, and by steamer by Gipps Land lake and river Avon, which is navigable for ocean-going vessels within 3 miles of Stratford ... Stratford has three hotels, a State school, and four churches. The district is a pastoral one, with some farms and a few mining claims. There are a tannery and flour-mill in the township. Population about 500.

TALLAROOK ... a village on the Beechworth road, 55 miles N. of Melbourne, and a station on the North-Eastern Railway ... The hotels are, the Railway, Tallarook, and Junction ... From here goods are forwarded to Yea, Alexandra, and Upper Goulburn, by Cobb's coach, which leaves daily, Sundays excepted. There is also a large trade doing in timber. Population about 300.

TANGIL ... is a postal township ... and is reached by Cobb's coach from Melbourne. There is one hotel, a State school, and two stores. The district is a mining one, and has a population of 290 persons, of whom 120 are located in the township itself.

VOILET TOWN ... a postal township and telegraph office on Honeysuckle creek and the Beechworth road.

WARRNAMBOOL ... a seaport municipal town ... The harbour is well protected from stormy weather ... A large trade is done from the port ; the principal exports are wool, potatoes, wheat, preserved meats, and dairy produce ... There are five flour-mills in or near the town. The population of the borough numbers between 4,000 and 5,000 ; the shire nearly 10,000. There are two newspapers, the Warrnambool Examiner and the Warrnambool Standard. The principal hotels are the Victoria, Commercial, Royal, Princess Alexandra, Royal Archer, Rising Sun, and Criterion.

YANDOIT ... a township on Jim Crow creek ... The communication is by coach and rail via Guildford ; via Kyneton would be much nearer, but there are no regular conveyances ... good agricultural land in the district ... To the NE. about 4 miles distant is an extensive bed of superior clay, fit for making superior earthenware. There is also a mineral spring, whose waters are said to be quite equal to those of Hepburn. The gold-bearing reefs, running near and through the township, when thoroughly tested, will make it a place of note." (The Australian handbook and almanac and shippers' and importers' directory, 1876)

18 July 1853 Post Office Hut, Ballarat, Victoria - Courtesy State Library Victoria

1861 Electric Telegraph & Post Office, Maldon, Tarrengower (Thomas Hannay, 1835-1897, photographer) - Courtesy State Library Victoria

1895 A Country Post Office (Edwin M. Sibly) - Courtesy State Library Victoria

1860-1870 Lilydale Post and Telegraph Office (Lightning Photographers) - Courtesy State Library Victoria

1954 Maryborough, Victoria, 1854-1954 : the story of a century (Harold. V. Nunn)
- Courtesy State Library Victoria

ca. 1860 Post office and telegraph station, Dunolly
(G. H. Jenkins, 186?-?, photographer) - Courtesy State Library Victoria

1853 The Post Office, Melbourne (James Buckingham Philip, 1830, lithographer) - Courtesy State Library Victoria

ca. 1880 General Post Office (John William Lindt, 1845-1926, photographer) - Courtesy State Library Victoria

Chapter Three

Cobb and Co. proprietors

Stage Coach Regulations

Act for regulating Stage Coaches and Carriages.

I. No person shall keep, use, or employ any stage carriage, unless licensed ...

II. Every coach, carriage, or vehicle, used, employed, or let out for conveying passengers, and which shall travel 3 miles or more within the hour ... each passenger shall pay a separate and distinct fare for his conveyance thereby.

III. Two or more Justices ... shall grant a license.

IV. Every stage carriage ... determine the number of inside and outside passengers which may be safely carried ...

V. Application for a license must be made and signed by the proprietor ...

VI. Every license must specify the Christian name, surname, and place of abode of the proprietor or proprietors, the names of the extreme places to which the stage carriage shall be licensed to go ...

VII. Every license ... renewed from year to year ...

VIII. The sum of five shillings to be charged for every license.

IX. Any person ... without having a license, shall forfeit £20.

X. Every stage carriage must have painted in some conspicuous part of each side ... proprietor ... the extreme places from and to which the same shall be licensed to travel ...

XI. No outside passenger, nor any luggage shall be carried on the roof or top of any stage carriage, the roof or top of which from the ground shall be more than 8 feet 9 inches, or the bearing of which on the ground shall be less than 4 feet 6 inches, under a penalty of £5.

XII. Every stage carriage with four wheels, or more, Licensed to carry:— 9 Passengers, not more than 5 to the outside ...

XIII. The driver and children in the lap not to be counted as passengers ...

XIV. Luggage carried on the top ... not to exceed 10 feet 9 inches in height from the ground ...

XV. No person to sit on luggage placed on the roof of any stage carriage, nor more than one person to sit on the box with the driver, under a penalty of £5.

XVI. If the number of passengers inside or outside of any stage carriage shall exceed the number allowed ... forfeit £5.

XVII. If a driver of a stage carriage shall carry above the number of passengers allowed by his license ... penalty of £5.

XVIII. Any driver of a stage carriage drawn by three or more horses, quitting the box without delivering the reins to some fit and proper person ... shall forfeit £5.

XIX. If any driver ... through intoxication or negligence ... or furious driving ... endanger the safety of any passenger or other person ... shall forfeit £5 ...

(Tegg's New South Wales pocket almanac and remembrancer, 1840, p.102)

ca. 1880-1890 Stage coach crossing bridge - Courtesy State Library Victoria

Proprietors of Cobb and Co. coaching lines, Victoria

Proprietors of Cobb and Co. — 1854

*Freeman Cobb, John B. Lamber/Lambert, James Swanton, John Murray Peck

Proprietors of Cobb and Co. — 1855

*Freeman Cobb, James Swanton, John Murray Peck, Arthur Blake

Proprietors of Cobb and Co. — 1856

*'Messrs. Cobb and Co.' [possibly Thomas Davies from this point in time]

Proprietors of Cobb and Co. — 1857

*Thomas Davies Pre-18 April 1857-23 Sep 1857 ... sold to *Alexander Walker

*Chas. Colclough

*Watson and Hewitt (George Watson and Cyrus Hewitt) ... sold lines to *Swanton, Blake, and Co. (James Swanton, Arthur Lincoln Blake)

*F. B. Clapp and Co. (Francis Boardman Clapp)

Proprietors of Cobb and Co. — 1858

*Watson and Hewitt ... sold lines to F. B. Clapp and Co.

*Swanton, Blake and Co. ... became Victoria Stage Company

*W. H. Brayton

Proprietors of Cobb and Co. — 1859

*Victoria Stage Company, partners Arthur Lincoln Blake (Head manager of business, Melbourne), Charles Culwell Gardiner, Jacob Rogers, Pegleg Whitford Jackson, George Loop Woodworth, John Francis Britton, Levi Rich, Oliver Blake Clapp, Christopher Ives, John Murray Peck, James Joseph Blake, McCormick, as at 19 Sep 1859 ... change of partners 30 Nov 1859

*F. B. Clapp and Co.

*W. H. Brayton ... left district

Proprietors of Cobb and Co. — 1860

*Victoria Stage Company, partners Arthur Lincoln Blake, Peleg Whitford Jackson, John Francis Britton, Oliver Blake Clapp, Christopher Ives, John Murray Peck, Charles Culwell Gardiner, as at 25 Jun 1860 ... company soon dissolved

*F. B. Clapp and Co.

*Watson and Hewitt

*William Warren

Proprietors of Cobb and Co. — 1861

*F. B. Clapp and Co. ... now known as *Australian Stage Company, 16 Jan 1861-25 Jan 1861, partners William Randle, Cyrus Hewitt, William Williams, Matthew M'Caw, John R. Ricards, jun., John Halfey, A. L. Blake, F. B. Clapp, G. B. Perkins, William Woods, Thomas Ogilvie, J. D. Robinson, Hugh M'Phillimy, C. C. Skarratt, T. A. Lascelles, J. T. Fallen, David Jones, Walter Craig, Alexander Kelly, Charles Croaker, B. H. Fernald, William Malcolm, Joel Tompkins, Oliver Cooper, J. L. Huntley, Francis Tozer, as at 7 May 1860

*Australian Stage Company, new partners 25 Jan 1861

*M'Phee & Co.

*Michel and Hughes by 13 Jun 1861-10 Jul 1861

*Henry Hoyt advertised 5 Jun 1861

*Robertson, Britton and Co. ... 1 Feb 1861 A. W. Robertson retired from Bendigo Stage Company that continued with partners William B. Bradley, Walter R. Hall, William F. Whitney, Edward Moore, Frank May ... which then sold plant to *Watson & Hewitt ... Watson and Hewitt ceased by 2 Apr 1861 ... selling to *Robertson, Britton and Co. by 3 Jun 1861

Proprietors of Cobb and Co.—1862

*Australian Stage Company

*Robertson, Britton and Co. partners A. W. Robertson and John Britton, as at 13 Jun 1862 … some, but not all, of Robertson and Britton's lines were then advertised as *Robertson, Wagner and Co. whose partners were A. W. Robertson, John Wagner, James Rutherford, W. B. Bradley, Wm. F. Whitney

*Henry Hoyt

*M'Phee & Co.

Note: Evidence not found to date, as to when James Rutherford, W. B. Bradley, and Wm. F. Whitney joined A. W. Robertson and John Wagner, trading under the style of Cobb and Co.

Proprietors of Cobb and Co.—1863

*Australian Stage Company

*Robertson, Britton and Co. & *Robertson, Wagner and Co.

*Henry Hoyt still being advertised 3 Dec 1863

*Meigs & Anderson advertised 5 Dec 1863

Proprietors of Cobb and Co.—1864

*Australian Stage Company

*Robertson, Britton and Co. & *Robertson, Wagner and Co.

*Meigs & Anderson

*J. J. Stiles

*R. Davey

*John Cawker

*A. Lane

*G. Whorlom

*M'Phee and Co./John M'Phee

*J. C. Horr

*Thomas Stoneman

*Cameron and Jones advertised from 17 Jun 1864-21 Sep 1864

Proprietors of Cobb and Co.—1865

*Australian Stage Company

*Robertson, Wagner and Co.

*Meigs & Anderson

*J. C. Horr line … to *M'Phee and Co./John M'Phee

*Ballarat Stage Company

*Thomas Stoneman

Proprietors of Cobb and Co.—1866

*Australian Stage Company

*Robertson, Wagner and Co.

*Meigs & Anderson/Meggs and Anderson

*M'Phee and Co.

*Ballarat Stage Company

*Thomas Stoneman

*E. Moore and Co.

*Meigs & Anderson, Thomas Stoneman, Joshua Vines … became *Western Stage Company 27 Dec 1866

Proprietors of Cobb and Co.—1867

*Australian Stage Company still advertised 9 Jan 1867

*Robertson, Wagner and Co.

*M'Phee and Co.

*Western Stage Company

Proprietors of Cobb and Co. —1868

*Robertson, Wagner and Co. partners Alexander W. Robertson, John Wagner, George John Watson, William James, as at 14 Jan 1868
*M'Phee and Co.
*Anderson and M'Phee
*Western Stage Company
*Matthew Veal and Co.
*Scott & Nugent

Proprietors of Cobb and Co. —1869

*Robertson, Wagner and Co.
*M'Phee and Co.
*Anderson & M'Phee
*Western Stage Company
*Matthew Veal and Co.

Proprietors of Cobb and Co. —1870

*Robertson, Wagner and Co.
*M'Phee and Co.
*Anderson & M'Phee
*Western Stage Company
*Matthew Veal and Co.

Proprietors of Cobb and Co. —1871

*Robertson, Wagner and Co. 15 Aug 1871 "Dissolution of 'Cobb and Co.' partnership in the colonies of Victoria, New South Wales, and Queensland, has been this day dissolved by mutual consent A. W. Robertson, J. Rutherford. W. B. Bradley, Wm. F. Whitney, John Wagner"

Note: Robertson and Wagner took Victoria; the Echuca, Deniliquin, Hay, Booligal, and Wilcannia road, and west of it (Cobb and Co., Melbourne)
*M'Phee and Co.
*Anderson & M'Phee
*Western Stage Company
*Matthew Veal and Co.

Proprietors of Cobb and Co. —1872

*Robertson, Wagner and Co., A. W. Robertson and J. Wagner listed on mail tenders not as Cobb & Co.
*M'Phee and Co.
*Anderson & M'Phee
*Western Stage Company
*Matthew Veal and Co.
*J. Cawker

Proprietors of Cobb and Co. —1873

*Robertson, Wagner and Co.
*M'Phee and Co.
*Anderson & M'Phee
*Western Stage Company
*Matthew Veal and Co.
*J. Cawker

Proprietors of Cobb and Co. —1874

*Robertson, Wagner and Co.
*M'Phee and Co.
*Anderson & M'Phee
*Western Stage Company
*Matthew Veal and Co.

Proprietors of Cobb and Co. —1875

*Robertson, Wagner and Co.
*M'Phee and Co.
*Anderson & M'Phee
*Western Stage Company
*Matthew Veal and Co.

Proprietors of Cobb and Co. —1876

*Robertson, Wagner and Co.
*M'Phee and Co.
*Anderson & M'Phee
*Western Stage Company partners Thomas Stoneman, Charles Anderson, Joshua Vine, as at 13 Dec 1876
*Matthew Veal and Co

Proprietors of Cobb and Co. —1877

*Robertson, Wagner and Co.
*M'Phee and Co.
*Anderson & M'Phee
*Western Stage Company
*Matthew Veal and Co.

Proprietors of Cobb and Co. —1878

*Robertson, Wagner and Co.
*M'Phee and Co.
*Anderson & M'Phee
*Western Stage Company
*Matthew Veal and Co.
Note: Death of Freeman Cobb

Proprietors of Cobb and Co. —1879

*Robertson, Wagner and Co.
*M'Phee and Co.
*Anderson & M'Phee
*Western Stage Company
*Seth Sharp

Proprietors of Cobb and Co. —1880

*Robertson, Wagner and Co.
*M'Phee and Co.
*Anderson & M'Phee
*Western Stage Company
*Seth Sharp/S. Sharp

Proprietors of Cobb and Co. —1881

*Robertson, Wagner and Co.
Note: A. W. Robertson & John Wagner lesses of Pericoota, Tattaila
*M'Phee and Co.
*Anderson & M'Phee
*Western Stage Company
*Seth Sharp/S. Sharp

Proprietors of Cobb and Co. —1882

*Robertson, Wagner and Co.
*M'Phee and Co.
*Western Stage Company
*Seth Sharp/S. Sharp
*Vines and M'Phee

Proprietors of Cobb and Co. —1883

*Robertson, Wagner and Co.
*M'Phee and Co.
*Anderson & M'Phee
*Western Stage Company
*Seth Sharp/S. Sharp
*Vines and M'Phee
*T. Cawker

Proprietors of Cobb and Co. — 1884

*Robertson, Wagner and Co.
*M'Phee and Co.
*Western Stage Company
*Vines and M'Phee

Proprietors of Cobb and Co. — 1885

*Robertson, Wagner and Co.
*M'Phee and Co.
*Western Stage Company
*Vines and M'Phee

Proprietors of Cobb and Co. — 1886

*Robertson, Wagner and Co.
*M'Phee and Co.
*Western Stage Company
*Vines and M'Phee

Proprietors of Cobb and Co. — 1887

*Robertson, Wagner and Co.
*M'Phee and Co.
*Western Stage Company
*Vines and M'Phee

Proprietors of Cobb and Co. — 1888

*Robertson, Wagner and Co.
*M'Phee and Co.
*Western Stage Company
*Vines and M'Phee

Proprietors of Cobb and Co. — 1889

*Robertson, Wagner and Co.
*M'Phee and Co.
*Western Stage Company
*Vines and M'Phee

Proprietors of Cobb and Co. — 1890

*Robertson, Wagner and Co.
*Western Stage Company
*Vines and M'Phee

Proprietors of Cobb and Co. — 1891

*Robertson, Wagner and Co.
*Western Stage Company
*Vines and M'Phee

Proprietors of Cobb and Co. — 1892

*Robertson, Wagner and Co.
*Western Stage Company
*Vines and M'Phee

Proprietors of Cobb and Co. — 1893

*Robertson, Wagner and Co.
*Western Stage Company
*Vines and M'Phee

Proprietors of Cobb and Co. — 1894

*Robertson, Wagner and Co.
*Western Stage Company
*Vines and M'Phee

Proprietors of Cobb and Co.—1895

*Robertson, Wagner and Co.
*Western Stage Company
*Vines and M'Phee

Proprietors of Cobb and Co.—1896

*Robertson, Wagner and Co.
*Western Stage Company
*Vines and M'Phee
*A. Grant
Note: Death of A. W. Robertson 16/18 Jul 1896

Proprietors of Cobb and Co.—1897

*Robertson & Wagner
*Western Stage Company
*Vines and M'Phee

Proprietors of Cobb and Co.—1898

*Robertson & Wagner
*Western Stage Company
*Vines and M'Phee

Proprietors of Cobb and Co.—1899

*Robertson & Wagner sold line to *George Alexander McGowan (Mac)
* Western Stage Company
* Vines and M'Phee

Proprietors of Cobb and Co.—1900-1904

* Robertson, Wagner and Co. dissolved with A. W Robertson's death (16/18 Jul 1896) but some lines still advertised as Robertson, Wagner and Co.
*Western Stage Company
*Vines and M'Phee
Note: Death of John Wagner 27 Jan 1901; Death of John Murray Peck 19 Nov 1903

Proprietors of Cobb and Co.—1905-1929

*A. N. Vines (1905-1919)
*H. Womersley (1919-1921)

18 Dec 1920 Cobb and Co.'s Charleville Factory closed

Cobb and Co. retired from coaching business in the west (Queensland)

By 14 Aug 1924 Yeulba and Surat ... Last Queensland horse-drawn coach owned by Cobb and Co. supplanted by a modern motor service

1929 Voluntary Liquidation of *Cobb and Co. Ltd, Queensland, Alfred Uhl, Liquidator

Note: 6 Sep 1920 Death of Francis Boardman Clapp

* * *

1 Nov 1963 "Victoria was the last state in which this occurred ... The Colac Herald has now been informed that Mr. William Thomas Fletcher, who still have relatives in this district, ran his Cobb & Co. coach from Deans Marsh to Lorne 'until at least 1925'. This certificate is to conduct the service which was issued by the deputy registrar general of Victoria was produced at the 'Colac Herald' office this week"

1 Dec 1823 "Lorne via Ocean Road. Large comfortable cars leave daily from garage at 8.30 a.m., arriving at Lorne midday. Coaches daily from Dean's Marsh to Lorne. Daily Service to Torquay ... Fletcher's Services Pty Ltd" Not listed as Cobb and Co. (Advertising, 1 Dec 1923, p.1)

18 Nov 1925 "Lorne Cars leave Garage daily ... for Great Ocean Road ... Fletcher's Services Pty Ltd. 29 Gheringhap St., Geelong, Telephone 2481 [?]." (Advertising, 18 Nov 1925, p.2)

Proprietors of Cobb and Co. coaching lines, New South Wales

Proprietors of Cobb and Co. —1862

28 May 1862 Messrs. *Robertson and Britton, with James Rutherford manager N.S.W.

13 Jun 1862 *Robertson, Britton and Co., partners A. W. Robertson and John Britton ... some, but not all, of Robertson and Britton's lines were then advertised as *Robertson, Wagner and Co. whose partners were A. W. Robertson, John Wagner, James Rutherford, W. B. Bradley, Wm. F. Whitney

Proprietors of Cobb and Co. —1868

*Robertson, Wagner and Co., partners Alexander W. Robertson, John Wagner, George John Watson, William James, as at 14 Jan 1868 ... (group possibly running 'Cobb and Co., Melbourne' before official Cobb and Co. partnership dissolution)

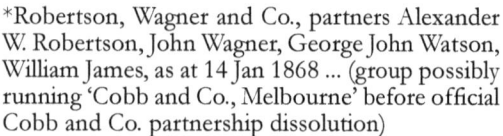

Proprietors of Cobb and Co. —1871

*Robertson, Wagner and Co. 15 Aug 1871 ... "Dissolution of 'Cobb and Co.' partnership in the colonies of Victoria, New South Wales, and Queensland, has been this day dissolved by mutual consent A. W. Robertson, J. Rutherford. W. B. Bradley, Wm. F. Whitney, John Wagner"

30 Dec 1871 New partnership James Rutherford, Walter R. Hall, William B. Bradley, William F. Whitney, Colin Robertson (Cobb and Co., Sydney)

Note: Robertson and Wagner took Victoria; the Echuca, Deniliquin, Hay, Booligal, and Wilcannia road, and west of it (Cobb and Co., Melbourne)

Proprietors of Cobb and Co. —1874

13 Jan 1874 William Brown Bradley retired from partnership known as Cobb & Co.

Partners James Rutherford, Walter R. Hall, Wm. F. Whitney, Colin Robertson, as at 13 Jan 1874

Proprietors of Cobb and Co. —1876

After 6 May 1876 partners James Rutherford, Walter Russell Hall, William Franklin Whitney

Proprietors of Cobb and Co. —1881

Note: James Rutherford, Walter R. Hall, William B. Bradley, William F. Whitney lessees of Woollagoola Beriarh, and Gooagoola

Proprietors of Cobb and Co. —1885

Partners James Rutherford, William Franklin Whitney ... dissolution of Cobb and Co. partnership 15 Oct 1885

Proprietors of Cobb and Co. —1887

Note: Cobb & Co. Mail Contracts address listed as Sydney

Proprietors of Cobb and Co. —1888

Note: Cobb & Co. Mail Contracts address listed as Bathurst

Proprietors of Cobb and Co. —1894

Note: Cobb and Co. listed on N.S.W. mail contracts; Death of William Franklin Whitney 31 Oct 1894

Proprietors of Cobb and Co. —1895

Note: James Rutherford and/or Cobb and Co. listed on N.S.W. mail contracts

Proprietors of Cobb and Co. —1898

Note: Cobb & Co. no longer listed on mail contracts in New South Wales

Proprietors of Cobb and Co. —1899

*Robertson, Wagner and Co., sold Hay and Deniliquin lines to *George Alexander McGowan (Mac)

Note: Death of James Rutherford 14 Sep 1911

Proprietors of Cobb and Co. coaching lines, Queensland

Proprietors of Cobb and Co. —1862

28 May 1862 Messrs. *Robertson and Britton, with James Rutherford manager N.S.W.

Proprietors of Cobb and Co. —1865

1 Jan 1865 Mr. Grant, Queensland managing director

Proprietors of Cobb and Co. —1871

*Robertson, Wagner and Co., partners prior to 15 Aug 1871 A. W. Robertson, J. Rutherford, W. B. Bradley, Wm. F. Whitney, John Wagner

30 Dec 1871 New partnership James Rutherford, Walter R. Hall, William B. Bradley, William F. Whitney, Colin Robertson

Proprietors of Cobb and Co. —1874

13 Jan 1874 William Brown Bradley retired from partnership known as Cobb & Co.; As at 13 Jan 1874 partners J. Rutherford, W. R. Hall, Wm. F. Whitney, Colin Robertson

Proprietors of Cobb and Co. —1876

After 6 May 1876 partners James Rutherford, Walter Russell Hall, William Franklin Whitney

Proprietors of Cobb and Co. —1881

*Qld Cobb and Co. Limited, Aug 1881 company was incorporated, shareholders were W. R. Hall, J. Rutherford, F. Shaw, I. T. Barthelomew, T. Gallagher, C. M. Kirk, F. C. Shaw, H. W. Shaw, H. B. Taylor, R. M'Master, J. Coyle, W. J. Richardson, L. Uhl, J. Coyle (Charters Towers), W. Jenkins, John Bock

Proprietors of Cobb and Co. —1907

"A special meeting of Cobb and Co., Limited, was held yesterday afternoon for the purpose of receiving the liquidator's report on the winding up of the old company ... Mr. J. Story presided ... it had been decided to form a new company under the name of Cobb and Co., Limited, the old company being styled Cobb and Co. The liabilities of the company's per balance book were £66,879 8s. 1d., and the assets £47,023 5s. 9d., showing a debit balance of £19,856 2s. 4d. The new company was formed with a capital of 30,000 shares for every £200 shares held in the old company, shareholders were allotted 100 £1 shares in the new company paid up to 15s. The report was adopted." (Messrs Cobb and Co, 18 Mar 1907, p.4)

Proprietors of Cobb and Co.—1920

Directors of Cobb and Co., Ltd., Queensland: A. Uhl (chairman), W. N. Morcom, Dr. E. D. Ahern, W. Ross Munro, and H. Uhl with Mr. G. W. F. Studdert, F.A.I.S. as secretary.

Proprietors of Cobb and Co. —1928

"Cobb and Company Limited. The days of vast coaching enterprises ... had gone ... A chain of stores in the Surat and St. George districts was opened, and certain coaching was done, but per motor car. Then the coaching was dropped and just the stores continued. Lately a fire destroyed the St. George stores and stock, and though business was continued in temporary premises the company has had enough if it ... they have put up a proposal to go into liquidation." (End of Cobb and Co., 15 Nov 1928, p.2)

Proprietors of Cobb and Co. —1931

"The report of the liquidator of Cobb and Co., Ltd ... Since the last report there have been further decreases in the price of wool. This, together with the present trade depression, has made it difficult to collect outstanding debts. The property at Surat was sold during the year for £200. Efforts have also been made to dispose of the Dirranbandi property at a satisfactory price without effect." (Cobb and Co., 23 Oct 1931, p.10)

Cobb and Co. Name—1948

"Right To Name ... Gordon Wallace Fitzgerald Studdert, merchant ... When the company voluntarily liquidated in 1929, he was general manager, and by agreement acquired the company's Surat business, together with the right to use name 'Cobb and Co,' for £5,100." (Historic Firm Recalled, 30 Nov 1948, p.6)

1880-1890 Tyers River Inn - The Gippsland and Regional Studies Collection (GRSC)
- Courtesy Federation University Australia

1890 Cobb & Co. Coach, Renmark - Courtesy State Library of South Australia

ca. 1890-1900 Tallandoon Station and mail coach (that travelled daily 70 miles from Wodonga to Mitta), driver George McLean? - Courtesy State Library Victoria

1902 Coach and police escort (Henry Goldman, photographer) - Courtesy State Library Victoria

> "So many 'Cobb and Co.'s' arose throughout the country that I am at a difficulty to say who were and who were not his legitimate successors."
> (Exit King Cobb, 27 Nov 1890, p.2)

Supporting evidence:

Cobb and Co. proprietors—Freeman Cobb, John B. Lamber, James Swanton, John Murray Peck & then came Arthur Lincoln Blake

- "The four 'Boys,' as they called themselves, raised all the capital they could, and on January 30, 1854, started, as Cobb and Co., their first coach from the Criterion Hotel, Collins street, Melbourne, for the Forest Creek diggings, now Castlemaine, under the title of, as advertised in 'The Argus' of the day, The American Telegraph Line of Coaches. Within 12 months Lamber retired and Arthur Blake went into the partnership. The new firm—Melbourne and Forest Creek, extended the lines to Bendigo, and opened branches to Maryborough and other centres, and later to Swan Hill. Soon other Americans and Canadians ('Yankees' and 'Canuks') followed, some joining Cobb and Co. as drivers." (a [?] Drive, 31 July 1937, p.4)

Cobb and Co. proprietor—Thomas Davies

- "PEOPLE'S LINE OF COACHES TO BALLAARAT.—Change of Route. The Proprietor of the above popular Line of Coaches has the pleasure to announce that, since the 1st inst., a new route has been travelled by them from Keilor to Ballan ... This line connects with the Daily Lines to Creswick and Fiery Creeks, Magpie, Chalk Hills, and Burnbank. Anticipating the approaching season, the proprietor is obliged to advance the fares above the present unremunerative rates. Fare to Ballan £3 Do. to Ballaarat. No exertions will be spared to render this the most desirable means of conveyance, and to retain the patronage of the travelling public. Agents : J. F. Britton, 23 Bourke-street east. A. Butler, 44 Bourke-street east; Office. Bull and Mouth Hotel. E. B. Covington, People's Booking Office, Bath's Hotel, Ballaarat. Thos. Davies, Proprietor. Melbourne, April 5th, 1856." (Advertising, 9 Apr 1856, p.3)

- "NOTICE—The undersigned, proprietor of the Telegraph line of Coaches, begs to inform the public on and after Monday, the 5th January, his offices for booking passengers and parcels for Castlemaine, Bendigo, Ballarat &c., will be closed every evening at 7 o'clock. Thomas Davies." (Advertising, 3 Jan 1857, p.1)

- "SALES BY AUCTION ... J. Henderon has been honoured with instructions from Thomas Davies, Esq., (Cobb and Co.) to offer by public auction, at George Watson's Bazaar ... the whole of his draught stock, together with drays and harness, consisting of 25 mares and geldings ... for positive and absolute sale, in consequence of the owner retiring that branch of his business and for no other reason ... Not the slightest reserve." (Advertising, 4 May 1857, p.3)

- "FAT CATTLE ... First-class pens ... 25s per 100 lbs ... Horses—All descriptions ... We have disposed of 43 head of Government condemned horses, at an average £22 ; also 23 heavy draught horses, the property of Thomas Davis, Esq., of the firm of Messrs. Cobb and Co., at an average of £130 ; they were a very superior lot, and caused a brisk competition." (Dalmahoy Campbell & Co's. Circular, 3 Jun 1857, p.2)

- "Cobb and Co.'s Telegraph Line Of Coaches, now running from Melbourne to Ballaarat direct, will be discontinued, and removed to the road from Geelong to Ballaarat. Thomas Davis, proprietor." (Advertising, 18 Jul 1857, p.3)

- "NOTICE.—Mr. Thomas Davies, having disposed of his entire interest in the Telegraph Stage Lines, both on the Melbourne and Castlemaine, and Geelong and Ballaarat Roads, to Alexander Walker, Esq., of Melbourne. In retiring from the business begs to tender his thanks to the public for the support hithorto granted him, and on behalf of his successor, who will ably sustain the reputation of Cobb and Co.'s Telegraph Lines, to ask a continuance of patronage. (Signed) Thomas Davies. 23 Bourke-street, Melbourne, September 19th, 1857." (Advertising, 26 Sep 1857, p.8)

- "An adjourned meeting of the trustees of Mr. Thomas Davies, formerly the proper action of Cobb's line of coaches to the gold-fields, was held at the Criterion. Two trustees stated that it was impossible to arrive at anything like a correct state of the insolvent's affairs, as fresh claims were constantly being made on the estate. At the last meeting the liabilities were stated at £10,000, and at the present, what with contingent claims, the trustees amid not out estimate them at less than £95,000. Large shipments of hides had been made by the insolvent to London, which were drawn against to the extent of nearly £7,500. It was said that large sums would be lost on these shipments, the hides having been invoiced at from 70 lbs. to 65 lbs per hide, and at 7d. per lb. These weights are extraordinary for Australian hides, and the shipments appear to require looking into. A very strong feeling appeared at one time to prevail among the creditors in favour of placing the estate at once under the authority of the Insolvent Court, but it was eventually arranged to further adjourn the meeting until the 18th instant, the trustees being empowered, in the meantime, to employ an efficient accountant to examine the books of the Insolvent and draw up a balance-sheet, also to report upon the position of the estate at the time that a settlement was made by the insolvent on his wife." (Mercantile and Money Article, 9 Feb 1858, p.8)

Cobb and Co. proprietor—Alexander Walker

- "Tenders are requested for the Lines Of Coaches, known as Cobb and Co.'s Telegraph and Estafette Lines, running between Geelong and Ballaarat, and between Melbourne and Castlemaine, Maryborough and Sandhurst. One-third of the purchase money at least must be paid in cash, and the balance by approved bills, at dates not exceeding three and six months. A cash tenderer in full will have preference. Parties may either tender for the one or both lines. Full particulars can be learned on application to the undersigned, with whom tenders are to be lodged. Tenders will be opened at Twelve noon, on Wednesday, 21st inst. The highest or any tender will not necessarily be accepted. Alex. Walker, Cobb and Co., Telegraph Coach Office, 23 Bourke-street, Melbourne, 8th October, 1857." (Advertising, 10 Oct 1857, p.8)

- "COBB & CO.'S TELEGRAPH LINE OF MAIL COACHES ... Melbourne, Sandhurst, Maryborough, and Dunolly ... Watson and Hewitt, Proprietors ... Cobb & Co.'s Coaches, 24th October, 1857. All claims against the undersigned as proprietor of the Telegraph Line of Coaches to be sent in within ten days from this date, or they cannot be recognised. Alexander Walker, 23 Bourke street." (Advertising, 26 Oct 1857, p.1)

Cobb and Co. proprietors— Watson & Hewitt (Cyrus Hewitt & George John Watson)

- "We beg to inform the Public that we have this day Disposed of our entire interest in the Lines of Coaches now running on the Castlemaine, Sandhurst and Maryborough roads (known as Cobb and Co.'s Telegraph Lines) to Messrs Swanston, Blake, and Co, who will continue running as usual. All claims against said lines to be sent in within one week from this date, otherwise they will not be liquidated. Watson & Hewitt, Per J. F. Sweeney, Castlemaine Hotel, Dec. 28, 1857." (Advertising, 1 Jan 1858, p.2)
- "This day disposed of our Lines of Mail Coaches, plying between Melbourne and Ballaarat and Geelong and Ballaarat ... to Messrs. F. B. Clapp and Co. ... Watson and Hewitt." (Advertising, 19 Jan 1858, p.8)
- "THE HORSE TAMING SECRET. Mr. Ferguson, The Only Authorised 'Rarey' (And Pupil of the world-famed American) Has Arrived In Tasmania ! Ferguson will commence his class in Launceston about 1st October. Testimionials To Mr. Ferguson, the first Australian 'Rarey,' Pupil of the world-famed American :—We, the undersigned, hereby record our perfect satisfaction of the sense, humanity, facility, and success of the Rarey treatment in horse taming, imparted to us by his pupil, Mr. Ferguson. Lieut. Colonel Robbins, Edward Row Stock Agent, Bowman breeder N.S.W., C. Hewitt horse purchaser for India, F. B. Clapp, Swanton and Blake, Victoria Stage Company, Dr. Thomson, W. P. Simons, Bell's Life in Victoria. And over eighty other gentlemen have also given their signatures." (Advertising, 9 Oct 1858, p.1)
- "COBB'S COACHES—We understand that Messrs. Watson and Hewitt, who have for so long been the proprietors of Cobb's Telegraph Line of Coaches, have disposed of all their interest in the line to Messrs. Robertson, Britton, and Co, both the principal partners in which firm have long been connected with coaching enterprise in Victoria. An advertisement, which appears in our columns, requests that all accounts against Messrs. Watson and Hewitt, in this district, may be sent in to Mr. C. D. Pollock, M'Ivor Hotel, Maryborough, for liquidation." (Advertising, 7 Jun 1861, p.3)
- "COURTNEY V. BENNETT AND ANOTHER. This was an action by Mr. Courtney, official assignee of the estate of Cyrus Hewitt, against Mr. J. B. Bennett and Mr. M. W. Taylor, who lately carried on business in partnership as solicitors, to recover £375, money received by them on behalf of the estate. Mr. Fellows appeared for the defendant Bennett; Mr. Dobson for the defendant Taylor. Hewitt was a coach proprietor and mail contractor, but in October last he came to the determination to sell off his plant and business. Robertson and Wagner became the purchasers of the property, but Hewitt authorised them to retain a cheque for £375 and a bill of exchange for £500, as security for any liens or securities on the plant which they might be called on to satisfy." (Law Report, 6 Aug 1867, p.6)
- "In the juries of four court, yesterday, before Mr Justice Williams, the sitting was occupied with two cases in which official assignees were concerned. The first, that of Courtney v. Bennett and another, was to recover a sum of £375 paid to the defendants, as solicitors for Cyrus Hewitt, and on account of the sale of a number of his coaches, horses and harness before his insolvency. The jury awarded £109, being the amount claimed, less certain moneys owing to the defendants, and others paid by them on Hewitt's account." (The News of the Day, 6 Aug 1867, p.5)
- "VICTORIA COURSING CLUB ... Stewards ... John Wagner, Geo. Watson ... A Piece of Plate, value £20, given by the club for competition amongst the six greyhounds beaten by Lavender Water (disqualified) in the St. Leger Stakes of 1874 ... there must have been close on 400 persons present to witness the sport, amongst them being all the leading patrons of the sport in the colony. At the outset hares were apparently scarce ... Owing to the unfavourable formation of the country over which the trials took place, it was impossible for reporters to obtain anything like a good view, and as it would not be policy to give imaginary descriptions of what others might have seen, coursing readers must be content with the following brief details of the running :— St. Leger.— My Idea and Lucy were unsighted at the first attempt. Next time Lucy led and disappeared over a rise, My Idea being again unsighted. After a few seconds absence the hare came in sight of the spectators, with My Idea next in pursuit, and the white bitch serving Lucy, the latter made a most determined drive, and killed — verdict for My Idea. In a beautiful slip D.O. instantly drew herself clear of Bellona, and striding away in grand style the daughter of Wizard was Virtually left standing still. When D.O. had placed something like fifteen to twenty lengths of daylight between herself and her opponent, the hare swerved across the brow of a hill, and the black got unsighted. Bellona, with her weather eye open, saw the tactics adopted by Puss, and, keeping well on the line of her game, disappeared in command. After making several casts, D.O. struck out in the direction of the judge, but whether she succeeded in taking any further part in the course the spectators were unable to observe. Shortly afterwards Mr. Gardner returned and decided for Bellona." (Victoria Coursing Club Second Meeting 1875, 15 May 1875, p.5)
- "George Watson and Cyrus Hewitt (trading as Watson and Hewitt) acquired the business from Davies ... The city agent was A. Butler, his brother was agent at Geelong, C. Miller at Castlemaine, J. Crowley at Sandhurst, J. Blake at Maryborough, J. H. Peck at Ballarat (afterwards the Ballarat agent was E. J. Brayton), John Wagner was superintendent in Melbourne ... After Mr. Hewitt's death A. W. Robertson and John Wager became partners with Mr. Watson, and subsequently Walter Hall and E. James. The title of the firm then became Robertson, Wagner, and Co. ... Much of this information was given, to me by the late Mr. George Watson many years ago." (Notes & Answers, 4 May 1918, p.25)

Cobb and Co. proprietors—F. B. Clapp and Co. (Francis Boardman Clapp)

- "NOTICE.—The Business heretofore carried on under the style or title of F. B. Clapp & Co. will in future be known as The Australian Stage Company. E. T. FOLEY, Agent." (Advertising, 28 Jan 1861, p.1)
- "ABBOT'S BUGGIES, Hill's celebrated American Harness, F. B. Clapp, agent, 11 and 13 Latrobe-street east." (Advertising, 19 Nov 1878, p.8)
- "EDWIN JOHN BRAYTON, DECEASED ... Francis Boardman Clapp, of the city of Melbourne, gentleman ... John Wagner, of the same place, coach proprietor, the executors named therein ... will distribute the whole of the assets." (Advertising, 13 Jan 1879, p.3)

- "MANY HAPPY RETURNS OF THE DAY ... On Thursday, June 27 :—To Mr. Francis Boardman Clapp, born 1833." (Table Talk, 21 Jun 1889, p.3)

- "The funeral of Mr Francis Boardman Clapp, formerly chairman of directors of the Melbourne Tramway and Omnibus Co., whose death occurred at his residence, at South Yarra, yesterday, will take place in the St. Kilda Cemetery tomorrow morning at 9.30. Mr Clapp, who was nearly 90 years of age, was a well-known figure in Melbourne transport circles, having founded lines of coaches as far back as 1855. He was a native of America, and arrived in Australia in 1853. Mr H. W. Clapp, one of his sons, is now on his way to Australia from America, to take up the position of Chairman of the Victorian Railway Commissioners. The Railway Commissioners have expressed to the members of the family their deep regret at the death of Mr Clapp." (Funeral of Mr Clapp, 7 Sep 1920, p.12)

- "News of the death of Mr. Francis Boardman Clapp, formerly chairman of directors of the Melbourne Tramway and Omnibus Company, which occurred at his residence, Domain road, South Yarra, yesterday, will be received with feelings of regret. Mr. Clapp had been awaiting the arrival of his son, Mr. H. W. Clapp, the new chairman of the Railways Commissioners, who is expected to arrive in Sydney next week from America, and Mrs. Clapp and Miss Clapp had gone to Sydney to meet the s.s. Ventura. For over 60 years Mr. Clapp was a leader in the transport business in Victoria, and, though for over twelve years he had been blind, it was only in the last few years that he was compelled to retire from business. He retained his position as chairman of the Tramway Company until its career was closed and its undertakings were transferred to the Old Tramway Board. Mr. Clapp was born at Holden, Massachusetts (U.S.A.), in 1833, and arrived in Victoria when twenty years of age. He had even then some experience in coaching, and shortly after his arrival opened up the Western district of Victoria by means of his coaches. He established lines of coaches from Geelong to Ballarat and Hamilton, and to Warrnambool and Portland in 1855, and the traffic was soon very large. Mr. Clapp believed in the products of his own country. He accordingly secured the Victorian agencies for Abbott buggies and for Hill's harness. Abbott buggies were built by Abbott Downing, and Co., of Boston, who provided many of the coaches in use in the Western States of America, and Mr. Clapp imported some to Australia. With these two side lines to the coaching business Mr. Clapp was a busy man. In 1867 Mr. Clapp sold out of the coaching business and visited America. When he returned in 1868, it was with the object of establishing omnibuses in Melbourne. While in America he had ordered half a dozen omnibuses, and on his return to Melbourne he organised a company to run omnibuses. He associated himself with Mr. Henry Hoyt, with whom he had been in partnership in his coaching days, and Mr. William McCulloch, the proprietor of Kirk's Bazaar. The American 'buses' arrived in Hobson's Bay on February 22 1869, and, strangely on the same day, another ship arrived from Boston with a number of immigrants, one of whom was just the man Mr. Clapp wanted. That was Mr. H. A. Wilcox, who brought letters of introduction to Mr. Clapp, and became the first clerk in the Omnibus Company, of which Messrs Clapp, Hoyt and McCulloch were the directors, and Mr. W. G. Sprigg was the secretary. Mr. Clapp being the general manager. The associations then formed have only been broken by death. Subsequent directors were Mr. A. W. Robertson and Mr J. M. Pratt, both of whom had previously been associated with Mr. Clapp in business. On March 23, 1869, the first line of omnibuses in Melbourne began to run. The route was from the corner of Swanston and Bourke streets, Melbourne, to the Birmingham Hotel, at the corner of Smith and Johnston streets, Collingwood. Traffic to the suburbs hitherto had been carried on by means of cabs, the fares being sixpence each way by day, and one shilling after 6 o'clock in the evening. The fare by omnibus was threepence each way day and night, and the new conveyances became popular at once. In order to cope with the heavy traffic the company purchased a number of 'buses in Sydney, and an order was given to McGregor and Co., coachbuilders of Melbourne, for 20 more 'buses on the American pattern but they were not built to specification, and the company refused to take delivery. McGregor and Co. thereupon put their 'buses on the roads, in opposition to the company, which had built others in its own shops. Mr. Clapp's business acumen, knowledge and determination soon brought him the victory in this competition and he was able to buy the rejected 'buses at a considerable reduction on the contract price. After the success of the initial line, it was not long before lines were opened to Richmond, Fitzroy, Simpson's road Carlton, North Melbourne, and Brunswick, in that order. In 1878 the company bought out a line of waggonettes with horses which had been run to Prahran and lines to St. Kilda, South Melbourne and Port Melbourne were established. Thus Mr. Clapp and his associates within ten years captured the whole of the street passenger traffic of Melbourne. Mr. Clapp was the life and soul of the business. He was a born organiser, a good business man, an excellent judge of men and of methods, his foresight and caution being remarkable. When in 1883, after long negotiations with the municipalities the Tramways Act was passed, Mr. Clapp's influence was dominant. He was in the forefront of the organisation which provided Melbourne with its network of cable trams, which gradually pushed the omnibus out. The story of Mr. Clapp's life is indissolubly bound up with that of the Tramway Company. Mr. Clapp leaves a widow, three sons, and four daughters. Mr. Harold Clapp, his eldest son is the recently appointed chief Railways Commissioner; his second son, Mr. T. B. Clapp was in charge of the work of electrifying the suburban railways. He returned to America some time ago, but recently arrived in Melbourne again. The third son, Mr. Leroy Clapp, is a notable metallurgist." (Death of Mr. F. B. Clapp, 7 Sep 1920, p.6)

- "His father, Francis Boardman Clapp, was born in Massachusetts (U.S.A.), and migrated to Australia in 1853 (a year before the first Australian railway line was opened, between Melbourne and Sandgate, now Port Melbourne). He came out in a 600-ton sailing ship, which was forced into Rio with yellow fever and a sprung leak, causing Clapp to mourn his selection of Australia instead of California. Clapp worked first with the historic Cobb and Co. coaches, which ran the gauntlet of bushrangers during the gold rush. There was a picturesque legend that he once drove Cobb's coaches. This earned Harold Clapp [son] the respect of romantic lad porters, but it was not true. His father was only a 'horse procurer.' Later Clapp, still providing a transport background for his second son, formed the Melbourne Tramway and Omnibus Company, and became managing director.

Isabelle Pierce, also born in Massachusetts, came out to Melbourne with her father and mother in 1869, and there married Francis Boardman Clapp. Harold Winthrop ... is one of three sons." (Clapp: Railwayman with a one-track mind, 25 Aug 1945, p.10)

Cobb and Co. proprietor—W. H. Brayton (Possibly Will, Ned Brayton's Brother)

- "TENDERS ACCEPTED ... Conveyance of mails from 1st October, to 31st December, 1857 ... between Cathcart and Pleasant Creek ... F. B. Clapp and W. H. Brayton." (Tenders Accepted, 30 Sep 1857, p.5)
- "NOTICE.—The undersigned, being about to leave the district, requests that all persons to whom he is indebted will send in their accounts to Mr. O. B. Clapp, M'Ivor Hotel, Maryborough, by the 1st March, otherwise they will not be recognised. W. H. Brayton." (Advertising, 1 Mar 1859, p.4)
- "DON'T READ THIS ! And forget that the Best Description of Carriages can be had at No. 90 Bourke-street east, opposite Theatre Royal. W. H. Brayton, Proprietor." while "The Imported Trotting Stallion. Vermont Boy ... 5 yrs. Old, 15½ hands ... Will stand this season, at L10 10s each mare. Vermont Boy is the first trotting entire ever brought to Australia, and was specially chosen by the undersigned after a careful search over the eastern states of America, and amongst the best known trotting studs. PEDIGREE: Vermont Boy is by the trotting stallion Kessuth, of a famous broad mare, got by the celebrated Boston Tiger out of a thoroughbred English dam ... W. H. Brayton and O. B. Clapp." (Advertising, 17 Jan 1860, p.1)
- "NEW ZEALAND ... Mr W. H. Brayton, one of the Melbourne firm of Cobb and Co., arrived by the Alhambra from Melbourne. This company has chartered the Ocean Bride. She will bring sixty horses, and a number of coaches and freight waggons. The firm intend running coaches from Invercargill." (New Zealand, 12 Feb 1863, p.3)

Cobb and Co. proprietor—Victoria Stage Company

- "GEORGE DEIHL M'CORMICK ... Arthur Lincoln Blake (Head manager of business at Melbourne), Charles Culwell Gardiner, Jacob Rogers, Peleg Whitford Jackson, George Loop Woodworth, John Francis Britton, Levi Rich, Oliver Blake Clapp, Christopher Ives, John Murray Peck, James Joseph Blake formed under the style 'Victorian Stage Company,' on the 1st December 1857 ... Very soon after the business was launched by the purchase of Watson and Hewitt's line of coaches from Melbourne to Castlemaine ... after the business was launched the plaintiff [McCormick] and Mr. A. L. Blake had violent personal differences ... The rest of the firm sided with Mr. Blake, and supported him ... to establish new lines, which Mr. McCormick opposed." (Advertising, 19 Sep 1859, p.2)
- "NOTICE.—All Claims against, and all Debts due to, the Victorian Stage Company up to the 30th November, inst., must be sent in to the head office, No. 23 Bourke-street east, on or before the 16th December, proximo, as the partnership expires on the 30th inst. by effluxion of time. Victorian Stage Company, per A. L. BLAKE, Manager." (Advertising, 25 November 1859, p.3)
- "NEW YORK LIVERY and LETTING STABLES. 90 Bourke-street east, adjoining the Royal Mail Hotel and Cobb and Co.'s new booking office, and opposite the Theatre Royal. Saddle horses for ladies and gentlemen, buggies, barouches, carryalls, chaises, waggons, tiburies, dog-carts, trotting-sulkies, cabs, and light comfortable Coaches for picnics, excursions, &c. Livery for horses by the day, week, or month, on reasonable terms. Baits. Private sale-yards of the Victorian Stage Company for matched and single horses, of which a number are constantly on hand. Persons visiting the Theatre Royal may have their horses carefully attended to, and brought to the door of the theatre at close of the performance, or at five minutes' notice. Baits, or not, as desired. All the above-named vehicles are new. The horses have been selected for the express purpose of letting and comprise light showy hacks, and carriage horses, strong roadsters for journeys, fast trotters, and slow steady animals for family use. Parties having homes at this establishment may have them brought to their residence by leaving their orders with the manager. The proprietor, formerly a partner in the Victorian Stage Company, desires the favour of a call from all old friends and patrons of the line. F. J. Rogers, Proprietor. J. M. Bradley, Manager." (Advertising, 16 Apr 1860, p.8)
- "We, the undersigned, do hereby give notice that the Partnership hitherto existing, between us, under the style of the Victorian Stage Company, Expired by effluxion of time on the 25th of June ult. All claims against the said company up to that date must be sent in to A. L. Blake, the manager, in Melbourne, or to one of the agents mentioned below on or before the 21st of August, or they will not be recognised. The names of the agents are as follows :—J. F. Britton, Sandhurst ; P. W. Jackson, Castlemaine ; J. M. Connoll, Digger's Rest ; C. D. Pollock, Maryborough ; H. T. Millie, Shamrock Hotel, Ararat ; A. Montegani, Creswick's Creek ; E. T. Foley, Ballarat ; James Hay, M'Ivor ; Wm. Jones, Echuca. (Signed) Arthur Lincoln Blake. Peley Whitford Jackson. John Francis Britton. Oliver Blake Clapp. Christopher Ives. John Murray Peck. Charles Culwell Gardiner." (Advertising, 21 Jul 1860, p.3)
- "The Victorian Stage Company, which comprised thirteen partners, all 'Yankees" and Canadians, which took over the Bendigo road branches in the later part of 1875, and carried on under the old name of Cobb and Co. ... The thirteen included Peck, Blake, and Swanton, Cagg's old partners, the others being mostly overseers, and some of the most trusted drivers of the original firm ... Mr. George Woodworth, who died only last year, was the last survivor of Cobb and Co.'s original drivers, and one of the thirteen partners of the Victorian Stage Co., and the first to drive a 'Jack' into Bendigo. He often related that when he first took the ribbons on a 'Jack' it happened he had a light load.

> *She rolled so 'like a ship at sea' that for the whole of his stage from Castlemaine to Bendigo the sensation of top heaviness was so strong that he felt all the time she was going to lurch over his wheelers. But, the old man added with pride, never a Jack was known to leave her braces or lose her centre of gravity."*

(Cobb and Co., 20 Jun 1922, p.13)

Cobb and Co. proprietor—Australian Stage Company

- "F. B. Clapp and Co. now known as Australian Stage Company." (Advertising, 28 Jan 1861, p.1)
- "PROSPECTUS of the Australian Stage Company. Capital, £75,000, in 15,000 Shares of £5 each, Preliminary deposit of £1 per share to be paid on application, and the remaining sum of £4 per share within 14 days of allotment, or deposits will be forfeited. Operations will be commenced as soon as the amount of 8,000 shares are subscribed and paid up. In the event of the required number of shares not being subscribed for, the Directors undertake to return the deposits in full. Provisional Directors : William Randle, Esq., Melbourne. Cyrus Hewitt, Esq., Melbourne. William Williams, Esq., Melbourne. Matthew M'Caw, Esq., Melbourne. John R. Ricards, jun., Esq, Melbourne. John Halfey, Esq., Melbourne. A. L. Blake, Esq., Melbourne. F. B. Clapp, Esq., Melbourne. G. B. Perkins, Esq., Swan Hill. William Woods, Esq., Sandhurst. Thomas Ogilvie, Esq., Geelong. J. D. Robinson, Esq., Geelong. Hugh M'Phillimy, Esq., Geelong. C. C. Skarratt, Esq, Geelong. T. A. Lascelles, Esq., Geelong. J. T. Fallen, Esq., Albury. David Jones, Esq., Ballarat. Walter Craig, Esq., Ballarat. Alexander Kelly, Esq., Ballarat. Frederick Taylor, Esq., Castlemaine. Edward Cay, Esq., Castlemaine. B. Butterworth, Esq., Castlemaine. Caleb Anderson, Esq., Castlemaine. Charles Croaker, Esq., Portland. B. H. Fernald, Esq, Pitfield. William Malcolm, Esq., Hamilton. Joel Tompkins, Esq., Raglan. Oliver Cooper, Esq., Ararat. J. L. Huntley, Esq., Belfast. Francis Tozer, Esq., Warrnambool. With power to add to their number. Bankers—Bank of New South Wales. Solicitor—W. H. Gatty Jones, Esq. Secretary—W. Kent Hall, Esq. The magnitude of the interests involved in the operations connected with the various stage lines for passenger and mail conveyance radiating from the cities of Melbourne and Geelong has engaged, for some time past, the attention of the projectors of this enterprise, with a view to concentrate under one co-operative management the various and often conflicting interests of individual proprietors. It is anticipated that under the auspices of a responsible and influential joint stock proprietary, and in contemplation of the opening of the Melbourne and Sandhurst, and Geelong and Ballarat lines of railway, the business would assume a permanent form, and the sphere of its operations be profitably extended. Overland communication with Sydney by a main trunk line, with branches diverging to the more important townships on the route, including the Snowy River district, would appear to be amongst the legitimate and immediate extensions of this enterprise, to accomplish which a very small additional out-lay will be needed, as a large quantity of surplus stock, the property of the present proprietors, is available for the purpose ... negotiations have been opened with the Victorian Stage Company, Messrs. F. B. Clapp and Co. (proprietors of the lines known as Cobb and Co.'s Telegraph Lines), and other coach proprietors ... As the receipts of this company will be in cash, and the whole of the stock being in a high state of efficiency, needing no outlay for present requirements, it may be confidently anticipated that a dividend will be declared at an early date. It is determined that no transfer of shares shall be recognized until the 1st January, 1861, when the transfer book of the company will be opened."

On the same page ... "HOLLOWAY'S OINTMENT.—Possessed of this remedy every man is his own family physician. If his wife or children are troubled with eruptions of the skin, sores, tumors, white swellings, sore throats, asthma, or any other external ailment, a persevering use of the Ointment is all that is necessary to produce a radical cure. It is invaluable to the population of this climate. BAD LEGS AND BAD BREASTS. In no case has this Ointment been known to fail either in the cure of bad legs or bad breasts ; thousands of persons of all ages have been effectually cured by it when discharged from hospitals as incurable. If the dropsy settles in the legs, the Ointment will cure it if used with the Pills." (Advertising, 7 May 1860, p.8)

- "AUSTRALIAN STAGE COMPANY ... The share-list will remain open until the 12th June, and the alotment made as soon after as practicable. The lines negotiated for include those set out in the schedule annexed. (See propectus.) All application for shares to be made to the Provisional Directors, at their offices, 3 Hall of Commerce, Melbourne. Forms of application may be obtained from the undermentioned agents, viz. : Ogilvie and Robinson, Geelong. S. C. Burt, Esq., Sydney. L. Macpherson, Sandhurst. B. Butterworth, Castlemaine. A. Kelly, Ballarat. Melbourne, May 6 1860." (Advertising, 28 May 1860, p.8)
- "NOTICE.—We, the undersigned, hereby give notice, that we have withdrawn our names from the published list of directors of the Australian Stage Company, and ceased to have any connexion therewith since the 22nd ult, Dated June 8, 1860. Benjamin Butterworth. Caleb Anderson. Edward Cay. F. Taylor" (Advertising, 11 Jun, 1860, p.8) Advertised the same week "INTRODUCTION OF AUSTRALIAN BIRDS INTO BRITAIN.—Gentleman desirous to aid in Mr. Edward Wilson's plan of introducing the Australian magpie and laughing jackass into Britain are requested to send birds of those species to the undersigned, who will be glad to arrange for their transmission to Europe. Ferd. Mueller, Melbourne Botanical and Zoological Gardens, January 18." (Advertising, 12 Jun, 1860, p.3)

Cobb and Co. proprietors—Robertson, Britton and Co. (Alexander William Robertson, John Britton)

- "BENDIGO STAGE COMPANY. A. W. Robertson, Manager." (Advertising, 15 Aug 1860, p.8)
- "NOTICE.—The partnership hitherto existing between Alexander W. Robertson, William B. Bradley, Walter R. Hall, William F. Whitney, Edward Moore, and Frank May, and trading under the name of the Bendigo Stage Company, has been this day dissolved, by mutual consent, that is so far as said Alexander W. Robertson is concerned, who retires from the firm, having disposed of his interest in the same to the above named W. B. Bradley, W. R. Hall, W. F. Whitney, Edward Moore, and F. May, who will still continue to carry on the business as heretofore. Alexander W. Robertson. William B. Bradley. Walter R. Hall. William F. Whitney. Edward Moore. Frank May. Witness—B. G. Teasdale." (Advertising, 1 Feb 1861, p.8)
- "£2 REWARD. LOST, from Cobb's Coach, which left Woodend at 9 a.m., on Monday, the 21st inst., between Woodend and Castlemaine, a bag containing Set of Double Buggy Harness, silver mounted. The finder will receive Two Pounds reward, on delivery of same, at any of Cobb's offices, Woodend, Kyneton, or Castlemaine. Robertson, Britton and Co., Commercial Hotel." (Advertising, 1 Nov 1861, p.8)

- "CASTLEMAINE MINING DIVISION ... Outstanding accounts. The following parties are requested to call at the Sub Treasury, for their accounts:—Robertson, Britton and Co." (Advertising, 17 Jan 1862, p.5)
- "FOR SALE. The well-known coach factory in Forest-street, now occupied by Messrs. Robertson, Britton, and Co., Stage Proprietor." (Advertising, 7 Apr 1862, p.3)
- "PRELIMINARY NOTICE. FOR THE LACHLAN GOLD FIELDS DIRECT. Cobb and Co. will despatch a number of Coaches for the Lachlan Diggings direct on or about the 28th of May. Intending passengers can be booked at any of Cobb and Co.'s offices in the Colony of Victoria. The Coaches will leave Ballarat on or about the 28th of May. The day of starting will be published in another advertisement. Fare from Sandhurst. £5. E. J. Brayton, Agent." (Advertising, 24 May 1862, p.1)
- "For The LACHLAN GOLDFIELDS. Special Notice. To prevent the travelling public from laboring under any misapprehension respecting the coaches which we intend sending to the Lachlan Goldfields, we to state that we despatch a number of coaches for there, one trip only, leaving Sandhurst (Bendigo) on Monday, the 2nd of June. Fare from Sandhurst, £5. Per COBB & Co. A. C. Brunig, Manager." (Advertising, 30 May 1862, p.5)
- "OFF TO THE LACHLAN.—On Monday morning last twelve coaches, well horsed, several forage waggons, and a lot of loose horses, belonging to Messrs. Robertson and Britton, the coach proprietors—the successors and present representatives, of Cobb and Co., of Victoria coaching celebrity—passed through Deniliquin en route to the Lachlan." (Deniliquin Police Court, 13 Jun 1862, p.3)

Cobb and Co. proprietors—Robertson, Wagner and Co. (Alexander William Robertson, John Wagner, George John Watson, William James/James Rutherford, W. B. Bradley, William Franklin Whitney)

- "Mr Britton sold his interest, and Mr John Wagner entered into partnership with Mr Robertson, since which Robertson, Wagner Co. have controlled and owned the business." (Reminiscences of Cobb and Co., 26 Jan 1898, p.4)
- "Cobb & Co.'s Telegraph Line of Mail Coaches in connection with the Melbourne & Mount Alexander Railway ... Robertson, Wagner & Co." (Advertising 28 May 1862, p.3)
- "Great changes, the Talbot Leader reports, have recently taken place in the coach proprietors of this district. A few weeks since Messrs. Cobb and Co. sold their plant on this line to Messrs. Robertson, Wagner, and Co., of Castlemaine, and two or three days ago the same firm purchased Messrs. Gasquoine and Co., the contractors for the mail ... By these arrangements Messrs. Robertson, Wagner, and Co. will secure a complete monopoly of the road from Ballarat to Talbot and Maryborough on the one side, and from Castlemaine to Inglewood on the other. We hope the new firm will inaugurate their career by placing better coaches on the line from Talbot to Ballarat than has been the case hitherto. For years a journey to Ballarat or Castlemaine has been a positive infliction, owing to the extremely uncomfortable nature of the coaches." (Advertising, 12 Mar 1866, p.5)
- "COBB AND CO.'S TELEGRAPH LINE.—Accommodation Coach.—Beaufort and Ballarat ... Robertson, Wagner and Co." (Advertising, 1 Apr 1867, p.1)
- "An extraordinary journey was made yesterday by Messrs. Robertson, Wagner, Geo. Watson, and James, proprietors of the Beechworth line of mail-coaches. The party, in buggy drawn by two horses (with changes) made the extraordinary trip of 163 miles, from Wangaratta to Melbourne, starting at four a.m., and reaching Melbourne at seven p.m By far the greater part of the journey was over bush roads, and Mr. George Watson drove all the way.

  The result shows the quality of Australian horses, and also the capacity of the driver.

  It may be added the party stopped not unfrequently to refresh the cattle [horses], and had a far from hasty dinner at Avenel, on the road." ('Tuesday, January 14, 1868', 14 Jan 1868, p.5)
- "Judgments have been signed in the Supreme Court against the Queen in favour of Elizabeth Wingate Grant, for £80, and £6 1s. 3d. costs; Alex. W. Robertson, George John Watson, Willian James, and John Wagner, for £132; and £6 1s. 6d. costs; John H. W. Pettiit, £52 10s., £6 6s. 4d. costs." (The Gippsland Times, 7 Jul 1868, p.2)
- "RUN OF CROWN LANDS ... Warrego District ... Back of Back Moodana ... Jas. Rutherford, J. Wagner & A. W. Robertson." (Run of Crown Lands, 31 Oct 1871, p.2495)
- "DISSOLUTION OF PARTNERSHIP.—Notice is hereby given, that the partnership heretofore existing between the undersigned, as station owners and coach proprietors, in the colonies of Victoria, New South Wales, and Queensland, has been this day dissolved by mutual consent. Dated 15th day of August, 1871 A. W. Robertson, J. Rutherford, W. B. Bradley, Wm. F. Whitney, John Wagner. Witness—Alf B. Malieson, solicitor and notary public, Melbourne." (Advertising, 23 Dec 1871, p.3)
- "LOST, near Opera-house, gold bracelet, diamond setting. Finder rewarded. A. W. Robertson, Cobb and Co." (Advertising, 19 Mar 1873, p.8)
- "ENTRIES FOR OAKS AND DERBY. The entries for the Victoria Coursing Club Oaks and Derby closed yesterday afternoon, at the office of the club, in Bank-place. For the Derby 49 entries were sent in the following names ... J. Wagner, G. Watson ... The entries for the Oakes were much better, there being 63 names sent in, the nominators being ... J. Wagner, G. Watson ... The sires best represented are Cumloden, Inverniven, Pilot, and Young King." (Entries for Oaks and Derby, 21 Nov 1874, p.12)
- "VICTORIA COURSING CLUB ... Stewards ... John Wagner, Geo. Watson ... A Piece of Plate, value £20, given by the club for competition amongst the six greyhounds beaten by Lavender Water (disqualified) in the St. Leger Stakes of 1874." (Victoria Coursing Club Second Meeting 1875, 15 May 1875, p.5)
- "NAME OF RUN. Woollagoola West, Woollagoola, Morbella, Morbella West, Goolagoola, Mara Creek, Waughgandary, Grahway, Beriarh, Wandabringey. From whom transferred. A. W. Robertson and J. Rutherford. To whom transferred.
- J. Rutherford, W. B. Bradley, W. F. Whitney, and W. R. Hall." (Transfer of Runs, 25 April 1876, p.1632)

- "NEW YORK LIFE INSURANCE CO., Purely Mutual. Accumulated funds ... £11,387,945 Surplus over all liabilities 2,139,335 ... RISKS accepted and claims paid in pounds sterling at branch office, 77 Collins-street west, Melbourne. Board of Reference for Victoria: Herbert James Henty, Esq., J.P., chairman (James Henty and Co.) R. J. Alcock, Esq., (James Service and Co.) R. J. Horsfall, Esq., (R. Goldsborough and Co., Limited) G. Fairburn, jun., Esq., (Wm. Sloane and Co.) Hon. J. F. Levies, M.L.A., Minister of Mines, B. J. Fink, Esq., M.L.A. A. W. Robertson, Esq., (Robertson Wagner and Co.) A. W. Fraser, Esq., J.P. (Fraser and Co.) James Robertson, Esq., M.D. C. W. Gibson, Esq., (Fisken, Gibson and Co.) Ed. Waters. Esq., Thomas Purves, Manager. Agent for Sale and district—S. Karan, Watchmaker, Foster-street. Medical Examiner—J. A. Reid, Esq., M.D., Cunninghame-street." (Advertising, 26 Jan 1885, p.1)
- "NOTIFICATION OF RESUMPTION OF LANDS FOR ROADS ... Land District of Deniliquin. Parish No. 70, 12, 13, 14, 4, 3, 2, 1, Parish Name Yarraman, Reputed Owner. A. W. Robertson and J. Wagner. Occupier. A. W. Robertson and J. Wagner ... widening of road." (Notification of Resumption of Lands for Roads, 11 Jan 1896, p.260)
- "DEPARTMENT OF LANDS ... Renewal of Occupation Leases for 1897 ... Telleraga ... Alexander William Robertson, Salathiel Booth, and John Wagner ... Estimated Area Available 5,325 Acres." (Renewal of Occupation Licenses for 1897, 30 Sep 1896, p.6871)
- "Mr. Alfred Deakin's father was for many years accountant in the Bourke-street, Melbourne, office of the firm, and had been previously partner in a Melbourne firm of coach proprietors. Mr. A. W. Robertson was living at Castlemaine, then the hub of the firm's Victorian activities, and Mr. John Wagner was at Bendigo, also a big centre." (Cobb & Co., 18 Jun 1918, p.4)

Death of A. W. Robertson

- "JOHN WAGNER DIED YESTERDAY ... Robertson and Wagner dissolved with A. W. Robertson's death in 1896." (Death of Mr. John Wagner, 28 Jan 1901, p.7)
- "It may here be stated that the two members of the firm, who originated the campaign in New South Wales in 1861—A. W. Robertson and John Wagner—were British Americans, being natives of Canada, and, were splendid types of the men who, in all new countries, are resolute and resourceful colonisers. As employers, they were just and liberal in all dealings with their vast army of employees, as evidence of which there was never during their 40 years of coaching business the slightest friction between them and their employees. It can truthfully be said, too, that never had a firm a more capable, loyal, and faithful body of servants. Several of them filled important positions in the public life of the Australian States; amongst whom may be mentioned Mr. John Taverner, the present Agent-General for Victoria in London, who was a stage coach driver on the Bendigo to Swan Hill Road in Victoria. Mr. A. R. Outtrim, the present M.L.A. for Maryborough, and ex-Minister for Mines in that State, and F. A. Byrne, driver, agent, and manager, and ex-M.L.A. for Hay, in New South Wales. In this connection it may be mentioned that the father of Mr. Alfred Deakin, an old coaching man, and member of the old-time firm of Bill and Deakin, was accountant to Robertson, Wagner, and Co. for several years." (The Contributor, 25 Nov 1908, p.1405)
- "Very few of the pioneers of Victoria were better known than Mr A W Robertson, and his numerous friends will learn with deep regret of his death, which occurred yesterday at his residence, Orrong-road ... Mr Robertson lived a comparatively quiet life for many years but in the gold digging era he was one of the most prominent energetic and enterprising of our business men. He came to the colony in the year 1853 from Hawkesbury, Ottawa, Canada. If he was not a native of Canada he was born on the voyage over from Scotland to that place, and he always regarded himself as a Canadian. He was attracted to Victoria by the richness of our alluvial gold diggings and for a few years after his arrival he sought fortune on the gold fields trying his luck at Fiery Creek (now known as Beaufort) and other places. After a few years he started business as a carrier. Those were the days when £100 a ton was given for cartage from Melbourne to Beechworth or to Bendigo, and Mr Robertson, who was a keen organiser, saw the possibilities of the situation. He soon had a number of teams under his control on the roads, and being himself stationed in Melbourne, was able to arrange for freights and keep his teams going constantly ... Robertson's teams became recognised as the most expeditious, punctual, and reliable on the roads, and he profited accordingly ... It was not long before the competing firms were amalgamated under the management of Mr. Robertson, who became the leading spirit of the whole concern. The new firm obtained the contracts for the carriage of Her Majesty's mails at a reduction of something like £40,000 on what had been paid the previous year.

> The story of the early days of coaching in the colonies has yet to be written and a most interesting and exciting narrative it would make.

The drivers were nearly all remarkable characters, possessing a marked individuality of their own. Many of them were, like Mr Robertson, British Americans. He showed keen insight in the choice of his drivers and other employees and in the management of the large business had full scope for his splendid organising faculty. The punctuality which was maintained in spite of many obstacles was remarkable, and was a thing in which Mr Robertson took an especial pride. Faith was kept with the public in the most careful manner and people could regulate their watches by the arrival or departure of Robertson and Wagner's coaches ... The firm had factories at Bendigo, Castlemaine and Kilmore, where they built their own coaches. Castlemaine was for years a principal centre of the coaching business and there Mr Robertson resided for a considerable time. The business under his management was very profitable until the railways cut off a great deal of the work ... He was a genial kindly man and was always popular with his employes and those connected with him in business. He took no part in public affairs, but was closely identified with the pastoral interest, and for some time was chairman of directors of Goldsbrough Mort, and Co Limited. As a sportsman he was connected with the Victoria Racing Club, of which body he was a committee man and steward. Mr Robertson was twice married but survived both his wives. He had a family of six children and three sons and two daughters survive him. He has been in failing health for the last two years and for the past two months his decease has been anticipated by his relatives." (Death of Mr A. W. Robertson, 17 Jul 1896, p.6)

- "THE DEATH OF MR A. W. ROBERTSON. We regret to have to announce the death of Mr A. W. Robertson, of the firm of Robertson and Wagner, one of the pioneers of coaching in this colony. Mr Robertson had been seriously ailing for the last two years, and for the three months prior to his decease had been confined to the house. His death, which occurred at midday on Thursday at his residence, Ontario, Balaclava road, Caulfield, was not due to any particular disease, but rather to general debility and break down of his constitution, he being 65 years of age. For some years he has had poor health, and his condition was rendered much more serious by an accident he had in a lift in the Hotel Australia, Sydney, some months ago, in which his ribs and collar bone were badly injured. During the past three days he had been insensible, and Dr T. N. Fitzgerald, who was unremitting in his attention, recognised at the beginning of the week that his patient's case was hopeless. He arrived in Melbourne in 1853 and was on the gold fields for several years, chiefly in the Castlemaine district. About this time he met Mr Wagner, who had also come from Canada, and the two entering into partnership bought a portion of Cobb and Co. coaching routes ... rapidly extending the routes in every direction,

  they were not only the pioneers of the gold fields, but of almost all parts of the colony.

  Castlemaine was made the headquarters, and with a line of waggons established between Melbourne and Bendigo they were very successful. The principal coach routes of the firm at the outset were to Castlemaine and Bendigo, and in the Echuca and North-Eastern districts. After coaching there for many years they extended their operations into Gippsland, and ultimately into New South Wales ... Mr Robertson, who lived at Castlemaine as managing partner, was considered one of the smartest business men in Victoria. For years the firm were the principal contractors for mails, and retain some of them to the present day. Several years ago they sold out of many of their routes, and remaining interested in coaching in Victoria only to a slight extent, although they still retain a few lines in New South Wales, in the Deniliquin and Hay districts. Mr Robertson was also largely interested in mining and pastoral pursuits. He possessed a large share in the Marathon Station in Queensland, and, in conjunction with Mr Wagner, held other large pastoral interests, notably Perricoota Station, near Echuca, Medkin Station, in the Moree district, and Orban, in Queensland. He was several times requested to stand for the Legislative Council, and although he held immense influence he preferred to devote his attention to private pursuits. He was considered one of the best 'whips' in the colony and a great lover of horses. Personally he was one of the most generous and liberal minded of men in all his dealings and a man of whom it is said by those who knew him most intimately that he never made an enemy." (The Death of Mr A. W. Robertson, 18 Jul 1896, p.2)

- "MR. A. W. ROBERTSON ... a shrewd, genial, and popular man ... His home for many years was Ottawa, Orrong-road, Caulfield." (Obituary, 18 Jul 1896, p.34)

- "MR. ROBERTSON ... possessed a large share in the Marathon Station in Queensland, and, in conjunction with Mr. Wagner, held other large pastoral interests." (Death of a Cobb's Coach Pioneer, 21 Jul 1896, p.2)

- "In private life Mr Robertson was held in affectionate esteem, and in his business dealings his word was his bond. The deceased gentleman took no part in the politics of the day, his position as a Government contractor rendering it impossible for him to do so." (Country Notes, 21 Jul 1896, p.3)

- "ROBERTSON AND WAGNER ... Pericoota, on the Murray, is one of their fine possessions. The Duke of Edinburgh got some good shooting there during his visit to Australia, and his Royal Highness, who never forgets an Australian face, was glad to renew Mr. Robertson's acquaintance in London in the eighties, when the owner of Pericoota gave a splendid at home and got Melba to sing to his distinguished guests. On the whole the firm were very successful in their ventures, and one of their happy purchases was a number of Mount Morgan shares before the mine had been developed." (Obituary, 18 Jul 1896, p.34)

- "The funeral took places on Saturday afternoon, starting from the late residence of the deceased, 'Ontario,' corner of Caulfield and Orrong roads, and proceeding thence to the Boroondara cemetery. There was a very large attendance, the mourners comprising many well known public men. Nearly 100 vehicles joined the cortège. The service at the grave was conducted by the Rev. W. Fellows, and when the massive oaken casket in which the remains of the deceased were enclosed was lowered into the family vault an immense number of wreaths and floral offerings were laid upon it, prominent among them being tributes from the Victoria Racing Club and the Victoria Amateur Turf Club. The pall bearers were Dr. Lloyd, Mr. J. A. Panton, Mr. T. N. Fitzgerald, Mr. C. H. Wagner, Mr. F. Clapp and Mr. Mitchell. The funeral arrangements were in the hands of Mr. W. G. Apps." (The Late A. W. Robertson, 25 Jul 1896, p.7)

- "The old scythe bearer has been busy during the past week. First came the death of Mr. A. W. Robertson ... The deceased gentleman was one of the links that connected the colony's present with its past ... More than one sensational incident was attached to the Robertson and Wagner coaching period. I remember 'Cabbage Tree Ned' driving his sixteen horse team along the Plank-road into Ballarat with the Government House party aboard, with the coach one mass of flags, and bands playing. Ballarat, despite its Eureka troubles, was essentially loyal then, and for many years after ... It was under Mr. Robertson's reign, too, that another sensational incident occurred, it was during the time of the American civil war. News had come of a northern victory, and the coach that drove up to the Exchange Hotel had the Stars and stripes flying 'fore and aft.' In addition, whether intentionally or by accident, was never known, the Union Jack was hung under the American flag. An Englishman in the crowd saw this, communicated it to his fellows, and at once there was a cry 'Up with the Union Jack.' Not mind you down with the Stars and Stripes. The driver, backed up by a number of American friends, at first refused, the crowd grew more clamorous, pistols and knives were talked of, and there were all the elements of a serious row. Mr. Robertson, however, opportunely put in an appearance, and the riot was quelled, by the two flags being hung amid cheers, side by side on the hotel walls and over the coaching office. Mr. Robertson had many anecdotes to tell of wild bushranging days when 'bail up' was a well known cry to the drivers.

Indeed, no man I suppose could have furnished more 'vivid' materials for the making of our early history. To the last he maintained the popularity his manliness and geniality had earned for him whether as a private friend, a business man or as a member of the V.R.C. Committee." (Our Melbourne Letter, 25 Jul 1896, p.3)

- "WILL OF THE LATE MR. A. W. ROBERTSON PROPERTY IN VICTORIA, £22,410. The registrar has received for probate the will of Alexander William Robertson, late of 'Ontario,' Balaclava, gentleman, who died on the 16th of July last, leaving a will dated February 2, 1895, and six codicils, dated respectively July 31, 1895, January 12, 1896, June 9, 1896, July 6, 1896, July 9, 1896, July 11, 1896. Value of property in Victoria—real £12,510, personal £9,900. With the exception of a legacy of 50 guineas to the Rev. Walter Fellows, testator leaves the whole of his property to his children and other relations." (Will of the Late Mr. A. W. Robertson, 15 Oct 1896, p.6)

- "THE GRAND SALE of Sumptuous art, furniture of The Late A. W. Robertson, Esq. To be held at His Late Residence, Ontario, Corner of Balaclava and Orrong Roads, East St. Kilda. To the elite of Melbourne, Lovers of Art, &c." (Advertising, 8 Jul 1897, p.2)

Death of John Wagner

- "Mr John Wagner, the well-known coach proprietor, died on Sunday afternoon at his residence, Stonington, Glenferrie, at the age of 74, after a painful illness extending over three years. Mr Wagner, who was a native of Canada, was born on an estate which had been in the possession of the family for several generations, which was originally a gift of royalty in recognition of the loyal support which the family had rendered to the Throne. When about 18 years of age he went to California to seek his fortune, but eventually he drifted over to Victoria among the earliest of the gold seekers. The difficulty of transport was one of the most serious that the prospector had to encounter, and Mr Wagner quickly saw the possibilities in good lines of coaches. He made a start in that direction in 1852, and a few years later had established several lines about Geelong. He went into partnership with Messrs Hewitt and Co., and married an American lady, a sister of Mr Hewitt. Later Mr Wagner joined Mr A. W. Robertson in establishing the firm of Robertson and Wagner, coach proprietors, and the new firm bought up several coaching lines, including the Bendigo service. This was, of course, before the introduction of railways, and the firm carried the mails for many years, the lines of coaches all being run under the title of Cobb and Co.'s. The partners were also engaged in pastoral pursuits, and at one time held a large interest in the famous Mount Morgan mine, before the formation of the company which purchased the property. The partnership was dissolved by Mr Roberson's death in 1896, and since that date Mr Wagner purchased several estates in New South Wales and Queensland. He was an enthusiastic sportsman, and in his early days kept a large kennel of greyhounds, and was noted as an excellent judge of horses. Mr Wagner leaves a family of two sons and three daughters. One of his daughters married Major Hamman, who retired from the army before the outbreak of war in South Africa, but was recalled last June, and is now quartered in Cornwall. Another daughter married Mr S. M'Culloch, of Melbourne. His eldest son, Mr John Wagner, practised for some time as a barrister in Melbourne and Sydney, but subsequently took up journalism as a profession, and is now literary editor of the 'New York Sun'." (Death of Mr John Wagner, 29 Jan 1901, p.2)

- "One of Hay's oldest industries has been closed, Messrs. Robertson, Wagner and Co. having discontinued the business of coach and buggy builders which they have carried on in connection with their coaching operations for many years. Cobb and Co.'s factory was started in 1877, and for many years was the leading local industry, over thirty men being employed at one time. The advent of the railway led to a diminution of the coaching business, and to a corresponding decrease in that of the factory, but a good number of men have been engaged up to the present. The standard of the work turned out by the firm has always been high, and the manufactures of the firm enjoy a nigh reputation. Mr Henry Proctor, who, for the past fifteen years, has managed the business, succeeds to the good-will, and will hereafter carry on operations in the premises opposite Tattersall's." (No Title, 10 Jul 1896, p.2)

- "Jack Wagner, the Australian barrister, has been living by his pen during the last few years in America, and some of his efforts at the playwright's art have brought him praise and money in the United States. Mr. Wagner is a son of one of the principals in the well-known coaching and squatting firm of Robertson and Wagner—Cobb and Company." (Personal, 18 Dec 1896, p.2)

Cobb and Co. proprietors—Henry Hoyt/H. Hoyt

- "FRANCIS BOARDMAN CLAPP ... associated himself with Mr. Henry Hoyt, with whom he had been in partnership in his coaching days, and Mr. William McCulloch, the proprietor of Kirk's Bazaar." (Death of Mr. F. B. Clapp, 7 Sep 1920, p.6)

- "NEW YORK and AUSTRALIAN HORSE and CARRIAGE MART and LIVERY and LETTING STABLES.—The proprietor of the above-named establishment, having at considerable expense supplied the stables with a splendid stock of horses and the best carriages in the colony, is prepared to contract with ladies and gentlemen for carriages and horses by the week, month, or year, on the most reasonable terms. Henry Hoyt, proprietor, 90 Bourke-street east, opposite Theatre Royal. Geo. Glasscock, manager." While appearing on the same page "Astrology & Chiromancy. Madame Siecle, late Madame Eckardt, is continually visited by persons of the highest standing, to whom she has revealed their past lives and future. 106 Lonsdale-street west." (Advertising, 3 Mar 1866, p.6)

- "RECEIVED FROM MR. HENRY HOYT, one of the promoters of the Melbourne Omnibus Company ... Sir,—I have the honour to intimate to you that being convinced in my mind of the very great necessity there exists of establishing in Sydney a complete omnibus reform. I frequently intended, if time would allow me, to pay a visit to this city for the purpose of laying my views before the Corporation, and, if possible, of introducing a system exactly similar to that carried out in Melbourne with such success by the Melbourne Omnibus Company. The system in Melbourne is now so complete, that there is not the slightest hitch. The aldermen are grateful, the public is delighted. And in consequence of the easy and frequent communication with the outskirts of the city, property in the suburbs has enhanced in value very considerably. I have imported from New York ten omnibuses, at a cost of £220 each, built on the latest and best principle, six of which are now in Sydney, and can be seen by you at any time you may appoint.

I enclose you the rules (for your perusal) of the Melbourne Omnibus Company, and will engage to run my omnibuses in strict accordance with these rules on the leading thorough-fares—say Queen's Wharf and Glebe—provided the Corporation give me the inducement I consider necessary, and which I do not consider a very great one, considering the vast expenditure I must incur as well as the many advantages the public will derive. My proposition is as follows:—I will place ten omnibuses, erected on the most perfect and convenient principle, between, say, Queen's Wharf and Glebe, with the best harness, horses, and drivers procurable, and run every five minutes up to 12 o'clock at night ; provided I am granted by the Corporation a separate and distinct stand at once, and the exclusive right to the road on the 1st of January, 1872. I will also provide a suitable waiting room for passengers in the centre of George-street, or in any place the Corporation may decide. If encouraged, I will also, before long, provide sufficient omnibuses on the same principle on the other lines of the city, I have the honour to be, Sir, your most obedient servant, Henry Hoyt." (Proposed New Lines of Omnibuses, 20 Sep 1871, p.5)

Cobb and Co. proprietors—M'Phee & Co./John M'Phee

- "FATAL ACCIDENT AT COBB AND CO.'S STABLES. An accident by which a young man named Frederick Halse, aged twenty-two, was suddenly deprived of life, occurred at two o'clock on Tuesday morning in a shop in Lydiard street, next to Cobb and Co.'s stables. It appears from the evidence taken at the inquest ... John M'Phee, coach proprietor, deposed that he was lessee of the premises in question, known as M'Phee and Company's stables." (Fatal Accident at Cobb and Co's Stables, 6 Apr 1870, p.2)

- "NEWS AND NOTES. Another big coach load of rushers went off from Cobb's Corner for Sandhurst on Wednesday morning, and the whole Corner adjourned to see the phenomenon. Instead of throwing old slippers after the voyagers, three or four dishonored cheques, drawn by some of them, were flouted before their eyes and the eyes of the sympathetic host of onlookers.

- A SERIOUS ACCIDENT happened on Wednesday to Mr John M'Phee, of M'Phee and Co., the well-known coach proprietors. At about half-past twelve o'clock in the afternoon Mr. M'Phee left his house at Soldiers' Hill in a buggy, and was driving down the hill in Armstrong street towards the Gnarr Creek bridge, when the horse tried to get away. The strain on the reins caused the one on the near side, to break, and the horse then went down the hill at a gallop. There is no thoroughfare over the Gnarr Creek bridge, and vehicles have to pass between the side of the bridge and the footpath. The side of the embankment has not been fenced, and fearing that the horse would drag the buggy into this hollow, Mr M'Phee threw himself out of the vehicle. He was picked up by several persons who were passing at the time, and then taken into the Corporation baths while Dr Whitcombe was sent for. Before the doctor arrived Mr M'Phee was removed to his own house. It was found that the small bone of the ankle joint was broken, and that Mr M'Phee had also, received a nasty cut on the temple. He was attended by Drs Whitcombe and Radcliffe. The horse bolted through the town with the buggy at a rapid pace, and ultimately ran against a heavy waggon, and came to grief. The buggy was considerably damaged, and the horse also sustained some injuries. It is high time that the City Council took action to have the Gnarr Creek embankment fenced." (Notes and News, 19 Oct 1871, p.2)

- "MARR v. M'PHEE & CO. The following is the Courier report of the case of Marr v. M'Phee :— This was an action brought by Dr. Marr, of Ballan, to recover from the defendants, who are owners of some of Cobb's coaches, £3,000 damages for injuries sustained by him while riding on the coach from Ballan to Melbourne ... On the 8th August he took his seat on the box of the coach to Melbourne, in company with the driver and Mr. Cheri Mars ...

  The driver was depressed, and said he had been up all night dancing.

  At the bottom of the hill, near Bacchus Marsh, down which they went at a great speed, the coach upset, and witness was thrown off ...

  Patrick O'Hagan gave evidence that the axle broke at a flaw in the iron. The iron, he considered, was of poor quality the grain being very coarse. The flaw could only have, been noticed after the breakage ... William Marshall, a blacksmith at Bacchus Marsh, deposed that a sudden jolt must have caused the accident. Morris Nash deposed that when the accident happened the coach was going at a reasonable speed. He knew the driver, who was a careful one ... Charles D. Pollock deposed he knew the driver Steele; and that he was always reckoned one of the best his Honour, proceeded to sum up, putting whether bad workmanship, bad iron, or bad driving had been proved. After less than half an hour's retiral, the jury returned into court. The foreman said they had agreed to give a verdict for the defendants, each party to pay their own costs. His Honour said he could not accept this, and a verdict was then given for the defendants." (Marr v. M'Phee & Co., 6 May 1876)

- "DEATH OF MR JOHN M'PHEE ... the well known coach proprietor and owner of Woodstock Estate, Lilicur, will cause profound regret amongst his vast circle of friends and aquaintances. Perhaps there was no more generally known man in the colony than the genial John M'Phee .. The deceased, who was 67 years of age, was an old and well-known colonist, being one of the coaching pioneers of Victoria, and in no little way helped to build up the colony. The following extract which we take from that well-known work 'Victoria and its Metropolis—: past and present will no doubt be read with interest ... John M'Phee, Ballarat, is a native of Scotland. He landed in Melbourne in 1852, and in company with two cousins made his way to Bendigo being amongst the first diggers at Ironbark and Pegleg gullies. He went to Ballarat at the commencement of Eureka lead and Little Bendigo, and left the diggings just before the Eureka Stockade riot, and was in Melbourne when the military left there for the scene of the disturbance ... He joined Cobb and Co in 1860 and has since occupied an important position in the Company's business in the Ballarat and Geelong divisions. The magnitude of Cobb and Co.'s coaching operations then is well and widely known, but it may not be generally known that the business was started by Mr Cobb in person, and that there were at one time five different companies running in conjunction, but each on its own account. Mr M'Phee was one of the few remaining of the original promoters of this business.

About 40 years ago he began to acquire land and some 20 yours ago bought Woodstock. He has had many adventures during his coaching career and was driving the leading coach of the caravan engaged to convoy a large body of Chinese from Creswick to Clunes to replace the Europeans during the strike on 9th of December 1873, when as the caravan neared Clunes it was stopped by a barricade, behind which were several hundred men and women, who sent forth such a volley of missiles that both caravan and police had to retreat to Ascot. The 'Excelsior', the coach driven by Mr M'Phee, though well preserved still bears marks of the affray." (Death of Mr John M'Phee, 3 Nov 1899, p.2)

- "Mr. Smiley's visit emphasised a note of personal interest, for he was able to tell me something of my grandfather, one 'Johnny' McLean, in his day among the best-known drivers in the State. In December, 1912, he laid down the reins after having handled them continuously for fifty-one years. Arriving from Fort William, Scotland, in '59, he became the picked driver of his cousin, John M'Phee, who, I believe, took over part of the plant and routes of Cobb and Co. I was interested to learn from Mr. Smiley that the grand old jack-coach, now in the Melbourne Museum, the only one now south of the line, was John M'Phee's." (Memories and Musings, 22 May 1941, p.14)

Cobb and Co. proprietors—Vines and M'Phee (Joshua Vines, Father of Arthur Nicolls Vines)

- "COACH ACCIDENT On The Queenscliff Road. An accident which might have resulted more seriously than it fortunately did occurred on Saturday afternoon on the Queenscliff road, east of Kensington Hill, one of Cobb and Co.'s coaches, laden with 21 passengers, overturning in the middle of the roadway and depositing its occupants in a heap in the dust. It appears that, in accordance with instructions received, the firm named despatched a four-horse coach, driven by Mr T. Vines (son of Mr. J. Vines, one of the proprietary) to the railway station at midday on Saturday, to meet a party of Wesleyan clergymen and laymen from Melbourne, who wished to be driven to Barwon Heads, to decide upon a site for a clergymen's sanatorium at Ocean Grove—the name given to a very picturesque part of the coast on the Geelong side of the Barwon Heads, where it is intended to erect a Grand Coffee Palace which is designed as an appropriate seaside retreat for metropolitans at suitable seasons of the year ... Everything went smilingly until Kensington Hill had been passed, when, as the team were bowling grandly along the level road,

> the near fore-axle suddenly broke at the collar washer and caused the near wheel to give way, the result being that the coach swerved and turned completely over, the passengers being thrown out in a huddled heap. The driver was precipitated between the wheelers and fell straddle-legs on the pole, but with immediate presence of mind he 'scrambled' over the back of the 'off-sider,' and leaped, clear of the team, to the ground ...

The horses bolted with the fore-carriage, which became detached, but their mad career was stopped suddenly by a mob of cattle which occupied the roadway about one hundred yards ahead. When the frightened animals were thus compelled to slacken their pace, two of the cattle drovers seized the heads of the leading pair and brought them to a standstill. Mr T. Vines having by this time arrived on the scene detached a horse from the team and rode on to the Wallington Hotel, about a mile and a half distant, from whence he despatched vehicles to convey the party thither. On arrival, at the hotel the reverend gentlemen and their lay friends were treated with the utmost kindness by Mr Key, the new proprietor, and the departing lessee (Mr. Thomson), all lavatory and other conveniences being freely placed at their disposal. After a good wash and a little rest the party determined to finish their trip ... Mr Vines rode back to town and reported the occurrence at the stables in Malop-street, where upon Mr. T. Moss (the working manager) got ready another coach and four." (Coach Accident on the Queenscliff Road, 21 Nov 1887, p.3)

- "The death occurred here to-day of Mr. Joshua Vines, senior partner in the well-known coaching firm of Vines and M'Phee ... came to Australia 1854, was roadmaster between Geelong and Ballarat for the original firm of Cobb and Co." (Obituary 1 Oct 1906, p.5)

Cobb and Co. proprietor—Arthur Nicholls Vines (Son of Joshua Vines)

- "We are instructed by Mr. Arthur N. Vines owner of the old-established business of Cobb and Co., Coach Proprietors, Livery-stables Keepers, 7c./ &c., to invite Tenders for the assets ... Ocean Grove, Barwon Heads, Torquay ... Geelong ... Queenscliff ... horses ... vehicles ... harnesses ... goodwill." (Advertising, 17 Jan 1914, p.23)

- "THE COBB CABLE. The cable to which reference was made yesterday was addressed 'Cobb, Geelong'. As soon as Mr. Arthur Vines of Cobb and Co., saw the paragraph in the 'Advertiser' yesterday, he knew the message was from his son, who is on active service. The Brett mentioned in the message is Mr. Brett, manager of the Commercial Bank, London, to whom, by arrangement, young Vines' letters have been sent. Evidently the latter was leaving for France, and desired to have his letters still addressed care of Mr. Brett ... The text of the message was—'France to-day, letters Brett, no rank or number—Vines.' Mr. Vines, sen., called at the depot yesterday, and received the cable." (The Cobb Cable, 11 Aug 1917, p.2)

- "PASSING OF COBB AND CO. Formal ratification has been given by the directors and shareholders of the Geelong and Cressy Trading Company in the purchase by the company of buildings situated in Malop street, and occupied as livery for between 69 and 70 years. For the last 35 of these they have been known as Cobb and Co.'s. The late Mr. Joshua Vines conducted the stables for many years under the management of Mr Robt. Purnell ... Later the business was conducted by Mr A. N. Vines, who a couple of years back, disposed of his interest in it to Mr. H. Womersley. The property was owned by the trustees in the estate of the late Mr. William Humble, who have completed the sale negotiations. It is expected that possession will he taken this week." (Geelong, 23 Feb 1921, p.6)

- "CR. ARTHUR NICHOLLS VINES, PRESIDENT OF THE SHIRE OF BELLARINE ... After leaving school he entered the office of his father, the late Mr. Joshua Vines (Cobb and Co., Geelong). On the death of his father he managed the Geelong coaching business known as Cobb and Co." (Cr. Vines Dies Suddenly, 16 May 1938, p.34)

Cobb and Co. proprietors—Meigs & Anderson (Jasper Bingham Meigs, Charles Anderson)

- "We learn by the Geelong papers that Messrs Meigs and Anderson, who have obtained mail contracts for the Western District for the year, have agreed to carry members of Parliament travelling to and from the district they represent free of charge." ('1866 Monday October 22', 22 Oct, 1866, p.4)

- "FUNERAL NOTICE. The Friends of the late Mr Jasper Bingham Meigs (of the firm of Cobb and Co.) are respectfully invited to follow his remains to the place of interment, the Ballarat Old Cemetery. The funeral procession will move from his late residence, 72 Armstrong street north, on Thursday, 13th inst, at Two o'clock precisely. Chas. Morris, Undertaker, Grenville street, near the Alfred Hall." While advertised on the same page "To Private Families ... For sale, Milch Cow ... £8 ... Apply at milking-time, 5 o'clock p.m." (Family Notices, 12 Jun 1872, p.3)

- "DUNKELD. (From our own correspondent.) July 31. Coaching days in Victoria are now almost memories of the past, in consequence of the extended railway system throughout the colony. My recollection carries me back to the good old times early in the fifties when Cobb and Co. monopolised the passenger traffic between Hamilton and Ballarat, when Meggs and Anderson carefully and fearlessly tooled their conveyance with that indomitable pluck and endurance characteristic of the Yankee. Sometimes the obstacles met with were rather of a formidable character. A large tree would often be found lying across the coach track, completely blocking it. When passing through thickly timbered country much watchfulness had to be exercised to escape falling branches and trees. Indeed in most coaching journeys great care, courage and nerve were required on the part of the drivers, as well as coolness and decision, in overcoming the difficulties and dangers of the road;

    but what could be more delightful than a drive through the bush on the box seat of a coach enlivened by the racy anecdotes and native wit of an American jehu?

    What a contrast to the present monotonous, but more rapid journey in a well appointed carriage behind the iron horse? Not only did Cobb and Co. enliven the road, but commercial travellers, bullock teams *et hoc genus omne* contributed their quota to an exciting, wholesome and profitable trade now mopped up by railway transit. Any thing that will relieve the dull monotony of our bush towns is welcome. We therefore duly appreciated a visit from the Wickcliffe footballers last Saturday." (Dunkeld, 2 Aug 1888, p.4)

Cobb and Co. proprietors—Western Stage Company (Jasper Bingham Meigs, Charles Anderson, Thomas Stoneman, Joshua Vines)

- "We find the following in the Warrnambool Sentinel:— Messrs. Meigs and Anderson having purchased the large plant of Messrs. Rounsevell and Co. (the Adelaide mail contractors) for £70,000, have entered into a combination with Mr. Thomas Stoneman, one of the oldest coach proprietors in this district, and also with Mr. Joshua Vines, formerly the contractor for the mails between Warrnambool and Geelong. The new company is to be called the Western Stage Company, and the principal depot of this powerful association is to be at Warrnambool." ('Tuesday Januarys 1867', 8 Jan 1867, p.5)

- SOUTH AUSTRALIA "Mr. H. R. Fuller has purchased the share of Mr. Jackson in the firm of Cobb & Co. Adelaide. The firm now consists of Messers. Fuller, B. Rounseville, Meigs, and Hill." (Summary of News 5 Aug 1868, p.3) "Before Mr. Justice Stow and a Jury. Mills v. Stoneman and others ... agreement ... Mrs. Meigs her one-fourth share ... The original partners of Cobb & Co. were Henry Hill and others." ('Tuesday, December 12,' 16 Dec 1876, p.10)

- "LAW AND CRIMINAL COURTS. ... Before His Honor Mr. Justice Stow and Juries. Mills V. Stoneman and Others ... two overdue bills of exchange ... The plaintiff was George Mills, and the defendants Thomas Stoneman, Charles Anderson, and Joshua Vine, sued as members of the firm of Cobb & Co. ... The bill was given to Mr. Vine for the Western Stage Company ... the money put into Cobb and Co. by Mr. Meigs, was the money borrowed from the Western Stage Company ... Meigs said the gentlemen were his partners ... His Honor pointed out that Meigs might have been put forward by the other gentlemen as representing an interest in the Western Stage Company, but that did not bind them. The deed of partnership should be produced." (Law and Criminal Courts, 13 Dec 1876, p.1)

Cobb and Co. proprietor—Alexander Allan Grant (Archie)

- "WALHALLA. It is said that competition is the life of trade, and accordingly Messrs Cobb and Co. on Monday last reduced the fares between Moe and Walhalla to 9s 6d return and 5s single ... On Tuesday Mr. A. Grant had his coach ticketed with 'Fares to Walhalla, 5s.' and on the following day Mr Bain had a placard thus 'Fares as usual, 8s single, return 13s 6d. No Sweating." It is needless to add that the rivalry is causing much amusement locally." (Walhalla, 5 Oct 1900, p.4)

- "DEATH OF MR. ARCHIE GRANT ... he called a spade a spade ... treating rich and poor with the greatest courtesy and respect, relieving coaching journeys with him of much of the fatigue and monotony attendant upon same, more particularly in the early days, when roads were bad and stages at long intervals. It is now about 13 years since deceased arrived in this district, when he founded Cobb and Co's. line of coaches from Moe to Walhalla ... His labours during the greater part of the above period were surrounded by hard work, worry and loss of money, and he left Moe a poorer, we regret to say, but wiser man ... On behalf of the residents of this district we tender profound condolence to Grant's bereaved relatives ... We are indebted to our contemporary at Tallangatta for the accompanying information ... Deceased, who came to Tallangatta about 14 months ago ... He was also a one time employ of Cobb and Co., having been in their service at Wood's Point ... He had, unfortunately, delayed railing in a doctor until too late, as he died soon after Dr. Patterson arrived. The cause of death was pneumonia. It was a surprise to a number of people to learn that the active and genial driver was bordering on 63 years of age. A pathetic incident occurred in connection with this death. Matthew Grant, who had not seen his brother for two and a half years, after travelling all the way from Linton, near Ballarat, arrived at the stables on Tuesday morning, too late to see him alive ... He leaves a brother and sister, both younger than himself." (Death of Mr. Archie Grant, 23 Jan 1906, p.3)

- "IN THE DAYS OF COBB AND CO. To The Editor Of The Argus. Sir,—On May 12 a correspondent at Leongatha, H.H.P., expressed wonder why the old drivers of Cobb and Company are not remembered. Most of them are dead. The first name he mentions is that of Archie Grant. His proper name was Alexander Allan Grant. I am his youngest son now 66 years of age. His oldest son David, was killed on one of Cobb and Company's coaches with a unicorn team, which bolted with him, more than 20 years ago at the bridge over the Murrumbidgee River at Hay, New South Wales. A. A. Grant was one of the drivers who were imported, like many of the coaches, at that time, and he drove to most of the gold rushes in Victoria. One of his best feats was when he drove a team of 18 horses attached to a coach through Melbourne at the celebration of the Duke of Edinburgh's visit. - Yours &c., C. C. GRANT. Eltham, May 13." (In the Days of Cobb and Co, 15 May 1929, p.11)

Cobb and Co. proprietors—Seth Sharp/S. Sharp

- "The Friends of the late Mr Seth Sharp, of New Town, are respectfully invited to follow his remains to the Smythesdale Cemetery. The funeral to leave his late residence, the Railway Hotel, on Tuesday, the 14th, at 3 o'clock p.m. Andrew Veitch, Undertaker, Smythesdale." (Family Notices, 14 Sep 1886, p.3)

Cobb and Co. proprietor—James Courtland Horr (Court)

- "NOTE: Post Office Tenders ... conveyance of mails between Hobart and Launceston in reply to public notice inviting the same ... J. C. Horr, Cobb and Co.'s Office, Ballaarat, £3496." (Tasmania, 16 Jun 1864, p.6)
- "QUESTIONABLE TURF PRACTICES.—We are sorry to see that Mr. Cort Horr, well known in this district in collection with Cobb & Co., has been getting into a turf difficulty at Ballarat. The horse named Oddstocking, which has been winning several races lately, was entered by him for the District Plate, and at starting was first favourite. His rider was young Bates, a lad that was for some time in the employment of Mr. James Wilson, and who was with him when Ebor broke down slightly under suspicious circumstances, just before the Ballarat Champion Race." (Local News, 7 Dec 1864)
- "COURT HORR. The above was a familiar name in Ballarat in the old days of Cobb and Cos., and many of the older residents will remember Court Horr the superintendent of that extensive coaching business between Ballarat and Melbourne, and Ballarat and Geelong, before the advent of railways. The following particulars, taken from a Californian paper, announces his death on the 10th March of this year, and will be of interest to old friends : — *Olympia, Wash., 10th March : Ex-Mayor James Courtland Horr died this morning. He was born at Waitsfield, Vt., on 17th January, 1832, removing with his parents to Lorraine county, O., in 1834, when two years of age. He worked hard during his younger days, and at the age of 21 went to Australia to seek his fortune, where he remained 12 years. While in Australia he was superintendent of Cobb and Co.'s stage coaches running to Ballarat. Returning again to the United States in 1865, he operated, with his brother, a cheese factory in Ohio. He removed to California for his health in 1868, and in February, 1871, was appointed special agent of the Treasury Department at San Francisco and Fort Townsend, which position he filled until 1885. Previous to his removal he had charge of the district including Oregon, Washington, and Alaska. In 1876 he was elected mayor of Olympia, and in 1877 a member of the Legislature. He was re-elected mayor in 1880. He represented Thurston county in the State senate in 1893-95. He was married in Australia in 1864 to Miss Elisabeth T. Upton.*" (Court Horr, 14 Jun 1899, p.4)

Cobb and Co. proprietor—James A. Lyall (Jas., possibly a sub-contractor)

- "Yesterday witnessed a complete change in the various mail contracts in this district. The old familiar Cobb and Co, on the Hamilton line, which had such a long and successful run for many years, with James Lyall in charge of the team ... the Western Stage Co. Coleraine to Harrow and Harrow to Noradjuha, the latter line being sublet to Mr. Lyall." (Harrow, 4 Jul 1918, p.3)

Cobb and Co. proprietor—George Alexander McGowan (Mac)

- "NOTICE. WE beg to thank the travelling public for the patronage received by the undersigned coach proprietors for many years, and now wish to announce that We have Sold (as from 1st April, 1899) all our Interest in the Hay and Deniliquin Line of Coaches—To—Mr. George A. McGowan, And we solicit for him a continuance of the support so liberally extended to us in the past. Robertson, Wagner & Co. With reference, to the above, I beg to assure the travelling community that no effort on my part shall be wanting to merit a continuance of the support so liberally granted to my predecesors, Cobb and Co. G. A. Mcgowan, Proprietor." (Advertising, 12 May 1899, p.4)
- "Mr George Alexander McGowan, a gentleman who was very prominently before the public of Hay and district in the seventies and early eighties, died at Collie, W. A., on Friday, at a ripe old age. Mr McGowan was a Canadian by birth, and came to Australia with his brother, Mr J. W. McGowan, an expert electrician, who was at one time deputy postmaster general of Victoria. Mr McGowan's father was city treasurer of New York in the sixties. After spending some time in Victoria with the firm of Robertson Wagner and Co. (Cobb and Co.) Mr McGowan was sent to this district and given charge of the mail coach road between Hay and Wagga. He was coach agent at Hay, when coaching was at the zenith of its prosperity, and lived here with his family. The club house of the Waradgery Club was built by him. He was also district representative for Messrs Powers, Rutherford and Co., and for Risby's Narrandera sawmills. When the rail way reached Hay, he went further west, to Broken Hill, where he speculated in mining and experienced the ups and downs of most mining speculators. Later, he returned to Hay and entered into partnership with Mr J. C. Smith, but he sold his interest in the firm to Mr Simpson after a brief term and retired—living first at Western port, Victoria, and afterwards at Collie, W.A., where he spent the evening of his days. For a brief period, during his residence at Hay, he lived at Te Aro (All press) between Hay and Gunbar. His death removes one of those, who, in the earlier days of the district, played his part in a worthy manner." (No Title, 4 Sep 1917, p.2)
- "GEORGE ALEXANDER, ANOTHER STURDY PIONEER ... 'Mac,' as he was known to his many friends ... His son, George, and daughters, Mrs. G. Harris and Mrs. J. Archer, still live in Collie ... George ... engaged in various enterprises in Victoria and New South Wales, but is best known as the proprietor of the celebrated Cobb and Co.'s Mail Coaches. This company ran coaches between Hay and Melbourne, and Hay to Balranald, One Tree, Booligal, Gunbar, Hillston, Boonoonban, Wanganella and Deliniquin ...

His family still recall the stories he told them, of the early days of Cobb and Co. ... His son, George, who retired from the Collie coal mining industry some years ago, was a driver on the famous Cobb and Co. coaches on the W.A. Goldfields in the early days. He was the last driver on the run between Sandstone and Boulder." (Stamp a Tribute to Pioneer, 29 Apr 1954, p.14)

Cobb and Co. proprietor—Charles Russell (Steve)

- "The late Mr. Russell, who was in his 58th year, was noted for his generous and retiring disposition, and had lived in the Merriwa district for upwards of forty years, during which time he had made a host of friends. For many years past he had engaged in a carrying business, and ran regular trips between Merriwa and Cassilis, and 'Steve,' as he was popularly known, was loved by practically everyone on the road. He carried on this business in the district before there were any railways, and roads were mere tracks in many instances. Born in the Denman district, he was a son of the late Mr. Charles Russell, who himself was connected with Cobb and Co. in the old coaching days ... Besides a sorrowing wife, the late Mr. Russell leaves a family of four daughters,

    Mary, Myra, Mabel and Maud,

    to mourn their loss. Brothers of deceased are Edward and Reginald (Merriwa), Frank and Norman (Baerami) and Stan. The latter served with the Light Horse on Gallipoli, and on the termination of the war did not return to Australia. He is at present managing a rubber plantation at Victoria Point, Burma. Sisters of deceased are Mrs. J. Kelman. (Merriwa), Mrs. K. Hennessey (Baerami), and Mrs. G. Cameron (Dubbo)." (Merriwa and District News, 26 Aug 1938, p.6)

Cobb and Co. proprietor—H. Womersley

- "COBB AND CO.'S CHANGES HANDS. Mr. H. Womersley, so well known as a motor car proprietor for many years past, has purchased the business of Cobb and Co, Malop-street. The travelling public, who for the past quarter of a century have been so efficiently served under the old management, will receive even greater benefits under the new, owing to the fact that motor services will be substituted for horse vehicles, thereby ensuring much quicker transit, and greater comfort in travelling. The favorite seaside resorts of Barwon Heads, Torquay and Ocean Grove will have an up-to-date motor service; cars will leave the office twice daily, returning to link up with the midday and evening trains. Anglesea and Airey's Inlet will have regular services, the former twice daily. In addition to these services, cars will be available at any hour required, either day or night. The facilities for obtaining through combined rail, boat and coach tickets will be continued under new management." (Cobb and Co.'s Changes Hands, 12 Dec 1919, p.2)

- "ASSIGNED ESTATE H. WOMERSLEY (Cobb and Co., Geelong). Tenders are invited for purchases of asset of goodwill, consisting of name of Cobb and Co. together with Mail Contract between Geelong and Ocean Grove." (Classified Advertising, 19 Feb 1921, p.5)

Cobb and Co. proprietor—Mr. Gardiner

- "KYNETON POLICE COURT ... Mr. Gardiner, part proprietor of the line of coaches known as 'Cobb and Co.'s' for carrying more passengers than the licence allowed, was called ... 11 passengers over the proper number ... fined him £55." ('Friday, May 4, 1860.', 4 May 1860, p.5)

Cobb and Co. proprietor—William Warren

- "YANDOIT.—The Creswick Advertiser of Friday says—Mr Warren, well-known as part proprietor of Cobb and Co.'s coaches, has bought an hotel at Yandoit, and the managers of the Victorian Stage Company have put on an extra coach between Yandoit and Castlemaine. There appears to be a great deal of speculation going on in disposing of shares in quartz reefs in that locality. Yandoit is in a direct line of road between Creswick and Castlemaine." (Serious Riot at the Parliament Houses, 30 Aug 1860, p.3)

Cobb and Co. proprietors—Crooke and Watt (James Elijah Crooke, James Watt)

- "BACCHUS MARSH ... A public meeting was held in this township on Saturday last, September 25th, when a large number of the inhabitants assembled to express their indignation at, and to call the attention of the Government to the present state of the Main road from Melbourne to Ballaarat ... The following resolutions were unanimously carried ... Proposed by Mr J. E. Crook, seconded by Mr Scott—That a memorial be presented to the Hon. President of the Board of Land and Works, drawing his attention to the state of the road, and urging ... the completion of the Main road. Proposed by Mr Watt, seconded by Mr Meikle—That the following memorial be presented to the Honorable the President of Board of Land and Works by a deputation from the inhabitants of Bacchus Marsh and Ballan." (Bacchus Marsh, 1 Oct 1858, p.6)

- "MESSRS CROOKE AND WATT, PUBLICANS, of Bacchus Marsh ran lines of coaches in the Ballarat district, keeping the style of Cobb and Co. Mr Crooke left a son, who is the present proprietor of the Aspendale racecourse, while Mr Watt, a quiet gentlemanly man, who first saw the light at the British Embassy in Copenhagen, was laid to rest many years later in Longwood. His son, a manager of the North eastern line of coaches for Cobb and Co. ran a small line of his own in the same district after the building of the Sydney Melbourne railway drove the old firm off the main road." (Cobb and Co., 5 Jun 1922, p.1)

- JAMES WATT "However, it is known that on October 6, 1851, James Watt, of the Border Inn, Bacchus Marsh, had a coach running between Melbourne and Ballarat. It ran four times a week, leaving Elizabeth street at 2 o'clock one day and arriving at 3 the next—a 25 hours' run—a good record considering that there was no road but only a bush track, with the daily incidents of boggings and other mishaps." (A Pioneer Comes to Town, 8 Sep 1934, p.9)

Drivers of Coaches are hereby notified of the following Rule:—

"No Ladies allowed on the Box Seat of the Coach."

A Fine of FORTY SHILLINGS *will be charged the Driver for breaking this Rule.*

ROBERTSON, WAGNER & CO.

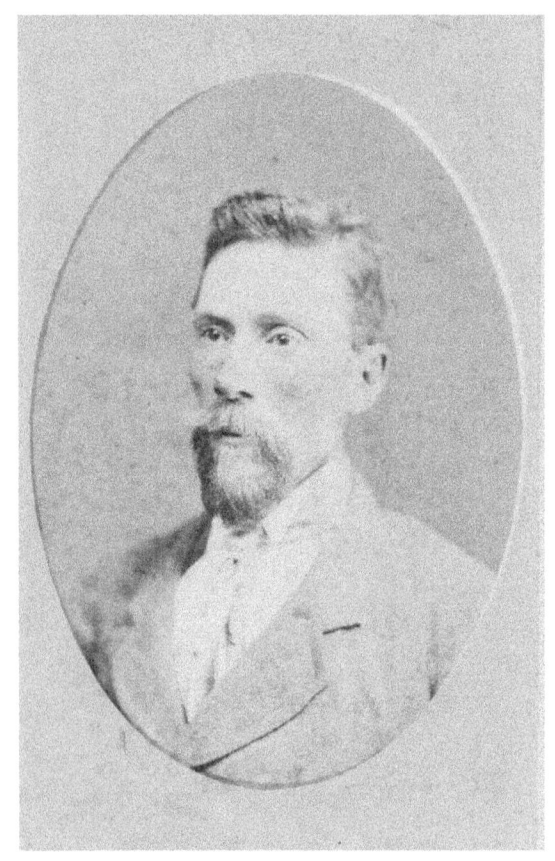

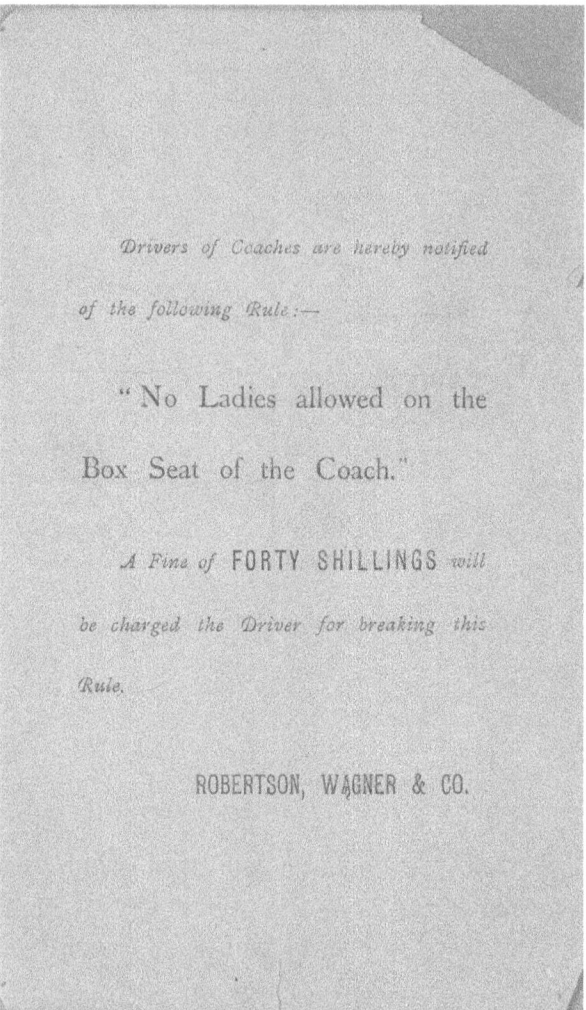

ca. 1878-1888 Archie Grant of Cobb & Co. (A. W. Burman, Melbourne photographer) - Courtesy State Library New South Wales

No Ladies allowed on the Box Seat of the Coach Poster [1938] - Courtesy State Library Victoria

Parker's Star Hotel (formly Conlan's), Walhalla - Courtesy of Public Record Office Victoria

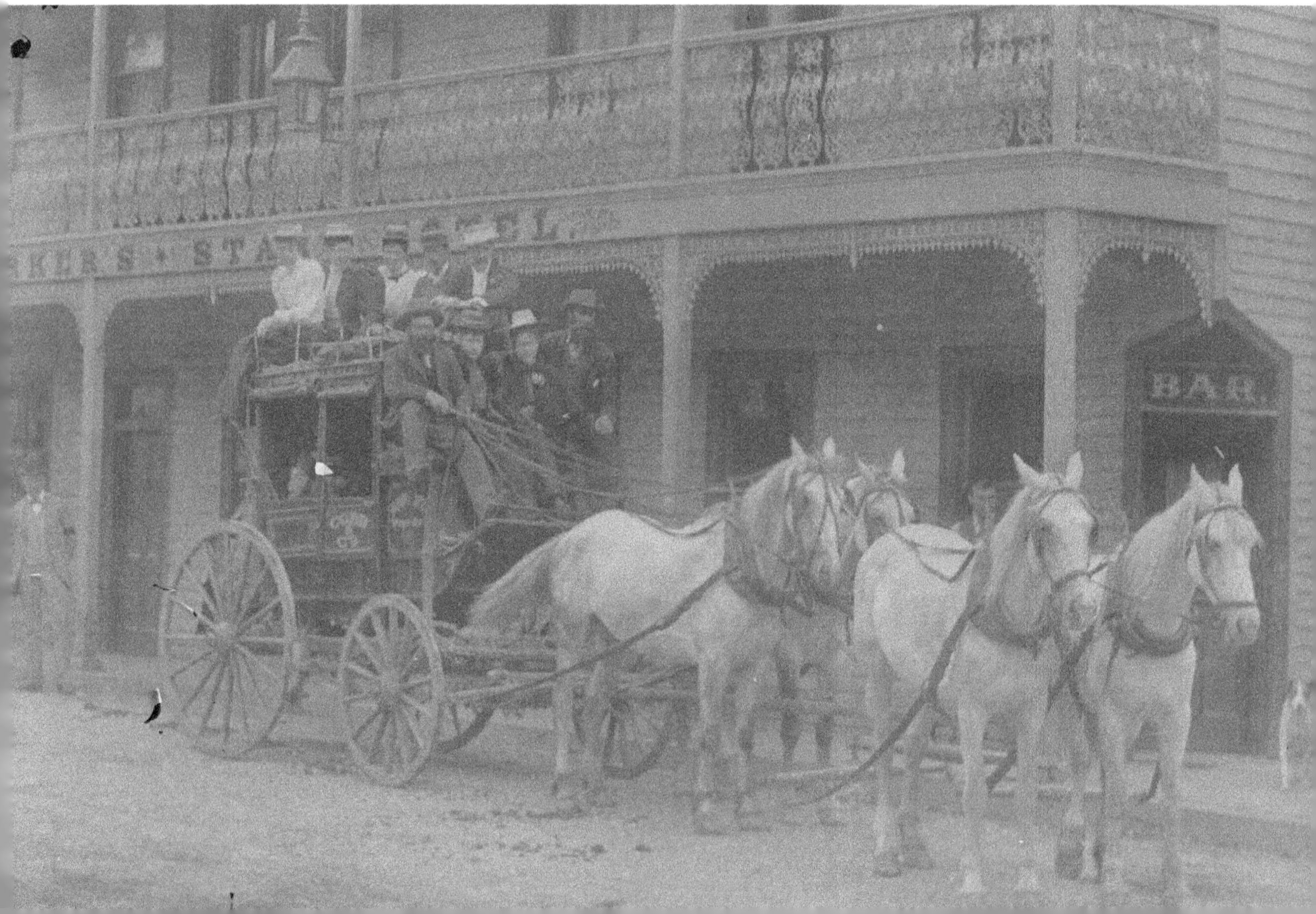

ca. 1890 Thomas Vines driving a Cobb & Company Coach, Geelong
District, Victoria - Courtesy Museums Victoria

1887-1896 Coach Road from Wollongong to Sydney - Courtesy University of Wollongong

Chapter Four

Coaching Victoria

1850s

Green and Gold

(Poem about The Yarra)

Green and smooth the Yarra flows
Between the grassy banks;
Through English trees the sunlight shows
In green and golden shafts.
Gold the shafts that pierce the deeps,
And waver in the weeds.
A golden tear the willow weeps
Beneath her tresses green.
The Yarra slips mid green and gold,
Through shadow and through light.
Singing a river-song of old.
So slow, so quiet, so deep.

By Moriet D'ombrain (14), 17 Powlett St., E- Melbourne. — Green Certificate.
(Poem About the Yarra, 23 May 1939, p.20)

1920-1930 [?] Collection of flexible base negatives showing the Yarra River in flood (Herbert Palmer, photographer) - Courtesy State Library Victoria

Examples of Cobb and Co. Coaching Lines, Victoria—1850s

1853

Adams & Co.—Express Carriers in Melbourne. Freeman Cobb worked for Adams and Co.

1854

Cobb and Co.—Freeman Cobb, John B. Lamber, James Swanton, John Murray Peck ... Change within 12 months ... Freeman Cobb, James Swanton, John Murray Peck, and Arthur Lincoln Blake

- 31 Jan 1854 American Telegraph Line of Coaches—Melbourne, Forest Creek, Bendigo (Cobb and Co.)
- Cobb and Co. coach—Geelong, Portland via Batesford, Shelford; Skipton and Streatham to meet at Streatham another coach which left Portland the same hour in the morning, and passed through Heywood, Branxholme, Hamilton, etc. Passengers and mails were exchanged at Streatham, after which each coach started on its return journey
- 25 Nov 1854 Telegraph Stage Line—Melbourne, Castlemaine via Essendon, Keilor, Gap, Gisborne, Woodend, Carlsruhe, Kyneton, Malmesbury, Elphinstone connecting with Bendigo, Maryborough
- 17 Aug 1854 Cobb and Co.'s express conveyances—To Pretty Sally's hill

1855

- 18 Feb 1855 American Telegraph Line of Stages—Melbourne, Ballarat, stopping at Keilor, Rockey Bank, Bacchus Marsh, Ballarat, connecting with the branch line of coaches for Creswick's Creek, through to Ballarat (Hewitt and Co. not advertised as Cobb and Co.)
- 30 May 1855 Cobb and Co.'s Telegraph Line of Stage Coaches/Cobb and Co.'s Telegraph Line—Castlemaine, Melbourne, Bendigo, Simson's passing by Keilor Gap, Gisborne, Five-Mile Creek, Carlsruhe, Kyneton, Coliban, Elphinstone, and connecting, at Castlemaine, with branch lines for Harcourt, Porcupine, Bendigo, Tarrengower, Carisbrook, Maryborough, Daisy Hill
- 5 Sep 1855 Cobb and Co.'s coaches—Castlemaine, Bendigo, Maryborough, Mount Blackwood
- 21 Sep 1855 Cobb and Co.'s Telegraph Line of American Coaches

1856 Jan-Apr

- 29 Apr 1856 Cobb and Co.'s Telegraph Line of Stage Coaches—Castlemaine, Melbourne, Bendigo, Maryborough via Elphinstone, Taradale, Malmsbury, Kyneton, Carlsruhe, Woodend, Gisborne, Keilor; Bendigo, Maryborough

1856 May-Dec

May 1856 Freeman Cobb left Australia; 'Cobb and Co.' now referred to as 'Messrs. Cobb and Co.'

- 29 May 1856 Cobb and Co.'s People's Telegraph Line of Covered Coaches—Ballaarat, via Staughton's Station, Ballan, &c.
- 29 May 1856 Messrs. Cobb & Co.'s Telegraph Line of Coaches—Castlemaine, Bendigo, Maryborough via Keilor, Gisborne, Five Mile Creek, Carlsruhe, Kyneton, Coliban, Back Creek, Elphinstone
- 3 Jun 1856 Cobb and Co.'s Telegraph Line of Stage Coaches—Castlemaine Melbourne, Bendigo, Maryborough
- 15 Jul 1856 Cobb and Co.'s coaches—Castlemaine, Bendigo, Maryborough, Ballaarat, &c., and per Royal Mail to Beechworth
- 15 Oct 1856 Messrs. Cobb and Co.—City and the Mount Alexander gold-fields
- 29 Nov 1856 Messrs. Cobb and Co.'s Coaches/Cobb and Co.'s Telegraph Line of Coaches—Castlemaine, Bendigo, Maryborough, Dunolly

Note: 8 Nov 1856 People's Telegraph Line of Coaches—Melbourne, Ballaarat, via Bacchus Marsh, Ballan (Thomas Davies) not advertised as a Cobb and Co.

1857 Jan-Aug

Cobb and Co.—Thomas Davies

- 12 Jan 1857 Messrs. Cobb & Co.'s—Castlemaine, Melbourne, Bendigo, Maryborough, Dunolly
- 30 Jun 1857 Cobb and Co.'s Telegraph Line Of Mail Coaches—Castlemaine, Sandhurst, Maryborough, Ballaarat, Geelong
- 1 Jul 1857 Cobb & Co.'s Telegraph Line of Coaches—Castlemaine, Bendigo, Maryborough, Dunolly
- 18 Jul 1857 Cobb & Co.'s Telegraph Line of Coaches—Melbourne, Ballaarat direct ... line changed to Geelong to Ballaarat
- 25 Jul 1857 Cobb and Co.'s Telegraph Line Of Mail Coaches—Night mail ... Kyneton, Castlemaine, Sandhurst
- 25 Jul 1857 Cobb and Co.'s Telegraphic Line of Mail Coaches—Castlemaine, Sandhurst, Maryborough, Ballaarat, Geelong
- 19 Aug 1857 Cobb and Co.'s Telegraph Line of Mail Coaches—Melbourne, Castlemaine, Sandhurst, Maryborough, Ballaarat via Geelong

1857 Aug-Sep

Cobb and Co.—Alexander Walker

- 23 Sep 1857 Telegraph Line of Mail Coaches.—Castlemaine, Sandhurst, Maryborough, Ballaarat, Geelong

Cobb and Co.—Chas. Colclough

- 11 Aug 1857 Cobb and Co.'s Telegraph Line Of Mail Coaches—Bacchus Marsh, Ballan

1857 Oct-Dec

Cobb and Co.—Watson and Hewitt

- 26 Oct 1857 Cobb & Co.'s Telegraph Line of Mail Coaches—Melbourne, Sandhurst, Maryborough, Dunolly
- 28 Oct 1857 Telegraph Line of Mail Coaches—Castlemaine, Sandhurst, Maryborough, Ballaarat; Mount Ararat
- 4 Nov 1857 Cobb & Co.'s Telegraph Line—Geelong, Melbourne
- 6 Nov 1857 Telegraph Line of Mail Coaches—Castlemaine, Sandhurst, Maryborough, Ballaarat, Geelong; Ballaarat direct passing through Melton, Bacchus Marsh, Ballan
- 21 Dec 1857 Cobb and Co.'s Telegraph Line of Coaches—Pleasant Creek by way of Maryboro', Avoca, Ararat

1858

Cobb and Co.—Watson and Hewitt

- 1 Feb 1858 Cobb and Co.'s Telegraph Line—Geelong and Melbourne
- 17 Jun 1858 Telegraph Line of Mail Coaches—Ballaarat; Beechworth ... Not advertised as Cobb and Co.

Cobb and Co.—Swanton, Blake and Co.

- 1 Jan 1858 Cobb & Co.'s Telegraph Line of Coaches—Melbourne, Sandhurst, Maryborough, Ararat, Pleasant Creek
- 23 Apr 1858 Cobb and Co.'s Telegraph Line of Mail Coaches—Melbourne, Sandhurst, Maryborough, Ararat, Pleasant Creek
- 27 Aug 1858 Cobb and Co.'s Telegraph Line of Mail

Coaches—Castlemaine, Sandhurst, Maryborough, Ararat, Pleasant Creek

Cobb and Co.—F. B. Clapp and Co.
- 4 Feb 1858 Telegraph Lines of Mail Coaches—Melbourne to Ballaarat direct; Ballaarat via Geelong
- 10 Feb 1858 Cobb and Co.'s Telegraph Line of Royal Mail Coaches—Geelong, Melbourne direct, running in connection with the Geelong and Melbourne Railway

Cobb and Co.—W. H. Brayton
- 14 May 1858 Cobb and Co.'s Telegraph Line Of Mail Coaches—Through to Pleasant Creek by way of Maryborough, Avoca, Ararat

1858 Aug-Dec

Cobb and Co.—Proprietors not listed
- Cobb and Co.'s Telegraph Line of Royal Mail Coaches—Eversley to Melbourne

Cobb and Co.—Victoria Stage Company (formerly Swanton, Blake and Co.)
- 8 Nov 1858 Cobb and Co.'s Telegraph Line Of Mail Coaches.—Summer arrangement ... Castlemaine, Sandhurst, Maryborough connecting with Echuca, Moama, Swan Hill, Maiden's Punt on the Murray and Dunolly, Avoca, Ararat, Pleasant Creek, Tarrangower
- 17 Nov 1858 Cobb and Co.'s Telegraph Line of Mail Coaches—Melbourne, Castlemaine; Night Coach ... Sandhurst, Castlemaine, Kyneton, Melbourne; Melbourne to Moama

Cobb and Co.—F. B. Clapp and Co.
- 30 Oct 1858 Cobb and Co.'s Telegraph Line of Royal Mail Coaches—For Melbourne, For Geelong ... run in connection with the Geelong and Melbourne Railway ... For Melbourne via Geelong ... Creswick, Daisy Hill, Clunes, Maryborough, Dunolly, Castlemaine, Chinaman's, Fiery Creek, Mount Ararat, Pleasant Creek, Smythe's Creek
- 6 Oct 1858 Telegraph Lines of Mail Coaches—Melbourne to Ballaarat direct, to Ballaarat via Geelong

Cobb and Co.—W. H. Brayton
- 27 Aug 1858 Cobb and Co.'s Telegraph Line of Mail Coaches—Through to Pleasant Creek by way of Maryboro', Avoca, Ararat

1859

Cobb and Co.—Proprietors not listed
- 1 Jan 1859 Cobb and Co.'s Telegraph Line of Royal Mail Coaches—Eversley to Melbourne
- 4 Jul 1859 Cobb and Co.'s Telegraph Line of Mail Coaches—Back Creek

Cobb and Co.—Victoria Stage Company
- 6 Jan 1859 Cobb and Co.'s Telegraph Line of Daily and Nightly Mail Coaches—Melbourne, Sandhurst
- 14 Jan 1859 Cobb and Co.'s Telegraph Line of Mail Coaches—Castlemaine, Sandhurst, Maryborough, Ararat, Ballarat; To Ballarat
- 5 Feb 1859 Telegraph Line of Mail Coaches—Castlemaine, Sandhurst, Maryborough, Tarrengower ... connecting with ... Echuca, Moama, Swan Hill, Maiden's Punt on the Murray and Dunolly, Avoca, Ararat, Pleasant Creek, Tarrengower
- 12 Feb 1859 Cobb and Co.'s Telegraph Line of Mail Coaches—Castlemaine, Sandhurst, and Maryborough etc., etc., will connect with Melbourne and Mount Alexander Railway at Digger's Rest Station
- 31 Oct 1859 Cobb and Co.'s Telegraph Line of Mail Coaches—Five Daily Coaches to Castlemaine ... Castlemaine, Sandhurst, Swan Hill, Maryborough, Ararat, Creswick Creek &c., connecting with Victoria Railways at Digger's Rest Station ... pass through ... Ararat, Avoca, Amphitheatre, Buckeye, Baringhup (Loddon), Castlemaine, Carlsruhe, Creswick Creek, Carisbrook, Durham Ox, Eversley, Elphinstone, Gap, Gisborne, Guildford, Harcourt, Kyneton, Kingston, Maryborough, Malmesbury, Muckleford, Ravenswood, Reedy Lake Station, Sandhurst, Swan Hill, Serpentine Creek, Tarrengower (Maldon), Woodend ... connect with ... Back Creek, Pleasant Creek, Dunolly, Moama, Echuca, Deniliquin, &c.

Cobb and Co.—F. B. Clapp and Co.
- 5 Feb 1859 Cobb and Co.'s Western Telegraph Line of Mail Coaches—Geelong, Portland passing through Bruce's Creek, Shelford, Rokewood, Pitfield, Skipton, Streatham, Portland; Geelong, Warrnambool, Belfast passing through Inverleigh, Cressy (Frenchman's), Darlington (Elephant Bridge), Mortlake (Mount Shadwell), Framlington (Hopkins), Woodford, Belfast; Geelong, Colac passing through Duneed, Winchelsea, Eicket's Marsh, Colac
- 18 Feb 1859 Cobb and Co.'s Telegraph Line of Mail Coaches—Ballarat via Bate's Ford, Separation, Clyde, Lethbridge, Meredith, Corduroy, Buninyong connecting with Mount Ararat, Fiery Creek, Creswick's Creek, Chines, Smythe's Creek, Amherst, Maryboro, Dunolly, Avoca
- 16 Mar 1859 Cobb and Co.'s Western Telegraph Line of Mail Coaches—Geelong and Portland passing through Bruce's Creek, Shelford, Rokewood, Pitfield, Skipton, Streatham, Wickliffe, Dunkeld, Hamilton, Branxholme, Green Hills, Heywood, Portland
- 17 Jun 1859 Telegraph Line of Mail Coaches—Ballaarat via Geelong
- 10 Sep 1859 Cobb and Co.'s Telegraph Coaches—Bacchus Marsh, Keilor, Melton

Cobb and Co.—W. H. Brayton
- 14 Jan 1859 Cobb and Co.'s Telegraph Line of Mail Coaches—Ararat

Cobb and Co.—Watson and Hewitt
- 5 Feb 1859 Cobb and Co.'s Telegraph Line of Mail Coaches—Whroo, Rushworth, Murchison, Somerton, Donnybrook, Kilmore, Pyalong, M'Ivor

Along the tracks—1850s

See *Appendix 2: Supporting evidence for Cobb and Co. coaching lines, Victoria*

1854 – "TELEGRAPH STAGE LINE, from Melbourne to Castlemaine, Bendigo and Maryborough, carrying Adams and Co. Inland Express, Daily. Cobb and Co, beg to announce that on and after Wednesday, October 11th, 1854, their regular line of stage coaches will leave the Criterion Hotel, Collins-street, every morning (Sundays excepted), at six o'clock precisely for Castlemaine and Essendon, Keilor, Gap, Gisborne, Wood End, Carlsruhe, Kyneton, Malmesbury, and Elphinstone, arriving at Castlemaine before sunset, and connecting with the Bendigo and Maryborough coaches, which leave the Victoria Hotel at six o'clock on the following morning. The proprietors of this line, having added largely to their stock of elegant coaches, which for comfort and convenience are acknowledged to be unsurpassed, can offer to the travelling public increased facilities, and their friends and patrons may confidently expect that the speed and regularity which marked the line with some degree of favor throughout the last season, will be observed in all their future operations. Cobb and Co., Proprietors. Melbourne, October 11th, 1854." (Advertising, 12 Oct 1854, p.8)

1855 – "COBB AND CO, would also announce, that, in view of the increased passenger traffic on the Mount Alexander Road, they have entered into an arrangement with Messrs. F. J. Rogers and Co., for the use of a portion of their new, elegant, and spacious premises, No. 23 Bourke-street, opposite the Union Hotel, and that, on and after Monday, June 4th, passengers who find it better suited to their convenience, can book and procure tickets of Messrs F. J. Rogers and Co., and start from their New Office, which will be opened every morning at five o'clock, for the special accommodation of the travelling public. Principal Offices and Agents. Melbourne ... Adams and Co.'s Office, No 69 Collins-street,—T. K. Newton, agent. Melbourne ... Telegraph Stage office, No. 23 Bourke-street,—F. J. Rogers, agent. Castlemaine ... Prince of Wales Hotel,—I. B. Lamber, agent. Bendigo ... Haycock's Office,—G. W. Haycock, agent. Maryborough, Telegraph Store,—Hewitt and Co., agents. Cobb and Co., Proprietors, Melbourne." (Advertising, 19 Jun 1855, p.2)

"VICTORIA BOOKING OFFICE, Bull and Mouth. Cobb & Co.'s Daily line of coaches to Castlemaine, Bendigo, Maryborough and Mount Blackwood. W. Jeune, Agent." (Advertising, 5 Sep 1855, p.2)

1856 – "COACH ACCIDENT. A few days ago an accident, which might have been attended with more serious consequences, occurred to Messrs. Cobb and Co.'s conveyance, a short distance from Castlemaine. It seems that some portion of the electric wire crossing the road at that place, not having as yet been elevated to its destined position, came in contact with the top of the vehicle, tearing it and slightly injuring more than one of the passengers. No blame appears to have attached to the driver. —Kyneton Herald. POISONING.— Our attention has been directed to a proceeding of a very dangerous character adopted in landing arsenic along with flour at the jetty. Casks of arsenic are placed on the top of bags of flour, and quantities of the poison have been seen scattered over the bags of flour. We are informed that it is the usual custom to land arsenic and flour together in this way, the latter placed below, so that it receives whatever of the poison escapes from the casks. It is quite time some check was put upon this practice ; otherwise we may expect to hear some day of instances of wholesale poisoning in Portland.—Portland Guardian." (Advertising, 12 Dec 1856, p.3)

1858 – "COBB AND CO.'S TELEGRAPH LINE OF MAIL COACHES ... Reduction of fares ... Through to Pleasant Creek by way of Maryboro', Avoca, and Ararat, in one day. W. H. Brayton" While on the same page "CASTLEMAINE HOSPITAL. Rules regarding the Admission of Patients. I.— All persons claiming admission must produce a receipt for their benefaction or subscription ... before being allowed to enjoy the benefits of the Hospital ... IV. In cases of accidents ... if able, be required to pay all reasonable charges for maintenance and medical treatments." (Advertising, 27 Aug 1858, p.2)

"COBB AND CO.'S TELEGRAPH LINE OF MAIL COACHES.—Castlemaine, Sandhurst, Maryborough ... connecting with ... Echuca, Moama, Swan Hill, and Maiden's Punt on the Murray and Dunolly, Avoca, Ararat and Pleasant Creek ... Agents—A. Butler, agent, 23 Bourke-street east, Melbourne ; Joseph Burrall, Shamrock Hotel, Sandhurst ; J. F. Sweeney Victoria Hotel, Castlemaine ; James J. Blake, Castlemaine Hotel, do. ; O. B. Clapp, M'Ivor Hotel, Maryborough. Victorian Stage Co. Per A. L. Blake, Manager." (Advertising, 30 Sep 1858, p.8) On the same page "FOR SALE, four roomed Cottage, Johnston street, Collingwood. Price £175. W. Daish, 82 Collins street, east." (Advertising, 1 Oct 1858, p.3)

"COBB AND CO.'S TELEGRAPH LINE OF MAIL COACHES—Melbourne, Castlemaine Night Coach ... Sandhurst, Castlemaine, Kyneton, Melbourne ... Melbourne to Moama ... Victorian Stage Company. Heffernan and Crowley, agents, Shamrock Hotel, Sandhurst." advertised on same page "MERCHANDISE ... Cricket bats, Balls, and Stumps, by the best makers ... Cutlery ... Razors ... Carpenter's tools ... Cross-cut saws, Wedges, Augers, Adzes ... Williams and Son's." (Advertising, 17 Nov 1858, p.1)

1859 – "COBB AND CO.'S WESTERN TELEGRAPH LINE OF MAIL COACHES between Geelong and Portland. F . B. Clapp and Co. Proprietors ... Passing through Bruce's Creek, Shelford, Rokewood, Pitfield, Skipton, Streatham, Portland ; Geelong to Warrnambool and Belfast ... Passing through Inverleigh, Cressy (Frenchman's), Darlington (Elephant Bridge), Mortlake (Mount Shadwell), Framlington (Hopkins), Woodford, Belfast ; Geelong to Colac ... Passing through Duneed, Winchelsea, Eicket's Marsh, Colac" Advertising appearing on the same page "CABBAGE-TREE HATS Original Cabbage-Tree Hat Shop, Wholesale and retail. N. B. Panama Hats blocked. 75 Swanston Street." (Advertising, 2 Apr 1859, p.4)

"COBB AND CO.'S TELEGRAPH LINE OF MAIL COACHES. In connection with the Melbourne and Mount Alexander Railway, From Digger's Rest Station to Melbourne ... Coaches for Melbourne, Sandhurst, Maryborough, Ararat, and Ballarat ... Victoria Stage Co. A. L. Blake, Manager" Appearing on the same page "SMITH'S PATENT CRINOLINE HATS. Made expressly for the Australian Colonies. The best ventilated and most suitable covering for the head ever produced. The first Shipment to arrive per Suffolk." (Advertising, 2 March 1859, p.4)

"MELBOURNE NEWS ... Messrs. Cobb and Co. have started a coach, which leaves Kilmore in the morning at seven, and Melbourne at three o'clock, reaching Kilmore again the same day. This gives the inhabitants of Kilmore the opportunity of spending three hours in the metropolis, and returning home within twelve hours ... THE POLICE AT BACK CREEK. The robbery of the Beechworth mail, and the escape of the prisoners from the Back Creek ... have naturally caused a deep sensation in all parts of the colony. It is some time now since lawlessness and ruffianism reached such a pitch, and were so glaringly manifested as of late.

The sticking-up of the mail, and the cool robbery of the passengers and mailbags, recal to mind the period of the robbery of the M'lvor escort ... in 1852. Yet these events occur now in the year 1859—seven years after when sufficient time, in all conscience, has been afforded for establishing an efficient police system throughout the colony, and giving to a monstrously over-taxed community at least the simple and ordinary requirements of society, the protection and security of life and property ... The robbery of the Beechworth mail may be allowed to pass without much comment, for no foresight can prevent a number of desperate men from committing such an outrage ... But this case of the prison-breaking at Back Creek, by which five or six of the greatest ruffians in the colony are let loose again upon society is of quite a different character ... at a time when the machinery of good government should have been established throughout the colony it is a disgrace of the most damning kind." (Melbourne News, 28 May 1859, p.2)

"TELEGRAPH LINE OF MAIL COACHES to Ballaarat via Geelong ... F. B. Clapp and Co., Proprietors." On the same page "PETER THOMSON'S CELEBRATED BRACELESS TROUSERS, large assortment (own make) ; samples in window." (Advertising, 17 Jun 1859, p.7)

"£6 REWARD. Lost from the neighborhood of Bryant's Crossing, Loddon, a Chestnut Mare, branded CE near shoulder, SC off shoulder. Also from Castlemaine, a Bay Mare, branded M near shoulder. AD conjoined. Three pounds each will be paid on recovery of the above. Victoria Stage Co. J. P. Sweeney, Agent." (Advertising, 7 Nov 1859, p.4)

Written in 1922 "THE PIONEERS. AND THEIR GLORIOUS WORK. Opening Up Gippsland. Hardships and Trials of the Early Settlers. (By E. J. Hutter.) In our youth one of our greatest pleasures is trying to look into the future ; of course with high hopes, which are seldom realised. But there comes a time when we lose faith in dreams of coming happiness and success, and take a greater pleasure in looking backward, and contemplating the past. In attempting to recall the early days of this part of Gippsland, I must ask you to remember I was only a child at the time ... BRANDY CREEK ... In 1872 diphtheria was very prevalent ... There was no anti-toxin ... my two brothers died ... the doctor ordered a complete change ... My father at once started for this new Eldorado, and arriving at Brandy Creek ... This new Eldorado soon became generally known ... described it as 'the finest land under the Canopy of Heaven' ... before ... this district was cut off from everywhere—on the north by the Baw Baw mountains, on the south by the Strezlecki ranges, and a howling wilderness between that and the sea ; on the west by the awful Koo wee rup swamp to the scrub, and a trembling bog, that nothing but a bird could cross, and on the east by the almost equally uncrossable Moe swamp ... People have often wondered how Brandy Creek got its name. The old road from Shady Creek to Cannibel Creek became very bad. A man named Campbell found a new track via Brandy Creek and the Bunyip. Mr. Wm. Pearson was the first to travel it. Campbell chanced to be camped at the creek when the former came along, and I am sorry to say was suffering from over indulgence in spring water. Mr. Pearson—like most old bushmen carried a pocket pistol of brandy. After same was emptied (for medicinal purposes, of course) it was thrown into the creek which was thereupon christened 'Brandy Creek.' The Government, finding this track much shorter than the told one, made a road for the Gippsland coach. The cattle drovers thereupon began to use it, and to prevent the track from being spoilt, the Government erected a toll gate at Brandy Creek and made a charge of 6d per head for all stock going through. This of course caused them to revert to the original track. It was shortly after this that Brandy Creek started to boom. A man named Smith bought an acre of land from Mr. Hann ; erected an accommodation house, and sold out in seven or eight months, netting £800. This man started with a capital of £4 10s. THE RICH FOREST. The rush to Brandy Creek set in 1874 ... new people were arriving every day. The track in was a blazed line, after a pack track known as Lardner's line—a due north and south survey, run by Mr. Lardner, district surveyor. This was an awful track in winter—mud up to the horses girths, and no get off it, as there was a solid wall of scrub on either side. But to call it scrub is a poor description. It was truly a magnificent forest of giant trees, with a luxuriant growth of jungle underneath—hazel, musk, blanket wood, orange, sassafras, blackwood, wattle, and other lovely shrubs, as well as fern trees of great beauty in the gullies ... A lot of tracks through the scrub were simply blazed lines—a description of a track almost unknown to the present residents of this district. These blazed lines generally led to some selectors' lonely hut ; surrounded by a square of cut off scrub, waiting for summer and a burn. In some cases I have heard of the selector placing his young children in a box and packing them in on horseback. The famous 'glue pot' was near Brandy Creek, on the old coach road. This was an awful hole where the coach regularly got stuck, and passengers were turned out in the middle of the night to help dig the coach out and then a walk a mile or more in the mud. The next improvement in the roads was corduroy, which made a barbarous road, and was only one degree better than the mud. The story is told of a hat seen on top of the mud, and when moved, the owner and his horse were found underneath! In the early days the animals in the forest had their own distinctiveness. Dingoes were of course very plentiful. The harmless native bear was rather alarming to the newcomer, with his awful screams like someone being murdered. The lyre bird was common ... However, the most striking and peculiar animal was the large earth worm, which I have often seen measure 5ft. long. Strangers found the worm story the hardest of all to believe. Brandy Creek was the only place within miles where there was anything in the way of a township, and it was the starting point for all selectors. Of course Cobb and Co.'s coach was the most popular mode of travelling to and from Melbourne. At that time John Meehan was in charge of Cobb and Co.'s stables at Brandy Creek, and my old friend Jack was well known and popular with all travellers and others ... About that time the late Mr. Ryan became postmaster at Brandy Creek. Later on he was in charge at Warragul ... GOLD RUSH. After we were settled at Lardner some years we went through an experience common to Australia—a gold rush! Gold was discovered at Sally's selection, caped [?] gold creek and now known as Tetoora. Everyone became very excited, and a canvas village sprang up, but it did not last long, the alluvial gold soon gave out, and all was quietness again ...

HONOR THE PIONEERS. There is much more that one could write of the early Warrgul district and early settlement in this part of Gippsland but perhaps sufficient has been written to remind some of the pioneers of the varied experiences & stirring times of 40 to 50 years ago ; while the younger men and women of the next generation will perhaps dwell for a moment in admiration of what has been accomplished by, their fathers and mothers as pioneers—members of 'the legion that never was listed' whose heroic, lion-hearted labor and womanly sacrifice has made the forest blossom with bounteous crops and pastures, and added a new and fertile province to the State of Victoria." (The Pioneers, 28 Feb 1922, p.3)

1890 Boyles Hotel, Fernshaw, Victoria - Courtesy Museums Victoria

1866 Tatchell's Royal Hotel, Inglewood (John Deslandes) - Courtesy State Library Victoria

ca. 1880-1881 Mac's Hotel, Portland (G. J. Nicholls, photographer) - Courtesy State Library Victoria

ca. 1861 Simpson's Bendigo Hotel, Dunolly; 'Cobb & Co. Telegraph Line' written on coach
(G. H. Jenkinson, 1836?- photographer) - Courtesy State Library Victoria

ca. 1880-1990 Bairnsdale showing Club and Orient Hotels, Main Street Gardens
(Walter Hodgkinson, photographer) - Courtesy State Library Victoria

1889 Clifton Springs Hotel (Reminiscence of a visit to Victoria,
Australia, April 1889 Part I) - Courtesy State Library Victoria

ca. 1861 Western Hotel, Mercer Street, Geelong; sign reads
'Depot for Cobb & Co.'s Telegraph Line of Coaches' - State Library Victoria

ca. 1853 Bath's Hotel, Ballarat - Courtesy State Library Victoria

ca. 1875 Shamrock Hotel, Sandhurst (N. J. Claire, 1837-1918, photographer) - Courtesy State Library Victoria

1861 Theatre Royal, Bendigo; signs 'Shamrock Hotel' and 'Cobb and Co. Booking Office'
(Benjamin Pierce Batchelder, 1826-1891, photographer) - Courtesy State Library Victoria

ca. 1870-1880 Castlemaine-Sandhurst coach outside [Railway Hotel],
a coach full of passengers being pulled by sixteen horses - Courtesy State Library Victoria

1861 Castlemaine Hotel, Hargraves Street, Castlemaine (Richard Daintree, 1832-1878) - Courtesy State Library Victoria

Chapter Five

Coaching Victoria

1860s

Gold!

Falsely alluring, I shimmer and shine
Over the millions that hold me divine,
Trampling each other, they rush to adore me,
Heaping the dearest of treasure before me—
Love and its blessedness, Youth and its wealth,
Honor, Tranquillity, Innocence, Health—
Buying my favor with evil and pain ;
Huge is the sacrifice, poor is the gain.
Naught but my effigy, passionless, cold,
God of a frenzied idolatry—Gold !

—Collier's.
(Worker, 5 Feb 1920, p.3)

1886 Gold store and hut (The Picturesque Atlas of Australasia, p. 211)
- Courtesy The University of Queensland

Examples of Cobb and Co. Coaching Lines, Victoria—1860s

1860 Jan-Jul

Cobb and Co.—Proprietors not listed
- 1 Jul 1860 Messrs. Cobb and Co.—About to start a line of coaches from Eden to Kiandra

Cobb and Co.—Victoria Stage Company
- 9 Apr 1860 Cobb and Co.'s Telegraph Line of Mail Coaches—Castlemaine, Melbourne ... M'Ivor, Moama, Swan Hill
- 13 July 1860 Cobb and Co.'s Telegraph Lines of Mail Coaches—Melbourne ... Sandhurst, Ballaarat ... Creswick ... Swan Hill

Cobb and Co.—F. B. Clapp and Co.
- 21 Jan 1860 Cobb and Co.'s Western Telegraph Lines of Royal Mail Coaches—Geelong, Portland passing through Bruce's Creek, Shelford, Rokewood, Pitfield, Skipton, Streatham, Wickliffe, Dunkeld, Hamilton, Branxholme, Green Hills, Heywood ... Geelong, Warrnambool, & Belfast passing through Murgheboluc, Inverleigh, Cressy (Frenchman's), Lismore, Brown's Water Holes, Elephant Bridge, Mortlake, Framlington, Woodford, Warrnambool, Tower Hill
- 24 Jan 1860 Cobb and Co.'s Telegraph Lines of Royal Mail Coaches—Geelong and Ballarat ... Smythe's Creek, Carngham, Brown's, Firey Creek, Ararat, Pleasant Creek, Creswick, Back Creek, Clunes, Daisy Hill, Maryboro', Castlemaine

Cobb and Co.—Victoria Stage Company + F. B. Clapp and Co.
- 27 Jan 1860 Cobb and Co.'s General Stage Office—Castlemaine, Sandhurst, Swan Hill, Euston, Echuca, Maryborough, Ararat, Pleasant Creek, Ballarat, Creswick's Creek, Hamilton, Portland, Casterton, Darlington, (Elephant Bridge), Warrnambool, Belfast
- 21 Jun 1860 Cobb and Co.'s General Stage Office—Castlemaine, Sandhurst, Swan Hill, Euston, Echuca, Maryborough, Ararat, Sandy Creek, Lamplough, Inglewood, via Sandhurst, Maryborough, Pleasant Creek, Ballarat, Creswick's Creek, Hamilton, Portland, Casterton, Darlington, (Elephant Bridge), Warrnambool, Belfast

1860 Aug-Dec

Cobb and Co.—Proprietors not listed
- 25 Oct 1860 Cobb and Co.'s Leviathan Coaches—commenced running for the summer ... Geelong, Ballarat; Cobb and Co.'s—Londonderry diggings, Black Ranges, near Ararat
- 13 Dec 1860 Cobb & Co.'s 4 horse coaches—[Ballarat] Clunes and Back Creek, Inglewood, and all intermediate stages; Cobb & Co.'s Royal Mail Coaches—[Ballarat] To Geelong; Cobb & Co.'s Leviathan 8-horse Coaches—[Ballarat] Geelong (Summer season); Cobb & Co.'s 4 horse coaches—[Ballarat] Creswick; Cobb & Co.'s 4 horse coaches—[Ballarat] Daylesford via Creswick, Deep Creek
- 8 Nov 1860 Cobb & Co.'s Royal Mail Six Horse Coaches—Geelong, Melbourne

Cobb and Co.—F. B. Clapp and Co.
- 12 Dec 1860 Cobb and Co.'s Western Telegraph Lines of Royal Mail Coaches—Geelong, Portland passing through Bruce's Creek, Shelford, Rokewood, Pitfield, Skipton, Streatham, Wickliffe, Dunkeld, Hamilton, Branxholme, Green Hills, Heywood ... Geelong, Warrnambool, & Belfast passing through Murgheboluc, Inverleigh, Cressy (Frenchman's), Lismore, Brown's Water Holes, Elephant Bridge, Mortlake, Framlington, Woodford, Warrnambool, Tower Hill
- 12 Dec 1860 Cobb and Co.'s Telegraph Lines of Royal Mail Coaches—Geelong and Ballarat ... Smythe's Creek, Brown's, Firey Creek, Ararat, Pleasant Creek, Creswick, Back Creek, Clunes, Daisy Hill, Maryboro', Castlemaine

Cobb and Co.—Watson and Hewitt
- 3 Aug 1860 Cobb and Co.'s Telegraph Line of Mail Coaches—Castlemaine, Melbourne; McIvor; Moama; Swan Hill
- 10 Aug 1860 Cobb and Co.'s Telegraph Line of Mail Coaches—Melbourne & Mount Alexander Railway ... Melbourne, Sandhurst, Maryborough, Ararat, Ballarat, Creswick Creek, Swan Hill, Back Creek, Lamplough, Inglewood, Newbridge, Dunolly, Sandy Creek
- 18 Oct 1860 Cobb and Co.'s Telegraph Line of Royal Mail Coaches—Alexander Temperance Hotel ... Hargreave's Royal Oak ... Digger's Rest Station

Cobb and Co.—F. B. Clapp and Co. + Watson and Hewitt
- 7 Aug 1860 Cobb and Co.'s General Stage Office, No. 74 Bourke-street east—Castlemaine, Sandhurst, Swan Hill, Euston, Echuca, Maryborough, Ararat, Sandy Creek, Lamplough, Inglewood, via Sandhurst, Maryborough, Pleasant Creek, Ballarat, Creswick's Creek, Hamilton, Portland, Casterton, Darlington, (Elephant Bridge), Warrnambool, Belfast
- 1 Jan 1861 Cobb and Co.'s General Stage Office, No. 35 Bourke street East—Castlemaine, Sandhurst, Swan Hill, Euston, Echuca, Maryboro', Ararat, Sandy Creek, Lamplough, and Inglewood, via Sandhurst and Maryborough, Pleasant Creek, Ballaarat, Creswick's Creek, Hamilton, Portland, Casterton, Darlington, (Elephant Bridge), Warrnambool and Belfast

1861 Jan-Jun

Cobb and Co.—Proprietors not listed
- 22 Mar 1861 Cobb and Co.'s Australian Express Parcels Delivery—Melbourne; Parcels will be delivered at any of Cobb and Co.'s offices, at the various townships in the interior ... additional rates for inland carriage

Cobb and Co.—Australian Stage Company
- 16 Jan 1861 Cobb and Co.'s Western Telegraph Line of Royal Mail Coaches—Geelong, Portland; Geelong, Warrnambool, Belfast
- 30 Jan 1861 Cobb and Co.'s Telegraph Line of Royal Mail Coaches—For Geelong ... connection with Geelong and Melbourne Railway, and passengers for Melbourne via Geelong; Mount Blackwood; Fiery Creek
- 23 Mar 1861 Cobb and Co.'s General Stage Offices—Geelong, Ballaarat, Raglan, Ararat, Pleasant Creek, Creswick Creek, Clunes, Back Creek, Amherst, Maryborough, Dunolly, Avoca, Lexton, M'Kinnon's, Inglewood, Sandy Creek, Lamplough, Daylesford, Portland, Hamilton, Belfast, Warrnambool, Elephant Bridge, Apsley, Harrow, Penola, Casterton, Coleraine,

Digby, Merino, Skipton, Streatham, Rokewood, Shelford, Wickliffe, Pitfield, Cavendish, Heywood, Melton, Bacchus Marsh, Ballan, Gordon's, and intermediate townships
- 21 Mar 1861 Cobb and Co.'s Telegraph Line of Royal Mail Coaches—Geelong ... to way stations and to other places beyond Ballarat, including Smythe's Creek, Brown's, Carngham, Linton's, Raglan, Ararat, Pleasant Creek, Horsham, Crowlands, Inglewood, Lamplough, M'Kinnon's, Avoca, Burbank, Maryboro', Amherst, Back Creek, Castlemaine, Creswick, Clunes
- 23 Mar 1861 Cobb and Co.'s Coaches—Ballaarat ... Melbourne to Ballarat via Keilor ... Melbourne to Ballaarat via Geelong
- 22 May 1861 Cobb & Co.'s Royal Mail Coaches—Geelong; Melbourne Direct; Mount Blackwood, Creswick, daily, Daisy Hill, Clunes, Maryborough, Dunolly, Sandy Creek, Inglewood, Castlemaine, Lamplough, Fiery Creek, Mount Ararat, Pleasant Creek, Smythe's Creek; Back Creek, Clunes, Creswick direct, Brown's, Daylesford, Deep Creek (Jim Crow), St. Arnaud, Mount Korong, Miners' Rest, Mt. Blowhard, Ascot
- 22 May 1861 Cobb & Co.'s Royal Mail Coaches—[Ballarat] Castlemaine, Bendigo ... Sandhurst
- 22 May 1861 Cobb & Co.'s coach—Fiery Creek (Raglan) to Ballarat
- 22 May 1861 Cobb & Co.'s Australian Express Parcel Delivery—Melbourne and Suburbs ... forwarded to Ballarat ... Delivered in Melbourne, Collingwood, Richmond, or Emerald Hill

Cobb and Co.—Watson and Hewitt
- 8 Jan 1861 Cobb and Co.'s Telegraph Line of Mail Coaches—Castlemaine, Sandhurst, Swanhill, Maryborough, Ararat, Ballarat, Creswick Creek etc., connecting with the Victorian Railway at the Digger's Rest Station ... pass through Ararat, Avoca, Amphitheatre, Buckeye, Barunhup, Loddon, Castlemaine, Carlsruhe, Creswick Creek, Carisbrook, Durham Ox, Eversley, Elphinstone, Gap, Gisborne, Guilford, Harcourt, Kyneton, Kingston, Maryborough, Malmsbury, Muckleford, Ravenswood, Reedy Lake Station, Sandhurst, Swan Hill, Serpentine Creek, Tarrangower (Maldon), Woodend connecting with Back's Creek, Pleasant Creek, Dunolly, Moama, Echuca, Deniliquin, etc. etc.
- 17 Jan 1861 Cobb and Co.'s Telegraph Line of Mail Coaches—Alexander's Temperance Hotel to Digger's Rest Station
- 8 Mar 1861 Cobb and Co.'s Telegraph Line of Royal Mail Coaches—In connection with the Melbourne & Mount Alexander Railway ... for Melbourne, Sandhurst, Maryborough, Ararat, Ballarat, Creswick Creek, Swan Hill, Back Creek, Lamplough, Inglewood, Newbridge, Dunolly, and Sandy Creek
- 14 Feb 1861 Cobb and Co.'s Telegraph Line of Mail Coaches—Castlemaine and Melbourne, M'Ivor, Moama, Swan Hill
- 18 Mar 1861 Cobb and Co.'s General Stage Office—Kyneton, Castlemaine, Sandhurst, Swan Hill, Euston, Echuca, Moama, Deniliquin, Maryborough, Ararat, Dunolly, Lamplough, Tarrangower (Maldon), Yandoit, Creswick

Cobb and Co.—Australian Stage Company & Watson and Hewitt
- 16 Jan 1861 Cobb and Co.'s Telegraph Line of Royal Mail Coaches—Geelong, Ballarat
- 16 Jan 1861 Cobb and Co.'s General Stage Office, No. 35 Bourke-street east—Passengers and parcels ... Castlemaine, Sandhurst, Swan Hill, Euston, Echuca, Maryborough, Ararat, Sandy Creek, Lamplough, and Inglewood, via Sandhurst and Maryborough, Pleasant Creek, Ballaarat, Creswick's Creek, Hamilton, Portland, Casterton, Darlington, (Elephant Bridge), Warrnambool and Belfast and all intermediate stations

1861 Jun-Dec

Cobb and Co.—Proprietors not listed
- 14 Jun 1861 Cobb & Co.'s Australian Express Parcels Delivery—To Collingwood, Fitzroy, Richmond, South Yarra, Prahran, Windsor, St. Kilda, Hawthorne, Kew, Tourak, Carlton, Flemington, and Emerald hill

Cobb and Co.—Robertson, Britton and Co.
- 5 Jun 1861 Cobb and Co.'s Telegraph Line of Mail Coaches—Maryborough, Melbourne, Castlemaine, Sandhurst, Ararat, Lamplough, Avoca, M'Kinnon's, Redbank
- 8 Jun 1861 Cobb and Co.'s General Stage Office—Kyneton, Castlemaine, Sandhurst, Swan Hill, Euston, Moama, Deniliquin, Maryboro', Ararat, Dunolly, Lamplough, Tarrangower (Maldon), Yandoit, Creswick and all intermediate stations
- 24 Jun 1861 Cobb and Co.'s Telegraph Line of Mail Coaches—Digger's Rest Station to Melbourne; Melbourne, Sandhurst, Maryborough, Ararat, Ballarat, Creswick Creek, Swan Hill, Back Creek, Lamplough, Inglewood, Newbridge, Dunolly, Sandy Creek
- 3 Oct 1861 Cobb and Co.'s Telegraph Line of Coaches—Castlemaine, Melbourne; Runnymede; M'Ivor; Swan Hill
- 1 Nov 1861 Cobb and Co.'s Telegraph Line of Mail Coaches—In connection with the Melbourne & Mount Alexander Railway; Melbourne, Sandhurst, Maryborough, Ararat, Ballarat, Creswick Creek, Swan Hill, Back Creek, Lamplough, Inglewood, Newbridge, Dunolly, Sandy Creek, Daylesford Direct

Cobb and Co.—Australian Stage Company
- 5 Jul 1861 Cobb and Co.'s Royal Mail Coaches—McKinnon's to Ballarat and Melbourne
- 5 Oct 1861 Cobb & Co—Creswick Creek, Melbourne; Bathurst, Geelong
- 19 Dec 1861 Cobb & Co's. Leviathan Coaches—Ballarat, Geelong

Cobb and Co.—Henry Hoyt/H. Hoyt
- 5 Jun 1861 Cobb and Co.'s Royal Mail Telegraph Line of Coaches—Eltham, St Andrew's and the new diggings
- 18 Jun 1861 Cobb and Co.'s Royal Mail Telegraph Line of Coaches—Caledonian, Mountain Diggings
- 22 Jun 1861 Cobb and Co.'s Telegraph Line Royal Mail of Coaches—Geelong for Portland, Belfast, Warrnambool, and all intermediate townships

Cobb and Co.—M'Phee & Co.
- Cobb and Co.'s Royal Mail Coaches—Mountain Creek to Ballarat daily ... McKinnon's Rush (Pilot Boat Hotel),

Avoca, Lamplough, Lexton, Lake Learmonth, Ballarat ... Geelong ... Melbourne

Cobb and Co.—Michel and Hughes
- 13 Jun 1861 Cobb and Co.'s Telegraph Line of Coaches—Dandenong

1862 Jan-Apr

Cobb and Co.—Proprietors not listed
- Cobb & Co.'s Australian Express Parcels Delivery—East Melbourne, Collingwood, East Collingwood, Fitsroy, Richmond, South Yarra, Prahran, Windsor, St Kilda, Hawthorn, Kew, Toorak, North Melbourne, Carlton, Flemington, Emerald Hill

Cobb and Co.—Australian Stage Company
- 10 Feb 1862 Cobb and Co.'s Royal Mail Coaches—Avoca, Lamplough, Back Creek, Clunes, Creswick, Castlemaine, Ballarat, Geelong, Melbourne; Dunolly, Sandy Creek, Inglewood

Cobb and Co.—Robertson, Britton and Co.
- 15 Jan 1862 Cobb and Co.'s General Stage Office, 35 Bourke street—Kyneton, Castlemaine, Sandhurst, Swan Hill, Euston, Moama, Deniliquin, Maryborough, Ararat, Dunolly, Lamplough, Tarrangower (Maldon), Yandoit, Creswick and all intermediate stations
- 27 Jan 1862 Cobb and Co.'s Telegraph Line of Mail Coaches—In connection with the Melbourne & Mount Alexander Railway ... Coaches for Melbourne, Sandhurst, Maryborough, Ararat, Ballarat, Creswick Creek, Swan Hill, Back Creek, Lamplough, Inglewood, Newbridge, Dunolly, and Sandy Creek; Coach to Daylesford
- 10 Feb 1862 Cobb and Co.'s Telegraph Line of Mail Coaches—[Maryborough] to Avoca, Moonambel Barkly (Navarre), Redbank, Lamplough, Amphitheatre, Eversley, Ararat, Pleasant Creek; Castlemaine, Sandhurst, Melbourne and intermediate places
- 21 Mar 1862 Cobb and Co.'s Telegraph Line of Mail Coaches—In connection with the Melbourne & Mount Alexander Railway; Melbourne, Sandhurst, Maryborough, Malden, Ararat, Ballarat, Creswick, Swan Hill, Back Creek, Lamplough, Inglewood, Dunolly, and Sandy Creek
- 21 Mar 1862 Cobb and Co.'s Royal Mail Coaches—Maldon, Ararat, Carisbrook, Dunolly, Lamplough and Maryborough; Newbridge, Sandy Creek and Inglewood

Cobb and Co.—Henry Hoyt
- 16 Jan 1862 Cobb and Co.'s Telegraph Line of Royal Mail Coaches—Geelong for Belfast; Geelong for Portland; Hamilton for Apsley; Casterton for Heywood; Hamilton for Belfast; Melbourne for Heidelberg; Melbourne, Elsham, Caledonia, and St Andrew's

1862 May-Dec

Cobb and Co.—Proprietors not listed
- 8 Nov 1862 Cobb and Co.'s Telegraph Line of Royal Mail Coaches—Geelong, Linton's, thence to Hamilton, Portland
- 29 Dec 1862 Cobb and Co.'s Western Telegraph Line of Royal Mail Coaches—Branch Coaches leave Hamilton for Apsley, via Cavendish, Balmoral, and Harrow ... leaving Hamilton for Penola, via. Coleraine and Casterton ... leaving Heywood for Casterton, via Hotspur, Digby, Merino, and Sandford ... Return Coaches leave the Company's Booking Offices ... Portland ... Apsley ... Penola

Cobb and Co.—Australian Stage Company
- 3 May 1862 Cobb and Co.'s Telegraph Lines—Geelong and Ballaarat; Melbourne to Ballaarat via Geelong
- 9 May 1862 Cobb and Co.'s Royal Mail Coaches—Avoca, Lamplough, Back Creek, Clunes, Creswick, Castlemaine, Ballarat, Geelong Melbourne; Dunolly, Sandy Creek, Inglewood
- 22 Dec 1862 V.R. Cobb and Co.'s Telegraph Line of Royal Mail Coaches, south-west corner of Sturt and Lydiard streets—To Melbourne direct ... Ballarat passing through Gordon, Ballan, and Bacchus Marsh ... to Creswick Creek, Clunes, Talbot (Back Creek), Amherst (Daisy Hill), Maryborough, Dunolly, Sandy Creek, Inglewood, Wedderbourne (Mount Korong) via Inglewood, St. Arnaud (New Bendigo), Kingston, Smeaton, Yandoit, Castlemaine, Sandhurst (Bendigo), Mount Prospect, Deep Creek (Jim Crow), Daylesford, Woodend via Daylesford, Miners' Rest, Blowhard, Lake Learmonth, Mount Bolton, Springs, Lexton, Lamplough, Avoca, Moonambel (M'Kinnon's), Redbank, Barkly (Navarre), Burrumbeet, Raglan (Fiery Creek), Ararat, Great Western, Pleasant Creek, Skipton, Hamilton, Portland, Gordons, Ballan, Pentland Hills, Bacchus Marsh, Melton, Keilor road, Mount Blackwood

Cobb and Co.—Robertson, Britton and Co.
- 1 Aug 1862 Cobb and Co.'s Telegraph Line of Mail Coaches—In connection with the Melbourne & Mount Alexander Railway; Digger's Rest Station to Melbourne; Melbourne, Sandhurst, Maryborough, Ararat, Ballarat, Creswick Creek, Swan Hill, Back Creek, Lamplough, Inglewood, Newbridge, Dunolly, Sandy Creek leave the Kangaroo Hotel, Maldon ... for Ararat, Carisbrook, Dunolly, Lamplough, Maryborough; Newbridge, Sandy Creek, and Inglewood
- 22 Nov 1862 Conveyance of mails to and from Castlemaine and Maryborough, daily, by way of Muckleford, Maldon, Baringhup, and Carisbrook; to and from Maldon, Dunolly

Cobb and Co.—Robertson, Wagner and Co.
- 5 May 1862 Cobb and Co.'s General Stage Office—Kyneton, Castlemaine, Sandhurst, Swan Hill, Euston, Moama, Deniliquin, Maryboro, Ararat, Dunolly, Lamplough, Tarrangower (Maldon), Yandoit, Creswick, and all intermediate stations
- 5 May 1862 Cobb and Co.'s Telegraph Line of Mail Coaches—In connection with the Melbourne & Mount Alexander Railway; From Woodend and Kyneton Station to Melbourne; Coaches for Melbourne, Sandhurst, Maryborough, Ararat, Ballarat, Creswick Creek, Swan Hill, Back Creek, Lamplough, Inglewood, Newbridge, Dunolly, Sandy Creek
- 9 May 1862 Cobb and Co.'s Telegraph Line of Mail Coaches—Maryborough, Avoca, Moonambel, Barkley (late Navarro), Redbank, Lamplough, Amphitheatre, Eversley, Ararat, Pleasant Creek; Castlemaine, Sandhurst, Melbourne and intermediate places
- 2 Jul 1862 Cobb and Co.'s Telegraph Line of Mail Coaches—Castlemaine, Melbourne, Swan Hill, Moama

or Echuca, Runnymede, Deniliquin, M'Ivor, Inglewood, Whipstick
- 24 Dec 1862 Contracts for Postal Lines—79. Robertson, Wagner & Co. Melbourne; Hay, Deniliquin; Deniliquin, Moama

Cobb and Co.—Henry Hoyt
- 29 Dec 1862 Cobb and Co.'s Western Telegraph Line of Royal Mail Coaches—Ballarat to Smythesdale, Linton, Skipton, Streatham, Wickliff, Dunkeld, Hamilton, Branxholme, Green Hills, Heywood, Portland

EXPANSION FURTHER INTO NEW SOUTH WALES:
Cobb and Co. (Melbourne)—28 May 1862 Messrs. Robertson and Britton, with James Rutherford, Manager N.S.W.
- 24 May 1862 Preliminary Notice—Ballarat, Lachlan Gold Fields
- 12 Jul 1862 Cobb and Co.'s Line of Coaches—Forbes, Bathurst
- 15 Jul Messers Cobb and Co. Melbourne—Sydney, Yass; Sydney, Bathurst

1863

Cobb and Co.—Proprietors not listed
- 11 Apr 1863 Cobb and Co.—Pleasant Creek; Clunes, Talbot (Back Creek) via Creswick, Ballarat; Blowhard, Learmonth, Springs
- 16 Jun 1863 Branch Coaches—leave Hamilton for Apsley, via Cavendish, Balmoral, and Harrow leaving Hamilton for Penola, via Coleraine and Casterton leaving Heywood for Casterton, via Hotspur, Digby, Merino, and Sandford ... Return Portland, Hamilton, Casterton, Apsley, Penola

Cobb and Co.—Australian Stage Company
- 11 Jul 1863 V.R. Cobb and Co.'s Telegraph Line of Royal Mail Coaches—Ballarat to Creswick, Clunes, Ascot (Coghill's Creek), Talbot (Back Creek), Amherst (Daisy Hill), Maryborough, Dunolly, Sandy Creek (Tarnagulla), Inglewood, St. Arnaud (New Bendigo), Kingston, Smeaton, Yandoit, Guildford, Castlemaine, Sandhurst (Bendigo), Mount Prospect, Deep Creek (Jim Crow), Daylesford, Woodend, Miners' Rest, Mount Blowhard, Lake Learmonth, Mount Bolton, Springs, Lexton, Avoca, Lamplough, Woodstock, Moonambel (Mountain Creek), Redbank, Barkly (Navarre), Landsborough (New Rush), Burrumbeet, Raglan (Fiery Creek), Buangor (M'Donald's), Ararat, Great Western, Pleasant Creek, Glenorchy, Horsham, Gordons, Ballan, Pentland Hills, Bacchus Marsh, Melton, Keilor

Cobb and Co.—Robertson, Britton and Co.
- 12 Jan 1863 Conveyance of Mails—Sandhurst to Inglewood, by way of Marong
- 20 Nov 1863 Cobb and Co.'s Royal Mail Coaches—Maldon, Ararat, Carisbrook, Dunolly, Lamplough, Maryborough; Newbridge, Sandy Creek, Inglewood

Cobb and Co.—Robertson, Wagner and Co.
- 31 Mar 1863 Cobb and Co.'s Telegraph Line of Mail Coaches—in connection with the Melbourne & Mount Alexander Railway ... leave the Kangaroo Hotel, Maldon ... Baringhup, Carisbrook, Maryborough, Ararat, Lamplough, Eddington, Dunolly, Tarnagulla, Burnt Creek; Castlemaine and Melbourne; Castlemaine Hotel and Railway Station for Carisbrook, Maryborough, Back Creek, Avoca, Moonambool, Landsborough, Barkly, Red Bank, Ararat, Eversley; Inglewood, Serpentine, Durham Ox, Swan Hill, M'Ivor, Echuca, Moama, Red Bank, Deniliquin, Hay; Yandoit, Creswick, Ballaarat; Daylesford
- 14 Apr 1863 Cobb and Co.'s General Stage Office—Kyneton, Castlemaine, Sandhurst, Swan Hill, Huston, Moama, Deniliquin, Maryborough, Ararat, Dunolly, Lamplough, Tarrengower (Maldon), Yandoit, Creswick, and all intermediate stations
- 30 May 1863 Coach Notice—Kyneton, Blue Mountains Rush

Cobb and Co.—Henry Hoyt
- 6 Feb 1863 Cobb and Co.'s Western Telegraph Line of Royal Mail Coaches—Ballarat to Smythesdale, Linton, Skipton, Streatham, Wickliff, Dunkeld, Hamilton, Branxholme, Green Hills, Heywood, Portland
- 3 Apr 1863 Mail Arrangements for 1863. Cobb and Co.'s Western Telegraph Line of Royal Mail Coaches—Ballarat to Hamilton & Portland, Hamilton to Portland ... from Hamilton; Ballarat via Dunkeld, Wickliffe, Streatham, Skipton; Portland via Branxholme, Green Hills, Heywood; Apsley via Cavendish, Balmoral, Harrow; Penola via Coleraine, Casterton, Fletcher's Store; Penhurst, Caramut, Hexham, Mortlake; Eumeralla, Orford, Belfast

Cobb and Co.—Meigs & Anderson
- 28 Dec 1863 Cobb and Co.'s Western Telegraph Line of Royal Mail Coaches—Reduction in fares, Ballarat to Smythesdale, Linton, Skipton, Streatham, Wickliff, Dunkeld, Hamilton, Branxholme, Green Hills, Heywood, Portland ... Head Office, Lydiard street for Smythes and Linton ... Mails and passengers for Ballarat, Portland, Apsley, Penola

1864 Jan-Jun

Cobb and Co.—Australian Stage Company
- 5 Jan 1864 V.R. Cobb and Co.'s Telegraph Line of Royal Mail Coaches, south-west corner of Sturt and Lydiard streets—Ballarat to Creswick, Clunes, Ascot (Coghill's Creek), Talbot (Back Creek), Amherst (Daisy Hill), Maryborough, Dunolly, Sandy Creek (Tarnagulla), Inglewood, St. Arnaud (New Bendigo), Kingston, Smeaton, Yandoit, Guildford, Castlemaine, Sandhurst (Bendigo) Mount Prospect, Deep Creek (Jim Crow), Daylesford

Cobb and Co.—Robertson, Britton and Co.
- 5 Jan 1854 V.R. Cobb and Co.'s Telegraph Line of Royal Mail Coaches, south-west corner of Sturt and Lydiard streets—CASTLEMAINE ROAD Kingston, Smeaton, Yandoit, Guildford, Castlemaine, Sandhurst (Bendigo) ...
- 22 Jan 1864 Cobb and Co.—Malden to Maryborough, Dunolly, Inglewood
- 12 Feb 1864 Cobb and Co.'s Royal Mail Coaches—leave the Kangaroo Hotel, Maldon for Ararat, Carisbrook, Dunolly, Lamplough and Maryborough; For Newbridge, Sandy Creek and Inglewood

Cobb and Co.—Robertson, Wagner and Co.
- 1 Feb 1864 Cobb & Co.'s Coaches—in connection with Victorian Railways ... start from Castlemaine Hotel and Railway Station for Newstead, Carisbrook, Maryborough, Back creek, Avoca, Moonambel, Landsborough, Barkly Red Bank, Eversly, Ararat, Maldon, Eddington, Dunolly, Tarnagulla, and Burnt Creek. Passengers booked, via Sandhurst, for Inglewood, Serpentine, Durham Ox, Swan Hill, M'lvor, Echuca, Moama, Red Bank, Deniliquin and Hay; For Yandoit, Creswick, Ballarat; Daylesford
- 12 Feb 1864 Cobb and Co.'s Telegraph Line of Mail Coaches—in connection with the Melbourne & Mount Alexander Railway ... Coaches of the above line will leave the Kangaroo Hotel, Maldon for Baringhup, Carisbrook, Maryborough, Ararat, Lamplough, Eddington, Dunolly, Tarnagulla, Burnt Creek; Castlemaine and Melbourne; Castlemaine Hotel and Railway Station for Maldon, Carisbrook, Maryborough, Back Creek, Avoca, Moonambool, Landsborough, Barkly, Red Bank, Ararat, Eversley via Sandhurst for Inglewood, Serpentine, Durham Ox, Swan Hill, M'Ivor, Echuca, Moama, Red Bank, Deniliquin, and Hay; For Yandoit, Creswick, Ballaarat; Daylesford

Cobb and Co.—Meigs & Anderson
- 5 Jan 1864 Cobb and Co.'s Western Telegraph Line of Royal Mail Coaches—Reduction in fares Ballarat to Smythesdale, Linton, Skipton, Streatham, Wickliff, Dunkeld, Hamilton, Branxholme, Green Hills, Heywood, Portland ... Head Office, Lydiard street; For Smythes, Linton ... Mails and passengers ... For Ballarat, Portland, Apsley, Penola

Cobb and Co.—J. J. Stiles
- 24 Jun 1864 Cobb and Co.'s Western Telegraph Line of Royal Mail Coaches—Hamilton, Portland via Branxholme, Green Hills, Heywood

Cobb and Co.—R. Davey
- 24 Jun 1864 Cobb and Co.'s Western Telegraph Line of Royal Mail Coaches—Hamilton, Apsley via Cavendish, Balmoral, Harrow; Hamilton, Eumeralla, Orford, Belfast

Cobb and Co.—John Cawker
- 24 Jun 1864 Cobb and Co.'s Western Telegraph Line of Royal Mail Coaches—Hamilton, Penola via Coleraine, Casterton, Fletcher's Station

Cobb and Co.—A. Lane
- 24 Jun 1864 Cobb and Co.'s Western Telegraph Line of Royal Mail Coaches—Hamilton, Penshurst, Caramut, Hexham, Mortlake

Cobb and Co.—M'Phee and Co.
- 5 Jan 1864 V.R. Cobb and Co.'s Telegraph Line of Royal Mail Coaches—AVOCA ROAD Miners' Rest, Mount Blowhard, Lake Learmonth, Mount Bolton, Springs, Lexton, Avoca, Lamplough, Woodstock, Moonambel (Mountain Creek), Redbank, Barkly (Navarre), Landsborough (New Rush)

Cobb and Co.—J. C. Horr
- 5 Jan 1864 V.R. Cobb and Co.'s Telegraph Line of Royal Mail Coaches—Burrumbeet, Raglan (Fiery Creek), Buangor (M'Donald's), Ararat, Great Western, Pleasant Creek

Cobb and Co.—Thomas Stoneman
- 4 Jan 1864 Cobb & Co's. Royal Mail Line of Coaches—Geelong, Warrnambool, Belfast
- 23 Jul 1864 Cobb & Co's. Royal Mail Line of Coaches—LEIGH ROAD to Shelford, Rokewood, Pitfield, Lintons

1864 Jul-Dec

Cobb and Co.—Australian Stage Company
- 2 Aug 1864 V.R. Cobb and Co.'s Telegraph Line of Royal Mail Coaches—Ballarat to Creswick, Clunes, Ascot (Coghill's Creek), Talbot (Back Creek), Amherst (Daisy Hill), Maryborough, Dunolly, Sandy Creek (Tarnagulla), Inglewood, St. Arnaud (New Bendigo), Mount Prospect, Deep Creek (Jim Crow), Daylesford

Cobb and Co.—Robertson, Wagner and Co.
- 2 Aug 1864 V.R. Cobb and Co.'s Telegraph Line of Royal Mail Coaches—CASTLEMAINE ROAD Kingston, Smeaton, Yandoit, Guildford, Castlemaine, Sandhurst (Bendigo)

Cobb and Co.—Meigs & Anderson
- 2 Aug 1864 V.R. Cobb and Co.'s Telegraph Line of Royal Mail Coaches—Ballarat to Smythesdale, Linton, Skipton, Streatham, Wickliff, Dunkeld, Hamilton, Portland

Cobb and Co.—M'Phee and Co./John M'Phee
- 2 Aug 1864 V.R. Cobb and Co.'s Telegraph Line of Royal Mail Coaches—AVOCA ROAD Miners' Rest, Mount Blowhard, Lake Learmonth, Mount Bolton, Springs, Lexton, Woodstock, Lamplough, Avoca, Moonambel (Mountain Creek), Redbank, Barkly), Landsborough, Redbank, Stuart Mill, St Arnaud
- 28 Nov 1854 V.R. Cobb and Co.'s Telegraph Line of Royal Mail Coaches—ARARAT ROAD Burrumbeet, Raglan (Fiery Creek), Buangor (M'Donald's), Ararat, Great Western, Pleasant Creek

Cobb and Co.—J. C. Horr
- 23 Jul 1864 V.R. Cobb and Co.'s Telegraph Line of Royal Mail Coaches—Burrumbeet, Raglan (Fiery Creek), Buangor (M'Donald's), Ararat, Great Western, Pleasant Creek

Cobb and Co.—Thomas Stoneman
- 23 Jul 1864 V.R. Cobb & Co's. Royal Mail Line of Coaches—LEIGH ROAD to Shelford, Rokewood, Pitfield, Lintons

Cobb and Co.—Cameron and Jones
- 2 Aug 1864 Cobb and Co.'s Criterion Line of Coaches—Beaufort, Ararat, and Pleasant Creek

1865

Cobb and Co.—Proprietors not listed
- 16 Jun 1865 Cobb and Co.—Sale to Port Albert

Cobb and Co.—Australian Stage Company
- 10 Jan 1865 V. R. Cobb and Co.'s Telegraph Line of Royal Mail Coaches—Ballarat to Creswick, Clunes, Ascot (Coghill's Creek), Talbot (Back Creek), Amherst (Daisy Hill), Maryborough, Dunolly, Sandy Creek (Tarnagulla), Inglewood, St. Arnaud (New Bendigo), Mount Prospect, Deep Creek (Jim Crow), Daylesford
- 11 Jan 1865 Cobb and Co.'s Royal Mail Line of Coach—Melbourne to Daylesford
- 4 Dec 1865 V.R. Cobb and Co.'s Telegraph Line of Royal Mail Coaches—Ballarat to Creswick, Clunes,

Ascot (Coghill's Creek), Talbot (Back Creek), Amherst (Daisy Hill), Maryborough, Dunolly, Sandy Creek (Tarnagulla), Inglewood, St. Arnaud (New Bendigo), Mount Prospect, Deep Creek (Jim Crow), Daylesford
Cobb and Co.—Robertson, Wagner and Co.
- 10 Jan 1865 V.R. Cobb and Co.'s Telegraph Line of Royal Mail Coaches—CASTLEMAINE ROAD Kingston, Smeaton, Yandoit, Guildford, Castlemaine, Sandhurst (Bendigo)
- 1 Jul 1865 Cobb & Co.'s Telegraph Line of Coaches—Echuca, Deniliquin
- 26 Aug 1865 Cobb & Co.'s Telegraph Line of Mail Coaches—Deniliquin, Sandhurst; Hay (Lang's Crossing Place) Murrumbidgee; Hay, Deniliquin
- 4 Dec 1865 V.R. Cobb and Co.'s Telegraph Line of Royal Mail Coaches—CASTLEMAINE ROAD Kingston, Smeaton, Yandoit, Guildford, Castlemaine, Sandhurst (Bendigo)

Cobb and Co.—Meigs & Anderson
- 10 Jan 1865 V.R. Cobb and Co.'s Telegraph Line of Royal Mail Coaches—HAMILTON ROAD Ballarat to Smythesdale, Linton, Skipton, Streatham, Wickliff, Dunkeld, Hamilton, Portland
- 3 May 1865 V.R. Cobb and Co.—Melbourne to Sale, Barnsdale, Bald Hills, by steamer and coach
- 4 Dec 1865 V.R. Cobb and Co.'s Telegraph Line of Royal Mail Coaches—HAMILTON ROAD Ballarat to Smythesdale, Linton, Skipton, Streatham, Lake Bolake, Wickliff, Mail Tent, Dunkeld, Hamilton

Cobb and Co.—M'Phee and Co./John M'Phee
- 10 Jan 1865 V.R. Cobb and Co.'s Telegraph Line of Royal Mail Coaches, south-west corner of Sturt and Lydiard streets—AVOCA ROAD Miners' Rest, Mount Blowhard, Lake Learmonth, Mount Bolton, Springs, Lexton, Woodstock, Lamplough, Avoca, Moonambel, Barkly, Landsborough, Redbank, Stuart Mill, St Arnaud
- 10 Jan 1865 V.R. Cobb and Co.'s Telegraph Line of Royal Mail Coaches, south-west corner of Sturt and Lydiard streets—ARARAT ROAD Burrumbeet, Raglan (Fiery Creek), Buangor (M'Donald's), Ararat, Great Western, Pleasant Creek
- 4 Dec 1865 V.R. Cobb and Co.'s Telegraph Line of Royal Mail Coaches—AVOCA & ST. ARNAUD'S Miners' Rest, Mount Blowhard, Lake Learmonth, Mount Bolton, Springs, Lexton, Woodstock, Lamplough, Avoca, Moonambel, Barkly, Landsborough, Redbank, Stuart Mill, St Arnaud

Cobb and Co.—Ballarat Stage Company
- 4 Dec 1865 V.R. Cobb and Co.'s Telegraph Line of Royal Mail Coaches—ARARAT, PLEASANT CREEK and HORSHAM ROAD Burrumbeet, Beaufort, Mount Colem, Buangor, Ararat, Great Western, Stawell, Glenorchy, Ashens, Longernong, Horsham

1866

Cobb and Co.— Proprietors not listed
- 8 Dec 1866 Kooringa and Redruth

Cobb and Co.—Australian Stage Company
- 5 Mar 1866 V.R. Cobb and Co.'s Telegraph Line of Royal Mail Coaches—Ballarat to Creswick, Clunes, Ascot (Coghill's Creek), Talbot (Back Creek), Amherst (Daisy Hill), Maryborough, Dunolly, Sandy Creek (Tarnagulla), Inglewood, St. Arnaud (New Bendigo), Mount Prospect, Deep Creek (Jim Crow), Daylesford

Cobb and Co.—Robertson, Wagner and Co.
- 5 Mar 1866 V.R. Cobb and Co.'s Telegraph Line of Royal Mail Coaches—CASTLEMAINE ROAD Kingston, Smeaton, Yandoit, Guildford, Castlemaine, Sandhurst (Bendigo)
- 12 Mar 1866 V.R. Cobb and Co.'s Telegraph Line of Royal Mail Coaches—ARARAT, PLEASANT CREEK and HORSHAM ROAD Burrumbeet, Raglan (Fiery Creek), Buangor, Ararat, Great Western, Pleasant Creek, Glenorchy, Ashens, Longernong, Horsham
- 23 May 1868 Cobb & Co.'s Line of Coaches—Deniliquin, Echuca; For Hay; Hay for Deniliquin; Leave Hay for Booligal

Cobb and Co.—Meigs & Anderson
- 5 Mar 1866 V.R. Cobb and Co.'s Telegraph Line of Royal Mail Coaches—HAMILTON ROAD Ballarat to Smythesdale, Linton, Skipton, Streatham, Lake Bolake, Wickliff, Mail Tent, Dunkeld, Hamilton

Cobb and Co.—M'Phee and Co.
- 5 Mar 1866 V.R. Cobb and Co.'s Telegraph Line of Royal Mail Coaches—AVOCA & ST. ARNAUD'S Miners' Rest, Mount Blowhard, Lake Learmonth, Mount Bolton, Springs, Lexton, Woodstock, Lamplough, Avoca, Moonambel, Barkly, Landsborough, Redbank, Stuart Mill, St Arnaud, Swam Water, Cop Cop, Richardson Bridge, Mount Jeffcot, Watcham, Morton Plains
- 12 Mar 1866 V.R. Cobb and Co.'s Telegraph Line of Royal Mail Coaches—MARYBOROUGH and DUNOLLY ROAD Ballarat to Creswick, Clunes, Ascot (Coghill's Creek), Talbot (Back Creek), Amherst (Daisy Hill), Maryborough, Dunolly, Sandy Creek (Tarnagulla), Inglewood, St. Arnaud (New Bendigo)

Cobb and Co.—Ballarat Stage Company
- 5 Mar 1866 V.R. Cobb and Co.'s Telegraph Line of Royal Mail Coaches—ARARAT, PLEASANT CREEK and HORSHAM ROAD Burrumbeet, Raglan (Fiery Creek), Buangor, Ararat, Great Western, Pleasant Creek, Glenorchy, Ashens, Longernong, Horsham

Cobb and Co.—Thomas Stoneman & Co.
- 5 Apr 1866 Cobb & Co's. Western Telegraph Line of Coaches—Mortlake, Hamilton and Penola ... Hamilton, Darlington, Mortlake, Penola, Caramut, Penshurst ... Inverleigh, Cressy, Hexham, Penshurst ... Coleraine, Casterton and Penola
- 27 Dec 1866 Cobb & Co's. Western Telegraph Line of Coaches—LEIGH ROAD Railway Station to Shelford and Rokewood Connecting thence with coaches to Bulldog, Lintons, Cape Clear, Smythesdale, Ballarat
- 27 Dec 1866 Cobb & Co's. Western Telegraph Line of Coaches—Geelong to Colac through Duneed, Winchelsea, Birregurra
- 27 Dec 1866 Cobb & Co's. Western Telegraph Line of Coaches—Darlington, Mortlake, Hamilton for Inverleigh, Cressy, Darlington, Mortlake and for Warrnambool, Belfast, Hepburn, Caramut, Penshurst, Hamilton

Cobb and Co.—E. Moore and Co.
- 12 Mar 1866 V.R. Cobb and Co.'s Telegraph Line of

Royal Mail Coaches, south-west corner of Sturt and Lydiard streets— DAYLESFORD and MALMSBURY ROAD Ballarat to Creswick, Mount Prospect, Deep Creek (Jim Crow), Daylesford, Coomoora, Dyers, Glenlyon, Red Hill, Germans, Kyneton road, Malmsbury

1867

Cobb and Co.—Australian Stage Company & Robertson, Wagner and Co.
- 9 Jan 1867 Cobb and Co.'s Telegraph Line of Mail Coaches—Maryborough, Avoca, Moonambel, Redbank, Barkly, Lamplough, Amphitheatre, Eversley, Crowlands, Landsborough, Ararat; Carisbrook, Joyce's Creek, Newstead, Castlemaine, Melbourne; Amherst, Talbot, Clunes, Creswick, Ballarat, Geelong; Carisbrook, Baringhup, Maldon, Castlemaine, Melbourne; Burnt Creek, Dunolly; M'Cullum's Creek, Majorca

Cobb and Co.—Robertson, Wagner and Co.
- 1 Apr 1867 V.R. Cobb and Co.'s Telegraph Line of Royal Mail Coaches—DAYLESFORD and MALMSBURY ROAD Ballarat to Creswick, Mount Prospect, Deep Creek (Jim Crow), Daylesford, Coomoora, Dyers, Glenlyon, Red Hill, Germans, Kyneton road, Malmsbury
- 1 Apr 1867 V.R. Cobb and Co.'s Telegraph Line of Royal Mail Coaches—CASTLEMAINE ROAD Kingston, Smeaton, Hepburns, Yandoit, Guildford, Castlemaine, Sandhurst (Bendigo); ARARAT, PLEASANT CREEK and HORSHAM ROAD Royal Mail Coach Burrumbeet, Raglan (Fiery Creek), Buangor (McDonald's), Ararat, Great Western, Pleasant Creek, Glenorchy, Ashens, Longernong, Horsham
- 1 Apr 1867 Cobb and Co.'s Telegraph Line.—Accommodation Coach.—Beaufort and Ballarat

Cobb and Co.—M'Phee and Co.
- 1 Apr 1867 V.R. Cobb and Co.'s Telegraph Line of Royal Mail Coaches—MARYBOROUGH and DUNOLLY ROAD Ballarat to Creswick, Clunes, Ascot (Coghill's Creek), Talbot (Back Creek), Amherst (Daisy Hill), Maryborough, Dunolly, Sandy Creek (Tarnagulla), Inglewood, St. Arnaud (New Bendigo); AVOCA & ST. ARNAUD'S DAILY Miners' Rest, Mount Blowhard, Lake Learmonth, Mount Bolton, Springs, Lexton, Woodstock, Lamplough, Avoca, Moonambel, Barkly, Landsborough, Redbank, Stuart Mill, St Arnaud, Swam Water, Cop Cop, Richardson Bridge, Mount Jeffcot, Watcham, Morton Plains

Cobb and Co.—Western Stage Company
- 5 Jan 1867 Cobb & Co.'s. Western Telegraph Line of Royal Mail Coaches—Geelong to Belfast, Hamilton ... passing through Inverleigh, Cressy, Lismore, Darlington, Caramut, Penshurst, Mortlake, Warrnambool, Belfast, Hexham, Framlington, Hamilton; Night Mail, Geelong and Belfast ... With Branch Line from Camperdown to Mortlake and Hamilton ... Camperdown, Terang, Warrnambool, Belfast, Mortlake, Hexham, Penshurst, Hamilton; Geelong and Camperdown passing through Winchelsea, Birregurra, Colac, Larpent, Stony Rises, Camperdown; Day Coach ... Geelong and Colac passing Mount Moriac, Winchelsea, Birregurra, Colac; LEIGH ROAD (Railway Station) and Smythesdale ... LEIGH ROAD Railway Station ... passing Teesdale, Shelford, Rokewood, Junction, Bulldog, Cape Clear, Scarsdale, Smythesdale; Geelong and Queenscliffe ... Geelong, Kensington, Wallington
- 1 Apr 1867 V.R. Cobb and Co.'s Telegraph Line of Royal Mail Coaches—HAMILTON ROAD Ballarat to Smythesdale, Linton, Skipton, Streatham, Lake Bolake, Wickliff, Mail Tent, Dunkeld, Hamilton
- 26 Oct 1867 Cobb & Co's. Western Telegraph Line of Royal Mail Coaches—On and after Monday, January 1st, 1867 ... Booking Office, opposite Victoria Hotel, Hamilton; For Ballarat via Dunkeld, Wickliffe, Streatham, Skipton, Lintons, Smythesdale; For Portland, via Branxholme, Green Hills, Heywood; For Mortlake, via Penshurst, Caramut, Hexham; For Apsley, via Cavendish, Balmoral, Harrow; For Penola, via Coleraine, Casterton, Fletcher's Station

1868

Cobb and Co.—Robertson, Wagner and Co.
- 7 Sep 1868 Cobb and Co.'s Telegraph Line of Royal Mail Coaches—DAYLESFORD and MALMSBURY ROAD ... Ballarat to Creswick, Mount Prospect, Deep Creek (Jim Crow), Daylesford, Coomoora, Dyers, Glenlyon, Red Hill, Germans, Kyneton road, Malmsbury; CASTLEMAINE ROAD Kingston, Smeaton, Hepburns, Yandoit, Guildford, Castlemaine, Sandhurst (Bendigo); ARARAT, PLEASANT CREEK and HORSHAM ROAD Burrumbeet, Raglan (Fiery Creek), Buangor (McDonald's), Ararat, Great Western, Pleasant Creek, Glenorchy, Ashens, Longernong, Horsham
- 15 Sep 1868 Cobb and Co.'s Telegraph Line of Royal Mail Coaches—Sale to Melbourne (Overland) ... Sale, Rosedale, Traralgon, Morewell, Moe, Shady Creek, Bunyip, Pakenham, Berwick, Dandenong, Springvale, Oakleigh, and Melbourne ... Sale to Bairnsdale ... Rosedale to Toongabbi, Mountain Queen Hotel, Happy-go-Lucky, and Royal Exchange Hotel, Stringer's Creek ... Cansick's Hotel, Rosedale

Cobb and Co.—M'Phee and Co.
- 7 Sep 1868 Cobb and Co.'s Telegraph Line of Royal Mail Coaches, south-west corner of Sturt and Lydiard streets—MARYBOROUGH and DUNOLLY ROAD Ballarat to Creswick, Clunes, Ascot (Coghill's Creek), Talbot (Back Creek), Amherst (Daisy Hill), Maryborough, Dunolly, Sandy Creek (Tarnagulla), Inglewood, St. Arnaud (New Bendigo); AVOCA & ST. ARNAUD'S Miners' Rest, Mount Blowhard, Lake Learmonth, Mount Bolton, Springs, Lexton, Woodstock, Lamplough, Avoca, Moonambel, Barkly, Landsborough, Redbank, Stuart Mill, St Arnaud, Swam Water, Cop Cop, Richardson Bridge, Mount Jeffcot, Watcham, Morton Plains
- 7 Sep 1868 Cobb and Co.'s Coaches—Ballarat to Dunolly, New Rush

Cobb and Co.—Anderson and M'Phee
- 7 Sep 1868 Cobb and Co.'s Line of Coaches—To and from Ballarat to Smythesdale ... Scarsdale ... Piggoreet, Carngham, Lintons, Staffordshire, Derwent Jacks ... Cape Clear ... Bulldog ... Rokewood Junction ...

Rokewood ... Break O'Day

Cobb and Co.— Western Stage Company
- 2 Jan 1868 HAMILTON ROAD Ballarat to Smythesdale, Linton, Skipton, Streatham, Lake Bolac, Wickliff, Mail Tent, Dunkeld, Hamilton
- 4 Mar 1868 Cobb & Co's. Western Telegraph Line of Royal Mail Coaches—Booking Office, opposite Victoria Hotel, Hamilton; For Ballarat via Dunkeld, Wickliffe, Streatham, Skipton, Lintons, Smythesdale; For Portland, via Branxholme, Green Hills, Heywood; For Mortlake, via Penshurst, Caramut, Hexham; For Apsley, via Cavendish, Balmoral, Harrow; For Penola, via Coleraine, Casterton, Fletcher's Station
- 22 Apr 1868 Cobb & Co's. Western Telegraph Line of Royal Mail Coaches—Night Mail ... Geelong and Belfast with Branch Line from Terang to Mortlake and Hamilton, thence to Mount Gambier and Adelaide passing Mount Duneed, Winchelsea, Camperdown, Terang, Yallock, Warrnambool, Belfast, Mortlake, Hexham, Caramut, Birregurra, Colac, Penshurst, Hamilton, Apsley, Penola, Casterton, Mount Gambier, Adelaide; Summer Arrangements. Colac and Camperdown ... for Winchelsea, Birregurra, Colac, Camperdown; Geelong to Belfast via Darlington and Mortlake passing through Inverleigh, Cressy, Lismore, Darlington, Caramut, Penshurst, Mortlake, Warrnambool, Belfast, Hexham, Framlington, Hamilton; LEIGH ROAD and ROKEWOOD ... Leigh Road Railway Station ... passing Teesdale and Shelford
- 7 Sep 1868 Cobb and Co.'s Telegraph Line of Royal Mail Coaches, south-west corner of Sturt and Lydiard streets—HAMILTON ROAD Ballarat to Smythesdale, Linton, Skipton, Streatham, Lake Bolake, Wickliff, Mail Tent, Dunkeld, Hamilton
- 7 Sep 1868 Cobb and Co.'s Royal Mail Line—Geelong to Queenscliff

Cobb and Co.— Matthew Veal and Co.
- 7 Sep 1868 Cobb and Co.'s Line of Coaches ... Break O'Day, Linton, Carngham to Ballarat via Smythesdale daily ... Linton, Piggoreet, Staffordshire, Scarsdale, Smythesdale, Break O'Day, Rokewood, Rokewood Junction, Bulldog, Cape Clear, Derwent Jacks

Cobb and Co.— Scott & Nugent
- 1 Feb 1868 Cobb and Co.'s Line of Coaches— Meredith, Steiglitz

1869

Cobb and Co.— Robertson, Wagner and Co.
- 26 Mar 1869 Cobb and Co.'s Telegraph Line of Royal Mail Coaches Johnson's Bridge, Deniliquin, Hay, Booligal
- 28 Sep 1869 Cobb and Co.'s Telegraph Line of Royal Mail Coaches, south-west corner of Sturt and Lydiard streets—DAYLESFORD and MALMSBURY ROAD Ballarat to Creswick, Mount Prospect, Deep Creek (Jim Crow), Daylesford, Coomoora, Dyers, Glenlyon, Red Hill, Germans, Kyneton road, Malmsbury
- 28 Sep 1869 Cobb and Co.'s Telegraph Line of Royal Mail Coaches—CASTLEMAINE ROAD Creswick, Kingston, Smeaton, Moorookyle, Glengower, Newstead, Green Gully, Castlemaine
- 28 Sep 1869 Cobb and Co.'s Telegraph Line of Royal Mail Coaches—ARARAT, PLEASANT CREEK and HORSHAM ROAD Burrumbeet, Raglan (Fiery Creek), Trawalla, Buangor (McDonald's), Ararat, Great Western, Pleasant Creek, Glenorchy, Ashens, Longernong, Horsham

Cobb and Co.—M'Phee and Co.
- 28 Sep 1869 Cobb and Co.'s Telegraph Line of Royal Mail Coaches—MARYBOROUGH and DUNOLLY ROAD Ballarat to Creswick, Clunes, Ascot (Coghill's Creek), Talbot (Back Creek), Amherst (Daisy Hill), Maryborough, Dunolly, Sandy Creek (Tarnagulla), Inglewood, St. Arnaud (New Bendigo)
- 28 Sep 1869 Cobb and Co.'s Telegraph Line of Royal Mail Coaches—AVOCA & ST. ARNAUD'S Miners' Rest, Mount Blowhard, Lake Learmonth, Mount Bolton, Springs, Lexton, Woodstock, Lamplough, Avoca, Moonambel, Frenchman's Landsborough, Redbank, Stuart Mill, St Arnaud, Swam Water, Cop Cop, Richardson Bridge, Mount Jeffcot, Watcham, Morton Plains
- 28 Sep 1869 Cobb and Co. Summer Arrangement—Ballarat, Miner's Rest, Learmonth, Mount Bolton (Talbot Inn), Flour Mill (Mount Bolton), Springs

Cobb and Co.—Anderson and M'Phee
- 28 Sep 1869 Cobb and Co.'s Line of Coaches—Ballarat to Smythesdale, Scarsdale, Piggoreet, Carngham, Lintons, Staffordshire, Derwent Jacks ... Cape Clear ... Bulldog ... Rokewood Junction ... Rokewood ... Break O'Day

Cobb and Co.—Western Stage Company
- 1 Jan 1869 Cobb & Co's. Western Telegraph Line of Royal Mail Coaches—Night Mail ... Geelong and Belfast with Branch Line from Terang, Mortlake, Hamilton, thence to Mount Gambier and Adelaide passing Mount Duneed, Winchelsea, Camperdown, Terang, Yallock, Warrnambool, Belfast, Mortlake, Hexham, Caramut, Birregurra, Colac, Penshurst, Hamilton, Portland, Apsley, Penola, Casterton, Mount Gambier, Adelaide; Cobb & Co.'s Summer Arrangements Geelong and Queenscliffe
- 28 Sep 1869 Cobb and Co.'s Telegraph Line of Royal Mail Coaches—HAMILTON ROAD Ballarat to Smythesdale, Linton, Skipton, Streatham, Lake Bolac, Wickliff, Mail Tent, Dunkeld, Hamilton, Warrenheip, Gordon, Ballan, Mernlong, Bacchus Marsh, Melton, Keilor; HAMILTON ROAD Ballarat to Linton, Skipton, Streatham, Lake Bolake, Wickliff, Mail Tent, Dunkeld, Hamilton, Portland, Adelaide; NEW MELBOURNE ROAD Ballarat to Warrenheip, Gordons, Ballan, Merniong, Bacchus Marsh, Melton, Keilor
- 28 Sep 1869 Cobb and Co.—Mount Blackwood, Ballarat; Ballarat to Adelaide via Penola and Mount Gambier

Cobb and Co.—Matthew Veal and Co.
- 26 Apr 1869 Cobb Co.'s Telegraph Line of Coaches—Break O'Day, Carngham to Ballarat via Smythesdale, Piggoreet, Staffordshire, Scarsdale, Rokewood, Rokewood Junction, Bulldog, Cape Clear, Derwent Jacks

Along the tracks—1860s

See *Appendix 2: Supporting evidence for Cobb and Co. coaching lines, Victoria*

1860 – "LATEST INTELLIGENCE ... At the Trial Sweepstakes to-day, Flying Buck cantered over the course, followed by Flatcatcher. The Turf Club Cup was won by Defence; Buck second, Yankee third. In the Steeplechase, Camel led once round, but fell, and came in a good second; Pop-goes-the-Weazel winning without making a false move; Charlie nowhere ... MINING ACCIDENT ... Hooper, while working in the claim belonging to the New Chum Company, in New Chum Gully, met with an accident which has terminated fatally. We understand that a quantity of stone fell on the head of the unfortunate man ... We hear that the ground in which the deceased was working was in a very rotten condition ... MUNICIPAL POLICE Court ... Thomas Connel, who had, after being duly warned, persisted in riding across the footbridge over the storm water channel ... he was let off at 5s. and the costs ... James M'Namara, charged with calling Ann Smith bad names, was discharged ... WHERE ARE THE POLICE ? ... Saturday night, or rather Sunday morning, was, for some two or three hours, the scene of a continued series of rows, men and women fighting and indulging in the most disgusting language, beside a number of dogs making the night more hideous by their howling and barking ... Some remarks as to the keeping beer shops open, and disorderly conduct therein, we decline to publish. The police will, no doubt, do all that is necessary, without any hint from us. RUNAWAY HORSE.—A horse, attached to a dray, made a bolt on Saturday from the Post office bridge ... endangering the lives and limbs of the lieges ... CRICKET.—The return match between the Sandhurst and Barker's Creek clubs is fixed ... Arrangements have been made with Cobb's to take our team down by the first coach that morning. The following gentlemen comprise the Bendigo eleven Messrs. Shum, Be?ham, Bruce, G. Ratcliffe, Hall, Hunt, Kerr, J. S. Crofts, Rainer, Porter, and Jackson. Mr. Brown, of Lockwood, will be scorer, and Mr. Lillywhite, stand umpire ... BURTON'S CIRCUS, which was pitched in the Reserve, opposite the Shamrock Hotel, was well filled on Saturday night ... The company also includes a witty and very good clown ... SURGICAL OPERATION.—Amputation of the right arm, immediately below the shoulder, has been successfully performed by Dr. Dow on a man named John Quirk, farm servant to Mrs House of Bullock Creek ... at Bendigo Gold District General Hospital, and we understand that the patient is going on excellently well." (Latest Intelligence, 26 Mar 1860, p.2)

"COBB AND CO.'S TELEGRAPH LINE OF MAIL COACHES. Shamrock Hotel and Abbott's Hotels ... For Castlemaine and Melbourne ... For M'Ivor ... For Moama ... For Swan Hill ... N.B.—No notice will be taken of Accounts against the above company, unless sent in for payment weekly on Saturdays, Watson & Hewitt, Proprietors, Heffernan and Crowley, Agents." (Advertising, 3 Aug 1860, p.1)

"BY COBB & CO.'S ROYAL MAIL SIX HORSE COACHES—Geelong ... before proceeding to Melbourne ... Booking Offices, Bath's and the George Hotels, Township ; North Grant, Exchange, London Tavern, Rock of Cashel, Duchess of Kent, Star, United States, and Rising Sun Hotels, Main Road. E. T. Foley Agent" (Advertising, 8 Nov 1860, p.1)

"COBB AND CO.'S TELEGRAPH LINE OF ROYAL MAIL COACHES. Between Lamplough, Back Creek, Maryborough, Dunolly, Sandy Creek, Inglewood, Castlemaine, Clunes, Creswick, Ballarat, Geelong and Melbourne ... For further particulars enquire of Mr. Frank Mansfield, United States and Foos's; Mr. W. B. Oats, Foos's Hotel, Sandy Creek; Mr. Geo. Simpson, Bendigo Hotel, Dunolly; Mr. C. D. Pollock, M'Ivor Hotel, Maryborough; Mr. C. F. Colerick, Commercial Hotel, Back Creek; Mr. C. Mulcahy, Shamrock Hotel, Lamplough." (Advertising, 9 Nov 1860, p.3)

"YANDOIT. The rush to Yandoit is exciting much interest, not only on this gold field, but among the miners of Ballarat ... Fifteen miles from Castlemaine, on the road to Ballarat—a road travelled twice daily by Cobb and Co.'s coaches—is the Yandoit hotel. At the rear of this hotel, running southward for a mile or two, is a rather narrow flat, known as the Forty Foot diggings. On the east this flat is hemmed in by a range, the quartz reefs on which are the immediate cause of the attraction to Yandoit." Reported on the same page "HIGHWAY ROBBERY WITH FIREARMS.—On Tuesday evening last, about three-quarters of an hour before sun down, a dealer named John Hurley, and a lad about fifteen or sixteen years of age, who was travelling with him, were stopped by four armed men about seven miles on the other side of Binalong, and robbed of a considerable sum of money ... Hurley and his companion were both mounted, but the robbers were on foot. It appears that Hurley is a dealer in stock, and resides at Beechworth. Previous to the robbery, he with the lad referred to, had been for some days in the neighborhood of Burrowa, whither they had gone with the view of purchasing about sixty head of cows and calves. Being unable to procure them, Hurley purchased seven pigs from a publican in the township. In paying for them, he exposed in the bar a considerable portion of the money be had about him, and the lad who was with him has subsequently stated that there he saw one of the four men by whom they were afterwards bailed up. They started from Burrowa for Binalong, driving the pigs before them, and when within seven miles of the latter place a man over took them ... with three other men, all of short stature and thick set ; one of them was armed with a double-barrelled fowling piece, and another with a Colt's revolver. The man who carried the gun presented it at Hurley, while the other, who had the revolver, covered the lad with it. Hurley was ordered to give up his money ... They were then tied to a tree and both searched, while one of the men stood over them with the revolver presented and cocked ... The robbers then took possession of the horses, and while the man who had the revolver in his hand was jumping on to one, one of the barrels went off, and the contents, supposed to be slugs, struck the ground close to the foot of one of his companions. The party then made off." (Yandoit, 10 Sep 1860, p.2)

"COBB AND CO.'S WESTERN TELEGRAPH LINES OF ROYAL MAIL COACHES between Geelong and Portland ... Geelong, Warrnambool, & Belfast F. B. Clapp & Co., Proprietors ... Additional Night Mail Coaches. On and after Saturday, December 8th ... Sunday Coach. Cobb and Co.'s Leviathan Coach will leave the Railway Station, Geelong, every Sunday morning, on arrival of 9 a.m. Train from Melbourne ... 11 a.m. Fares 15s." (Advertising, 24 Dec 1860, p.1)

"COBB & CO.'S 4 HORSE COACHES ... Clunes and Back Creek, Inglewood, and all intermediate stages ... Cobb & Co.'s Royal Mail Coaches ... To Geelong ...

Cobb & Co.'s Leviathan 8 horse Coaches ... Geelong (Summer season) ... Cobb & Co.'s 4 horse coaches ... Creswick ... Cobb & Co.'s 4 horse coaches ... Daylesford via Creswick and Deep Creek ... Leviathan Coaches. Cobb & Co.'s Leviathan 8 horse Coaches for Geelong have now commenced for the Summer season. Fare 10s. E. T. Foley, Agent." (Advertising, 13 Dec 1860, p.1)

"SPECIAL NOTICE. In consequence of the Damage Sustained by the Geelong and Melbourne Railway, during the late Severe Storm, preventing (for the present) Traffic by that route, Messrs. Cobb & Co. have made Arrangements to Convey their Passengers, Leaving Ballarat at 5.45 a.m., by Steamer, to Melbourne. The Second Coach will leave at eleven o'clock, a.m., in lien of 7.45 as herefore. Fare, 10s. E. T. Foley, Agent." (Advertising, 13 Dec 1860, p.1)

1861 – "M'IVOR HOTEL—W. C. Wilson, proprietor Family and Commercial Hotel. Booking Office for Cobb & Co.'s line of Coaches, which arrive and start daily for all parts of the Colony." (Advertising, 14 Jan 1861, p.1)

"COBB AND CO.'S AUSTRALIAN EXPRESS PARCELS DELIVERY. PRINCIPAL OFFICES : No. 90 Bourke street east. No. 81 Collins street west. Express Waggons leave the Company's Central Depot, No. 90 Bourke street east, to deliver parcels throughout Melbourne ... Australian Stage Co. Proprietors. C. Russell, Manager; Australian Livery and Letting Stables. No. 90 Bourke Street east ... The Proprietors of the Australian Stage Company having purchased the abovenamed stables, beg to inform the public that they have always on hand vehicles of every description, and a choice selection of horses ... Australian Stage Co. Proprietors. Anthy. Riggs, Superintendent." (Advertising, 23 Mar 1861, p.8)

"COBB & CO.'S TELEGRAPH LINE OF ROYAL MAIL COACHES ... This Line of Coaches run in connection with the Geelong and Melbourne Railway, and passengers for Melbourne via Geelong can be booked through at the Office next to Bath's Hotel at an additional charge of 4s second class, and 7s first class. ... TO MELBOURNE DIRECT—Through in Nine Hours,—leaving at 8 a.m. Fare, 13s 6d. Arriving in Melbourne at 5 p.m. Only a limited number of passengers taken. Australian Stage Company, Proprietors ... Luggage and parcels bearing the Australian Express Company's Stamps delivered anywhere in Melbourne or the suburbs, on arrival of the Trains at the Spencer-street Railway Station. Shilling and Six-penny Express Stamps on sale at this office. Office hours, from 5 a.m. to 9 p.m.; Sundays, from 4 p.m. to 9 p.m. A. C. Brunig, Manager, Ballarat. C. Russell, Manager, Geelong and Melbourne." Advertised on the same page "Winter Goods! Winter Goods! DAVID JONES ... Direct Importation ... Upwards of 175 Cases, trunks and Bales ... French-felt hats ... Tartan all-Wool Scarf Shawls ... Flounced Silk Robes ... Sewed Muslin Goods ... Gent's Drab, Brown, and Black Reversible Coats ... Gent's Coloured Doe Pants ... Scarlet Blankets ... Tapestry Carpets with Hearth-Rugs to Match ... Crinoline Skirt Steel ... Braided Silk and Bead Hair Nets ... Criterion Store, Main Road, Ballarat." (Advertising, 22 May 1861, p.1)

"COBB & CO.'S LEVIATHAN COACHES ... Bathurst to Geelong ... Australian Stage Co." (Advertising, 5 Oct 1861, p.1)

"THE POST-OFFICE REVENUES for the past year (1861) amounted to 127,869/., and the expenditure to 109,479/. In the conveyance of the inland mails the number of miles travelled was 1,511,381. The number of post-offices in Victoria is 365 ; 5,166,149 letters, and 2,818,761 newspapers were posted in the course of the year. 1,762,566 letters, and 2,086,979 newspapers received and despatched by ship during the above time." (A few particulars supplementary to the catalogue of the products of the Colony of Victoria, Australia/compiled by J. G. Knight, p.12)

1862 – "TWENTY-TWO OF GEELONG AND THE WESTERN DISTRICT V. THE ALL ENGLAND ELEVEN. The Eleven arrived by the first train from Melbourne yesterday morning, and were received at the railway-station by the majority of their western antagonists. Cobb and Co.'s leviathan coach, drawn by twelve splendid greys, and driven by a famous whip, conveyed them and their friends to Gosling's British Hotel where they reside during their sojourn. Pending their preparations for taking the field, the Twenty-two held a meeting, and Mr. S. S. Rennie was unanimously elected captain. All these preliminaries being adjusted, the whole of the persons engaged were driven to the new ground, at the east end of the Botanical Gardens where, the wickets were pitched without delay." (Twenty-two of Geelong and the Western District V. the All England Eleven, 27 Jan 1862, p.3)

"COBB & CO.'S AUSTRALIAN EXPRESS PARCELS DELIVERY. Parcels can now be booked at COBB & CO.'s office, M'Ivor Hotel, Maryborough, for delivery at any of the following Suburbs of Melbourne:—East Melbourne, Collingwood, East Collingwood, Fitsroy, Richmond, South Yarra, Prahran, Windsor, St Kilda, Hawthorn, Kew, Toorak, North Melbourne, Carlton, Flemington, and Emerald Hill." (Advertising, 10 Feb 1862, p.1)

"COBB AND CO.'S TELEGRAPH LINE OF MAIL COACHES—In connection with the Melbourne & Mount Alexander Railway. From the Digger's Rest Station to Melbourne ... Three daily lines of coaches to Melbourne ... Coaches for Melbourne, Sandhurst, Ballarat &c ... Coaches for Melbourne, Sandhurst, Maryborough, Ararat, Ballarat, Creswick Creek, Swan Hill, Back Creek, Lamplough, Inglewood, Newbridge, Dunolly, and Sandy Creek ... leave the Booking Offices, Victoria and Castlemaine Hotels ... Robertson, Britton and Co. ... Cobb and Co.'s Royal Mail Coaches leave the Kangaroo Hotel, Maldon ... for Ararat, Carisbrook, Dunolly, Lamplough, Maryborough ... For Newbridge, Sandy Creek, and Inglewood ... Robertson, Britton and Co." While advertised on the same page "PERRY'S PATENT concentrated essence of Copaiba and cubeb, sugar-coated globules. Composed of rare and valuable gums, and also extracts of copaiba and cubebs, for the cure of obstinate gleet, gonorrhoea, and all urethral affections ... In all cases of Gonorrhoea, Gleet, Strictures &c., a single trial will prove the efficacy of this invaluable remedy." (Advertising, 1 Aug 1862, p.4)

1863 – "NEWS AND NOTES. On Wednesday evening a violent assault was committed at the Springs, near Mount Bolton, by an ostler, in the service of the landlord of the Springs Hotel, on Henry Pape, the driver of Cobb and Co.'s Ballarat and Springs coach. The assault, which appears to have been quite unprovoked, was committed with a pitchfork with which the ostler charged Pape who, while warding off the attack, received a severe wound from one of the prongs of the fork on his right hand, the little finger of which was almost severed from the hand. Dr Leman, of Learmonth, sewed up the wound and rendered all needful assistance.

A warrant was speedily obtained from Learmonth, and was very promptly executed during the night by senior Constable Nelson, the prisoner Martin Brontie being lodged in the Learmonth watch-house till Monday, when he will be bought before the Bench." (News and Notes, 7 Mar 1863, p.2)

PLEASANT CREEK "On and after Tuesday, 31st March, Cobb and Co. will despatch a coach … arriving in Pleasant Creek same day. The mail coach will leave heretofore at 12.30 a.m. daily … E. J Brayton, Agent … Cobb and Co.—On and after this date, Cobb and Co. will despatch a coach to Clunes and Talbot (Back Creek) via Creswick … arrive in Ballarat at 11 a.m., giving them two hours to transact business and return same day. E. J Brayton, Agent … Reduction of Fares Cobb and Co.—A coach will leave Cobb and Co.'s Office daily … for Blowhard, Learmonth, and Springs … E. J Brayton, Agent." While "PREPARED LIQUID GLUE, useful in every house; mends China, glass, wood, books, boots and shoes, &c. H. Fortune, Victoria street." (Advertising, 11 Apr 1863, p.1)

1864 – "V.R. COBB AND CO.'S TELEGRAPH LINE OF ROYAL MAIL COACHES, south-west corner of Sturt and Lydiard streets—Burrumbeet, Raglan (Fiery Creek), Buangor (M'Donald's), Ararat, Great Western, Pleasant Creek … J. C. Horr … THE LEVIATHAN is the largest Tailoring, Clothing, Outfitting, and Boot and Shoe Establishment in Melbourne … Squatters and settlers supplied at wholesale prices … Established 14 years." (Advertising, 23 Jul 1864, p.1)

"COBB & CO'S. ROYAL MAIL LINE OF COACHES …. Geelong to Belfast … Leigh Road to Shelford, Rokewood, Pitfield, Lintons … Offices and agents: Cobb's & Co.'s office, Melbourne and Geelong, and at the Leigh Road Station. Cobb & Co's. Livery and Letting Stables. Back of Union Hotel, Malop-street, Geelong and opposite Messrs Synnot and Guthrie, Wool Stores. Sadle horses, buggies, carryalls carriages, and every description of vehicle to be had at a moment's notice. Horses taken in to bait or stand at livery by the day, week, or month, on reasonable terms. Also at Queenscliff, for which place a coach leaves daily … Thomas Stoneman, Proprietor." (Advertising, 20 Jul 1864, p.1)

1865 – "EFFECTS OF THE DROUGHT AT SANDHURST.—The Committee of the Sandhurst Mining Board appointed to compile statistics relative to the necessity of water supply for this gold-field, reported that there were no fewer than 350 puddling machines stopped up to the present time through the want of water, which averaged at four men to the mill, gave a total of 1400 men thus thrown out of employment. There were also twenty-eight crushing machines at a standstill, each with an average of ten men, thus giving 280, which added to the other make a total of 1860 men idle. So many crushing machines being stopped had been the means of throwing other men out of employment, such as carters, woodcutters, and claimholders, who have been compelled to stop work through not being able to have their quartz crushed. Therefore the committee were of opinion that the number of men unemployed at the present time could not be short of 3000, and these were the producers of the staple of the district.—*Advertiser*." Meanwhile "WANTED a boy as generally useful; Victoria Hotel, Armstrong street. Wanted hair-pickers. Daws, upholsterer, Lydiard street, near Railway Station … Wanted an experienced assistant, one accustomed to the slops. Apply, with references, to Twentyman and Stamper. Wanted smart lad to take charge of buggy and horse; must be accustomed to horses. Apply to Mr Lamb, first brick house in Errard street … Wanted Muscular Christians to take their daily exercise at the John O'Groat Skittle Hall, Main road … TO BUTCHERS.—Wanted, a steady Man, who understands the business. Apply William Wright, Durham Lead … NOTICE.—Strayed into the Junction Hotel tables, Smythesdale road, Chesnut Horse, branded Ys near shoulder, off fore and hind feet white, blazed. The owner can have the same by paying expenses." (Advertising, 29 Mar 1865, p.3)

"THE GROOM'S FORTUNE … A person named Donald Cameron, lately employed as a groom at Cobb and Co.'s stables, received intimation on Friday, that owing to the death of a relation of his wife he was in receipt of about £7,000. Cameron is well known as a careful, steady man, and his improved position in life is considered to be well." (St. Arnaud Police Court, 16 Jun 1865, p.3)

1866 – "KOORINGA AND REDRUTH … The inhabitants here hope that now Messrs. Cobb and Co. have the superintendence of the Northern portion of the passenger traffic of the colony, they will see the propriety of at once placing on the road dust-proof and water-proof vehicles." (Kooringa and Redruth, 8 Dec 1866, p.7)

1868 – "COBB AND CO.'S LINE OF COACHES between Meredith and Steiglitz … Scott & Nugent, Proprietors … THE GEELONG SEA BATHING COMPANY BATHS … favourite and fashionable … First-class … Second-class … First-class ticket, per dog … N. B.—Any male of families unable to pay for bathing, may on application … obtain free tickets of admission for the third-class baths." (Advertising, 1 Feb 1868, p.1)

"COBB AND CO.'S TELEGRAPH LINE OF ROYAL MAIL COACHES leave the booking-office, Club Hotel, Sale … To Melbourne (Overland) … Sale, Rosedale, Traralgon, Morewell, Moe, Shady Creek, Bunyip, Pakenham, Berwick, Dandenong, Springvale, Oakleigh, and Melbourne … Sale to Bairnsdale … Rosedale to Toongabbi, Mountain Queen Hotel, Happy-go-Lucky, and Royal Exchange Hotel, Stringer's Creek … Cansick's Hotel, Rosedale … Robertson, Wagner & Co., Proprietors. J. Robertson, Manager." Advertised on the same page "GIPPSLAND STEAM NAVIGATION COMPANY (LIMITED.) Steam to Melbourne… Passengers booked through to Melbourne at the Company's Office, Foster-street, Sale." (Advertising, 15 Sep 1868, p.1)

1869 – "COBB & CO.'S LIVERY, LETTING AND BAIT STABLES … Great Malop-street, Geelong … Western Stage Company … TOBACCO. TOBACCO ON SALE, by the Undersigned. Aromatic Tobacco : Gold Bar, Atlantic Cable, Pocket Pieces, May, Apple. &c. Twist Tobaccoes : Barrett's Anchor Brand, Eagle, Emu, Raven, Queen of the South. Cavendish : Two Seas, Star Light, Venus, Lennox, Bocknor's, and Buchanan's. Our Own Mixture : Fresh Cut Daily. Warranted Genuine. CIGARS : The Finest Havannah, Manila, and Swiss. SNUFFS : English and Colonial. MATCHES : All kinds of Bell and Black and Palmer's make, Taylor's, Page's, etc. etc. A select assortment of Fancy Goods, cheap. CRICKETING GOODS AND FISHING TACKLE. The best Makers E. Sander & Co., Wholesale and Retail Tobacconists, 52 Moorabool-street." (Advertising, 20 Jan 1869, p.1)

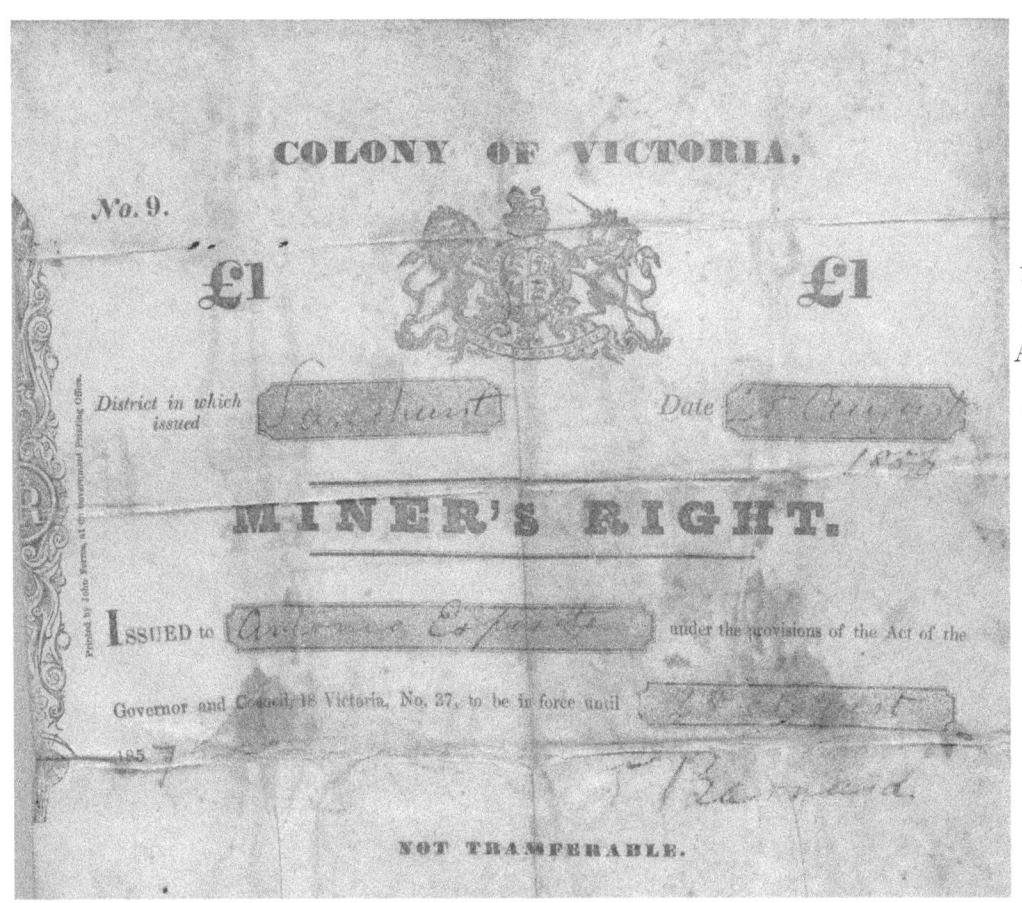

1856 Colony of Victoria, Miner's Rights, Issued to Antonio Esposito, 28 August 1856 and valid for one year in the district of Sandhurst - Courtesy State Library Victoria

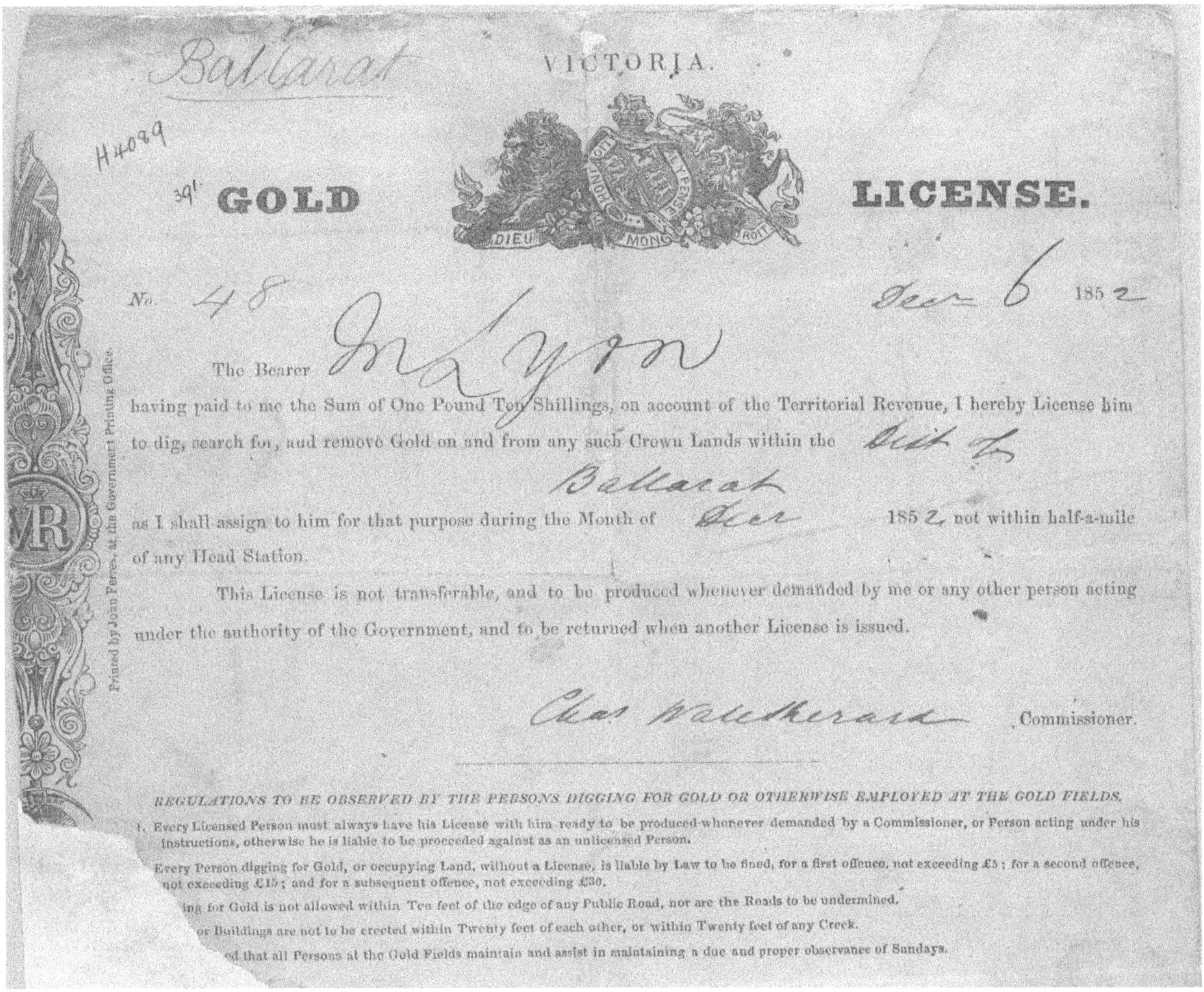

1852 Victoria Gold License - Courtesy State Library Victoria

1858 Old Post Office Hill. Forest Creek (Richard Daintree, 1832-1878, photographer) - Courtesy State Library Victoria

1860 [?] View of horse and puddling machine (John H. Jones, 1817?-1872, photographer) - Courtesy State Library Victoria

September 1889 Republic Gold Mine, Warburton (Reminiscence of a visit to Victoria, Australia, April 1889 Part II, John Steel Jnr.) - Courtesy State Library Victoria

Gold escort leaving Walhalla (Fredrick Cornell) - Courtesy Federation University

ca. 1859-1863 A tunnel at Jim Crow diggings, Victoria (Richard Daintree, 1832-1878, photographer)
- Courtesy State Library Victoria

ca. 1869-1869 Independent claim, Buninyong, Mullock heap and logs in foreground - Courtesy State Library Victoria

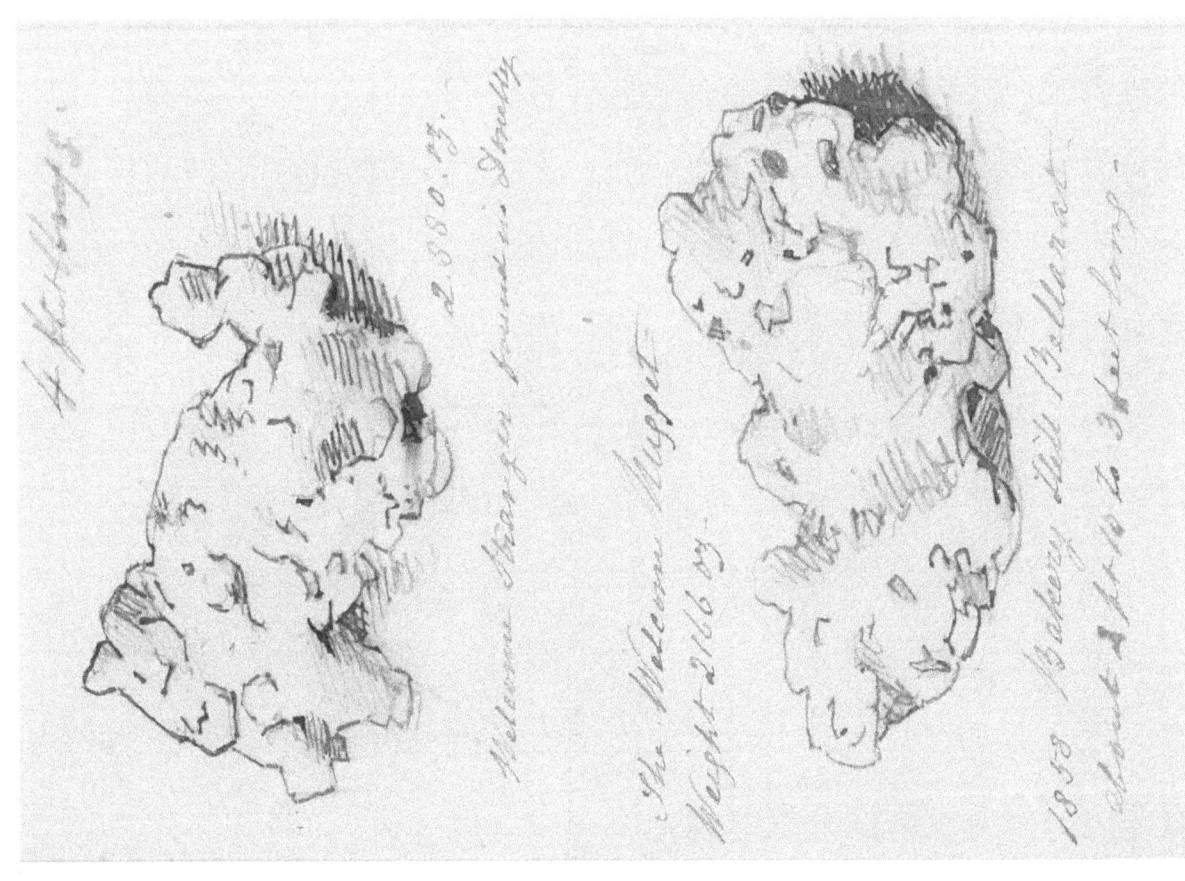

A collection of drawings in watercolour, ink and pencil : illustrative of the life, character & scenery of Melbourne 1850-1862. Third series / drawn by William Strutt

GOLD YIELD OF CLUNES—1857 to 1901.
* * * * *

NAME OF COMPANY, ETC.	TOTAL GOLD WON.	
	oz. of gold.	Value in £.
The Clunes Quartz Company	514,886	2,123,905
New North Clunes Quartz Company	253,373	1,045,164
South Clunes Quartz Company	124,521	513,649
South Clunes United Quartz Company	68,083	280,842
New Lothair Quartz Company	29,665	122,368
Yankee Quartz Company (approximate)	45,000	185,625
Victoria Quartz Company (approximate)	70,000	288,750
Criterion Quartz Company	47,560	190,240
Clunes United Quartz Company	16,270	67,114
Bute and Downes Alluvial Company	14,378	59,462
Clunes Central Quartz Company (approximate)	5,146	21,227
Alluvial, &c. (approximate)	50,000	200,000
Miscellaneous Parties (approximate)	100,000	400,000
Grand total	1,338,882	5,498,346

1902 The Clunes mines, past history, future prospects : being information collected by the Clunes Borough Council, Victoria, p.5 (Edited by Arthur James Giddings, 1868?-1943) - Courtesy National Library Australia

Chapter Six

Coaching Victoria

1870s & 1880s

Long Jim of Cobb & Co.

Then its lights, ho ! of the township.
How the whip cracks at its glancing
Hound the heads of all five horses midst the rattle, for they must
Know the stage is over, and they reef almost to prancing
As they're drawn up to the office in a steam of sweat and dust.

All the people know the driver And he's very much alive. Sir,
To the smiles of township beauties, for with them he's quite the beau,
For his coming some hearts gladden,
Ah '. and many too twill sadden,
For he carries good and bad news, does Long Jim of Cobb & Co.

(The Poet's Corner, 20 Nov 1900, p.10)

Cobb's coach, below Fernshaw, Black's Spur, Victoria, Australia, (J.W. Lindt: Master Photographer)
- Courtesy National Gallery of Australia

Examples of Cobb and Co. Coaching Lines, Victoria—1870s & 1880s

1870

Cobb and Co.—Proprietors not listed
- 2 Jul 1870 Cobb and Co.'s Line of Coaches—Meredith and Steiglitz ... in time for the mid-day trains to Melbourne, Geelong, and Ballarat

Cobb and Co.—Robertson, Wagner and Co.
- 14 Apr 1870 Cobb and Co.'s Telegraph Line of Royal Mail Coaches—DAYLESFORD and MALMSBURY ROAD Ballarat to Creswick, Mount Prospect, Deep Creek (Jim Crow), Daylesford, Coomoora, Dyers, Glenlyon, Red Hill, Germans, Kyneton road, Malmsbury; Cobb and Co.'s Telegraph Line of Royal Mail Coaches—CASTLEMAINE ROAD Creswick, Kingston, Smeaton, Moorookyle, Glengower, Newstead, Green Gully, Castlemaine; PLEASANT CREEK AND HORSHAM ROAD Burrumbeet, Raglan (Fiery Creek), Trawalla, Buangor (McDonald's), Ararat, Great Western, Pleasant Creek, Glenorchy, Ashens, Longernong, Horsham
- 27 May 1870 Cobb and Co.'s Telegraph Line of Royal Mail Coaches—ARARAT, PLEASANT CREEK AND HORSHAM ROAD Burrumbeet, Raglan (Fiery Creek), Buangor (McDonald's), Ararat, Great Western, Pleasant Creek, Glenorchy, Ashens, Longernong, Horsham

Cobb and Co.—M'Phee and Co./John M'Phee
- 14 Apr 1870 Cobb and Co.'s Telegraph Line of Royal Mail Coaches—MARYBOROUGH and DUNOLLY ROAD Ballarat to Creswick, Clunes, Ascot (Coghill's Creek), Talbot (Back Creek), Amherst (Daisy Hill), Maryborough, Dunolly, Sandy Creek (Tarnagulla), Inglewood, St. Arnaud (New Bendigo); AVOCA & ST. ARNAUD'S Miners' Rest, Mount Blowhard, Lake Learmonth, Mount Bolton, Springs, Lexton, Woodstock, Lamplough, Avoca, Moonambel, Frenchman's Landsborough, Redbank, Stuart Mill, St Arnaud, Swam Water, Cop Cop, Richardson Bridge, Mount Jeffcot, Watcham, Morton Plains

Cobb and Co.—Anderson and M'Phee
- 14 Apr 1870 Cobb and Co.'s Line of Coaches—Ballarat to Smythesdale, Scarsdale, Piggoreet, Carngham, Lintons, Staffordshire; Derwent Jacks, Cape Clear, Bulldog, Rokewood Junction, Rokewood

Cobb and Co.—Western Stage Company
- 14 Apr 1870 Cobb and Co.'s Telegraph Line of Royal Mail Coaches—HAMILTON ROAD Ballarat to Linton, Skipton, Streatham, Lake Bolac, Wickliff, Mail Tent, Dunkeld, Hamilton, Portland, Adelaide; MELBOURNE ROAD Ballarat to Warrenheip, Gordons, Ballan, Merniong, Bacchus Marsh, Melton, Keilor; Cobb and Co.—Ballarat to Gordon, Egerton, Ballan; Cobb Co.'s Telegraph Line of Coaches—Geelong to Queenscliff
- 27 May 1870 Cobb Co.'s Telegraph Line of Coaches—Geelong to Queenscliff
- 2 Jul 1870 Cobb & Co's. Western Telegraph Line of Royal Mail Coaches—Night Mail ... Geelong to Belfast and Mortlake with Branch Line from Mortlake to Caramut, Penshurst and Hamilton, thence to Mount Gambier and Adelaide passing Mount Duneed, Winchelsea, Camperdown, Terang, Yallock, Warrnambool, Belfast, Mortlake, Hexham, Caramut, Birregurra, Colac, Penshurst, Hamilton, Portland, Apsley, Penola, Casterton, Mount Gambier, Adelaide, Coleraine, Balmoral, Cavendish, Branxholme, Edenhope, Heywood, Portland, Narracoote, Strathalbyn, Panmure; Cobb & Co.'s Telegraph Line of Coaches—Ballarat to Hamilton thence to Penola and Adelaide passing through Smythesdale, Lintons, Skipton, Streatham, Lake Bolac, Glen Thompson, Wickliffe

Cobb and Co.—Matthew Veal and Co.
- 27 May 1870 Cobb Co.'s Telegraph Line of Coaches—Rokewood, Carngham to Ballarat via Smythesdale, Staffordshire Reef, Bulldog, Cape Clear, Derwent Jacks, Scarsdale

1871

Cobb and Co.—Proprietors not listed
- 22 May 1871 Cobb and Co.'s Line of Coaches—Meredith and Steiglitz in time for the mid-day trains to Melbourne, Geelong, and Ballarat, returning from the Royal Hotel, Meredith; Geelong and Portarlington Line passing through Curlewis, Drysdale, and Bellarine
- 7 Sep 1871 Cobb & Co's. Royal Mail Telegraph Line of Coaches—Geelong and Queenscliffe ... Night Mail, Geelong to Warrnambool and Belfast with Branch Line from Mortlake, Caramut, Penshurst and Hamilton, thence to Mount Gambier and Adelaide via Penola passing Mount Duneed, Winchelsea, Camperdown, Terang, Yallock, Warrnambool, Belfast, Mortlake, Hexham, Caramut, Birregurra, Colac, Penshurst, Hamilton, Portland, Apsley, Penola, Casterton, Mount Gambier, Adelaide, Coleraine, Balmoral, Cavendish, Branxholme, Edenhope, Heywood, Portland, Narracoorte, Strathalbyn, Panmure; Day Coach to Colac; Geelong and Mortlake via Darlington passing through Murgheboluc, Inverleigh, Warrambine, Cressy, Lismore, Tooliorook; LEIGH ROAD and ROKEWOOD ... Leigh Road Railway Station

Cobb and Co. (Melbourne)—Robertson, Wagner and Co.
- 1 Mar 1871 Cobb and Co.'s Telegraph Line of Royal Mail Coaches—DAYLESFORD and MALMSBURY ROAD Ballarat to Creswick, Mount Prospect, Deep Creek (Jim Crow), Daylesford, Coomoora, Dyers, Glenlyon, Red Hill, Germans, Kyneton road, Malmsbury; CASTLEMAINE ROAD Creswick, Kingston, Smeaton, Moorookyle, Glengower, Newstead, Green Gully, Castlemaine; ARARAT, PLEASANT CREEK and HORSHAM ROAD Burrumbeet, Raglan (Fiery Creek), Buangor (McDonald's), Ararat, Great Western, Pleasant Creek
- 16 Sep 1871 Cobb and Co.—Ballarat to Daylesford ... Deep Creek, Mount Prospect; DAYLESFORD and MALMSBURY ROAD; CASTLEMAINE ROAD
- 4 Nov 1871 Cobb and Co.'s Telegraph Line of Royal Mail Coaches—ARARAT, PLEASANT CREEK and HORSHAM Burrumbeet, Raglan (Fiery Creek), Buangor (McDonald's), Ararat, Great Western, Pleasant Creek connecting with Little Wimmers, Boga Lakes, Gelorchy, Ashens, Longernong to Horsham

Cobb and Co.—M'Phee and Co.

- 1 Mar 1871 Cobb and Co.'s Telegraph Line of Royal Mail Coaches—MARYBOROUGH and DUNOLLY ROAD Ballarat to Creswick, Clunes, Ascot (Coghill's Creek), Talbot (Back Creek), Amherst (Daisy Hill), Maryborough, Dunolly, Sandy Creek (Tarnagulla), Inglewood, St. Arnaud (New Bendigo); AVOCA & ST. ARNAUD'S daily Miners' Rest, Mount Blowhard, Lake Learmonth, Mount Bolton, Springs, Lexton, Woodstock, Lamplough, Avoca, Moonambel, Frenchmans, Landsborough, Redbank, Stuart Mill, St Arnaud, Swam Water, Cop Cop, Richardson Bridge, Mount Jeffcot, Watcham, Morton Plains
- 16 Sep 1871 Cobb and Co.—MARYBOROUGH and DUNOLLY ROAD; AVOCA and ST. ARNAUD'S ROAD Ballarat to Clunes; Summer Arrangement ... Ballarat and Springs Road

Cobb and Co.—Anderson and M'Phee
- 1 Mar 1871 Cobb and Co.'s Telegraph Line of Royal Mail Coaches—HAMILTON ROAD Ballarat to Linton, Skipton, Streatham, Lake Bolake, Wickliff, Mail Tent, Dunkeld, Hamilton, Portland, Adelaide; MELBOURNE ROAD Ballarat to Warrenheip, Gordons, Ballan, Merniong, Bacchus Marsh, Melton, Keilor
- 16 Sep 1871 Cobb and Co.'s Telegraphic Line of Coaches—Ballarat and Smythesdale; Mount Blackwood, Ballarat; HAMILTON ROAD, MELBOURNE ROAD; Ballarat to Melbourne via Ballan, Bacchus Marsh
- 4 Nov 1871 Cobb and Co.'s Telegraphic Line of Coaches—Ballarat and Smythesdale; Scarsdale, Piggoreet, Carngham, Chepstowe, Lintons, Staffordshire, Derwent Jacks, Cape Clear, Bulldog, Rokewood Junction, Rokewood

Cobb and Co.—Western Stage Company
- 7 Sep 1871 Cobb and Co.'s Telegraph Line of Coaches—Ballarat to Hamilton thence to Penola and Adelaide passing through Smythesdale, Lintons, Skipton, Streatham, Lake Bolac, Glen Thompson, Wickliffe, Dunkeld
- 16 Sep 1871 Cobb and Co. Special Coach to Skipton; Cobb Co.'s Royal Mail Line—Geelong to Queenscliff

Cobb and Co.—Matthew Veal and Co.
- 4 Nov 1871 Cobb and Co.'s Telegraphic Line of Coaches—Rokewood, Carngham to Ballarat via Smythesdale daily, Staffordshire Reef, Smythesdale, Rokewood, Rokewood Junction, Bulldog, Cape Clear, Derwent Jacks, Scarsdale

1872

Cobb and Co.—Proprietors not listed
- 12 Mar 1872 Cobb and Co.'s Line of Coaches—Meredith and Steiglitz; Geelong and Portarlington Line, passing through Curlewis, Drysdale and Bellarine
- 22 Jun 1872 Telegraph Line of Coaches. Cobb & Co.—From Wagga to Tarcutta, Albury, Sydney and Melbourne
- 28 Sep 1872 Cobb and Co.—Broadford and Alexandra

Cobb and Co. (Melbourne)—Robertson, Wagner and Co.
- 4 Jan 1872 Cobb and Co.—Ballarat to Daylesford
- 21 Sep 1872 Cobb and Co.'s Telegraph Line of Royal Mail Coaches—Daylesford and Malmsbury Road; Ararat, Pleasant Creek and Horsham Road; Castlemaine Road

Cobb and Co.—M'Phee and Co.
- 21 Sep 1872 Cobb and Co.'s Telegraph Line of Royal Mail Coaches—MARYBOROUGH AND DUNOLLY ROAD; AVOCA & ST. ARNAUD'S

Cobb and Co.—Anderson and M'Phee
- 4 Jan 1872 Cobb and Co.'s Telegraphic Line of Coaches—Ballarat and Smythesdale; Ballarat to Melbourne
- 21 Sep 1872 Cobb and Co.'s Telegraph Line of Royal Mail Coaches—HAMILTON ROAD AND MELBOURNE ROAD

Cobb and Co.—Western Stage Company
- 12 Mar 1872 Cobb and Co.—Geelong, Queenscliffe; Night Mail ... Geelong, Warrnambool, Belfast with Branch Line from Mortlake, Caramut, Penshurst, Hamilton thence to Mount Gambier and Adelaide via Penola; Hamilton Branch through Penshurst, Caramut, Hexham, Mortlake connect with Belfast Line ... Geelong following mornings; Mount Duneed, Winchelsea, Camperdown, Terang, Yallock, Warrnambool, Belfast, Mortlake, Hexham, Caramut, Birregurra, Colac, Penshurst, Hamilton, Portland, Apsley, Penola, Casterton, Mount Gambier, Adelaide, Coleraine, Balmoral, Cavendish, Branxholme, Edenhope, Heywood, Portland, Narracoorte, Strathalbyn, Panmure; Day Coach To Colac And Camperdown; To and from Geelong and Lady of the Lake, Winchelsea, Birregurra, Colac, Larpent, Stoneyford, Camperdown; Geelong and Mortlake via Darlington passing through Murgheboluc, Inverleigh, Warrambine, Cressy, Lismore, Tooliorook; Leigh Road and Rokewood; Cobb and Co.'s Telegraph Line of Coaches Ballarat to Hamilton thence To Penola and Adelaide passing through Smythesdale, Lintons, Skipton, Streatham, Lake Bolac, Glen Thompson, Wickliffe, Dunkeld
- 13 Mar 1872 Cobb & Co's. Western Telegraph Line of Royal Mail Coaches—Conveyance of Mails, Passengers, and Parcels, For Ballarat, via Dunkeld, Glen Thompson, Wickliffe, Lake Bolac, Streatham, Skipton, Lintons, and Smythesdale; For Penola, via Wannon, Coleraine, Casterton, and Fletcher's Station; For Casterton, via Wannon and Coleraine; For Apsley, via Cavendish, Balmoral, and Harrow; For Warrnambool and Belfast, via Caramut and Koroit; For Portland, via Branxholme and Heywood; For Ararat, via Wickliffe and Kiora; For Mortlake, via Penshurst, Caramut, and Hexham

Cobb and Co.—Matthew Veal and Co.
- 4 Jan 1872 Cobb and Co.'s Telegraphic Line of Coaches—Rokewood, Carngham to Ballarat via Smythesdale

Cobb and Co.—J. Cawker
- 1 Jan 1872 Cobb & Co.'s line of coaches—[Portland] leave Mac's Hotel for Casterton

1873

Cobb and Co.—Proprietors not listed
- 3 Jan 1873 Cobb and Co.'s Line of Coaches between Meredith and Steiglitz; Geelong and Portarlington line, passing through Curlewis, Drysdale and Bellarine
- 31 May 1873 Telegraph Line of Coaches. Cobb & Co.—From Wagga to Tarcutta, Adelong, Albury, Sydney and

Melbourne
- 18 Jan 1873 Cobb and Co.—Alexandra and Tallarook

Cobb and Co. (Melbourne)—Robertson, Wagner and Co.
- 14 Jun 1873 Cobb and Co.'s Telegraph Line of Royal Mail Coaches—DAYLESFORD AND MALMSBURY ROAD; CASTLEMAINE ROAD; Ararat, Pleasant Creek and HORSHAM ROAD
- 14 Jun 1873 Cobb and Co.—Ballarat to Beaufort

Cobb and Co.—M'Phee and Co.
- 14 Jun 1873 Cobb and Co.'s Telegraph Line of Royal Mail Coaches—Maryborough and DUNOLLY ROAD; AVOCA AND ST ARNAUD'S ROAD ; Cobb and Co.—Ballarat to Clunes; Summer Arrangement ... Ballarat and Springs Road ... Ballarat to Miner's Rest, Learmonth, Mount Bolton (Talbot Inn), Flour Mill (Mount Bolton), Springs

Cobb and Co.—Anderson and M'Phee
- 14 Jun 1873 Cobb and Co.'s Telegraph Line of Royal Mail Coaches—HAMILTON AND MELBOURNE ROAD; Cobb and Co.—Ballarat to Melbourne; Mount Blackwood to Ballarat; Cobb and Co.'s Telegraph Line of Coaches—Ballarat and Smythesdale

Cobb and Co.—Western Stage Company
- 3 Jan 1873 Cobb and Co.'s Telegraph Line of Coaches—Ballarat to Hamilton thence to Penola and Adelaide, passing through Smythdale, Linton, Skipton, Streatham, Lake Bolake, ? Thompson, Wickliff, Dunkeld
- 18 Mar 1873 Cobb and Co.—Geelong and Queenscliffe connected with Sorrento, by steamer Pioneer; Night Mail ... Geelong to Warrnambool, Belfast, Mortlake with Branch Line to Hexham, Caramut, Penshurst, Hamilton thence to Mount Gambier and Adelaide via Penola; Hamilton Branch through Penshurst, Caramut, Hexham, Mortlake connect with Belfast Line at Terang ... Geelong following mornings; Day Coach to Colac, Camperdown, Geelong , Mortlake via Darlington passing through Murgheboluc, Inverleigh, Warrambine, Cressy, Darlington, Lismore, Tooliorook; LEIGH ROAD and Rokewood ... Leigh Road Railway Station; Ballarat to Hamilton thence to Penola and Adelaide
- 22 Mar 1873 Cobb & Co's. Western Telegraph Line of Royal Mail Coaches—Hamilton ... For Ballarat; For Penola; For Geelong, via Hochkirch, Penshurst, Caramut, Mortlake, Terang, Camperdown, Stonyford, Colac, Birregurra, and Winchelsea; For Casterton; For Apsley; For Portland; For Ararat

Cobb and Co.— Matthew Veal and Co.
- 30 Jun 1873 Cobb and Co.'s Telegraphic Line of Coaches—Rokewood, Carngham to Ballarat via Smythesdale

Cobb and Co.—J. Cawker
- 27 Mar 1873 Cobb & Co.'s Line of Coaches—[Portland] leave Mac's Hotel for Casterton

1874

Cobb and Co.—Proprietors not listed
- Cobb and Co.'s Line of Coaches—Meredith and Steiglitz ... starting from Scott's ... returning from the Royal Hotel, Meredith
- Cobb and Co.'s—Geelong and Portarlington Line, Passing through Curlewis, Drysdale and Bellarine

Cobb and Co. (Melbourne)—Robertson, Wagner and Co.
- 16 Jan 1874 Cobb and Co.'s Telegraph Line of Royal Mail Coaches—Daylesford and MALMSBURY ROAD; CASTLEMAINE ROAD; Ararat, Pleasant Creek and HORSHAM ROAD; Cobb and Co.—Ballarat to Beaufort
- 3 Oct 1874 Cobb and Co.'s Telegraph Line of Royal Mail Coaches—Leave Shamrock Hotel ... Sandhurst to Haywood, Tarnagulla, Swan Hill, Heathcote, Inglewood

Cobb and Co.—M'Phee and Co.
- 16 Jan 1874 Cobb and Co.'s Telegraph Line of Royal Mail Coaches—Maryborough and DUNOLLY ROAD; AVOCA AND ST ARNAND'S ROAD
- 16 Jan 1874 Cobb and Co.—Ballarat to SPRING ROAD
- 7 Mar 1874 Cobb and Co—Ballarat to Clunes

Cobb and Co.—Anderson and M'Phee
- 16 Jan 1874 Cobb and Co.'s Telegraph Line of Royal Mail Coaches—HAMILTON ROAD; MELBOURNE ROAD; Cobb and Co.—Ballarat to Melbourne
- 7 Mar 1874 Cobb and Co.'s Telegraphic Line of Coaches—Ballarat and Smythesdale; Cobb and Co.—Ballarat to Mount Blackwood; Ballarat to Gordon ... Ballan

Cobb and Co.—Western Stage Company
- 3 Jan 1874 Cobb & Co.'s Western Telegraph Line of Royal Mail Coaches—[Hamilton] For Ballarat via Dunkeld, Glen Thomson, Wickliffe, Late Bolac, Streatham, Skipton, Lintons and Smythesdale; For Penola, via Wannon, Coleraine, Casterton, and Fletcher's station; For Geelong, via Hochkirch, Penshurst, Caramut, Mortlake, Terang. Camperdown, Stonyford, Colac, Birregurra and Winchelsea; For Casterton, via Wannon and Coleraine; For Apsley, via Cavendish, Balmoral, and Harrow; For Portland via Branxholme and Heywood; For Ararat, via Wickliffe and Kiora; Hamilton to Ballarat; Hamilton to Warrnambool
- 7 Jan 1874 Cobb and Co.—Geelong and Queenscliffe; Night Mail ... Geelong to Warrnambool, Belfast, Mortlake with Branch Line to Hexham, Caramut, Penshurst and Hamilton thence to Mount Gambier and Adelaide via Penola; HAMILTON BRANCH through Penshurst, Caramut, Hexham, Mortlake connecting with Belfast Line at Terang ... Geelong following mornings; Day coach to Colac and Camperdown; Geelong and Mortlake via Darlington; LEIGH ROAD and Rokewood ... Leigh Road Railway Station; Cobb and Co.'s Telegraph Line of Coaches—Ballarat to Hamilton thence to Penola and Adelaide
- 22 Jun 1874 Cobb and Co.'s Royal Mail Line—Geelong to Queenscliff

Cobb and Co.— Matthew Veal and Co.
- 1 Jan 1874 Cobb and Co.'s Telegraphic Line of Coaches—Rokewood, Carngham to Ballarat via Smythesdale

1875

Cobb and Co.—Proprietors not listed
- 10 Aug 1875 Cobb and Co.'s—Geelong and Portarlington line passing through Curlewis, Drysdale, Bellarine
- 10 Aug 1875 Cobb and Co.'s Line of Coaches—

Meredith, Steiglitz

Cobb and Co. (Melbourne)—Robertson, Wagner and Co.
- 4 Feb 1875 Cobb and Co.'s Telegraph Line of Royal Mail Coaches—DAYLESFORD and MALMSBURY ROAD; CASTLEMAINE ROAD; Ararat, Stawell, And Horsham

Cobb and Co.—M'Phee and Co.
- 4 Feb 1875 Cobb and Co.'s Telegraph Line of Royal Mail Coaches—MARYBOROUGH and DUNOLLY ROAD; BALLARAT AND ST ARNAUD ROAD; AVOCA AND ST ARNAUD'S ROAD; Cobb and Co.— Night Mail ... Talbot and Maryborough and Dunolly
- 11 Mar 1875 Cobb and Co.—BALLARAT AND SPRINGS ROAD

Cobb and Co.—Anderson and M'Phee
- 30 Jan 1875 Cobb and Co.—Ballarat to Gordon; Ballan; Cobb and Co.'s Telegraph Line of Royal Mail Coaches—HAMILTON ROAD and MELBOURNE ROAD
- 4 Feb 1875 Cobb and Co.'s Telegraph Line of Coaches—To and from Ballarat to Smythesdale; Scarsdale, Piggoreet, Carngham, Chepstowe, Linton, Staffordshire; Derwent Jacks, Cape Clear, Bulldog, Rokewood Junction, Rokewood

Cobb and Co.—Western Stage Company
- 30 Jan 1875 Cobb Co.'s Royal Mail Line—Geelong to Queenscliff
- 10 Aug 1875 Cobb & Co.—Geelong and Queenscliffe; Geelong to Warrnambool, Belfast, and Mortlake via Winchelsea, Birregurra, Colac, Camperdown, and Terang; Sunday Mortlake, Warrnambool, and Belfast with branch line to Hexham, Caramut, Penshurst, Hamilton thence to Mount Gambier and Adelaide via Penola, and all intermediate post towns; Day coach ... Geelong to Winchelsea, Birregurra, Colac, Camperdown; HAMILTON BRANCH. Hamilton through Penshurst, Caramut, Hexham, Mortlake connect with Belfast line at Terang, Geelong ... Mount Duneed, Winchelsea, Camperdown, Terang, Yallock, Warrnambool, Belfast, Mortlake, Hexham, Caramut, Birregurra, Colac, Penshurst, Hamilton, Portland, Apsley, Penola, Casterton; Mount Gambler, Adelaide, Coleraine, Balmoral, Cavendish, Branxholme, Edenhope, Heywood, Portland, Narracoorte, Strathalbyn, Panmure; Geelong to Warrnambool via Cressy, Darlington, and Mortlake passing through Murgheboluc, Darlington, Inverleigh, Mortake, Hesse, Ellerslie, Cressy, Ballangeich, Lismore, Purnim, Derinallum, Woodford; LEIGH ROAD TO ROKEWOOD Leigh Road Railway Station, Rokewood
- 10 Aug 1875 Cobb & Co.'s Telegraph Line of Coaches—Ballarat to Hamilton thence to Penola and Adelaide passing through Smythesdale, Lake Bolac, Lintons, Glen Thompson, Skipton, Wickliffe, Streatham, Dunkeld

Cobb and Co.—Matthew Veal and Co.
- 30 Jan 1875 Cobb and Co.'s Telegraphic Line of Coaches—Rokewood, Carngham to Ballarat and Smythesdale

1876

Cobb and Co. (Melbourne)—Robertson, Wagner and Co.
- 15 Feb 1876 Cobb and Co.'s Telegraph Line of Royal Mail Coaches—Ballarat and ST. ARNAUD ROAD; CASTLEMAINE, DAYLESFORD; DAYLESFORD and MALMSBURY ROAD; Cobb and Co.—Stawell and Horsham
- 29 Sep 1876 V. R. Cobb and Co.'s Telegraph Line of Royal Mail Coaches—CASTLEMAINE ROAD; ARARAT ROAD

Cobb and Co.—M'Phee and Co.
- 15 Feb 1876 Cobb Co.—Ballarat, LEXTON ROAD
- 6 May 1876 Cobb and Co. coach—Ballan, Melbourne
- 29 Sep 1876 V. R. Cobb and Co.'s Telegraph Line of Royal Mail Coaches—BALLARAT ROAD; ST. ARNAUD ROAD

Cobb and Co.—Anderson and M'Phee
- 15 Feb 1876 Cobb and Co.'s Telegraph Line of Royal Mail Coaches—Ballarat, Smythesdale, SKIPTON AND WICKLIFFE ROADS; MELBOURNE ROAD
- 6 Mar 1876 Cobb and Co.—Ballarat, Blackwood

Cobb and Co.—Western Stage Company
- 15 Feb 1876 Cobb and Co.'s Telegraph Line of Royal Mail Coaches—ARARAT AND HAMILTON ROAD; Cobb Co.'s Royal Mail Line—Geelong to Queenscliff
- 11 Mar 1876 Cobb & Co.'s Western Telegraph Line of Royal Mail Coaches—[Hamilton] For Ararat, via Dunkeld, Glen Thomson, Kiora, and Maroona; For Penola, via Wannon, Coleraine, Casterton, and Fletcher's station; For Geelong via Hochkirch, Penhurst, Caramut, Mortlake, Terang, Camperdown, Stonyford, Colac, Birregurra and Winchelsea; For Casterton via Wannon -and Coleraine; For Narracoorte and Apsley via Cavendish, Balmoral, Harrow and Edenhope; For Portland, via Branxholme and Heywood; Cobb and Co.—Portland to Casterton via Heywood, Hotspur, Digby, Merino and Sandford; Cobb and Co.—Hamilton to Warrnambool
- 13 Apr 1876 Cobb and Co.'s Western Telegraph Line—Day Coaches ... Camperdown and Geelong passing through Colac; Night Mail ... Belfast to Geelong via Camperdown; Mortlake, Hexham, Caramut, Penshurst and Hamilton thence to Mount Gambier and Adelaide, via Penola, and all intermediate post towns ... Mount Duneed, Winchelsea, Camperdown, Terang, Yallock, Warrnambool, Belfast, Mortlake, Hexham, Caramut, Birregurra, Colac, Penshurst, Hamilton, Portland, Apsley, Penola, Casterton, Mount Gambier, Adelaide, Coleraine, Balmoral, Cavendish, Branxholme, Edenhope, Heywood, Portland, Naracoorte, Strathalbyn, Panmure; Mortlake to Geelong, via Darlington passing through Murghebolac Inverleigh Warrambine Cressy Darlington Lismore Tooliorook

Cobb and Co.—Matthew Veal and Co.
- 11 Feb 1876 Cobb and Co.'s Telegraph Line of Coaches—Rokewood, Carngham, Staffordshire Reef
- 6 Mar 1876 Cobb and Co.'s Telegraphic Line of Coaches—To and from Ballarat to Smythesdale,

Scarsdale, Piggoreet, Carngham, Chepstowe, Linton, Staffordshire ... Derwent Jacks, Cape Clear, Bulldog, Rokewood Junction, Rokewood

1877

Cobb and Co.—Proprietors not listed
- 5 Oct 1877 Cobb and Co.—Melbourne, Mulgrave, Dandenong, Berwick, Bunyip, Whiskey Creek, Brandy Creek

Cobb and Co.—Robertson, Wagner and Co.
- 31 Jan 1877 Cobb and Co.'s Telegraph Line of Royal Mail Coaches—DAYLESFORD AND MALMSBURY ROAD
- 10 May 1877 Cobb and Co. Horsham, Glenorchy, Karkarooc, Longerenong, Murtoa; Castlemaine and Daylesford

Cobb and Co.—M'Phee and Co.
- 10 May 1877 Cobb and Co.—Geelong to Donald; Cobb and Co.—Ballarat and LEXTON ROAD ... Miner's Rest, Blowhard, Learmonth, Mount Bolton, Flour Mill, Springs

Cobb and Co.—Anderson and M'Phee
- 31 Jan 1877 Cobb and Co.'s Telegraph Line of Royal Mail Coaches—MELBOURNE ROAD
- 10 May 1877 Cobb and Co.—Smythesdale and Linton Road; Buninyong to Egerton; Ballarat and Skipton

Cobb and Co.—Western Stage Company
- 10 May 1877 Cobb and Co.—Geelong to Queenscliff; Skipton, Streatham, Bolac, Wickliffe, and Junction Road

Cobb and Co.—Matthew Veal and Co.
- 10 May 1877 Cobb and Co.'s Telegraph Line of Coaches—Rokewood, Carngham, Chepstowe, Linton, Staffordshire Reef

1878

Cobb and Co.— Proprietors not listed
- 11 Jul 1878 Cobb and Co.—Through Maffra to Melbourne

Cobb and Co.—Robertson, Wagner and Co.
- 11 Jan 1878 Cobb and Co.—Horsham, Glenorchy, Karkarooc, Longerenong, Murtoa; Castlemaine and Daylesford

Cobb and Co.—M'Phee and Co.
- 11 Jan 1878 Cobb and Co.—Ballarat and LEXTON ROAD; Ballarat to Learmonth

Cobb and Co.—Anderson and M'Phee
- 11 Jan 1878 Cobb and Co.'s Telegraph Line of Royal Mail Coaches—MELBOURNE ROAD Ballarat to Warrenheip, Gordon, Ballan, Merniong, Bacchus Marsh, Melton, KEILOR ROAD Station; Cobb and Co.—Smythesdale and LINTON ROAD; Buninyong Station to Egerton; Ballarat and BLACKWOOD ROAD, Red Hill, Barry's Reef; WICKLIFFE ROAD; Ballarat and Skipton; Gordons to Egerton

Cobb and Co.—Western Stage Company
- 11 Jan 1878 Cobb and Co.—Loutit Bay to Winchelsea
- 30 May 1878 Cobb & Co.—Geelong and Queenscliffe; Night Mail ... in connection with the Victorian Railways Colac to Warrnambool, Koroit, Belfast and Mortlake via Camperdown and Terang; Day coach ... in connection with the Victorian Railways Colac to Camperdown, Terang and Warrnambool with branch to and from Terang and Mortlake; HAMILTON BRANCH Hamilton through Penshurst, Caramut and Hexham, and from Mortlake; Camperdown, Penshurst, Coleraine, Terang Hamilton, Balmoral, Yallock, Portland, Cavendish, Warrnambool, Apsley, Branxholme, Bedfast, Penola Edenhope, Mortlake, Casterton, Heywood, Hexham, Mount Gambier, Portland, Caramut, Adelaide, Narracoorte, Birregurra, Panmure, Strathalbyn; GEELONG TO WARRNAMBOOL via Cressy, Darlington, and Mortlake passing through Murgheboluc, Darlington, Inverleigh, Mortake, Hesse, Ellerslie, Cressy, Ballangeich, Lismore, Purnim, Derinallum, Woodford; HAMILTON TO CASTERTON via Wannon and Coleraine, thence to Penola, Mt. Gambier, and Adelaide. BALLARAT AND WICKLIFFE, passing through Smythesdale, Streatham, Linton, Lake Bolac, Skipton; 141bs of luggage allowed to each passenger at owner's risk, excess luggage chargeable at the rate of 2d per lb for any distance not exceeding 50 miles. Carriage on all parcels must he prepaid. The proprietors do not hold themselves responsible for parcels exceeding £10 in value, unless the same shall have been declared at the time of booking, and paid for accordingly

Cobb and Co.—Matthew Veal and Co.
- 11 Jan 1878 Cobb and Co.'s Telegraph Line of Coaches—Rokewood, Carngham, Chepstowe, Linton, Staffordshire Reef

1879

Cobb and Co.—Proprietors not listed
- 17 Jan 1879 Cobb and Co.'s coaches—Lorne
- 8 May 1879 Cobb and Co. Cobb—Will start a coach on the Haddon line, commencing probably on Monday next
- 21 Nov 1879 Cobb and Co. Ballarat to Adelaide—Ballarat by train to Hamilton, thence Cobb and Co.'s coach and rail from Narracoorte

Cobb and Co.—Robertson, Wagner and Co.
- 28 Jan 1879 Cobb and Co.—Horsham, Glenorchy, Karkarooc, Longerenong, Murtoa—Coaches leave, Stawell for Hersham ... Glenorchy ... for Longerenong and Murtoa ... for Karkarooc and Minyip
- 21 Nov 1879 Cobb and Co.'s Telegraph Line of Royal Mail Coaches—Castlemaine to Daylesford

Cobb and Co.—M'Phee and Co.
- 28 Jan 1879 Cobb and Co.—Ballarat to Learmonth; Ballarat and LEXTON ROAD
- 21 Nov 1879 Cobb and Co.—Summer Arrangement ... Ballarat to St. Arnaud
- 21 Nov 1879 Cobb and Co.'s Telegraph Line of Royal Mail Coaches—Ballarat to St. Arnaud

Cobb and Co.—Anderson and M'Phee
- 28 Jan 1879 Cobb and Co.—Ballarat and BLACKWOOD ROAD ... Red Hill ... Barry's Reef ... Gordon's to Egerton ... Ballarat and Skipton ... Buninyong Station to Egerton; Cobb and Co.'s Telegraph Line of Royal Mail Coaches—Melbourne Road
- 21 Nov 1879 Cobb and Co.—SMYTHESDALE ROAD and Ballarat discontinued at the present; Cobb and Co.'s

Telegraph Line of Royal Mail Coaches—Smythesdale and LINTON ROAD; Ballarat and Skipton; WICKLIFFE ROAD

Cobb and Co.—Western Stage Company
- 18 Oct 1879 Cobb & Co.'s Western Telegraph Line of Royal Mail Coaches—[Hamilton] For Casterton via Wannon and Coleraine; For Penola, Mount Gambier, Narracoote, Adelaide via Wannon, Coleraine, Casterton; For Colac (in connection with the Victorian Railways), via Hochkirch, Penshurst, Caramut, Mortlake, Terang, Camperdown, Stonyford, Birregurra; For Narracoorte and Apsley, via Cavendish, Balmoral, Harrow, and Edenhope; For Belfast, Koroit, and Warrnambool, via Byaduk, Macarthur, and Orford; For WarrnambooL via Caramut; For Penshurst; For Mount Gambier, via Coleraine, Casterton, Lindsay; For Lorne (Loutit Bay), coaches leave Winchelsea ... Connecting with Victorian railways. Special Arrangements. Commercial Travellers and others may arrange for Private Conveyances to any part of the Western District
- 18 Nov 1879 Cobb and Co.'s Western Telegraph Line—Day Coaches. Colac and Warrnambool; Night Mail ... Belfast to Geelong via Camperdown with branch line to Mortlake, Hexham, Caramut, Penshurst, Hamilton thence to Mount Gambier and Adelaide via Penola, and all intermediate post towns; Mortlake to Geelong

Cobb and Co.—Seth Sharp
- 28 Jan 1879 Cobb and Co.—Discontinuance of Coach. Piggoreet Road. On and after the 1st August, 1878, the coach formerly leaving Piggoreet ... for Ballarat will cease running. Also, the coach formerly leaving Smythesdale ... will cease running; Piggoreet Road.—Coaches leave Ballarat ... for Piggoreet; ROKEWOOD ROAD.—Coaches leave Ballarat for Rokewood; KANGAROO ROAD.—Coaches leave Ballarat for Kangaroo via Staffordshire Reef; CHEPSTOWE ROAD.—Coaches leave Ballarat via Carngham, for Chepstowe

1880

Cobb and Co.—Proprietors not listed
- 22 Jun 1880 Cobb and Co.—Benalla, Yarrawonga
- 18 Sep 1880 Cobb and Co.—Ballarat to Adelaide ... Ballarat ... train to Hamilton ... Cobb and Co.'s Coach and rail from Narracoorte

Cobb and Co.—Robertson, Wagner and Co.
- 18 Sep 1880 Castlemaine and Daylesford (Robertson, Wagner and Co. ... Not listed as Cobb and Co.)

Cobb and Co.—M'Phee and Co.
- 18 Sep 1880 Cobb and Co.—ST ARNAUD ROAD; Morning coach to Learmonth; BALLARAT AND LEXTON ROAD Ballarat, Miner's Rest, Blowhard, Learmonth, Mount Belton, Flour Mill, Springs, Lexton; Cobb and Co.—BALLARAT, ST ARNAUD AND LANDSBOROUGH ROAD Ballarat to Miner's Rest, Blowhard, Learmonth, Mount Bolton, Springs, Lexton, Lamplough, Avoca, Moonambel, Frenchmans, Landsborough, Redbank, Stuart Mill, St Arnaud, Cope Cope, Swan Water, Donald ... Leaving St Arnaud for East Charlton

Cobb and Co.—Anderson and M'Phee
- 18 Sep 1880 Cobb and Co.'s Telegraph Line of Royal Mail Coaches—Ballarat, Blackwood, and KEILOR ROAD; Cobb and Co.—Gordon and Egerton Railway Station; MELBOURNE ROAD Ballarat, Warrenheip, Ballan, Myrniong, Bacchus Marsh, Melton, Keilor Road Station; Ballarat, Smythesdale, Scarsdale, Newton, Linton; Ballarat and Blackwood Road; Ballarat, Red Hill; Ballarat to Barry's Reef; Ballarat and Skipton

Cobb and Co.—Western Stage Company
- 18 Sep 1880 Cobb and Co.—Royal Mail Line Geelong to Queenscliff
- 29 Jan 1880 Cobb & Co.'s Western Telegraph Line of Royal Mail Coaches—[Hamilton] Conveyance of Mails, Passengers and Parcels ... For Casterton, via Wannon and Coleraine; For Penola, Mount Gambier, Narracoorte, and Adelaide, via Wannon, Coleraine, and Casterton; For Colac (in connection with the Victorian Railways), via Hochkirch, Penshurst, Caramut, Mortlake, Terang, Camperdown, Stonyford, and Birregurra; For Narracoorte and Apsley, via Cavendish, Balmoral, Harrow, and Edenhope; For Belfast, Koroit, and Warrnambool, via Byaduk, Macarthur, and Orford; For Warrnambool via Caramut; For Penshurst; For Mount Gambier, via Coleraine, Casterton, and Lindsay; For Lorne (Loutit Bay).—Coaches leave Winchelsea daily on arrival of first train from Melbourne; Not advertised as 'Cobb and Co.' coach conveying Hamilton Spectator to Redruth, Coleraine and Casterton; Branxholme to Merino; Coleraine to Harrow

Cobb and Co.—Seth Sharp/S. Sharp
- 18 Sep 1880 Cobb and Co.—Ballarat, ROKEWOOD ROAD; Ballarat to Piggoreet; Kangaroo Line ... Staffordshire Reef to Smythesdale; Smythesdale to Staffordshire; Kangaroo to Smythesdale; CHEPSTOWE ROAD ... Ballarat via Carngham for Chepstowe

1881

Cobb and Co.—Proprietors not listed
- 19 Mar 1881 Cobb and Co.—Ballarat to Adelaide, overland in 56 hours ... Ballarat ... train to Hamilton ... Cobb and Co.'s Coach and rail from Narracoorte
- 11 Nov 1881 Cobb and Co.—Winchelsea to Lorne (Messrs. Mountjoy Brothers will run their coaches from Birregurra to Lorne)

Cobb and Co.—Robertson, Wagner and Co.
- 19 Mar 1881 Cobb and Co.'s Telegraph Line of Royal Mail Coaches ... Castlemaine and Daylesford
- 7 Jun 1881 Cobb and Co.'s Coaches—Sandhurst to Raywood, Tarnagulla, Heathcote; Cobb and Co.'s Inglewood coach SWAN HILL LINE—Inglewood to Swan Hill and Kerang, to Boort, via Powlett Plains, to Wychetella, via Powlett Plains, to Wychetella and Boort, via Wedderburn, to East and West Charlton, to Towaninnie

Cobb and Co.—M'Phee and Co.
- 19 Mar 1881 Cobb and Co.—Ballarat, St. Arnaud, and Landsborough; Ballarat and Lexton Road; Morning coach to Learmonth

Cobb and Co.—Anderson and M'Phee
- 19 Mar 1881 Cobb and Co.'s Telegraph Line of Royal Mail Coaches—Ballarat, Blackwood, and KEILOR ROAD; Ballarat to Newtown; Smythesdale and

LINTON ROAD; WICKLIFFE ROAD; Gordon and Egerton Railway Station; Ballarat and Skipton; Cobb and Co.—Ballarat to Warrenheip; Gordon, Ballan, Myrniong, Bacchus Marsh, Melton, Keilor Road Station

Cobb and Co.—Western Stage Company
- 19 Mar 1881 Cobb and Co.—Geelong to Queenscliff
- 6 Oct 1881 Cobb & Co.'s Western Telegraph Line of Royal Mail Coaches—[Hamilton] For Casterton via Wannon and Coleraine; For Penola, Mount Gambier, Narracoote, Adelaide via Wannon, Coleraine, Casterton and Heathfield; For Colac (in connection with the Victorian Railways), via Hochkirch, Penshurst, Caramut, Mortlake, Terang, Camperdown, Stonyford; For Narracoorte and Apsley, via Cavendish, Balmoral, Harrow, and Edenhope; For Belfast, Koroit, and Warrnambool, via Byaduk, Macarthur, and Orford; For Mount Gambier (in connection with T. Cawker's coaches from Casterton); Branxholme to Merino and Casterton; Penshurst to Dunkeld; Coleraine to Harrow; Belfast to Portland

Cobb and Co.—Seth Sharp/S.Sharp
- 19 Mar 1881 Cobb and Co.'s Telegraph Line of Royal Mail Coaches—Ballarat, ROKEWOOD ROAD; Ballarat to Piggoreet; Cobb and Co.—CHEPSTOWE ROAD; Kangaroo Line ... Staffordshire Reef to Smythesdale ... Smythesdale to Staffordshire ... Kangaroo to Smythesdale

1882

Cobb and Co.—Proprietors not listed
- 17 Mar 1882 Cobb and Co.—BALLARAT TO ADELAIDE Ballarat ... train to Hamilton ... Cobb and Co.'s Coach and rail from Narracoorte; Ballarat to Streatham; Winchelsea and Lorne; Metropolis to Geelong by train, thence to Winchelsea, on board a Cobb and Co's. coach destined for Loutit Bay, Dean's Marsh, Lorne
- 16 Dec 1882 Cobb and Co.—Lilydale to Fernshaw, Healesville, Marysville, Yarra-flats, Warburton, &c.

Cobb and Co.—Robertson, Wagner and Co.
- 25 Aug 1882 Cobb and Co.'s Telegraph Line of Royal Mail Coaches—To Percydale; Ararat Road

Cobb and Co.—M'Phee and Co.
- 17 Mar 1882 Cobb and Co.—Ballarat to Learmonth Road; Ballarat, St Arnaud, and LANDSBOROUGH ROAD; Cobb and Co.'s Telegraph Line of Royal Mail Coaches—Ballarat and Lexton Road
- 25 Aug 1882 Cobb and Co.'s Telegraph Line of Royal Mail Coaches—BALLARAT ROAD; Landsborough & PLEASANT CREEK ROAD; ST ARNAUD ROAD

Cobb and Co.—Western Stage Company
- 17 Mar 1882 Cobb and Co.—Royal Mail Line Geelong to Queenscliff
- 26 Oct 1882 Cobb & Co.'s Western Telegraph Line of Royal Mail Coaches—[Hamilton] For Casterton via Wannon and Coleraine; For Penola, Mount Gambier, Narracoote, Adelaide via Wannon, Coleraine, Casterton and Heathfield; For Colac (in connection with the Victorian Railways), via Hochkirch, Penshurst, Caramut, Mortlake, Terang, Camperdown, Stonyford; For Narracoorte and Apsley, via Cavendish, Balmoral, Harrow, and Edenhope; For Belfast, Koroit, and Warrnambool, via Byaduk, Macarthur, and Orford; For Mount Gambier (in connection with T. Cawker's coaches from Casterton); Branxholme to Merino and Casterton; Penshurst to Dunkeld; Coleraine to Harrow; Belfast to Portland; Winchelsea to Lorne; Cobb & Co.'s—[Hamilton] Coach and Rail, 1st Class ... Casterton and Melbourne; Mt. Gambier and Melbourne; Penola and Melbourne; Narracoorte and Melbourne, Warrnambool and Melbourne, Belfast and Melbourne; Heywood and Mount Gambier

Cobb and Co.—Seth Sharp/S. Sharp
- 17 Mar 1882 Cobb and Co.—Ballarat to St. Arnaud; CHEPSTOWE ROAD; BALLARAT AND ROKEWOOD ROAD; Ballarat, PIGGOREET ROAD
- 17 Mar 1882 Cobb and Co—Kangaroo Line

Cobb and Co.—Vines and M'Phee
- 17 Mar 1882 Cobb and Co.—Blackwood to Ballan ... Gordon and Egerton Railway Station ... WICKLIFFE ROAD ... Ballarat and Newtown ... MELBOURNE ROAD; Cobb and Co.'s Telegraph Line of Royal Mail Coaches ... Ballarat and BLACKWOOD ROAD ... Ballarat and KEILOR ROAD Station

1883

Cobb and Co.—Proprietors not listed
- 22 Mar 1883 Cobb and Co.—Ballarat to Adelaide ... Overland in 56 hours ... Ballarat ... train to Hamilton ... Cobb and Co.'s Coach and rail from Narracoorte
- 6 Apr 1883 Cobb & Co.—Alexandra to Tallarook
- 2 Nov 1883 Cobb & Co.—Intention to run Yea to Mansfield via Doon and from Jamieson to Yea via Alexander
- 16 Oct 1883 Cobb & Co.—Heywood and Mount Gambier via Casterton; Coach and Rail, 1st Class ... Casterton and Melbourne, Mt. Gambier and Melbourne, Penola and Melbourne, Narracoorte and Melbourne, Warrnambool and Melbourne, Belfast and Melbourne
- 4 Dec 1883 Cobb & Co.—St. James, Hill Plain, Yarrawonga

Cobb and Co.—Robertson, Wagner and Co.
- 25 Aug 1882 Cobb and Co.'s Telegraph Line of Royal Mail Coaches—To Percydale; ARARAT ROAD

Cobb and Co.—M'Phee and Co.
- 22 Mar 1883 Cobb and Co.—Ballarat to Learmonth and Lexton; Ballarat to St Arnaud and LANDSBOROUGH ROAD
- 25 Aug 1882 Cobb and Co.'s Telegraph Line of Royal Mail Coaches—BALLARAT ROAD; Landsborough & PLEASANT CREEK ROAD; ST ARNAUD ROAD

Cobb and Co.—Western Stage Company
- 22 Mar 1883 Cobb and Co.—Royal Mail Line ... Summer Arrangements ... Special arrangements night or day ... Geelong to Queenscliff
- 23 Aug 1883 Cobb & Co.—Geelong to Wallington via Moolap and Kensington; Winchelsea and Lorne on application; Livery, Letting and Bait Stables Geelong, Queenscliff, Hamilton, Ballarat, Camperdown, St. Arnaud; Camperdown to Koroit via Terang, Panmure, and Warrnambool reaching Camperdown in time for the afternoon train to Geelong, Melbourne, Ballarat; Night Mail Camperdown to Terang, Warrnambool, Koroit, Belfast, Mortlake, and Hamilton; Camperdown and

Lismore; Camperdown for Darlington and Mortlake thence to Ballangeich and Warrnambool
- 16 Oct 1883 Cobb & Co.'s Western Telegraph Line of Royal Mail Coaches—For Casterton, via Wannon and Coleraine; For Penola, Mount Gambier, Narracoorte, Adelaide via Wannon, Coleraine, Casterton and Heathfield; For Camperdown (in connection with the Victorian Railways), via Hochkirch. Penshurst, Caramut, Mortlake and Terang; For Narracoorte and Apsley, via Cavendish, Balmoral, Harrow, and Edenhope; For Belfast, Koroit, and Warrnambool, via Byaduk. Macarthur, Orford; For Mount Gambier (in connection with T. Cawker's coaches from Casterton); Branxholme to Merino and Casterton; Penshurst to Dunkeld; Coleraine to Harrow; Belfast to Portland

Cobb and Co.—Seth Sharp/S. Sharp
- 22 Mar 1883 Cobb and Co.—Chepstowe Road; Kangaroo Line

Cobb and Co.—Vines and M'Phee
- 22 Mar 1883 Cobb and Co.—Gordon and Egerton Railway Station; Ballarat to Blackwood, Newberry and Trentham via Gordon and Ballan
- 22 Mar 1883 Cobb and Co.'s Telegraph Line of Royal Mail Coaches—Ballarat to Streatham; Ballarat and Keilor Road via Gordon, Ballan and Bacchus Marsh

Cobb and Co.—T. Cawker
- 5 Sep 1883 Cobb and Co.—Mount Gambier to Melbourne (Coach and Rail first-class)

1884

Cobb and Co.—Proprietors not listed
- 29 Mar 1884 Cobb and Co.—Pyramid Hill to Kerang
- 1 Jul 1884 Cobb and Co.—Coach to run Casterton to Harrow, via Chetwynd and Brimboal
- 24 Sep 1884 Cobb and Co.—Ballarat to Adelaide ... Overland in 56 hours ... Cobb and Co.'s Coach and rail from Narracoorte
- 11 Nov 1884 Cobb and Co.—Dimboola, NHill, Bordertown
- 14 Nov 1884 Cobb and Co.—The Mansfield to EUROA ROAD

Cobb and Co.—Robertson, Wagner and Co.
- 23 Sep 1884 Cobb and Co. Coaches—Sale to Bairnsdale; Sale to Omeo

Cobb and Co.—M'Phee and Co.
- 4 Feb 1884 Cobb and Co. Cobb and Co.'s Telegraph Line of Royal Mail Coaches—BALLARAT TO ST. ARNAUD Ballarat to Charlton ... Ballarat, St. Arnaud, and Landsborough Road (Minersrest, Blowhard, Learmonth, Mount Bolton, Springs, Lexton, Lamplough, Avoca, Moonambel, Frenchmans, Landsborough, Redbank, Stuart Mill, St. Arnaud); Ballarat, Learmonth, and Lexton (Minersrest, Blowhard, Learmonth, Addington, Springs, Lexton

Cobb and Co.—Western Stage Company
- 5 Jan 1884 Cobb and Co.—Geelong to Wallington via Moonlap and Kensington; Geelong and Queenscliff; Winchelsea and Lorne; Camperdown to Koroit via Tera, Panmure, and Warrnambool; Night Mail in connection with the Victorian Railways. Camperdown, Terang, Warrnambool, Koroit, Belfast, Mortlake, and Hamilton (Yallock Warrnambool Belfast Mortlake Hexham Caramut Penshurst Hamil Apsley Penola Casterton Mount Gambier Adelaide Panmure Coleraine Balmoral Cavendish Edenhope Portland Narracoorte Stratham); Camperdown and Lismore; Camperdown and Mortlake via Darlington
- 4 Feb 1884 Cobb and Co.'s Telegraph Line of Royal Mail Coaches—Geelong to Queenscliff
- 23 Sep 1884 Cobb & Co.'s Western Telegraph Line of Royal Mail Coaches—[Hamilton] Conveyance Of Mails, Passengers and Parcels ... For Casterton via Wannon and Coleraine; Casterton to Penola thence to Narracoorte and Adelaide; For Camperdown (in connection with the Victorian Railways) via Hochkirch, Penshurst, Caramut, Mortlake and Terang; For Narracoorte and Apsley, via Cavendish, Balmoral, Harrow and Edenhope; For Belfast, Koroit, and Warrnambool, via Byaduk, Macarthur, and Orford; For Mount Gambier (in connection with T. Cawker's coaches); Penshurst to Dunkeld; Coleraine to Harrow; Casterton and Harrow; Belfast to Portland; Heywood to Merino

Cobb and Co.—Vines and M'Phee
- 4 Feb 1884 Cobb and Co.'s Telegraph Line of Royal Mail Coaches—Ballan and Gordon Railway Station; To and from Scarsdale and Linton; To and from Scarsdale and Skipton; To and from Scarsdale and Streatham; Ballarat to KEILOR ROAD via Gordon, Ballan, and Bacchus Marsh; Lake Bolac to WICKLIFFE ROAD Railway Station; Gordon and Egerton Railway Station

1885

Cobb and Co.—Proprietors not listed
- 24 Mar 1885 Cobb and Co.—Ballarat to Adelaide ... Ballarat ... train to Casterton; coach and rail from Narracoorte
- 24 Mar 1885 Cobb and Co.—Excursion coach to Learmonth; To and from Scarsdale and Linton, O'Meara's Junction, Skipton, Streatham
- 23 May 1885 Cobb and Co.—Healesville, Fernshaw and Marysville
- 31 Aug 1885 Cobb & Co. are prepared to make special arrangements Winchelsea and Lorne
- 3 Sep 1885 Cobb and Co.—St. James, Yarrawonga

Cobb and Co.—Robertson, Wagner and Co.
- 27 Feb 1885 Cobb and Co.'s Telegraph Line of Royal Mail Coaches—Kilmore, Sandhurst
- 28 Mar 1885 Cobb and Co. Coaches leave Club Hotel—Sale to Bairnsdale; Sale to Omeo
- 9 Jun 1885 Cobb and Co.'s Royal Mail Coaches—Sandhurst to Heathcote Hotel; Pyramid Hill, Kerang, Swan Hill; Pyramid Hill; Euston, Wentworth

Cobb and Co.—M'Phee and Co.
- 13 Oct 1885 Cobb and Co.—Ballarat to Learmonth and Lexton; Ballarat to St Arnaud and LANDSBOROUGH ROAD

Cobb and Co.—Western Stage Company
- 6 Feb 1885 Cobb and Co.'s Royal Mail Coaches—Heywood and Casterton, leave Commercial Hotel Heywood ... via Hotspur, Digby, Merino [?], and Sandford; Heywood and My. Gambier via Casterton; Portland and Belfast ... connecting with coach to Koroit,

Warrnambool and Colac; Casterton and Branxholme connecting with train to Hamilton; Hamilton and Penola passing through Coleraine and Casterton
- 24 Mar 1885 Cobb and Co.'s—Excursion through Tickets. Coach and Rail from Ballarat to Warrnambool and Belfast
- 13 Oct 1885 Cobb and Co.—Special arrangements, night or day Geelong to Queenscliff
- 24 Nov 1885 Cobb & Co.'s Western Telegraph Line of Royal Mail Coaches—[Hamilton] Conveyance of Mails, Passengers and Parcels ... For Wannon and Coleraine; Casterton to Penola thence to Narracoorte and Adelaide; For Camperdown (in connection with the Victorian Railways) via Hochkirch, Penshurst, Caramut, Mortlake and Terang; For Narracoorte and Apsley, via Cavendish, Balmoral, Harrow and Edenhope; For Belfast, Koroit, and Warrnambool, via Byaduk, Macarthur, and Orford; Casterton to Mount Gambier; Penshurst to Dunkeld; Coleraine to Harrow; Casterton and Harrow; Belfast to Portland

Cobb and Co.—Vines and M'Phee
- 31 Aug 1885 Cobb & Co. Rokewood ... leave Leigh Station passing through Teesdale, Shelford, Warrambine thence to Rokewood Junction, Cape Clear, Derwent Jack's, Scarsdale meeting train for Ballarat
- 13 Oct 1885 Cobb and Co.—Gordon and Egerton Railway Station

1886

Cobb and Co.—Proprietors not listed
- 4 Mar 1886 Cobb and Co.—Lilydale, Healesville, Warburton, Yarra Flats
- 10 Mar 1886 Cobb and Co.'s Coaches.— Connect with Victorian Railways ... Scarsdale and Linton, Scarsdale and Skipton and Streatham; Ballarat to Adelaide, train to Hamilton, Cobb and Co.'s Coach and rail from Narracoorte
- 6 May 1886 Cobb and Co.—Yarrawonga for Tungamah, St. James
- 22 Sep 1886 Cobb's—Healesville, Fernshaw, Marysville, Warburton, Yarra-flats (from Lilydale Hotel)

Cobb and Co.—Robertson, Wagner and Co.
- 23 Jan 1886 Cobb and Co. Coaches—Sale to Bairnsdale; Sale to Omeo
- 10 Feb 1886 Cobb and Co.—Sandhurst to Heathcote Hotel; Kerang to Swan Hill; Kerang to Euston and Wentworth; Kerang to Bairanald
- 21 Jul 1886 Cobb and Co.'s Telegraph Line of Royal Mail Coaches—via Hay to Pine Ridge, Wangarella, Deniliquin, Booligal, Mossgeil, Ivanhoe, Wilcannia, Silverton, Gunbar, Hillston, Maude, Oxley, Balranald, Euston, Wentworth, Menindie, and Mount Gipps
- 29 Oct 1886 Cobb and Co.'s Telegraph Line of Royal Mail Coaches—Kilmore; Sandhurst

Cobb and Co.—M'Phee and Co.
- 10 Mar 1886 Cobb and Co.—Ballarat, Miners' Rest, Blowhard, Learmonth, Addington, Springs, Lexton; Ballarat to St Arnaud and Landsborough Road & Charleton

Cobb and Co.—Western Stage Company
- 10 Mar 1886 Cobb and Co.—Geelong to Swampy Creek, Anglesea River; Special arrangements, night or day ... Geelong to Queenscliff
- 7 Dec 1886 Cobb & Co.'s Western Telegraph Line of Royal Mail Coaches—[Hamilton] Conveyance Of Mails, Passengers and Parcels ... For Wannon and Coleraine; Casterton to Penola thence to Narracoorte; For Camperdown (in connection with the Victorian Railways), via Hochkirch, Penshurst, Caramut, Mortlake and Terang; For Apsley, via Cavendish, Balmoral, Harrow and Edenhope; For Belfast, Koroit, and Warrnambool, via Byaduk, Macarthur, and Orford; Penshurst to Dunkeld; Coleraine to Harrow; Penshurst and Belfast; Belfast to Portland

Cobb and Co.—Vines and M'Phee
- 10 Mar 1886 Cobb and Co—Gordon and Egerton Railway Station

1887

Cobb and Co.—Proprietors not listed
- 26 Oct 1887 Connect with Victorian Railways Cobb and Co.'s Coaches—Scarsdale and Linton, O'Meara's Junction, Skipton, Streatham
- 14 Jan 1887 Cobb and Co.—Healesville
- 25 Mar 1887 Cobb's—Healesville, Fernshaw, Marysville, Warburton, Yarra-flats (from Lilydale Hotel)

Cobb and Co.—Robertson, Wagner and Co.
- 8 Jan 1887 Cobb and Co.—Echuca, Shepparton
- 29 Jan 1887 Cobb & Co.—Bairnsdale, Bruthen, Omeo, Sale
- 28 Mar 1887 Cobb and Co.—Echuca, Mooroopna, Shepparton
- 8 Jul 1887 Cobb and Co.'s Telegraph Line of Royal Mail Coaches—Kilmore, Sandhurst

Cobb and Co.—M'Phee and Co.
- 26 Oct 1887 Cobb and Co.—Ballarat to Charlton; Ballarat to St Arnaud and LANDSBOROUGH ROAD; Ballarat, Learmonth, and Lexton

Cobb and Co.—Western Stage Company
- 6 Sep 1887 Cobb & Co.'s Western Telegraph Line of Royal Mail Coaches—[Hamilton] Conveyance Of Mails, Passengers and Parcels ... For Wannon and Coleraine; Casterton to Penola thence to Narracoorte and Adelaide; For Terang via Hochkirch, Penshurst, Caramut, Mortlake; For Apsley, via Cavendish, Balmoral, Harrow and Edenhope; For Port Fairy, Koroit, and Warrnambool, via Byaduk, Macarthur, and Orford; Penshurst to Dunkeld; Coleraine to Harrow; Casterton to Harrow; Penshurst and Koroit; Port Fairy to Portland
- 26 Oct 1887 Cobb and Co.—Geelong to Queenscliff

Cobb and Co.—Vines and M'Phee
- 26 Oct 1887 Cobb and Co.—Blackwood and Bacchus Marsh via Ballan and Myrniong ... train to Gordons, thence by coach ... Trentham
- 26 Oct 1887 Cobb and Co.—Gordon and Egerton Railway Station

1888

Cobb and Co.—Proprietors not listed
- 6 Mar 1888 Cobb and Co.'s Coaches—Bruthen to Tambo Crossing, Bairnsdale to Tambo Crossing
- 9 May 1888 Cobb's—Healesville, Fernshaw, Marysville,

Warburton, Yarra-flats (from Lilydale Hotel)
- 24 Jul 1888 Connect with Victorian Railways Cobb and Co.'s Coaches—Scarsdale and Linton, O'Meara's Junction, Skipton, Streatham; Ocean Grove
- 18 Dec 1888 Cobb and Co.'s coaches left this hotel (Edgcumbe's Hotel, late Royal Mail, Healesville) for Fernshaw, Narbethong, and Marysville

Cobb and Co.—Robertson, Wagner and Co.
- 6 Mar 1888 Cobb & Co. Bairnsdale to Bruthen, Bairnsdale to Omeo, Sale to Stratford
- 21 Dec 1888 Cobb and Co.'s Telegraph Line of Royal Mail Coaches—Kilmore

Cobb and Co.—M'Phee and Co.
- 24 Jul 1888 Cobb and Co.—Ballarat, St. Arnaud and LANDSBOROUGH ROAD ... Ballarat to Charlton ... Ballarat, Learmonth, and Lexton

Cobb and Co.—Western Stage Company
- 3 Apr 1888 Cobb and Co.—Geelong to Ocean Grove via Wallington
- 24 Jul 1888 Cobb and Co.—Including Coach and Rail ... To and from Warrnambool and Port Fairy; To or from Melbourne and Koroit; To or from Geelong and Koroit; Geelong to Queenscliff
- 6 Sep 1887 Cobb & Co.'s Western Telegraph Line of Royal Mail Coaches—[Hamilton] Conveyance Of Mails, Passengers and Parcels ... For Terang via Hochkirch, Penshurst, Caramut, Mortlake; For Apsley, via Cavendish, Balmoral, Harrow and Edenhope; For Port Fairy, Koroit, and Warrnambool, via Byaduk, Macarthur, and Orford; Penshurst to Dunkeld; Coleraine to Harrow; Casterton to Harrow; Penshurst and Koroit; Port Fairy to Portland; WICKLIFFE ROAD Railway Station and Lake Bolac

Cobb and Co.—Vines and M'Phee
- 3 Apr 1888 Cobb and Co.—LEIGH ROAD to Rokewood
- 24 Jul 1888 Cobb and Co.—Backwood and Bacchus Marsh via Ballan and Myrniong; Gordon and Egerton Railway Station

1889

Cobb and Co.—Proprietors not listed
- 21 Jan 1889 Cobb and Co.—Connect with Victorian Railways Cobb and Co.'s Coaches ... Scarsdale and Linton, O'Meara's Junction, Skipton, Streatham
- 16 Feb 1889 Cobb and Co.'s coaches—Left this hotel (Edgcumbe's Hotel, late Royal Mail, Healesville) for Fernshaw, Narbethong, and Marysville
- 27 Apr 1889 Cobb and Co.—Healesville, Fernshaw
- 2 May 1889 Cobb and Co.'s Coaches—Bairnsdale to Sarsfield, Bruthen and Omeo

Cobb and Co.—Robertson, Wagner and Co.
- 22 Aug 1889 Cobb and Co. Telegraph Line of Mail Coaches—Kilmore

Cobb and Co.—M'Phee and Co.
- 21 Jan 1889 Cobb and Co.—Ballarat to Learmonth and Lexton; Ballarat to St Arnaud and LANDSBOROUGH ROAD

Cobb and Co.—Western Stage Company
- 21 Jan 1889 Cobb and Co.—Special arrangements, night or day ... Geelong to Queenscliff; Seaside Excursion Tickets. Including Coach and Rail ... To Warrnambool, Port Fairy from Melbourne, Sandhurst, Geelong and Ballarat ... Ocean Grove; Coach and Rail ... summer months ... Cobb and Co.'s offices, Melbourne, Geelong, Ballarat and Sandhurst
- 12 Feb 1889 Cobb & Co.—Apsley and Hamilton via Edenhope, Harrow and Balmoral; Coach and Rail to and from Melbourne

Cobb and Co.—Vines and M'Phee
- 21 Jan 1889 Cobb and Co.—Gordon and Egerton Railway Station; Blackwood and Bacchus Marsh via Ballan and Myrniong

---

"LAKE MUNDI ... The great drawback that the present Border duty is to farmers living on the border, was plainly and rather painfully illustrated here a few days ago. A Mr. Stark, a most energetic farmer who has resided here for many years, has long seen and felt the want of a steam engine in the district for thrashing and chaff cutting purposes. Some time ago he purchased a four-horse-power engine in Adelaide, which he used for cutting a considerable quantify of chaff in and about Penola. But having some chaff of his own to cut on the Victorian side of the border, he thought he would cross the engine over last week, and as he had used it for so long a time in South Australia, he naturally imagined he could cross into Victoria and back without paying duty. However, he was ordered by the Customs officer stationed at Penola, to pay the duty (£50) before he dare cross it.

Now, is not that hard-lines for a man who wishes to make an honest penny, and also benefit his neighbours ? I do not know what the Government will expect next ! If Mr. Stark can be charged for the steam-engine that be has used is South Australia, why not charge me or anyone else who may bring across a buggy, cart, or waggon that we have used in South Australia ?

Do they charge Cobb and Co. duty every time they bring a coach back from. Penola to convey passengers from Casterton to Hamilton ? I say why not charge for one as well as the other ? I understand that Mr. Stark has left his engine on the South Australian side, and has written to Mr. Shiels to see what can be done in the matter, as he considers it very hard to have to pay £50 for being allowed to cut his own chaff with his own machine. It will be a great loss, not only to Mr. Stark himself, but to the whole neighbourhood, if he cannot cross this engine, as many depend on getting their work done by it." (Lake Mundi, 22 Mar 1883, p.3)

1853 Cobb & Cos. Leviathan coach, carrying 98 passengers, running between Ballarat & Geelong (H. Deutsch, Ballarat lithd. & pubd.) - Courtesy National Library Australia

Along the tracks—1870s & 1880s

See *Appendix 2: Supporting evidence for Cobb and Co. coaching lines, Victoria*

1870 – CONTRACTS "The principal contracts for the conveyance of mails during 1870 have been obtained by Messrs Robertson, Wagner and Co. They are two in number, and amount in the whole to £56,635 10s. [Ballarat]." (News and Notes, 21 Feb 1870, p.2)

"DOUBLE COACH ACCIDENT ... We observe that Mr. Collins, the only person who sustained severe injury, has since had to undergo amputation at the hospital :— It is not often that we hear of accidents to Messrs. Cobb and Co.'s mail coaches, which start from Adelaide ; but a serious catastrophe occurred on Monday afternoon near the Eagle on the Hill, on the Mount Barker-road better known as Fordham's. It appears from what our reporter could learn ... that the Strathalbyn omnibus, which was driven by Mr. S. Hall, was standing in front of the inn, when the Mount Barker coach, which leaves town about a quarter of an hour after the other, came up, Mr. Rooke driving ... Rooke refused to allow any one to take his reins, stating that he did not intend leaving his seat, but subsequently jumped off the box for the purpose we understand, of looking after a fare that had not been paid. Whilst he was on the ground the horses moved on and although having the reins Rooke had little or no control over them—the result was they went up against Hall's horses, starting them, and the ostler not being able to hold the animals they drew the coach over the sideling. The bus came into collision with a stout telegraph post, which it knocked down, after which it turned over on to a fence, but that offered no resistance ... so there were two mail coaches overturned within a few yards of each other. Rooke maintained his hold of his horses to the end. It is a singular circumstance that not one of the horses of either team was in the least injured. The Mount Barker omnibus being but slightly damaged it was soon righted, and Rooke proceeded on his journey. With regard to Hall's coach, however the damage sustained was more serious ... Hall borrowed a horse from Mr. W. Morcomb, who was riding by at the time, and proceeded as fast as possible to town to procure medical assistance and to obtain another coach, immediately on the information reaching Messrs. Cobb and Co. a vehicle was dispatched." (Double Coach Accident, 18 May 1870, p.4)

1872 – "COBB & CO.'S LINE OF COACHES—J. Cawker ... leave Mac's Hotel for Casterton" on the same page "PUBLIC HOLIDAYS. Monday, 1st January-New Year's Day, Sunday, 17th March-St. Patrick's Day, Friday, 29th March-Good Friday, Saturday, 30th March-Easter Eve, Monday, 1st April-Easter Monday, Tuesday, 2nd April-Easter Tuesday, Tuesday, 23rd April-St. George's Day, Monday, 20th May-Whit Monday, Friday, 24th May-Her Majesty's Birthday, Thursday, 20th June-Her Majesty's Accession, Monday, 1st July-Separation Day, Saturday, 9th November-Prince of Wales' Birthday, Saturday, 23rd November-Proclamation of New Constitution, Saturday, 30th November-St. Andrew's Day, Wednesday, 25th December-Christmas Day." (Portland Guardian Almanac, 1 Jan 1872, p.1)

"COBB & CO'S. WESTERN TELEGRAPH LINE OF ROYAL MAIL COACHES ... Conveyance of Mails, Passengers, and Parcels ... Booking Office, opposite Victoria Hotel, Hamilton ... For Ballarat ... Penola ... Casterton ... Apsley, ... Warrnambool And Belfast ... Portland ... Mortlake ... Western Stage Company, Proprietor. George Tillyer, Agent. Cobb and Co.'s General Booking Office, Gray-street, Hamilton." While "JOHN CREED, CARPENTER AND UNDERTAKER, is prepared to execute funerals either in Plain or First-class Styles, at greatly reduced prices. A First-class Hearse and Plumes on hire, one, two, or four horses." (Advertising, 13 Mar 1872, p.1)

1874 – "COBB AND CO.'S TELEGRAPH LINE OF ROYAL MAIL COACHES—Leave Shamrock Hotel ... Sandhurst to Haywood, Tarnagulla, Swan Hill, Heathcote, Inglewood Jno. Robertson, Manager, Robertson, Wagner and Co." (Advertising, 3 Oct 1874, p.4)

1875 – DEAD BODY "On Tuesday morning the mailboy, when about five miles from Carngham, on the Chepstowe road, discovered the dead body of a lad lying on the road, with one wheel of a four-horse waggon resting upon it. He procured assistance and upon extricating the body life was found to be quite extinct ... THE FIRST CONVICTION AGAINST PERSONS TAKING FISH under 4 oz in weight from Lake Wendouree was obtained at the City Police-court on Tuesday. Mr Jas. Orr, lately from up-country, did not know that there were fishing regulations in Ballarat, and he took a lot of small perch from the lake. A nominal fine of one shilling and half-a-crown costs was inflicted." (Notes and News, 17 Feb 1875, .2)

1876 – "COBB AND CO.'S WESTERN TELEGRAPH LINE. Arrangements for 1876 ... Camperdown and Geelong. Day Coaches leave Wiggins' Leura Hotel ... Night Mail ... Belfast to Geelong ... Mortlake, Hexham, Caramut, Penshurst and Hamilton thence to Mount Gambier And Adelaide, Via Penola, and all intermediate post town ... Western Stage Company, Proprietors, Cobb and Co.'s General Booking-office. ... AUSTRALIAN BONE MILL COMPANY. Late Askunas and Co., and Robertson, Wagner and Co. Per Ton. Bone dust, guaranteed unadulterated £6 10. Phosphatic guano, 75 per cent phosphates £6 10. Animal guano, an article of great value £6 10. Super-phosphate, a most valuable manure, £9 0. Neatsfoot oil and antifriction grease." (Advertising, 13 Apr 1876, p.1)

1877 – RAILWAY TRAIN "*The Gippsland Mercury* vouches for the truth of the following :—An amusing incident occurred at Sandy Creek the other day. A girl, who had never before seen a railway train, observed one approaching, and fearful that a fluttering of clothes, hung out on a line to dry, might frighten the engine. She ran to a man who was working close by, and asked if such would be the case. He laughingly replied in the affirmative, but the girl was not satisfied, and asked the landlady of the hotel the same question. Seeing the fun of the thing she also answered 'yes,' whereupon, to her great astonishment, the girl cut down the line, letting the clean linen fall into the mud. Although rather annoyed at the result of the joke she could not blame the girl, and could but indulge in a hearty laugh." (News and Notes, 23 Jun 1877, p.3)

1878 – "COBB AND CO. Horsham, Glenorchy, Karkarooc, Longerenong, Murtoa ... Castlemaine and Daylesford ... Robertson, Wagner and Co.; Ballarat and Lexton Road ...

Ballarat to Learmonth ... M'Phee and Co. ... E. D. McMillian, agent; Cobb and Co.'s Telegraph Line of Royal Mail Coaches—Melbourne Road ... Cobb and Co. Smythesdale and Linton Road ... Buninyong Station to Egerton ... Ballarat and Blackwood Road, Red Hill, Barry's Reef ... Wickliffe Road ... Ballarat and Skipton ... Gordons to Egerton ... Anderson and M'Phee; Cobb and Co. Loutit Bay to Winchelsea ... Western Stage Company E. D. McMillian, agent; Cobb and Co.'s Telegraph Line of Coaches—Rokewood, Carngham, Chepstowe, Linton, Staffordshire Reef ... Matthew Veal and Co.; MEANWHILE VICTORIAN RAILWAYS TIME TABLE: From Ballarat to Melbourne. From Melbourne to Ballarat. From Ballarat to Castlemaine and Sandhurst. From Castlemaine to Ballarat. From Ballarat to Stawell. From Stawell to Ballarat. Ararat to Portland. Maryborough to Dunolly. Dunolly to Maryborough. Maryborough to Avoca. Avoca to Maryborough. Geelong to Colac. Colac to Geelong. Trains stop at Geelong fifteen minutes for refreshments. Passengers can stop at any intermediate Station, but must proceed to their destination on the day their ticket was issued. Children under Four Years old." (Advertising, 11 Jan 1878, p.1)

1879 – "COBB AND CO.'S COACHES will in future leave Lorne on Saturdays at 10 a.m., in lieu of Sundays ... Passengers may rely upon obtaining superior accommodation at Mountjoy's boarding establishment, or Gosney's Lorne hotel. Passengers are conveyed by Cobb and Co. to either house." (News & Notes, 17 Jan 1879, p.3)

1880 – "COBB AND CO.'S TELEGRAPH LINE OF ROYAL MAIL COACHES—Ballarat, Blackwood, and Keilor Road ... Cobb and Co.—Gordon and Egerton Railway Station; Melbourne Road ... Ballarat, Warrenheip, Ballan, Myrniong, Bacchus Marsh, Melton, Keilor Road Station; Ballarat, Smythesdale, Scarsdale, Newton, Linton; Ballarat and Blackwood Road ... Ballarat, Red Hill, Ballarat to Barry's Reef; Ballarat and Skipton ... E. D. M'Millan Agent ... Anderson and M'Phee; St Arnaud Road; Morning coach to Learmonth; Ballarat and Lexton Road ... Ballarat, Miner's Rest, Blowhard, Learmonth, Mount Belton, Flour Mill, Springs, Lexton ... Ballarat, St Arnaud and Landsborough Road ... Ballarat to Miner's Rest, Blowhard, Learmonth, Mount Bolton, Springs, Lexton, Lamplough, Avoca, Moonambel, Frenchmans, Landsborough, Redbank, Stuart Mill, St Arnaud, Cope Cope, Swan Water, Donald ... Leaving St Arnaud for East Charlton ... E. D. M'Millan Agent ... M'Phee and Co.; Cobb and Co.—Ballarat to Adelaide—Ballarat ... train to Hamilton ... Cobb and Co.'s Coach and rail from Narracoorte (?); Castlemaine and Daylesford ... E. D. M'Millan Agent ... Robertson, Wagner and Co. (Not listed as Cobb and Co.); Cobb and Co.—Ballarat, Rokewood Road; Ballarat to Piggoreet; Kangaroo Line ... Staffordshire Reef to Smythesdale; Smythesdale to Staffordshire; Kangaroo to Smythesdale; Chepstowe Road ... Ballarat via Carngham for Chepstowe ... Seth Sharp; Cobb and Co.—Royal Mail Line Winter Arrangement ... Geelong to Queenscliff ... E. D. M'Millan Agent ... Western Stage Company." While advertised "KEATING'S COUGH LOZENGES. Cough, Asthma, Bronchitis, Accumulation of Phlegm. Composed of the purest articles. These lozenges contain no opium nor deleterious drug ... speedy and certain." (Advertising, 18 Sep 1880, p.4)

1881 – "THE BEST MEAT PIE IN THE CITY, 2d ; a Tea, Coffee, Chocolate, Cocoa or Boiled Milk, 2d. 124 and 126 Bourke street, opposite Waxworks. We have received from Mr P. G. Dixon samples of sodawater made from water specially brought from Mount Macedon. The sodawater is excellent, and is of course free from that nauseating taste so clearly discernable in sodawater or other cordials made from the filthy Yan Yean. We have also received from Mr Dixon a sample of the Mount Macedon water, which it is quite a treat to drink, after having for some time to put up with the beastly stuff supplied by the Public Works Department ... THE SCIENTIFIC AGE ... Everything seems to be done by the telephone now-a-days. If a man gets taken ill, the doctor physics him by telephone. If a girl wants to do a bit of courting, she does it by the telephone—in fact, everything is telephoned. The other day I'm blessed if wasn't measured for a suit of clothes by telephone. I looked in at the Wholesale Clothing Company's Gertrude-street, to ask what time it was, when before I could say knife, the man switched on to the factory, whipped a tape round my waist, and sang out through the telephone, 33, 18, 34, ... Somehow or other the instrument did not work well, because ... the cutter had got my measurement ... mixed up ... 93 ins around the waist ... he called out *what sort of an animal have you got down there?* The cutter thought ... the tape gentleman ... was measuring a hippopotamus." (News and Notes, 2 Jun 1881, p.4)

1882 – "COBB AND CO.'S TELEGRAPH LINE OF ROYAL MAIL COACHES ... Ballarat and Lexton Road ... M'Phee and Co.; Cobb and Co. ... Chepstowe Road ... Ballarat and Rokewood Road ... Ballarat, Piggoreet Road ... Seth Sharp; Kangaroo Line ... S. Sharp; Cobb and Co.—Blackwood to Ballan ... Gordon and Egerton Railway Station ... Wickliffe Road ... Ballarat and Newtown ... Melbourne Road ... Vines and M'Phee; Cobb and Co.—Royal Mail Line ... Winter Arrangements ... Geelong to Queenscliff ... Western Stage Company; Cobb and Co.—Ballarat to Adelaide—Overland in 56 hours ... Ballarat ... train to Hamilton ... Cobb and Co.'s Coach and rail from Narracoorte; Cobb and Co.—Ballarat to Streatham; Cobb and Co.—Winchelsea and Lorne Leave Sharp's Hotel, Newtown. Leave O'Farrell's Hotel, Scarsdale. Leave Eldorado Hotel, Smythes Agent K. Gallass, Winchelsea." (Advertising, 17 Mar 1882, p.4)

"CAMELS FOR COBB'S COACHES. The wretched state of the Mount Browne road ... Messrs. Cobb and Co. ... they have hitherto managed to struggle through with the mail. But horse flesh and blood cannot stand it any longer ... Mr. Byrne, manager of the firm, during his last trip, to the diggings, was forced to the conclusion that the mail by ordinary means could no longer be carried, and with considerable fore-thought he at once set about and succeeded in securing several camels to relieve the worn-out mail horses and secure a continuance of the service." (Camels for Cobb's Coaches, 22 Apr 1882, p.4)

1883 – DELIVERY TIMES "As you are, no doubt aware, sir, the traffic between Alexandra and Tallarook is something enormous ... goods dispatched from the metropolis ... arrives in Alexandra somewhere about the 28th day ... allowing 3 days for the transit between Tallarook and Alexandra ... it takes about 25 days to get therm delivered to the carrier after arrival at Tallarook ... whilst parcels dispatched from Melbourne via Tallarook, thence by Cobb & Co. to Alexandra, are delivered to the coachman 14 days after being sent off, thus taking only 15 days to be delivered here by the quickest route we are blessed with." (Management at Tallarook Station, 6 Apr 1883, p.2) while "I understand that it is the intention of Cobb & Co., as soon as the railway from Tallarook to Yea is open, to run lines of coaches direct from Yea to Mansfield via Doon, and from Jamieson to Yea via Alexandra ...

It appears, however, Cobb is not going to have it all to himself ; for I observe that Mr F. G. Seaton, of Alexandra, intends, on the opening of the Yea line, to run an express between Alexandra and Yea—fares, 4s. I hear that Mr McLeish, butcher at the King Parrot, intends opening a shop, in High-street, opposite Mr Purcell's store—the ground, about ¼ acre, cost £80." (Yea, 2 Nov 1883, p.2)

"SERIOUS ACCIDENT ... happened to Cobb and Co.'s coach on Saturday afternoon, at Hill Plain, half way between St. James and Yarrawonga. It appears that after the groom had hitched the pole-straps one of the horses became unmanageable, and before the driver had taken hold of the reins the horses bolted ... Mrs Atkins jumped out with her baby soon after the horses bolted, and fell under the coach, the wheel passing over both her legs which are supposed to be broken. The baby was not hurt." (The Ovens District Hospital, 4 Dec 1883, p.2)

"ST. ARNAUD ... After several days of fine weather it rained from morning to evening yesterday, 110 points being recorded during that time. The crops throughout the district are promising good yields. They have not looked so well at this time of the year for the past six years. At the Charlton Pastoral and Agricultural Society show yesterday the whole ground was a perfect puddle. Messrs. Cobb and Co.'s four-horse special. coach, which left Charlton for St Arnaud yesterday with 16 passengers, sank bodily on the road in water 2 feet in depth. The coach remains stuck, and it will be necessary to procure a team of bullocks to remove it." (Country News, 14 Sep 1883, p.7)

1884 – TOM THUMB COACH "We started from Lilydale under luxurious conditions, having chartered for the use of our party, six in all, the comfortable 'Tom Thumb' coach of Cobb and Co., which, with its well-padded sides and back, is to the ordinary coach what a first-class railway carriage is to a second-class ... Yarra Flats ... Healesville, with its richly-laden fruit gardens, its grand populars and its luxuriant blackberry hedges ... Fernshaw ... Black Spur ... Indeed, one of our number had been for some time seeing in the long swinging strips of bark peeling off from the huge gum-trees suggestions of dangling bell-pulls, with genial but illusory associations of whisky and sodawater. These ideas gave zest to the drink we took from the cool rushing stream down under the fern trees on the left of the road ... The little settlement of Narbethong, at Fisher's Creek, a few miles beyond the top of the Black Spur, has become a favourite resort of tourists during the last year or two ... We descended to the pretty little village of Marysville ... Mr. Keppel's Hotel and then those who are so disposed make acquaintance with his wonderful bath, where a cold sparkling rill of mountain water is led into a large, square bath neatly slabbed round, and big enough to swim in. An untimely cold prevented me from sharing in the enjoyment of this bath ... Nobbly Spur ... The road along this part is a very adventurous one. It is well made but narrow, and we always have a deep and precipitous declivity on one side and a bank notched into the hill on the other ... Tommy's Bend ... a view of Sassafras Gully ... beech forest ... we camped for lunch in a delightful spot ... The pleasant rippling stream ran within a couple of yards of our fire ... Driver Newman hitched the horses ... as we parted at the end of our journey we felt that we had spent three very pleasant and well-filled days." (Sketches Pen with, 9 Apr 1884, p.55)

1885 – "COBB AND CO.'S TELEGRAPH LINE OF ROYAL MAIL COACHES to Kilmore ... Sandhurst. Leave the Heathcote Hotel ... Booking-office, Heathcote Hotel, Robertson, Wagner & Co., Proprietors, Kearney & Co., Agents ... NEW RATES FOR POSTAGE ... Victorian Rates. Letters.—For every 1 oz, or under, 2d ... Intercolonial rates. New South Wales, New Zealand, Queensland, South Australia, Tasmania, Western Australia, and Fiji. Letters.—For every 1 oz, or under, 2d. Post Cards.—Additional stamp, 1d." (Advertising, 27 Feb 1885, p.4)

"COBB AND CO.'S LIVERY AND LETTING STABLES, George Hotel, Lydiard street, Ballarat. Cobb and Co. ... Vines and M'Phee; Cobb and Co.'s Excursion coach to Learmonth; Cobb and Co.'s Excursion through Tickets. Coach and Rail ... from Ballarat to Warrnambool and Belfast ... Western Stage Company." Meanwhile "Steam to Sydney and all Queensland Ports and Fiji." (Advertising, 24 Mar 1885, p.1)

"COBB AND CO. COACHES LEAVE CLUB HOTEL—Sale to Bairnsdale ... Sale to Omeo ... Booking Office Mrs. Bryant's Club Hotel, Sale (Robertson, Wagner & Co.)" While hotels advertising on the same page were "Club Hotel, Sale, Royal Exchange Hotel, Sale, Criterion Hotel, Sale, Crown Hotel, Sale, Railway Refreshment Rooms, Sale, Victorian Hotel, Sale, Albion Hotel, Sale, Sale Hotel, Sydney Hotel, Melbourne, Rosedale Hotel, Rosedale, Exchange Hotel, Rosedale, Morwell Hotel, Morwell Railway Station, Club Hotel, Toongabbie, Prince of Wales Hotel, Club Hotel, Jemmy's Point, Grand Junction Hotel, Traralgon, Crown Hotel, Traralgon, Criterion Hotel, Trafalgar, Western Port Hotel, Mirboo North, Omeo Hotel, Omeo, Traveller's Rest, Port Albert Road, Hunt Club Hotel, Wurruk, Shakespeare Hotel, Stratford, Grand Junction Hotel, Traralgon, Druids' Hotel, South Melbourne, Club Hotel, Boolara, Commercial Hotel, Mirboo, Gippsland Hotel, Melbourne, Kirk's Bazaar Hotel, Melbourne, Commercial Hotel, Heyfield." (Advertising, 28 Mar 1885, p.1)

1886 – "NOTES AND NEWS. France claims the honour of establishing the first post-office. It was invented for the use of the Government in 1463 ... In Switzerland no child who cannot present a certificate of vaccination is permitted to attend a public or private school ... The oldest specimen of hosiery is probably a pair of lambswool socks, recently found in an Egyptian tomb, wherein they had lain for two thousand years ... It is rather curious to reflect that the London Post Office now carries letters, transmits telegrams, conveys our parcels, and receives deposits, and that all this work is done under the superintendence of a blind man, whose chief assistant has but one leg ... Husband and wife had been warmly but good-humouredly discussing a matter of domestic economy, but the wife was very positive, and her husband said at last: *Well, I see that your mind is made up, so I will not press the matter further. Still you are not infallible. Yes, I am*, was the prompt answer ... The German authorities add a peculiar terror, not known at Oxford or Cambridge, to the penalty of expulsion from a university. The delinquent's name is posted in every university in Prussia, until his name and offences are familiar as household words throughout the length and breadth of the land ... It appears that Martin Luther's wedding ring is yet in existance. A few years ago it was on exhibition at a jeweller's shop in Dusseldorf; Germany.

On it is represented the crucifiction of Christ, a small bright ruby standing for a drop of blood. The inscription is: 'Catherine von Boba to Dr. Martin Luther, 13 June, 1525' ... HERE ARE SOME INSTANCES OF TERRIBLE OVERCROWDING :—In Robert-street, Lower Gornal, Birmingham, seven persons, including two women, a man, and a youth 16 years of age, sleep in one bed, in a room 8 feet by 9 feet. A family of seven, in Rock-street, Upper Gornal, two of them being grown-up daughters, and one of them a son of 10, occupy two beds in one room, which is used as a shoemake's shop, and measures 9 feet by 11 feet (says *Truth*) ... As the most lately formed colony, Queensland will stand well in the front among her sisters at the Colonial Exhibition of 1886 ... in no industry will she appear to better advantage than in the display to be made in mining exhibits. With a wealth of mineral resources the extent of which is as yet unknown to the best geological judges in the colony." (Notes and News, 1 Jan 1886, p.3)

LILYDALE "The old coaching days were not altogether without their charm, a fact which was, testified to by the numbers of visitors who during the summer months flocked to Lilydale, a hot, dusty drive of nearly four hours was compensated for by the scenery at the finish ... For some considerable time Cobb and Co. who throughout have maintained the a supremacy of the roads, have been opposed by Hoyt and Co., a Melbourne firm, the latter carrying the mails. Cobb and Co., dispatch two coaches daily for Healesville, one for Warburton and one for Yarra Flats." (Lilydale, 4 Mar 1886, p.2)

"RAILWAYS OVERLAND. Melbourne, Ballarat and Ararat to Adelaide by Rail: Twenty-three Hours Actual Travelling from Melbourne. Night's Rest on the Road. Good Hotel Accommodation, Through Fares: Melbourne to Adelaide: First class, £4 41; second class, £3 3s. Ballaarat to Adelaide: First class, £2 13s.; second Class, £2 16s. Ararat to Adelaide: First class, £3 6s. 6d. second class, £2 11s. Booking Offices: Melbourne: Albion Hotel, Bourke-street East. Ballarat: Cobb and Co.'s Office, Lydiard-streets East. Ararat: Tusons's Hotel. Robertson, Wagner and Co., Agents for C. and E. Millar." (Advertising, 27 Aug 1886, p.1)

"COBB AND CO.'S COACHES leave Club Hotel Sale to Bairnsdale ... Cobb and Co.'s Booking Office, T. Hunter, Sale. Robertson, Wagner & Co." Also advertised "FOR THE TOILET. AYER'S HAIR VIGOR is indispensable to complete a toilet. It is an agreeably perfumed dressing ... It stimulates weak and thin hair to renewed growth, and restores faded or gray hair to its original color and beauty." (Gippsland Mercury, 30 Dec 1886, p.1)

1887 – "THE COACHES.—Monday last was a black letter day with the Healesville coaches. On the trip down in the morning Cobb and Co. and Hoyt and Co. came into collision the other side of the Yarra Grange gate, with the result that the swingle bar attached to the latter was broken. On the first up trip of Hoyt's coach, one of the horses commenced to prance round at Hill's, and nearly freed himself from the fastenings. On the evening trip down of Cobb and Co. one of the horses gave out through the excessive heat and fell at Park's Sportsman's Arms Hotel, considerably knocking itself about, and had to be left behind. THE LATE ACCIDENT.—On Friday last Messrs. Cobb and Co. despatched a special conveyance to Narbethong in charge of Mr. W. Newman, for the purpose of conveying Mr. Josephs, who was recently so severely injured near that place, to Lilydale and thence to Melbourne.

A start was made from Miller's Hotel at 4 a.m. on Saturday, and the 'spur' was crossed in due course, weights being attached to the vehicle coming down the incline, and Edgecumbe's Hotel, Healesville, was reached in time for breakfast, after which the party indulged in a good rest, and Lilydale was reached in time for the evening train, from whence Mr. Josephs was conveyed to Melbourne, and then on to his home at St. Kilda. Mr. Josephs, notwithstanding his severe injuries, is progressing very favorably, and the little boy, who it was at first thought had sustained concussion of the brain, is now apparently all right." (No Title, 14 Jan 1887, p.2)

"THE EASTERN DIVISION OF VICTORIA ... Leaving Melbourne for Frankston by the train ... Prince's Bridge station ... Richmond, South Yarra, Hawthorn and Toorak ... the sandy plateau of Caulfield, with its racecourse ... Glen Huntly and the embryonic suburban towns of North Road and McKinnon ... Between South Brighton and Mordialloc, a distance of six miles, Highett, Cheltenham and Mentone intervene ; the first and second of these places have recently sprung into existence, and the third is an old established town surrounded by market gardens ... Beyond this, the railway skirts the great Carrum Swamp for a distance of nine miles and terminates for the present at Frankston ... A good coach road crosses a somewhat uninteresting tract of country between Frankston and Hastings. The latter is a straggling village, lying on the edge of a salt marsh which stretches down to the shallow waters of an extensive lagoon flecked with the white wings of the sea-birds that perch on the green islets left bare by the receding tide." (Picturesque atlas of Australasia/ edited by Andrew Garran, p.293)

1888 – "THE MELBOURNE EXHIBITION ...The attendance at the Centennial International Exhibition during the week ending October 20 was 60,691 a slight improvement only on that of the preceding week. THE CAUFIELD RACES are credited with having detracted from the attendance on Saturday ... luncheon ... about 60 gentlemen attended ... Mr. W. A. B. Gellibrand, President of the Legislative Council of Tasmania ... The only toast was that of 'The Queen,' after which the chairman offered a cordial welcome to the visitors. He stated that Mr. Gellibrand's father was one of a party of gentlemen who in the early days made a treaty with the [First Nations People] for the purchase of 350,000 acres of land, including the whole of the site of the city of Melbourne ... In acknowledging the welcome Mr. Gellibrand said that the circumstances to which Sir James MacBain had alluded, were subjects upon which he could not reflect with pleasure, for when his father came to this colony he was lost, and no trace of him was ever found, and the treaty concluded with the [First Nations Peoples] was annulled by the New South Wales Government, and the result was disastrous to his family." (The Melbourne Exhibition, 30 Oct 1888, p.3)

1900 Tarcoola mail coach - Courtesy State Library South Australia

1870 Northeast Tasmana, Horse stuck in the mud - Courtesy Libraries Tasmania

1928 The camel mail on the Cordillo run, in the far north. The vehicle shown is probably the last of the old 'Cobb's coaches' now in use - Observer, Adelaide, 23 Jun 1928, p.36

1900 Pacifying the horses after they bolted and detached themselves from the mail coach - Courtesy National Archives Australia

Chapter Seven

Coaching Victoria

1890s & 1900s

'Old Jack' of Coaching Days

Lor', yes! my coaching days are 'done!' I'm but a worn-out horse
That raced to win—but ended lame upon Life's stony course,
Time was when no one drove a coach with steadier hand than I;
O'er rough or smooth—'twas in the blood—I made the horses fly.
The townsfolk took a pride in me; and I in my good name;
I never took a drop too much, whatever went or came …

My heart was soft to helpless things—I'd a little girl, you see,
That always kept the balance straight between the road and me.
She knew the horses, every one, and called them all by name—
'Boxer,' 'Trumps,' and 'Killaloe,' 'Old Ranger,' 'Bob,' and 'Game.'
And never yet the coach was in, but she was standing there,
With the light from out the stables like a glory on her hair …

Her eyes were blue as heaven above; her hair was rings of gold;
They used to say the like of her was never meant grow old.,
Well, one wild winter came our way, and cut the roads up rough,
For once, I found work pretty stiff, and luck out, sure enough!
The trees were falling thick as leaves with every blast that blew.
And many a tiring job I had to cut my passage through.

The flats were like a glue-pot; but, driving rain or gale,
Late or early must arrive the Queen's own Royal Mail …
And never captain loved his boat with stronger love than I.
Loved that old coach of Cobb and Co.'s I pulled through wet or dry …

My little one fell ill that year, she'd caught a feverish cold;
The doctor said her case was bad, on life she'd little hold …

She loved to hear my voice, I knew, a singing her to sleep—
She'd never mind how loud it was; how rough-and coarse and deep!
My little maid, she leaned on me as trusting as a dove;
She knew the height and breadth, you see, of her old father's love!
One morning when I had to go, she did not seem so bright,
But whispered, 'I will clap my hands when you come home to-night!'

All day it rained without a break, and, on the journey back,
I saw a giant gum-tree fall right crash across the track …
I reached the town. It seemed to me all voices sounded queer.
Less hearty in their greetings—and my heart stood still with fear …

And though she could not hear my voice, I held her to my breast;
And sang the songs I used to sing, the songs she loved the best …

* * * *

That's many a long, long year ago!—I never thought to tell,
The sorrow of a worn-out heart that kept old secrets well!
I wish the Boss above would give His order for the track.
Where the old are let down lightly, and the tired ones don't go back.
I'm old and tired enough, He knows! No need to further roam—
Ah, God, to hear her clap her hands, and cry 'My Daddy's home!'

By Marion Miller Knowles.
(Original Poetry, 25 Jan 1908, p.51)

1889 Horses, Black Hill, Port Arlington, "When shall we three meet again" - Courtesy State Library Victoria

Examples of Cobb and Co. Coaching Lines, Victoria—1890s & 1900s

1890

Cobb and Co.—Proprietors not listed
- 7 Feb 1890 Cobb and Co.—Connect with Victorian Railways to Ballarat ... Scarsdale to Linton ... O'Meara's Junction ... Skipton ... Streatham; Special Tickets ... Queenscliff, Ocean Grove and Brougham Loch
- 26 Sep 1890 Cobb and Co.—Connect with Victorian Railways to Ballarat, Scarsdale, Skipton, Streatham; Waubra, Avoca, St. Arnaud; Ballarat and Miner's Rest
- Cobb and Co.—Molesworth to Alexandra

Cobb and Co.—Robertson, Wagner and Co.
- 29 Apr 1890 Cobb & Co.—Hay to Hillston and Gunbar; Carrathool and Hillston

Cobb and Co.—Western Stage Company
- 26 Sep 1890 Cobb and Co.—Special arrangements, night or day Geelong to Queenscliff; Geelong to Ocean Grove and Barwon Heads; Coach and Rail ... summer months ... Cobb and Co.'s offices, Melbourne, Geelong, Ballarat and Sandhurst
- 21 Oct 1890 Cobb & Co.'s Western Telegraph Line of Royal Mail Coaches—For Mortlake via Hochkirch, Penhurst, Caramut, Hexham; For Apsley, via Cavendish, Balmoral, Harrow, and Edenhope; For Port Fairy, Koroit, and Warrnambool via Byaduk, Macarthur, and Orford; Koroit and Kirkstall; Penshurst Railway Station to township; Coleraine to Harrow; Casterton and Harrow; Port Fairy to Portland; WICKLIFFE ROAD Railway Station and Lake Bolac

Cobb and Co.—Vines and M'Phee
- 7 Feb 1890 Cobb and Co.—Ballan, Blackwood, Trentham, Myrniong, Bacchus Marsh; Ballarat and Lexton; Lake Bolac to Wickliffe Road Railway Station in time for Hamilton and Ballarat trains
- 26 Sep 1890 Cobb and Co.—Gordon and Egerton Railway Station

1891

Cobb and Co.—Proprietors not listed
- 1891 Cobb and Co.'s Coaches—Linton to Skipton, Streatham, O'Meara's; Seaside Excursion Tickets ... Ballarat to Ocean Grove, Barwon Heads, Clifton Springs, Portarlington
- 25 Mar 1891 Cobb and Co.—Waubra, Avoca, and St. Arnaud; Ballarat and Miner's Rest; Connect with Victorian Railways
- 28 Mar 1891 Cobb and Co.—Clifton Springs ... meet all trains at Drysdale and Melbourne steamers at Portarlington
- 24 Dec 1891 Cobb and Co.—connecting with train [Ballarat] to and from Linton and Skipton, Linton and Streatham, Linton and O'Meara's Junction; Ballarat and Miners' Rest; Ballarat and Mount Blowhard

Cobb and Co.—Robertson, Wagner and Co.
- 26 Feb 1891 Cobb & Co.—Swan Hill to Euston, Mildura and Wentworth, Swan Hill to Bairanald

Cobb and Co.—M'Phee and Co.
- 21 Jan 1889 No longer listed as Cobb and Co.—Ballarat and Lexton

Cobb and Co.—Western Stage Company
- 25 Mar 1891 Cobb and Co.—Geelong to Queenscliff
- 31 May 1891 Cobb and Co.—Geelong and Barwon Heads via Marshalltown; Geelong to ocean Grove via Wallington ... Railway Platform and Ocean Grove
- 22 Sep 1891 Cobb & Co.'s Western Telegraph Line of Royal Mail Coaches—For Croxton East, via Hochkirch; For Apsley, via Cavendish, Balmoral, Harrow, and Edenhope; For Port Fairy, Koroit, and Warrnambool via Byaduk, Macarthur, and Orford; Penshurst and Mortlake; Penshurst Railway Station. Conveyance to the township meets each train. Special arrangements for commercial gentlemen; Coleraine to Harrow; Casterton and Harrow ; Port Fairy to Portland; WICKLIFFE ROAD Railway Station and Lake Bolac; Special Notice Livery and Letting Stable at Penshurst
- 15 Nov 1901 Cobb and Co.—Ballarat to Pitfield via Smythesdale and Cape Clear ... leaves Craig's Stables, Ballarat, Telephone 188
- 14 Dec 1891 Cobb and Co.—Portarlington and Drysdale Railway Station

Cobb and Co.—Vines and M'Phee
- 25 Mar 1891 Cobb and Co.—Gordon Egerton and railway station
- 31 May 1891 Cobb and Co.—LEIGH ROAD to Rokewood passing through Teesdale, Shelford, and Warrambine ... connecting with trains to Geelong
- 24 Dec 1891 Cobb and Co.—By Rail and Coach Ballarat and Port Campbell ... coaches leave Camperdown on arrival of first train; Geelong to Queenscliff ... special arrangements day or night; Ballarat and Clifton Springs and Portarlington; Gordon Egerton and railway station (Vines and M'Phee); Lake Bolac to WICKLIFFE ROAD Railway Station not listed as Cobb and Co.

1892

Cobb and Co.—Proprietors not listed
- 20 May 1892 Cobb and Co.—Waubra, Avoca, and St. Arnaud (Lexton, Lamplough, Moonambel, Landsboro, Redbank, Stuart Mill); Ballarat and Miner's Rest; Connect with Victorian Railways Cobb and Co.'s Coaches ... Linton to Skipton, Streatham, O'Meara's
- 12 Jul 1892 Cobb and Co.—Moe, Walhalla

Cobb and Co.—Western Stage Company
- 20 May 1892 Cobb and Co.—Geelong to Queenscliff
- 2 Aug 1892 Cobb & Co.'s Western Telegraph Line of Royal Mail Coaches—For Apsley, via Cavendish, Balmoral, Harrow and Edenhope; For Macarthur, via North and South Byaduk; Mortlake, Caramut; Coleraine to Harrow; Casterton and Harrow; Port Fairy to Portland; WICKLIFFE-ROAD Railway Station and Lake Bolac; Casterton to Mount Gambier ... horses carefully driven
- 20 Dec 1892 Cobb and Co.—Portarlington for Geelong and Drysdale

Cobb and Co.—Vines and M'Phee
- 19 Jan 1893 Cobb and Co.—LEIGH ROAD to Rokewood
- 20 May 1892 Cobb and Co.—Through Tickets by Rail or Coach ... Ballarat and Port Campbell via Camperdown; Gordon Egerton and railway station

1893

Cobb and Co.—Proprietors not listed
- 19 Jan 1893 Cobb and Co.—Geelong and Ocean Grove, via Wallington; Ocean Grove, Barwon Heads, and Spring Creek
- 20 May 1892 Cobb and Co.—Waubra, Avoca, and St. Arnaud (Lexton, Lamplough, Moonambel, Landsboro, Redbank, Stuart Mill); Ballarat and Miner's Rest; Connect with Victorian Railways Cobb and Co.'s Coaches ... Linton to Skipton, Streatham, O'Meara's

Cobb and Co.—Robertson, Wagner and Co.
- 18 Apr 1893 Cobb and Co.—Hay to Melbourne

Cobb and Co.—Western Stage Company
- 19 Jan 1893 Cobb and Co.—Portarlington and Drysdale Railway Station
- 11 Apr 1893 Cobb and Co.—Queenscliff, Moolap, Leopold and Wallington on the QUEENSCLIFF-ROAD, and the other for Drysdale via Moolap, Leopold, and Curlewis
- 8 Aug 1893 Cobb & Co.'s Western Telegraph Line of Royal Mail Coaches—For Apsley, via Cavendish, Balmoral, Harrow and Edenhope; For Macarthur, via North and South Byaduk; Mortlake, Caramut; Coleraine to Harrow; Casterton and Harrow; Fort Fairy to Portland; WICKLIFFE-ROAD Railway Station and Lake Bolac; Macarthur and Port Fairy; Port Fairy and Warrnambool

Cobb and Co.—Vines and M'Phee
- 19 Jan 1893 Cobb and Co.—LEIGH ROAD to Rokewood
- 20 May 1892 Cobb and Co..—Through Tickets, By Rail or Coach ... Ballarat and Port Campbell via Camperdown; Gordon Egerton and railway station

1894

Cobb and Co.—Proprietors not listed
- 1 May 1894 Cobb and Co.—Geelong and Ocean Grove; Geelong to Barwon Heads; Geelong to Drysdale

Cobb and Co.—Robertson, Wagner and Co.
- 5 Jan 1894 Cobb and Co.—Great Reduction in Fares. Hay to Melbourne

Cobb and Co.—Western Stage Company
- 11 Jan 1894 Cobb & Co.'s Western Telegraph Line of Royal Mail Coaches—For Apsley, via Cavendish, Balmoral, Harrow and Edenhope; For Macarthur, via North and South Byaduk; Mortlake, Caramut; Coleraine to Harrow; WICKIFFE-ROAD Railway Station and Lake Bolac; Macarthur and Port Fairy; Port Fairy and Koroit
- 1 May 1894 Cobb and Co.—Drysdale, Portarlington, and Clifton Springs

Cobb and Co.—Vines and M'Phee
- 1 May 1894 Cobb and Co.—LEIGH ROAD to Rokewood, connecting with trains to and from Geelong

1895

Cobb and Co.—Robertson, Wagner and Co.
- 17 Sep 1895 Cobb & Co.—Deniliquin; Hay to Melbourne

Cobb and Co.—Western Stage Company
- 5 Jan 1895 Cobb & Co.'s Western Telegraph Line of Royal Mail Coaches—For Apsley, via Cavendish, Balmoral, Harrow, and Edenhope; For Macarthur, via North and South Byaduk; Mortlake, Caramut; Coleraine to Harrow; WICKIFFE-ROAD Railway Station and Lake Bolac; Macarthur and Port Fairy; Port Fairy and Koroit
- 20 Dec 1895 Cobb and Co.—Geelong and Ocean Grove; Geelong and Queenscliff

Cobb and Co.—Vines and M'Phee
- 20 May 1892 Cobb and Co.—Through Tickets, By Rail or Coach ... Ballarat and Port Campbell via Camperdown; Gordon Egerton and railway station

1896

Cobb and Co.—Proprietors not listed
- 14 Jan 1896 Cobb and Co.—LEIGH ROAD to Rokewood, Ballarat and Rokewood; Barwon Heads and Ocean Grove; Geelong and Ocean Grove; Geelong to Drysdale and Portarlington; Drysdale, Portarlington, and Clifton Springs; Portarlington and Drysdale; Geelong to Steiglitz
- 22 May 1896 Cobb & Co.'s Cab—Meredith and Steiglitz
- 6 Oct 1896 Cobb and Co.—Ballarat to Miner's Rest
- 17 Oct 1896 Cobb & Co.'s Coaches—Mansfield to Wood's Point; Mansfield, Jamieson, connecting with Sheehan's coach to Wood's Point; Cobb & Co.'s Telegraph Line of Coaches—Moe, Walhalla

Cobb and Co.—Robertson, Wagner and Co.
- 7 Jan 1896 Cobb and Co.—Bairnsdale & Omeo
- 21 Jan 1896 Cobb & Co.—Booligal & Hay; Hay to Melbourne (Robertson, Wagner and Co.)
- 7 Feb 1896 Cobb & Co.—Discontinuance of the Deniliquin day coach between Hay and Deniliquin
- 25 Mar 1896 Cobb & Co. Royal Mail Coaches—Balranald for Oxley and Hay

Cobb and Co.—Vines and M'Phee
- 6 Oct 1896 Cobb and Co.—Ballarat and Rokewood

Cobb and Co.—Western Stage Company
- 14 Jan 1896 Cobb and Co.—Queenscliff stables; Ocean Grove Coach meets Melbourne steamers at Jetty
- 6 Oct 1896 Cobb and Co.—Geelong and Queenscliff; Ballarat to Barwon Heads or Ocean Grove
- 24 Oct 1896 Cobb & Co.'s Royal Mail Coaches—For Hamilton and Balmoral; For Macarthur, via North and South Byaduk; Coleraine to Harrow; WICKLIFFE ROAD Railway Station and Lake Bolac; Casterton to Penola thence to Narracoorte and Adelaide; Casterton to Mount Gambier; Macarthur and Port Fairy; Koroit and Port Fairy; exclusive right of entry with cabs to Hamilton Station ... Thos. Vines, District Manager

Cobb and Co.—A. Grant
- 17 Oct 1896 Cobb & Co.'s Telegraph Line of Coaches—Moe and Walhalla

Cobb and Co.—Jas. A Lyall
- 24 Oct 1896 Cobb & Co.—Harrow to Noradjuha

1897

Cobb and Co.—Proprietors not listed
- 15 Apr1897 Cobb & Co.'s Telegraph Line of Coaches—Moe and Walhalla

- 19 May 1897 Cobb and Co. CAB—Meredith to Steiglitz

Cobb and Co.—Robertson & Wagner
- 24 Feb 1897 Cobb & Co. Royal Mail Coaches—Balranald for Oxley and Hay

Cobb and Co.—Vines and M'Phee
- 19 May 1897 Cobb and Co.—Ballarat and Rokewood

Cobb and Co.—Western Stage Company
- 25 Jan 1897 Cobb and Co.—Special coaches ... Ocean Grove, Barwon Heads and Torquay
- 19 May 1897 Cobb and Co.—Geelong and Queenscliff
- 24 Oct 1896 Cobb & Co.—Harrow to Noradjuha

1898

Cobb and Co.—Proprietors not listed
- 7 Jun 1898 Cobb and Co.—Meredith to Steiglitz

Cobb and Co.—Robertson & Wagner
- 24 Feb 1897 Cobb & Co. Royal Mail Coaches—Balranald for Oxley and Hay

Cobb and Co.—Western Stage Company
- 8 Oct 1898 Cobb & Co.—Korite Inn Stables, Coleraine

Cobb and Co.—Vines and M'Phee
- 7 Jun 1898 Cobb and Co.—Barwon Heads, Ocean Grove, Torquay; Ballarat and Rokewood; Rokewood and LEIGH ROAD; Meet each train to and from Gordon and Egerton and Railway Station

1899

Cobb and Co.—Proprietors not listed
- 10 Feb 1899 Cobb and Co.—The Tyres, Moondarra, Walhalla
- 22 Mar 1899 Cobb's (steamer or rail and coach)—Ocean Grove, Barwon Heads, Clifton Springs, Anglesea, Airey's Inlet, Torquay; Rokewood, Mount Mercer; Ballarat, Rokewood; Cobb and Co.'s four-horse Coach—Moe, Walhalla

Cobb and Co.—Robertson & Wagner
- Continued until 1 April 1899

Cobb and Co.—Vines and M'Phee
- 12 Jan 1899 Cobb and Co.—Combined Rail and Coach ... Ballarat, via Geelong, Barwon Head; Ballarat to Mount Mercer, via Buninyong; Ballarat and Rokewood; Rokewood and LEIGH ROAD; Meet each train to and from Gordon and Egerton and Railway Station

Cobb and Co.—Western Stage Company
- 12 Jan 1899 Cobb and Co.—Geelong and Queenscliff
- 8 Jul 1899 Cobb and Co.—Livery, Letting & Coaching Stables ... Hamilton and Coleraine; Cabs available all hours during the day or night ... Cab rank opposite Post-office; Hamilton to Macarthur passing through Byaduk North, and South en route

1900

Cobb and Co.—Proprietors not listed
- 10 Jan 1900 Cobb & Co.—Geelong, Drysdale, Portarlington, via Moolap, Curlewis; combined steamer and coach tickets issued from Melbourne to Ocean Grove, Barwon Heads, Anglesea and Airey's Inlet, Clifton Springs, and Queenscliff
- 1Aug 1900 Cobb and Co.'s Coaches—Mount William Rush via Wickliffe
- 6 Sep 1900 Cobb and Co.—Cape Clear, Pitfield, Ballarat
- 22 Nov 1900 Cobb & Co.—Wickliffe, Lake Bolac

Cobb and Co.—Vines and M'Phee
- Cobb & Co.'s Coaches—LEIGH ROAD, Shelford, and Rokewood connects with train to Geelong and Melbourne; Ballarat, Napoleons and Rokewood; Ballarat, Pitifield, Glenfine Mines

Cobb and Co.—Western Stage Company
- 21 Aug 1900 Cobb and Co.'s Coaches—Mount William Rush ... WICKLIFFE ROAD, Mt. William; Livery, Letting & Coaching Stables ... Hamilton and Coleraine.; Cabs available all hours during the day or night ... Cab rank opposite Post-office; Hamilton to Macarthur passing through Byaduk North, and South en route

Cobb and Co.—Alexander Allan Grant/Grant, Sheehan & Co.
- 2 Jan 1900 Cobb & Co.'s Coaches—Healesville to Marysville and Walker's Yarra Track
- 5 Oct 1900 Messers Cobb and Co.—Moe to Walhalla

1901

Cobb and Co.—Proprietors not listed
- 15 Jan 1901 Cobb and Co.'s Coaches—Mount William Rush ... WICKLIFFE ROAD, Mt. William; Wickliffe, Lake Bolac
- 22 Jun 1901 Cobb & Co.'s Royal Mail Daily Line Coaches—Toongabbie and Walhalla

Cobb and Co.—Vines and M'Phee
- 3 Apr 1901 Cobb & Co.'s Coaches—LEIGH ROAD, Shelford, and Rokewood; Ballarat, Napoleons and Rokewood; Ballarat, Pitifield, Glenfine Mines ... Craig's Stables, Ballarat

Cobb and Co.—Western Stage Company
- 15 Jan 1901 Cobb and Co.'s Coaches—Mount William Rush ... WICKLIFFE ROAD, Mt. William; WICKLIFFE ROAD, Lake Bolac
- 15 Nov 1901 Cobb & Co.'s Coaches—Geelong, Torquay (leaves Palace Hotel) via Mt. Duneed and Germantown; Geelong, Anglesea and Airey's Inlet; Geelong, Ocean Grove via Moolap, Leopold and Wellington; Geelong, Barwon Heads via Marshall town and Connewarre; Geelong, Clifton Springs ... Leaves Portarlington on arrival of steamers, returning to connect with steamers to Melbourne ... Leaves Drysdale on arrival of trains; Portarlington, Bellarine, Drysdale via Moolap and Curlewis; Drysdale, Portarlington and Clifton Springs; LEIGH ROAD to Rosewood via Teesdale and Shelford; Ballarat to Pitfield Plains via Smythesdale and Cape Clear

1902

Cobb and Co.—Western Stage Company
- 14 Feb 1902 Cobb & Co.—Seaside Coaches ... Geelong, Torquay, Anglesea, Barwon Heads, Ocean Grove, Clifton Springs, Queenscliff, Portarlington, and Drysdale; LEIGH ROAD to Rokewood, via Teesdale and Shelford; Ballarat to Pitfield Plains via Smythesdale and Cape Clear

1903

Cobb and Co.—Western Stage Company
- 3 Feb 1902 Cobb & Co.—Central Stables ... Baits, stands, and liveries a speciality ... Man always in attendance at night ... Seaside Coaches ... Geelong, Torquay, Anglesea, Barwon Heads, Ocean Grove, Clifton Springs, Drysdale, Bellarine and Portarlington ... Parcels carried at special rates ... Cobb and Co.'s Head Office, Malop-street, Geelong. Telephone 1... Ballarat to Pitfield Plains Via Smythesdale and Cape Clear ... LEIGH ROAD to Rokewood, Via Teesdale and Shelford

1904

Cobb and Co.—Proprietors not listed
- 20 Jan 1904 Cobb & Co.—Geelong, Torquay, Anglesea and Airey's Inlet, Barwon Heads, Ocean Grove, Clifton Springs, Drysdale, Bellarine and Portarlington; Ballarat to Pitfield Plains via Scarsdale

1905

Cobb and Co.—Proprietors not listed
- 6 Feb 1905 Cobb and Co.'s—Ballarat to Torquay, Barwon Heads, Ocean Grove, Anglesea, and Airey's Inlet, Geelong, Torquay, Anglesea and Airey's Inlet; Ballarat and Smythesdale Ballarat and Newtown, Scarsdale, Ballarat and Cape Clear, Ballarat and Pitfield, Ballarat and Illabarook, Ballarat and Junction, Ballarat and Rokewood; Ballarat to Skipton and Streatham
- 22 May 1905 Cobb and Co.—Mail Service. Tenders Accepted ... P.O. and R.S. Geelong; clearing Geelong letter boxes; Geelong, Ocean Grove; Ocean Grove, Marcus Hill; Geelong, Curlewis; Geelong, Torquay and Torquay, Anglesea River; P.O. and R.S. Queenscliff; Queenscliff, Point Lonsdale

1906

Cobb and Co.—Proprietors not listed
- 23 Jan 1906 Cobb & Co.—Summer Time Table ... Geelong to Torquay, Geelong to Anglesea and Airey's Inlet, Geelong to Barwon Heads, Geelong to Ocean Grove, Queenscliff to Ocean Grove through Combined Steamer or Rail and Coach
- 13 Nov 1906 Cobb and Co.—Ballarat and Pitfield via Cape Clear, thence to Illabarook, Rokewood Junction, Rokewood; Ballarat and Smythesdale, Newtown. Scarsdale, Cape Clear, Pitfield, Illabarook, Junction, Rokewood

1907

Cobb and Co.—Proprietors not listed
- 8 Jun 1907 Cobb & Co.—Geelong to Torquay, Geelong to Anglesea and Airey's Inlet, Geelong to Barwon Heads, Geelong to Ocean Grove, Queenscliff and Portarlington through combined steamer and coach tickets
- 24 Jun 1907 Cobb and Co.—Ballarat and Pitfield via Cape Clear, thence to Illabarook, Rokewood Junction, Rokewood; Ballarat and Smythesdale, Newtown. Scarsdale, Cape Clear, Pitifield, Illabarook, Junction, Rokewood

1908

Cobb and Co.—Proprietors not listed
- 22 Apr 1908 Cobb's Combined Tickets—Torquay, Barwon Heads, Ocean Grove, Anglesea, Airey's Inlet
- 8 Aug 1908 Cobb and Co.—Ballarat and Pitfield via Cape Clear, thence to Illabarook, Rokewood Junction, Rokewood; Ballarat and Smythesdale, Newtown. Scarsdale, Cape Clear, Illabarook, Junction, Rokewood

1909

Cobb and Co.—Proprietors not listed
- 8 Jun 1907 Cobb & Co.—Drag Excursions ... Geelong, Torquay, Barwon Heads, Anglesea and Airey's Inlet, Ocean Grove

Along the tracks—1890s & 1900s

See *Appendix 2: Supporting evidence for Cobb and Co. coaching lines, Victoria*

1890 – ACCIDENT "An accident happened to Cobb's coach on Wednesday while journeying from Molesworth to Alexandra. When within a mile and a half of the latter township the horses swerved off the road, coming in contact with a culvert railing, and throwing the driver from his seat. The horses then dashed on at a 'terrific pace,' running over the bank of Johnson's Creek, 10 feet high. The driver was picked up in an unconscious state. Fortunately there were only two male passengers, who just managed to jump out before reaching the creek, and were not hurt beyond receiving a shaking. The coach was smashed badly." (No Title, 18 Apr 1890, p.2)

"COBB & CO. Hay to Hillston and Gunbar ... Carrathool and Hillston ... Robertson, Wagner & Co." while "Rabbit skins bought in any quantity ... Sydney ... AMERICAN LEAF ... Tobacco. Dixson & Sons. The largest Factory ... Cigarettes are fast securing this market 10,000 per hour—far outrivalling all other patents in the world ... the choicest of imported goods ... Elegant slide boxes and packets of 40, 20 and 10 Cigarettes." (Advertising, 29 Apr 1890, p.1)

"A WINTER TRIP TO OMEO. By Horresco Referens That it is the unexpected which happens, is, I believe, a very true saying, and undoubtedly in my case the unexpected did happen, for I should have considerably doubted the sanity of any person who told me when I left Princes' Bridge station last Monday morning en route for Omeo, that I should have to complete my journey to that place by a thirty odd miles walk over ranges and fording creeks. The weather looked gloomy enough when the train glided out of the station, but at Caulfield the sun was shining ... Warragul was reached, the rain was pouring down, and from there to Bairnsdale it never ceased. A speedy drive brought me to Cobb and Co.'s office ... guess my dismay when the genial proprietor Mr. Norton, of the hotel, informed me this could not be done, as all the places were already filled ... I implored to be taken on, even if I rode on the roof, in the terrible downpour which was then going on ; but as I spoke the coach drove off ... the next best thing appeared to me was to go back ; so I wended my way to the telegraph office ... when Mr. Norton rushed in, said he had made a mistake, that, there was one seat vacant in the coach, and if I took his cab it would overtake it. In the twinkling of an eye I rushed to the cab and away we went after the coach. It was a stiff chase though not a long one because ere three miles had been covered we came up with it, and I and my baggage were duly transferred. The interior was pretty crowded and its struck me that all the passengers were of the opinion that my room would have been more acceptable than my company, but they were too polite to express their sentiments ... Bruthen was reached ... I was in the midst of my tea when, the coach driver announced to me that after all there had been no mistake, and all the places from Bruthen to Omeo had been booked ... owing to the kindness of a lady ... hearing that it was of some importance I should reach Omeo without delay, generously gave me her seat consenting to remain at Bruthen till next day. With the feeling that I had at last triumphed over all difficulties, I retired to rest and rose refreshed at 4 o'clock to resume the journey. The morning was as black as Erebus—like a waterspout the rain fell ... Away we went in the darkness ... An early start on a wet morning is not conducive to make persons look cheerful, and a two hours ride in a close coach, over a rough road,

with a passenger or two suffering from coach sickness,

affect the complexion of most persons, and all the insides looked, even if they did not feel so, pretty seedy. It is wonderful, however, what a restorative a nip of whisky is. I passed a flask round, there was not a refusal ... On arriving at the old Tambo crossing ... the river was rushing ... in two hours Fraser's crossing was reached ... the river was deep, and running fast and furious ... if I wished to proceed I had to 'pad the hoof.' ... The younger members of the party were not persuaded from leaving Frazer's ... we lost sight of the horsemen ... the work was hard ... we came to a mountain torrent ... by means of clambering over the bough of a tree which leaned over it, we succeeded in getting over it ... Range after range had to be clambered in quick succession, innumerable mountain torrents to be forded, till our bodies were becoming thoroughly exhausted, and frequent rests had to be made. Fortunately our 'spirits' did not fail, as it was a piece of fair fortune that I carried a goodly flask ... we caught the glimmer of a light at Quinn's. A few minutes walk enabled us to reach the hotel ... We were warmly congratulated on all sides on our safe arrival, and the fact that we had made the journey in so short a time, viz., four and a half hours ... Capital accommodation and a night's rest made one as fresh as a lark ... I started by myself for a 20-mile tramp ... the rain never ceased falling ... The roar of the Tambo was almost deafening ; the sight was grand in the extreme ; every now and again trees would be undermined, and fall into the river with a sound like that of a park of artillery being fired ... As night closed in, I reached Omeo ... Wet and tired I soon found dry clothes and repose at my old friend Bazeley's Hotel and I had the proud satisfaction of feeling that I by using the pedertrian powers I have been favoured with I was enabled to ... keep my engagement with the public." (A Winter Trip to Omeo, 17 Jul 1890, p.8)

1891 – "COBB AND CO.'S LIVERY AND LETTING STABLES ... P. Hodgetts, Manager. (Vines and M'Phee) ... Telephone Craig's Royal Hotel Stables—No. 188. Forester's George Hotel Stables—No. 188; Cobb and Co. ... Seaside Excursion Tickets ... Ballarat to Ocean Grove, Barwon Heads, Clifton Springs, Portarlington ... Cobb and Co.'s Office, Craig's Stable; Cobb and Co. ... Gordon Egerton and railway station (Vines and M'Phee); Cobb and Co. ... Geelong to Queenscliff (Western Stage Company); Cobb and Co. Waubra, Avoca, and St. Arnaud; Cobb and Co. Ballarat and Miner's Rest; Connect with Victorian Railways Cobb and Co.'s Coaches ... Linton to Skipton, Streatham, O'Meara's; Railway Time-Table for March ... Ballarat to Melbourne, Geelong to Ballarat, Geelong to Melbourne, Ballarat to Stawell, Ballarat to Maryborough, Ballarat to Buninyong, Ballarat to Waubra, Ballarat to Linton, Ballarat to Daylesford, Ballarat to Portland" Advertised on the same page "BALLARAT SANITARY AND DEODORISING COMPANY ... Emptying pans ... Dead horses removed ... Manufacture of the Jubilee Disinfectant ... All orders promptly attended to" (Advertising, 25 Mar 1891, p.1)

"THE OMEO ROAD AGAIN BLOCKED. COACH TRAFFIC SUSPENDED. Yesterday morning, Mr J. Norton, the Bairnsdale agent for Cobb and Co., received a telegram from Tambo Crossing, instructing him not to book passengers beyond Bruthen until further notice, the recent rains having again rendered the Tambo Valley road impassable for wheel traffic." (The Omeo Road again blocked, 17 Sep 1891, p.2)

1892 – STRUCK BY LIGHTNING "A drover named Major, who was in charge of Cobb and Co.'s sheep, was stuck dead by lightning at Wellington." (Odds and Ends, 16 Jan 1892, p.2)

1893 – SPECIAL EXCURSION TRIPS "Next Wednesday special excursion trips at reduced fares will be made by Cobb and Co.'s coaches to Ocean Grove, Barwon Heads, and Spring Creek" while written on the same page "A novel display in connection with the manufacture of HATS FROM RABBIT FUR and wool is now being made in the show window of Messrs Bright and Hitchcocks' establishment, in Moorabool-street.

In regard to the industry for profitably turning to account the fur of the rabbit, which has long figured conspicuously in the list of vermin, the firm named exhibit in a cage a pair of live wild rabbits, and on a line with the rodents the various processes by which their skins and fur become sources of profit and comfort are well illustrated, splendid samples of the hats made from the rabbit fur being shown as the final stage. It is a very interesting exhibit and the fact that the Victorian manufactured hats, made from fur, are driving out of the market the English make from the same material, owing to the cheapness of the article, which is as durable and as attractively manufactured as the imported, should prove doubly so to all who are anxious to support Austral products." (Town Talk, 19 May 1893, p.2)

"ALLEGED LARCENY FROM A LIVERY STABLE An unappreciated visit to the Steiglitz goldfields was paid on Saturday evening by four young men from Geelong, who were arrested on a charge of vagrancy by Constables O'Sullivan and M'Guigan ... They were charged at the watchhouse with larceny as bailees of a horse, buggy and harness, the property of the Western Stage Company. On Saturday afternoon ... two of the prisoners ... went to Cobb and Co.'s stables in Malop-street and hired the horse and a double-seated buggy, for the purpose of driving to the railway station to meet a special train from Melbourne with the Carlton football players, in order to convey couple of their friends to the football ground. The authorities at the stables were apparently unaware of the fact that owing to the continued want of success this season of the Carlton football club's representatives the club is not in a financial position to engage special trains. The Carlton players and supporters came from Melbourne by the steamer Edina, and it is quite evident that the hirers of the horse and buggy had made up their minds to enjoy a trip into the country ... On the way down they met Cobb and Co's. coach returning from the goldfields, and the fact that they put the buggy rugs over their heads when driving past the coach aroused the suspicions of the coach driver, who reported the matter on arrival in Geelong, and the local police were apprised of the affair. The quartette enjoyed themselves in the Steiglitz township on Saturday night, and after the closing of the business places there they sought shelter in a shed. After midnight the attention of the Steiglitz police was attracted to the shed ... These resulted in the police deciding at one o'clock on Sunday morning to place the gang under arrest ... The party had a very cold journey back to Geelong, and returned to Moorabool-street in anything but a happy mood—cold and hungry." (Alleged Larceny From a Livery Stable, 25 Sep 1893, p.4)

1896 – "COBB & CO. To and from Booligal & Hay ... Cobb & Co. Great Reduction in fares. Hay to Melbourne ... Passengers may break their journey on a single or return ticket at any stage between Deniliquin and Melbourne. Return tickets available for three months ... Robertson, Wagner & Co." Advertised on the same page "AYER'S SARSAPARILLA —CURES— Indigestion, Sleeplessness, Loss of Strength and Appetite, and Nervous Disorders" (Advertising, 21 Jan 1896, p.1)

"COBB & CO. ... Coach between Hay and Deniliquin has been discontinued for the present, but will be resumed in the cool weather. Robertson, Wagner & Co." (Advertising, 7 Feb 1896, p.3)

"THE MAIL CONTRACTS. LOST BY COBB AND Co. ... The loss of the contract from Bairnsdale to Omeo by, Messrs. Cobb and Co. may. be a very serious matter to those residents of Omeo, if the new contractor does not perform his work satisfactorily for there is no doubt, that Messrs. Cobb and Co. have done a very great deal towards the opening up of the Omeo district ... The Bairnsdale to Omeo service is no light undertaking, as 40 horses and 7 coaches are required either on the road or ready for emergency."

While "On Monday a very HEAVY STORM occurred on the Divide between the Bundarrah and Middle Creek. The rain poured down for an hour and a small creek there rose 15 ft. Logs of great length came rushing down and the flood made a wreck of one big flat on Middle Creek." (The Mail Contracts, 19 Feb 1896, p.2)

Other news of the day ... "OLD MATURED AUSTRALIAN WINES ... Bulk and Bottle ... can highly recommend for Invalids' use; FRENCH P D CORSETS ... Awarded 10 Gold Medals ... are unrivalled for perfect fit, beauty of finish, and style ... Obtainable from all leading drapers in every variety of shape and style. Many inferior imitations being offered under similar sounding names, purchasers are requested to see that each pair bears the Manufacturers Trade Mark on brand inside; VIGOR PILLS for men, 5s 6d.per box, posted. Write W. N. Garfield. Collins-street. Melbourne; RABBIT DESTRUCTION. Arsenic, Strychnine, Phosphorous, Bisulphide of Carbon, Phosphorized Wheat, &C. Sold At Lowest Rates By Bull & Owen, Chemists, Malop-Street; Centrl College 'Knowle House,' FOR BOYS and GIRLS. Principal: Miss Clanchy ... Latin ... French and Arithmetic ... English ... Geography and Physiology ... Geometry. Vacancies for Boarders; WATER WATER WATER TANKS. TANKS. TANKS ... R. H. Sennett, Ryrie-street ... Washing copper, boilers and frames ... Meat safes ... Cockatoo stands ... Telephone 210; Sheepskins, hides, calfskins, tallow, horsehair, and beeswax wanted in any quantities, at highest current rates. W. B. WILTON, Leather Merchant; For Sale.—Cobb And Co. have for sale several useful vehicles, waggonettes, waggons, and buggies at low prices ; also, some useful horses. Apply at Bay View Stables (late Walker's) or at Malop street stables. Western Stage Co.; PUBLICATIONS AND LITERATURE FIREWORKS ! FIREWORKS ! Queen's Birthday, 1896. Henry Franks and Co., Stationers, Etc., Have received a New Supply of all the latest novelties in fireworks; Thacker Bookseller and Stationer ... Has on hand ... New Birth day, Condolence and Wedding Cards; THOMAS' SHEEP DIPPING SPECIFIC. These magnificent preparations are quite, unequalled by any other maker for the eradication of tick, lice, or scab, and really improve the quality of the wools; H. Blomfield Brown & Co., Little Malop-street Geelong; MONEY TO LEND.—Any sums large and small amounts, at moderate rates of interest and without delay. Apply to W. P. Carr. Auctioneer, Ryrie-street, Geelong." (Advertising, 22 May 1896, p.1)

"EDUCATING THE HORSE.—Professor Lichtwark gave a very interesting exhibition at the Western Stage Company's factory yesterday afternoon ... Mr. Lichtwark ... who have had a great deal of experience with horses very much impressed. The Professor took a fractious chestnut filly of Mr. Vines' in hand, and in a very short space of time completely subdued the animal and rendered it tractable by most easy methods. Every movement was easy for both horse and man, and the Professor quietly made the filly lie down without using the slightest force. Another exhibition will be given at the same place on Wednesday afternoon, when a larger attendance is hoped for. Mr. Lichtwark will also give an exposition of horsemanship tonight, at 7.30, at Cobb and Co.'s stables." (Items of News, 18 Aug 1896, p.2)

CABS "During the season Cobb and Co. will have cabs running to the principal sights of the district of Warrnambool. Their telephone number is 65. The charges made by the firm are strictly moderate. The district manager is Mr Thomas Vines." (Cobb and Co., 5 Dec 1896, p.9)

1897 – EXCURSION "To-morrow special excursion trips will be made to and from Melbourne via Portarlington by the steamers Excelsior and Courier ... The Western Stage Company will despatch special coaches to-morrow to Ocean Grove, Barwon Heads and Torquay, leaving Cobb and Co's. office in Malop-street at 9.15 a.m., and returning from the seaside resorts at 4 p.m.

The steamer Bellarine will make numerous excursions to Point Henry tomorrow, and passengers will have an excellent opportunity of viewing at close range the racing of the yachts engaged in the sailing regatta." (Town Talk, 25 Jan 1897, p.2)

"COBB AND CO. Orchardists and others will do well to visit the stand of Messrs Cobb and Co., and inspect their latest improved spray pumps, which were so favorably commented on at last year's show by all who saw them, for their simplicity, durability, effectiveness, and cheapness. They are this year showing 'The Gem' pump for household gardens to their 'Champion' pump for large orchards, the 'Challenge' and 'Favorite' for small orchards. Messrs Cobb and Co. are also exhibiting square and corrugated iron tanks, and their patent water-carting tank, 'specially designed for country use,' as well as wire nettings, wire strainers, and other farming requisites." (Cobb and Co., 4 Sep 1897, p.5)

1901 – "COBB'S THROUGH TICKETS, RAIL AND STEAMER. Ocean Grove, Barwon Heads, Torquay, Anglesey, Airey's Inlet, Clifton Springs. Agents, Huddart, Parker, Hutchison's, Cook's, L. White." Advertised on the same page "MATRIMONY. A.—MARRIAGES CELEBRATED by Ordained Clergymen, ANY denomination with due solemnity, in strictest privacy, at Holt's Matrimonial Agency, 448 Queen street, Melbourne, opposite the Old Cemetery, or elsewhere, from 10 am till 9 p.m. daily, Saturdays included (no notice required) Fee, 10/6; or marriage, with guaranteed gold wedding ring, and necessary witnesses provided, pound1 / 1 /. P.S.—No other charges whatever. All sizes more costly wedding rings kept in stock if required." (Advertising, 12 Aug 1901, p.10)

1902 – MEMORIES "I have received a letter from two of my lifelong friends ... asking me to refresh their memories of the Cobb and Co. days of long ago ... I well remember an incident that happened in 1902. One of the drivers could not blow a bugle—better known as a mailhorn—and every mailman was compelled to carry one of the mail horns strapped on the driving side of his coach. This particular driver could not blow the bugle and our postmaster ... asked him why he did not blow the bugle coming into town. The driver, told him he couldn't but the postmaster told him that was no excuse, and he (the driver) would have to learn. Strange to say, a chap named Sam ... was returning to the town by coach and the driver ... was telling him about his trouble and Sam replied, *Oh, don't worry about that, we'll fix it.* Sam always carried his cornet with him ... When within about 900 yards of the post office, Sam played 'Yankee Doodle,' 'Pop goes the Weasel' and one or two other snappy tunes on his cornet. Needless to say, he put it away when he was close to the post office. When the driver pulled ... the PM rushed out, rubbing his eyes and looking at the driver, asked him to show him his bugle. Of course the driver had the bugle in his hand, and was puffing like a steam engine, carrying out the joke to a 'T.' That was the joke of the town for quite awhile ... NO MADE ROADS There was no such thing as made-up roads. At a very bad swamps and sandy patch, a few pine logs were laid to act as corduroy ... SLY GROG There were plenty of sly grog shops in those days and one of the drivers in with a sly grog chap got 15 [?] a bottle landed ... This particular driver would buy two cases at a time and pack the 24 bottles in straw envelopes and put them into a large empty mail bag, tie, seal and stamp the bag with a post office stamp, and put the bag in the bottom of the boot of the coach and pack mailbags on top. As time passed, this driver was suspected of carrying grog for this certain sly grog shop, so a young policeman was sent to meet the coach and search it. He examined all the mailbags in the coach excepting the one with the whisky. He picked up the mouth of the bag, saw the post office seal on it and remarked to the driver, *Well, I am on a wild goose chase.* Had he lifted the bag the weight would, have told him that it was not mail ... Many of the incidents I have forgotten, as a lot of water has passed under the bridge since they happened." (In the Days of Cobb & Co., 19 Jan 1951, p.2)

1905 – "COBB AND CO.'S—Ballarat to Torquay, Barwon Heads, Ocean Grove, Anglesea, and Airey's Inlet. Geelong, Torquay, Anglesea and Airey's Inlet ... Cobb and Co.'s Office, Craig's Stables, Cook and Son, also Ballarat Railway Station. Telephone No. 188 ... Craig's Stables, Lydiard street, Ballarat ... Ballarat and Smythesdale Ballarat and Newtown, Scarsdale, Ballarat and Cape Clear, Ballarat and Pitfield, Ballarat and Illabarook, Ballarat and Junction, Ballarat and Rokewood ; Ballarat to Skipton and Streatham ... Cobb and Co., Craig's Royal Stables ... cash purchases of all suitable horses, vehicles and harness ... Geo. O. Cole, Manager." (Advertising, 6 Feb 1905, p.4)

HEATHCOTE HOTEL "Mr Daniel Pammenter, one of the widely known and much respected proprietors of the Heathcote Hotel, will learn with regret of his decease ... In addition to medical treatment, everything was done in the way of careful nursing but without avail. Mr Pammenter had reached the age of 73 years, and was a native of Linton, Cambridge, England. Previous to coming to this country he had been about 10 years in America. He was resident in Victoria for about 50 years, having been nearly 50 years at the Heathcote Hotel. In the first part of that period, while at the hotel, during the proprietorship of the late Mr James Hay, he was representing the well known firm of coach proprietors, Messrs. Cobb and Co., having about 30 horses under his charge here and elsewhere. Just before the Spring Creek (Graytown) Rush, in 1867, he and Mr John Kearney became proprietors of the Hotel, having purchased it from the late Mr Hay, and were the proprietors of it ever since ... Mr Pammenter was married to Miss Alice Christina Anderson ... and whom he has left with a grown up family of one son and three daughters to mourn their sad loss. As a proprietor of the Hotel Mr Pammenter was commercially and favorably known throughout the State, and his uniform courtesy, kind and generous nature and other good qualities gained for him the esteem of all who knew him." (Obituary, 19 Jan 1905, p.3)

1908 – "FIGHT WITH A TIGER SNAKE. Louie Myers, accompanied by his wife, recently proceeded to take charge of Cobb & Co.'s Middle Creek mail change. The building is an old one, and just before erecting a bedstead Myers came into contact with a monster tiger snake, 7 ft. 6 in. long. The brute showed fight and worked its way out of the room, and noticing Mrs. Myers, who had a small baby in arms, chased her in a savage manner with his fangs out. Mrs. Myers screamed with terror ; her husband and another man meanwhile were in hot haste after the monster, and succeeded in hitting him with a big stone just before the reptile had an opportunity to do any harm." while in Sydney "THE ROTTEN EGG TRADE. There is at present a set of men carrying on business in Sydney against whom the public should be warned (says the Sydney Morning Herald). These people frequent the whole sale dairy produce stores in Sussex street, and buy bad eggs. These eggs are absolutely rotten, and are usually destroyed by agents. But the egg fiend purchases a few cases for almost nothing, and by washing in acids removes all stains, and makes the eggs look fresh and new. These 'sick' eggs, as they are termed in the street, are hawked about the suburbs, and the unsuspecting housewife eagerly purchases them at a price considerably lower than that at which the legitimate traders can supply good eggs." (Fight with a Tiger Snake, 14 Mar 1908, p.15)

ca. 1880-1900 Snow covered Omeo, Victoria (Walter Hodgkinson, photographer) - Courtesy State Library Victoria

ca. 1900 Omeo-Bruthen Mail Coach, Cassilis-Swifts Creek Road, Ensay; Coach was driven and owned by the Haylock Brothers - Courtesy State Library Australia

1880 Lilydale with the Dandenong forest in the distance, Victoria
(Charles Nettleton, 1826-1902) - Courtesy National Library Australia

Club Hotel, Bairnsdale (F. W. FL. Eastwood, 1888-1900, photographer) - Courtesy State Library Victoria

1890-1900 View of Lorne, Victoria (Michael J. Drew, 1873-1943, (photographer) - Courtesy State Library Victoria

1899 Leaving Lorne - Courtesy State Library Victoria

Chapter Eight

Coaching Victoria

1910 onwards

Good-Bye to Cobb & Co.

No move across the salt bush plains,
through Mulga clumps and Yarran,
The old red coach no longer strains
across the ridges barren.
How oft, in little lawns out back, we'd
watch it come and go,
With straining eyes along the track,
to welcome Cobb and Co.

No more we'll see it rushing down
the steep and rocky ranges;
For where it went soon grew a town,
about the old horse changes.
Still out it pushed to no man's land,
thru' dusk and dawn's grey glow,
It made the tracks through hills of
sand, the coach of Cobb and Co.

No more through townships once a
week, past squatters and selectors;
To fossickers along the creek, up hills
to old prospectors.
Through forests thick it blazed the
trails, and always sure if slow;
To lonely men it brought the mails,
The coach of Cobb and Co.

No more in sunshine, or in rain, no
more in rivers flooded,
We'll ever see such teams again, by
pure bred sires blooded.
The railway lines pushed further out,
the old-time coach must go.
Now motor cars which fear no drought,
displaces Cobb and Co.

But memory will oft fly back, when
cars fast by are dashing,
We'll miss the drivers' old whip crack,
and see bright headlights flashing.
And far out where my old mates lie,
they'll see pass to and fro,
A silent team go slowly by, the ghosts
of Cobb and Co.

By Steve Hart.
(Good-Bye To Cobb & Co, 5 Sep 1924, p.4)

1889 Sorrento on Port Phillip Bay,
Road to Back Reach - Courtesy State Library Victoria

Examples of Cobb and Co. Coaching Lines, Victoria—1910s & 1920s

1910

Cobb and Co.—Proprietors not listed
- 22 Mar 1910 Cobb & Co.—Seaside, Drag and Coach Arrangements (Telephone 1) ... Torquay, Barwon Heads; Ocean Grove

1911

Cobb and Co.—Proprietors not listed
- 18 Jan 1911 Cobb & Co.—Excursions This Week. Telephone No. 1. Barwon Heads ... Seaside Coaches ... Anglesea and Airey's Inlet, Torquay, Barwon Heads, Ocean Grove, Queenscliff

1912

Cobb and Co.—Proprietors not listed
- 1 Jun 1912 Cobb and Co.'s Royal Mail Telegraph Line. Coaches—Geelong, Warrnambool, Belfast ... passing through Murghebolac, Inverleigh, Warrambine, Frenchman's, Lismore, Darlington, Mortlake, Framlingham, Woodford and Warrnambool arriving at Belfast early the second day. Passengers and parcels can be booked through at the Melbourne or Ballarat office. Reduced fares: Geelong to Warrnambool

Cobb and Co.—V. N. Vines
- 3 Jan 1912 Cobb & Co.—Seaside Coaches ... Anglesea and Airey's Inlet, Torquay, Barwon Heads, Queenscliff ... Coach Office

1913

Cobb and Co.—V. N. Vines
- 4 Jan 1913 Cobb & Co.—Coaching Arrangement ... Torquay, Barwon Heads, Ocean Grove, Queenscliff, Anglesea and Airey's Inlet ... Ambulance for Hire and Ambo box, Weewondilla, and Warrandoo

1914

Cobb and Co.—Proprietors not listed
- 8 Jun 1914 Cobb & Co.—Telephone, 1001 ... Special Excursion Drags ... Torquay, Barwon Heads, Ocean Grove, Queenscliff, Anglesea and Airey's Inlet ... Ambulance for Hire
- 1 Apr 1914 Woolnough's Line of Coaches (Late of Cobb & Co.)—Portarlington, Clifton Springs, and Drysdale to Geelong

1915

Cobb and Co.—Proprietors not listed
- 5 Jan 1915 Cobb & Co.—Telephone, 1001 ... Office and Stables, Malop-street east ... Torquay, Barwon Heads, Ocean Grove, Anglesea and Airey's Inlet ... Passengers travel by Queenscliff train alight at Marcus Station ... Coach meets all ordinary trains at Marcus

1916

Cobb and Co.—Proprietors not listed
- 4 Feb 1916 Cobb & Co.—Motor Cars for Hire, Day or Night. Ring 1001 ... Torquay, Barwon Heads, Ocean Grove, Anglesea and Airey's Inlet
- 16 Dec 1916 Cobb's Coaches—Barwon Heads, Torquay, Ocean Grove, Anglesea and Airey's Inlet ; through excursion tickets issued Spencer street railway

1917

Cobb and Co.—Proprietors not listed
- 16 May 1917 Cobb's Coaches—Barwon Heads, Torquay, Ocean Grove, Anglesea and Airey's Inlet

1918

Cobb and Co.—Proprietors not listed
- 20 Feb 1819 Cobb's Coaches—Barwon Heads, Torquay, Ocean Grove, Anglesea and Airey's Inlet

1919

Cobb and Co.—Proprietors not listed
- 6 Feb 1919 Cobb & Co.—Seaside Conveyance ... Torquay, Barwon Heads, Airey's Inlet, Queenscliff, Ocean Grove, Anglesea

1920

Cobb and Co.—H. Womersley
- 9 Apr 1920 Cobb & Co.—Seaside Conveyance ... Queenscliff, Point Lonsdale, Torquay, Airey's Inlet, Ocean Grove (Sunday Picnics by Motor), Anglesea, Barwon Heads ... advertised 17 Apr 1920 Cobb and Co.—Seaside Motor Conveyances

1921–1929

No evidence found to date

Dates unknown

Cobb and Co.—Myrtleford and Bright

COBB AND CO.'S CHANGES HANDS.

"Mr. H. .Womersley, so well known as a motor car proprietor for many years past, has purchased the business of Cobb and Co., Malop-street. The travelling public, who for the past quarter of a century have been so efficiently served under the old management, will receive even greater benefits under the new, owing to the fact that motor services will be substituted for horse vehicles, thereby ensuring much quicker transit, and greater comfort in travelling.

The favorite seaside resorts of Barwon Heads, Torquay and Ocean Grove will have an up-to-date motor service; cars will leave the office twice daily, returning to link up with the midday and evening trains. Anglesea and Airey's Inlet will have regular services, the former twice daily. In addition to these services, cars will be available at any hour required, either day or night. The facilities for obtaining through combined rail, boat and coach tickets will be continued under new management."
(Cobb and Co. Changes Hands, 12 Dec 1919, p.2)

Along the tracks—1910s onwards

See *Appendix 2: Supporting evidence for Cobb and Co. coaching lines, Victoria*

1910 – "ANGLESEA RIVER HOTEL. Ocean, mountain, fishing, boating, shooting; Cobb's coach daily. Mrs. Jackson, proprietress." (Advertising, 2 Feb 1910, p.16)

"COBB & CO.—SEASIDE, Drag and Coach Arrangements (Telephone 1) ... Torquay, Barwon Heads; Ocean Grove; Special Conveyances Can Be Arranged For At Any Time, Day Or Night." (Advertising, 22 Mar 1910, p.1)

1912 – "THE PALACE HOTEL, Torquay ... to sell by auction ... together with all the magnificent furniture, 2 pianos, linen, cutlery, etc., as a going concern ... over 50 rooms ... everything in perfect order ... The hotel is lighted with acetylene gas, Telephone laid on, asphalt tennis court, good water supply bore, windmill, and ten tanks ... very large stabling, now let to Cobb and Co., whose coaches call daily at the Hotel all the year round." (Advertising, 28 Sep 1912, p.6)

1915 – "MR. CHARLES WATT ... The late Mr. Watt was one of the band of pioneers who came to Australia in the early fifties. At one time he was manager at Deniliquin for Robertson, Wagner and Co., the well-known coach proprietors, but in the seventies he came to Benalla as manager for Cobb and Co., of whose business right throughout the North-Eastern district he had charge ... The deceased was the possessor of many sterling qualities, and was highly respected." (Mr. Charles Watt, 8 Jan 1915, p.3)

"DRAG AXLE BREAKS. In the descent of Yarra-street hill yesterday afternoon the back axle of one of Cobb's large drags, returning from Torquay, broke, and the wheels, bulging in, gripped the sides of the vehicle and prevented its collapse. Some ladies aboard were terrified., but their fears were allayed by Mr. J. Rowe, who had warned the driver of the danger and afterwards assisted the occupants to alight. A repair gang took charge of the vehicle, and had a tough job in lifting it for removal to the stables at 5 p.m." Meanwhile "CARTER'S LEG BROKEN. In the descent of the hill in Buckland Avenue yesterday at midday, the harness of a wood cart driven by George Burr gave way, the two shafts snapped off short, and the vehicle, which was fully laden, tipped up. Burr fell clear but the cart rolled back, and one of the wheels passed over his left leg. He was conveyed to the Geelong Hospital in a motor car." (Drag Axle Breaks, 26 Jan 1915, p.3)

1917 – "COBB'S COACHES, Barwon Heads, Torquay, Ocean Grove, Anglesea and Airey's Inlet ... FOR SALE Several Vehicles in First-Class Order and Good, Useful Horses for all classes of light work." (Advertising, 16 May 1917, p.1)

1918 – "COBB'S COACHES—Barwon Heads, Torquay, Ocean Grove, Anglesea and Airey's Inlet" Advertised on the same page "EXCEPTIONAL OPPORTUNITY, owner leaving Geelong.—Newly-erected up-to-date W. B. Villa, all ready for sewerage, containing 5 rooms, pantry, bathroom, vestibule, electric light, bath heater ... £700." (Advertising, 20 Feb 1918, p.1)

"THE OLD COACHING DAYS. SOME REMINISCENCES. (By 'Old Resident.') ... There are not left amongst us now many whose recollections of the district can go back to the old coaching days of the period of Mr Keays' arrival in Daylesford ... Going back to the early part of '62, I have no occasion to dilate upon the roads we had at that period, for the theme has been constantly written about and all sorts of anecdotes relative to the depth of the mud on highways of the old days, and hairbeadth escapes of travellers thereon from being buried alive, have been related by the hundred. A notable one concerned the finding of a hat, from beneath which, when the discoverer essayed to pick it up, a voice was heard to protest *Hold on, that's my hat*. The discoverer there upon endeavored to drag from his burial ground the person beneath the hat, whereupon the submerged exclaimed, *Wait till I get my feet out of the stirrups, my horse is beneath me*. The yarn is a little far fetched, but still there were places on our main roads where the sinking out of sight could easily have occurred ... Although present day vehicles are well built for lightness and strength, and a credit to the builders, yet I think the American pattern through-brace—that is the leather springs—was what was wanted for the rough roads. I see we have still one of the old identities laying up in Cobb and Co.'s yard.

Although discarded my friend, you lived through a hard life,

I would like to see you preserved if there was a museum for your kind, so that the coming generations could see the style of vehicle our forefathers journeyed by." (The Old Coaching Days, 10 Sep 1918, p.3)

1919 – "OCEAN GROVE Messrs. Cobb and Co. start their motor service of twice daily to-day, and mails and papers will be delivered much earlier. Mr. Foyster is also running a char-a-banc Daily." Advertised on the same page "FOR WASHING DAINTY CURTAINS USE LUX Few things do more to make a room bright and cheery than dainty, clean curtains ... Lux coaxes the dirt out ... won't shrink woolens ... DODGE BROTHERS MOTOR CAR The merits of these are too well known to comment upon Balfour's Garage ... KODAK–your best Christmas and New Year companion ... Give Kodaks to the grown-up friends you wish to please the most ... There is no gift for a child to compare with a Brownie." (Country News, 16 Dec 1919, p.5)

"HOW RABBITS CAME TO VICTORIA. It is claimed that the introduction of rabbits into Victoria was at a place in the bush near Guildford still known locally as the Rabbit Warren. The following extract from a Tasmanian paper ... bears on the subject : — Relative to the discussion which is proceeding on the introduction of rabbits into Victoria, Mr Leslie N. Murdoch forwards the following extract from the 'Castlemaine Advertiser,' 1863 : — Rabbit Growing. — *In these days when so much attention is directed to the introduction of new industries it will be interesting to our readers to know that for the last two or three years there has been started a most novel and useful speculation, which, while it will return a very handsome profit, we hope, to the spirited originators, will prove a vast service to the community. We allude to the large rabbit warren established by Messrs Gravenor and others beyond Guildford. Upwards of 200 acres of land, hill and dale, have been fenced in with 7-foot palings sunk 2 feet in the ground, and originally about 50 couples of rabbits were turned out about two years ago. With the extraordinary fecundity for which bunny is celebrated, these fifty have increased to so many thousands. So much so that in a few weeks the proprietors will be in a position to regularly supply the neighboring markets of Castlemaine and Daylesford, and will soon extend their operations to Sandhurst and the great metropolis. The great relief, in summer time, especially, of being able to obtain some unusual food other than the eternal mutton and beef of the good old times, makes this enterprise of considerable interest to the public, and the large revenues which the owners of extensive rabbit warrens in England obtain, point to the speculation as one which ought to amply repay its spirited originators. We should not omit to state that the most extreme care is exercised to prevent depredations either by wild dogs or dishonest men. A night watch is systematically kept.*

This new industry has been introduced unaided by the State, the land having been purchased by the proprietors. We can only say that we trust that their pluck and patience will reap the reward so eminently due. On being interviewed on the subject, an old resident of the Guildford township said that the statements are absolutely true, but a bush fire came along and having destroyed the paling fence, the rabbits were liberated, and escaped to the surrounding country, eventually spreading all over the district." (How Rabbits Came to Victoria, 17 Sep 1918, p.2)

1920 – "MOTOR SERVICE. Cobb & Co.'s Cars. Run to all Seaside and other places for Business or Pleasure. Charges Strictly Moderate. Cars Garaged Day or Night. Accessories, Tyres, Tubes etc., always on hand. We do all Repairs to any make of Cars. All Work done promptly and at lowest rates. Workmanship Guaranteed. Phone, 1001, Day. Phone, 1440, Night." (Advertising, 5 Aug 1920, p.1)

Mail delivery using camels

1880 – "CAMELS FOR COBB'S COACHES. The wretched state of the Mount Browne road has taxed the energy and resources of Messrs. Cobb. and Co. to the utmost of late. In spite of every difficulty that want, food and water could put in their way, they have hitherto managed to struggle through with the mail. But horse flesh and blood cannot stand it any longer. The horse, the animal *par excellence* of modern Australia, is played out so far as keeping up mail communications on a waterless road goes, and camels have to be employed. Mr. Byrne, manager of the firm, during his last trip, to the diggings, was forced to the conclusion that the mail by ordinary means could no longer be carried, and with considerable forethought he at once set about and succeeded in securing several camels to relieve the worn-out mail horses and secure a continuance of the service. These useful animals have hitherto been unpopular in this part of the country, but, on this occasion, we are sure that their advent will be welcome. It is of the utmost importance that the isolation of Mount Browne should be prevented, with regard to letters as well as food, and camels only can do it. It certainly is not pleasant for a smart five-in-hand coach-driver to have to take to camel driving, but we believe that an Australian or two will have to turn Afghan or Arab until rain comes.—Western Grazier." (Camels for Cobb's Coaches, 22 Apr 1882, p.4)

1925 – HORSES RELINQUISHED "Coaching ... No one is a greater authority on the subject than Mr. James Nicholas, of Peron Peninsula Station, Shark Bay, and in an interview ... Mr. Nicholas has given us a narrative of coaching in Australia as he has seen it during the last 50 years ... out west in New South Wales ... There was a very bad drought ... sheep and stock dying in thousands, as also did the coach horses ... As to keep them working would have meant carting chaff some 500 miles, an impossible proposition, Cobb and Co. had for the first time to relinquish horses and get camels to carry the mails, and they did it well. I think that was the first time in Australia that camels had carried mails. Kidman and Nicholas ran Esperance to Norseman with camels for a month in 1896, while I was obtaining a coaching plant to put on that road, and they did it first rate, running to time always." (Coaching in the Commonwealth, 17 May 1925, p.9)

1928 – IMAGE in Observer, Adelaide, SA "The camel mail on the Cordillo run in the far north. The vehicle shown is probably the last of the old 'Cobb's coaches' now in use." (Mails by Camels, 23 Jun 1928, p.36)

1929 – IMAGE in The Register News Pictorial, Adelaide, SA "A Cobb & Coy. Coach ... here is a photograph of a Cobb & Coy. coach ... it used to be drawn by the famous Blanche water horses, bred by the late Sir Thomas Elder, and which bore the T.E. brand. The horses are all gone, and the old homestead, is deserted, but this coach still runs. The driver told me that the wheels of the old bus are as good as the day they were made, and the vehicle has never been under cover ... This old royal mail is now drawn by camels, and it runs over the very bad stretch on the Strzelecki, between Mount Hopeless and Innamincka, and is met at each 'end' of the track by a motor-lorry." (Out Among the People, 29 Jul 1929, p.6)

1947 – ONLY MAN WHO EVER DROVE A TEAM OF CAMELS IN A COACH "Old drivers recalled nostalgically the stories of some of the other old-timers. Of John Conway Burke, who drove the first passenger coach from Melbourne to Sydney 108 years ago. Of Arthur Harman, still living in South Australia, who claims to be the only man who ever drove a team of camels in a coach ... In recognition of his long service in the cause of transport, Jim Conroy was awarded the Imperial Service Medal by King Edward VII—the first time this decoration had been awarded to an Australian. One of the youngest of the Cobb and Co. drivers was Sidney Coleman, for many years Mayor of Bourke." (First Coach, 20 Jun 1947, p.2)

And let's not forget the mail boys and a few bushrangers

HARDSHIPS OF MAIL BOYS "The Mail Boys of Other Days. To the Editor of the Age. Sir,—In reference to the hardships of Cobb and Co.'s. coach drivers, with all due respect to them, I would like to draw attention to the hardships of the poor mail boys in the early days. They had no one to attend to their horses when they came to change them, as had the coach drivers. They had to go into a paddock and catch their own horses, and ride long, lonely journeys. There were no roads, only bush tracks, with mud up to the stirrups. The poor horses suffered with mud rot, the hair falling off their legs. They were only grass fed. I give my experience as mail boy in Gippsland in the [18]seventies and early eighties:

I rode the mail to Merriman's Greek, Woodside, Lillie's Leaf, Tarraville, Port Albert and Stockyard Creek (now named Foster). On the long stage between Woodside and Merriman's Creek, 28 miles, I only saw two persons in two years. One was a stockman camped at the twelve-mile yard, and the other was, a young woman, who rode through with me from Rosedale to Woodside. I would arrive at Port Albert from Rosedale after dark, and Mr. Ferris, the post master, was very good to me. He would make up my Stockyard Creek mail while I waited, so that I could get an early start on my journey next morning. The road to Stockyard Creek was very bad; there were no bridges over the creeks in those days. You had to plough the horse through them. The township of Welshpool was then called Shady Creek, I would cross the Agnes River and change horses at the old saw mill paddock, Muddy Creek, where the township of Toora is now. One of the oldest settlers in South Gippsland, John Amy, of the Franklin River, told me that the old saw mill was built there in the forest close to the beach to evade the police. In those days there were timber poachers, who had no licence. I left Port Albert early one morning for Stockyard Creek with the mail. The rivers were all in flood, as it had been raining for days. The old Alberton-bridge was undergoing repairs, and they had built a temporary bridge further up in the narrow part of the river. When I arrived at the Alberton post office the post mistress said: *You can't get your horse over the river, as the bridge is under water, but there is a foot bridge, made in the early days from a fallen tree, further up the river. You may be able to cross there. Let your horse go; he will come back here, as we reared him. Walk to the Gelliondale cattle station, three miles; they will supply you with a horse.* So I let my horse go, and crossed the log and walked to the station.

They lent me a good old horse, and told me not to take the Shady Creek track, but follow the Wilson's Promontory telegraph line along the beach to Port Welsh pool, then cross the plains to the Agnes River. When I arrived at the Agnes River the bridge was out of sight, so I got off on to a stump, took some of my clothes off, tied them in a bundle around my neck with a slip knot, got into the saddle, patted old Gelliondale on the neck and put him to the river. He crossed it like a seagull. I then dressed myself, pushed along till I came to the old saw mill paddock, changed horses, crossed Muddy Creek with the water nearly up to the horse's back. I then pushed him as hard as I could, as I was afraid of being marooned on the east side of the Franklin River, where I might have perished in the night. But when I got to the river there was about eighteen inches of water on the bridge, so I crossed all right. Old John Amy was on the look out for me, as he did not think I would get through. I then pushed on for all I was worth to the diggings before dark. I arrived at Stockyard Creek more mud than clothes. I used to stay at Granny McMillan's, sister-in-law of Angus McMillan, who discovered Port Albert. She was waiting for me with a change of clothes, a big fire and a big feed. Next morning I went to the post office for the Melbourne mail. The post master said: *Well, boy, I have just got word from O'Dea's that the Franklin River has risen four feet during the night, and is still rising. So I do not think you will get through to-day. But I must send you on your journey; be careful and take no risks.* I started on my journey. It was raining hard when I came to Bennison Creek-bridge, there being about two feet of water over it. I got off my horse, put the reins over my arm, held on to the rail of the bridge and led him across in case some of the decking was washed away. When I came to the Franklin River John Amy was on the look out for me. He said: *Boy, your cake is dough. There is the river. Where is the bridge? Turn in the gate, put your horse in the stable, get a change of clothes and wait till the flood water recedes off the bridge, as some of the decking is washed away.* On the second morning the water was off the bridge. We put some planks across it, so as to get the horse over. I arrived at Port Albert two days late. My wages were to be 2/6 per week, but when I was paid off after two years mail-boy work, my wages did not average 1/6 per week. Could the coach drivers beat this ?— Yours, &c., Dick Pullen, North Richmond, 28th June." (The Mail Boys of Other Days, 1 Jul 1933, p.6)

BUSHRANGER—HARRY POWER

1870 – "POWER THE BUSHRANGER. Considerable excitement was created in Bourke-street early yesterday morning, in consequence of it having oozed out that Power the bushranger would be brought down in the Beechworth coach in charge of Superintendent Hare, en route to Pentridge, where he will undergo the sentence awarded him ... The mail coach was due at the post office at seven a.m., but in consequence of the heavy state of the roads it was three hours behind time, and did not arrive at Cobb and Co.'s office until ten o'clock ... By ten o'clock a large crowd had assembled ... to gratify their curiosity by a sight of the bushranger. As the coach stopped at the post-office to put out the mail-bags, there was a rush to that place ... he [Power] pushed his head outside, and lifted his hat to those assembled, as if anxious to exhibit himself as the notoriety of the hour ... lifted his hat two or three times to the onlookers, as he was driven off to the Melbourne gaol ... upon entering the gaol started back at the sight of the murder Smith, whose body was hanging from the gallows ... he appeared rather cowed at this sight, and turned his head, but very soon recovered his nonchalant demeanor ... The appearance of the prisoner was very different to what most people expected ... He was wrapped up in a comfortable drab cloth coat, with a muffler round his neck, and a light low-crowned felt hat on. His appearance was that of a yeoman farmer, or cattle-dealer, and any one riding along the road in the country would have no hesitation in joining him for company as far as his looks were concerned. His face is pleasant rather ... he is of great muscular power, and capable of long endurance ... On the road out Power was very chatty, and appeared quite willing to detail his exploits ... His first question when he got inside was to know whether any ' tucker' was to be had ... the minimum of his term of imprisonment, he will then be seventy years of age, and almost incapable of doing further mischief ... He says that he has never shed any blood, and never intended to do so ... He accounted for sending back Mr. M'Bain's watch and horse by saying that he wished to have some friends when he came out of gaol ... He is very bitter in his feelings towards the Quinns, whose house it will be recollected was at no great distance from the place where he was captured. He declares that they gave information about him, as they know when he was in his mia-mia and asleep. At the same time he pays a high tribute to his captors ; he states that he was very sound asleep on the morning of his capture, and when he awoke and found Mr. Nicholson standing over him and Mr. Hare with a hold of his hand, he 'knew it was all up. It was no go'." (Power the Bushranger, 5 Aug 1870, p.3)

"Early pioneers, herdsmen, or gold-diggers, who gave Feathertop its name, must have been possessed of a poetic vein. But I remember how Feathertop evolved poetry from the lips of Harry Power, the bushranger. Many years ago when he was under my medical charge at Pentridge, this noted outlaw would describe to me the glories of camping out on these ranges, with 'Feathertop shining in the sun in the early morning.' I was a new chum then, and had not the most remote idea where Feathertop was. The knowledge that there was snow in Australia came to me years afterwards, and it is still a novelty to many in Melbourne." (Across the Australian Alps, 20 Apr 1889, p.13)

BUSHRANGER—MORGAN (MAD DOG)

1864 – "MORGAN. BUSHRANGER AND MURDERER. When and where is it to end? ... Are we never to hear the end of Morgan? ... We have still another week of Morgan's murders and misdeeds .... Is this a third murder we shall have to put down to Morgan's fearful account within a week? When is he to be shot as a native dog ? — Albury Banner. July 2nd." (Morgan. Bushranger and Murderer, 7 Jul 1864, p.2)

BUSHRANGER—GYPSEY SMITH

1879 – "DEATH OF A BUSHRANGER 'Gypsey Smith, whose name is associated with some of the most daring bushrangers in the early days of the goldfields in Victoria, died in the Melbourne Hospital last week. According to the prison records he was transported from England when a mere youth to Van Diemen's Land. Being a refractory convict he was subsequently sent to Port Arthur, where the worst class of criminals were confined. In the year 1853, he with six others escaped in a whaling boat, and after a perilous voyage landed at Brighton. Being an absconded, he said it would be useless to go to the diggings, as he would soon be discovered, and at once decided on a course of bushranging. In those days the assistance rendered by the police for the security of life and property was but limited, which encouraged desperate criminals to commit acts which have furnished a long catalogue of crimes in the early days of the goldfields and subsequent years. Smith was often seen in a spirit of bravado passing among the diggers with a red sash round his waist, in which were exhibited a brace of pistols. On one occasion he was arrested by a young trooper, who was taking him to the lockup. In a lonely part of the road Smith asked the trooper to take off the handcuffs for a moment, which the officer consented to do. As soon as the prisoners hands were free he seized the officer's sword and attacked him.

The trooper at the same moment drew the scabbard from his belt, and at once stood on his defence. The two fought for some time, and the prisoner finding he was getting the worst of the fight struck the officer's horse, which bolted into the bush, and Smith escaped. Smith always spoke of the trooper as one of the best men he had ever met with in an encounter. On another occasion, when Smith and his mate, named M'Nally, were surrounded by the police, the latter was shot dead, and the former escaped. In the year 1857, Smith was arrested at Ballarat, and would have been lynched by the diggers, but they were prevented by a few of the police. Smith was tried and sentenced to 15 years on the roads of the colony. In those days the Pentridge stockade was very insecure, and Smith was sent to the hulk President. Afterwards be was transferred to Pentridge, and placed in a position of trust in one of the divisions, where he conducted himself to the satisfaction of the authorities. After he was discharged from prison he was taken in hand by Mr Lang, son of the late Dr Lang, of Sydney, who appears to have placed considerable confidence in Smith's honesty. He was often entrusted by Mr Lang to bring mobs of cattle from New South Wales to Melbourne market to sell, and in subsequent years he was placed in charge of a station.—*Argus*."(Death of a Bushranger, 19 Jul 1879, p.2)

BUSHRANGERS—TOKE, ARMSTRONG & CHAMBERLAIN

"I was staying at Melbourne in December, 1858, after a long overland journey from South Australia, when business summoned me to visit the Omeo gold-field, situated at the extreme eastern end of the colony of Victoria, in the neighbourhood of the Australian Alps ... The district was in a state of excitement consequent upon the murder of a Mr Green, a well known gold-buyer, who was returning from Omeo accompanied by a gentleman and lady. They had gone only a mile or two from Omeo, when they were fired at from a clump of trees, near the track. Green was struck, and fell to the ground ; his male companion was untouched, and carried out of danger by his frightened horse ; but the lady was thrown from her saddle and broke her arm. While Green lay on the ground, one of the murderers rushed up and despatched the halpless victim with a tomahawk. For some reason or other, the lady was left unmolested, and finally returned to Omeo ... In due time I reached Omeo with out meeting any of the murderous gang. As I rode down its one straggling street I saw an excited crowd gathered about a building, which turned out to be the court-house. On inquiry, I was informed that three men were being examined on the charge of murdering Mr. Green ... I soon learned that the accused were notorious characters in that neighbourhood, and were known under the names of Toke, Armstrong, and Chamberlain. Toke, or Tom Toke as he was commonly called, succeeded in proving an alibi ; but the other two were committed for trial to Melbourne where they were afterwards convicted, and hanged." (With Tom Toke, The Australian Bushranger, 20 Aug 1883, p.3)

BUSHRANGERS—KELLY GANG—EDWARD & DANIEL KELLY, STEPHEN HART AND JOSEPH BYRNE

"*Were you ever stuck up?* I asked of Bob Grover, of Wagga, aged 87. *Me? No, said Bob, but I've had some encounters with real bushrangers. In the Kelly days passengers and drivers alike were all keyed up and expecting the worst. I drove in the Kelly country, but I was never stuck up, because I always carried a bottle of brandy in the boot. More than once or twice I've swung round a bend to see Ned Kelly himself with his hand up to stop me. All he wanted was a stiff nip, and he always got it from me, and we'd swap a word or two. He was always alone. I fancy he was inclined to keep Dan, and Steve Hart and Joe Byrne in the background a bit. They were a bit too flash for Ned.*" (Those were the Days!, 8 May 1928, p.6)

1944 – "Death of Mr. George Wells DROVE COACH FOR COBB & CO ... in his 83rd year. The late Mr. Wells was born in Gippsland, Victoria, and in his youth was apprenticed to a coach builder. The driving of coaches appealed more to him so he left this to go driving for Cobb & Co. in the Ballarat district, over roads upon which the Kelly gang operated. He was unmolested by this gang on condition he did not carry police escorts. This information was conveyed to him by Kate Kelly, with whom he claimed to have danced on many occasions." (Death of Mr. George Wells, 27 Oct 1944, p.1)

"A short HISTORY OF THE GANG. In the month of April, 1878, Con. Fitzpatrick proceeded to Greta with the intention of arresting Daniel Kelly for house stealing, but was overpowered by various members of the family, and received a wound in the wrist from the revolver of the brother Edward, and the prisoner escaped. Mrs. Kelly, Williams and Skillion, for aiding and abetting in the escape were tried and sentenced to long terms of imprisonment, but the two Kellys evaded the police and found a hiding place in the ranges. It came to the ears of the police that the gang were in the seclusion amongst the Wombat ranges, and three parties of police started out in different directions for the purpose of capturing them. One of these parties headed by Sergeant Kennedy, and Cons. Scanlan, Lonigan, and McIntyre closed upon the band in October 1878, but instead of stealing upon them unawares the tables were turned, and four men, Edward and Daniel Kelly, Stephen Hart and Joseph Byrne, rushed on the police and committed a crime hitherto unparalleled in the history of the colony, by brutally murdering the Sergeant, Lonigan, and Scanlan, McIntyre alone escaping to tell the tale. Parties of police and civilians immediately went out to effect an arrest of the murderers. To offer sufficient inducement, a reward of £8000 was offered and the band declared outlaws, but they escaped from everything, and were neither heard of nor seen until one morning in December 1879. The whole country was thrown into a state of excitement with the announcement that the four men had stuck up the bank at Euroa, and robbed it of £2000, locked up the inhabitants in a neighboring station, and broke down the telegraph wires. Returning again to their hiding place, a perfect fortress, they were not heard of until February 1879, when they appeared at Jerilderie, in New South Wales, and for the second time bailed up a town and threw the population into a state of helpless terror, and after effecting their purpose, once more escaped. After being kept at bay for upwards of a year, the Kellys turned their attention to those whom they believed were betraying them, and made a raid on the house of Aaron Sherrit, and commenced what was probably intended to be a series of reprisals by a cowardly and dastardly act of revenge—his murder. Four of the police force were in the hut at the time, but they lifted neither hand nor sword. Knowing that all they could do would be required to prevent their capture after such an act, the gang, with all speed possible, rode to Glenrowan, with the intention of wrecking a train, which they knew would be sent with police on the deed becoming known. Of the frustration of their design and subsequent fight, in which Daniel Kelly, Hart, and Byrne perished in the flames, the facts are too well known to need recapitulation. Suffice it that Edward Kelly, the leader of the gang, was captured alive ... had the awful sentence of death passed on him." (Execution of Edward Kelly, 13 Nov 1880, p.3)

1878 – "THE ENCOUNTER AT GLENROWAN ... the murders of the police near Mansfield occurred as long ago as the 26th of October, 1878, the Euroa outrage on the 9th December of the same year, and the Jerilderie affair on the 8th and 9th of February, 1879.

The lapse of time induced many to believe that the gang was no longer in the colony, but these sceptics must now be silent. The outlaws demonstrated their presence in a brutally effective manner by the murder of the unfortunate Aaron Sherritt at Sebastopol. Immediately on the news being spread the police were in activity. A special train was despatched from Melbourne at 10.15 on Sunday night ... ... We were now about to enter the Kelly country, and caution was necessary. As the moon was shining brightly, a man was tied on upon the front of the engine to keep a look-out for any obstruction of the line. Just before starting, however, it occurred to the authorities that it would be advisable to send a pilot engine in advance, and the man on the front of our engine was relieved. A start was made from Benalla at 2 o'clock, and at 25 minutes to 3, when we were travelling at a rapid pace, we were stopped by the pilot engine. This stoppage occurred at Playford and Desoyre's paddocks, about a mile and a quarter from Glenrowan. A man had met the pilot and informed the driver that the rails were torn up, about a mile and a half beyond Glenrowan, and that the Kellys were waiting for us near at hand ... the Kellys ... were at that moment in possession of Jones' public-house, about a hundred yards from the station. He called upon the police to surround the house, and his advice was followed without delay. Superintendent Hare with his men, and Sub-inspector Connor with his [First Nation] trackers, at once advanced on the building. They were accompanied by Mr. Rawlins, a volunteer from Benalla, who did good service. Mr. Hare took the lead, and charged right up to the hotel. At the station were the reporters of the Melbourne press, Mr. Carrington, of The Sketcher, and the two ladies who had accompanied us. The latter behaved with admirable courage, never betraying a symptom of fear although bullets were whizzing about the station and striking the building and train ... Sub-inspector O'Connor and Senior-constable Kelly took charge, and kept pelting away at the outlaws all the morning ... Mrs. Jones ... removing her wounded boy from the building ... sending him on to Wangaratta for medical treatment. The firing continued intermittently ... At daybreak police reinforcements arrived from Benalla, Beechworth, and Wangaratta ... Before daylight Senior-constable Kelly found a revolving rifle and a cap lying in the bush, about 100 yards from the hotel. The rifle was covered with blood, and a pool of blood lay near it. This was evidently the property of one of the bushrangers, and a suspicion therefore arose that they had escaped ... When day was dawning the women and children who had been made prisoners in the hotel were allowed to depart ...

CAPTURE OF NED KELLY ... Close attention was paid to the hotel, as it was taken for granted that the whole gang were there. To the surprise of the police, however, they soon found themselves attacked from the rear by a man dressed in a long grey overcoat and wearing an iron mask. The appearance of the man presented an anomaly, but a little scrutiny of his appearance and behaviour soon showed that it was the veritable leader of the gang Ned Kelly himself. On further observation it was seen that he was only armed with a revolver. He, however, walked coolly from tree to tree, and received the fire of the police with the utmost indifference, returning a shot from his revolver when a good opportunity presented itself. Three men went for him, viz., Sergeant Steele of Wangaratta, Senior-constable Kelly, and a railway guard named Dowsett. The latter, however, was only armed with a revolver. They fired at him persistently, but to their surprise with no effect. He seemed bullet-proof. It then occurred to Sergeant Steele that the fellow was encased in mail, and he then aimed at the outlaw's legs. His first shot of that kind made Ned stagger, and the second brought him to the ground with the cry, *I am done—I am done*. Steele rushed up along with Senior-constable Kelly and others. The outlaw howled like a wild beast brought to bay, and swore at the police

... Kelly became gradually quiet and it was soon found that he had been utterly disabled. He had been shot in the left foot, left leg, right hand, left arm, and twice in the region of the groin. But no bullet had penetrated his armour. Having been divested of his armour he was carried down to the railway station, and placed in the guard's van. Subsequently he was removed to the stationmaster's office, and his wounds were dressed there by Dr. Nicholson, of Benalla ... In the meantime the siege was continued without intermission, that the three other outlaws were still in the house was confirmed by remarks made by Ned, who said they would fight to the last, and would never give in ... A rumour got abroad that Byrne was shot when drinking a glass of whisky at the bar of the hotel about half-past 5 o'clock in the morning, and the report afterwards turned out to be true. The remaining two kept up a steady defence from the rear of the building during the forenoon, and exposed themselves recklessly to the bullets of the police. They, however, were also clad in mail, and the shot took no effect. At 10 o'clock a white flag or handkerchief was held out at the front door, and immediately afterwards about 30 men, all prisoners, sallied forth holding up their hands. They escaped whilst Dan Kelly and Hart were defending the back door ... The siege was kept up all the forenoon, and till nearly 3 in the afternoon ... At 10 minutes to 3 o'clock another and the last volley was fired into the hotel, and under cover of the fire Senior-constable Charles Johnson, of Violet Town, ran up to the house with a bundle of straw which (having set fire to) he placed on the ground at the west side of the building ... Just at this juncture Mrs. Skillian, sister of the Kellys, attempted to approach the house from the front ... Her object in trying to reach the house was apparently to induce the survivors, if any, to come out and surrender ... Not very many minutes elapsed, however, before smoke was seen coming out of the roof, and flames were discerned through the front window on the western side ... and as the building was lined with calico, the fire spread rapidly ... Father Gibney, at much personal risk from the flames, hurried into a room to the left, and there saw two bodies lying side by side ... the bodies of Dan Kelly and Hart ... Whether they killed one another or whether both or one committed suicide, or whether both being mortally wounded by the besiegers, they determined to die side by side, will never be known ... As to Byrne's body, it was found in the entrance to the bar-room, which was on the east side of the house, and there was time to remove it from the building, but not before the right side was slightly scorched ... The armour in which each member of the gang was clad was of a most substantial character. It was made of iron a quarter of an inch thick, and consisted of a long breast-plate, shoulder plates, back-guard, and helmet. The helmet resembled a nail can without a crown, and with a long slit at the elevation of the eyes to look through ... Ned Kelly's armour alone weighed 97lb., a considerable weight to carry on horseback. There are five bullet marks on the helmet, three on the breast-plate, nine on the back-plate, and one on the shoulder plate. His wounds, so far as at present known, are :—Two on the right arm, several on the right leg, one on the left foot, one on the right hand, and two near the groin." (The Encounter at Glen Rowan, 1 Jul 1880, p.2)

1880 – "EDWARD KELLY. The outlaw Edward Kelly is still a patient in the hospital of the Melbourne gaol. He maintains the same quiet demeanor, and his health continues to improve. He cannot be brought to the City Police Court on Monday next." (Edward Kelly, 23 Jul 1880, p.3)

"TRIAL OF EDWARD KELLY ... Kelly, who was dressed in a new suit of clothes, and looked hale and hearty ... Kelly has considerably improved in appearance since he was at Glenrowan. He hopped from the gaol (as he has a wounded foot) to the waggonette ...

Dr. O'Brien dressed Kelly's wounds in the gaol this morning. He has 23 gunshot wounds" (Trial of Edward Kelly, 7 Aug 1880, p.4)

"TRIAL OF EDWARD KELLY ... Edward Kelly was placed on his trial for having, in October, 1878, at Stringy Bark Creek, near Mansfield, murdered Constable Thomas Lonigan ... Mr. C. A. Smyth opened the case. He stated the circumstances under which the party of police, consisting of Sergeant Kennedy, and Constables Lonigan, Scanlan and M'Intyre, in October of 1878, left in search of the prisoner and his brother, Dan Kelly, in order to arrest them on the charge of shooting at Constable Fitzpatrick; how the police camp was surprised by the prisoner, at the head of a gang of three others; how Lonigan was thereupon shot, and how the search for the outlaws was continued, and ended in the events which transpired at Glenrowan, in June last ... The following evidence was then called: — Detective Ward produced a warrant dated 15th March, 1878, for the arrest of the prisoner on a charge of horse stealing. He also produced a warrant to apprehend Daniel Kelly for the same offence. Cross-examined: He had been connected with the pursuit of the Kelly gang since the 29th September, 1879. He was chiefly stationed in the ranges. Constable P. Day produced a warrant for the apprehension of the prisoner for the attempted murder of Constable Fitzpatrick. Constable Thomns M'Intyre deposed that on the 25th October, 1878, he left Mansfield with a party of police in charge of Sergeant Kennedy. The party consisted of Michael Seaman, Thomas Lonigan and witness. They were organised to search for the Kelly robbers. On the 25th October they got about twenty miles into the Wombat Ranges, where they camped for the night. Kennedy and Scanlan left the camp on horseback, to patrol. During the afternoon witness, with his fowling-piece, shot at a couple of parrots. About four p.m. a fire was lit, principally to guide Kennedy and Scanlan to the camp. Nearly an hour afterwards he was standing with his face to the fire, and heard a voice say, *Bail up; hold up your hands.* Witness was unarmed at the time. Turning round he saw four men, each armed with a gun, which were presented at Lonigan and witness. [Edward Kelly] was one of the four, who were partly concealed in the spear grass, which was about 5 feet high. Witness ... saw [Edward Kelly] ... point it at Lonigun and fire. Lonigan fell, and sang out, *O, Christ, I'm shot.* The four men then said, *Keep your hands up,* and then walked towards the camp. [Edward Kelly] ... said, *Dear, dear, what a pity that man tried to get away.* [Edward Kelly] told witness that he had better get Kennedy arid Scanlan to surrender, *because if they don't surrender, we will shoot you, and if they get away we will shoot you* ... [Edward Kelly] said, *Hist, lads, here they come.* Kennedy was advancing in front ... [Edward Kelly] jumped up and said *bail up.* Kennedy put his hand on his revolver and [Edward Kelly] then fired a shot, which did not take effect. Scanlan was dismounting, and got somewhat flurried; he missed his footing, and, to save himself from failing, he let go his Spencer rifle which he had grasped, and fell upon his hands and knees. While in this position he received a shot, fired by [Edward Kelly]. Scanlan rolled over on the ground. Kennedy at the same time put his face on his horse's neck and rolled off on the off side. Witness then caught Kennedy's horse, and he succeeded in mounting it ... and getting away into the bush. He heard several other shots fired afterwards. After riding about two miles, he was thrown off the horse. He remained in the bush all night, and reached Mansfield on the following day (Sunday) about noon. A search party was organised, and on Monday morning the bodies of Scanlan and Lonigan were found. Kennedy's body was not discovered until two days afterwards. The tent had been burnt ... George Stephens, groom, deposed that ... [Edward Kelly] narrated to witness what took place in the Wombat Ranges ... He said he had shot Lonigan through the head, and also that he had wounded Scanlan, who fell on his head. Kennedy retreated to the trees and kept up a fire. While retreating in this manner, [Edward Kelly] said he followed him, and at last shot him through the chest ... Robert Macdougall, warehouseman, gave corroborative evidence. J. Gloster, hawker, deposed that he was amongst the men who were stuck-up on Young-husband's station. [Edward Kelly] told him that he shot both Kennedy and Lonigan." (Trial of Edward Kelly, 29 Oct 1880, p.3)

1880 – "EDWARD KELLY. There is nothing new to report concerning the condemned man Edward Kelly. He sleeps and eats well, and is quiet and orderly in his demeanor. Persons in the yard of the Supreme Court to-day about noon could hear the clanking of the convict's chains, as he took his hour's exercise in the yard adjoining the old wing of the gaol." (Edward Kelly, 1 Nov 1880, p.4)

1880 – "TRIAL OF EDWARD KELLY ... Throughout both days the court was densely crowded, and the progress of the trial was watched with the closest interest. A large crowd of people were also assembled in front of the courthouse anxiously awaiting an opportunity to catch a glimpse of the prisoner. Kate Kelly and Mrs. Skillian were present, and an unusually large contingent of constables was stationed in the court to guard all the means of exit. The evidence did not in any material point differ from that given by the witnesses who were examined at the preliminary police court investigations ...

The prisoner had himself confessed his guilt. After an absence from court of half-an-hour, the jury brought in a verdict of guilty.

Upon the judge's associate asking the prisoner whether he had anything to say why sentence should not be passed upon him, Kelly said ... *No one knows anything about my case but myself. I'm sorry I did not ask my counsel to sit down, and examine the witnesses myself. I could have made things look different, I'm sure. No one understands my case ...* His Honor : *The facts against you are so numerous and so conclusive, not only as regards the offence which you are now charged with, but also for the long series of criminal acts which you have committed during the last eighteen months, that I do not think any rational person could have arrived at any other conclusion ...* Prisoner : *I do not fear death, and I am the last man in the world to take a man's life away. I believe that two years ago, before this thing happened, if a man pointed a gun at me to shoot me, I should not have stopped him, so careful was I of taking life. I am not a murderer, but if there is innocent life at stake, then I say I must take some action. If I see innocent life taken, I should certainly shoot if I was forced to do so, but I should first want to know whether this could not be prevented, but I should have to do it if it could not be stopped in any other way.* His Honor : *Your statement involves wicked and criminal reflection of untruth upon the witnesses who have given evidence.* Prisoner : *I dare say the day will come when we shall all have to go to a bigger court than this. Then we will see who is right and who is wrong. As regards anything about myself, all I care for is that my mother, who is now in prison, shall not have it to say that she reared a son who could not have altered this charge if he had liked to do so.* His Honor : *... You confessed it to them and you stand self-accused. It is also proved that you committed several attacks upon the banks, and you seem to have appropriated large sums of money—several thousands of pounds. It has also come within my knowledge that the country has expended about £50,000 in consequence of the acts of which you and your party have been guilty. Although we have had such examples as Clarke, Gardiner, Melville, Morgan and Scott, who have all met ignominious deaths, still the effect has, apparently, not been to hinder others from following in their foot-steps. I think that this is much to be deplored, and some steps must be taken to have society protected. Your unfortunate and miserable associates have met with deaths which you might envy ... May the Lord have mercy on your soul.* Prisoner : *Yes ; I will meet you there.*" (Trial of Edward Kelly, 6 Nov 1880, p.203)

"EXECUTION OF EDWARD KELLY ... At the time appointed for the execution, an immense crowd assembled in the road in Victoria-street, fronting the gaol.

They stared vacantly at the walls of the building and engaged in conversation. There was no demonstration. Immediately after sentence of death was passed on Kelly, additional precautions were taken to ensure his safe custody in the Melbourne gaol. He was placed in one of the cells in the old wing, and irons were riveted upon his legs, leather pads being placed round his ankles to prevent chafing. The cell had two doors—an outer one of solid iron, and an inner one of iron bars. The outer door was always kept open, a lamp was kept burning overhead, and a warder was continually sitting outside watching the prisoner. During the day he was allowed to walk in the adjoining yard for exercise, and on these occasions two warders had him under surveillance. He continued to maintain his indifferent demeanour for a day or two, professing to look forward to his execution without fear, but he was then evidently cherishing a hope of reprieve.

When he could get any one to speak to, he indulged in brag, recounting his exploits and boasting of what he could have done when at liberty had he pleased.

Latterly, however, his talkativeness ceased, and he became morose and silent. Within the last few days he dictated a number of letters for the Chief Secretary, in most of which he simply repeated his now well-known garbled version of his career and the spurious reasons he assigned for his crimes. He never, however, expressed any sorrow for his crimes; on the contrary, he always attempted to justify them. In his last communication he made a request that his body might be handed over to his friends—an application that was necessarily in vain. On Wednesday he was visited by his relatives, and bade them farewell. At his own request his portrait was also taken for circulation amongst his friends. He went to bed at half-past 1 o'clock on Thursday morning, and was very restless up to half-past 2, when he fell asleep. At 5 o'clock he awoke and arose, and falling on his knees prayed for 20 minutes, and then lay down again. He rose finally at about 8 o'clock, and at a quarter to 9 a blacksmith was called in to remove his irons. The rivets having been knocked out, and his legs liberated, he was attended by Father Donaghy, the Roman Catholic clergyman of the gaol. Immediately afterwards, he was conducted from his cell in the old wing to the condemned cell alongside the gallows in the new or main building. In being thus removed, he had to walk through the garden which surrounds the hospital ward, and to pass the handcart in which his body was in another hour to be carried back to the dead-house. Making only a single remark about the pretty flowers in the garden, he passed in a jaunty manner from the brilliant sunshine into the sombre walls of the prison. In the condemned cell the last rites of the Roman Catholic Church were administered to him by Father Donaghy and Dean O'Hea. In the meantime a large crowd of persons had commenced to gather in front of the gaol, and the persons who had received cards of admission assembled in the gaol yard. A few minutes before 10 o'clock, the hour fixed for the execution ... and the onlookers stood on the basement floor in front of the drop ... The governor asked for his warrant, and having received it, in due form bowed in acquiescence. The new hangman, an elderly grey-headed, well-conditioned looking man, named Upjohn, who is at present incarcerated for larceny ... Kelly ... merely said,

Ah, well, I suppose it has come to this,

as the rope was being placed round his neck. He appeared as in court, with beard and whiskers, never having been shaved. The priests in their robes followed him out of the cell repeating prayers, and another official of the Church stood in front of him with a crucifix ... his death was instantaneous ... The outside crowd had increased by 10 o'clock to about 4,000— men, women, and children; but a large proportion of them were larrikin-looking youths ... One woman, as the hour struck, fell on her knees in front of the entrance, and prayed for the condemned man." (Execution of Edward Kelly, 15 Nov 1880, p.3)

EDWARD KELLY'S LETTER "The miscreant sent to Mr Cameron about 20 pages of MS., which upon examination turns out to be the letter spoken of by Mrs Fitzgerald as having been written by him at Faithful Creek station. The packet bore the Glenrowan post-mark of 16th inst., and must have been posted on that day or the preceding Sunday ... The letter is cleverly written, and starts with the statement that the writer despairs of justice, unless the public listen to his wrongs. He goes on to narrate the manner in which he has been continually harassed by the police in petty ways, and how they annoyed his family and knocked his sisters about. Great complaint is made of the way in which Fitzpatrick and a certain publican gave their evidence about the Greta affair, which led to Kelly's mother with her baby and two men, who Kelly states were incorrect (innocent?), being sent to gaol for assaulting Fitzpatrick. Kelly swears he was not at Greta then, but four hundred miles away, and that Fitzpatrick was not shot by Dan Kelly; that Fitzpatrick had no warrant, and that was why Mrs Kelly and Dan threw him out of the house. On returning home Kelly found himself proscribed with £100 reward offered for him, and then he went off with his brother to Bullock Creek, where they worked at mining. Hearing that the police had turned out, and that the country was 'woven' with police sent after them, they thought it the best plan to surprise the police in their camp, and get their arms, ammunition and horses, as they had only two small guns, and then to make a rush and get through the circle. Kelly then describes fully the Wombat Creek massacre. They sneaked upon the camp after hearing the firing of guns, and when he appeared they called on Macintyre to surrender, which he did, but Lonigan ran behind a log, and was raising his hand to shoot Kelly when the latter shot him dead. On the return of Scanlan and Kennedy, the former was shot while shooting at the Kellys, and the latter ran behind a tree firing. Kelly shot him in the arm, when he at once rushed into the open, dropping his pistol. Kelly, however, did not see this, and when Kennedy turned, no doubt to surrender, he shot him through the chest. Kelly's letter concluded with violent threats that if justice is not done to his relatives and the innocent men in prison,

he would turn tiger, and war against all human kind.

He has no wish to kill civilians, but if the police go about in disguise he cannot distinguish between them, and he threatens to cause a great railway disaster. The letter concludes with four lines of original poetry, signed 'with a sweet good-bye, from Edward Kelly, a forced outlaw.' Curiously enough, in another part of the Mercury, from which the foregoing is extracted, Mr Cameron, referring respectfully to himself, expresses a fervent hope *that the letter will not see the light until Ned Kelly is shot, as there is too much sympathy for the bloodthirsty ruffians*; and then proceeds to dish up another slander against the courage and capacity of the police." (Edward Kelly's Letter, 20 Dec 1878, p.3)

1883 – "A MAIL COACH STUCK UP ... News has been received in town tonight stating that Cobb's coach with the mails for Inverell, Bundara, and Tingha was stuck up by a man armed with a pistol, who called himself Kelly, the bushranger. The mails were stolen, but the passengers were not molested." (A Mail Coach Stuck Up, 24 May 1883, p.2)

1880 Ned Kelly, the bushranger ... taken day before execution
(Charles Nettleton, 1826-1902) - Courtesy National Library Australia

1880 The Trial of Edward Kelly, the bushranger - Courtesy State Library Victoria

ca. 1910-1920 Victorian Railways guard Jesse Dowsett holding Ned Kelly's pistol
(Victorian Railways, photographer) - Courtesy State Library Victoria

ca. 1900-1940 Horse drawn vehicle (State Rivers and Water Supply Commission, photographer) - Courtesy State Library Victoria

1896 Main Street, Walhalla, Victoria (Herbert Percival, photographer) - Courtesy State Library Victoria

1900-1920 Stage Coach with Passengers, Lorne, Victoria
(S. Anderson, photographer) - Courtesy Museums Victoria Collections

1890 W. Mountjoy's Coach, Erskine River, Lorne, Victoria
(William S. Anderson, photographer) - Courtesy Museums Victoria

Chapter Nine
Livery and bait stables

To Mr Pat Gooley, of Messrs Cobb and Co.

We miss the old coach, and the seven o'clock post,
With its letters and packets of news ;
The railway is gained, but how much, hath been lost,
Is a quantum for differing views.

Though the gathering crowd forgot, one and all,
To present you with tickets to banquet and ball,
We'll toast your good health in compliment true—
There's many a worse driver, believe me, than you.

Up hill, and down dale, and on dry, dusty level,
In hail, rain, and shine, you have driven us well ;
Often thirsty and heated—but well-mannered and civil :
A few eyes will moisten when we bid you farewell.

When down life's steep incline your chariot doth tend,
And the fast-flying coachman speeds to the end ;
Keep a steady look-out through the changing view,
And say, 'I am here !' when the Mailman is due.

When we, on our last trip, are called to embark,
When the daylight expires and the shadows grow dark :
May we 'fix up our lamps,' and 'all a-board !' take,
And 'pull up' at a grave with our foot on the brake.

By J. Addison White.
(To Mr Pat Gooley, of Messrs Cobb and Co., 13 May 1886, p.3)
ca. 1901 Union Hotel (Thomas Henry Armstrong, photographer) - Courtesy State Library Victoria

Livery and Bait Stables, examples

BALLARAT

1860 – "TENDERS required for Supplying Coach Stable Ballarat, for Messrs F. B, Clapp & Co , with 100 tons of first class sweet Oaten Hay, to be delivered as required. Tenders will be taken for part, or the lot,—and sureties required. For particulars, apply to William Eaves, Armstrong street. Tenders will be opened 15th March." (Advertising, 7 Mar 1860, p 4)

1863 – "TO FARMERS, CORN MERCHANTS AND OTHERS. Tenders For Supplying Forage. Tenders will be received until 31st instant, for supplying Oats, Barley, Hay, and Hay chaff of prime quality at the coaching stables of the Australian Stage Company ... Barley, unless delivered at Ballarat, must be crushed. Samples will be required ... Oats or Barley. Hay Chaff. Bran ... Ararat Avoca Ballarat Buangor Burrumbeet Ballan Bacchus Marsh Creswick Creek Clunes Dunolly Deep Creek Daylesford Keilor Station Landsborough Learmonth Lexton Moonambel Maryborough Moorabool Melton Raglan Stawell Talbot Western (Armstrongs) ... Australian Stage Company, Cobb and Co.'s Offices ... TO BLACKSMITHS. Tenders are invited for Shoeing the Australian Stage Company's Coach Horses at Ballarat, for a period of one year ... To Ironmongers, Saddlers, and Others, Tenders will be received, until 31st instant, for supplying the undermentioned articles at the coach stables of the Australian Stage Company, Ballarat. Samples may be seen on application ... dander brushes ... body brushes ... water brushes ... mane combs ... stable brooms ... buckets (iron) ... neatsfoot oil ... dungforks ... chamois leather ... brown soap ... Castile soap ... soft soap ... sponge ... 6 large-sized reflector coach lamps. Tenders to be addressed Australian Stage Company. Cobb and Co.'s Offices, Ballarat, 14th January, 1863." (Advertising, 16 Jan 1863, p.3)

1868 – "FIRE IN ARMSTRONG STREET. A fire broke out at about half-past eight o'clock on Tuesday night in the stable occupied by Mr Suley, veterinary surgeon, at the rear of Cutter and Lever's coach factory in Armstrong street. The stable was, however, closer to Lydiard than Armstrong street, being close to the back of Mr Mullen's printing office on that side, and close on the north side to the yard immediately behind Craig's hotel, and separating the hotel from the range of brick stables, iron-roofed, that open into Bath street. The stable where the fire broke out was once Cobb and Co.'s night stable or part of it, and was attached to other stables, to Cutter and Lever's workshops, and a large series of great wooden barn-like buildings, within and about which there was a perfect wilderness of old coaches, new coaches, buggies, gigs, and all the materials which go to make new or mend old vehicles of all kinds. Strange to say, it seems that neither on Cutter and Lever's highly combustible premises nor about any of the stables was there a domestic water service, or if there were one it was not used. Had there been one, and had it been used at once, the fire might easily have been subdued or kept where it broke out." (Fire in Armstrong Street, 11 Mar 1868, p.2)

1870 – "FATAL ACCIDENT AT COBB AND CO.'S STABLES. An accident by which a young man named Frederick Halse, aged twenty-two, was suddenly deprived of life, occurred at two o'clock on Tuesday morning in a shop in Lydiard street, next to Cobb and Co.'s stables. It appears from the evidence taken at the inquest ... deceased rented a small fruit shop and sleeping room of Mr M'Phee, the lessee of the premises, and that a loft above the sleeping room had been used for the storage of oats ... a groom named William Cochrane, who works in the stables ... saw a crack in the boards in the end stall of the stable, which led him to suspect there was something wrong, and on looking again at daylight he found that the loft had fallen in. He gave the alarm, and on Sergeant M'Cullagh going to the spot he found that deceased usually slept in the room below the loft and after half-an-hour's shovelling out of the oats by himself and three other constables, they found the body of deceased below ... Mr. M'Phee, in accounting for the accident, said that as deceased had recently papered and canvassed out his room he must have removed the blocks which supported the joists ... John M'Phee, coach proprietor, deposed that he was lessee of the premises in question, known as M'Phee and Company's stables." (Fatal Accident at Cobb and Co's Stables, 6 Apr 1870, p.2)

1882 – "GENERAL NEWS ... Fire at Cobb and Co.'s Stables. Ballarat, Thursday Evening. A fire broke out in Cobb and Co.'s stables, Lydiard street, next to the Royal George hotel, this evening, at about half-past 5 o'clock. At the time there were thirteen horses and a number of vehicles on the premises, valued altogether at about £1,200. All the traps were got out safely, also the horses. Most of the horse feed was destroyed by fire and water, and the interior of the building on the northern side was completely destroyed. All the damage is covered by insurance. Mr. M'Phee, the owner, thinks the fire was caused by the gas igniting the straw." On the same page "IN THE DISTRICT COURT on Thursday, a young man named Henry Richards was proceeded against for smoking at the Hobson's Bay railway station. From the evidence given by the officials it appeared that he was not only smoking and thereby infringing the regulations, but was puffing the smoke into the faces of females who were waiting at the station" ... Other news on the same page ... "THE SIX RAILWAY CARRIAGES which arrived recently from England have been delivered at the railway workshops. One is a first-class, and the others are second class carriages. They are all very well finished, and were built in accordance with the requisitions of the locomotive superintendent, Mr. Mirls. A noticeable feature is that all the compartments are very roomy. The first-class carriage contains four compartments (one being for smoking), and the second-class fire compartments. Each are fitted with Venetian blinds, spring curtains, hat racks, etc., and the seats and backs are well padded. The carriages are fitted with electric apparatus for communicating with the guards. The apparatus cannot now be utilised, as some of the fittings have yet to arrive. Continuous footboards are provided. The builders were Messrs. Brown, Marshall, and Co., of Birmingham, and the workmanship has given every satisfaction. Four more carriages to arrive are overdue, and ten others are expected to arrive at any moment. The new railway carriages which have recently arrived from England, and which were placed on the lines on Saturday, have been put to a good test. On Saturday they ran two journeys to Sandhurst and back, and since that they have been as far as Albury and back. They ran with great smoothness and steadiness, notwithstanding opinions expressed in certain quarters in regard to that matter, and officers of the department are greatly pleased with them ... THE PRISONERS AT THE PENTRIDGE STOCKADE, according to the custom of several years back, were permitted to have plum pudding and tea on Christmas Day." (Fire at Cobb and Co.'s Stables, 30 Dec 1882, p.14)

1884 – "COBB AND CO.'S LIVERY AND LETTING STABLES, George Hotel, Lydiard street, Ballarat. Cobb and Co. having leased these commodious Stables, the public may now rely upon being well served at this establishment ... Vines and M'Phee; Cobb and Co. Ballarat to Adelaide Overland in 56 hours ... Cobb and Co.'s Coach and rail from Narracoorte; Cobb and Co. ... Ballarat to St Arnaud ... Ballarat to Charlton ... M'Phee and Co." (Advertising, 24 Sep 1884, p.1)

1886 – "COBB AND CO LIVERY AND LETTING STABLES, George Hotel, Lydiard street, Ballarat. COBB and CO. having Leased these commodious Stables, the public may rely upon being well served at this establishment. Commercial gentlemen liberally dealt with. Horses taken in to livery by the day, week, or month. Horses and Vehicles for Hire. Telephone to George Hotel, No. 130. Vines and M'Phee, Proprietors." (Advertising, 10 Mar 1886, p.1)

1887 – "COBB AND CO.'S LIVERY AND LETTING STABLES ... George Hotel, Lydiard street, Ballarat ... Branch Letting Stables. Geelong, Queenscliff, Hamilton, St. Arnaud, Daylesford, Sandhurst, Belfast, Beechworth, &c. Vines and M'Phee." (Advertising, 26 Oct 1887, p.1)

1888 – "COBB AND CO.'S LIVERY AND LETTING STABLES (Vines and M'Phee) ... Telephone Craig's Royal Hotel Stables—No. 1888 Forester's George Hotel Stables—No. 188." While advertised on the same page "Ok The Blood Is The Life. CLARKE'S WORLD-FAMED BLOOD MIXTURE. Largest Sale Of Any Medicine In The World. Overwhelming Testimony Accompanies Every Bottle, Proving This To Be The Greatest Medicine Ever Discovered. For Cleansing And Clearing The Blood. From All Impurities, whether the result of Contagious Disease, hereditary taint, or foul matter of any description, it cannot be too highly recommended. For Scrofula, Scurvy, Eczema, Skin and Blood Diseases, and Sores of all kinds, it is a never-failing and permanent cure. It Cures Old Sores Cures Sores on the Neck Cures Sore Legs Cures Blackheads, or Pimples on the Face Cures Scurvy Cures Ulcers Cures Blood and Skin Diseases Cures Glandular Swellings Clears the Blood from all Impure Matter, From whatever cause arising. As this Mixture is pleasant to the taste, and warranted free from anything injurious to the most delicate constitution of either sex, the Proprietors solicit sufferers to give it a trial to test its value." (Advertising, 16 Aug 1888, p.1)

1893 – "A MAN NAMED HENRY WILHELM, a groom employed at Cobb and Co.'s livery stables, Ballarat, was admitted into the hospital on Monday, having fractured some of his ribs through a heavy fall. Wilhelm formerly lived at Ballan." (Local and General News, 2 Nov 1893, p.3)

1903 – "COBB & CO.—CENTRAL STABLES ... Baits, stands, and liveries a speciality ... Man always in attendance at night ... Seaside Coaches ... Geelong, Torquay, Anglesea, Barwon Heads, Ocean Grove, Clifton Springs, Drysdale, Bellarine and Portarlington ... Parsels carried at special rates ... Cobb and Co.'s Head Office, Malop street, Geelong. Telephone 1... Ballarat to Pitfield Plains Via Smythesdale and Cape Clear ... Leigh Road to Rokewood, Via Teesdale and Shelford ... Western Stage Co." (Advertising, 13 Feb 1903, p.1)

1905 – "COBB AND CO.'S OFFICE, Craig's Stables, Cook and Son, Also Ballarat Railway Station. Telephone No 188 ... Craig's Stables, Lydiard street, Ballarat ... Cobb and Co., Craig's Royal Stables ... cash purchases of all suitable horses, vehicles and harness ... Geo. O. Cole, Manager." (Advertising, 6 Feb 1905, p.4)

1906 – Ballarat "COBB AND CO.'S EXCURSIONS. Cobb and Co. announce the following excursions for this week:—Thursday next, moonlight drive; a drag will leave the stables, Bath street, about 7.30 p.m., returning at 9.30. Friday—Grocers' picnic. Burrmubeet, 9 a.m, Saturday—Moorabool Falls, 2.15 p.m.; hot water provided. Sunday—Trip to Daylesford; a drag will leave the stables at 9 a.m. Fares are published in the advertising columns." (Cobb and Co.'s Excursions, 7 Mar 1906, p.1)

1913 – "LIVERY STABLE WAGES. Charges of unpaying an employee. Messrs. Cobb and Co. livery stable keepers, of Ballarat, were charged with a breach of the Factory Act, was heard before Messrs C. Walker and J. Fraser, J.'sP, at the City Court yesterday morning. The charge was that on the 19th April defendants employed Geo. Perryman and Geo. Watson at a rate lower than that determined by the Livery Stable Board." (Livery Stables Wages, 21 Jun 1913, p.3)

BEAUFORT

1869 – EARTHQUAKE "A distinct shock of earthquake was felt at Bombala, last Tuesday morning, at ten minutes past five, followed by a rumbling sound proceeding in a westerly direction. The shock was sufficiently violent to awaken several persons in bed ... Two severe shocks of earthquake were felt at Gipps Land, last Monday morning ... COBB AND CO.'S STABLES, at Beaufort, Victoria, have been destroyed by fire ; the horses were saved ... A PROLIFIC GOAT.—A circumstance which is, I believe, very uncommon, occurred on Thursday to a goat, the property of a Mr. Collier, of this city. The goat, which is about the general size, gave birth, on that day, to five fine kids, four of whom are living, and in good health ; the fifth has since died." (General, 4 Sep 1869, p.3)

CASTLEMAINE

1860 – "TENDERS are requested for the supply of best Tartarian Oats, of Colonial growth, at the undermentioned places, for a period of twelve months, from the 1st of March 1860, to 1st March 1861. Specifications may be had upon application to Mr. P. W. Jackson, Victoria Hotel ; Castlemaine ; C.C. Gardiner ; Victoria Hotel, Kyneton, and J. M. Peck, Old Bush Inn, Gisborne: Castlemaine - 10,800 bushels Elphinstone 3,780 " Taradale 1,800 " Kyneton 11,340 " Woodend 8,040 " Gisborne 11,400 " Digger's Rest 5,000 ", Tenders will be received for portions, or the whole of the above contract. Bonds to be given and taken for the faithful performance of same. Tenders received until the 25th inst., and to be addressed to Mr. A. L. Blake, Manager, Victorian Stage Company, No. 23, Great Bourke street east." (Advertising, 27 Feb 1860, p.1)

COLERAINE

1898 – "SPECIAL ANNOUNCEMENT. Cobb & Co. wish to intimate to their customers that they have leased the Korite Inn Stables, Coleraine, where they will in future carry on their business, and hope to receive a fair share of public patronage. Western Stage Co." (Advertising, 8 Oct 1898, p.2)

DAYLESFORD

1875 – ACCIDENT "We (Daylesford Mercury) regret to state that an accident occurred on Tuesday afternoon which has resulted in the death of a young man named C. W. H. Symons. On Wednesday; deceased hired a saddle horse at Cobb and Co.'s livery stables, and went for a ride towards Glenlyon ... Symon's horse swerved at a waterhole, and dashed his rider against a tree. Deceased was taken up insensible and conveyed to the Junction hotel .... no doctor was sent for ... About 8 p.m. on the same evening, Mr Moore, proprietor of the Royal Mail hotel, where deceased had been staying for the past five of six weeks, received a message that Symons was hurt. Early yesterday morning Mr Moore drove out Dr Massy to the Junction hotel, and the latter, on examination, found that deceased's skull was fractured, and ordered his removal to the Hospital. The poor fellow, however, expired on the way ... He was nearly 21years of age, and would of come into a fortune of £3000 on attaining his majority" while "A bad accident occurred to a boy, named Richard Ellis, aged 13 years, at Egerton Wednesday, 19th May.

It appears that instead of going to school, as he was told, he went a little way from his residence into the bush, where a man was passing with a gun. The man asked young Ellis to hold his gun for a few minutes, which he did. He then rested the but end on the ground and placed the middle finger of his left hand on the top of the barrel, and he states that whilst holding it steady it went off, taking with it the whole of his finger. The man, who is not known, gave the boy the large sum of threepence and left him to do the best he could without any attempt to relieve him, though the man's carelessness most probably caused the loss of the finger. The boy's father was at work in the Egerton Company's mine when the accident occurred. Dr Griffiths dressed the wound." (News and Notes, 21 May 1875, p.2)

1900 – "COBB AND CO. What a world of happy memories is inspired by the name of the great coaching firm! It was in 1864 that Mr John Keays was transferred from Talbot to take charge of the business at Daylesford, and his energy and capability soon became evident. The business flourished apace, and four years later the livery and letting branch was started. Since then it has gained and gained, until now there are coaching, livery and carrying departments at the rear of the Commercial Hotel, in portion of which is the office. It is like a visit to the Agricultural Show to see the show of vehicles of all kinds in the yards and coach-houses, and as many as thirty well-trained and sturdy horses are stabled. The 'whips' are tried and true, some of them experts of the old coaching days, and it is a pleasure, as the writer knows from experience, to see them handle the ribbons." (Cobb and Co., 1 Dec 1900, p.1)

1917 – "OUTBREAK OF FIRE COBB AND CO.'S STABLES GUTTED. Daylesford, Wednesday. An outbreak of fire occurred to-day at Cobb and Co.'s stables, at the rear of the Commercial Hotel. The back of the stables was badly gutted, but the timely arrival of the firemen saved the front portion of the building" while "RETURNED SOLDIER WELCOMED A number of residents assembled at the Beaufort railway station on Tuesday to welcome Sergt Gilbert Smith, of Waterloo, who has been invalided home. He was previously invalided home from Gallipoli, and acted as recruiting sergeant here for some time before returning to the Front about 18 months ago." (Outbreak of Fire, 22 Nov 1917, p.5)

"COBB & CO.'S STABLES ON FIRE. At 3 o'clock on Wednesday afternoon a fire broke out in Cobb and Co.'s (Silbereisen's) stables in Duke streets Mr. Foster, clerk of courts was proceeding down Albert street from the Court House on his way to the Bank, when he observed dense smoke issuing from the buildings. He promptly rushed into the office of Mr R. W. Shellard solicitor, and phoned to the Post Office asking some of the officials to ring the alarm bell at the fire Station. The belt was rung and the firemen were very prompt in responding and thanks to their energetic efforts soon had the flames under control and extinguished them before a great deal of damage was done. A very large crowd assembled to view the conflagration. Fortunately, only two horses and a pony were in the stables at the time. Mr Silbereisen released the horses and got them out safely, but the pony ran back and there was, great danger of it being burnt to death. Happily, however after considerable effort it was rescued. All Mr Silbereisen's harness, was saved, but a considerable amount of chaff and other food was destroyed. It is not known how the fire originated. At 11.30 two men unloaded fodder at the stables and everything was then apparently safe. The fire evidently broke out in the loft. The stables are the property of Mr J. Stubbs, of the Commercial Hotel and are insured in the Commercial Union Insurance Co. for £200. The contents were insured for £200 in the New Zealand Insurance Co. by Mr Silbereisen." (Cobb & Co.'s Stables on Fire, 23 Nov 1917, p.3)

1922 – DAYLESFORD SALE "of the Commercial Hotel ... include the commodious stables, which at present are let to Cobb and Co. at the rental of 52 per annum." (Classified Advertising, 15 April 1922, p.2)

1928 – "IN THE DAY'S OF COBB & CO. By Norman Campbell ... the mere mention of the famous firm stirs romantic memories of other days ... Cobb & Co.'s office at the Albion Hotel, in Bourke street, was closed in 1890. To-day the name of Cobb & Co. is perpetuated at Daylesford, where a livery stable is conducted under that title. It is the only Cobb & Co. stable remaining in Victoria. Ichabod! the glory is departed." (In the Days of Cobb & Co., 23 Jun 1928, p.3)

Frankston

"SHADES OF COBB AND CO. Discussion ensued this week in Frankston as to who was Frankston's original blacksmith. The honor was given to John Cameron, blacksmith and vet who opened a smithy in Bay Street, where Gray's garage now stands, for the main purpose, then of shoeing the Cobb and Co. coach horses. Mr. Hugh Cameron, of Frankston, is a son of the pioneer village smith." (Shades of Cobb and Co., 16 May 1946, p.1)

Geelong

1866 – "COBB & CO.'S LIVERY, LETTING, AND BAIT STABLES ... Geelong ... Hesse-street, Queenscliff ... Thomas Stoneman & Co." (Advertising, 27 Dec 1866, p.1)

"TO HAY AND CORN MERCHANTS. Tenders For Forage. Tenders, addressed to the proprietors of the Western Stage Company, will be received until noon, on Saturday, 29th instant, for supplying their Geelong Stables with the best description of Horse Feed to include Hay, Straw and Bedding, in such quantities as may be from time to time required, for three months, commencing on the 1st January, 1867. Accounts to be rendered monthly. Cobb and Co.'s Coach Office, Great Malop street, Geelong. December 23rd, 1866." (Advertising, 27 Dec 1866, p.1)

1868 – "COBB & CO.'S LIVERY, LETTING, AND BAIT STABLES, Opposite Messrs. Synnot & Guthrie's Wool Warehouse, Union Hotel, Great Malop-street, Geelong." (Advertising, 3 Jan 1868, p.1)

"COBB & CO.'S LIVERY AND LETTING STABLES ... Geelong ... Western Stage Company, Cobb and Co.'s Booking Office, Geelong." (Advertising, 22 Apr 1868, p.1)

1894 – "FIRE IN MALOP-STREET. A fire which broke out at seven minutes to one this morning in a carpenter's shop belonging to Mr Frank Ebery, builder and contractor, nearly led to the destruction of the extensive stables of the Western Stage Company. It is fortunate that a perfect calm prevailed, for had the flames been fanned by a westerly wind nothing but the most superhuman efforts could have saved the stables from ruin. As it was the side of the office became ignited through the heat, and was blazing merrily when the firemen arrived. The alarm was given in the first instance by Ned Hands, the watchman at the stables, and almost simultaneously the alarm at Purdie's corner and that near the wool stores of Dennys, Luscelles, Austin and Co. were put into operation by Constables Sullivan and Patullo.

Exactly seven minutes later the firemen, under the command of Captain Keon, had the water, at intense pressure, playing upon the flames, which were extinguished in a few minutes. The conflagration while it lasted brilliantly illuminated the town, and attracted a great crowd of spectators, many of whom assisted the members of the Salvage Corps in removing the horses and vehicles from the stables. All the office books were removed to a place of safety by the Salvage Corps, which got to work very expeditiously under the direction of Lieutenant Davies. Before the arrival of the firemen Senior-constable Mulloy did some useful work inside the stables by playing two ordinary hoses upon the walls of the loose boxes nearest the fire, so as to keep them cool. Except for the charred office wall and the disturbance of the furniture, there was nothing to indicate that the stable had been in such grave danger. The salvage of the buildings illustrated in a convincing manner the value of an efficient body of firemen like the Geelong brigade in a large centre of population. Mr Ebery's shop and its contents were entirely consumed. The loss is covered by insurance for £100 in the South British Fire Insurance Company. The stables of the Western Stage Company are owned by Mr W. Humble, who has them insured in the Lion office, of which Mr Tully is agent, and policies running close into the neighborhood of £1000 are hold by the Guardian office over the stock-in-trade of the company. This office has met several calls lately in Geelong. Mr W. Abraham, its popular agent, was congratulated this morning upon its escape on this occasion." (Fire in Malop-street, 31 Jan 1894, p.2)

1895 – TANKS "Wanted to Sell ... square, round, cheapest in city, 200 gallon round, for water carting, with hose and frame; 40s. Cobb & Co., Latrobe-st [Melbourne]." (Advertising, 20 Apr 1895, p.5)

1896 – "COBB & CO.'S ... LIVERY, LETTING, & BAIT STABLES, Malop-Street East, Geelong, And Bay View Stables, Corio-Terrace. Largest and Best Assortment of Conveyances and Horses on hire. Special Arrangements for Picnic Parties, Stock and Station Agents, Mining Brokers, Commercial Travellers. Horses hired to Ocean Grove. Barwon Heads, Clifton Springs, Drysdale, Queenscliff, Portarlington, Leigh Road, Steiglitz, Rokewood. Careful attention given, and stabling free of cost. Good Grooms employed and special attention given to horses left at Livery and Bait." (Advertising, 22 May 1896, p.1)

1912 – "FIRE IN A BUS. Mr. C. Podger's bus had a narrow escape from destruction by fire last evening. While on the stand in Moolabool-street at about nine o'clock, the candle in the lamp set fire to the wood works and the flames had secured a good hold before being noticed by the owner, who made desperate efforts to smother them. Some passers-by noticed Mr. Podger's predicament, and Mr. Ward ran to Cobb and Co.'s stable and secured a bucket of water, which had the desired effect." (Fire in a Bus, 5 Jan 1912, p.2)

1921 – "GEELONG. PASSING OF COBB AND CO. Formal ratification has been given by the directors and shareholders of the Geelong and Cressy Trading Company in the purchase by the company of buildings situated in Malop street, and occupied as livery for between 69 and 70 years. For the last 35 of these they have been known as Cobb and Co.'s ... It is expected that possession will be taken this week." (Geelong, 23 Feb 1921, p.6)

"CLEARING SALES. Norman Belcher and Co. report a highly successful clearing sale of motor cars and accessories, etc. at Cobb and Co.'s garage, Malop-street, on Wednesday last. The sale was conducted under instructions from Mr. P. Neilson (of Neilson and Neilson), public accountants, Geelong, as trustee of the assigned estate of H. Womersley. The whole of the fleet of seven Studebaker motor cars together with a large quantity of machinery, etc., were disposed of." (Commercial, 12 Mar 1921, p.8)

Hamilton

1882 – "WANTED. — a Lad, for the stable. Apply to Cobb and Co., Hamilton." (Advertising, 16 Dec 1882, p.3)

1896 – "MOUNTED RIFLES. The following Company Order has been issued: The inspection of H Company by Major-General Sit C. Holled - Smith, Military Commandant, will take place at Hamilton, on Thursday, 3rd December, r896. Fall-in at 1.30 p.m. Dress-Full Marching Order. This parade is compulsory, every man is to attend, those sick or on duty only excepted, when a certificate from a Medical Officer must be forwarded. The following will be the train arrangements : Narrawong detachment ... Heywood Detachment ... Milltown Detachment ... Casterton Detachment ... Branxholme Detachment ... Byaduk Detachment.— To march by road. All horses to be at the different stations at least half-an-hour before the time appointed, and every assistance is to be given to get the horses trucked as soon as possible. On arrival at Hamilton the horses will be taken to Cobb and Co.'s stables at Thomson-street, were arrangements will be made to have them fed while the men are at dinner. Immediately each man has finished his dinner he should proceed to the stables and look after his horse, kit, &c., and all ranks must be ready to move off at the time appointed." (Mounted Rifles, 11 Nov 1896, p.2)

Horsham

1953 – "HAD COBB AND STABLE Mr. Hermann Kuhne, of Rainbow, is amazed at the changes that have taken place in Horsham and district over the last 80 years ... Now 91 years old, he first came to Horsham in 1890 when the site of the present city was a mere settlement of two small hotels, two stores, smithy, a Cobb and Co. stable, and a few other buildings. One of the stores was a brick building, still standing in Hamilton Street, which was built by one of Horsham's first pioneers, Mr. George Langlands. The building at that time housed Langlands' store and Post Office ... CARRIED WATER At the time Mr. Kuhne arrived here in Horsham district was recovering from the drought of 1869 and residents had to carry water from Wimmera River to their homes and properties." (Remembers when had Cobb and Co. Stable, 14 Oct 1953, p.2)

Kilmore

1950 – VISIT TO KILMORE "Cobb & Co. Old Drivers ... Prior to reaching Kilmore the party stopped at Wallan to inspect the old Inverlochy Hotel now delicensed 40 years, and built 100 years ago by the grandfather of the present owner, Mr. Leo Laffan. In the coaching days Wallan was the last stage before reaching Melbourne ... visitors were guests of their President (Mr. Wallace Mitchell) at the Royal Oak Hotel for lunch ... In the afternoon the visitors adjourned to Moore Park ... It was particularly fitting that the spot in the Park ... was once the private garden of the Kilmore Hotel—a recognised stage coach depot. Of greatest interest to the visitors was perhaps the inspection of the old Cobb & Co. blue stone stables and coach sheds at the rear of the post office and now the property of Mr. C. Dillon ... The address was presented to the late Mr. Hugh Mitchell by the citizens of Kilmore when he retired as driver for Cobb & Co. 78 years ago ...

That there was no intention of allowing the party to become dull was very evident from the fact that, one of their guests for the trip was Smoky Dawson, who provided fitting entertainment at Kilmore—and Wallan—with his hillbilly songs and guitar." (Cobb & Co. Old Drivers, 2 Nov 1950, p.5)

MELBOURNE

1859 – "AMERICAN LIVERY AND LETTING STABLES ... with a line of omnibuses in connection with every train to and from the railway station ... James Swanton, proprietor". (Advertising, 2 Jun 1859, p.7)

"AMERICAN LIVERY AND LETTING STABLES, Stephen street, between Bourke and Little Bourke street east (late Ford's). American buggies, carryalls, gigs, dog-carts, chaisos, ladies' and gentlemen's saddle horses, always on hire. Horses kept by the day, week, or month, on the most reasonable terms. James Swanton, Proprietor." (Advertising 9 Jul 1859, p.1)

1861 – "TENDERS will be received until the 15th instant, for the supply of the following stores, at the Australian Stage Company's Stables at Melbourne : 50 boxes coach candles, sperm, sixes 50 do Belmont sperm candles, do 50 lb. sponge 20 kegs coach grease, prepared 5cwt. best Liverpool soap 5cwt. rock salt 6 dozen body-brushes, best quality 1 gross strong hemp halters 1 do light do do 6 dozen strong stable lanterns 6 gross dander-brushes, best quality ... C. Russell, Manager. Cobb and Co.'s Offices, 35 Bourke-street east, Melbourne. Tenders will be received until the 28th instant, for SHOEING THE HORSES belonging to the Australian Stage Company, as often as may be required, during a period of six months, at the undermentioned coach stations : Geelong, Ballarat, Raglan, Ararat, Creswick Creek, Back Creek, Dunolly. Particulars as to number of horses at each station, and terms of contract, &c., may be had on application to the manager. Australian Coach Company. C. Russell, Manager. Cobb's Coach Offices, Melbourne. Tenders will be received until the 26th inst. for SUPPLY OF OATS, HAY, CHAFF, AND BRAN, at the undermentioned coach stations, monthly or otherwise, as may be required, during a period of nine months : Geelong, Spread Eagle, Burrumbeet, Creswick's Creek, Clyde, Ballan, Raglan, Clunes, Meredith, Bacchus Marsh, M'Donald's, Back Creek. Corduroy, Melton, Ararat, Maryborough. Ballarat, Keliorroad, Pleasant Creek, Dunolly, Sandy Creek, Inglewood. Particulars as to terms of contract and quantities required, &c, may be had on application to the manager, to whom tenders must be addressed. Australian Stage Company. C. Russell, Manager. Cobb and Co.'s Offices, Melbourne." (Advertising, 11 Feb 1861, p.8)

MEREDITH

1926 – ROYAL HOTEL "The old stable which has stood 65 years at the rear of the Royal Hotel, Meredith, has been demolished. This was the stable that accommodated the coaching teams of Cobb and Co. on the Geelong-Ballarat road in the early days. The new stable will be associated with a motor car garage." (Australasian News in a Nutshell, 6 Feb 1926, p.8)

MOE

1904 – HORSE GORED BY COW "The Rev. L. Fieiding, after celebrating a marriage at Moe on Wednesday evening last, left his horse in Lloyd street, opposite the residence of Mrs Stratton, for a brief period. On his return he discovered that the animal was suffering from a severe wound under the shoulder on the near foreleg, evidently caused by having been gored by a cow, a number of which nightly parade our streets. The horse was so badly hurt that Mr Fielding had to leave it at Cobb and Co.'s stables for treatment, and had to return to Trafalgar on a bike." (No Title, 26 Apr 1904, p.2)

MORWELL

1877 – "THE FIRE AT COBB & CO.'S STABLES, MORWELL ... magisterial inquiry ... we submit this course was not followed ... It could have been proved that there were more than one safe and good lamp for the use of the grooms ... It has been sought to throw most of the blame on one groom, Matthew Cooney, but evidence could have been, forthcoming to prove that this man was not at all to blame, or, at least, not more, so than the other. Cooney has been in the employ of Cobb and Co. for many years, always a night groom, and no charge of carelessness has hitherto been made against him ... We have little doubt that if all the evidence obtainable had been produced the fire would have been shown to be the result of pure accident instead of gross carelessness ... We are, Sir, yours, &c., The Drivers." (Correspondence, 5 Dec 1877, p.3)

PENHURST

1891 – "COBB & CO'S WESTERN TELEGRAPH LINE OF ROYAL MAIL COACHES ... We wish to inform our numerous customers that we have opened a Livery and Letting Stable at rear of W. Moorman's Penshurst Hotel, Penshurst, and that every effort will be made to promote the public convenience, and to give general satisfaction ... Horses and Buggies, and other conveyances always on Hire at our Letting Stables, Victoria Hotel, Hamilton ; also at Star of the West Stables, Port Fairy ; George Hotel, Craig's Hotel, and Irwin's Provincial Hotel, Ballarat, Geelong, Daylesford. Queenscliff, Koroit, Macarthur, Penhurst, etc ... Western Stage Company, Proprietors, Cobb and Co.'s General Booking Office, Thompson street. Hamilton." (Advertising, 3 Sep 1891, p.1)

PRAHAN

1934 – "OLD STABLES BURNT. Used by Cobb and Co. A relic of the old coaching days in Victoria was destroyed yesterday when stables adjoining a delicensed hotel in Commercial road, Prahran, caught fire. Once the stables were used by the coaching firm of Cobb & Co. A dog which had been tied up in the stables was released by Mr. Thomas Hawkless, an occupant of the adjoining building, which was saved by the prompt action of boarders and others living on the premises." While "USA ... Sir Charles Kingsford-Smith, the Australian airman, who has arrived here, will inspect Lockheed aeroplanes. Possibly he will purchase one for the London-Melbourne Centenary Air Race." (Old Stables Burnt, 22 May 1934, p.8)

QUEENSCLIFF

1868 – "COBB & CO.'S LIVERY, LETTING, AND BAIT STABLES ... at Hesse-street, (Near Adman's Hotel), Queenscliff." (Advertising, 3 Jan 1868, p.1)

ROSEDALE

1927 – "COBB AND CO. LINK GOING ROSEDALE, Wednesday. —One of Rosedale's oldest landmarks—a brick stable and loft—has boon demolished. It was attached to the Rosedale hotel, and was erected more than 65 years ago, being used as a central depot for Cobb and Co.'s coaches when they were running from Walhalla to Port Albert. The bricks are in perfect order, and are to be used in extensive additions to the Rosedale Hotel." (Cobb and Co. Link Going, 10 Feb 1927, p.8)

SALE

1878 – "COBB & CO.'S LIVERY & LETTING STABLES, Raymond Street, Sale. First Class Single and Double-seated Buggies, Coaches and Drags for Hire, also Saddle Horses. Horses broken to Single and Double Harness and Saddle. Finest Loose Boxes in Gippsland. Charges Moderate. Robertson, Wagner, & Co., Proprietors ... CAUTION. My Greyhound 'Ferryman' strayed, or was enticed away, from Cobb's Stables in Raymond-street ... He had a collar bearing my name. If promptly returned a Reward will be given. If detained after this notice any person in whose possession he may be found will get into trouble, as the matter is in the hands of the police. J. F. SWEENEY. Cobb's Office, Sale" (Advertising, 16 Sep 1878, p.2)

SANDHURST/BENDIGO

1867 – "FATAL RESULT OF A SLIGHT ACCIDENT.— About a fortnight ago a man named Edmund Foley, 35 years of age, employed at Messrs Cobb & Co.'s. stables in Mundy-street, had a splinter driven into his thumb while at work. Little attention was paid to what was then considered a trivial accident, but in a few days alarming symptoms appeared and medical advice was sought. Gangrene, however, supervened, and it was deemed expedient on Thursday last to have the unfortunate man removed to the hospital, where, despite every attention, he expired a few minutes before nine o'clock yesterday morning. We regret to learn that the deceased leaves a widow and family to deplore his untimely death, the cause of which will probably form the subject of further inquiry." On the same page "A METEOR.—Last night, about nine o'clock, a brilliant meteor appeared in the sky to the east, descending in an oblique direction towards the south, and then suddenly vanishing." (The Alleged Truck System at Harcourt, 7 Sep 1867, p.2)

1870 – "SANDHURST POLICE COURT ... stealing ... From the evidence of the prosecutor—a coach driver in the employ of Cobb and Co. it appeared that he had a bedroom attached to the company's stables in Mundy street. He left the property referred to safe in a box in his bedroom ... to take the coach to Spring Creole. Meeting with an accident he was not able to return to Sandhurst before the expiration of about a week or eight days ... Prisoner was employed as a sort of odd man about the stables, and had access to prosecutor's bedroom; and had opportunities of seeing his property ... He [Thomas Gough] might have invited other persons about the premises to enter his bedroom; but no one could have access in his absence, as it was always locked, and he took the key with him. The bedroom was only canvas-partitioned off from the hay-loft. Entrance to the bedroom had been effected by an aperture cut in the canvas sufficiently large to admit a man ... The Police Magistrate thought there were some slight suspicious circumstances attached to the case, and, although he thought it was a weak one, he believed it ought to be decided by a jury. The prisoner was committed for trial." (Sandhurst Police Court, 14 Sep 1870, p.3)

1893 – "H. RYNHART, VETERINARY SURGEON, has Purchased those large brick stables (late Cobb and Co.), corner of Mundy and Mollison Streets, three minutes' walk from railway station, and is now in possession." Advertised on the same page "RABBIT SKINS 100,000 DOZEN Wanted at once. Cash Paid. H. D. Anderson, Leather and Grindery Merchant, Hargreaves-street, next Manning's. Highest Prices for Sheep and Opossum Skins, Beeswax and Horsehair." (Advertising, 18 Aug 1893, p.1)

WARRNAMBOOL

1896 – "COBB AND CO. The Western Stage Company, better known by the name of Cobb and Co., has now fine livery and letting stables in Warrnambool, at the Western Hotel, situate at the corner of Timor and Kepler streets." (Cobb and Co., 5 Dec 1896, p.9)

OTHER LOCATIONS OF STABLES

1879 – "MINHAMITE SHIRE COUNCIL ... tenders be called for draining, forming and metalling 20 chains of Hamilton to Belfast road, between Orford and Deep Creek, immediately to the north of Cobb and Co.'s stables, to the west of section 58, Broadwater." (Minhamite Shire Council, 31 Jul 1879, p.3)

1884 – "BRICKS— Sixty thousand, new and old ; Rubble Doors, Windows, Flooring Joists. Cobb's stables, Lonsdale-street west." (Advertising, 15 Mar 1884, p.7)

1890 – "COBB AND CO. ... Tenders for oats, chaff and straw ... as required at the stables ... Learmonth, Lexton, Avoca, Junction Ararat and Crowlands road, Ararat, Moonabel, Landsborough, Kelvin, near Stuart Mill, St. Arnaud, Avon Plains, Rupanyup, Donald, Morton Plains, Charlton, Wooroonook, Wycheproof, Scarsdale, Linton, Skipton, Streatham, Wickliffe, Rokewood, Shelford, Gordon, Myrniong, Bacchus Marsh, Ballarat." (Advertising, 22 Feb 1890, p.4)

1901 – "COBB and CO.' S LIVERY LETTING, and BAIT STABLES ... Hamilton ... Portarlington, Drysdale, Ocean Grove, Barwon Heads, Gordons, Rokewood, Coleraine." (Family Notices, 15 Nov 1901, p.1)

1916 – ANCIENT MONEY "A remarkable find of ancient money was made in Mr. Penrose Johnson's garden at North Armidale the other morning (says the 'Armidale Express'). Mr. Johnson was digging in his garden when the pick struck something hard. The something turned out to be an iron pot, and under the pot were two tins, which were found to contain £421 in five and one pound notes. The notes were in a fairly good state of preservation, though 20 or 30 years old. How the notes got there is a mystery. The garden is the old site of Gill's coaching stables and later of Cobb and Co.'s stables." (Personal, 11 Mar 1916, p.6)

> "AH, YES ! THEY WERE GOOD DAYS—
> the days of Cobb and Co. ; but now Cobb and Co. have gone further back, leaving a few miserable two-horse bone-shakers to ply their calling along cross roads and bye-ways ; but along the roads there still remain old and ruined "Travellers' Rests" and "Squatters' Arms" to remind us of the days that are gone ; at the rear of these old ruins, with their broken, rusty, and crooked lamp-posts and sign-boards, now hanging dejected and useless, are big tottering wrecks that once were barns and stables ; old slab structures that once accommodated coach-horses and sheltered commercials' buggies ; but they have out-lived their usefulness. In some there are the remains of old coaches, and at evening when the light is soft, when the hot sun has sunk behind the hills in the west, little children climb upon the box seat, and clamber inside and play at Cobb and Co. ... "
> (Cobb and Co., 10 Jan 1903, p.1)

1900 Cobb and Co.'s Livery Stables, Weekly Times (Melbourne, Vic. : 1869 - 1954), 1 Dec 1900, p.2

1908 Advertising Poster, Cobb & Co.
Clearing Sale, Moorabool Street, Geelong, Victoria,
18 Dec 1908 - Courtesy Museums Victoria

1886 Horse Bazaar (The Picturesque Atlas of Australasia, p.275) - Courtesy The University Queensland

Chapter Ten

Cobb and Co. faded into the shadows

Shadow of Cobb & Co.

(Suggested by the passing of the last Queensland Cobb & Co. coach).

It stands beside an old cow bail,
   Where tied-up Rover howls;
A coach that was the Royal Mail
   A roosting place for fowls;
A special perch has a Leghorn,
   A Langshan roosts below;
A crowing couple ev'ry morn
   From off a Cobb & Co.

Along the back a Spanish hen
   Mates with a Wyandotte,
Though a big Dorking now and then
   Disputes the black bird's spot.
And when long shadows speak the sun
   Its setting time doth show,
On the box seat an Orpington
   Roosts high on Cobb & Co.

And there it stands of glory shorn
   That was a driver's pride
When creaking past the fields of corn
   It made the mountain side,
Or moved o'er plains with flashing lights
   That set the track aglow
When through the mud on winter's nights
   It splashed for Cobb & Co.

Now 'gone the days' when its four wheels
   Went rumbling down the road,
Or through the bush when 'Jack's' loud peals
   Greeted its human load.
The lamps are smashed that gleamed afar,
   Its axles bent and low:
'Base uses' since the motor car
   Disposed of Cobb & Co.

I sit and look at it sadly,
   A battered thing on wheels,
No leaders pulling reins madly.
   No polers lashing heels,
No driver with his vice-like grip
   Waiting the word to go,
No 'All aboard!' no cracking whip—
   Shadow of Cobb & Co.

By Hugh Stone.
(Shadow of Cobb and Co., 10 Sep 1025, p.18)

ca. 1910-1930 Small country town, with hotel and bank on elevated side road, Cobb and Co. coach parked in yard - Courtesy State Library Victoria

On the box seat

"Rat-a-tat-tat! A silence, Rat-a-tat! Still no reply. Rat-a-tat-TAT!! And as if in answer to the last thundering knock came a sleepy groan,—and waking from a dreamless slumber, I could not imagine where I was. Gleaming rays of light shone through the cracks above and below the door; hurrying footsteps echoed along the sounding verandah, an occasional voice could be heard and I sleepily turned again, when *Time to get up! Coach is nearly ready!* Then, in a flash, I remembered that I was a passenger, and springing out of bed, hurried through a toilet, performed with freezing fingers, and soon issued forth in search of breakfast.

A dimly lighted room ; a table spread near a smoky five: a sleepy looking waitress ; it looked dreary enough, but it was now or never, so the only thing was to set to work at once, and it did not seem many minutes before a rumble was heard, and to the cry of *All aboard*, luggage was stowed away, passengers climbed to their seats, and we rattled off to the Post Office to get the mails for which we were kept waiting for some minutes. It was freezing bitterly, and every available rug and wrap was called into requisition; but soon the last bag was packed in, and the waybill handed to the driver, who slackened the reins and swung his whip. But the horses, grown restive with waiting, refused to start. With a plunge, the offside leader shot forward as the others hung back, then backed on to the bars, lashing out furiously as they touched her heels. The long whip flew out, and from shoulder to hip scored a long line on the glossy hide, and before the report of the crack died away, one and all were going strong, with the reins stretched like fiddle-strings in the driver's hands. But

He swings his reefing leaders like a man who knows the game

and in a moment the gleaming Post Office lights were far behind, as with a rattle of wheels and clacking bars we tore down the straggling township street with its occasional flickering lamps, and out into the open country with a freezing wind in our faces, and the silver moonlight streaming down on the ground white with frost. There was not a sign of daylight ; but just clearing the horizon, hung the morning star—a globe of fire—scarcely paling in the light of the moon.

On and on we rattled, crossing the rolling downs, here cresting a high ridge, there plunging down into the darkness of a hollow ; now crossing a shallow creek, clattering over its stony bed, or slashing through a bore stream ; then out on a bare clay pan, where the eager horses snatched and reefed at their bits, and made the pace hot in spite of the brake hard down and the steady pull on the reins. But after a few more ridges, they warmed to their work and settled into a good swinging trot, as the breaking day showed us a world sheeted with hoar frost. All the plains were an expanse of white, and, so still had been the night just over, that the tops of all the trees were drooping beneath the same chilly covering, which, for a few moments, as the rising sun desired the horizon, caught the rays and sparkling frostily in their light ... But suddenly, just when at its greatest beauty and brilliance, the scarcely perceptible warmth of the sun proving too much, a change was quickly visible, and the crests of the rises melted into a dull, purple shade, with the frost for a few moments longer still clinging in the shadows and hollows. Then it was all gone, leaving only the monotonous rise and fall of the dust-coloured downs, and we shivered in the piercing dawn-wind which seemed easily to penetrate every wrap.

A moment's pause to leave a mail-bag in a box on a station gate, then away against for about ten miles, when we came to a 'change,' where close to the road was a little iron-roofed hut, with the usual horse-yards near the door. Scarcely had the smoking horses come to a standstill when all the passengers were out and trying to stamp some warmth into their half-frozen feet; but all too soon the fresh horses were harnessed and we must take our places once more as they were led up to be hooked in. The wheelers, although a little fidgety, were soon in, but the leaders, two brown mares, were not so amenable, one, Mulga Mag by name, starting off with a rear and a plunge before her traces were hooked, and for fifty yards we tore along with double brakes hard on, and the mare doing her best to get away, but her efforts were unavailing, for the driver, although his arms were nearly wrenched from their sockets, succeeded in turning and stopping the excited team. In a moment the groom was at their heads, and soon had the traces hooked, then stood aside at the word *Let them go!* For a moment they stood motionless, then Mag, after a slight movement, stood upright on her hind legs, pawing wildly in the air, and came down with her feet over the other leader's back, which in turn began to plunge, and rearing, threw Mulga Mag down on her side, where for a second she lay struggling and kicking, with the wheelers trampling over her. Wildly floundering she got on her feet, and with another rear plunged forward. At last we were off!

Out across a level plain, over a road almost as hard as iron, beaten down as it was by many feet, we sped, and there on the left our driver pointed out his tracks inside only a couple of months before, when, during heavy wet weather, he had taken all day to traverse two miles! The plain was crossed, then a broad belt of myalls, from which, as we emerged, we came on a flock of travelling sheep. How they scurried across the road to avoid us, as with never a halt we held our way, coming soon to high, stony ridges, from the first of which, as we reached the summit, could be seen a vista of blue hills stretching away for many miles. In the foreground was a wide sweep of amber ridges, waving with golden grasses, rising sharply out from the deep, tender blue of the distant hills, with deeper shadows in the gorges and here and then a red sandstone cliff, all standing out against the brilliantly clear winter sky. From a turn in the road a glimpse was caught of the clustering white roofs of a homestead, lying apparently at the foot of the ranges, but in reality many miles from them, and with a wide sweep of downs before. Another mail box, and then a long descent, until the road, leaving the open country, swept down along the banks of the river, shadowed by huge gums hanging over the glistening white sandy bed. Close above the steep banks wound the road, and at last in the shelter of the timber, we began to get the benefit of the sunshine, and by the time the half-way house was reached, had quite thawed. Thirty-five miles of our journey over in less than five hours, and we were, glad of an hour's rest, free from the rattle and jerk of the heavy leather-swung coach. Soon we were ready for the road once more, our fractious leaders again giving some trouble in starting, but their run was nearly over, as in a few miles we came to another change by a long, lily covered lagoon, this time merely a tent and yard by the road-side.

Through the short, perfect afternoon we bowled merrily along, the road keeping chiefly through timbered country, at times touching the river, until among the heavy, green trees we caught sight of more roofs, and soon pulled up at the station gate to deliver the mails. Leaving the river, once more we emerged on the high, open downs, and sped along to the accompaniment of stories of reckless driving, of narrow escapes, and the

Jest and the laughter that shorten the way

with, of course, a good game of "bottle-loo," in which the driver always scored highest. The last change! In half-an-hour the sun set, and in the gathering darkness a silence fell on the erstwhile merry travellers, and mile followed mile with never a word uttered ; no sound but the rattle, of gear and the clacking bars. An occasional question ; a short reply ; a crack of the whip ; then again that silence which always seems to come at the close of a long coach drive, no matter how pleasant the day, or how congenial the companions, and as the flickering township lights gleamed redly through the darkness, promising warmth and comfort, our long day came to an end, and with the beat, beat of the horses' feet, and the swing and rattle of the coach still in our ears, half regretfully we took our leave of the driver, who, with skilful hand and never-failing courtesy, had carried us through a day of

Risks Maybe more than we dream ;

for after all, there are many worse things than a long day behind such, teams as those we watched making short work of the flying miles." (A Day with Cobb & Co., 2 Sep 1904, p.12)

Drove for Cobb and Co.

See also 'Along the tracks of Cobb and Co. - Cobb's Coach Drivers'

The experience of driving for Cobb and Co. emerges vividly in a 1904 account: "The driver put back the brake noisily, and swung the whip as the horses went up into the collar, and the nondescript vehicle that is called a 'coach,' because anything that carries mails is a coach, according to Cobb, surged through the gluey mud. The 'coach' had evidently been designed for a waggonette, but after the builder had laid the foundations of the forecarriage the material had run out, and the hindcarriage had been cut off short, so that the longitudinal seats were ridiculously short for the width of the vehicle. Ahead the weak July sun struggled with the mist that had been the rain of yesterday; the big-boned, unbeautiful, reliable horses trotted tirelessly up hill and down hill, and on the level, never varying the pace on stone, gravel, sand, or quag ... there was damp in the air, a grey greenness to the eye, and a dozen miles of wattles breaking into yellow, and sick with over-budding. The coachdriver, a hairless-faced north easterner, of 30 or so, was hard to begin speech, but harder to stop. He gave his views on many subjects, displaying a great range of superficial knowledge ... We stopped at every half mile or so to pick up or deliver letters from the loose bag, and for these moments business was unconsiderate enough to stop pleasure ... The land was dotted with dairy cows standing in the grass of the paddocks ... The irregular Cobb rattled over a stony patch of the road ... crossed a creek by a crazy moss-eaten bridge, and pulled up by two great Norfolk pines flanking the gate-posts of a farmhouse ... A slip of a girl ... ran down to the coach, she gave a letter to the driver ... *And when you're coming out again will you bring three reels of black cotton, No. 1, and two packets of pins; and if you can see a nice book bring that* ... She handed him a buttonhole of violets and one of daphne, and he thanked her and looked at us and grinned uneasily as he avoided the eyes of the passengers and settled the reins between his fingers as the coach began to move ... When we were out of ear-shot he handed the violets to me ... *I get plenty of 'em—every house y' come to the girls give me flowers. You are to be envied*, said I. *No, no, it isn't me. It's because I drive the coach, and if they want anything from the store I bring it, y' see. Ger-r-y up.*" (Country Sketcher, 8 Oct 1904, p.50)

Likewise, stories of Miles, the driver from Portland, offer insight into the skill and confidence expected of Cobb's coachmen: "Miles, the driver from Portland, had on is last stage into Streatham (or Hopkins, as it was then called) a team of six light coloured chestnuts, as nearly alike as it was possible to get them. For the Portland end he had six greys, and used to come into Portland at a gallop. From Julia Street he swept into Bentwick Street, and would hardly slacken pace until he landed the coach, passengers and all in the yard of Mac's Hotel. He often disturbed the minds of nervous passengers, but I do not think he ever made a mistake ...

As he pulled up his team he sat on the box with a satisfied smile on his face, like a man who has had a good dinner and subsided into an armchair.

I rode once in the 'fifties ... Miles being the driver. We had a rowdy team of four bays at Green Hill, and one of the traces, slipping out of the swingle-bar ring ... the team made off at a gallop for four miles over a half-cleared road, before Miles pulled them to a dancing standstill ... in my hurry to get out, I fell heavily ... I ruptured a vein internally and sprained my ankle ... Jimmy Miles ... When Cobb and Co. sold out here, they transferred their business to New Zealand, and Miles was sent there as one of the drivers. My brother, John, told me ... ... Drivers of vehicles had to blow a horn before entering a steep decline ... Miles heard no signal ... came face to face with a heavily-loaded waggon ... he turned his team almost at right angles over the bank, landing safely far below in the valley. An aunt of Miles died in America, leaving him a large sum of money ... to started to ride to a port where he would get a ship to America. Poor Miles never reached his destination, for he was drowned in one of the fast-running streams over there ... OTHER FAMOUS DRIVERS ... 'Cabbage Tree Ned', 'Bendigo Ike', Jim Redfern, Frank Rutherford ... Cobb and Co. sold their Western lines to Meggs and Anderson ... driving themselves on important lines." (1948/49 Annual report and balance sheet / Cobb & Co.'s Old Coach Drivers' Association, p.11)

Cobb and Co. drivers often had careers of significant length and variety, such as Robert Scott, who drove routes to Myrtleford and Bright after emigrating from Scotland: "At 18 years, of age, Robert Scott left his native Dumferline, in Scotland, and came to Australia. We next find him working on a farm in Indigo. Later he joined the service of the well-known firm of Cobb and Co. and drove a coach to Myrtleford and Bright ... A genial, trustworthy, honourable man, he enjoyed the respect and esteem of all who knew him ... he is survived by two sons, Robert and John, and three daughter, Margaret, Elizabeth (Mrs. J. Jones), Jeannie (Mrs. Bidstrup) Queensland" On the same page "GOLD FROM NEW GUINEA. Twelve thousand ounces of New Guinea gold arrived in Sydney to-day including a nugget weighing two hundred ounces." (Obituary, 3 Oct 1928, p.2)

In other cases, coach driving formed part of a broader, often colourful life. "A man whose colourful career included a period as a coach driver for Cobb and Co. in Victoria and N.S.W. ... Mr. F. W. Wallace, who was born in Sussex (Eng.) ... came to Australia with his parents at the age of two years and spent his boyhood at Macquarie Plains. As a young man he moved to Queensland, where he worked as a boundary and stock rider. He was also employed by Cobb and Co. as a driver in Victoria and N.S.W. ... Mr. Wallace has always enjoyed very good health and still enjoys life to the 'full' His chief pleasures are his pipe and listening to cricket and football broadcasts.

He claims that

hard work kills no one ...

his family, Robert (Hobart), Ena (Mrs. E. Neilson, Brisbane), George (Launceston), Eva (Mrs. E. Lee, Launceston), Phil (Burnie)." (Drove Coaches For Cobb & Co., 3 Mar 1953, p.7)

Still others, like George McDonald, combined their driving with other jobs. "As a driver of Cobb and Co.'s coaches, Mr. George McDonald, who has died in Camperdown, assisted to guard the telegraph lines at the time of the Kelly gang outrages. Mr. McDonald, who had lived in Camperdown for 22 years, was born in Scotland 90 years ago. He came to Melbourne at the age of eight and later went to Violet Town, where he assisted in land surveying. It was while in this district that he was employed by Cobb and Co. He later took up dairying in Gippsland." (The Church and the People, 18 Jun 1942, p.3)

The end of Cobb and Co.

As the 20th century progressed, the heyday of Cobb and Co. began to fade, giving way to a wave of nostalgia. "The time has come ... Great Days of Cobb & Co. ... In October 1934, two great historic events coincided—the Centenary Air Race from London to Melbourne and a conference of drivers of Cobb and Co's. famous old horse coaches ... The first reunion of Cobb coach men was held in the Melbourne Exhibition Building on May 5, 1925. Most of the men were in their seventies, some were in their eighties and nineties. The ages of five of the elders aggregated 437 years. How they talked and toasted old days! And their talk was priceless, for they handled the ribbons, cracked the whip and sounded the merry horn from the days of the hectic gold rush onward.

Through the wild bush country from the rich digging of Ballarat and Bendigo, their flashing six-in-hands had brought untold treasure to the growing city.

Records attest that at one time and another, no less than 36 Cobb coaches were bailed up by bushrangers. LANDMARKS. The Melbourne terminus in Little Lonsdale street, near Elizabeth street, is still landmarked by stables and stalls and by the historic Buck's Head Hotel building. Another nearby hostelry of the past, the Robert Burns (Shades of Tam O'Shanter) is said to have sheltered the redoubtable Ned Kelly himself at times. In those days the coach run from Ballarat to Melbourne was made in the scorching time of 25 hours. A modern plane could do it in 25 minutes. But what of that. In point of efficiency, Cobb's coachmen were as superlative in their day as the haughtiest air-ace of our time. From the motor trade sprang the happy inspiration to muster the old coach drivers and link the coaching era by way of tradition with road transport of to-day and to-morrow ... Time runs on and the ranks of the old drivers thin out." (The Time has Come, 1 Mar 1948, p.4)

Looking further back, the decline had been underway in regional centres for some time. "The noted coaching firm of Cobb and Co., so far as Sandhurst is concerned, is dead killed by the railway ... The Sandhurst office was in the Mall about where the shop of Mr. Osborne, watchmaker, stands, next the Shamrock hotel. Three remarkably skilful drivers—J. Pack, J. R. Lambert and J. Swanston—were engaged. They were important men in those days, for owing to the dangers of the road, life and limb depended on their skilful handling of the reins. Reminiscences of these early travels are amongst the pleasant and exciting memories of all old Bendigonians.

The swimming of the coach in seas of mud and the bumping over the corduroy road, when hats and heads, it is said, used to go through the roof of the vehicle, can be amply testified to ... Mr. Crowley, of the Albion Hotel, Sandhurst ... was their agent in Sandhurst ... About 1864, the office of the company in Sandhurst was shifted to the Williamson-street side of the Shamrock Hotel, and it there remained until it finally closed the other day ... This firm attended to the public wants with a faithfulness worthy of all praise, and by their energy and enterprise the high repute of Cobb and Co., was firmly established in this and the surrounding districts. They extended the coaching to Inglewood, Heathcote, and Swan Hill. An extraordinary thing in connection with the Cobb and Co. firm, of this and, we believe, of other districts, was its reliability. Ten miles an hour was the travelling rate, and time was kept to the minute, so to speak, no matter what the difficulties or dangers to be overcome. Particular attention was paid to employing only first class men as drivers, and it is most creditable to the Sandhurst branch that very few accidents ever happened, the only serious one we believe, being that at the steep and dangerous gully of the Buckeye, when the coach was capsized and the driver killed. The opening of the Heathcote

railway is the last straw that brought this famous company to an end

on Sandhurst, that being the only route on which a coach was running from this centre." (The End of Cobb and Co. in Sandhurst, 8 Sep 1888, p.5)

In Queensland, the formal end of Cobb and Co.'s operations came in early 1924. However, "with the final passing of Cobb and Co. at the end of 1921 another link with the old days had snapped. On January 10, F. Palmer, mail contractor, between Charleville and Tambo (Queensland) took over the remaining plant of Cobb and Co." (Cobb and Co., 9 Feb 1922, p.4)

Meanwhile, the company itself sought ways to adapt to changing times. "*The lights of Cobb and Co.* although dimmed, have not yet been extinguished. The activities of the original company were intimately associated with early Australian history, but the advent of the railway drove coaching out of the arena of profitable enterprises, and nowadays the company has, we are told in its latest report, changed from

the erratic and risky coaching business to the more stable and lucrative one of storekeeping.

At least, that change has been 'practically accomplished.' The report, which is for the year ended June 30 last, shows net profit of £3507, after providing for depreciation of horses and plant. In the coaching section there was a loss of £2235, caused by the cost of feed during July, August, and September, 1920. The directors state that all of the company's mail contracts will terminate on December 31 next, and that they have renewed contracts for only three services, which are of great assistance to the stores in the delivery of goods, inwards and outwards. Subsidy for these contracts is £1485 per annum, or an increase of £225. Sales of coaching properties, such as paddocks and cottages, are reported to have been satisfactory, showing a net profit of £1290, and several properties remain to be sold. Stocks, etc., of the five stores are said to constitute a valuable asset, representing the profits of the last few years, cash realised from the sale of the coaching and factory properties, and new capital subscribed.

The board expresses the opinion that payment of regular annual dividends should be started before the end of the present year." (Cobb and Co., Ltd., 14 Nov 1921, p.9)

Despite efforts to diversify, the business did not survive. "A chain of stores in the Surat and St. George districts [Queensland] was opened, and certain coaching was dropped and just the stores continued. Lately a fire destroyed the St. George stores and stock, and though business was continued in temporary premises the company has had enough of it. Dividends have lately been paid at quite a respectable figure, the capital intact, and the company has a very capable general manager; but the directors say that trade in the south-west is precarious and risky, and they have put up a proposal to go into liquidation. That probably will mean the end of Cobb and Company in Queensland—of course except historically—if not in Australia." (End of Cobb and Co., 15 Nov 1928, p.2)

Symbolically, the last Queensland coach run marked the final chapter in an era of overland mail and passenger travel. "The last Coach ... Slowly but surely of late years the horse coach has been disappearing from many parts, of the State Queensland, until earlier in the week there appeared in our columns, that

on August 14,
the last horse-coach trip of the world-renowned
firm of Cobb and Co. had been run
from Surat to Yeulba ...

The motor coach has come in its place, but memory of the old conditions will long survive. Who will forget, the coach driver's cheery voice ... 'the elite' sitting up on the box seat ... The arrival and departure ... it was not an uncommon sight to see practically the whole populace awaiting the coach at the post offices of those localities ... The coach, with its leather springs and six to eight horses ... portion of the journey was that over corduroy ... The coach driver ... the bushman's news paper ... In most cases the driver would place the mail in the receptacle provided by the selector or station owner, as the case may be, and the receptacle varied from a biscuit tin to a zinc-lined box placed about the height from the ground that would allow of the driver placing the letters in it without getting off his seat ... The greatest bugbear to travellers was the gate-opening business ; no two gates would be alike, and possibly each had a style of opening patent to itself ...

Who will forget the meal served at Lodor's mail change? Roasted goat, prickly pear jam and jelly, splendid home-made bread, to say nothing of the hot scones and 'nanny's' butter, which made up a really 'rich' meal, and that cheered the heart of the traveller for the next stage of the journey."(The Last Coach, 5 Sep 1924, p.16)

The Coach's Story

Half-hidden in a tangle of tussock and bracken, and bent low to earth as if to hide in shame from curious eyes, it lay — the forlorn relic of what had once been the pride of the road — her Majesty's mail coach ...

Two crazy and nearly spokeless wheels alone remained to save it from utter collapse. Shafts, splashboard, seats, windows, fittings, all had disappeared. With its arms folded on the rail of a rickety fence ...

What times I have had on the open road; glorious nights when under a full moon the shining quartz track stretched ahead like a silver ribbon, and in the frosty air the sharp ring of eight pairs of shoes made the sparks fly. Drab nights, when thick fog laid a clammy hand on coach and passengers alike ...

Days of storm and flood, when my passengers, huddled together in my cosy interior, were startled by a sudden opening of the door ... I served this district faithfully, carrying its people to and fro with comfort and safety ... That was before speed became the god that most travellers worship ...

My limbs were now sending forth ominous creaks and groans with the weight of years, and my once handsome coat was sadly the worse for wear. One dreary evening the horses were taken out of the shafts for the last time, and I was dragged to this unused paddock among other worn-out servants of man ...

Here I am useless and forgotten; yet I had my day — a long one, too — but it has closed. The whisper died away to silence." (The Coach's Story, 2 Jun 1934, p.4)

2024 Groomsmens quarters and
1 of 4 double stables, 1857,
The Evans Hotel, Bealiba
- Courtesy John Maher

1925 The last stage coach
of the famous Cobb & Co.,
now the property of Asbett
Bros., of Scarsdale – '
The Last of its Kind',
The Herald, 4 April, p.4.

1860 Cobb & Co. Coach at Queenscliff (Simpson, photographer) - Courtesy State Library Victoria

ca. 1900-1920 View at Queenscliff, Victoria - Courtesy State Library Victoria

1886 Queenscliff (The Picturesque Atlas of Australasia, p. 254) - Courtesy The University of Queensland

1901[?] Barwon Heads coach - Courtesy State Library Victoria

ca. 1880-1938 Coach and horses and a motor bus with passengers
(John Henry Harvey, 1855-1938, photographer - Courtesy State Library Victoria

ca. 1883 Looking west on Flinders Lane from the intersection with Swanston Street, Melbourne (N. J. Caire, 1837-1918) - Courtesy State Library Victoria

ca. 1891-1914 Motor vehicles lining Flinders Lane, Melbourne - Courtesy State Library Victoria

ca. 1930 Cobb & Co. Coach - Courtesy State Library South Australia

ca. 1901 Remains of a gig after a smash (Thomas Henry Armstrong, 1857-1930 - Courtesy State Library Victoria

Appendices

Appendix 1: The Americans

> **1853 THE AMERICANS WHO CAME TO MELBOURNE:**
> - George Mowton (Partner of Adams & Co.)
> - Freeman Cobb (Worked for Adams & Co.)
> - Elisha Winslow Cobb (Freeman's Brother)
> - George Francis Train ("I advanced the money for Freeman Cobb to commence a line [coaching] from Melbourne to Sandhurst")
>
> **1853 "ADAMS & CO. (EXPRESS CARRIERS) COMMENCED IN MELBOURNE:**
> "They commenced carrying from Liardet's (Port Melbourne) to the City of Melbourne for a start but 'no road' across the swamp between Emerald Hill, now South Melbourne, and the river was such a quagmire that their waggons sank to the hubs ... They advised their principals in the United States against the carrying business, but told them that there was a good opening for a real up-to-date line of coaches to the diggings ... The United States companies turned down the coaching proposition."
>
> **1854 FREEMAN COBB COMMENCED CARRYING FROM MELBOURNE TO THE GOLDFIELDS**

George Mowton & Adams & Co. (1853-1855)
- American
- Partner who established Adams and Co. Express Carriers in Melbourne

"GEORGE MOWTON, Merchant, aged 35, arrived in Australia 1 April 1853; Native place USA; Ship master: Cummings E.; Ship name: Fanny. Also listed as arriving were Caroline Mowton (aged 31), Nelson Mowton (aged 8), Caroline Mowton (aged 4)." (Inward Overseas Passenger Lists) George Mowton was soon identified as "Resident Partner of Adams And Co., in Australia. Melbourne." (Advertising, 24 Nov 1854, p.6)

"SHIPPING INTELLIGENCE ... Adams & Co., with their usual energy and foresight, sent out a messenger by the New Orleans, to establish a branch of their business in Australia. It will undoubtedly prove of great importance in process of time. Mr. Myers, the gentleman who goes out, is well known here for his promptitude and efficiency" (Shipping Intelligence, 7 May 1853, p.2) "ADAMS AND CO.'S Great American and European Express.—The public are respectfully informed, that the undesigned will Start their express to Europe, America, and California ... Mr. George Mowton, our resident partner, may be found for the present, at the Royal Hotel, Great Collins-street, private entrance. Adams and Co., of New York. Melbourne, 26th, 1853." (Advertising, 26 Apr 1853, p.8)

"COMMUNICATION BETWEEN AMERICA AND THESE COLONIES.—Among our recent commercial undertakings we notice the establishment of a branch of the house of Messrs. Adams & Co., the Express agents of New York. This is a description of business so novel with us that it is scarcely understood. The Company undertake the conveyance of gold-dust and packages of every description from one country to another, for which purpose they have established agencies in all the chief towns of America, England and her colonies ; but more particularly in the United States, which is the head quarters from whence they have radiated their operations ... Despatch combined with economy is their principle of business, which in an active community like ours, will no doubt be readily appreciated and taken advantage of, particularly by those who would rather prefer paying for the security of certain and speedy delivery, than have their goods delayed for an indefinite period, and tossed from hand to hand till they are almost destroyed, if not altogether lost. Besides the speed, the security of this mode of conveyance also seems strongly to recommend it ; at least, it must have the confidence of the Government of the United States, when we mention that, during the Mexican war, this Company transmitted coin from the Government mint to New Orleans, to the extent of 20,000,000 dollars—an extent of transactions which speaks highly of their standing and utility." (Homebush Races, 11 Jun 1853, p.3)

"ADAMS & CO.'S, Great American and European Express, North-east corner Collins and Queen-streets, Nos. 1, 2, and 3. We would respectfully inform the Public that we have taken the above offices, for the transaction of the Express, Exchange, and general Commission Business ... We are prepared to ... draw for any amount on England or America in sums to suit. Treasure entrusted to our care is fully covered by open policies in the Indemnity Mutual Marine, Marine Assurance, Alliance Marine, and Royal Exchange Insurance Companies London, and Sun, New York and Atlant Companies, New York. To persons desirous of sending to their friends at home, we offer the best facilities ... Alvin Adams, Boston, W. B. Dinemore, New York, E. S. Sanford, Philadelphia, S. M. Shoemaker, Baltimore, George Mowton, Melbourne. Melbourne May 6th, 1853." (Advertising, 13 May 1853, p.11)

"UNITED STATES.—We are indebted to the Melbourne branch of Adams and Co.'s Express for Boston and New York papers to the 17th February. The intelligence is not later than previously received by way of England. The Boston Daily Atlas, February 17, says :—The subscription which was opened a few days since, to the Australian Steam Ship Company, in New York, it is stated is progressing satisfactorily; and sufficient has been secured to pay for and fit out the first steamer by May next. She is to be called the Golden Age, and was originally launched by Mr. W. H. Brown, as the fifth boat of the Collins' line. Her first voyage will be direct to Sydney and Port Phillip, where she will take her place in the trade between Australia and Panama. Several fresh vessels were laid on for these colonies, and the papers contain numerous advertisements in relation to the Australian trade growing up.—Empire." (Sydney News, 1 Jun 1853, p.2)

"COLT'S REVOLVERS—A few of these unrivalled Pistols for sale, by Adams and Co., corner of Collins and Queen-streets, upstairs." (Advertising, 14 May, 1853, p.5) "Adams & Co.'s, American and European Express Clipper ship Glance. We shall despatch our next Express to England, United States, Canada, and South America, by the above ship ... Adams & Co., North-east corner of Queen and Collins-streets, Melbourne. For further Information, apply Mr. Myers, Victoria Hotel, Geelong." (Advertising, 9 Jun 1853, p.1)

"THE QUICKEST ROUTE TO THE UNITED STATES. For Callao. THE A 1 American Clipper Ship Glance. 600 tons register, E. C. Taylor, commander, having been unavoidably detained, will sail in a few days for the above port. Has a few berths left. For passage, apply to the agents. THOMAS GARDNER & CO., 81 Flinders-lane, west. N.B. This vessel will carry Messrs. Adam's and Co.'s first American Express via the Isthmus of Panama, and parties may rely on despatch." (Advertising, 21 Jun 1853, p.6)

"STEAM TO SYDNEY. The magnificent steam-ship New Orleans, 1200 tons burthen, 450 horse power, Captain Edgar Wakeman, will leave for Sydney on Wednesday, 22nd June, 1853. Passengers to leave the Queen's wharf at 4 p.m by a steamer provided to carry them to the New Orleans, which will proceed to sea at daybreak on Thursday morning. Captain H. F. Fox, well known on this coast for many years, proceeds in her as coast pilot. The New Orleans is unrivalled for sea qualities, and comfortable accommodations for cabin and steerage passengers. Fares—Cabin, £12 10s. ; Steerage, £6 10s For freight or passage, apply to George Wilson, at the office of Adams & Co., North-east corner of Queen and Collins-streets." (Advertising, 22 Jun 1853, p.4)

"VICTORIA GOLD-MINING COMPANY.—Capital £50,000, in 10,000 shares of £5 each ... Directors. The Right Worshipful J. T. Smith, Esq., M.L.C. John O'Shanassy, Esq., M.L.C. Alderman Hodgson, Esq., M.L.C. A. F. A. Greeves, Esq., M.L.C., Henry Jennings, Esq., John Stephen, Esq., Alderman, Henry Ginn, Esq., George Mowton, Esq., James Fraser, Esq. Chief Director of the Works, Charles Kinnear, Esq. Bankers. The Bank of Victoria. Solicitor. S. M. South, Esq. Provisional Secretary. James Fraser, Esq. This Company has been formed for working scientifically, by the aid of patented machinery and skilled labor, the boundless Gold Fields of this colony ... The Directors propose to engage experienced men now on the diggings, at current daily wages, with the addition of 10 per cent, on the gross proceeds of their labor, thereby affording a guarantee for their zeal and integrity. It is proposed to unite with the great Australian Gold Company of London, 0.1 terms to be agreed upon, retaining in the hands of this Company the entire Colonial management. Two of the Directors will be in attendance on Monday, Wednesday, and Friday of each week until further notice ... for the purpose of receiving applications for shares, at the office of Messrs. Adams and Co., 69, Collins-street, west. A deposit of £2 per share is to be paid on application, and the remainder by two equal instalments, at intervals of not less than two months ... Dated Melbourne, Aug. 25, 1863." (Advertising, 10 Sep 1853, p.8)

"TO MINERS AND RESIDENTS AT THE MINES.—The undersigned beg leave to inform their patrons ... With the exception ... of Mr. George W. Haycock, at the Bendigo, no person is authorized to act in any capacity for the undersigned. Parties desirous of forwarding gold, gold dust, valuable parcels, or of remitting by bills of exchange to the United States, or England, can communicate by post or Government Escort, fully assured their wishes will meet with prompt attention. We forward an Express bi-monthly, by first class sailing vessels, to the United States, via Callao and the Isthmus of Panama (acknowledged to be the shortest route to the States), and by sailing vessels and steamers to our agents in Liverpool and London. All Treasure covered by insurance also parcels, when desirable, and duplicate papers furnished. Gold dust forwarded to the Mint at Philadelphia, or the Bank of England, and placed to account of the skipper. Bills of Exchange ... issued till within a few hours of the sailing of each vessel.—Adams and Co., 69, Collins street, west." (Advertising, 27 May 1854, p.1)

"AMERICAN TELEGRAPH LINE OF STAGES ... starting ... Adams and Co.'s office, 69 Collins-street west (Hewitt and Co., not Cobb and Co.)" (Advertising, 30 Nov 1854, p.8)

"NOTICE. —The Public are respectfully informed that, during the absence of Mr, George Mowton to the United States, Mr. Dyer Ames will represent the firm of Adams and Co. in Australia, and is fully authorised to sign the name said firm. (Signed), ALVIN ADAMS. WM B. DINSMORE. EDW. S. SANFORD. SAM. M. SHOEMAKER. GEO. MOWTON." (Advertising, 23 May 1854, p.3)

"NOTICE.—The undersigned, being about to leave in the Norna, for England and the United States for a short period, would respectfully inform the public that, during his absence, Messrs. Samuel L. Cutter and Freeman Cobb, will attend to the business of Adams and Co., in Australia ; the former will have superintendence of the Banking and Exchange business, and the latter the General Business of the House, in the Express department, George Mowton, Resident Partner of Adams and Co., in Australia. Melbourne." (Advertising, 25 Nov 1854, p.6)

"THE FAILURE OF MESSRS ADAMS AND CO., OF SAN FRANCISCO. In the extracts we gave from the California papers some weeks ago, concerning the stoppage of this house, it was made to appear that the gold dust, coin, &c., of which the firm was possessed, had been taken away by certain interested parties for their own benefit. The following official letters, which we quote from the Daily Alta of 20th March, give a very different complexion to the affair. Having published the erroneous statement, we deem it but fair to give the true one ... Mr Fredrick Billings ... the firm which he is a member obtained from the house of Adams and Co. the sum of 10,000 dollars as a retaining fee for their services in the emergency in which the house was placed ... Mr Billings discloses the fact that on the same night and after he had been thus retained, he found Mr King, Mr Cohen, and others, moving the gold dust and coin into a wagon on Merchant street ...

It is true that on the night of the 22nd the gold dust and coin were removed by me from the vaults of Adams and Co. to a place of greater security. This removal was considered a proper and judicious step, in view of the excitement which the announcement on the morrow, of the failure of the house of Adams and Co. could not fail to produce ... The books of Adams and Co., will show the amount they had on hand when the suspension took place ... There are gentlemen in this city of the highest respectability in no way connected with Adams and Co., who, when called on as witnesses, will testify as to the disposition that was made of the funds, and will show that the object was not to defraud creditors, but to protect the funds for their benefit ... The removal of coin, gold dust; and bullion, from the office of Adams and Co., on the night of the 22nd ult., to a place of security, was made as a measure of precaution, by the advice of the undersigned, and with their full knowledge: — Eugene Casserly, H. P. James, Edward P. Flint; San Francisco, March 19, 1855." (The Failure of Messrs. Adams and Co., of San Francisco, 25 Jun 1855, p.3)

"NOTICE.—The Copartnership existing between the undersigned, under the name of

Adams and Co., in Australia, was dissolved

on the 1st day of March last. A. Adams, W. B. Dinsmore, E. G. Sanford, S. M. Shoemaker, Geo. Mowton. By their Attorney and Agent, Dyer Ames." (Advertising, 6 Nov 1855, p.7)

"NOTICE.—Removal.—After Monday, the 29th instant, the Agent of Adams and Co., Mr. Dyer Ames, may be found at the office of Messrs. E. W. Cobb and Co., No. 112, Collins-street west. All parties holding certificates of deposit will please present them before the 1st day of December next. Adams and Co., by their Agent and Attorney. Dyer Ames." (Advertising, 20 Nov 1855, p.3)

Freeman Cobb
- **Gentleman**
- **Worked for Adams & Co.**
- **Elisha Winslow Cobb's brother**
- **Freeman, or Freeman & Elisha Cobb, started Cobb and Co.**

"Freeman Cobb is an American, born near Boston. In May 1853, then being about 35 years of age, he arrived in Melbourne, having come out as agent for Adams and Co., the well known express company of New York." (Cobb's Box, 1875)

"Arrivals. 8 May 1854, Golden Age, U.N.'S. (s.), barque, 264 tons, Stiles, from Melbourne ... Passengers for Panama ... E. W. Cobb ... For Sydney ... 13 May 1854 Mr. George Mowton, Mr. F. Cobb." (Shipping Intelligence, 13 May 1854, p.2)

"Many of us witnessed the first efforts of Freeman Cobb to establish communication between the metropolis and the interior, and know how pluckily he in his two-horse conveyance conveyed half a dozen passengers from Melbourne to Sandhurst in three days, through difficulties that were deemed at the time almost insurmountable." (Title Deeds, 16 Sep 1859, p.3)

"NOTICE.—The undersigned, being about to leave in the Norma, for England and the United States for a short period, would respectfully inform the public that, during his absence, Messrs Samuel L. Cutter and Freeman Cobb will attend to the business of Adams and Co., in Australia ... the latter the General Business of the House, in the express department. George Mowton, Resident Partner of Adams and Co., in Australia. Melbourne." (Advertising, 24 Nov 1854, p.6)

"The following, by Mr James Hickey, foreman of the brigade, was read, approved of, and enclosed :—Dearest Madam, From the fact of a new formation of Volunteer Fire Brigade Company, No. 1, I have not had the satisfaction of the personal acquaintance of your much lamented son, Charles L. Clapp; at the same time I look back with much regret and grief upon the sad catastrophy that befel our brave and unfortunate elder brother ... the enclosed casket of relics, accompanied by full explanation furnished by the gentlemen who treasured them for this the only object on behalf of the entire brigade, with every condoling sentiment, I am, dear Madam, your most respectfully, James Hickey. To Mrs. D Clapp. The relics were then enclosed in a Japan casket inlaid with pearl, lined with silver foil, presented by Mr William Warren Cartwright, Assistant Foreman of Volunteer Fire Brigade/No 1 and for the melancholy purpose, then submitted to the care of Mr Freeman Cobb, who kindly volunteered to forward it with safety, despatch, and without remuneration per Adams and Co.'s Express. At the unanimous desire of the Committee, a vote of thanks was tendered to the gentlemen donors, to Mr Freeman Cobb, and to the Chairman of the Special Committee." (The Late Mr. Charles Clapp, 28 Nov 1854, p.5)

Earlier that year ...

30 Jan 1854 "Freeman Cobb, James Swanson, John Lamber, and John M. Peck ... formed themselves into a company, and started a line to Castlemaine and Bendigo, the fares then being £0 10s. to the former, and £8 to the latter place, none too much either, when we consider the wear and tear of horseflesh over the roads, or rather no roads, of those days, and the fact that hay on the wharf in Melbourne was £35 a ton, and cost another £30 to take to Bendigo." (Cobb's Box, 1875)

"The Telegraph Line of Coaches ... we venture to say that no one, not even Cobb himself, imagined that his enterprise would so rapidly approach the magnificent development lately, witnessed, when the humble half dozen passenger conveyance was represented by a gigantic car, holding fifty travellers and harnessed to fourteen greys, as fine specimens of horse flesh as one can hope to find in the southern hemisphere, 'tooled' by whips who are equalled by few, and excelled by none ... going direct to Swan Hill, communicating with Deniliquin and Moama, and performing daily journeys to Melbourne, Ballarat, Ararat, and the intermediate places. Twenty-six coaches belonging to this firm arrive at and depart from Castlemaine daily ; and the horses they possess number over 600. To these great dimensions has Freeman Cobb's 'speculation' expanded in the course of a few years.—M. A, Mail." (Title Deeds, 16 Sep 1859, p.3)

"Sale of Handsome Furniture, & SYMONS and PERRY have received in instructions from Freeman Cobb, Esq. (who is leaving the colony per Royal Charter) to sell by auction, at the Telegraph Coach Office, 23 Bourke-street east, on Thursday, 22nd inst., at twelve o'clock" (Advertising, 20 May 1856, p.4)

"The Undersigned, intending to leave this colony, requests that all Unsettled Accounts, and Claims of every description, be presented at the Booking Office, No. 23 Bourke-street east, on or before Thursday next, 22nd inst., for settlement, after which date they will not be recognised. Freeman Cobb. Melbourne, May 16th, 1856." (Advertising, 19 May 1856, p.7)

"Forfeited Conditional Purchases ... Wagga Wagga ... Freeman Cobb, 40 acres." (Destructive Fire, 9 Apr 1875, p.2)

NOTE: Benjamin Cobb and Co. was exporting timbers to India.

E.W. Cobb (Elisha Winslow Cobb)
- **American**
- **Merchant in Melbourne**
- **Brother of Freeman Cobb**
- **Freeman, Elisha, or Freeman & Elisha Cobb, started Cobb and Co.**

Cobb and Bowles Merchants "For Calcutta, via Madras.— The A1 Clipper Ship RADUGA, Charles W. Samson, Esq., Commander, will positively sale for the above ports on the 5th May. Having the most elegant accommodations for two cabin passengers, she presents an eligible opportunity for any person wishing to proceed to the indies. For passage apply to Cobb and Bowles, Collins-street west." (Advertising, 3 May 1854, p.2) while "COBB and BOWLES have for sale, now landing ex ships Raduga, Edward, and Buena Vista 70 cases Collin D handle shovels, 20 do. Hunt's do. Do, 10 do. handled axes, 28 do. Collins' picks, 100 bundles pails, 100 cases boots, and brogans, 60 do. counter scales, 7 do. Clocks, 30 do. Stoves, 125 do. chocolate, 284 do. Brandy, 42 do. brandy peaches, 175 do. Baltimore oysters, 60 do. fresh peaches, 30 do. water crackers, 20 do. apple marmalade, 200 tins herrings, Underwood's preserves and pickles. Great Collins Street, West." (Advertising, 27 Jun 1854, p.13)

"The copartnership heretofore existing between the undersigned, is this day dissolved by mutual consent, Mr. E. W. Cobb is authorized to settle all the affairs of the late firm. COBB & BOWLES. E. W. Cobb, Wm. B. Bowles. Melbourne, Jan. 10, 1855. The undersigned will continue the Business of the late firm of Cobb and Bowles, under the name and style of E. W. Cobb and Co. E. W. COBB, 112 Collins Street, West, Melbourne." (Advertising, 18 Jan 1855, p.8)

"E. W. Cobb and Co. PARTNERSHIP.—Henry Driver and Thomas R. Levitt, are partners in our house from this date.

E. W. Cobb and Co. Melbourne, Feb. 1st, 1854." (Advertising, 1 Feb 1855, p.8) ... "By mutual consent, Mr. Thomas R. Leavitt Retires from our house this day. (Signed), E. W. Cobb and Co. Thos. R. Leavitt. Melbourne, Nov 30,1855." (Advertising, 4 Dec 1855, p.3)

"SALES BY AUCTION, Friday, 4th April. Sale of Household Furniture at Grey-street St. Kilda ... at the house of E. W. Cobb, Esq ... The whole of that gentleman's household furniture, comprising Drawingroom furniture, including an excellent pianoforte Diningroom furniture Bedchamber furniture Kitchen utensils, &c. For full particulars of which see catalogues. The whole to be sold without any reserve. Observe-Sale takes place at Two o'clock." (Advertising, 3 Apr 1856, p.2)

"BENEVOLENT ASYLUM—Total number of inmates, including children, 136; under medical treatment, 62; receiving outdoor relief, 21. The Committee beg to acknowledge from Mr. Forsyth, £120; Mr. Dakin, £2 2s.; Dr. Howitt, £5 5s.; Mr. Cargill, £2 2s.: Messrs. Were, Kent and Co., £5 5s.; Mr. J. Fulton, £2 2s. ; Mr. R. Smith, £2 2s. ; Messrs. Smith, Merry and Co., £5 6s. ; Mr. D. R. Long, £2 2s. ; Messrs. E. W. Cobb and Co., £2 2s.; Messrs. Dove and Oswald, £2 2s. J. HAYNES, Secretary." (Advertising, 31 May 1856, p.3)

"IN THE INSOLVENT ESTATE of Elisha Winslow Cobb and Henry Driver, of Melbourne, in the colony of Victoria, merchants, trading under the style or firm of E. W. Cobb and Co. ... Elisha Winslow Cobb and Henry Driver, to appear before the said Supreme Court, to show cause why their estate should not by sentence of the said court be adjudged to be sequestrated for the benefit of their creditors." (Advertising, 3 Feb 1857, p.6)

MERCHANDISE & PACKETS—E. W. COBB AND CO.

"Ringleader, from Boston ... CARRIAGES, marked Thomas Greenoug ... LOBSTERS ... E. W. Cobb and Co., 112 Collins-street west." (Advertising, 17 Jan 1855, p.8) ... "DOORS AND SASHES." (Advertising, 25 Jan 1855, p.3) ... "For freight or Charter, the American brig, CARBON" (Advertising, 30 Jan 1855, p.1) ... "MACHINERY, AGRICULTURAL IMPLEMENTS ... SAW MILLS" (Advertising, 16 Feb 1855, p.2) ... "NEW ZEALAND POTATOES" (Advertising, 8 Jun 1855, p.7) ... "CORN MEAL ... for Sale ... E. W. Cobb, Agent for the company, 112 Collins street west." (Advertising, 20 Oct 1855, p.7) "Merchandise ... EXPRESS WAGGONS.— Three of very superior make for Sale by E. W. Cobb and Co., Collins street" while on the same page "Missing friends ... Thomas Richard Tracy will hear from his friends in London— his mother is still living—by applying Office of this paper." (Advertising, 9 Nov 1855, p.1) ...

"ICE. ICE. ICE. ICE. The Melbourne Ice Company ... Delivered to families 28 lbs. per week, six guineas per quarter ... Company, 112 Collins-street west. (Advertising, 1 Jan 1856, p.?) ... "STEAM ENGINE ... To be sold cheap for cash. E. W. Cobb, 112 Collins street west." While written on the same page "STATIONS AND LIVE STOCK ... Cockatoos, Canaries, all kinds, Parrots, Fowls, Turkeys, Rabbits, Pigeons, at 133 Little Collins-street east." (Advertising, 22 Apr 1856, p.10)

"For San Francisco direct. The A1 clipper barque Fettercairn ... This beautiful vessel is a very fast sailer, and is in excellent order. Her accommodations are unequalled by any on the berth, and an experienced surgeon accompanies her ... for FREIGHT OR PASSAGE ... apply to E. W. Cobb and Co., 118 Collins-street west, Melbourne; B. H. Hall and Co., Three-mile Creek, Ovens; George W. Haycock, View Point, Bendigo; John Gardiner, Castlemaine Hotel, Castlemaine; A. B. Covington, Bath's Hotel, Ballaarat; F. B. Clapp, Fiery Creek." (Advertising, 1 May 1856, p.1) ... "Vessels in Hobson's Bay, Saturday 5th April, 1856, with the destinations and agents ... Ocean Eagle, A. s , 590, Boot, from Boston, for Singapore. E. W. Cobb and Co." (Vessels in Hobson's Bay, 9 Apr 1856, p.4)

George Francis Train
- **American**
- **Merchant in Melbourne**
- **Said he financed first coach for Freeman Cobb**

"George Francis Train, is a young merchant of great promise. Indeed he has already made his mark in the commercial world. In the brief space of two years, as a commission merchant in Melbourne, Australia, he has been eminently successful, and accumulated a fortune sufficient to retire upon ... He sailed in August last for Liverpool, where, we believe, he intends establishing a mercantile house. His house in Melbourne is still in the full tide of successful experiment." (G. F. Train at Home, 7 Feb 1857, p.3)

"NOTICE.—The PARTNERSHIP existing since 1st November, 1855, between Geo. Francis Train, Joshua Crane, and Goe. Starbuck, Jun. EXPIRES this day by fluxion of time. The business will be continue as usual by Mr. Train, under the name and style of Geo. F. Train and Co." (Advertising, 6 Nov 1857, p.8)

"George F. Train lectured in Boston ... He claimed to be the only good man in the world, as well as the only wise one, and his goodness had rendered him the enemy of all mankind ... As a prophet he claimed to be superior to Moses ... He reckoned he had taken 30,000 baths, and had, in consequence 200 years to live. He had never shaken hands with a man for five years, and was consequently the healthiest man in the world without exception." (George F. Train on Himself, 8 Sep 1877, p.3)

MERCHANDISE & PACKETS—GEO. F. TRAIN

Geo. F. Train "The First Coaches.—I was able to introduce into Australia a great, many articles and ideas from America. I brought over from Boston a lot of 'CONCORD' WAGONS, of the same type as the one that 'Ben' Holliday drove across the continent, and I told Freeman Cobb who was then with Adams & Co., that I wanted him to start a line of coaches between Melbourne and the gold mines, a distance of about 100 miles. I advanced the money for the enterprise, and a line was established, the first in Australia, to Geelong. Ballarat, Bendigo, and Castlemaine. These were the first coaches seen in that continent. The coaches cost in Australia £3,000 apiece." (Death of Mr. G. F. Train, 21 Jan 1904, p.6)

"White Star Line of Liverpool PACKETS. For freight or passage, apply to Geo. F. Train and Co., Flinders-street east, opposite the railway station." (Advertising, 23 Nov 1854, p.7) ... "White Star Line of Australian PACKETS. Persons desirous of sending for their friends in England can obtain certificates of passage, cabin, second cabin, or steerage, by any of the clippers belonging to this celebrated line by applying at this office ... Those packets are all first class ... A liberal dietary scale is provided, of the best quality of provisions, and a qualified surgeon is appointed to each ship ... White Star, the Blue Jacket, and the Antipodes ; all of which are of the largest size, and of the Red Jacket's model ... For plans of cabin passage, certificates, bills of exchange and every information relative to the White Star line of packets, apply to Geo. F. Train, & Co., 7 Queen Street." (Advertising, 2 Nov 1854, p.1) "For Sale, by the Undersigned ... SALMON ... OYSTERS ... PEPPER SAUCE ... ASSORTED PICKLES ... QUARTS Geo F. Train and Co., Flinders-street east opposite the railway station." (Advertising, 25 Nov 1854, p.6)

Appendix 2: Supporting evidence for Cobb and Co. coaching lines, Victoria

1850s

"American Telegraph Line of Coaches.—Daily Communication between Melbourne, Forest Creek and Bendigo—Cobb and Co. beg to announce to the public that they have determined to run a line of well-appointed Coaches between the above places, starting from the Criterion Hotel every morning, (Sunday excepted) at 6 o'clock, and from Forest Creek, daily, at the same hour. The vehicles intended to run are the new American coaches, recently imported, and acknowledged to be the easiest conveyances in the colony. The first coach will start from the Criterion, on Monday, January 30th, and every attention will be given to ensure punctuality Cobb and Co., Proprietors." (Advertising, 31 Jan 1854, p.3)

"Telegraph Stage Line, from Melbourne to Castlemaine, Bendigo, and Maryborough, via Essendon, Keilor, Gap, Gisborne, Woodend, Carlsruhe, Kyneton, Malmesbury, and Elphinstone, carrying Adams and Co.'s Inland Express daily. Cobb and Co." (Advertising, 25 Nov 1854, p.8)

"American Telegraph Line of Stages ... Melbourne to Ballaarat ... Adam and Co.'s Office, Great Collins-street, Melbourne ... Hewitt and Co." (Advertising, 30 Nov 1854, p.8)

"Telegraph Stage Office, 23 Bourke-street east, and General Agency Depot. Booking Office for Cobb and Co.'s Telegraph Line to Castlemaine, Bendigo, Simson's, &c. Also, Hewett and Co.'s Line to Ballarat and Creswick's Creek. Depot for merchants and carriers for the transmission of all descriptions of merchandise to the various diggings ... Registry for addresses, Post Office delivery &c. Missing friends advertised for, and communicated with when found. Letters by order obtained from the Post Offices, and forwarded through all parts of the colonies." (Advertising, 27 Jun 1855, p.2)

"The People's Line of Coaches will, from this date, start from the Telegraph Stage Office, 23 Bourke street east ... passengers will be booked and parcels forwarded to Ballarat, Creswick, Fiery Creek, and all the way stations. THOMAS DAVIES, Proprietor." (Advertising, 20 Feb 1856, p.1)

"Cobb and Co.'s Telegraph Line of Stage Coaches, from Melbourne to Castlemaine, Bendigo, and Simson's Daily. Winter Arrangement. The successful operation of this line being in no way impeded by the state of the roads, the proprietors beg to announce that their coaches will continue their daily trips as above, starting from the office of Messrs. Adams and Co., No 69 Collins-street west, every morning ... passing by Keilor Gap, Gisborne, Five-Mile Creek, Carlsruhe, Kyneton, Coliban, and Elphinstone, and connecting, at Castlemaine, with branch lines for Harcourt, Porcupine, and Bendigo, Tarrengower, Carisbrook, Maryborough, and Daisy Hill." (Advertising, 19 Jun 1856, p.2)

"Telegraph Line of Mail Coaches ... Castlemaine, Sandhurst, Maryborough, Ballaarat ... Watson and Hewitt, proprietors. A. Butler, agent, 23 Bourke-street east. N. L. Butler, agent, 28 Great Malop-street, Geelong. C. W. B. Miller, agent, Commercial Hotel, Castlemaine. John Crowley, agent, Shamrock Hotel, Sandhurst. James J. Blake, agent, M'Ivor Hotel, Maryborough. A. B. Covington, agent, Bath's Hotel, Ballaarat." (Advertising, 29 Oct 1857, p.8)

"TELEGRAPH STAGE OFFICE AND GENERAL AGENCY DEPOT. 23 Bourke-street east opposite the Union Hotel. Goods, Merchandise, and Luggage Forwarded to the various diggings, at the lowest rates. Passengers and parcels booked for Cobb and Co.'s daily lines to Castlemaine, Bendigo and Maryborough. Also the Peoples' Line, to Ballaarat, Creswick, and Fiery Creek. Passengers forwarded to the Ovens by the daily coaches, also upon American waggons. An American and European Express mail up per White Star Line of Packets. Storage for merchandise and luggage. T. K. NEWTON AND CO., Proprietors." (Advertising, 27 Feb 1856, p.8)

"We, the Undersigned, Proprietors of the Telegraph, Despatch, and Argus Mail lines of Stage Coaches, beg to notify the public that on and after the 1st of May, 1856, the fares between Melbourne, Castlemaine, Bendigo, and Maryborough will be as follows : Melbourne to Castlemaine ... £4 ... Bendigo ... Maryborough £6. Cobb and Co. Foster and Vinge. Howard and Co. Melbourne, April 26,1856." (Advertising, 28 Apr 1856, p.8)

"Cobb & Co.'s Telegraph Line of Stage Coaches—Castlemaine to Melbourne, Bendigo and Maryborough via Elphinstone, Taradale, Malmsbury, Kyneton, Carlsruhe, Woodend, Gisborne and Keilor ; Bendigo and Maryborough ... J. B. Lamber, agent, Castlemaine Hotel." (Advertising, 29 Apr 1856, p.3)

"Bendigo to Melbourne in one day ! ! ! Cobb and Co.'s Telegraph Line of Coaches—Castlemaine, Bendigo, Maryborough ... G. W. Haycock, View Point." (Advertising, 16 May 1856, p.1)

"MESSRS. COBB & CO.'S TELEGRAPH LINE OF COACHES—Castlemaine, Bendigo, and Maryborough via Keilor, Gisborne, Five Mile Creek, Carlsruhe, Kyneton, Coliban, Back Creek, Elphinstone ... Messrs. Cobb and Co. solicit a continuance of their former patronage ... John F. Britton, Agent, No. 23 Bourke-street, Melbourne; Anthony Butler, 44 Bourke-street, Melbourne; Cobb and Co.'s People's Telegraph Line of Covered Coaches, To Ballaarat, via Staughton's Station, Ballan, &c. Leave the Bull and Mouth Booking Office, No. 44 Bourke-street ... Great attention paid to the comfort of Passengers, and every care taken in the safe delivery of Parcels. Passengers and Parcels booked by A. Butler, Agent, 44 Bourke street east. J. F. Britton, Agent, 23 Bourke-street east. Cobb and Co. ... Notice.—On and after Monday, the 2nd June, the coach now leaving Melbourne at 8 ½ a.m., will start at 8 a.m. precisely. Cobb and Co." (Advertising, 29 May 1856, p.8)

"Cobb & Co.'s Telegraph Line of Stage Coaches from Castlemaine to Melbourne, Bendigo, and Maryborough, daily. The proprietors beg to announce that their coaches are still making their daily trips, starting from the Castlemaine Hotel every morning (Sundays excepted) at six o'clock precisely, for Melbourne, via Elphinstone, Taradale, Malmsbury, Kyneton, Carlsruhe, Woodend, Gisborne, and Keilor. Their regular line of coaches for Bendigo and Maryborough leave the Castlemaine Hotel every morning at the same hour. Passengers booked, and parcels received by J. Gardner, agent, Castlemaine Hotel." (Advertising, 3 Jun 1856, p.4)

"23 Bourke-street becomes the Telegraph Stage Office and General Forwarding Depot ... Goods, Merchandise, and Luggage ... to the various Goldfields. Passengers booked ... per Cobb and Co.'s coaches to Castlemaine, Bendigo, Maryborough, Ballaarat, &c., and per Royal Mail to Beechworth ... T. K. Newton and Co." (Advertising, 15 Jul 1856, p.8)

"MESSRS. COBB AND CO. beg to inform the public that the Afternoon Coach for Castlemaine and Melbourne will, for the future, leave the Shamrock Hotel at half-past Two o'clock p. m., instead of Two as heretofore. John Crowley, Agent; 331-213 Shamrock Hotel, Sandhurst." (Advertising, 18 Oct 1856, p.1)

"Messrs. Cobb and Co.'s Coaches will leave their Booking Office, No. 23 Bourke-street East for Castlemaine, Bendigo, Maryborough, and Dunolly ... until further notice ... Cobb & Co." (Advertising, 29 Nov 1856, p.1)

"Cobb and Co.'s Telegraph Line of Coaches ... for Castlemaine, Bendigo, Maryborough, and Dunolly ... John F. Britton, agent, 23 Bourke-street east ; Anthony Butler, 44 Bourke-street east, Melbourne." (Advertising, 29 Nov 1856, p.1)

"Cobb and Co.'s Telegraph Line of Coaches ... Summer Arrangement ... Castlemaine, Bendigo, Maryborough, Dunolly." (Advertising, 8 Nov 1856, p.1)

"Messrs. Cobb & Co.'s—Castlemaine to Melbourne, to Bendigo, to Maryborough, to Dunolly ... The above coaches leave the Commercial Hotel, Castlemaine, calling at the Castlemaine and Victoria Hotels, as above. J. Gardner, Agent, Commercial Hotel." (Advertising, 12 Jan 1857, p.4)

"Cobb & Co.'s Telegraph Line of Coaches ... on and after 1st June, the coaches will leave the Commercial and Castlemaine hotels ... C. W. B. Miller, Commercial Hotel, J. F. Sweeney, Castlemaine Hotel." (Advertising, 22 Jun 1857, p.3)

"Cobb and Co.'s Telegraph Line of Mail Coaches ... Castlemaine ... Sandhurst ... Maryborough ... Ballaarat ... Geelong ... Booking Office, No 23 Bourke-street Thomas Davis, Proprietor." (Advertising, 30 Jun 1857, p.8)

"Night Mail. KYNETON, CASTLEMAINE, and SANDHURST Cobb And Co.'s Telegraph Line Of Mail Coaches, On and after Wednesday, the 1st July, 1857, a night coach will leave the Booking Office, No. 23 Bourke-street east, at Five o'clock in the Evening, for Kyneton, Castlemaine, and Sandhurst ... Those Coaches being all strong now, covered coaches, drawn by stock second to none in the colony, the most careful men employed to drive them ... Thomas Davies, Proprietor." (Advertising, 1 Jul 1857, p.8)

"Cobb & Co.'s Telegraph Line of Coaches ... Castlemaine, Bendigo, Maryborough, Dunolly." (Advertising, 10 Jul 1857, p.2)

"Cobb and Co.'s Telegraph Line of Mail Coaches—Melbourne, Castlemaine, Sandhurst, Maryborough, Ballaarat via Geelong ... Thomas Davies ... On Monday next the 20th inst., Cobb and Co.'s Telegraph Line of Coaches, now running from Melbourne to Ballaarat, direct, will be discontinued, and removed to the road from Geelong to Ballaarat." (Advertising, 22 Jul 1857, p.3)

"Night Mail Kyneton; Castlemaine, and Sandhurst. Cobb and Co.'s Telegraph Line of Mail Coaches; The People's Telegraph Line of Coaches—Ballaarat via Bacchus Marsh and Ballan; Cobb and Co.'s Telegraphic Line of Mail Coaches ... Castlemaine, Sandhurst, Maryborough, Ballaarat, Geelong ... Thomas Davies, Proprietor." (Advertising, 25 Jul 1857, p.1)

"Cobb and Co.'s Telegraph Line of Mail Coaches run daily to Bacchus Marsh and Ballan ... leave 23 Bourke-street east Chas. Colclough, Proprietor." (Advertising, 11 Aug 1857, p.8)

"Telegraph Line of Mail Coaches ... Castlemaine, Sandhurst, Maryborough, Ballaarat, Geelong ... Alexander Walker, Proprietor. A. Butler, agent, 23 Bourke-street east. N. L. Butler, agent., Criterion Coach Office, Moorabool-street, Geelong. C. W. Miller, agent, Commercial Hotel, Castlemaine. John Crowley, agent, Shamrock Hotel, Sandhurst. James J. Blake, agent, M'Ivor Hotel, Maryborough. A. B. Covington, agent, Bath's Hotel, Ballaarat." (Advertising, 23 Sep 1857, p.8)

"Clark and Co.'s Estafette Line of Coaches. Melbourne to Castlemaine ... John Wagner, manager.—Book Office, next door to Union Hotel, Bourke-street." (Advertising, 30 Sep 1857, p.3)

"Telegraph Line of Mail Coaches ... Castlemaine, Sandhurst, Maryborough, Ballaarat, Geelong ... Alexander Walker, Proprietor." (Advertising, 13 Oct 1857, p.8)

"Cobb & Co.'s Telegraph Line of Mail Coaches to Mount Ararat. On and after Wednesday Sept. 2nd, the above Line of Coaches will run ... C. W. B. Miller, agent." (Advertising, 28 Oct 1857, p.4)

"Geelong and Melbourne. Cobb & Co.'s Telegraph Line. Watson and Hewitt, On and after Thursday, July 23, the Coaches for Geelong and Melbourne, will leave Bath's and the George Hotel, Township, and United States Hotel ... J. M. Peck, Agent. [Ballaarat]" (Advertising, 4 Nov 1857, p.1)

"Cobb & Co.'s Telegraph Line of Mail Coaches ... Melbourne, Sandhurst, Maryborough, Dunolly ... Watson and Hewitt, proprietors. C. W. B. Miller, agent, Commercial Hotel and J. F. Sweeny, Castlemaine Hotel ... Cobb & Co.'s Telegraph Line of Mail Coaches to Mount Ararat. On and after Wednesday Sept. 2nd, the above Line of Coaches will run ... C. W. B. Miller, agent." (Advertising, 4 Nov 1857, p.3)

"Cobb and Co.'s Telegraph Line of Coaches to Ballaarat direct, leave No. 23 Bourke-street very morning at six o'clock, passing through Melton, Bacchus Marsh, Ballan. Fare £8. Watson and Hewitt, proprietors, A. Butler, agent." (Advertising, 6 Nov 1857, p.8)

"Telegraph Line of Mail Coaches ... Castlemaine, Sandhurst, Maryborough, Ballaarat, Geelong ... Watson and Hewitt, Proprietors. A. Butler, agent, 23 Bourke-street east. N. L. Butler, agent, Criterion Coach Office, Moorabool-street, Geelong. C. W. B. Miller, agent, Commercial Hotel, Castlemaine. John Crowley, agent, Shamrock Hotel, Sandhurst. James J. Blake, agent, M'Ivor Hotel, Maryborough. J. M. Peck, agent, Bath's Hotel, Ballaarat." (Advertising, 6 Nov 1857, p.8)

"Cobb and Co.'s Telegraph Line of Coaches ... through to Pleasant Creek by way of Maryboro', Avoca, and Ararat ... J. F. Sweeney, Agent, Castlemaine Hotel." (Advertising, 21 Nov 1857, p.4)

"Cobb & Co.'s Telegraph Line of Coaches ... Melbourne, Sandhurst, Maryborough, Ararat, and Pleasant Creek, leave the booking offices, Commercial and Castlemaine Hotels ... Swanton & Blake. Proprietors ... J. F. Sweeny, Agent, Castlemaine Hotel, or W. R. Hall, Commercial Hotel." (Advertising, 1 Jan 1858, p.2)

"Geelong and Melbourne. Cobb and Co.'s Telegraph Line. F. B. Clapp & Co., proprietors." (Advertising, 1 Feb 1858, p.1)

"[Ballarat] To Geelong By Cobb & Co.'s Royal Mail Telegraph Line. The fare by this old established and favourite line of six Horse Covered Coaches, has been reduced ... E. Foley, Agent." (Advertising, 4 Feb 1858, p.1)

"[Ballarat] to Geelong and Melbourne. Cobb & Co.'s Telegraph Line of Royal Mail Coaches ... This is the only Line of Coaches running in connection with the Geelong and Melbourne Railway ... F. B. Clapp & Co., proprietors." (Advertising, 10 Feb 1858, p.1)

"Cobb and Co.'s Telegraph Line of Mail Coaches [Mount Alexander] To Melbourne, To Sandhurst, To Maryborough, To Ararat and To Mount Pleasant ... Swanton, Blake & Co. Proprietors." (Advertising, 23 Apr 1858, p.2)

"Cobb and Co.'s Telegraph Line of Mail Coaches. Through to Pleasant Creek by way of Maryborough, Avoca and Ararat ... W. H. Brayton, Proprietor." (Advertising, 14 May 1858, p.2)

"Cobb & Co.'s Telegraph Line of Mail Coaches ... The proprietors of the above Line have removed their Booking Office from the Commercial to Victoria Hotel" On the same page "Commercial Hotel. Offices and Stabling to let. N.B.—No persons connected with the firm styling itself Cobb and Co. need apply." (Advertising, 21 May 1858, p.8)

"Telegraph Line of Mail Coaches to Ballaarat ... F. B. Clapp & Co., proprietors. ... Telegraph Line of Mail Coaches to Beechworth ... A Coach will leave our Booking Office, 23 Bourke-street east, at 2 p.m. Watson & Hewitt, Telegraph Line of Mail Coaches ... Castlemaine, Maryborough, and Sandhurst ... Swanton, Blake & Co. Agents—A. Butler, 23 Bourke-street east, Melbourne ; Joseph Burrall, Shamrock Hotel, Sandhurst ; J. F. Sweeney, Victoria Hotel, Castlemaine ; O. B. Clapp, M'Ivor Hotel, Maryborough." (Advertising, 17 Jun 1858, p.8)

"Cobb and Co.'s Telegraph Line of Coaches/Cobb and Co.'s Telegraph Line of Daily and Nightly Coaches Sandhurst, Melbourne, Kyneton, Castlemaine, Bendigo." (Advertising, 19 Jul 1858, p.1)

"Cobb and Co.'s Telegraph Line of Mail Coaches ... Castlemaine, Sandhurst, Maryborough, Ararat, and Pleasant Creek ... Swanton, Blake & Co. ... J. F. Sweeney ... J. M. Peck Agents." (Advertising, 19 Jul 1858, p.1)

"Cobb and Co.'s Telegraph Line of Mail Coaches ... Castlemaine Sandhurst Maryborough, Ararat, and Pleasant Creek ... Swanton, Blake & Co. ... A. L. Blake, Manager." (Advertising, 27 Aug 1858, p.2)

"Telegraph Lines of Mail Coaches ... 23 Bourke-street east, Ballaarat direct ... 26 Great Malop-street ... To Ballaarat via Geelong ... F. B. Clapp and Co." (Advertising, 29 Sep 1858, p.6)

"Cobb and Co.'s TELEGRAPH LINE OF MAIL COACHES ... Castlemaine, Sandhurst, Maryborough, Tarrengower ... connecting with ... Echuca, Moama, Swan Hill, and Maiden's Punt on the Murray and Dunolly, Avoca, Ararat, Pleasant Creek and Tarrengower ... Agents— A. Butler, agent, 23 Bourke-street east, Melbourne ; Heffernan and Crowley, Shamrock Hotel, Sandhurst ; J. F. Sweeney Victoria Hotel, Castlemaine ; James J. Blake, Castlemaine Hotel, do. ; G. B. Clapp, M'Ivor Hotel, Maryborough. Victorian Stage Co. Per A. L. Blake, Manager." (Advertising, 29 Oct 1858, p.8)

"Cobb and Co.'s TELEGRAPH LINE OF MAIL COACHES.— Summer arrangement ... Castlemaine, Sandhurst, Maryborough ... connecting with ... Echuca, Moama, Swan Hill, and Maiden's Punt on the Murray and Dunolly, Avoca, Ararat and Pleasant Creek and Tarrengower." (Advertising, 8 Nov 1858, p.8)

"Telegraph Line of Mail Coaches—Ballaarat ... F. B. Clapp and Co., Proprietors." (Advertising, 8 Nov 1858, p.8)

"Cobb and Co.'s TELEGRAPH LINE OF MAIL COACHES.— Summer arrangement ... Castlemaine, Sandhurst, Maryborough ... connecting with ... Echuca, Moama, Swan Hill, and Maiden's Punt on the Murray and Dunolly, Avoca, Ararat and Pleasant Creek and Tarrengower." (Advertising, 8 Nov 1858, p.8)

"Geelong and Melbourne. Cobb & Co.'s Telegraph Line ... Watson & Hewitt ... J. M. Peck, Agent, Bath's and George Hotel, Township." (Advertising, 3 Dec 1858, p.1)

"Messrs Cobb & Co. beg to inform the public (that notwithstanding the reports circulated to the contrary) they have as yet plenty of room in their covered coaches to carry intending passengers to Geelong and Melbourne, leaving Bath's Hotel daily ... E. T. FOLEY, Agent. N.B. Booking Office, next Bath's Hotel." (Advertising, 11 Dec 1858, p.1)

"Cobb and Co.'s Telegraph Line of Royal Mail Coaches ... Eversley to Melbourne W. R. Mitchell, agent Ararat." (Advertising, 1 Jan 1859, p.8)

"Cobb and Co.'s Telegraph Line of Daily and Nightly Mail Coaches—Melbourne ... start from Shamrock Hotel, Sandhurst ... Victoria Stage Company ... Heffernan and Crowley, Agents, Shamrock Hotel." (Advertising, 6 Jan 1859, p.1)

"Cobb and Co.'s TELEGRAPH LINE OF MAIL COACHES ... to Ararat ... J. F. Sweeney, Agent, Victoria Hotel, J. J. Blake, Agent, Castlemaine Hotel ... W. H. Brayton; Cobb and Co.'s Telegraph Line of Mail Coaches ... Cheap and Expeditious travelling ... To Ballarat ... Victoria Stage Co. ... A. L. Blake, Manager, J. F. Sweeney, Agent, Victoria Hotel; Cobb and Co.'s Telegraph Line of Mail Coaches ... Summer arrangements ... Castlemaine, Sandhurst, Maryborough, Ararat, Ballarat ... Victorian Stage Co. ... A. L. Blake, Manager, J. F. Sweeney, Agent, Victoria Hotel, J. J. Blake, Agent, Castlemaine Hotel." (Advertising, 14 Jan 1859, p.8)

"Cobb and Co.'s Telegraph Line of Mail Coaches From Eversley to Melbourne ... W. R. Mitchell, agent, Ararat." (Advertising, 19 Jan 1859, p.8)

"TELEGRAPH LINE OF MAIL COACHES To Beechworth ... via Kilmore, Broadford, Seymour, Avenel, Longwood, Euroa, Violet Town, Benalla, Wangaratta. Watson and Hewitt, proprietor. A. Butler, agent." (Advertising, 19 Jan 1859, p.8)

"TELEGRAPH LINE OF MAIL COACHES ... Castlemaine, Sandhurst, Maryborough, Tarrengower ... connecting with ... Echuca, Moama, Swan Hill, and Maiden's Punt on the Murray and Dunolly, Avoca, Ararat, Pleasant Creek and Tarrengower ... Agents—A. Butler, agent, 23 Bourke-street east, Melbourne ; Heffernan and Crowley, Shamrock Hotel, Sandhurst ; J. F. Sweeney, Victoria Hotel, Castlemaine ; James J. Blake, Castlemaine Hotel, do. ; O. B. Clapp, M'Ivor Hotel, Maryborough. Victorian Stage Co. Per A. L. Blake, Manager." (Advertising, 5 Feb 1859, p.4)

"Cobb and Co.'s Telegraph Line of Mail Coaches—Summer Arrangement ... coaches for Castlemaine, Sandhurst, and Maryborough ... Tarrengower ... Victoria Stage Company." (Advertising, 10 Feb 1859, p.8)

"Cobb and Co.'s Telegraph Line of Mail Coaches ... coaches for Castlemaine, Sandhurst, and Maryborough etc., etc., will connect with Melbourne and Mount Alexander Railway at Digger's Rest Station ... Agents : Melbourne A. Butler. Diggers' Rest J. M. Peck. Castlemaine J. T. Sweeney, Victoria Hotel, Sandhurst Heffernan and Crowley, Shamrock Hotel. Maryborough O. B. Clapp, M'Ivor Hotel ... Victoria Stage Company." (Advertising, 12 Feb 1859, p.4)

"Cobb and Co.'s TELEGRAPH LINE of MAIL COACHES TO M'IVOR ... Whroo, Rushworth, Murchison, passing through Somerton, Donnybrook, Kilmore, and Pyalong ... M'Ivor in nine hours Watson and Hewitt. C. R. Gordon, Agent, M'Ivor. A. Butler, Agent, Melbourne." (Advertising, 12 Feb 1859, p.4)

"Travelling ... Cobb and Co.'s Telegraph Line of Mail Coaches to BALLARAT, DAILY, VIA Bate's Ford, Separation, Clyde, Lethbridge, Meredith, Corduroy, Buninyong, Connecting with Daily Lines to Mount Ararat, Fiery Creek, Creswick's Creek, Chines, Smythe's Creek, Amherst, Maryboro, Dunolly, Avoca ... F. B. Clapp & Co., Proprietors." (Advertising, 18 Feb 1859, p.1)

"Railways ... Melbourne to Sunbury ; Melbourne to Williamstown ... Cobb and Co's., coaches to Sandhurst, Castlemaine &c." (Advertising, 22 Feb 1859, p.1)

"Cobb and Co.'s Western Telegraph Line of Mail Coaches between Geelong and Portland. F . B. Clapp and Co. Proprietors ... Passing through Bruce's Creek, Shelford, Rokewood, Pitfield, Skipton, Streatham, Wickliffe, Dunkeld, Hamilton, Branxholme, Green Hills, Heywood, Portland." (Advertising, 16 Mar 1859, p.1)

"Passengers for Cobb & Co.'s Coaches to Melbourne, Geelong, Fiery Creek, Ararat, Pleasant Creek, Creswick, Clunes, Back Creek, Maryborough. Castlemaine, Avoca, Smythe's Creek, and all intermediate places, can be booked at Bath's Hotel at any time on Sundays and after nine o'clock p.m. on week days." (Advertising, 25 Apr 1859, p.3)

"COBB and CO.'S TELEGRAPH LINE of MAIL COACHES. Castlemaine, Sandhurst, Maryborough ... will connect with the Melbourne, Mount Alexander Railway ... A coach also leaves the Diggers' Rest ... for Kyneton and intermediate stations. Victoria Stage Company, Proprietors. A. L. BLAKE, Manager." (Advertising, 10 May 1859, p.8)

"American Livery and Letting Stables, Stephen street, between Bourke and Little Bourke street east (late Ford's). American buggies, carryalls, gigs, dog-carts, chaises, ladies and gentlemen's saddle horses, always on hire. Horses kept by the day, week, or month, on the most reasonable terms. A line of omnibuses in connection with every train to and from the Railway Station, Batman's Hill, to the Builders' Arms, Collingwood. Fares from either Terminus to Swanston street or Cafe de Paris, 3d ; through fare, 6d. James Swanton, Proprietor." (Advertising, 17 Jun 1859, p.7)

"Cobb and Co.'s Telegraph Line of Mail Coaches From Back Creek ... A. D. Shepard, Agent." (Proprietor unknown)

(Advertising, 4 Jul 1859, p.1)

"Cobb and Co.'s Telegraph Line of Daily and Nightly Mail Coaches … Melbourne … Castlemaine … Swan Hill … Victoria Stage Co." (Advertising, 16 Aug 1859, p.1)

"Cobb and Co.'s TELEGRAPH LINE OF MAIL COACHES … Sandhurst, Melbourne, Castlemaine, Swan Hill … Night coaches … Melbourne, Castlemaine … Victoria Stage Co. A. L. Blake, Manager." (Advertising, 10 Sep 1859, p.3)

"Cobb and Co.'s Telegraph Coaches Bacchus Marsh, Keilor, Melton … F. B. Clapp & Co." (Advertising, 10 Sep 1859, p.3)

"Cobb and Co.'s Telegraph Line of Mail Coaches Geelong, Ballarat … J. B. Clapp & Co., Proprietors … Cobb and Co.'s Western Telegraph Line of Mail Coaches Geelong, Portland F. B. Clapp & Co., Proprietors." (Advertising, 29 October 1859, p.1)

"Cobb and Co.'s Telegraph Line of Mail Coaches, Five Daily Coaches to Castlemaine … Castlemaine, Sandhurst, Swan Hill, Maryborough, Ararat, Creswick Creek &c., connecting with Victoria Railways at Digger's Rest Station … pass through … Ararat, Avoca, Amphitheatre, Buckeye, Baringhup (Loddon), Castlemaine, Carlsruhe, Creswick Creek, Carisbrook, Durham Ox, Eversley, Elphinstone, Gap, Gisborne, Guildford, Harcourt, Kyneton, Kingston, Maryborough, Malmesbury, Muckleford, Ravenswood, Reedy Lake Station, Sandhurst, Swan Hill, Serpentine Creek, Tarrangower(Maldon), Woodend. And connect with coaches to Back Creek, Pleasant Creek, Dunolly, Moama, Echuca, Deniliquin, &c … Victoria Stage Company." (Advertising, 31 Oct 1859, p.8)

"Cobb and Co.'s TELEGRAPH LINE OF Daily and Nightly MAIL COACHES….Castlemaine, Sandhurst, Maryborough, Ararat, Kyneton, Woodend, Gisborne … Victoria Stage Co. A. L. Blake, Manager." (Advertising, 1 Nov 1859, p.1)

"Cobb and Co.'s Western Telegraph Lines of Royal Mail Coaches, Between Geelong and Portland. F. B. Clapp and Co." (Advertising, 31 Dec 1859, p.2)

"Telegraph line of mail coach TO BALLAARAT F. B. CLAPP and CO." (Advertising, 31 Dec1859, p.2)

"Cobb and Co.'s Western Telegraph Lines of Royal Mail Coaches, Between Geelong and Portland. F. B. Clapp and Co." (Advertising, 31 Dec 1859, p.2)

"ALTERATION OF TIME. COBB AND CO.'s TELEGRAPH LINES OF MAIL COACHES, FIVE DAILY COACHES TO Castlemaine. These Lines of Coaches to Castlemaine, Sandhurst, Swan Hill, Maryborough, Ararat, Creswick's Creek, &c., connecting with the Victorian railways at the Diggers' Rest Station. These Lines of Coaches pass through the following townships Ararat, Avoca, Amphitheatre, Buckeye, Baringhup (Loddon), Castlemaine, Carlsruhe, Creswick's Creek, Carisbrook, Durham Ox, Eversley, Elphinstone, Gap, Gisborne, Guilford, Harcourt, Kyneton, Kingston, Maryborough, Malmsbury, Muckleford, Ravenswood, Reedy Lake Station, Sandhurst, Swan Hill, Serpentine Creek, Tarrengower (Maldon), Woodend. And connect with coaches to Back Creek, Pleasant Creek, Dunolly, Moama, Echuca, Deniliquin &c., … Victorian Stage Company A. L. BLAKE, Manager." Meanwhile Advertising shows "James Swanton, proprietor of American Livery and Letting Stables with a line of omnibuses in connection with every train to and from the railway station." (Advertising, 2 Jun 1859, p.7)

1860s

"Cobb and Co.'s Western Telegraph Lines of Royal Mail Coaches between Geelong and Portland … Geelong, Warrnambool, & Belfast … F. B. Clapp and Co." (Advertising, 21 Jan 1860, p.1)

"Geelong and Ballarat … Cobb and Co.'s Telegraph Lines of Royal Mail Coaches … N. L. Butler, Booking Clerk. E. J. Foley, Booking Clerk, Ballarat. W. R. Mitchell, Booking Clerk, Ararat and Pleasant Creek … F. B. Clapp and Co." (Advertising, 24 Jan 1860, p.1)

"Cobb and Co.'s General Stage Office, No. 23 Bourke-street east … Passengers and parcels … Castlemaine, Sandhurst, Swan Hill, Euston, Echuca, Maryborough, Ararat, Pleasant Creek, Ballarat, Creswick's Creek, Hamilton, Portland, Casterton, Darlington, (Elephant Bridge), Warrnambool and Belfast. F. B. Clapp and Co. Victorian Stage Company." (Advertising, 27 Jan 1860, p.8)

"Cobb and Co.'s General Stage Office, No. 74 Great Bourke street east … Passengers and parcels … Castlemaine, Sandhurst, Swan Hill, Euston, Echuca, Maryboro', Ararat, Sandy Creek, Lamplough, and Inglewood, via Sandhurst and Maryborough, Pleasant Creek, Ballaarat, Creswick's Creek, Hamilton, Portland, Casterton, Darlington, (Elephant Bridge), Warrnambool and Belfast. F. B. Clapp and Co. Victorian Stage Company A. Butler, Agent." (Advertising, 22 Mar 1860, p.3)

"Cobb and Co.'s TELEGRAPH LINE OF MAIL COACHES Leave the Shamrock and Abbott's Hotel for … Castlemaine, Melbourne … M'Ivor, Moama, Swan Hill … Victoria Stage Company, Heffernan and Crowley, Agents." (Advertising, 9 Apr 1860, p.1)

"Cobb and Co.'s General Stage Office, No. 23 Bourke-street east … Passengers and parcels … Castlemaine, Sandhurst, Swan Hill, Euston, Echuca, Maryborough, Ararat, Sandy Creek, Lamplough, and Inglewood, via Sandhurst and Maryborough, Pleasant Creek, Ballarat, Creswick's Creek, Hamilton, Portland, Casterton, Darlington, (Elephant Bridge), Warrnambool and Belfast. F. B. Clapp and Co. Victorian Stage Company." (Advertising, 21 Jun 1860, p.8)

"Cobb and Co.'s General Stage Office, No. 74 Bourke-street west … Passengers and parcels … Castlemaine, Sandhurst, Swan Hill, Euston, Echuca, Maryborough, Ararat, Sandy Creek, Lamplough, and Inglewood, via Sandhurst, Maryboro', Pleasant Creek, Ballarat, Creswick's Creek, Hamilton, Portland, Casterton, Darlington, (Elephant Bridge), Warrnambool and Belfast. F. B. Clapp and Co. Victorian Stage Company." (Advertising, 1 Jul 1860, p.3)

"COBB AND CO.'s TELEGRAPH LINES OF MAIL COACHES … FIVE DAILY COACHES TO Melbourne … Coaches for Melbourne, Sandhurst, Ballaarat … Creswick … Swan Hill … Victorian Stage Co. … A. L. Blake, Manager, J. F. Sweeney, Agent, Victoria Hotel, Castlemaine." (Advertising, 13 Jul 1860, p.1)

"Cobb and Co.'s General Stage Office, No. 74 Bourke-street east … Passengers and parcels … Castlemaine, Sandhurst, Swan Hill, Euston, Echuca, Maryborough, Ararat, Sandy Creek, Lamplough, and Inglewood, via Sandhurst and Maryborough, Pleasant Creek, Ballarat, Creswick's Creek, Hamilton, Portland, Casterton, Darlington, (Elephant Bridge), Warrnambool and Belfast, and all intermediate townships. F. B. Clapp and Co. Watson & Hewitt, Proprietors. A. Butler, Agent." (Advertising, 7 Aug 1860, p.8)

"COBB AND Co.'s Telegraph Line of Mail Coaches. In connection with the Melbourne & Mount Alexander Railway … Coaches for Melbourne, Sandhurst, Maryborough, Ararat, Ballarat, Creswick Creek, Swan Hill, Back Creek, Lamplough, Inglewood, Newbridge, Dunolly, and Sandy Creek, leave the Booking Offices, Victoria and Castlemaine … Watson & Hewitt, Proprietors, J. F. Sweeney, Agent, Victoria Hotel." (Advertising, 10 Aug 1860, p.2)

"Cobb and Co.'s General Stage Office, No. 35 Bourke-street East … Passengers and parcels … Castlemaine, Sandhurst, Swan Hill, Euston, Echuca, Maryborough, Ararat, Sandy Creek, Lamplough, and Inglewood, via Sandhurst and Maryborough, Pleasant Creek, Ballarat, Creswick's Creek, Hamilton, Portland, Casterton, Darlington, (Elephant Bridge), Warrnambool and

Belfast. F. B. Clapp and Co. Watson & Hewitt, Proprietors. A. Butler, Agent." (Advertising, 14 Sep 1860, p.3)

"COBB AND CO.'S Telegraph Line of Mail Coaches. Shamrock Hotel ... For Castlemaine and Melbourne ... For McIvor ... For Moama ... For Swan Hill ... N.B.—No notice will be taken of Accounts against the above company, unless sent in for payment [?] on Saturdays, Watson & Hewitt, Proprietors, Heffernan and Crowley, Agents." (Advertising, 5 Oct 1860, p.8)

"COBB AND CO.'S Telegraph Line of Royal Mail Coaches ... Alexander Temperance Hotel ... Hargreave's Royal Oak .... Digger's Rest Station ... Watson & Hewitt." (Advertising, 18 Oct 1860, p.1)

"COBB AND CO.'S Telegraph Line of Mail Coaches. These lines of Coaches to Castlemaine, Sandhurst, Swanhill, Maryborough, Ararat, Creswick Creek, etc., connecting with the Victorian Railways at Digger's Rest Station ... These lines of coaches pass through ... Ararat, Avoca, Amphitheatre, Buckeye, Barunhup (Loddon) Castlemaine, Carlsruhe, Creswick Creek, Carisbrook, Durham Ox, Eversley, Elphinstone, Gap, Gisborne, Guilford, Harcourt, Kyneton, Kingston, Maryborough, Malmsbury, Muckleford, Ravenswood, Reedy Lake Station, Sandhurst, Swan Hill, Serpentine Creek Tarrangower (Maldon), Woodend. And connect with coaches to Back Creek, Pleasant Creek, Dunolly, Moama, Echuca, Deniliquin, etc., etc. A. L. Blake, Manager." (Advertising, 18 Oct 1860, p.1)

"COBB AND CO.'S LEVIATHAN COACHES Have commenced running for the summer, Between Geelong and Ballarat. Fare, 10s. Booking-office, 35 Bourke-street, next to Albion Hotel. A. Butler, Agent. Notice.—Cobb and Co.'s coaches are now running to the Londonderry diggings, Black Ranges, near Ararat ... Booking-office, 35 Bourke-street, next to Albion Hotel. A. Butler, Agent." (Advertising, 25 Oct 1860, p.8)

"Cobb and Co.'s General Stage Office, 35 Bourke-street east ... Passengers and parcels ... Castlemaine, Sandhurst, Swan Hill, Euston, Echuca, Maryborough, Ararat, Sandy Creek, Lamplugh, and Inglewood, via Sandhurst and Maryborough, Pleasant Creek, Ballarat, Creswick's Creek, Hamilton, Portland, Casterton, Darlington, (Elephant Bridge), Warrnambool and Belfast ... F. B. Clapp and Co. Watson & Hewitt, Proprietors. A. Butler, Agent." (Advertising, 12 Nov 1860, p.8)

"Geelong and Ballarat ... Cobb and Co.'s Telegraph Lines of Royal Mail Coaches ... N. L. Butler, Booking Clerk. E. T. Foley, Booking Clerk, Ballarat. W. R. Mitchell, Booking Clerk, Ararat and Pleasant Creek. F. B. Clapp & Co., Proprietors." (Advertising, 24 Dec 1860, p.1)

"Cobb and Co.'s Telegraph Lines of Royal Mail Coaches ... Geelong and Ballarat ... Smythe's Creek, Brown's, Firey Creek, Ararat, Pleasant Creek, Creswick, Back Creek, Clunes, Daisy Hill, Maryboro', Castlemaine ... F. B. Clapp and Co." (Advertising, 12 Dec 1860, p.1)

"Cobb and Co.'s Night Coach to Ballaarat will run as usual, Saturdays, on the arrival of the 7.15 p.m. train. A. Butler." (Advertising, 13 Dec 1860, p.1)

"Cobb and Co.'s General Stage Office, No. 35 Bourke street East ... Passengers and parcels ... Castlemaine, Sandhurst, Swan Hill, Euston, Echuca, Maryboro', Ararat, Sandy Creek, Lamplough, and Inglewood, via Sandhurst and Maryborough, Pleasant Creek, Ballaarat, Creswick's Creek, Hamilton, Portland, Casterton, Darlington, (Elephant Bridge), Warrnambool and Belfast. F. B. Clapp and Co. Watson & Hewitt, Proprietors." (Advertising, 1 Jan 1861, p.7)

"COBB AND CO.'S Telegraph Line of Mail Coaches, Connecting with the Victorian Railway at the Digger's Rest Station ... Coaches for Melbourne, Sandhurst, Castlemaine, Ararat, Daisy Hill and Ballarat ... Watson & Hewitt. Chas. D. Pollack, Agent." (Advertising, 2 Jan 1861, p.1)

"Summer Arrangement. COBB AND CO.'S Royal Mail Coaches between Ballarat and Inglewood." (Advertising, 2 Jan 1861, p.1)

"Alteration of Time. Reduced Fares. On and after Monday, the 26th instant, Cobb & Co.'s 4-horse Coaches will leave for Clunes and Back Creek, Inglewood, and all intermediate stages ... Returning ... E. T. Foley, Agent, Office—Next Bath's Hotel. Alteration of Time To Geelong for 15s. COBB & CO.'S ROYAL MAIL COACHES will in future be despatched from Bath's and the George Hotels, Township, and the several hotels on the Flat, at a quarter before 6 a. m. E. T. FOLEY, Agent. Midday Coach to Geelong. On and after Monday, 31st December, 1860, Messrs Cobb & Co. will despatch a Coach to Geelong daily ... Coach will also leave Geelong for Ballarat on arrival of the 12.45 p.m. train from Melbourne. E. T. FOLEY, Agent; Cobb and Co.'s Telegraph Line of Royal Mail Coaches ... Portland, Geelong and Melbourne in 36 hours F . B. Clapp and Co. Proprietors." (Advertising, 14 Jan 1861, p.1)

"Geelong and Melbourne. COBB AND CO.'S Telegraph Line of Royal Mail Coaches Australian Stage Company, Proprietors ... E. T. Foley, Booking Clerk, Bath's and George Hotels, Township." (Advertising, 15 Jan 1861, p.1)

"Cobb and Co.'s Western Telegraph Line of Royal Mail Coaches Between Geelong and Portland,, and between Geelong, Warrnambool, & Belfast ... The Australian Stage Company ... Cobb and Co.'s Telegraph Line of Royal Mail Coaches ... Geelong ... Ballarat ... The Australian Stage Company. F. B. Clapp & Co." (Advertising, 16 Jan 1861, p.1)

"Cobb and Co.'s General Stage Office, No. 35 Bourke-street east ... Passengers and parcels ... Castlemaine, Sandhurst, Swan Hill, Euston, Echuca, Maryborough, Ararat, Sandy Creek, Lamplough, and Inglewood, via Sandhurst and Maryborough, Pleasant Creek, Ballaarat, Creswick's Creek, Hamilton, Portland, Casterton, Darlington, (Elephant Bridge), Warrnambool and Belfast and all intermediate stations. The Australian Stage Company. Watson & Hewitt, A. Butler, Agent." (Advertising, 16 Jan 1861, p.8)

"Cobb and Co.'s Western Telegraph Line of Royal Mail Coaches. Between Geelong and Portland and between Geelong, Warrnambool, & Belfast ... The Australian Stage Company ... Cobb and Co.'s Telegraph Line of Royal Mail Coaches ... Geelong ... Ballarat ... The Australian Stage Company. F. B. Clapp & Co." (Advertising, 16 Jan 1861, p.1)

"COBB AND CO.'s TELEGRAPH LINE OF MAIL COACHES A coach of this line, for the convenience of the public in this district will start from Alexander's Temperance Hotel ... Digger's Rest Station ... Watson & Hewitt." (Advertising, 17 Jan 1861, p.4)

"Cobb and Co.'s Telegraph Line of Royal Mail Coaches ... Australian Stage Company ... THE Coaches for Geelong leave Bath's and the George Hotels, Township, United States and Rising Sun Hotels, Main road, daily, as follows. For Geelong ... This Line of Coaches run in connection with the Geelong and Melbourne Railway, and passengers for Melbourne via Geelong ... To Mount Blackwood ... To Fiery Creek ... Australian Stage Company." (Advertising, 30 Jan 1861, p.1)

"Cobb and Co.'s Telegraph Line of Mail Coaches—Five Daily Coaches ... to Castlemaine, Sandhurst, Swanhill, Maryborough, Ararat, Creswick Creek etc., connecting with the Victorian Railway at the Digger's Rest Station ... pass through Ararat, Avoca, Amphitheatre, Buckeye, Barunhup (Loddon), Castlemaine, Carlsruhe, Creswick Creek, Carisbrook, Durham Ox, Eversley, Elphinstone, Gap, Gisborne, Guilford, Harcourt, Kyneton, Kingston, Maryborough, Malmsbury, Muckleford, Ravenswood, Reedy Lake Station, Sandhurst, Swan Hill, Serpentine Creek, Tarrangower (Maldon), Woodend. And connect with coaches to Back's Creek, Pleasant Creek, Dunolly, Moama, Echuca, Deniliquin, etc. etc. ... Watson & Hewitt." (Advertising, 31 Jan 1861, p.1)

"COBB AND CO'S Telegraph Line of Royal Mail Coaches from Portland to Geelong and Melbourne in 36 hours!!! ... To Geelong, 5s. Cobb & Co.'s Leviathan coaches leave Bath's and George Hotels." (Advertising, 4 Mar 1861, p.3)

"COBB AND CO.'S Telegraph Line of Royal Mail Coaches In connection with the Melbourne & Mount Alexander Railway ... Coaches for Melbourne, Sandhurst, Maryborough, Ararat, Ballarat, Creswick Creek, Swan Hill, Back Creek, Lamplough, Inglewood, Newbridge, Dunolly, and Sandy Creek ... Watson & Hewitt." (Advertising, 8 Mar 1861, p.2)

"Cobb and Co.'s General Stage Office, No. 35 Bourke street East ... Passengers and parcels ... Kyneton, Castlemaine, Sandhurst, Swan Hill, Euston, Echuca, Moama, Deniliquin, Maryborough, Ararat, Dunolly, Lamplough, Tarrangower (Maldon), Yandoit, Creswick ... Watson & Hewitt, proprietors. A. Butler, Agent." (Advertising, 18 Mar 1861, p.8)

"Public Conveyances. COBB and CO.'S GENERAL STAGE OFFICES, 35 Bourke street east. Coaches run to and from Geelong, Ballaarat, Raglan, Ararat, Pleasant Creek, Creswick Creek, Clunes, Back Creek, Amherst, Maryborough, Dunolly, Avoca, Lexton, M'Kinnon's, Inglewood, Sandy Creek, Lamplough, Daylesford, Portland, Hamilton, Belfast, Warrnambool, Elephant Bridge, Apsley, Harrow, Penola, Casterton, Coleraine, Digby, Merino, Skipton, Streatham, Rokewood, Shelford, Wickliffe, Pitfield, Cavendish, Heywood, Melton, Bacchus Marsh, Ballan, Gordon's, and intermediate townships ... Australian Stage Company, Proprietors, A. Butler, Agent." (Advertising, 23 Mar 1861, p.8)

"Cobb and Co.'s General Stage Office, No. 35 Bourke street East ... Passengers and parcels ... Kyneton, Castlemaine, Sandhurst, Swan Hill, Euston, Moama, Deniliquin, Maryboro', Ararat, Dunolly, Lamplough, Tarrangower (Maldon), Yandoit, Creswick and all intermediate stations ... Watson & Hewitt." (Advertising, 6 Apr 1861, p 8)

"Further Redaction of Fares to Castlemaine and Bendigo COBB & CO.'S Royal Mail Coaches, LEAVING Bath's and George Hotels daily ... to Sandhurst. Australian Stage Company, Proprietors. Office next Bath's Hotel." (Advertising, 11 Apr 1861, p.1)

"GEELONG AND MELBOURNE. COBB & CO.'S TELEGRAPH LINE OF ROYAL MAIL COACHES, (AUSTRALIAN STAGE COMPANY, PROPRIETORS.) ... Coaches for Geelong leave Bath's and the George Hotels, Township, United States and Rising Sun Hotels, Main road, daily ... This Line of Coaches run in connection with the Geelong and Melbourne Railway ... Further Reductions of Fares by Cobb & Co.'s Royal Mail Coaches. TO MELBOURNE DIRECT— Through in Nine Hours ... Only a limited number of passengers taken; To Mount Blackwood, Creswick, Daisy Hill, Clunes, Maryborough, Dunolly, Sandy Creek, Inglewood, Castlemaine, Yandoit, Lamplough, Fiery Creek, Mount Ararat, Pleasant Creek, Smythe's Creek ... To Back Creek (Sundays excepted), Clunes direct, Creswick direct, Brown's direct, Daylesford, Deep Creek (Jim Crow), St. Arnaud, Mount Korong, Miners' Rest, Mt. Blowhard, M'Kinnon's ... No responsibility incurred for parcels or passengers' luggage beyond the amount paid for carriage. Office hours, from 5 a.m. to 9 p.m. ; Sundays, from 4 p.m. to 9 p.m. A. C. BRUNIG, Manager, Ballarat. C. RUSSELL, Manager, Geelong and Melbourne." (Advertising, 22 May 1861, p.1)

"COBB & CO.'S AUSTRALIAN EXPRESS PARCEL DELIVERY. PARCELS and LUGGAGE booked for Delivery anywhere in Melbourne and Suburbs at the usual rates per coach and rail to Spencer street Railway Station, and the addition of one of the Australian Express Company's Stamps ensures delivery of the same at the consignee's address in Melbourne or suburbs. Orders for parcels to be called for in Melbourne or suburbs and forwarded to Ballarat, must be left at the Coach Office ... Delivered in Melbourne, Collingwood, Richmond, or Emerald Hill or brought from any of these suburbs to Spencer street Station SIXPENCE ... Coach between Ballarat and Fiery Creek. ON and after Monday, the 29th of April, Cobb & Co. will despatch a Coach from Fiery Creek (Raglan) to Ballarat every morning ... arriving in time ... coach to Geelong, returning same day, leaving Ballarat at 2 p.m., allowing passengers 2 hours to transact business in Ballarat. Australian Stage Company, Proprietors; Afternoon Coach to Geelong. ON and after this date Cobb & Co. will despatch a Five-Horse Coach to Geelong daily, at half-past 1 o'clock p.m. Fare 10s. Australian Stage Co., Proprietors. Office, next Bath's Hotel, 26th March. 1861." (Advertising, 22 May 1861, p.1)

"Cobb and Co.'s Telegraph Line of Mail Coaches ... Coaches leave the Booking Office, Maryborough ... Melbourne ... including first class ... second class railway ticket, Castlemaine, Sandhurst, Ararat, Lamplough, Avoca, McKinnon's, Redbank ... Robertson, Britton and Co., Proprietors. Chas. D. Pollack, Agent; Cobb and Co.'s Royal Mail Telegraph Line of Coaches ... for Eltham, St Andrew's and the new diggings ... Henry Hoyt, Proprietor; Cobb and Co.'s Telegraph Line of Mail Coaches ... Coaches leave the Booking Office, Maryborough ... Melbourne ... including first class ... second class railway ticket, Castlemaine, Sandhurst, Ararat, Lamplough, Avoca, McKinnon's, Redbank ... Robertson, Britton and Co., Proprietors. Chas. D. Pollack, Agent." (Advertising, 5 Jun 1861, p.1)

"Cobb and Co.'s General Stage Office, No. 35 Bourke street East ... Passengers and parcels ... Kyneton, Castlemaine, Sandhurst, Swan Hill, Euston, Moama, Deniliquin, Maryboro', Ararat, Dunolly, Lamplough, Tarrangower (Maldon), Yandoit, Creswick and all intermediate stations ... Robertson, Britton and Co.; Cobb and Co.'s Telegraph Line of Mail Coaches In connection with the Melbourne & Mount Alexander Railway ... Coaches for Melbourne, Sandhurst, Maryborough, Ararat, Ballarat, Creswick Creek, Swan Hill, Back Creek, Lamplough, Inglewood, Newbridge, Dunolly, and Sandy Creek ... Robertson, Britton and Co., J. F. Sweeney, Agent, Victoria Hotel P.S.—Cobb & Co.'s Australian Express Parcels Delivery ... to Collingwood, Fitzroy, Richmond, South Yarra, Prahran, Windsor, St. Kilda, Hawhorne, Kew, Tourak, Carlton, Flemington, and Emerald hill." (Advertising, 14 Jun 1861, p.2)

"Cobb and Co.'s Telegraph Line of Coaches to Dandenong.— Four horse coach ... from Cobb and Co.'s office, 35 Bourke-street east. Leave Bowman's Hotel, Dandenong ... Small parcels and packages carefully attended to. Michel and Hughes, proprietors." (Advertising, 13 Jun 1861, p.8)

"Cobb and Co'.s Royal Mail Telegraph Line of Coaches ... Caledonian, Mountain Diggings H. Hoyt Proprietor." (Advertising, 18 Jun 1861, p.8)

"Cobb and Co.'s Telegraph Line—Royal Mail of Coaches for the western district ... leave Geelong ... N. L. Butler, Agent.... Henry Hoyt, Proprietor." (Advertising, 1 July, p.8)

"Cobb and Co.'s TELEGRAPH LINE OF MAIL COACHES Digger's Rest Station to Melbourne ... Coaches for Melbourne, Sandhurst, Maryborough, Ararat, Ballarat, Creswick Creek, Swan Hill, Back Creek, Lamplough, Inglewood, Newbridge, Dunolly, and Sandy Creek ... Robertson, Britton and Co., Proprietors." (Advertising, 24 Jun 1861, p.3)

"Cobb and Co.'s Telegraph Line of Mail Coaches for the western district ... Geelong, Portland, Belfast, Warrnambool and all intermediate townships. N. L. Butler, Agent, Malop Street, Geelong. Royal Mail Coaches for Elsham, St Andrew's and Caledonian Diggings leave the office No. 35 Bourke street east, Melbourne ... Anthony Butler, Agent ... Parcels Delivery. Head Office, 90 Bourke street east ... Melbourne and suburbs ... C. B. Kingman, Manager. Livery and Letting stables, 90 Bourke street east ... Henry Hoyt, Proprietor. New Diggings. Cobb and Co.'s Royal Mail Line of Coaches will leave the Booking Office, 35 Great Bourke street, Melbourne, for Caledonian and Mountain Diggings ... H. Hoyt, proprietor. " (Advertising, 1 Jul 1861, p.8)

"McKinnon's to Ballarat and Melbourne ... Cobb and Co.'s Royal Mail Coaches ... Australian Stage Company." (Advertising, 5 Jul 1861, p.1)

"COBB and CO.'S Telegraph Line of Coaches Leaves the Shamrock Hotel for the undermentioned places as follows, viz.; For Castlemaine and Melbourne ... For Runnymede ... For M'Ivor ... For Swan Hill ... Robertson, Britton and Co., Proprietors." (Advertising, 3 Oct 1861, p.3)

"Cobb and Co.'s Telegraph Line of Mail Coaches In connection with the Melbourne & Mount Alexander Railway ... Coaches for Melbourne, Sandhurst, Maryborough, Ararat, Ballarat, Creswick Creek, Swan Hill, Back Creek, Lamplough, Inglewood, Newbridge, Dunolly, and Sandy Creek ... Robertson, Britton and Co., J. F. Sweeney, Agent, Commercial Hotel." (Advertising, 1 Nov 1861, p.2)

"COBB and CO.'S Telegraph Line of Mail Coaches. Daylesford Direct ... Fare Ten Shillings. Robertson, Britton and Co., Proprietors. J. F. Sweeny, Agent." (Advertising, 1 Nov 1861, p.2)

"COBB & CO'S. LEVIATHAN COACHES leaving their office, next Bath's Hotel ... arriving in Geelong in time for the ... train ... Booking Offices—George Lester's, Geelong Exchange, Yarrowee, Duchess of Kent, Star, United States, and Rising Sun Hotels. E. T. FOLEY, Agent, Australian Stage Company, Proprietors." (Advertising, 19 Dec 1861, p.1)

"COBB and CO.'S GENERAL STAGE OFFICE, 35 Bourke street ... Passengers and parcels ... Kyneton, Castlemaine, Sandhurst, Swan Hill, Euston, Moama, Deniliquin, Maryborough Ararat, Dunolly, Lamplough, Tarrangower (Maldon), Yandoit, Creswick and all intermediate stations ... Robertson, Britton and Co, Proprietor, A. Butler, Agent." (Advertising, 15 Jan 1862, p.1)

"Cobb and Co.'s Telegraph Line of Royal Mail Coaches ... mails and passengers ... Geelong for Belfast ... Geelong for Portland ... Hamilton for Apsley ... Casterton for Heywood ... Hamilton for Belfast ... Melbourne for Heidelberg ... Melbourne, Elsham, Caledonia, and St Andrew's ... Henry Hoyt, Proprietor." (Advertising, 16 Jan 1862, p.8)

27 Jan 1862 "Cobb and Co.'s Telegraph Line of Mail Coaches In connection with the Melbourne & Mount Alexander Railway ... Coaches for Melbourne, Sandhurst, Maryborough, Ararat, Ballarat, Creswick Creek, Swan Hill, Back Creek, Lamplough, Inglewood, Newbridge, Dunolly, and Sandy Creek; Coach to Daylesford ... On and after Jan 1st, a coach will leave the Commercial Hotel at 11.30 a.m. ... returning there every morning ... Robertson, Britton and Co, J. F. Sweeney, Agent, Commercial Hotel." (Advertising, 27 Jan 1862, p.3)

"Cobb and Co.'s Royal Mail Coaches—for Avoca, Lamplough, Back Creek, Clunes, Creswick, Castlemaine, Ballarat, Geelong and Melbourne ... For Dunolly, Sandy Creek, and Inglewood ... Australian Stage Company." (Advertising, 10 Feb 1862, p.1)

"Cobb and Co.'s Telegraph Line of Mail Coaches In connection with the Melbourne & Mount Alexander Railway ... Three Daily Lines of Coaches to Melbourne ... Sandhurst, Maryborough, Malden, Ararat, Ballarat, Creswick, Swan Hill, Back Creek, Lamplough, Inglewood, Dunolly, and Sandy Creek ... Robertson, Britton and Co., J. F. Sweeney, Agent, Victoria Hotel, Castlemaine." (Advertising, 21 Mar 1862, p.5)

"Malden to Maryborough Dunolly and Inglewood. COBB and CO.'S Royal Mail Coaches leave the Kangaroo Hotel, Maldon ... for Ararat, Carisbrook, Dunolly, Lamplough and Maryborough. For Newbridge, Sandy Creek and Inglewood. Robertson, Britton and Co, Proprietors." (Advertising, 21 Mar 1862, p.5)

"Cobb and Co.'s Telegraph Lines Geelong and Ballaarat ... Melbourne to Ballaarat via Geelong ... Australian Stage Company, Proprietors." (Advertising, 3 May 1862, p.1)

"Cobb and Co.'s Telegraph Line of Mail Coaches In connection with the Melbourne & Mount Alexander Railway. From Woodend and Kyneton Station to Melbourne. Four daily lines of coaches to Melbourne ! ! ... Coaches for Melbourne, Sandhurst, Maryborough, Ararat, Ballarat, Creswick Creek, Swan Hill, Back Creek, Lamplough, Inglewood, Newbridge, Dunolly, and Sandy Creek leave the Booking Offices, Commercial and Castlemaine Hotels ... Robertson, Wagner and Co., Proprietors. J. F. Sweeny, Agent, Commercial Hotel." (Advertising, 5 May 1862, p.3)

"COBB and CO.'S GENERAL STAGE OFFICE, 35 Bourke street East ... Passengers and parcels ... Kyneton, Castlemaine, Sandhurst, Swan Hill, Euston, Moama, Deniliquin, Maryboro, Ararat, Dunolly, Lamplough, Tarrangower (Maldon), Yandoit, Creswick, and all intermediate stations ... Robertson, Wagner and Co., Proprietor, A. Butler, Agent, Melbourne." (Advertising, 5 May 1862, p.1)

"Cobb and Co.'s Telegraph Line of Mail Coaches. Leave the Booking Office, M'Ivor Hotel, Maryborough, daily ... Avoca, Moonambel, Barkley (late Navarro), Redbank, Lamplough, Amphitheatre, Eversley, Ararat, Pleasant Creek ... Castlemaine, Sandhurst, Melbourne and intermediate Places ... Robertson, Wagner and Co. Proprietors; McKinnon's to Ballarat and Melbourne. Daily. Cobb and Co.'s Royal Mail Coaches leave the Shamrock Hotel, McKinnon's ... for Avoca, Lamplough, Back Creek, Clunes, Creswick, Castlemaine, Ballarat, Geelong and Melbourne ... Dunolly, Sandy Creek, and Inglewood ... Australian Stage Company, Proprietors. J. Lamont, Agent. Commercial Hotel, McKinnon's." (Advertising, 9 May 1862, p.1)

"Cobb and Co.'s Telegraph Lines. Geelong and Ballaarat ... leave Geelong Railway Terminus for Ballarat ... Australian Stage Company, Proprietors." (Advertising, 13 May 1862, p.1)

"V.R. Cobb and Co.'s Telegraph Line of Royal Mail Coaches— To Melbourne Direct ... Ballarat, passing through Gordon, Ballan, and Bacchus Marsh, Australian Stage Company, E. J Brayton, Agent." (Advertising, 13 Sep 1862, p.1)

"Geelong to Linton's, thence to Hamilton and Portland. Winter arrangements ! ! Cobb and Co.'s Telegraph Line of Royal Mail Coaches ... Passengers and parcels can be booked through at the Melbourne or Ballarat offices. Cobb and Co.'s Coach Office, Union Hotel, Great Malop-street, Geelong. & Winter Arrangements ! ! Geelong to Warrnambool and Belfast. Cobb and Co.'s Royal Mail Telegraph Line ... Passengers and parcels can be booked through at the Melbourne or Ballarat offices. Cobb and Co.'s Coach Office, Union Hotel, Great Malop-street, Geelong." (Advertising, 8 Nov 1862, p.1)

"V.R. Cobb and Co.'s Telegraph Line of Royal Mail Coaches, Australian Stage Company ... Head Office—south-west corner of Sturt and Lydiard streets—To Melbourne direct ... Ballarat passing through Gordon, Ballan, and Bacchus Marsh ... to Creswick Creek, Clunes, Talbot (Back Creek), Amherst (Daisy Hill), Maryborough, Dunolly, Sandy Creek, Inglewood, Wedderbourne (Mount Korong) via Inglewood, St. Arnaud (New Bendigo), Kington, Smeaton, Yandoit, Castlemaine, Sandhurst (Bendigo), Mount Prospect, Deep Creek (Jim Crow), Daylesford, Woodend via Daylesford, Miners' Rest, Blowhard, Lake Learmonth, Mount Bolton, Springs, Lexton, Lamplough, Avoca, Moonambel (M'Kinnon's), Redbank, Barkly (Navarre), Burrumbeet, Raglan (Fiery Creek), Ararat, Great Western, Pleasant Creek, Skipton, Hamilton, Portland, Gordons, Ballan, Pentland Hills, Bacchus Marsh, Melton, Keilor road, Mount

Blackwood ... Luggage and parcels bearing the Australian Express Company's Stamps delivered anywhere in Melbourne or the suburbs, on arrival of the Trains at the Spencer-street Railway Station. Shilling and Sixpenny Express Stamps on sale at this office ... E. J. Brayton." (Advertising, 22 Dec 1862, p.1)

"Cobb and Co.'s Western Telegraph Line of Royal Mail Coaches—Ballarat to Smythesdale, Linton, Skipton, Streatham, Wickliff, Dunkeld, Hamilton, Branxholme, Green Hills, Heywood, Portland ... Henry Hoyt; Branch coaches leave Hamilton for Apsley, via Cavendish, Balmoral, and Harrow ... leaving Hamilton for Penola, via Coleraine and Casterton ... leaving Heywood for Casterton, via Hotspur, Digby, Merino, and Sandford ... Return Coaches leave the Company's Booking Offices ... Portland ... Apsley ... Penola ... Every information regarding Fares, &c, to be had on application at the Office, corner of Lydiard and Sturt streets. E. J. BRAYTON, Agent." (Advertising, 29 Dec 1862, p.1)

"CONTRACT ACCEPTED.—Conveyance of mails to and from Sandhurst to Inglewood, by way of Marong, six days a week, from the 1st April to 31st December, 1862, at the rate of £175 per annum in lieu of contract No. 105 of 1862, transferred from Wm. Wood ... £131 5s., Robertson, Britton, and Co." (Advertising, 12 Jan 1863, p.2)

"Cobb and Co.'s Western Telegraph Line of Royal Mail Coaches ... Ballarat to Smythesdale, Linton, Skipton, Streatham, Wickliff, Dunkeld, Hamilton, Branxholme, Green Hills, Heywood, Portland ... Henry Hoyt." (Advertising, 6 Feb 1863, p.1)

"Cobb and Co.'s Telegraph Line of Mail Coaches In connection with the Melbourne & Mount Alexander Railway ... Coaches of the above line will leave the Kangaroo Hotel, Maldon ... Baringhup, Carisbrook, Maryborough, Ararat, Lamplough, Eddington, Dunolly, Tarnagulla, Burnt Creek ... Castlemaine and Melbourne ... Castlemaine Hotel and Railway Station ... for ... Carisbrook, Maryborough, Back Creek, Avoca, Moonambool, Landsborough, Barkly, Red Bank, Ararat, Eversley ... Inglewood, Serpentine, Durham Ox, Swan Hill, M'Ivor, Echuca, Moama, Red Bank, Deniliquin, and Hay ... For Yandoit, Creswick, and Ballaarat ... Daylesford ... Booking Office, adjoining Castlemaine Hotel ... Robertson, Wagner, and Co., J. F. Sweeney, Agent." (Advertising, 31 Mar 1863, p.1)

"Mail Arrangements for 1863. Cobb and Co.'s Western Telegraph Line of Royal Mail Coaches ... Ballarat to Hamilton & Portland, Hamilton to Portland ... Coaches will be despatched for the conveyance of Mails and Passengers ... from Hamilton ... For Ballarat via Dunkeld, Wickliffe, Streatham, Skipton ... Portland via Branxholme, Green Hills, Heywood ... Apsley via Cavendish, Balmoral, Harrow ... Penola via Coleraine, Casterton, Fletcher's Store ... Penhurst, Caramut, Hexham, Mortlake ... Eumeralla, Orford, Belfast ... Return coaches leave from Company's booking office, Ballarat, Mac's Hotel, Portland, Botterill's hotel, Apsley, Cawker's hotel, Penola, Malcolm's Victoria Hotel. Henry Hoyt, proprietor. J. R. Webb Agent." (Advertising, 3 Apr 1863, p.1)

"Cobb and Co.'s General Stage Office No. 35 Bourke Street east. Passengers and parcels booked to Kyneton, Castlemaine, Sandhurst, Swan Hill, Huston, Moama, Deniliquin, Maryborough, Ararat, Dunolly, Lamplough, Tarrengower (Maldon), Yandoit, Creswick, and all Intermediate stations. Full particulars as to fare, times of starting, etc, to be had on application to the agent. No responsibility for parcels beyond the amount of Five Pounds (L5) sterling, unless value is declared and paid for at the time of booking. Passengers' luggage at owners' risk, and 14lb weight only allowed each free of charge. Robertson, Wagner, and Co., B. Teasdale." (Advertising, 14 Apr 1863, p.1)

"Great Reduction in Fares! Mail Cobb and Co.'s Western Telegraph Line of Royal Mail Coaches—Ballarat to Hamilton, Portland ... Henry Hoyt, proprietor. Booking-office Mac's Hotel, Portland." (Advertising, 16 Apr 1863, p.1)

"V. R. Cobb and Co.'s Telegraph Line of Royal Mail Coaches, south-west corner of Sturt and Lydiard streets—Ballarat to Creswick, Clunes, Ascot (Coghill's Creek), Talbot (Back Creek), Amherst (Daisy Hill), Maryborough, Dunolly, Sandy Creek (Tarnagulla), Inglewood, St. Arnaud (New Bendigo), Kingston, Smeaton, Yandoit, Guildford, Castlemaine, Sandhurst (Bendigo) Mount Prospect, Deep Creek (Jim Crow), Daylesford, Woodend, Miners' Rest, Mount Blowhard, Lake Learmonth, Mount Bolton, Springs, Lexton, Avoca, Lamplough, Woodstock, Moonambel (Mountain Creek), Redbank, Barkly (Navarre), Landsborough (New Rush), Burrumbeet, Raglan (Fiery Creek), Buangor (M'Donald's), Ararat, Great Western, Pleasant Creek, Glenorchy, Horsham, Gordons, Ballan, Pentland Hills, Bacchus Marsh, Melton, Keilor ... Australian Stage Company, Proprietors; Cobb and Co.'s Western Telegraph Line of Royal Mail Coaches—Ballarat to Smythesdale, Linton, Skipton, Streatham, Wickliff, Dunkeld, Hamilton, Branxholme, Green Hills, Heywood, Portland ... Henry Hoyt; Branch coaches leave Hamilton for Apsley, via Cavendish, Balmoral, and Harrow ... leaving Hamilton for Penola, via Coleraine and Casterton ... leaving Heywood for Casterton, via Hotspur, Digby, Merino, and Sandford ... Return Coaches leave the Company's Booking Offices ... Portland ... Apsley ... Penola ... Every information regarding Fares, &c, to be had on application at the Office, corner of Lydiard and Sturt streets ... COBB and CO.—Blowhard, Learmonth, and Springs; COBB and CO.—Clunes and Talbot (Back Creek) via Creswick, at 1 p.m. Passengers leaving Talbot and Clunes in the morning will arrive in Ballarat at 11 a.m., giving them two hours to transact business and return same day; COBB and CO.—Day coach to Ararat and Pleasant Creek ... E. J. BRAYTON, Agent ... MONSTER SALE David Jones ... All goods will be marked in plain figures in red ink to prevent confusion." (Advertising, 13 May 1863, p.1)

"Coach Notice.—On and after this date a coach will leave Kyneton for the Blue Mountains Rush daily ... on arrival of the 7.15 train from Melbourne ... Passengers and parcels booked at Cobb and Co.'s office, 35 Bourke-street east. Robertson, Wagner, and Co., proprietors. B. Teasdale agent." (Advertising, 30 May 1863, p.8)

"Malden to Maryborough Dunolly and Inglewood. COBB and CO.'S Royal Mail Coaches leave the Kangaroo Hotel, Maldon ... for Ararat, Carisbrook, Dunolly, Lamplough and Maryborough. For Newbridge, Sandy Creek and Inglewood. Robertson, Britton and Co, Proprietors." (Advertising, 23 Jun 1863, p.1)

"Cobb & Co's. Royal Mail Line of Coaches Geelong to Warrnambool and Belfast ... Thomas Stoneman." (Advertising, 4 Jan 1861, p.4)

"V. R. Cobb and Co.'s Telegraph Line of Royal Mail Coaches, south-west corner of Sturt and Lydiard streets, as under—Ballarat to Creswick, Clunes, Ascot (Coghill's Creek), Talbot (Back Creek), Amherst (Daisy Hill), Maryborough, Dunolly, Sandy Creek (Tarnagulla), Inglewood, St. Arnaud (New Bendigo), Mount Prospect, Deep Creek (Jim Crow), Daylesford ... Australian Stage Co., Proprietor; Burrumbeet, Raglan (Fiery Creek), Buangor (M'Donald's), Ararat, Great Western, Pleasant Creek ... J. C. Horr Proprietor; CASTLEMAINE ROAD Kingston, Smeaton, Yandoit, Guildford, Castlemaine, Sandhurst (Bendigo) ... Robertson, Britton and Co.; AVOCA ROAD Miners' Rest, Mount Blowhard, Lake Learmonth, Mount Bolton, Springs, Lexton, Avoca, Lamplough, Woodstock, Moonambel (Mountain Creek), Redbank, Barkly (Navarre), Landsborough (New Rush) ... M'Phee and Co., Proprietors; HAMILTON ROAD Ballarat to Smythesdale, Linton, Skipton, Streatham, Wickliff, Dunkeld, Hamilton ... Meigs & Anderson, Proprietors; Day coach to Ararat and Pleasant Creek ... E. J. Brayton, Agent." (Advertising, 14 Jan 1864, p.1)

"Cobb & Co.'s Coaches In connection with Victorian Railways ... start from Castlemaine Hotel and Railway Station for ... Newstead, Carisbrook, Maryborough, Back Creek, Avoca, Moonambel, Landsborough, Barkly Red Bank, Eversly, Ararat, Maldon, Eddington, Dunolly, Tarnagulla, and Burnt Creek. Passengers booked, via Sandhurst, for Inglewood, Serpentine, Durham Ox, Swan Hill, M'Ivor, Echuca, Moama, Red Bank, Deniliquin and Hay ... For Yandoit, Creswick, and Ballarat ... Daylesford ... Booking Office adjoining Castlemaine Hotel. Robertson, Wagner, & Co., J. F. Sweeney, Agent." Business advertisement on the same page "BAKER'S TEMPERANCE HOTEL. Hargreave Street, Castlemaine, Next door to Cobb & Co.'s office ... Dr. Preshaw SURGEON AND ACCOUCHEUR, Kirk Hill Villa, Lyttleton Street." (Advertising, 16 Jun 1864, p.1)

"Cobb and Co.'s Telegraph Line of Mail Coaches. In connection with the Melbourne & Mount Alexander Railway. Coaches of the above line will leave the Kangaroo Hotel, Maldon ... Baringhup, Carisbrook, Maryborough, Ararat, Lamplough, Eddington, Dunolly, Tarnagulla, Burnt Creek ... Castlemaine and Melbourne ... Castlemaine Hotel and Railway Station ... for ... Maldon, Carisbrook, Maryborough, Back Creek, Avoca, Moonambool, Landsborough, Barkly, Red Bank, Ararat, Eversley ... Passengers booked, via Sandhurst, for Inglewood, Serpentine, Durham Ox, Swan Hill, M'Ivor, Echuca, Moama, Red Bank, Deniliquin, and Hay ... For Yandoit, Creswick, and Ballaarat ... Daylesford ... Booking Office, adjoining Castlemaine Hotel ... Robertson, Wagner and Co., J. F. Sweeney, Agent; ... Kangaroo Hotel, High-street, Maldon ... Cobb's Coaches ... Maryborough, Dunolly, Sandy Creek, Back Creek, Daisy Hill, Kingower, Korong, Pleasant Creek, Ararat, and Lamplough ... Edward Ellis, Proprietor" while "FREE & EASY Every Saturday Evenings at the Kangaroo Hotel." (Advertising, 19 Jan 1864, p.1)

"Cobb and Co.'s Criterion Line of Coaches—leave Unicorn Hotel for Beaufort, Ararat, and Pleasant Creek ... Cameron and Jones, Proprietors. W. Stevenson, Agent." (Advertising, 2 Aug 1864, p.1)

"V. R. Cobb and Co.'s Telegraph Line of Royal Mail Coaches, south-west corner of Sturt and Lydiard streets ... Ballarat to Smythesdale, Linton, Skipton, Streatham, Wickliff, Dunkeld, Hamilton, Portland ... (Meigs & Anderson) ... E. J. Brayton, Agent." (Advertising, 2 Aug 1864, p.1)

"Cobb & Co's. Royal Mail Line of Coaches ... Geelong to Belfast ... Leigh and Lintons ... Leigh Road to Shelford, Rokewood, Pitfield, Lintons ... Offices and agents: Cobb's & Co.'s office, Melbourne and Geelong, and at the Leigh Road Station. Cobb & Co's. Livery and Letting Stables. Back of Union Hotel, Malop-street, Geelong and opposite Messrs Syrnot and Guthrie, Wool Stores. Sadle horses, buggies, carryalls carriages, and every description of vehicle to be had at a moment's notice. Horses taken in to bait or stand at livery by the day, week, or month, on reasonable terms ... Also at Queenscliff, for which place a coach leaves daily ... Thomas Stoneman, Proprietor." (Advertising, 6 Aug 1864, p.1,)

"V. R. Cobb and Co.'s Telegraph Line of Royal Mail Coaches, south-west corner of Sturt and Lydiard streets ... CASTLEMAINE ROAD Kingston, Smeaton, Yandoit, Guildford, Castlemaine, Sandhurst (Bendigo) ... Robertson, Wagner and Co.; AVOCA ROAD Miners' Rest, Mount Blowhard, Lake Learmonth, Mount Bolton, Springs, Lexton, Woodstock, Lamplough, Avoca, Moonambel (Mountain Creek), Redbank, (Barkly), Landsborough, Redbank, Stuart Mill, St Arnaud ... M'Phee and Co., Proprietors; Ballarat to Creswick, Clunes, Ascot (Coghill's Creek), Talbot (Back Creek), Amherst (Daisy Hill), Maryborough, Dunolly, Sandy Creek (Tarnagulla), Inglewood, St. Arnaud (New Bendigo), Mount Prospect, Deep Creek (Jim Crow), Daylesford ... Australian Stage Co., Proprietor." while "CASTLEMAINE ELECTION. Langley, Barford. October 4, 1864 ... A. W. Robertson, of Robertson, Wagner & Co." (Advertising, 6 Oct 1864, p.3)

"V. R. Cobb and Co.'s Telegraph Line of Royal Mail Coaches, south-west corner of Sturt and Lydiard streets—ARARAT ROAD Burrumbeet, Raglan (Fiery Creek), Buangor (M'Donald's), Ararat, Great Western, Pleasant Creek ... John M'Phee, Proprietor." (Advertising, 28 Nov 1864, p.1)

"V. R. Cobb and Co.'s Telegraph Line of Royal Mail Coaches, south-west corner of Sturt and Lydiard streets—Ballarat to Creswick, Clunes, Ascot (Coghill's Creek), Talbot (Back Creek), Amherst (Daisy Hill), Maryborough, Dunolly, Sandy Creek (Tarnagulla), Inglewood, St. Arnaud (New Bendigo), Mount Prospect, Deep Creek (Jim Crow), Daylesford ... Australian Stage Co., Proprietor; ARARAT ROAD Burrumbeet, Raglan (Fiery Creek), Buangor (M'Donald's), Ararat, Great Western, Pleasant Creek ... John M'Phee; HAMILTON ROAD Ballarat to Smythesdale, Linton, Skipton, Streatham, Wickliff, Dunkeld, Hamilton, Portland ... Meigs & Anderson." (Advertising, 10 Jan 1965, p.1)

"Cobb and Co.'s Royal Mail Line of Coach ... Melbourne to Daylesford and back in one day ... Australian Stage Company." (Advertising, 11 Jan 1865, p.8)

"V. R. Cobb and Co. Messrs Cobb and Co. have made arrangements to book passengers and parcels from Melbourne to Sale, Bairnsdale, and Bald Hills, by steamer and coach. Meigs & Anderson." (Advertising, 3 May 1865, p.1)

"Cobb & Co.'s Telegraph Line of Coaches leave Iron's Bridge Hotel, Echuca ... for Deniliquin. Robertson, Wagner, & Co., Proprietors. J. W. Stodart, Agent." (Advertising, 1 Jul 1865, p.4)

"COBB & CO.'S TELEGRAPH LINE OF MAIL COACHES, leave Taylor's Royal Hotel, Deniliquin, for Sandhurst ... For Hay (Lang's Crossing Place) Murrumbidgee ... Hay for Deniliquin ... ROBERTSON, WAGNER, & CO., Proprietors. HENRY SALOSHIN, Agent." (Advertising, 26 Aug 1865, p.1)

"V. R. Cobb and Co.'s Telegraph Line of Royal Mail Coaches, south-west corner of Sturt and Lydiard streets—Ballarat to Creswick, Clunes, Ascot (Coghill's Creek), Talbot (Back Creek), Amherst (Daisy Hill), Maryborough, Dunolly, Sandy Creek (Tarnagulla), Inglewood, St. Arnaud (New Bendigo), Mount Prospect, Deep Creek (Jim Crow), Daylesford ... Australian Stage Co.; CASTLEMAINE ROAD Kingston, Smeaton, Yandoit, Guildford, Castlemaine, Sandhurst (Bendigo) ... Robertson, Wagner and Co.; AVOCA & ST. ARNAUD'S DAILY Miners' Rest, Mount Blowhard, Lake Learmonth, Mount Bolton, Springs, Lexton, Woodstock, Lamplough, Avoca, Moonambel, Barkly, Landsborough, Redbank, Stuart Mill, St Arnaud ... M'Phee and Co.; ARARAT, PLEASANT CREEK AND HORSHAM ROAD DAILY Burrumbeet, Beaufort, Mount Colem, Buanger, Ararat, Great Western, Stawell, Glenorchy, Ashens, Longernong, Horsham ... Ballarat Stage Company; ... HAMILTON ROAD Ballarat to Smythesdale, Linton, Skipton, Streatham, Lake Bolake, Wickliff, Mail Tent, Dunkeld, Hamilton ... Meigs & Anderson." (Advertising, 4 Dec 1865, p.1)

"V. R. Cobb and Co.'s Telegraph Line of Royal Mail Coaches, south-west corner of Sturt and Lydiard streets ... Ballarat to Creswick, Clunes, Ascot (Coghill's Creek), Talbot (Back Creek), Amherst (Daisy Hill), Maryborough, Dunolly, Sandy Creek (Tarnagulla), Inglewood, St. Arnaud (New Bendigo), Mount Prospect, Deep Creek (Jim Crow), Daylesford ... Australian Stage Co.; CASTLEMAINE ROAD Kingston, Smeaton, Yandoit, Guildford, Castlemaine, Sandhurst (Bendigo) ... Robertson, Wagner and Co.; AVOCA & ST. ARNAUD'S DAILY Miners' Rest, Mount Blowhard, Lake Learmonth, Mount Bolton, Springs, Lexton, Woodstock, Lamplough, Avoca, Moonambel, Barkly, Landsborough, Redbank, Stuart Mill, St Arnaud, Swam Water, Cop Cop, Richardson Bridge, Mount Jeffcot, Watcham, Morton Plains ... M'Phee and Co.; ARARAT, PLEASANT CREEK AND HORSHAM ROAD ROYAL MAIL COACH

Burrumbeet, Raglan (Fiery Creek), Buangor, Ararat, Great Western, Pleasant Creek, Glenorchy, Ashens, Longernong, Horsham ... Ballarat Stage Company; HAMILTON ROAD Ballarat to Smythesdale, Linton, Skipton, Streatham, Lake Bolake, Wickliff, Mail Tent, Dunkeld, Hamilton ... Meigs & Anderson." (Advertising, 5 Mar 1866, p.1)

"V.R. Cobb and Co.'s Telegraph Line of Royal Mail Coaches, south-west corner of Sturt and Lydiard streets... DAYLESFORD and MALMSBURY ROAD ... Ballarat to Creswick, Mount Prospect, Deep Creek (Jim Crow), Daylesford, Coomoors, Dyers, Glenlyon, Red Hill, Germans, Kyneton road, Malmsbury ... E. Moore and Co.; MARYBOROUGH and DUNOLLY ROAD ... Ballarat to Creswick, Clunes, Ascot (Coghill's Creek), Talbot (Back Creek), Amherst (Daisy Hill), Maryborough, Dunolly, Sandy Creek (Tarnagulla), Inglewood, St. Arnaud (New Bendigo) ... M'Phee and Co.; CASTLEMAINE ROAD Kingston, Smeaton, Yandoit, Guildford, Castlemaine, Sandhurst (Bendigo) ... Robertson, Wagner and Co.; AVOCA & ST. ARNAUD'S DAILY Miners' Rest, Mount Blow-hard, Lake Learmonth, Mount Bolton, Springs, Lexton, Woodstock, Lamplough, Avoca, Moonambel, Barkly, Landsborough, Redbank, Stuart Mill, St Arnaud, Swam Water, Cop Cop, Richardson Bridge, Mount Jeffcot, Watcham, Morton Plains ... M'Phee and Co.; ARARAT, PLEASANT CREEK and HORSHAM ROAD ROYAL MAIL COACH Burrumbeet, Raglan (Fiery Creek), Buangor, Ararat, Great Western, Pleasant Creek, Glenorchy, Ashens, Longernong, Horsham ... Robertson, Wagner and Co.; HAMILTON ROAD Ballarat to Smythesdale, Linton, Skipton, Streatham, Lake Bolake, Wickliff, Mail Tent, Dunkeld, Hamilton ... Meigs & Anderson, E. J. Brayton, Agent." (Advertising, 12 Mar 1866, p.1)

"Cobb & Co's. Western Telegraph Line of Coaches ... Leigh Road Railway Station to Shelford and Rokewood Connecting thence with coaches to Bulldog, Lintons, Cape Clear, Smythesdale, and Ballarat ... Thomas Stoneman & Co.; Cobb & Co's. Western Telegraph Line of Coaches ... Geelong to Colac ... through Duneed, Winchelsea, Birregurra ... Thomas Stoneman & Co.; Cobb & Co's. Western Telegraph Line of Coaches ... Darlington, Mortlake, and Hamilton ... for Inverleigh, Cressy, Darlington, Mortlake ... and for Warrnambool, Belfast, Hepburn, Caramut, Penshurst, and Hamilton ... Thomas Stoneman & Co., Cobb & Co.'s Coach Office, Union Hotel, Geelong ... Cobb & Co.'s Livery, Letting, and Bait Stables ... Geelong ... Hesse-street, Queenscliff ... Thomas Stoneman & Co. " (Advertising, 27 Dec 1866, p.1)

"Cobb & Co's. Western Telegraph Line of Royal Mail Coaches ... GEELONG TO BELFAST AND HAMILTON ... passing through Inverleigh, Cressy, Lismore, Darlington, Caramut, Penshurst, Mortlake, Warrnambool, Belfast, Hexham, Framlington, Hamilton ... Night Mail, GEELONG AND BELFAST ... With Branch Line from Camperdown to Mortlake and Hamilton ... Camperdown, Terang, Warrnambool, Belfast, Mortlake, Hexham, Penshurst, Hamilton ... GEELONG AND CAMPERDOWN ... passing through Winchelsea, Birregurra, Colac, Larpent, Stony Rises, Camperdown ... Day Coach ... GEELONG AND COLAC ... passing Mount Moriac, Winchelsea, Birregurra, Colac ... LEIGH ROAD (Railway Station) AND SMYTHESDALE ... Leigh Road Railway Station ... passing Teesdale, Shelford. Rokewood, Junction, Bulldog, Cape Clear, Scarsdale, Smythesdale ... GEELONG AND QUEENSCLIFF ... Geelong, Kensington, Wallington ... Cobb & Co.'s Livery, Letting, and Bait Stables ... Geelong ... Western Stage Company Cobb and Co.'s Booking Office, Geelong." (Advertising, 5 Jan 1867, p.1)

Cobb and Co.'s Telegraph Line of Mail Coaches—Leave McIvor Hotel, Maryborough ... Avoca Moonambel Redbank Barkly Lamplough Amphitheatre Eversley Crowlands Landsborough Ararat; Carisbrook Joyce's Creek Newstead Castlemaine Melbourne; Amherst Talbot Clunes Creswick Ballarat Geelong; Carisbrook Baringhup Maldon Castlemaine Melbourne; Burnt Creek and Dunolly; M'Cullum's Creek Majorca ... Robertson, Wagner and Co. & Australian Stage Company." (Advertising, 9 Jan 1867, p.1)

"V. R. Cobb and Co.'s Telegraph Line of Royal Mail Coaches, south-west corner of Sturt and Lydiard streets ... DAYLESFORD and MALMSBURY ROAD ... Ballarat to Creswick, Mount Prospect, Deep Creek (Jim Crow), Daylesford, Coomoora, Dyers, Glenlyon, Red Hill, Germans, Kyneton road, Malmsbury ... Robertson, Wagner and Co.; MARYBOROUGH and DUNOLLY ROAD ... Ballarat to Creswick, Clunes, Ascot (Coghill's Creek), Talbot (Back Creek), Amherst (Daisy Hill), Maryborough, Dunolly, Sandy Creek (Tarnagulla), Inglewood, St. Arnaud (New Bendigo) ... M'Phee and Co.; CASTLEMAINE ROAD Kingston, Smeaton, Hepburns, Yandoit, Guildford, Castlemaine, Sandhurst (Bendigo) ... Robertson, Wagner and Co.; AVOCA & ST. ARNAUD'S DAILY Miners' Rest, Mount Blowhard, Lake Learmonth, Mount Bolton, Springs, Lexton, Woodstock, Lamplough, Avoca, Moonambel, Barkly, Landsborough, Redbank, Stuart Mill, St Arnaud, Swam Water, Cop Cop, Richardson Bridge, Mount Jeffcot, Watcham, Morton Plains ... M'Phee and Co.; ARARAT, PLEASANT CREEK and HORSHAM ROAD ROYAL MAIL COACH Burrumbeet, Raglan (Fiery Creek), Buangor (McDonald's), Ararat, Great Western, Pleasant Creek, Glenorchy, Ashens, Longernong, Horsham ... Robertson, Wagner and Co.; HAMILTON ROAD Ballarat to Smythesdale, Linton, Skipton, Streatham, Lake Bolake, Wickliff, Mail Tent, Dunkeld, Hamilton ... Western Stage Company, E. J. Brayton, Agent." (Advertising, 1 Apr 1867, p.1)

"Cobb & Co's. Western Telegraph Line of Royal Mail Coaches ... Booking Office, opposite Victoria Hotel, Hamilton ... For BALLARAT, via Dunkeld, Wickliffe, Streatham, Skipton, Lintons, and Smythesdale; For PORTLAND, via Branxholme, Green Hills and Heywood; For MORTLAKE, via Penshurst, Caramut, and Hexham; For APSLEY, via Cavendish, Balmoral, and Harrow; For PENOLA, via Coleraine, Casterton, and Fletcher's Station ... Return Coaches Company's booking office, Ballarat; From Mac's Hotel, Portland; From Botterill's Hotel, Apsley; From Royal Oak Hotel, Penola; Western Stage Company, Gray-street, Hamilton, J. Tucker, Agent." (Advertising, 4 Mar 1868, p.1)

"Cobb & Co's. Western Telegraph Line of Royal Mail Coaches ... Night Mail, GEELONG AND BELFAST ... With Branch Line from TERANG TO MORTLAKE AND HAMILTON, Thence to Mount Gambier and Adelaide ... passing Mount Duneed, Winchelsea, Camperdown, Terang, Yallock, Warrnambool, Belfast, Mortlake, Hexham, Caramut, Birregurra, Colac, Penshurst, Hamilton, Apsley, Penola, Casterton, Mount Gambier, Adelaide; SUMMER ARRANGEMENTS ... COLAC AND CAMPERDOWN ... for Winchelsea, Birregurra, Colac, and Camperdown ... GEELONG TO BELFAST via DARLINGTON AND MORTLAKE ... passing through Inverleigh, Warrambine, Cressy, Lismore, Darlington, Mortlake, Warrnambool, Belfast; LEIGH ROAD and ROKEWOOD Leigh Road Railway Station ... passing Teesdale and Shelford; GEELONG AND QUEENSCLIFFE ... Western Stage Company; Cobb and Co.'s Line of Coaches between Meredith and Steiglitz, starting from Scott's Hotel ... Scott & Nugent, Proprietors." (Advertising, 3 Apr 1868, p.1)

"Cobb and Co.'s Telegraph Line of Royal Mail Coaches, south-west corner of Sturt and Lydiard streets... DAYLESFORD and MALMSBURY ROAD ... Ballarat to Creswick, Mount Prospect, Deep Creek (Jim Crow), Daylesford, Coomoora, Dyers, Glenlyon, Red Hill, Germans, Kyneton road, Malmsbury ... Robertson, Wagner and Co.; MARYBOROUGH and DUNOLLY ROAD ... Ballarat to Creswick, Clunes, Ascot (Coghill's Creek), Talbot (Back Creek), Amherst (Daisy Hill), Maryborough, Dunolly, Sandy Creek (Tarnagulla), Inglewood, St. Arnaud (New Bendigo) ... M'Phee and Co.; CASTLEMAINE

ROAD Kingston, Smeaton, Hepburns, Yandoit, Guildford, Castlemaine, Sandhurst (Bendigo) ... Robertson, Wagner and Co.; AVOCA & ST. ARNAUD'S DAILY Miners' Rest, Mount Blowhard, Lake Learmonth, Mount Bolton, Springs, Lexton, Woodstock, Lamplough, Avoca, Moonambel, Barkly, Landsborough, Redbank, Stuart Mill, St Arnaud, Swam Water, Cop Cop, Richardson Bridge, Mount Jeffcot, Watcham, Morton Plains ... M'Phee and Co., ARARAT, PLEASANT CREEK AND HORSHAM ROAD ROYAL MAIL COACH Burrumbeet, Raglan (Fiery Creek), Buangor (McDonald's), Ararat, Great Western, Pleasant Creek, Glenorchy, Ashens, Longernong, Horsham ... Robertson, Wagner and Co.; HAMILTON ROAD Ballarat to Smythesdale, Linton, Skipton, Streatham, Lake Bolake, Wickliff, Mail Tent, Dunkeld, Hamilton ... Western Stage Company, E. J. Brayton, Agent." (Advertising, 7 Sep 1868, p.1)

"Cobb and Co.'s Line of Coaches ... Break O'Day, Linton, Carngham to Ballarat via Smythesdale daily ... Linton, Piggoreet, Staffordshire, Scarsdale, Smythesdale, Break O'Day, Rokewood, Rokewood Junction, Bulldog, Cape Clear, Derwent Jacks ... Matthew Veal and Co.; New Rush near Dunolly.—Quick Travelling Cobb and Co.'s Coaches directly to Dunolly ... Cobb's and Co.'s Mail Coach will leave their office, Ballarat, at 12 night ... M'Phee and Co.; Cobb and Co.'s Royal Mail Line ... Geelong to Queenscliff ... Omnibuses despatched from Cob and Co.'s office Geelong ... Western Stage Company; Cobb and Co.'s Line of Coaches ... To and from Ballarat to Smythesdale ... Scarsdale ... Piggoreet, Carngham, Lintons, Staffordshire, Derwent Jacks ... Cape Clear ... Bulldog ... Rokewood Junction ... Rokewood ... Break O'Day ... Anderson and M'Phee, E. J. Brayton." (Advertising, 7 Sep 1868, p.1)

"Cobb & Co's. Western Telegraph Line of Royal Mail Coaches ... Melbourne Booking Office for Passengers and Parcels:—Cobb and Co.'s General Coach Office, Great Bourke street. Night Mail, GEELONG AND BELFAST ... With Branch Line from TERANG TO MORTLAKE AND HAMILTON, Thence to Mount Gambier and Adelaide ... passing Mount Duneed, Winchelsea, Camperdown, Terang, Yallock, Warrnambool, Belfast, Mortlake, Hexham, Caramut, Birregurra, Colac, Penshurst, Hamilton, Portland, Apsley, Penola, Casterton, Mount Gambier, Adelaide; Cobb & Co.'s Summer Arrangements GEELONG AND QUEENSCLIFFE; Cobb & Co.'s Livery and Letting Stables ... Great Malop-street, Geelong ... Western Stage Company, Cobb and Co.'s Booking Office, Geelong." (Advertising, 1 Jan 1869, p.1)

"Cobb and Co.'s Telegraph Line of Royal Mail Coaches—Johnson's Bridge, Deniliquin, Hay, Booligal ... Robertson, Wagner and Co." (Advertising, 26 Mar 1869, p.4)

1870s

Cobb Co.'s Telegraph Line of Coaches ... Geelong to Queenscliff ... despatched from Cobb and Co.'s Booking Office, Great Malop street, Geelong ... Western Stage Company." (Advertising, 13 Apr 1870, p.1)

"Cobb and Co.'s Telegraph Line of Royal Mail Coaches, south-west corner of Sturt and Lydiard streets... DAYLESFORD and MALMSBURY ROAD ... Ballarat to Creswick, Mount Prospect, Deep Creek (Jim Crow), Daylesford, Coomoora, Dyers, Glenlyon, Red Hill, Germans, Kyneton road, Malmsbury ... Robertson, Wagner and Co.; MARYBOROUGH and DUNOLLY ROAD ... Ballarat to Creswick, Clunes, Ascot (Coghill's Creek), Talbot (Back Creek), Amherst (Daisy Hill), Maryborough, Dunolly, Sandy Creek (Tarnagulla), Inglewood, St. Arnaud (New Bendigo) ... M'Phee and Co.; CASTLEMAINE ROAD Creswick, Kingston, Smeaton, Moorookyle, Glengower, Newstead, Green Gully, Castlemaine ... Robertson, Wagner and Co; AVOCA & ST. ARNAUD'S DAILY Miners' Rest, Mount Blowhard, Lake Learmonth, Mount Bolton, Springs, Lexton, Woodstock, Lamplough, Avoca, Moonambel, Frenchman's Landsborough, Redbank, Stuart Mill, St Arnaud, Swam Water, Cop Cop, Richardson Bridge, Mount Jeffcot, Watcham, Morton Plains ... M'Phee and Co.; ARARAT, PLEASANT CREEK AND HORSHAM ROAD ROYAL MAIL COACH Burrumbeet, Raglan (Fiery Creek), Trawalla, Buangor (McDonald's), Ararat, Great Western, Pleasant Creek, Glenorchy, Ashens, Longernong, Horsham ... Robertson, Wagner and Co.; HAMILTON ROAD Ballarat to Linton, Skipton, Streatham, Lake Bolake, Wickliff, Mail Tent, Dunkeld, Hamilton, Portland Adelaide ... [NEW] MELBOURNE ROAD ... Ballarat to Warrenheip, Gordons, Ballan, Merniong, Bacchus Marsh, Melton, Keilor Western Stage Company; Cobb and Co. ... Ballarat to Gordon, Egerton, Ballan; Cobb and Co.'s Line of Coaches—To and from Ballarat to Smythesdale, Scarsdale, Piggoreet, Carngham, Lintons, Staffordshire ... Derwent Jacks, Cape Clear, Bulldog, Rokewood Junction, Rokewood ... Anderson and M'Phee, E. J. Brayton; Cobb Co's Telegraph Line of Coaches ... Geelong to Queenscliff Western Stage Company." (Advertising, 14 Apr 1870, p.1)

"Cobb & Co's. Western Telegraph Line of Royal Mail Coaches ... Melbourne Booking Office for Passengers and Parcels:—Cobb and Co.'s General Coach Office, Great Bourke street; Night Mail, GEELONG to BELFAST and MORTLAKE ... With Branch Line from MORTLAKE TO CARAMUT, PENSHURST AND HAMILTON Thence to Mount Gambier and Adelaide; LEIGH ROAD and ROKEWOOD ... Leigh Road Railway Station (Not listed as Cobb and Co); GEELONG AND QUEENSCLIFFE ... Cobb and Co.'s Line of Coaches between MEREDITH AND STEIGLITZ ... in time for the mid-day trains to Melbourne, Geelong, and Ballarat ... Western Stage Company's Booking Office, Leura Hotel, Camperdown ... Western Stage Company." (Advertising, 7 May 1870, p.1)

"Cobb & Co's. Western Telegraph Line of Royal Mail Coaches ... Melbourne Booking Office for Passengers and Parcels:—Cobb and Co.'s General Coach Office, Great Bourke street. Night Mail, GEELONG to BELFAST and MORTLAKE ... With Branch Line from MORTLAKE TO CARAMUT, PENSHURST AND HAMILTON Thence to Mount Gambier and Adelaide ... passing Mount Duneed, Winchelsea, Camperdown, Terang, Yallock, Warrnambool, Belfast, Mortlake, Hexham, Caramut, Birregurra, Colac, Penshurst, Hamilton, Portland, Apsley, Penola, Casterton, Mount Gambier, Adelaide, Coleraine, Balmoral, Cavendish, Branxholme, Edenhope, Heywood, Portland, Narracoote, Strathalbyn, Panmure GEELONG TO DARLINGTON ... passing through Murgheboluc, Inverleigh, Warrambine, Cressy, Lismore, Toolirook (Not listed as Cobb and Co.) LEIGH ROAD and ROKEWOOD ... Leigh Road Railway Station (Not listed as Cobb and Co.) GEELONG AND QUEENSCLIFFE ... (Not listed as Cobb and Co.) Western Stage Company; Cobb & Co's. Telegraph Line of Coaches. Ballarat to Hamilton thence to Penola and Adelaide Passing through Smythesdale, Lintons, Skipton, Streatham, Lake Bolac, Glen Thompson, Wickliffe ... Western Stage Company; Cobb and Co.'s Line of Coaches between MEREDITH AND STEIGLITZ ... in time for the mid-day trains to Melbourne, Geelong, and Ballarat" (Advertising, 2 Jul 1870, p.1)

"Cobb and Co.'s Telegraph Line of Royal Mail Coaches Leave their south-west corner of Sturt and Lydiard streets... DAYLESFORD and MALMSBURY ROAD ... Ballarat to Creswick, Mount Prospect, Deep Creek (Jim Crow), Daylesford, Coomoora, Dyers, Glenlyon, Red Hill, Germans, Kyneton road, Malmsbury ... Robertson, Wagner and Co.; MARYBOROUGH and DUNOLLY ROAD ... Ballarat to Creswick, Clunes, Ascot (Coghill's Creek), Talbot (Back Creek), Amherst (Daisy Hill), Maryborough, Dunolly, Sandy Creek (Tarnagulla), Inglewood, St. Arnaud (New Bendigo) ... M'Phee and Co.; HAMILTON ROAD Ballarat to Smythesdale, Linton, Skipton, Streatham, Lake Bolac, Wickliff, Mail Tent, Dunkeld, Hamilton, Portland, Adelaide ... MELBOURNE ROAD ... Ballarat to Warrenheip, Gordons, Ballan, Merniong, Bacchus Marsh, Melton, Keilor ...

Western Stage Company; CASTLEMAINE ROAD Creswick, Kingston, Smeaton, Moorookyle, Glengower, Newstead, Green Gully, Castlemaine ... Robertson, Wagner and Co.; AVOCA & ST. ARNAUD'S DAILY Miners' Rest, Mount Blowhard (Talbot Inn), Lake Learmonth, Flour Mill (Mount Bolton), Springs, Lexton, Woodstock, Lamplough, Avoca, Moonambel, Frenchman's, Landsborough, Redbank, Stuart Mill, St Arnaud, Swan Water, Cop Cop, Richardson Bridge, Mount Jeffcot, Watcham, Morton Plains ... M'Phee and Co.; ARARAT, PLEASANT CREEK AND HORSHAM ROAD ROYAL MAIL COACH Burrumbeet, Raglan (Fiery Creek), Buangor (McDonald's), Ararat, Great Western, Pleasant Creek, Glenorchy, Ashens, Longernong, Horsham ... Robertson, Wagner and Co.; Cobb and Co.—Ballarat to Clunes ... M'Phee and Co., E. J. Brayton, Agent; Cobb Co.'s Telegraph Line of Coaches ... Rokewood, Carngham to Ballarat via Smythesdale ... Staffordshire Reef, Bulldog, Cape Clear, Derwent Jacks, Scarsdale ... Matthew Veal and Co.; Mount Blackwood Cobb and Co. ... Anderson and M'Phee; Cobb and Co. ... Ballarat and Castlemaine ... Robertson, Wagner and Co." (Advertising, 25 Nov 1870, p.1)

"Cobb and Co.'s Telegraph Line of Royal Mail Coaches, south-west corner of Sturt and Lydiard streets... DAYLESFORD and MALMSBURY ROAD ... Ballarat to Creswick, Mount Prospect, Deep Creek (Jim Crow), Daylesford, Coomoora, Dyers, Glenlyon, Red Hill, Germans, Kyneton road, Malmsbury ... Robertson, Wagner and Co.; MARYBOROUGH and DUNOLLY ROAD ... Ballarat to Creswick, Clunes, Ascot (Coghill's Creek), Talbot (Back Creek), Amherst (Daisy Hill), Maryborough, Dunolly, Sandy Creek (Tarnagulla), Inglewood, St. Arnaud (New Bendigo) ... M'Phee and Co.; HAMILTON ROAD Ballarat to Linton, Skipton, Streatham, Lake Bolac, Wickliff, Mail Tent, Dunkeld, Hamilton, Portland, Adelaide ... MELBOURNE ROAD ... Ballarat to Warrenheip, Gordons, Ballan, Merniong, Bacchus Marsh, Melton, Keilor ... Anderson and M'Phee; CASTLEMAINE ROAD Creswick, Kingston, Smeaton, Moorookyle, Glengower, Newstead, Green Gully, Castlemaine ... Robertson, Wagner and Co.; AVOCA & ST. ARNAUD'S DAILY Miners' Rest, Mount Blowhard, Lake Learmonth, Mount Bolton, Springs, Lexton, Woodstock, Lamplough, Avoca, Moonambel, Frenchman's Landsborough, Redbank, Stuart Mill, St Arnaud, Swan Water, Cop Cop, Richardson Bridge, Mount Jeffcot, Watcham, Morton Plains ... M'Phee and Co.; ARARAT, PLEASANT CREEK AND HORSHAM ROAD ROYAL MAIL COACH Burrumbeet, Raglan (Fiery Creek), Buangor (McDonald's), Ararat, Great Western, Pleasant Creek ... Robertson, Wagner and Co., E. J. Brayton, Agent." (Advertising, 1 Mar 1871, p.1)

"Cobb & Co's. Royal Mail Telegraph Line of Coaches ... GEELONG AND QUEENSCLIFFE ... Night Mail, GEELONG to WARRNAMBOOL and BELFAST ... With Branch Line from MORTLAKE, CARAMUT, PENSHURST AND HAMILTON, Thence to Mount Gambier and Adelaide via Penola ... passing Mount Duneed, Winchelsea, Camperdown, Terang, Yallock, Warrnambool, Belfast, Mortlake, Hexham, Caramut, Birregurra, Colac, Penshurst, Hamilton, Portland, Apsley, Penola, Casterton, Mount Gambier, Adelaide, Coleraine, Balmoral, Cavendish, Branxholme, Edenhope, Heywood, Portland, Narracoorte, Strathalbyn, Panmure DAY COACH TO COLAC GEELONG AND MORTLAKE via DARLINGTON ... passing through Murgheboluc, Inverleigh, Warrambine, Cressy, Lismore, Tooliorook, LEIGH ROAD and ROKEWOOD ... Leigh Road Railway Station ... Livery, Letting and Bait Stables ... Great Malop-street, Geelong ... Western Stage Company; Cobb and Co.'s Telegraph Line of Coaches BALLARAT TO HAMILTON thence to PENOLA AND ADELAIDE passing through Smythesdale, Lintons, Skipton, Streatham, Lake Bolac, Glen Thompson, Wickliffe, Dunkeld ... Western Stage Company; Cobb & Co.'s General Coach Office, Great Malop-st, Geelong, Cobb & Co.'s General Coach Office,

Great Bourke street, Melbourne, Cobb and Co.'s General Coach Office, corner of Sturt-st and Lydiard-st, Ballarat; Cobb and Co.'s Line of Coaches between MEREDITH AND STEIGLITZ ... in time for the mid-day trains to Melbourne, Geelong, and Ballarat; Cobb and Co.'s GEELONG AND PORTARLINGTON LINE passing through Curlewis, Drysdale, and Bellarine." (Advertising, 7 Sep 1871, p.1)

"Cobb and Co.'s Telegraphic Line of Coaches ... Ballarat and Smythesdale ... Anderson and M'Phee, E. J. Brayton, Agent; Cobb and Co.—Ballarat to Daylesford ... Deep Creek, Mount Prospect ... Robertson, Wagner and Co.; Cobb and Co. Mount Blackwood ... Ballarat ... Anderson and M'Phee; Cobb and Co. Special Coach to Skipton ... Western Stage Company, Proprietors, E. J. Brayton, Agent; Cobb and Co.'s Telegraph Line of Royal Mail Coaches, south-west corner of Sturt and Lydiard streets ... DAYLESFORD and MALMSBURY ROAD ... Robertson, Wagner and Co.; MARYBOROUGH and DUNOLLY ROAD ... M'Phee and Co.; HAMILTON ROAD MELBOURNE ROAD ... Anderson and M'Phee; CASTLEMAINE ROAD ... Robertson, Wagner and Co.; AVOCA and ST. ARNAUD'S ROAD... M'Phee and Co.; ARARAT, PLEASANT CREEK AND HORSHAM ROAD ROYAL MAIL COACH ... Robertson, Wagner and Co.; E. J. Brayton, Agent; Cobb and Co.'s Telegraphic Line of Coaches ... Rokewood, Carngham to Ballarat via Smythesdale daily, Staffordshire, Smythesdale, Rokewood, Rokewood Junction, Bulldog, Cape Clear, Derwent Jacks, Scarsdale ... Matthew Veal and Co.; Cobb and Co. Ballarat to Clunes ... M'Phee and Co.; Cobb Co.'s Royal Mail Line ... Geelong to Queenscliff ... Western Stage Company, E. J. Brayton, Agent; Cobb and Co.'s Summer Arrangement ... Ballarat and Springs Road ... M'Phee and Co.; E. J. Brayton, Agent; Cobb and Co. Ballarat to Melbourne via Ballan, Bacchus Marsh ... Anderson and M'Phee, E. J. Brayton, Agent." (Advertising, 16 Sep 1871, p.1)

"Cobb and Co.'s Telegraph Line of Royal Mail Coaches— ARARAT, PLEASANT CREEK AND HORSHAM ROAD ROYAL MAIL COACH Burrumbeet, Raglan (Fiery Creek), Buangor (McDonald's), Ararat, Great Western, Pleasant Creek connecting with Little Wimmers, Boga Lakes, Gelorchy, Ashens, Longernong, to Horsham ... Robertson, Wagner and Co.; Cobb and Co.'s Telegraphic Line of Coaches—Rokewood, Carngham to Ballarat via Smythesdale daily, Staffordshire Reef, Smythesdale, Rokewood, Rokewood Junction, Bulldog, Cape Clear, Derwent Jacks, Scarsdale ... Matthew Veal and Co.; Cobb and Co.'s Telegraphic Line of Coaches ... leaves Cobb's Office and Watson's Town Hall Hotel, Armstrong street ... Ballarat and Smythesdale; Scarsdale, Piggoreet, Carngham, Chepstowe, Lintons, Staffordshire, Derwent Jacks, Cape Clear, Bulldog, Rokewood Junction, Rokewood ... Anderson and M'Phee, Cobb and Co.'s ... Ballarat and Springs Road ... M'Phee and Co.; Cobb and Co.'s Royal Mail Line. Geelong and Queenscliff ... Western Stage Company; Cobb and Co. ... Extra coach to Castlemaine ... Robertson, Wagner and Co.; Cobb and Co. ... Ballarat to Daylesford ... Robertson, Wagner and Co." (Advertising, 4 Nov 1871, p.1)

"Cobb and Co.—Ballarat to Daylesford ... Robertson, Wagner and Co.; Cobb and Co.'s Telegraphic Line of Coaches ... Rokewood, Carngham to Ballarat via Smythesdale ... Matthew Veal and Co.; Cobb and Co.—Ballarat to Melbourne ... Anderson and M'Phee." (Advertising, 4 Jan 1872, p.1)

"Cobb and Co. Reduced Fares ! Geelong and Queenscliffe Night Mail, GEELONG to WARRNAMBOOL and BELFAST ... With Branch Line from MORTLAKE, CARAMUT, PENSHURST AND HAMILTON thence to Mount Gambier and Adelaide via Penola HAMILTON BRANCH ... THROUGH Penshurst, Caramut, Hexham, Mortlake ... connect with Belfast Line ... Geelong following mornings. Intermediate Towns. Mount Duneed, Winchelsea, Camperdown, Terang, Yallock, Warrnambool, Belfast, Mortlake, Hexham, Caramut,

Birregurra, Colac, Penshurst, Hamilton, Portland, Apsley, Penola, Casterton, Mount Gambier, Adelaide, Coleraine, Balmoral, Cavendish, Branxholme, Edenhope, Heywood, Portland, Narracoorte, Strathalbyn, Panmure DAY COACH TO COLAC AND CAMPERDOWN ... To and from Geelong and Lady of the Lake, Winchelsea, Birregurra, Colac, Larpent, Stoneyford, Camperdown GEELONG AND MORTLAKE via DARLINGTON ... passing through Murgheboluc, Inverleigh, Warrambine, Cressy, Lismore, Tooliorook LEIGH ROAD and ROKEWOOD ... Leigh Road Railway Station; Livery, Letting and Bait Stables ... Great Malop-street, Geelong; Cobb and Co.'s Telegraph Line of Coaches BALLARAT TO HAMILTON thence to PENOLA AND ADELAIDE passing through Smythesdale, Lintons, Skipton, Streatham, Lake Bolac, Glen Thompson, Wickliffe, Dunkeld ... Western Stage Company; Cobb and Co.'s Line of Coaches between Meredith and Steiglitz ... starting from Scott's ... returning from the Royal Hotel, Meredith ... Cobb and Co.'s Geelong and Portarlington Line, Passing through Curlewis, Drysdale and Bellarine." (Advertising, 12 Mar 1872, p.1)

"Cobb and Co.'s Telegraph Line of Royal Mail Coaches, south-west corner of Sturt and Lydiard streets... DAYLESFORD and MALMSBURY ROAD ... Robertson, Wagner and Co.; MARYBOROUGH and DUNOLLY ROAD ... M'Phee and Co.; HAMILTON ROAD and MELBOURNE ROAD ... Anderson and M'Phee; CASTLEMAINE ROAD ... Robertson, Wagner and Co.; AVOCA & ST. ARNAUD'S DAILY ... M'Phee and Co.; ARARAT, PLEASANT CREEK AND HORSHAM ROAD ROYAL MAIL COACH ... Robertson, Wagner and Co., E. J. Brayton, Agent; Cobb and Co.'s Telegraph Line of Coaches ... Ballarat and Smythesdale ... Anderson and M'Phee and Co.; Cobb and Co. ... Ballarat to Melbourne ... Anderson and M'Phee.; Cobb and Co.'s Telegraph Line of Coaches ... Rokewood, Carngham to Ballarat via Smythesdale ... Matthew Veal and Co.; Cobb and Co. Ballarat to Daylesford ... Robertson, Wagner and Co." (Advertising, 21 Sep 1872, p.1.)

"Cobb and Co. ... Cobb & Co.'s General Coach Office, Great Bourke-street, Melbourne. Cobb & Co.'s General Coach Office, corner of Sturt and Lydiard streets, Ballarat. Cobb & Co.'s General Coach Office, Great Malop-street (next to Union Hotel), Geelong; Cobb and Co.'s Telegraph Line of Coaches. Ballarat to Hamilton thence to Penola and Adelaide, passing through Smythdale, Linton, Skipton, Streatham, Lake Bolake, ? Thompson, Wickliff, Dunkeld ... Western Stage Company; Cobb and Co.'s Line of Coaches between Meredith ... Cobb and Co.'s Geelong and Portarlington Line, Passing through Curlewis, Drysdale and Bellarine." (Advertising, 3 Jan 1873, p.1)

"Cobb and Co.'s General Booking Office, opposite the Victoria Hotel, Gray-street, Hamilton, General Booking Office, Ballarat, Booking Office, Mac's Hotel, Penola, Cobb and Co.'s Booking Office ... Leave Gleneig Inn, Casterton; Leave the Border Inn, Apsley; Leave Mac's Hotel, Portland ... Cobb and Co.'s Booking Office, Ararat George Tillyer, Agent. Cobb and Co.'s General Booking Office, Gray-street, Hamilton." (Advertising, 25 Jan 1873, p.1)

"Cobb and Co. Reduced Fares ! GEELONG AND QUEENSCLIFFE ... Connected with Sorrento, by steamer Pioneer. Night Mail, GEELONG to WARRNAMBOOL, BELFAST and MORTLAKE ... With Branch Line to HEXHAM, CARAMUT, PENSHURST AND HAMILTON, Thence to Mount Gambier and Adelaide via Penola HAMILTON BRANCH ... Through Penshurst, Caramut, Hexham, Mortlake ... connect with Belfast Line at Terang ... Geelong following mornings DAY COACH TO COLAC AND CAMPERDOWN GEELONG AND MORTLAKE via DARLINGTON passing through Murgheboluc, Inverleigh, Warrambine, Cressy, Darlington, Lismore, Tooliorook LEIGH ROAD and ROKEWOOD ... Leigh Road Railway Station ... Western Stage Company; Cobb and Co.'s Telegraph Line of Coaches BALLARAT TO HAMILTON thence to PENOLA AND ADELAIDE ... Western Stage Company." (Advertising, 18 Mar 1873, p.1)

"Cobb & Co's. Western Telegraph Line of Royal Mail Coaches ... Conveyance of Mails, Passengers, and Parcels ... Booking Office, opposite Victoria Hotel, Hamilton ... For BALLARAT For PENOLA For Geelong, via Hochkirch, Penshurst, Caramut, Mortlake, Terang, Camperdown, Stonyford, Colac, Birregurra, and Winchelsea ... For CASTERTON ... For APSLEY For PORTLAND For ARARAT ... Western Stage Company, Proprietor, George Tillyer, Agent. Cobb and Co.'s General Booking Office, Gray-street, Hamilton." (Advertising, 22 Mar 1873, p.1)

"Cobb & Co.'s Line of Coaches—leave Mac's Hotel for Casterton ... J. Cawker ... Jas. Lowe, Agent. Portland, 28th Dec 1871." (Advertising, 27 Mar 1873, p.1)

"Cobb and Co.'s Telegraph Line of Royal Mail Coaches Daylesford and Malmsbury Road ... Robertson, Wagner and Co.; Cobb and Co.'s Telegraph Line of Royal Mail Coaches Maryborough and Dunolly Road ... M'Phee and Co.; Cobb and Co.'s Telegraph Line of Royal Mail Coaches Hamilton and Melbourne Road ... Anderson and M'Phee and Co.; Cobb and Co.'s Telegraph Line of Royal Mail Coaches Castlemaine Road ... Robertson, Wagner and Co.; Cobb and Co.'s Telegraph Line of Royal Mail Coaches Avoca and St Arnand's Road ... M'Phee and Co.; Royal mail Coach ... ARARAT, PLEASANT CREEK AND HORSHAM ROAD ... Robertson, Wagner and Co.; Cobb and Co—Ballarat to Melbourne ... Anderson and M'Phee and Co.; Cobb and Co.'s Summer Arrangement ... Ballarat and Springs Road ... Ballarat to Miner's Rest, Learmonth, Mount Bolton (Talbot Inn), Flour Mill (Mount Bolton), Springs ... M'Phee and Co.; Cobb and Co.'s Telegraph Line of Coaches ... Ballarat and Smythesdale ... Anderson and M'Phee; Cobb and Co. ... Mount Blackwood to Ballarat ... ... Anderson and M'Phee; Cobb and Co. ... Ballarat to Beaufort ... Robertson, Wagner and Co.; Cobb and Co. ... Ballarat to Clunes ... M'Phee and Co.; Cobb and Co.'s Telegraph Line of Coaches ... Rokewood, Carngham to Ballarat via Smythesdale ... Matthew Veal and Co." (Advertising, 14 Jun 1873, p.1)

"Cobb and Co.'s Telegraphic Line of Coaches ... Rokewood, Carngham to Ballarat via Smythesdale ... Matthew Veal and Co." (Advertising, 30 Jun 1873, p.1)

"Cobb and Co.'s Telegraphic Line of Coaches ... Rokewood, Carngham to Ballarat via Smythesdale ... Matthew Veal and Co." (Advertising, 1 Jan 1874, p.1)

"Cobb and Co. Reduced Fares ! GEELONG AND QUEENSCLIFFE Night Mail, GEELONG to WARRNAMBOOL, BELFAST and MORTLAKE ... With Branch Line to HEXHAM, CARAMUT, PENSHURST AND HAMILTON, Thence to Mount Gambier and Adelaide via Penola HAMILTON BRANCH ... Through Penshurst, Caramut, Hexham, Mortlake ... connect with Belfast Line at Terang ... Geelong following mornings, DAY COACH TO COLAC AND CAMPERDOWN, GEELONG AND MORTLAKE via DARLINGTON, LEIGH ROAD and ROKEWOOD ... Leigh Road Railway Station ... Western Stage Company; Cobb and Co.'s Telegraph Line of Coaches BALLARAT TO HAMILTON thence to PENOLA AND ADELAIDE ... Western Stage Company; Cobb and Co.'s Line of Coaches between Meredith and Steiglitz ... starting from Scott's ... returning from the Royal Hotel, Meredith (Proprietor not listed); Cobb and Co.'s Geelong and Portarlington Line, Passing through Curlewis, Drysdale and Bellarine." (Advertising, 7 Jan 1874, p.1)

"Cobb and Co.'s Telegraph Line of Royal Mail Coaches Daylesford and Malmsbury Road ... Robertson, Wagner and Co.; Maryborough and Dunolly Road ... M'Phee and Co.; Hamilton and Melbourne Road ... Anderson and M'Phee;

Castlemaine Road ... Robertson, Wagner and Co.; Avoca and St Arnand's Road ... M'Phee and Co.; ARARAT, PLEASANT CREEK AND HORSHAM ROAD ROYAL MAIL COACH ... Robertson, Wagner and Co., E.J. Brayton, Agent; Cobb and Co. ... Ballarat and Springs Road ... M'Phee and Co.; Ballarat to Melbourne ... Anderson and M'Phee; Ballarat to Beaufort ... Robertson, Wagner and Co." (Advertising, , 16 Jan 1874, p.1)

"Cobb and Co.'s Telegraph Line of Coaches ... Ballarat and Smythesdale ... Anderson and M'Phee; Cobb and Co. ... Mount Blackwood to Ballarat ... Anderson and M'Phee; Cobb and Co. ... Ballarat to Melbourne ... Anderson and M'Phee; Cobb and Co.'s Telegraph Line of Coaches ... Rokewood, Carngham to Ballarat via Smythesdale ... Matthew Veal and Co.; Cobb and Co. ... Ballarat to Clunes ... M'Phee and Co.; Cobb and Co. Ballarat to Beaufort ... Robertson, Wagner and Co." (Advertising, 7 Mar 1874, p.1)

"Cobb Co.'s Royal Mail Line ... Geelong to Queenscliff ... Western Stage Company; Cobb and Co... Ballarat to Gordon ... Ballan... Anderson and M'Phee; Cobb and Co.'s Telegraph Line of Royal Mail Coaches—Hamilton Road and Melbourne Road ... E.J. Brayton, Agent ... Anderson and M'Phee; Cobb and Co.'s Telegraphic Line of Coaches—ROKEWOOD, CARNGHAM TO Ballarat AND Smythesdale ... Matthew Veal and Co." (Advertising, 30 Jan 1875, p.1)

"Cobb and Co.'s Telegraph Line of Royal Mail Coaches. Daylesford and Malmsbury Road ... Robertson, Wagner and Co.; Maryborough and Dunolly Road ... M'Phee and Co.; Castlemaine Road ... Robertson, Wagner and Co.; Ballarat and St Arnaud Road ... M'Phee and Co.; Avoca and St Arnand's Road ... M'Phee and Co.; ARARAT, Stawell, and HORSHAM ... Robertson, Wagner and Co.; Hamilton Road ... Anderson and M'Phee, E .J. Brayton, Agent; Cobb and Co. Talbot and Maryborough and Dunolly Night Mail Coach ... M'Phee and Co.; Cobb and Co. ... Castlemaine. Daylesford ... Robertson, Wagner and Co.; Cobb and Co.'s Telegraph Line of Coaches.—Rokewood, Carngham to Ballarat via Smythdale ... Matthew Veal and Co.; Cobb and Co.'s Line of Coaches—To and from Ballarat to Smythesdale, Scarsdale, Piggoreet, Carngham, Chepstowe, Linton, Staffordshire ... Derwent Jacks, Cape Clear, Bulldog, Rokewood Junction, Rokewood ... Anderson and M'Phee ... E. J. Brayton; Cobb Co.'s Royal Mail Line ... Geelong to Queenscliff ... Western Stage Company." (Advertising, 4 Feb 1875, p.1)

"Cobb and Co.—Summer Arrangement ... Ballarat and Springs Road ... M'Phee and Co." (Advertising, 11 Mar 1875, p.1)

"Cobb and Co.'s Telegraph Line of Royal Mail Coaches—Ballarat and St. Arnaud Road ... Castlemaine, Daylesford; Daylesford and Malmsbury Road ... Robertson, Wagner and Co.; Cobb and Co. Stawell and Horsham ... Robertson, Wagner and Co.; Cobb and Co.'s Telegraph Line of Royal Mail Coaches—Ballarat, Smythesdale, Skipton and Wickliffe Roads ... Melbourne Road ... Anderson and M'Phee; Cobb Co.'s Royal Mail Line ... Geelong to Queenscliff ... Western Stage Company; Cobb Co. Ballarat and Lexton Road ... M'Phee and Co.; Cobb and Co.'s Telegraph Line of Royal Mail Coaches—Ararat and Hamilton Road ... Western Stage Company." (Advertising, 15 Feb 1876, p.1)

"Cobb and Co.'s Telegraphic Line of Coaches—To and from Ballarat to Smythesdale, Scarsdale, Piggoreet, Carngham, Chepstowe, Linton, Staffordshire ... Derwent Jacks, Cape Clear, Bulldog, Rokewood Junction, Rokewood ... Matthew Veal and Co.; Cobb and Co. ... Ballarat ... Blackwood ... Anderson and M'Phee." (Advertising, 6 Mar 1876, p.1)

"Cobb and Co.'s Telegraph Line of Royal Mail Coaches Daylesford and Malmsbury Road ... Robertson, Wagner and Co.; Melbourne Road ... Anderson and M'Phee; Cobb and Co.'s Telegraph Line of Coaches—Rokewood, Carngham, Chepstowe, Linton, Staffordshire ... Derwent Jacks, Cape Clear, Bulldog, Rokewood Junction, Rokewood ... Matthew Veal and Co.; Cobb and Co. ... Ballarat and Lexton Road ... M'Phee and Co." (Advertising, 31 Jan 1877, p.1)

"Cobb and Co. Horsham, Glenorchy, Karkarooc, Longerenong, Murto ... Castlemaine and Daylesford ... Robertson, Wagner and Co.; Geelong to Donald ... Ballarat and Lexton Road ... Miner's Rest, Blowhard, Learmonth, Mount Bolton, Flour Mill, Springs ... M'Phee and Co., E. D. McMillian, agent; Smythesdale and Linton Road ... Buninyong to Egerton ... Ballarat and Skipton ... Anderson and M'Phee; Geelong to Queenscliff ... Skipton, Streatham, Bolac, Wickliffe, and Junction Road ... Western Stage Company E. D. McMillian, agent; Cobb and Co.'s Telegraph Line of Coaches—Rokewood, Carngham, Chepstowe, Linton, Staffordshire Reef ... Matthew Veal and Co." (Advertising, 10 May 1877, p.1)

"Cobb and Co.—HORSHAM, GLENORCHY, KARKAROOC, LONGERENONG, MURTOA—Coaches leave, Stawell for Horsham ... Glenorchy ... for Longerenong and Murtoa ... for Karkarooc and Minyip Robertson, Wagner and Co.; Ballarat and Blackwood Road .. Red Hill ... Barry's Reef ... Gordon's to Egerton ... Ballarat and Skipton ... Buninyong Station to Egerton ... Anderson and M'Phee; NOTICE.—Discontinuance of Coach.—Cobb and Co.—Piggoreet Road.—On and after the 1st August, 1878, the coach formerly leaving Piggoreet ... for Ballarat will cease running. Also, the coach formerly leaving Smythesdale ... will cease running ... Piggoreet Road.—Coaches leave Ballarat ... for Piggoreet ... ROKEWOOD ROAD.—Coaches leave Ballarat for Rokewood ... KANGAROO ROAD.—Coaches leave Ballarat for Kangaroo via Staffordshire Reef ... CHEPSTOWE ROAD.—Coaches leave Ballarat via Carngham, for Chepstowe ... Seth Sharp." (Advertising, 28 Jan 1879, p.1)

"Cobb and Co.'s Western Telegraph Line. Arrangements for 1879 Day Coaches. Colac and Warrnambool ... Night Mail ... Belfast to Geelong via Camperdown ... with branch line to MORTLAKE, HEXHAM, CARAMUT, PENSHURST and HAMILTON thence to MOUNT GAMBIER and ADELAIDE, via PENOLA, and all intermediate post town ... MORTLAKE to GEELONG ... WESTERN STAGE COMPANY, Proprietors, Cobb and Co.'s General Booking-office, Colac." (Advertising, 18 Nov 1879, p.1)

1880s

"Cobb and Co.'s Telegraph Line of Royal Mail Coaches ... Ballarat, Rokewood Road ... Ballarat to Piggoreet ... Seth Sharp; Cobb and Co.—Kangaroo Line ... Staffordshire Reef to Smythesdale ... Smythesdale to Staffordshire ... Kangaroo to Smythesdale ... S. Sharp; Cobb and Co.—Chepstowe Road ... Seth Sharp, Cobb and Co.'s Telegraph Line of Royal Mail Coaches ... Ballarat, Blackwood, and Keilor Road ... Ballarat to Newtown ... Smythesdale and Linton Road ... Wickliffe Road ... Gordon and Egerton Railway Station ... Ballarat and Skipton ... Anderson and M'Phee; Cobb and Co.—Ballarat to Warrenheip ... Gordon, Ballan, Myrniong, Bacchus Marsh, Melton, Keilor Road Station ... Anderson and M'Phee; Cobb and Co.'s Telegraph Line of Royal Mail Coaches ... Castlemaine and Daylesford ... Robertson, Wagner and Co.; Cobb and Co.—Ballarat, St. Arnaud, and Landsborough ... Ballarat and Lexton Road ... Morning coach to Learmont ... M'Phee and Co.; Cobb and Co. ... Geelong to Queenscliff ... Western Stage Company E. D. M'Millian, agent." (Advertising, 19 Mar 1881, p.4)

"General Conveyances. COBB AND CO.'S COACHES Leave the SHAMROCK HOTEL ... Sandhurst to Raywood ... Sandhurst to Tarnagulla ... Sandhurst to Heathcote; COBB AND CO.'S INGLEWOOD (Swan HILL LINE) COACHES Leave TATCHELL'S ROYAL HOTEL Inglewood, as follows: Inglewood to Swan Hill and Kerang Daily ... Inglewood to Boort, via Powlett Plains ... Inglewood to Wychetella, via Powlett Plains ... Inglewood to Wychetella and Boort, via Wedderburn

... Inglewood to Wedderburn ... Inglewood to East and West Charlton ... Inglewood to Towaninnie ... ROBERTSON, WAGNER, and CO, Proprietors. JOHN ROBERTSON. Manager." (Advertising, 7 Jun 1881, p.1)

"Cobb and Co. ... Ballarat to Learmonth Road ... Ballarat, St Arnaud, and Landsborough Road ... M'Phee and Co.; Cobb and Co.'s Telegraph Line of Royal Mail Coaches ... Ballarat and Lexton Road ... M'Phee and Co.; Cobb and Co. ... Chepstowe Road ... Ballarat and Rokewood Road ... Ballarat, Piggoreet Road ... Seth Sharp; Kangaroo Line ... S. Sharp; Cobb and Co.— Blackwood to Ballan ... Gordon and Egerton Railway Station ... Wickliffe Road ... Ballarat and Newtown ... Melbourne Road ... Vines and M'Phee; Cobb and Co.'s Telegraph Line of Royal Mail Coaches ... Ballarat and Blackwood Road ... Ballarat and Keilor Road Station ... Vines and M'Phee; Cobb and Co.—Royal Mail Line ... Winter Arrangements ... Geelong to Queenscliff ... Western Stage Company; Cobb and Co.—Ballarat to Adelaide—Overland in 56 hours ... Ballarat ... train to Hamilton ... Cobb and Co.'s Coach and rail from Narracoorte; Cobb and Co.—Ballarat to Streatham; Cobb and Co.—Winchelsea and Lorne Leave Sharp's Hotel, Newtown. Leave O'Farrell's Hotel, Scarsdale. Leave Eldorado Hotel, Smythes. Agent K. Gallass, Winchelsea." (Advertising, 17 Mar 1882, p.4)

"Cobb and Co.'s Telegraph Line of Royal Mail Coaches ... Booking Office, Avoca Hotel, Avoca ... To Percydale ... Ararat Road ... Robertson, Wagner and Co.; Ballarat Road ... Landsborough & Pleasant Creek Road ... St Arnaud Road ... M'Phee and Co., W. R. Smith, Agent." (Advertising, 25 Aug 1882, p.3)

"Lilydale to Fernshaw, Healesville, Marysville, Yarra-Flats, Warburton. &c. Cobb and Co.'s Coaches leave Lilydale Daily (Sundays excepted) at 9 a.m. for Healesville, Fernshaw, Fisher's Creek, Marysville, Warburton, &c., and for Yarra-flats at 6 p.m. daily (Sundays excepted). Return Fares :—Fernshaw, 11s. ; Marysville, 20s. ; Yarra-flats, 5s. ; Warburton, 10s. Full information at COBB and CO'.S offices, Bourke street east, where passengers and parcels may be booked." (Advertising, 16 Dec 1882, p.1)

"Cobb and Co. ... Ballarat to Learmonth and Lexton ... Ballarat to St Arnaud and Landsborough Road ... M'Phee and Co.; Cobb and Co. Royal Mail Line ... Summer Arrangements ... Special arrangements night or day ... Geelong to Queenscliff ... Western Stage Company; Cobb and Co. ... Gordon and Egerton Railway Station ... Ballarat to Blackwood, Newberry and Trentham Via Gordon and Ballan ... Vines and M'Phee; Cobb and Co.'s Telegraph Line of Royal Mail Coaches ... Ballarat to Streatham ... Ballarat and Keilor Road via Gordon, Ballan and Bacchus Marsh ... Vines and M'Phee; Cobb and Co. ... Chepstowe Road ... Seth Sharp; Kangaroo Line ... S. Sharp; Cobb and Co. ... Ballarat to Adelaide ... Overland in 56 hours ... Ballarat ... train to Hamilton ... Cobb and Co.'s Coach and rail from Narracoorte." (Advertising, 22 Mar 1883, p.4)

"Cobb and Co.'s Telegraph Line of Royal Mail Coaches ... Booking Office, Avoca Hotel, Avoca ... To Percydale ... Ararat Road ... Robertson, Wagner and Co.; Ballarat Road ... Landsborough & Pleasant Creek Road ... St Arnaud Road ... M'Phee and Co., W. R. Smith, Agent." (Advertising, 1 May 1883, p.1)

"Cobb and Co. Mount Gambier to Melbourne (Coach and Rail first-class) ... Booking Office—Thurston's Hotel ... T. Cawker." (Advertising, 5 Sep 1883, p.1)

"Cobb and Co. Geelong to Wallington via Moonlap and Kensington ... Geelong and Queenscliff ... Winchelsea and Lorne ... Camperdown to Koroit via Tera, Panmure, and Warrnambool ... Night Mail In connection with the Victorian Railways. Camperdown, Terang, Warrnambool, Koroit, Belfast, Mortlake, and Hamilton (Yallock, Warrnambool, Belfast, Mortlake, Hexham, Caramut, Penshurst, Hamil, Apsley, Penola, Casterton, Mount Gambier, Adelaide, Panmure, Coleraine, Balmoral, Cavendish, Edenhope, Portland, Narracoorte, Stratham ... Camperdown and Lismore ... Camperdown and Mortlake via Darlington ... Western Stage Company." (Advertising, 5 Jan 1884, p.1)

"Cobb and Co. Cobb and Co.'s Telegraph Line of Royal Mail Coaches leave their Booking-office, 27 Lydiard street ... Ballan and Gordon Railway Station ... To and from Scarsdale and Linton, To and from Scarsdale and Skipton, To and from Scarsdale and Streatham ... Ballarat to Keilor Road via Gordon, Ballan, and Bacchus Marsh; Lake Bolac to Wickliffe Road Railway Station; Gordon and Egerton Railway Station ... Vines and M'Phee; Ballarat to St. Arnaud, Ballarat to Charlton ... Ballarat, St. Arnaud, and Landsborough Road (Minersrest, Blowhard, Learmonth, Mount Bolton, Springs, Lexton, Lamplough, Avoca, Moonambel, Frenchmans, Landsborough, Redbank, Stuart Mill, St. Arnaud ... Ballarat, Learmonth, and Lexton ... Minersrest, Blowhard, Learmonth, Addington, Springs, Lexton ... M'Phee and Co.; Geelong to Queenscliff ... Western Stage Company." (Advertising, 5 Feb 1884, p.1)

"Cobb and Co. Coaches leave Club Hotel—Sale to Bairnsdale ... Sale to Omeo ... Booking Office Mrs. Bryant's Club Hotel, Sale ... Robertson, Wagner & Co." (Advertising, 23 Sep 1884, p.1)

"Cobb and Co.'s Royal Mail Coaches—Heywood and Casterton, leave Commercial Hotel Heywood ... via Hotspur, Digby, Merino [?], and Sandford; Heywood and Mt. Gambier via Casterton; Portland and Belfast ... connecting with coach to Koroit, Warrnambool and Colac; Casterton and Branxholme connecting with train to Hamilton; Hamilton and Penola passing through Coleraine and Casterton ... Andrew Stewart, Agent for Western Stage Co., Mac's Hotel, Portland." (Cobb and Co.'s, 6 Feb 1885, p.1)

"Cobb and Co.'s Royal Mail Coaches Sandhurst to Heathcote Hotel ... Pyramid Hill to Kerang and Swan Hill ... Pyramid Hill to Euston and Wentworth ... Robertson, Wagner & Co., J. Robertson, Manager; Livery and Letting Stables ... Corner of Mundy and Mollison Streets Sandhurst ... Particulars may be obtained at Cobb and Co.'s office, Shamrock Chambers." (Advertising, 9 Jun 1885, p.1)

1895 "Cobb & Co. ... a coach will leave our office, Lachlan-street, for Deniliquin ... Cobb & Co. Great Reduction in fares. Hay to Melbourne ... Passengers may break their journey on a single or return ticket at any stage between Deniliquin and Melbourne. Return tickets available for three months ... Robertson, Wagner & Co." (Advertising, 17 Sep 1895, p.1)

"Cobb and Co. ... Ballarat to Learmonth and Lexton ... Ballarat to St Arnaud and Landsborough Road ... M'Phee and Co." (Advertising, 13 Oct 1885, p.1)

"Cobb and Co. Coaches leave Club Hotel—Sale to Bairnsdale ... Sale to Omeo ... Booking Office Mrs. Bryant's Club Hotel, Sale ... Robertson, Wagner & Co." (Advertising, 23 Jan 1886, p.1)

"Cobb and Co.'s Sandhurst to Heathcote Hotel ... Kerang to Swan Hill ... Kerang to Euston and Wentworth ... Kerang to Bairanald ... Robertson, Wagner & Co." (Advertising, 10 Feb 1886, p.1)

"Cobb and Co.'s Telegraph Line of Royal Mail Coaches ... Leave the Heathcote Hotel ... to Sandhurst ... to Kilmore ... Booking-office, Heathcote Hotel, Robertson, Wagner & Co., Proprietors, Kearney & Co., Agents." (Advertising, 24 Feb 1886, p.1)

"COBB AND CO. LIVERY AND LETTING STABLES, George Hotel, Lydiard street, Ballarat. COBB and CO. having LEASED these commodious Stables, the public may rely upon being well served at this establishment. Commercial gentlemen liberally dealt with. Horses taken in to livery by the day, week, or month. Horses and Vehicles for Hire. Telephone to George Hotel, No. 130. VINES and M'PHEE, Proprietors; CONNECT WITH VICTORIAN RAILWAY. COBB and CO.'S COACHES. Daily (Sundays excepted) To and from SCARSDALE and LINTON, three times a day, connecting with each train. To and from SCARSDALE and SKIPTON, twice a day, in connection with first and last trains to and from Ballarat. To and from SCARSDALE and STREATHAM, once a day, in connection with last trains to and from Ballarat. Scarsdale to Linton... O'Meara's Junction ... Skipton ... Streatham. Any further information may be obtained at Cobb and Co.'s office, Ballarat; COBB and CO.—BALLARAT, ST. ARNAUD and LANDSBOROUGH ROAD ... M'PHEE and CO., Proprietors; COBB AND CO—BALLARAT, ST ARNAUD. The coach for St. Arnaud leaves Cobb and Co.'s office, Ballarat, at 11.36 pm., connecting with the 2.20 p.m. train at St. Arnaud for Donald's. Ballarat, St. Arnaud; Ballarat, Charlton M'PHEE and CO., Proprietors; Cobb and Co. ... Geelong to Swampy Creek, Anglesea River; Special arrangements, night or day ... Geelong to Queenscliff ... Western Stage Company; COBB and CO.—BALLARAT TO ADELAIDE ... Ballarat daily, train to Casterton hence by Cobb and Co.'s coach and rail from Narratoorte; Cobb and CO.—GORDON and EGERTON RAILWAY STATION. Conveyance meet each train to and from Gordon and Egerton, and Railway Station. VINES and M'PHEE, Proprietors; COBB and CO.—Reduced Fares. Reduced Fares.—BALLARAT, LEARMONTH, and LEXTON, daily (Sundays included), as follows:—Ballarat ... Miners' Rest ... Blowhard ... Ballarat to Learmonth ... Addington ... Springs ... Lexton ... M'PHEE and CO., Proprietors." (Advertising, 10 Mar 1886, p.1)

"Cobb and Co. ...Martin's Commercial Hotel, Echuca for Shepparton ... C. Roberts, Agent, Robertson, Wagner & Co." (Advertising, 8 Jan 1887, p.3)

"Cobb & Co. ... Bairnsdale, Bruthen, Omeo to Sale (Robertson, Wagner & Co.) ... Public Notice ... The Sale Office ... is now at the Club Hotel, Foster-street, Sale." (Advertising, 29 Jan 1887, p.1)

"Cobb and Co. ... Doran's Echuca Hotel for Mooroopna and Shepparton ... C. Roberts, Agent, Robertson, Wagner & Co." (Advertising, 28 Mar 1887, p.3)

"Cobb and Co.'s Telegraph Line of Royal Mail Coaches to Kilmore ... to Sandhurst ... Robertson, Wagner & Co., Kearney & Co., Agents." (Advertising, 8 Jul 1887, p.4)

"Cobb and Co.'s Livery and Letting Stables ... George Hotel, Lydiard street, Ballarat ... Branch Letting Stables. Geelong, Queenscliff, Hamilton, St. Arnaud, Daylesford, Sandhurst, Belfast, Beechworth, &c. ... Vines and M'Phee; Connect with Victorian Railways Cobb and Co.'s Coaches ... Scarsdale and Linton, O'Meara's Junction, Skipton, Streatham; Cobb and Co. ... Geelong to Queenscliff ... Western Stage Company; Cobb and Co. ... Ballarat to Charlton ... Ballarat to St Arnaud and Landsborough Road ... Ballarat, Learmonth, and Lexton ... M'Phee and Co.; Cobb and Co. Blackwood and Bacchus Marsh via Ballan and Myrniong. Passengers for Ballan, Blackwood, Myrniong and Bacchus Marsh leave Ballarat by train to Gordons, thence by coach ... Trentham ... Vines and M'Phee." (Advertising, 26 Oct 1887, p.1)

"Cobb & Co. ... Bairnsdale to Bruthen ... Bairnsdale to Omeo ... Sale to Stratford ... Robertson, Wagner & Co. ... LOOK OUT ! RAILWAY COFFEE TAVERN, Main Street. You can get a cup of coffee and a pie for 4d." (Lakes Navigation Co., Limited, 6 Mar 1888, p.1)

"Cobb and Co. ... Leigh Road to Rokewood ... Vines and M'Phee; Cobb and Co. ... Geelong to Ocean Grove via Wallington ... Western Stage Company; Victorian Railway Time Tables. Melbourne to Geelong, Geelong to Ballarat, Geelong to Melbourne, Geelong to Camperdown, Geelong to Terang, Geelong to Queenscliff, Geelong to Adelaide." (Advertising, 3 Apr 1888, p.1)

1888 "Cobb and Co. ... Ballarat, St. Arnaud and Landsborough Road ... Ballarat to Charlton ... Ballarat, Learmonth, and Lexton ... M'Phee and Co.; Cobb and Co. Including Coach and Rail ... To and from Warrnambool and Port Fairy ... To or from Melbourne and Koroit ... To or from Geelong and Koroit ... Cobb and Co.'s Office, Geringhap street ... Western Stage Company; Cobb and Co. Geelong to Queenscliff ... Western Stage Company; Cobb and Co. Backwood and Bacchus Marsh via Ballan and Myrniong ... Gordon and Egerton Railway Station ... Vines and M'Phee; Connect with Victorian Railways Cobb and Co.'s Coaches ... Scarsdale and Linton, O'Meara's Junction, Skipton, Streatham; Cobb and Co. Ocean Grove." Advertised on same page "Coal. Coal ... DOUBLE SCREENED HOUSEHOLD COAL ... delivered promptly ... received weekly from our Steamers discharging at Geelong ... THREE ENAMELLED CABINET PHOTOS, in any style, for 5s. Flegeltaub, School of Photography, Ballarat." (Advertising, 24 Jul 1888, p.1)

"Cobb and Co.'s Telegraph Line of Royal Mail Coaches to Kilmore ... Robertson, Wagner & Co., Kearney & Co., Agents." (Advertising, 21 Dec 1888, p.4)

"Cobb and Co.'s Coaches. BAIRNSDALE TO OMEO. ON and after Monday, the 17th, Cobb and Co's. coach to Sarsfield, Bruthen and Omeo will leave Norton's Bairnsdale Club Hotel at 4.30 p.m. in place of 5.30 p.m. as formerly." (Cobb and Co.'s Coaches, 2 May 1889, p.2)

"Cobb and Co.—Telegraph Line of Mail Coaches to Kilmore ... Leave the Heathcote Hotel ... Booking Office, Heathcote Hotel ... Kearney & Co., Agents. Robertson, Wagner & Co." (Advertising, 22 Aug 1889, p.4)

1890s

"Cobb and Co.—Blackwood and Bacchus Marsh via Ballan and Myrniong ... Vines and M'Phee." (Advertising, 19 Feb 1890, p.1)

"Cobb and Co. Special arrangements, night or day ... Geelong to Queenscliff ... Western Stage Company; Cobb and Co. ... Gordon and Egerton Railway Station ... Vines and M'Phee; Connect with Victorian Railways Cobb and Co.'s Coaches ... Scarsdale, Skipton, Streatham; Cobb and Co. ... Geelong to OCEAN GROVE and Barwon Heads ... Coach and Rail ... summer months ... Cobb and Co.'s offices, Melbourne, Geelong, Ballarat and Sandhurst ... Western Stage Company; Cobb and Co. Waubra, Avoca, and St. Arnaud; Cobb and Co. Ballarat and Miner's Rest." (Advertising, 26 Sep 1890, p.1)

"Cobb and Co. ... Clifton Springs and Portarlington; Cobb and Co. ... Geelong and Barwon Heads via Marshalltown ... Geelong to Ocean Grove via Wallington ... Railway Platform and Ocean Grove ... Cobb and Co.'s Office, Great Malop-street ... Western Stage Coy.; Cobb and Co. ... Leigh Road to Rokewood passing through Teesdale, Shelford, and Warrambine ... connecting with trains to Geelong ... Vines and M'Phee." (Advertising, 13 May 1891, p.1)

"Cobb and Co. Portarlington and Drysdale Railway Station ... Western Stage Co." (Advertising, 14 Dec 1891, p.4)

"Cobb and Co. ... Through Tickets, By Rail or Coach ... Ballarat and Port Campbell via Camperdown ... Vines and M'Phee, Craig's stable. (And Livery and Letting Stables); Cobb and Co. ... Geelong to Queenscliff ... Western Stage Company; Cobb and Co. Waubra, Avoca, and St. Arnaud (Lexton, Lamplough, Moonambel, Landsboro, Redbank, Stuart Mill); Cobb and Co. ... Gordon Egerton and railway station ... Vines and M'Phee; Connect with Victorian Railways Cobb and Co.'s Coaches ... Linton to Skipton, Streatham, O'Meara's; Cobb and Co. Ballarat and Miner's Rest. Connect with Victorian Railways Cobb and Co.'s Coaches ... Linton and Skipton ... Streatham." (Advertising, 20 May 1892, p.1)

"Cobb and Co. Portarlington for Geelong and Drysdale ... Western Stage Company." (Advertising, 20 Dec 1892, p.1)

"Note: Victorian Railway Time Table. Melbourne To Geelong. Geelong To Ballarat. Geelong To Queenscliff. Geelong To Wensleydale. Birregurra To Forrest. Geelong To Colac. Geelong To Terang. Geelong To Warrnambool. Geelong To Fort Fairy. Colac To Beeac. Terang To Mortlake. Melbourne To Adelaide, Via North Geelong. Camperdown To Timboon." (Advertising, 19 Jan 1893, p.1)

"Cobb and Co. Owing to the discontinuance of the mid-day train to Drysdale and Queenscliff arrangements have been made by the Western Stage Company (Cobb and CO.) to run two coaches every afternoon. One coach for the 'Cliff will leave at two o'clock via Moolap, Leopold and Wallington on the Queenscliff-road, and the other for Drysdale via Moolap, Leopold, and Curlewis." (Town Talk, 11 Apr 1893, p.2)

"Cobb and Co. Great Reduction in Fares. Hay to Melbourne ... Robertson, Wagner & Co." (Advertising, 18 Apr 1893, p.3)

"Cobb & Co., Oxford Chambers, Bourke-street, Melbourne; Cobb & Co.'s stables Malop-street, east, Geelong; Cobb and Co. Bourke-street, Melbourne." (Advertising, 1 May 1894, p.1)

"Cobb and Co. ... Bairnsdale & Omeo Daily Coach ... Robertson, Wagner & Co." (Advertising, 7 Jan 1896, p.1)

"Cobb and Co. Leigh Road to Rokewood, Ballarat and Rokewood ... Leave Craig's Stables ... W. Flahive, agent, Leigh Road; W. McKenzie, agent, Craig's Stables, Ballarat; A. Vines, agent, Cobb and Co.'s, office Geelong; Cobb and Co. Barwon Heads and Ocean Grove ... M. L. Hutchinson, Little Collins-street, Melbourne, Cobb & Co., Oxford Chambers, Bourke-street, Melbourne, Cobb & Co., Craig's Stables, Ballarat, Cook & Son, Melbourne, Bendigo, Ballarat; Cobb and Co. Geelong and Ocean Grove; Cobb and Co. Geelong to Drysdale and Portarlington; Cobb and Co. Drysdale, Portarlington, and Clifton Springs ... Portarlington and Drysdale; Cobb and Co. Geelong to Steiglitz ... Melbourne agents ... Huddart, Parker and Co., 305 and 307, Little Collins-street." (Advertising, 14 Jan 1896, p.1)

"Cobb & Co. Royal Mail Coaches Leave Balranald for Oxley and Hay ... ROBERTSON & WAGNER. W. Mackenzie, Agent." (Advertising, 25 Mar 1896, p.4)

"COBB & CO.'S COACHES—GEELONG TO OCEAN GROVE Coach passes through Moolap, Leopold, Wellington; TO BARWON HEADS Coach passes through Marshalltown, Connewarre, Connewarre East; TO STEIGLITZ via DARRIWIL Coach passes through Batesford, Gheringhap, Darriwil and Maude; TO DRYSDALE, PORTARLINGTON, and CLIFTON SPRINGS Coach passes through Moolap, Leopold, Curlewis, Bellarine; TO ROKEWOOD via LEIGH ROAD Coach passes through Teesdale, Shelford, Warrambine; COBB & CO.'S STABLES, STEIGLITZ. Conveyances of every description for hire; COBB & CO.'S GOODS WAGGON Goods and general merchandise carted to country towns at low rates; COBB and CO.'S Queenscliff stables First-class Stock. Quiet and Reliable Horses, Pony Carriages. Family Conveyances. Drags and Special Coaches for Picnics. Waggonettes meet Trains and Steamers. DAILY COACH TO PORTARLINGTON Connects with Conner and Excelsior, leaves Queenscliff ... Daily conveyances to Point Lonsdale. Cabs and Waggonettes obtainable at any hour; COBB & CO. DRYSDALE, PORTARLINGTON, AND CLIFTON SPRINGS. Waggonettes meet trains at Drysdale, conveying visitors to Portarlington or Clifton Springs. PORTARLINGTON AND ST. LEONARDS. Waggonettes meet steamers to convey visitors direct to St. Leonards; COBB & Co. ... STEAMER and COACH INCLUDED ... Melbourne to OCEAN GROVE, BARWON HEADS, CLIFTON SPRINGS via Portarlington, Queenscliff via Portarlington, Steiglitz via Geelong, AGENTS—Victorian Railways, Spencer-street, Melbourne. Ballarat. Bendigo. M. L. Hutchinson, 204, 207 Little Collins-street, Melbourne. Cook and Son, Melbourne. Cobb and Co., Melbourne. Huddart, Parker and Co., Melbourne. Vines and M'Phee, Ballarat. Cook and Son, Ballarat. J. Watts, Bendigo. Cranstoune and Simson, Queenscliff; Cobb and CO.'S—GEELONG TO STEIGLITZ, MELBOURNE to STEIGLITZ, including Steamer and Coach ... Cobb and Co., Oxford Chambers, Bourke ... Cobb & Co.'s Cab will commence running daily on Wednesday ... between Meredith and Steiglitz, connecting with trains at Meredith." (Advertising, 22 May 1896, p.1)

"Cobb & Co. Royal Mail Coaches ... Balranald for Oxley and Hay ... ROBERTSON & WAGNER. W. Mackenzie, Agent." (Advertising, 16 Sep 1896, p.4)

"Cobb and Co. Geelong and Queenscliff; Ballarat to Barwon Heads or Ocean Grove ... Western Stage Company." (Advertising, 6 Oct 1896, p.1)

"Mansfield to Wood's Point. Cobb & Co.'s Coaches leave Mansfield daily for Jamieson, connecting with Sheehan's coach to Wood's Point; Walhalla. Cobb & Co.'s Telegraph Line of Coaches runs daily between Moe and Walhalla ... A. Grant, proprietor." (Advertising, 17 Oct 1896, p.10)

"Walhalla. Cobb and Co.'s four-horse Coach leaves Moe daily ... P. Larkin, agent." (Advertising, 25 Nov 1896, p.1)

"Cobb & Co. Royal Mail Coaches ... Balranald for Oxley and Hay ... ROBERTSON & WAGNER. W. Mackenzie, Agent." (Advertising, 24 Feb 1897, p.4)

"Cobb and Co. ... Ballarat and Rokewood ... Vines & M'Phee; Cobb and Co. ... Geelong and Queenscliff ... Western Stage Company." (Advertising, 19 May 1897, p.1)

"Cobb and Co. Ballarat and Rokewood ... Rokewood and Leigh Road ... Vines & M'Phee, W. M'Kenzie manager, Telephone No. 188; Cobb and Co. Meet each train to and from Gordon and Egerton and Railway Station ... Vines & M'Phee; Cobb and Co. Meredith to Steiglitz; Cobb and Co. Barwon Heads, Ocean Grove, Torquay ... Agents: Vines & M'Phee, Craig's Stables; F. W. Niven and Co., Ballarat." (Advertising, 7 Jun 1898, p.1)

"Cobb and Co. Combined Rail and Coach ... Ballarat, via Geelong, Barwon Heads; Ballarat to Mount Mercer, via Buninyong; Ballarat and Rokewood ... Rokewood and Leigh Road ... Telephone No. 188; Meet each train to and from Gordon and Egerton and Railway Station ... Vines & M'Phee; Cobb and Co.—Geelong and Queenscliff ... Western Stage Company." (Advertising, 12 Jan 1899, p.1)

"Cobb's Combined Seaside Excursion TICKETS (steamer or rail and coach), Ocean Grove, Barwon Heads, Clifton Springs, Anglesea, Airey's Inlet, Torquay. Agents—Hutchinson, Cook's, Huddart, Parker ... Rokewood, Mount Mercer.—Cobb's daily COACHES leave Craig's stables, Ballarat, Rokewood, 7 a.m.; Mount Mercer, 7.30 a.m. ... Walhalla; Cobb and Co.'s four-horse COACH leaves Moe daily for Walhalla on arrival of midday train. Civility and attention. P. Larkin, agent." (Advertising, 22 Mar 1899, p.1)

1900s

"Cobb & Co.—Head Office, Moorabool-street east, Geelong. Telephone—Geelong, Drysdale, Portarlington, via Moolap, Curlewis; Leigh Road to Shelford and Rokewood; Ballarat to Napoleons and Rokewood; Ballarat to Pitfield and Glenfine Mines ... combined steamer and coach tickets issued from Melbourne to Ocean Grove, Barwon Heads, Anglesea and Airey's Inlet, Clifton Springs, and Queenscliff ... Livery Letting and Bait Stables." (Advertising, 10 Jan 1900, p.1)

"COBB AND CO.'S COACHES ... SUMMER ARRANGEMENTS. COACHES LEAVE BOOKING OFFICE, MALOP-STREET EAST, GEELONG.

TELEPHONE NO. 1. TORQUAY. Via Mt. Duneed and Germantown: Leaves Geelong daily ... returning leaves Palace Hotel, Torquay ... Fares: single 3s ; return, 5s. Horses and vehicles for hire at Torquay Stables. ANGLESEA and AIREYS INLET. Leaves Geelong daily ... Fares: Airey's Inlet, single 7s 6d: return, 14s. Anglesea, single 5s ; return, 9s. Hastey's coach conveys passengers from Anglesea to Airey's Inlet OCEAN GROVE. Via Moolap, Leopold and Wallington. Leaves Geelong daily ... Single fare, 3s ; return, 5s. Horses and vehicles for hire at Ocean Grove stables. BARWON HEADS Via Marshalltown and Connewarre : Leaves Geelong daily ... Single fare, 3s ; return, 5s. Horses and vehicles for hire at Barwon Heads stables. CLIFTON SPRINGS. Leaves Geelong daily ... Fares : Single 2s 6d ; return 4s. Leaves Portarlington on arrival or steamers, returning to connect with steamers to Melbourne. Fares : Single Is 6d, return 2s 6d. Leaves Drysdale on arrival of trains. Single 1s, return 2s. PRIVATE COACHES SUPPLIED WHEN REQUIRED. THROUGH COMBINED RAIL, STEAMER AND COACH. Issued at Melbourne by M. L. Hutchinson, Huddart, Parker and Co., Cook and Son, Spencer-street station, L. White ; Ballarat, Cobb and Co., Lydiard-street, Niven and Co., railway station ; Bendigo, Cook and Son and railway station. Coaches meet steamers and trains at Geelong, Queenscliff, Portarlington, Drysdale. PORTARLINGTON, BELLARINE, AND DRYSDALE. Via Moolap and Curlewis. Leaves Geelong daily at 3 p.m., returning Portarlington 7.30 a.m., Bellarine 8 a.m., Drysdale 8.30 a.m. Fares : Portarlington, single 2s, return 3s ; Bellarine, single 2s, return 3s : Drysdale, single 1s 6d. return 2s. DRYSDALE, PORTARLINGTON and CLIFTON SPRINGS. Regular cabs to and from Portarlington, Drysdale, and Clifton Springs. Cabs leave Drysdale. Cabs leave Portarlington. 9.15 a.m. 6 a.m. 4 p.m. 12.30 p.m. 7 p.m. 3 p.m. Saturdays only, cabs leave Drysdale at 3 p.m. Fares. Portarlington and Drysdale, single 1s, return 2s. Parcels carried at moderate rates. Cobb & Co.'s Coaches—Leigh Road, Shelford, and Rokewood; Ballarat, Napoleons and Rokewood; Ballarat, Pitifield, Glenfine Mines ... Vines & M'Phee, Craig's Stables, Ballarat." (Advertising, 22 Jan 1901, p.1)

"Cobb & Co.—Seaside Coaches ... Geelong, Torquay, Anglesea, Barwon Heads, Ocean Grove, Clifton Springs, Queenscliff, Portarlington, and Drysdale ... Cobb and Co.'s Head Office, Malop-street, Geelong. Telephone 1 ... Leigh Road to Rokewood, Via Teesdale and Shelford ... Ballarat to Pitfield Plains Via Smythesdale and Cape Clear ... Western Stage Co." (Advertising, 14 Feb 1902, p.1)

"Cobb & Co.—Geelong, Torquay, Anglesea and Airey's Inlet, Barwon Heads, Ocean Grove, Clifton Springs, Drysdale, Bellarine and Portarlington ... Ballarat to Pitfield Plains via Scarsdale." (Advertising, 20 Jan 1904, p.1)

"Cobb & Co.—Summer Time Table ... Coaches leave Booking Office, Moorabool-street. Telephone—No 1. Geelong to Torquay ... Geelong to Anglesea and Airey's Inlet ... Geelong to Barwon Heads ... Geelong to Ocean Grove ... Queenscliff to Ocean Grove ... Through Combined Steamer or Rail and Coach ... Horses and vehicles for hire." (Discovery of Bombs, 23 Jan 1906, p.1)

"Cobb & Co.—Coaches leave Booking Office, Moorabool-street. (Telephone—No 1.) Geelong to Torquay ... Geelong to Anglesea and Airey's Inlet ... Geelong to Barwon Heads ... Geelong to Ocean Grove ... Queenscliff and Portarlington ... Through combined steamer and coach tickets." (Advertising, 8 Jun 1907, p.1)

1910s

"EXCURSIONS THIS WEEK. TELEPHONE—No. 1. BARWON HEADS ... SEASIDE COACHES ... Anglesea and Airey's Inlet, Torquay, Barwon Heads, Ocean Grove, Queenscliff ... Ring up No. 1 for Picnic, Drags and Private Conveyance. Coach Office Moorabool-street. Stables Malop-street." (Advertising, 18 Jan 1911, p.1)

"COACH FARES. Geelong to Warrnambool and Belfast. Cobb and Co.'s Royal Mail Telegraph Line. Coaches leave the booking office, Great Malop-street, Geelong, for Warrnambool and Belfast every Tuesday and Friday at 5 a.m., passing through Murghebolac, Inverleigh, Warrambine, Frenchman's, Lismore, Darlington, Mortlake, Framlingham, Woodford and Warrnambool arriving at Belfast early the second day. Passengers and parcels can be booked through at the Melbourne or Ballarat office. Reduced fares: Geelong to Warrnambool, £2/10/-; Geelong to Belfast. £3. Cobb and Co.'s office, 28 Great, Malop-street, Geelong." (Coach Fares, 1 Jun 1912, p.10)

"Cobb & Co. ... Barwon Heads." (Cobb's Legal Puzzle, 2 Apr 1913, p.4)

"Cobb & Co.—Coaching Arrangement ... Torquay, Barwon Heads, Ocean Grove, Queenscliff, Anglesea and Airey's Inlet ... Ambulance for Hire ...V. N. Vines, proprietor." (Advertising, 4 Jan 1913, p.1)

"Cobb & Co.—Telephone, 1001 ... Special Excursion Drags ... Torquay, Barwon Heads, Ocean Grove, Queenscliff, Anglesea and Airey's Inlet ... Ambulance for Hire." (Advertising, 8 Jun 1914, p.1)

"Cobb & Co.—Telephone, 1001 ... Office and Stables : Malop-street east ... Special Excursion ... Torquay, Barwon Heads, Ocean Grove, Anglesea and Airey's Inlet ... Passengers travel by Queenscliff train alight at Marcus Station. Coach meets all ordinary trains at Marcus." (Advertising, 5 Jan 1915, p.1)

"COBB'S COACHES, Barwon Heads, Torquay, Ocean Grove, Anglesea, Airey's Inlet; through excursion tickets issued Spencer street railway. Government Tourist Bureau, Huddart, Parker." (Classified Advertising, 3 Jan 1917, p.1)

"TO LET.—Two Fine Unfurnished Rooms, right on the best corner at Barwon Heads (Cobb and Co.'s old Waiting Rooms). Very suitable for Shop or Tea Room. A fine opportunity to make good money during the coming holidays." (Advertising, 19 Dec 1917, p.6)

"COBB & CO. Telephone 1001 ... To Torquay, Ocean Grove, Barwon Heads ... Malop street East ... Regular Mail Coach Services ... Torquay, Barwon Heads, Ocean Grove, Anglesea, Airey's Inlet." (Advertising, 23 Mar 1918, p.1)

1920s

"Cobb & Co. 'Phone 1001 SEASIDE MOTOR CONVEYANCE ... Torquay, Barwon Heads, Airey's Inlet, Ocean Grove, Anglesea ... Cars leave office Malop-street ... Special Trip to Portarlington ... Drag ... car ... H. WOMERSLEY, Proprietor." (Advertising, 20 Jan 1920, p.1)

"Cobb & Co.—Cheap Excursions to Seaside Resorts ... Queenscliff, Point Lonsdale, Torquay, Airey's Inlet, Ocean Grove, Anglesea and Barwon Heads. Further particulars Phone 1001 ... we are Running a Series of Sunday Picnics per Motor. Fare, 6/- Return ; including Dinner and Afternoon Tea. Telephone 1001 or Ocean Grove H. Womersley, Proprietor." (Advertising, 11 Mar 1920, p.1)

Reference List

1851 'Bush Fires—Mount Macedon.', The Argus (Melbourne, Vic.: 1848-1957), 12 Feb, p.2., viewed 12 Mar 2024, http://nla.gov.au/nla.news-article4776139

1853 'Advertising', Geelong Advertiser and Intelligencer (Vic.: 1851-1856), 9 Jun, p.1., viewed 20 Jun 2023, http://nla.gov.au/nla.news-article94360681

1853 'Advertising', The Argus (Melbourne, Vic.: 1848-1957) 26 Apr, p.8., viewed 20 Jun 2023, http://nla.gov.au/nla.news-article4791988; 13 May, p.11., viewed 18 Jun 2023, http://nla.gov.au/nla.news-article4792582; 14 May, p.5., viewed 20 Jun 2023, http://nla.gov.au/nla.news-article4792592; 13 Jun, p.2., viewed 29 May 2023, http://nla.gov.au/nla.news-article4793468; 10 Sep, p.8., viewed 18 Jun 2023, http://nla.gov.au/nla.news-article255612063; 27 Sep, p.2., viewed 29 Jul 2023, http://nla.gov.au/nla.news-article4797469

1853 'Homebush Races.', The Goulburn Herald and County of Argyle Advertiser (NSW: 1848-1859), 11 Jun, p.3., viewed 20 Jun 2023, http://nla.gov.au/nla.news-article101736086

1853 'Inward Overseas Passenger Lists' (see Microfiche Copies: VPRS 7666 United Kingdom Ports; VPRS 7667 Foreign Ports; VPRS 13439 New Zealand Ports) https://prov.vic.gov.au/search_journey/select?keywords=george%20mowton&iud=true

1853 'Shipping Intelligence', The Moreton Bay Courier (Brisbane, Qld.: 1846-1861), 7 May, p.2., viewed 20 Jun 2023, http://nla.gov.au/nla.news-article3710114

1853 'Sydney News.', The Maitland Mercury and Hunter River General Advertiser (NSW: 1843-1893), 1 Jun, p.2., viewed 20 Jun 2023, http://nla.gov.au/nla.news-article667698

1854 'Advertising', Mount Alexander Mail (Vic.: 1854-1917), 27 May, p.1., viewed 30 Jul 2023, http://nla.gov.au/nla.news-article202633264

1854 'Advertising', The Age (Melbourne, Vic.: 1854-1954), 17 Nov, p.3., viewed 16 Jul 2023, http://nla.gov.au/nla.news-article154852524; 25 Nov, p.8., viewed 02 Aug 2023, http://nla.gov.au/nla.news-article154849193

1854 'Advertising', The Argus (Melbourne, Vic.: 1848-1957), 31 Jan, p.3., viewed 20 Jun 2023, http://nla.gov.au/nla.news-article4802637; 3 May, p.2., viewed 01 Aug 2023, http://nla.gov.au/nla.news-article4806812; 12 Oct, p.8., viewed 05 May 2024, http://nla.gov.au/nla.news-article4798863; 24 Nov, p.6., viewed 29 May 2023, http://nla.gov.au/nla.news-article4800754; 25 Nov, p.6., viewed 18 Jun 2023, http://nla.gov.au/nla.news-article4800795; 30 Nov, p.8., viewed 30 Jul 2023, http://nla.gov.au/nla.news-article4801034

1854 'Advertising', The Banner (Melbourne, Vic.: 1853-1854), 27 Jun, p.13., viewed 01 Aug 2023, http://nla.gov.au/nla.news-article179813811

1855 'Advertising', Bendigo Advertiser (Vic.: 1855-1918), 6 Oct, p.1., viewed 23 Jun 2023, http://nla.gov.au/nla.news-article88047637

1855 'Advertising', Mount Alexander Mail (Vic.: 1854-1917), 28 Sep, p.4., viewed 23 Jun 2023, http://nla.gov.au/nla.news-article202634720

1855 'Advertising', The Age (Melbourne, Vic.: 1854-1954), 18 Jan, p.8., viewed 01 Aug 2023, http://nla.gov.au/nla.news-article154851540; 24 Jan, p.2., viewed 30 Jul 2023, http://nla.gov.au/nla.news-article154852282; 30 Jan p.1., viewed 01 Aug 2023, http://nla.gov.au/nla.news-article154849461; 16 Feb, p.2., viewed 01 Aug 2023, http://nla.gov.au/nla.news-article154850551; 17 Feb, p.2., viewed 30 Jul 2023, http://nla.gov.au/nla.news-article154854348; 19 Jun, p.2., viewed 21 Jun 2023, http://nla.gov.au/nla.news-article154893884; 27 June, p.2., viewed 10 May 2024, http://nla.gov.au/nla.news-article154891015; 5 Sep, p.2., viewed 02 Aug 2023, http://nla.gov.au/nla.news-article154891515; 9 Nov, p.1., viewed 01 Aug 2023, http://nla.gov.au/nla.news-article154865702; 21 Nov, p.8., viewed 01 Aug 2023, http://nla.gov.au/nla.news-article154862697

1855 'Advertising', The Argus (Melbourne, Vic.: 1848-1957), 15 Jan, p.7., viewed 16 Jul 2023, http://nla.gov.au/nla.news-article4803099; 1 Feb, p.8., viewed 20 Jun 2023, http://nla.gov.au/nla.news-article4803854; 2 Jun, p.1., viewed 29 Jul 2023, http://nla.gov.au/nla.news-article4809029; 8 Jun, p.7., viewed 01 Aug 2023, http://nla.gov.au/nla.news-article4809300; 21 Sep, p.1., viewed 21 Jun 2023, http://nla.gov.au/nla.news-article4818873; 20 Oct, p.7., viewed 01 Aug 2023, http://nla.gov.au/nla.news-article4821369; 2 Nov p.7., viewed 01 Aug 2023, http://nla.gov.au/nla.news-article4822318; 26 Nov, p.8., viewed 02 Aug 2023, http://nla.gov.au/nla.news-article4824259; 4 Dec, p.3., viewed 01 Aug 2023, http://nla.gov.au/nla.news-article4824926

1855 'Extensive Fire in Flinders-Lane.', Bendigo Advertiser (Vic.: 1855-1918), 1 Nov, p.3., viewed 20 Feb 2024, http://nla.gov.au/nla.news-article88047876

1855 'Local Intelligence.', The Age (Melbourne, Vic.: 1854-1954), 13 Oct, p.5., viewed 16 Jul 2023, http://nla.gov.au/nla.news-article154893320

1856 'The Argus.', The Argus (Melbourne, Vic.: 1848-1957), 11 Sep, p.4., viewed 01 Aug 2023, http://nla.gov.au/nla.news-article7136414

1856 'Advertising', Bendigo Advertiser (Vic.: 1855-1918), 16 May, p.1., viewed 02 Aug 2023, http://nla.gov.au/nla.news-article88050079; 23 May, p.3., viewed 20 Jun 2023, http://nla.gov.au/nla.news-article88050197; 18 Oct, p.1., viewed 01 Aug 2023, http://nla.gov.au/nla.news-article87994962; 12 Dec, p.3., viewed 16 Jul 2023, http://nla.gov.au/nla.news-article87996066

1856 'Advertising', Mount Alexander Mail (Vic.: 1854-1917), 29 Apr, p.3., viewed 01 Aug 2023, http://nla.gov.au/nla.news-article202630915; 27 May, p.4., viewed 21 Jun 2023, http://nla.gov.au/nla.news-article202633964; 3 Jun, p.4., viewed 25 Jun 2023, http://nla.gov.au/nla.news-article202631463

1856 'Advertising', The Age (Melbourne, Vic.: 1854-1954), 20 Feb, p.1., viewed 30 Jul 2023, http://nla.gov.au/nla.news-article154865541; 31 May, p.1., viewed 21 Jun 2023, http://nla.gov.au/nla.news-article154864100; 23 Jun, p.1., viewed 23 Jun 2023, http://nla.gov.au/nla.news-article154861515; 25 Jun, p.1., viewed 27 Jun 2023, http://nla.gov.au/nla.news-article154860465; 3 Dec, p.8., viewed 03 Aug 2023, http://nla.gov.au/nla.news-article154870266

1856 'Advertising', The Argus (Melbourne, Vic.: 1848-1957), 1 Jan, p.2., viewed 26 Jun 2023, http://nla.gov.au/nla.news-article4827056; 27 Feb, p.8., viewed 26 Jun 2023, http://nla.gov.au/nla.news-article4831751; 13 Mar, p.3., viewed 26 Jun 2023, http://nla.gov.au/nla.news-article4832911; 3 Apr, p.2., viewed 01 Aug 2023, http://nla.gov.au/nla.news-article4834595; 9 Apr, p.3., viewed 29 Jun 2023, http://nla.gov.au/nla.news-article4835040; 22 Apr, p.10., viewed 01 Aug 2023, http://nla.gov.au/nla.news-article4836108; 24 Apr, p.1., viewed 01 Aug 2023, http://nla.gov.au/nla.news-article4836307; 28 Apr, p.8., viewed 03 Aug 2023, http://nla.gov.au/nla.news-article4836557; 1 May, p.1., viewed 20 Jun 2023, http://nla.gov.au/nla.news-article4836838; 19 May, p.7., viewed 25 Jun 2023, http://nla.gov.au/nla.news-article4838155; 29 May, p.8., viewed 30 Jul 2023, http://nla.gov.au/nla.news-article4839004; 31 May, p.3., viewed 01 Aug 2023, http://nla.gov.au/nla.news-article4839161; 15 Jul, p.8., viewed 25 Jun 2023, http://nla.gov.au/nla.news-article7133151

1856 'Advertising', Williamstown Chronicle (Vic.: 1856-1954), 8 Nov, p.1., viewed 03 Aug 2023, http://nla.gov.au/nla.news-article68568851; 29 Nov, p.1., viewed 25 Jun 2023, http://nla.gov.au/nla.news-article68568875

1856 'Domestic Intelligence.', The Argus (Melbourne, Vic.: 1848-1957), 15 Oct, p.5., viewed 23 Jun 2023, http://nla.gov.au/nla.news-article7138358

1856 'Mr. Geo. W. Haycock.', Bendigo Advertiser (Vic.: 1855-1918), 26 Sep, p.2., viewed 03 Aug 2023, http://nla.gov.au/nla.news-article88053027

1856 'Select Poetry.', The Argus (Melbourne, Vic.: 1848-1957), 7 Jun, p.6., viewed 03 Aug 2023, http://nla.gov.au/nla.news-article4839764

1856 'Supreme Court.', The Argus (Melbourne, Vic.: 1848-1957), 8 Nov, p.5., viewed 03 Aug 2023, http://nla.gov.au/nla.news-article7139744

1856 'The Dream Of Gold.', Colonial Times (Hobart, Tas. : 1828-1857), 25 Jun, p.3., viewed 18 Feb 2024, http://nla.gov.au/nla.news-article8782416

1856 'Vessels in Hobson's Bay,', The Argus (Melbourne, Vic.: 1848-1957), 9 Apr, p.4., viewed 01 Aug 2023, http://nla.gov.au/nla.news-article4835021

1857 'Advertising', The Argus (Melbourne, Vic.: 1848-1957), 26 Sep, p.8; 30 September, p.3., viewed 10 May 2024, http://nla.gov.au/nla.news-article7139509; 10 Oct, p.8.

1857 'Advertising', The Star (Ballarat, Vic.: 1855-1864), 2 Nov, p.1

1857 'Advertising', Bell's Life in Victoria and Sporting Chronicle (Melbourne, Vic.: 1857-1868), 6 Jun, p.1., viewed 12 Jun 2023, http://nla.gov.au/nla.news-article201380908; 25 Jul, p.1., viewed 13 Jun 2023, http://nla.gov.au/nla.news-article201376237

1857 'Advertising', Mount Alexander Mail (Vic.: 1854-1917), 12 Jan, p.4., viewed 01 Aug 2023, http://nla.gov.au/nla.news-article202634292; 22 Jun, p.3., viewed 27

Feb 2024, http://nla.gov.au/nla.news-article197084259; 22 Jun, p.3., viewed 30 May; 28 Oct p.4., viewed 27 Jun 2023, http://nla.gov.au/nla.news-article197088520; 10 Jul, p.2., viewed 13 Jun 2023, http://nla.gov.au/nla.news-article197084618; 4 Nov, p.3., viewed 27 Jun 2023, http://nla.gov.au/nla.news-article197087080; 21 Dec, p.4., viewed 27 Jun 2023, http://nla.gov.au/nla.news-article197088811

1857 'Advertising', The Age (Melbourne, Vic.: 1854-1954), 3 Jan, p.1., viewed 03 Aug 2023, http://nla.gov.au/nla.news-article154824488; 14 Jan, p.1., viewed 03 Aug 2023, http://nla.gov.au/nla.news-article154826058;18 Jul, p.3., viewed 23 Jun 2023, http://nla.gov.au/nla.news-article154833008; 22 July, p.3., viewed 10 May 2024, http://nla.gov.au/nla.news-article154835408; 26 Oct, p.1., viewed 17 Jul 2023, http://nla.gov.au/nla.news-article154831201

1857 'Advertising', The Argus (Melbourne, Vic.: 1848-1957), 3 Feb, p.6., viewed 12 Jun 2023, http://nla.gov.au/nla.news-article7144020; 27 Apr, p.8., viewed 03 Aug 2023, http://nla.gov.au/nla.news-article7148629; 4 May, p.3., viewed 12 Jun 2023, http://nla.gov.au/nla.news-article7149005 1 Jul, p.8., viewed 12 Jun 2023, http://nla.gov.au/nla.news-article7134547; 30 Jun p.8., viewed 12 Jun 2023, http://nla.gov.au/nla.news-article7134458; 11 Aug, p.8., viewed 03 Aug 2023, http://nla.gov.au/nla.news-article7136842; 23 Sep, p.8., viewed 13 Jun 2023, http://nla.gov.au/nla.news-article7139157; 13 Oct, p.8., viewed 13 Jun 2023, http://nla.gov.au/nla.news-article7140210; 29 Oct, p.8., viewed 27 Jun 2023, http://nla.gov.au/nla.news-article7141177; 6 Nov, p.8., viewed 13 Jun 2023, http://nla.gov.au/nla.news-article7141591; 10 Nov, p.3., viewed 09 Jul 2023, http://nla.gov.au/nla.news-article7141773; 30 Dec, p.3., viewed 03 Aug 2023, http://nla.gov.au/nla.news-article7144241

1857 'Advertising', The Star (Ballarat, Vic.: 1855-1864), 1 Sep, p.4., viewed 24 Jul 2023, http://nla.gov.au/nla.news-article66045875; 2 Nov, p.1., viewed 27 Jun 2023, http://nla.gov.au/nla.news-article66044973; 4 Nov, p.1., viewed 27 Jun 2023, http://nla.gov.au/nla.news-article66045010

1857 'Tenders Accepted.', The Age (Melbourne, Vic.: 1854-1954), 30 Sep, p.5., viewed 25 Feb 2024, http://nla.gov.au/nla.news article154830760

1858 'Advertising', Bendigo Advertiser (Vic.: 1855-1918), 19 Jul p.1., viewed 21 Jun 2023, http://nla.gov.au/nla.news-article87981950; 17 Nov, p.1., viewed 03 Aug 2023, http://nla.gov.au/nla.news-article87984948

1858 'Advertising', Launceston Examiner (Tas.: 1842-1899), 9 Oct, p.1. (Afternoon), viewed 04 Aug 2023, http://nla.gov.au/nla.news-article38993520

1858 'Advertising', Mount Alexander Mail (Vic.: 1854-1917), 1 Jan, p.2., viewed 27 Jun 2023, http://nla.gov.au/nla.news-article197087957; 23 Apr, p.2., viewed 21 Jun 2023, http://nla.gov.au/nla.news-article197084143; 14 May, p.2., viewed 21 Jun 2023, http://nla.gov.au/nla.news-article197087837; 21 May, p.8., viewed 21 Jun 2023, http://nla.gov.au/nla.news-article197085601; 28 Jul, p.4., viewed 22 Jun 2023, http://nla.gov.au/nla.news-article197087278; 23 Aug, p.4., viewed 22 Jun 2023, http://nla.gov.au/nla.news-article199050338; 27 Aug, p.2., viewed 22 Jun 2023

1858 'Advertising', The Age (Melbourne, Vic.: 1854-1954), 6 Jan, p.2., viewed 21 Jun 2023, http://nla.gov.au/nla.news-article154857787; 17 Jun, p.8., viewed 12 Jul 2023, http://nla.gov.au/nla.news-article7296248; 29 September, p.6., viewed 10 May 2024, http://nla.gov.au/nla.news-article154878360; 30 Sep, p.8., viewed 13 Jun 2023, http://nla.gov.au/nla.news-article7302003; 29 Oct, p.8., viewed 13 Jun 2023, http://nla.gov.au/nla.news-article7303588; 8 Nov, p.8., viewed 04 Aug 2023, http://nla.gov.au/nla.news-article7304183

1858 'Advertising', The Star (Ballarat, Vic.: 1855-1864), 1 Feb, p.1., viewed 21 Jun 2023, http://nla.gov.au/nla.news-article66048351; 4 Feb, p.1., viewed 21 Jun 2023, http://nla.gov.au/nla.news-article66046406; 10 Feb, p.1., viewed 21 Jun 2023, http://nla.gov.au/nla.news-article66046490; 11 December, p.1., viewed 10 May 2024, http://nla.gov.au/nla.news-article66332727

1858 'Bacchus Marsh,', The Age (Melbourne, Vic.: 1854-1954), 1 Oct, p.6., viewed 05 May 2024, http://nla.gov.au/nla.news-article154875941

1858 'Mercantile and Money Article.', The Sydney Morning Herald (NSW: 1842-1954), 9 Feb, p.8., viewed 29 Jun 2023, http://nla.gov.au/nla.news-article13006035

1859 'Advertising', Maryborough and Dunolly Advertiser (Vic.: 1857-1867 ; 1914-1918), 1 Mar, p.4.

1859 'Advertising', The Argus (Melbourne, Vic.: 1848-1957), 25 Nov, p.3.

1859 'Title Deeds.', Mount Alexander Mail (Vic.: 1854-1917), 16 Sep, p.3., viewed 26 Jul 2023, http://nla.gov.au/nla.news-article199046906

1859 'Advertising', Bell's Life in Victoria and Sporting Chronicle (Melbourne, Vic.: 1857-1868), 5 Feb, p.4., viewed 14 Jun 2023, http://nla.gov.au/nla.news-article201376672; 12 Feb, p.4., viewed 27 Jul 2023, http://nla.gov.au/nla.news-article201379318; 2 April, p. 4. , viewed 22 May 2024, http://nla.gov.au/nla.news-article201379576; 9 Jul, p.1., viewed 4 Aug 2023, http://nla.gov.au/nla.news-article201371802

1859 'Advertising', Bendigo Advertiser (Vic.: 1855-1918), 6 Jan, p.1., viewed 27 Jul 2023, http://nla.gov.au/nla.news-article87986095;
16 Aug, p.1., viewed 01 Jul 2023, http://nla.gov.au/nla.news-article87991418; 1 Nov, p.1., viewed 01 Jul 2023, http://nla.gov.au/nla.news-article87993208

1859 'Advertising', Geelong Advertiser (Vic.: 1859-1929), 18 Feb, p.1., viewed 14 Jun 2023, http://nla.gov.au/nla.news-article150075958; 16 Mar, p.1., viewed 14 Jun 2023, http://nla.gov.au/nla.news-article150076479; 29 Oct, p.1., viewed 14 Jun 2023, http://nla.gov.au/nla.news-article146567931

1859 'Advertising', Maryborough and Dunolly Advertiser (Vic.: 1857-1867 ; 1914-1918), 1 Mar, p.4., viewed 04 Aug 2023, http://nla.gov.au/nla.news-article253593165; 4 Jul, p.1., viewed 04 Aug 2023, http://nla.gov.au/nla.news-article253597905

1859 'Advertising', Mount Alexander Mail (Vic.: 1854-1917), 14 Jan, p.8., viewed 01 Jul 2023, http://nla.gov.au/nla.news-article199052471; 2 Mar, p.4., viewed 14 Jun 2023, http://nla.gov.au/nla.news-article199048455; 21 Oct, p.2., viewed 03 Jul 2023, http://nla.gov.au/nla.news-article199049838; 7 Nov, p.4., viewed 03 Jul 2023, http://nla.gov.au/nla.news-article199047323

1859 'Advertising', The Age (Melbourne, Vic.: 1854-1954), 2 Jun, p.7., viewed 17 Jul 2023, http://nla.gov.au/nla.news-article154828064; 17 Jun, p.7., viewed 23 Jun 2023, http://nla.gov.au/nla.news-article154829324; 10 Sep, p.3., viewed 14 Jun 2023, http://nla.gov.au/nla.news-article154828163; 31 Dec, p.2., viewed 01 Jul 2023, http://nla.gov.au/nla.news-article154880579

1859 'Advertising', The Argus (Melbourne, Vic.: 1848-1957), 1 Jan, p.8., viewed 04 Aug 2023, http://nla.gov.au/nla.news-article7307269; 19 Jan, p.8., viewed 01 Jul 2023, http://nla.gov.au/nla.news-article7308296; 10 Feb, p.8., viewed 27 Jul 2023, http://nla.gov.au/nla.news-article7309565; 22 Feb, p.1., viewed 14 Jun 2023, http://nla.gov.au/nla.news-article5676769; 10 May, p.8., viewed 04 Aug 2023, http://nla.gov.au/nla.news-article5680899; 25 Nov, p.3., viewed 03 Jul 2023, http://nla.gov.au/nla.news-article5692413

1859 'Advertising', The Star (Ballarat, Vic.: 1855-1864), 25 Apr, p.3., viewed 14 Jun 2023, http://nla.gov.au/nla.news-article66335365; 8 Mar, p.1., viewed 02 May 2024, http://nla.gov.au/nla.news-article66334435

1859 'Cobb and Co's. Conveyances.', Bendigo Advertiser (Vic.: 1855-1918), 28 Apr, p.3., viewed 28 Feb 2024, http://nla.gov.au/nla.news-article87988673

1859 'Family Notices', The Argus (Melbourne, Vic.: 1848-1957), 31 Oct, p.8., viewed 04 Aug 2023, http://nla.gov.au/nla.news-article5690897

1859 'Geelong Labour Market.', Portland Guardian and Normanby General Advertiser (Vic.: 1842-1843; 1854-1876), 15 Jun, p.2., viewed 28 Feb 2024, http://nla.gov.au/nla.news-article64511272

1859 'Inquests.', Mount Alexander Mail (Vic.: 1854-1917), 19 Sep, p.3., viewed 27 Feb 2024, http://nla.gov.au/nla.news-article199050380

1859 'Kyneton.', Bendigo Advertiser (Vic.: 1855-1918), 16 Sep, p.3., viewed 01 Aug 2023, http://nla.gov.au/nla.news-article87992186

1859 'Melbourne News.', Bendigo Advertiser (Vic.: 1855-1918), 28 May, p.2., viewed 05 May 2024, http://nla.gov.au/nla.news-article87989411

1859 'Supreme Court.', Mount Alexander Mail (Vic.: 1854-1917), 19 Sep, p.2., viewed 21 Jun 2023, http://nla.gov.au/nla.news-article199050382

1860 'Advertising' Bendigo Advertiser (Vic.: 1855-1918) 3 Aug 1860: 1. Web. 5 Aug 2023, http://nla.gov.au/nla.news-article87945575

1860 'Advertising', The Argus (Melbourne,Vic.: 1848-1957), 16 Apr, p.8.

1860 'Advertising', Bell's Life in Victoria and Sporting Chronicle (Melbourne, Vic.: 1857-1868), 3 Nov, p.1., viewed 03 Jul 2023, http://nla.gov.au/nla.news-article201378290

1860 'Advertising', Bendigo Advertiser (Vic.: 1855-1918), 9 Apr, p.1., viewed 03 Jul 2023, http://nla.gov.au/nla.news-article87942930

1860 'Advertising', Geelong Advertiser (Vic.: 1859-1929), 21 Jan, p.1., viewed 27 Jul 2023, http://nla.gov.au/nla.news-article148788147; 24 Jan, p.1., viewed 27 Jul 2023, http://nla.gov.au/nla.news-article148788215; 4 Dec, p.1., viewed 01 Jul 2023, http://nla.gov.au/nla.news-article148888263; 12 Dec, p.1., viewed 05 Aug 2023, http://nla.gov.au/nla.news-article148694666; 24 Dec, p.1., viewed 04 Jul 2023, http://nla.gov.au/nla.news-article148694962

1860 'Advertising', Maryborough and Dunolly Advertiser (Vic.: 1857-1867 ; 1914-1918), 9 Nov, p.3., viewed 04 Jul 2023, http://nla.gov.au/nla.news-article253597522

1860 'Advertising', Mount Alexander Mail (Vic.: 1854-1917), 27 Feb, p.1., viewed 03 Jul 2023, http://nla.gov.au/nla.news-article199600981; 11 Jun, p.1., viewed 12 Jul 2023, http://nla.gov.au/nla.news-article199606799 (13 Jul 1860 & 20 Jul 1860 & 27 Jul 1860); 10 Aug, p.2., viewed 03 Jul 2023, http://nla.gov.au/nla.news-article199604156; 7 Nov, p.4., viewed 02 Jul 2023, http://nla.gov.au/nla.news-article199606545

1860 'Advertising', The Age (Melbourne, Vic.: 1854-1954), 22 Mar, p.3., viewed 03 Jul 2023, http://nla.gov.au/nla.news-article154880815; 4 Jul, p.3., viewed 01 Jul 2023, http://nla.gov.au/nla.news-article154843337; 14 Sep, p.3., viewed 03 Jul 2023, http://nla.gov.au/nla.news-article154886434; 13 Dec, p.1., viewed 04 Jul 2023, http://nla.gov.au/nla.news-article154883235

1860 'Advertising', The Argus (Melbourne, Vic.: 1848-1957), 27 Jan, p.8., viewed 01 Jul 2023, http://nla.gov.au/nla.news-article5695876; 16 Apr, p.8., viewed 03 Jul 2023, http://nla.gov.au/nla.news-article5680688; 7 May, p.8., viewed 03 Jul 2023, http://nla.gov.au/nla.news-article5681867; 28 May, p.8., viewed 11 Jul 2023, http://nla.gov.au/nla.news-article5683255; 13 Jun, p.8., viewed 12 Jul 2023, http://nla.gov.au/nla.news-article5684194; 21 Jun, p.8., viewed 01 Jul 2023, http://nla.gov.au/nla.news-article5684731; 27 Jul, p.3., viewed 03 Jul 2023, http://nla.gov.au/nla.news-article5686869; 7 Aug, p.8., viewed 05 Aug 2023, http://nla.gov.au/nla.news-article5687464; 15 Aug, p.8., viewed 01 Jul 2023, http://nla.gov.au/nla.news-article5687954; 5 Oct, p.8., viewed 03 Jul 2023, http://nla.gov.au/nla.news-article5690976; 25 Oct, p.8., viewed 03 Jul 2023, http://nla.gov.au/nla.news-article5692169; 12 Nov, p.8., viewed 04 Jul 2023, http://nla.gov.au/nla.news-article5693163

1860 'Advertising', The Kyneton Observer (Vic.: 1856-1900), 18 Oct, p.1., viewed 03 Jul 2023, http://nla.gov.au/nla.news-article240850286; 10 Nov, p.1., viewed 01 Jul 2023, http://nla.gov.au/nla.news-article240850466

1860 'Advertising', The Star (Ballarat, Vic.: 1855-1864), 7 Mar, p 4., viewed 03 Jul 2023, http://nla.gov.au/nla.news-article72465438; 21 Jul, p.3; 8 Nov, p.1., viewed 05 Aug 2023, http://nla.gov.au/nla.news-article66335650; 13 Dec, p.1., viewed 07 Aug 2023, http://nla.gov.au/nla.news-article66336288

1860 'Advertising', The Tarrangower Times and Maldon District Advertiser (Vic.: 1858-1862), 13 Jul, p.1., viewed 01 Jul 2023, http://nla.gov.au/nla.news-article265420071

1860 'Friday, May 4, 1860.', The Argus (Melbourne, Vic.: 1848-1957), 4 May, p.5., viewed 25 Feb 2024, http://nla.gov.au/nla.news-article5681735

1860 'Kyneton.', Mount Alexander Mail (Vic.: 1854-1917), 8 Oct, p.2., viewed 18 May 2024, http://nla.gov.au/nla.news-article199605976

1860 'Latest Intelligence.', Bendigo Advertiser (Vic.: 1855-1918), 26 Mar, p.2., viewed 06 May 2024, http://nla.gov.au/nla.news-article87942625

1860 'Serious Riot at the Parliament Houses.', Mount Alexander Mail (Vic.: 1854-1917), 30 Aug, p.3., viewed 11 Apr 2024, http://nla.gov.au/nla.news-article199605565

1860 'Tuesday, July 31, 1860.', The Argus (Melbourne, Vic.: 1848-1957), 31 Jul, p.4., viewed 04 Aug 2023, http://nla.gov.au/nla.news-article5687095

1860 'Yandoit.', Mount Alexander Mail (Vic.: 1854-1917), 10 Sep, p.2., viewed 11 Apr 2024, http://nla.gov.au/nla.news-article199604617

1861 'Advertising', Portland Guardian and Normanby General Advertiser (Vic.: 1842-1843; 1854-1876), 14 Jan, p.1., viewed 15 Jun 2023, http://nla.gov.au/nla.news-article65445513

1861 '[Copy.]', The Age (Melbourne, Vic.: 1854-1954), 20 Nov, p.6., viewed 02 Jul 2023, http://nla.gov.au/nla.news-article154900827

1861 'Advertising', The Age (Melbourne, Vic.: 1854-1954) 29 Jun 1861, p.8. Web. 15 Jun 2023 http://nla.gov.au/nla.news-article154899570; 1 Jul 1861, p.8. Web. 5 Jul 2023 http://nla.gov.au/nla.news-article154901475

1861 'Advertising', Bendigo Advertiser (Vic.: 1855-1918), 3 Oct, p.3., viewed 15 Jun 2023, http://nla.gov.au/nla.news-article87377582

1861 'Advertising', Maryborough and Dunolly Advertiser (Vic.: 1857-1867 ; 1914-1918), 2 Jan, p.1., viewed 04 Jul 2023, http://nla.gov.au/nla.news-article253599613; 14 Jan, p.1., viewed 04 Jul 2023, http://nla.gov.au/nla.news-article253599920; 5 Jun, p.1., viewed 05 Jul 2023, http://nla.gov.au/nla.news-article253604031; 5 Jul, p.1., viewed 06 Jul 2023, http://nla.gov.au/nla.news-article253604773

1861 'Advertising', Mount Alexander Mail (Vic.: 1854-1917), 1 Nov, p.2., viewed 06 Jul 2023, http://nla.gov.au/nla.news-article197098383

1861 'Advertising', Mount Alexander Mail (Vic.: 1854-1917), 8 Mar, p.2., viewed 01 Jul 2023, http://nla.gov.au/nla.news-article199606986; 14 Jun, p.2., viewed 05 Jul 2023, http://nla.gov.au/nla.news-article199602207; 24 Jun, p.3., viewed 21 Jun 2023, http://nla.gov.au/nla.news-article199605768; 1 Nov, p.8., viewed 06 Jul 2023, http://nla.gov.au/nla.news-article197098358

1861 'Advertising', The Age (Melbourne, Vic.: 1854-1954), 1 Jan, p.7., viewed 02 Jul 2023, http://nla.gov.au/nla.news-article154884064; 22 Mar, p.8., viewed 06 Aug 2023, http://nla.gov.au/nla.news-article154889194; 23 Mar, p.8., viewed 02 Jul 2023, http://nla.gov.au/nla.news-article154887619; 6 Apr, p 8., viewed 04 Jul 2023, http://nla.gov.au/nla.news-article154887165; 16 Aug, p.1., viewed 06 Jul 2023, http://nla.gov.au/nla.news-article154902677;

1861 'Advertising', The Argus (Melbourne, Vic.: 1848-1957), 16 Jan, p.8., viewed 04 Jul 2023, http://nla.gov.au/nla.news-article5696716; 11 Feb, p.8., viewed 04 Jul 2023, http://nla.gov.au/nla.news-article5697479; 18 Mar, p.8., viewed 02 Jul 2023, http://nla.gov.au/nla.news-article5698543; 2 Apr, p.8., viewed 08 Jul 2023, http://nla.gov.au/nla.news-article5698946; 18 Jun, p.8., viewed 06 Jul 2023, http://nla.gov.au/nla.news-article5701134; 5 Jun, p.8., viewed 09 Jul 2023, http://nla.gov.au/nla.news-article5700774; 22 Jun, p.8., viewed 09 Aug 2023, http://nla.gov.au/nla.news-article5701273; 1 Jul, p.8., viewed 09 Jul 2023, http://nla.gov.au/nla.news-article5701516

1861 'Advertising', The Herald (Melbourne, Vic.: 1861-1954), 22 Mar, p.1., viewed 02 May 2024, http://nla.gov.au/nla.news-article244311504; 22 Apr, p.1., viewed 15 Jun 2023, http://nla.gov.au/nla.news-article244311748; 4 Jun, p.1., viewed 05 Jul 2023, http://nla.gov.au/nla.news-article244244827

1861 'Advertising', The Kyneton Observer (Vic.: 1856-1900), 17 Jan, p.4., viewed 01 Jul 2023, http://nla.gov.au/nla.news-article240850993; 31 January, p.1., viewed 10 May 2024, http://nla.gov.au/nla.news-article240851116

1861 'Advertising', The Star (Ballarat, Vic.: 1855-1864), 14 Jan, p.1., viewed 04 Jul 2023, http://nla.gov.au/nla.news-article66336826 ; 28 Jan, p.1; 15 Jan, p.1., viewed 04 Jul 2023, http://nla.gov.au/nla.news-article66336845; 16 Jan, p.1., viewed 04 Jul 2023, http://nla.gov.au/nla.news-article66336879; 30 Jan, p.1., viewed 05 Aug 2023, http://nla.gov.au/nla.news-article66337128; 4 Mar, p.3., viewed 15 Jun 2023, http://nla.gov.au/nla.news-article66337723; 14 Mar, p.3., viewed 04 Jul 2023, http://nla.gov.au/nla.news-article66337934; 22 May, p.1., viewed 04 Jul 2023, http://nla.gov.au/nla.news-article66339401; 5 Oct, p.1., viewed 07 Aug 2023, http://nla.gov.au/nla.news-article66342539

1861 'County Court Of Grant.', Geelong Advertiser (Vic.: 1859-1929), 7 Jun, p.3., viewed 22 Feb 2024, http://nla.gov.au/nla.news-article150305873

1861 'Late Coaches.', Bendigo Advertiser (Vic.: 1855-1918), 2 Jul, p.2., viewed 26 May 2023, http://nla.gov.au/nla.news-article87375659

1861 Map Victoria. Department of Crown Lands and Survey. 1861.https://viewer.slv.vic.gov.ity=IE15491636&mode=browse

1861 'The Comet.', Maryborough and Dunolly Advertiser (Vic.: 1857-1867 ; 1914-1918), 7 Jun, p.3., viewed 27 Jul 2023, http://nla.gov.au/nla.news-article253604076

1862 "Advertising" Maryborough and Dunolly Advertiser (Vic.: 1857-1867 ; 1914-1918) 11 Jun 1862, p.1. Web. 8 Aug 2023 http://nla.gov.au/nla.news-article253513402

1862 'A few particulars supplementary to the catalogue of the products of the Colony of Victoria, Australia', compiled by J.G. Knight, Pethpam 2712, [London? : s.n.], 1862 printing, Trove Digital Library

1862 'Deniliquin Police Court.', The Pastoral

Times and Southern Courier (Deniliquin, N.S.W : 1861 - 1862), 13 Jun, p.3., viewed 20 Aug 2023, http://nla.gov.au/nla.news-article270951190

1862 A few particulars supplementary to the catalogue of the products of the Colony of Victoria, Australia / compiled by J.G. Knight, [London? : s.n.], 1862 printing

1862 'Advertising', Geelong Advertiser (Vic.: 1859-1929), 8 Nov, p.1., viewed 25 Jul 2023, http://nla.gov.au/nla.news-article148903866

1862 'Advertising', Maryborough and Dunolly Advertiser (Vic.: 1857-1867 ; 1914-1918), 10 Feb, p.1., viewed 08 Aug 2023, http://nla.gov.au/nla.news-article253504208; 9 May, p.1., viewed 07 Jul 2023, http://nla.gov.au/nla.news-article253511180; 14 May, p.1., viewed 07 Jul 2023, http://nla.gov.au/nla.news-article253511467

1862 'Advertising', Mount Alexander Mail (Vic.: 1854-1917), 27 Jan, p.3., viewed 07 Jul 2023, http://nla.gov.au/nla.news-article197098574; 28 May, p.3., viewed 04 May 2024, http://nla.gov.au/nla.news-article197097414; 5 May, p.3., viewed 07 Jul 2023, http://nla.gov.au/nla.news-article197094816; 7 Apr, p.3., viewed 09 Jul 2023, http://nla.gov.au/nla.news-article197095742

1862 'Advertising', The Age (Melbourne, Vic.: 1854-1954), 16 Jan, p.8., viewed 06 Jul 2023, http://nla.gov.au/nla.news-article5708548; 5 May, p.1., viewed 06 Jul 2023, http://nla.gov.au/nla.news-article154847517; 13 May, p.1., viewed 07 Jul 2023, http://nla.gov.au/nla.news-article155008225

1862 'Advertising', The Herald (Melbourne, Vic.: 1861-1954), 15 Jan, p.1., viewed 07 Jul 2023, http://nla.gov.au/nla.news-article244180965; 15 Mar, p.1., viewed 07 Jul 2023, http://nla.gov.au/nla.news-article244182594; 3 May, p.1., viewed 07 Jul 2023, http://nla.gov.au/nla.news-article244226310

1862 'Advertising', The Star (Ballarat, Vic.: 1855-1864), 13 Sep, p.1., viewed 24 Jul 2023, http://nla.gov.au/nla.news-article66327138; 29 Dec, p.1., viewed 09 Aug 2023, http://nla.gov.au/nla.news-article66329832

1862 'Advertising', The Sydney Morning Herald (NSW: 1842-1954), 21 Mar, p.2., viewed 25 Jul 2023, http://nla.gov.au/nla.news-article13226119

1862 'Advertising', The Tarrangower Times and Maldon and Newstead Advertiser (Vic.: 1862-1873), 21 Mar, p 5., viewed 07 Jul 2023, http://nla.gov.au/nla.news-article265387439; 1 Aug, p.4., viewed 27 Jul 2023, http://nla.gov.au/nla.news-article265362427

1862 'Castlemaine Mining Division.', Mount Alexander Mail (Vic.: 1854-1917), 17 Jan, p.5., viewed 07 Jul 2023, http://nla.gov.au/nla.news-article197096150

1862 'Government Gazette.', The Age (Melbourne, Vic.: 1854-1954), 22 Nov, p.7., viewed 09 Jul 2023, http://nla.gov.au/nla.news-article154969422

1862 'The Gold Fields.', Geelong Advertiser (Vic.: 1859-1929), 25 Sep, p.1. (Supplement to The Geelong Advertiser), viewed 25 Feb 2024, http://nla.gov.au/nla.news-article149830475

1862 'To the Editor of the Gippsland Times.', Gippsland Times (Vic.: 1861-1954), 12 Sep, p.3., viewed 07 Feb 2024, http://nla.gov.au/nla.news-article65361908

1862 'Twenty-Two of Geelong and the Western District V. The All England Eleven.', The Mercury (Hobart, Tas. : 1860-1954), 27 Jan, p.3., viewed 04 May 2024, http://nla.gov.au/nla.news-article8803900

1863 'Advertising', Bell's Life in Victoria and Sporting Chronicle (Melbourne, Vic.: 1857-1868), 17 Jan, p.1., viewed 05 Aug 2023, http://nla.gov.au/nla.news-article199059632

1863 'Advertising', Hamilton Spectator and Grange District Advertiser (Vic.: 1860-1870), 20 Mar, p.1., viewed 25 Jul 2023, http://nla.gov.au/nla.news-article194859329; 3 Apr, p.1., viewed 09 Aug 2023, http://nla.gov.au/nla.news-article194861933; 10 Apr, p.1., viewed 25 Jul 2023, http://nla.gov.au/nla.news-article194861904

1863 'Advertising', Portland Guardian and Normanby General Advertiser (Vic.: 1842-1843; 1854-1876), 16 Apr, p.1. (Evening), viewed 25 Jul 2023, http://nla.gov.au/nla.news-article64628582

1863 'Advertising', The Argus (Melbourne, Vic.: 1848-1957), 30 May, p.8., viewed 09 Aug 2023, http://nla.gov.au/nla.news-article6486191

1863 'Advertising', The Herald (Melbourne, Vic.: 1861-1954), 14 Apr, p.1., viewed 25 Jul 2023, http://nla.gov.au/nla.news-article244294628

1863 'Advertising', The Star (Ballarat, Vic.: 1855-1864), 16 Jan, p.3., viewed 09 May 2024, http://nla.gov.au/nla.news-article72554202 6 Feb, p.1., viewed 27 Feb 2024, http://nla.gov.au/nla.news-article72554696 ; 27 Feb p.1., viewed 25 Jul 2023, http://nla.gov.au/nla.news-article72555203; 11 Apr, p.1., viewed 09 Aug 2023, http://nla.gov.au/nla.news-article72556206; 13 May, p.1., viewed 12 May 2024, http://nla.gov.au/nla.news-article72556973; 11 Jul, p.1., viewed 09 Aug 2023, http://nla.gov.au/nla.news-article72515649

1863 'Advertising', The Tarrangower Times and Maldon and Newstead Advertiser (Vic.: 1862-1873), 31 Mar, p.1., viewed 07 Jul 2023, http://nla.gov.au/nla.news-article265365168; 23 Jun, p.1., viewed 07 Jul 2023, http://nla.gov.au/nla.news-article265365646; 20 Nov, p.1., viewed 07 Jul 2023, http://nla.gov.au/nla.news-article265366501

1863 'Inglewood.', Bendigo Advertiser (Vic.: 1855-1918), 21 Feb, p.2., viewed 24 Jul 2023, http://nla.gov.au/nla.news-article87934556 ; 2 Apr, p.2., viewed 17 Feb 2024, http://nla.gov.au/nla.news-article87935433

1863 'Lyceum Theatre.', Bendigo Advertiser (Vic.: 1855-1918), 12 Jan, p.2., viewed 09 Jul 2023, http://nla.gov.au/nla.news-article87933744

1863 'New South Wales Parliament.', The Sydney Morning Herald (NSW: 1842-1954), 19 Aug, p.5., viewed 26 Jul 2023, http://nla.gov.au/nla.news-article28621466

1863 'New Zealand.', Mount Alexander Mail (Vic.: 1854-1917),12 Feb, p.3., viewed 07 Feb 2024, http://nla.gov.au/nla.news-article200382795

1863 'News and Notes.', The Star (Ballarat, Vic.: 1855-1864), 7 Mar, p.2., viewed 05 May 2024, http://nla.gov.au/nla.news-article72555362

1864 'Advertising', Geelong Advertiser (Vic.: 1859-1929), 20 Jul, p.1., viewed 06 May 2024, http://nla.gov.au/nla.news-article150463872; 6 August, p.1., viewed 12 May 2024, http://nla.gov.au/nla.news-article150464304

1864 'Advertising', Mount Alexander Mail (Vic.: 1854-1917), 16 June, p.1., viewed 12 May 2024, http://nla.gov.au/nla.news-article197443721

1864 'Advertising', The Star (Ballarat, Vic.: 1855-1864), 14 January, p.1., viewed 12 May 2024, http://nla.gov.au/nla.news-article72512853

1864 'Advertising', The Tarrangower Times and Maldon and Newstead Advertiser (Vic.: 1862-1873), 19 January, p.1., viewed 12 May 2024, http://nla.gov.au/nla.news-article265366841

1864 'Castlemaine.', Leader (Melbourne, Vic.: 1862-1918, 1935), 20 Aug, p.17., viewed 28 Feb 2024, http://nla.gov.au/nla.news-article197293594

1864 'General Intelligence.', Hobart Town Advertiser : Weekly Edt. (Tas.: 1859-1865), 18 Jun, p.1., viewed 27 Feb 2024, http://nla.gov.au/nla.news-article264702971

1864 'Local News.', Hamilton Spectator and Grange District Advertiser (Vic.: 1860-1870), 7 Dec, p.2., viewed 24 Feb 2024, http://nla.gov.au/nla.news-article194724269

1864 'Morgan. Bushranger And Murderer.', Mount Alexander Mail (Vic.: 1854-1917), 7 Jul, p.2., viewed 09 May 2024, http://nla.gov.au/nla.news-article197546195

1864 'No title', Hamilton Spectator and Grange District Advertiser (Vic.: 1860-1870), 24 Jun, p.2. (Supplement To The Hamilton Spectator), viewed 16 Feb 2024, http://nla.gov.au/nla.news-article194723815

1864 'Tasmania.', The Age (Melbourne, Vic.: 1854-1954), 16 Jun, p.6., viewed 19 Feb 2024, http://nla.gov.au/nla.news-article155012816

1864 'The Report of the Yarra Flood Commission', (Robert Adams) p.2. Viewed 19 Apr 2024. https://viewer.slv.vic.gov.1877 'Correspondence.', Gippsland Times (Vic.: 1861-1954), 5 Dec, p.3. (Morning.), viewed 01 Mar 2024, http://nla.gov.au/nla.news-article61830731

1877 'News and Notes.', The Kyneton Observer (Vic.: 1856-1900), 23 Jun, p.3., viewed 06 May 2024, http://nla.gov.au/nla.news-article240926208

1878 'Miscellaneous.', Warwick Examiner and Times (Qld.: 1867-1919), 5 Oct, p.6., viewed 14 Oct 2022L19026913&mode=browse

1865 'Advertising', The Ballarat Star (Vic.: 1865-1924), 29 Mar, p.3., viewed 06 May 2024, http://nla.gov.au/nla.news-article112885686

1865 'Local.', Gippsland Guardian (Vic.: 1855-1868), 16 Jun, p.2., viewed 07 Feb 2024, http://nla.gov.au/nla.news-article109909205

1865 'St. Arnaud Police Court.', Maryborough and Dunolly Advertiser (Vic.: 1857-1867 ; 1914-1918), 16 Jun, p.3., viewed 20 Apr 2024, http://nla.gov.au/nla.news-article253588217

1866 'Kooringa and Redruth, Dec. 6.', South Australian Weekly Chronicle (Adelaide, SA: 1858-1867), 8 December, p.7., viewed 13 May 2024, http://nla.gov.au/nla.news-article94743579

1867 'The News Of The Day.', The Age (Melbourne, Vic.: 1854-1954), 6 Aug, p.5., viewed 13 Sep 2023, http://nla.gov.au/nla.news-article185504663

1867 'Advertising', Hamilton Spectator and Grange District Advertiser (Vic.: 1860-1870), 26 Oct, p.1., viewed 21 Jan 2024, http://nla.gov.au/nla.news-article194476984

1867 'Country News.', Leader (Melbourne, Vic.: 1862-1918, 1935), 22 Jun, p.19., viewed 16 Feb 2024, http://nla.gov.au/nla.news-article196632988

1867 'The Alleged Truck System at Harcourt.', Bendigo Advertiser (Vic.: 1855-1918), 7 Sep, p.2., viewed 02 Mar 2024, http://nla.gov.au/nla.news-article87954741

1868 'Fire in Armstrong Street.' The Ballarat Star (Vic.: 1865-1924) 11 Mar 1868: 2. Web. 2 Mar 2024, http://nla.gov.au/nla.news-article113601714

1868 'Advertising', Geelong Advertiser (Vic.: 1859-1929), 3 Jan, p.1., viewed 02 Mar 2024, http://nla.gov.au/nla.news-article147776312; 3 April 1868: 1. Web. 12 May 2024 <http://nla.gov.au/nla.news-article150466196; 13 April, p.1., viewed 12 May 2024, http://nla.gov.au/nla.news-article148794733

1868 'Advertising', Hamilton Spectator and Grange District Advertiser (Vic.: 1860-1870), 4 Mar, p.1., viewed 20 Jan 2024, http://nla.gov.au/nla.news-article194475969

1868 'Summary of News.', Border Watch (Mount Gambier, SA: 1861-1954), 5 Aug, p.3., viewed 19 Feb 2024, http://nla.gov.au/nla.news-article77165508

1868 'Yatta Creek. Barossa.', Adelaide Observer (SA: 1843-1904), 17 Oct, p.7., viewed 07 Feb 2024, http://nla.gov.au/nla.news-article158933834

1869 'Under the Verandah.', Leader (Melbourne, Vic.: 1862-1918, 1935), 27 Mar, p.17., viewed 13 Oct 2022, http://nla.gov.au/nla.news-article196482306

1869 'Hurricane in Sale.', The Manaro Mercury, and Cooma and Bombala Advertiser (NSW: 1862-1931), 2 Apr, p.7., viewed 25 Feb 2024, http://nla.gov.au/nla.news-article113958512

1869 'Melbourne Business Men', The Cornwall Chronicle (Launceston, Tas. : 1835-1880), 15 May, p.2., viewed 07 Mar 2024, http://nla.gov.au/nla.news-article65984206

1869 'The Floods.', The Argus (Melbourne, Vic.: 1848-1957), 19 Oct, p.5., viewed 24 Feb 2024, http://nla.gov.au/nla.news-article5816660

1870 'Advertising', The Ballarat Star (Vic.: 1865-1924), 25 November, p.1., viewed 12 May 2024, http://nla.gov.au/nla.news-article218800300

1870 'Double Coach Accident.', Border Watch (Mount Gambier, SA: 1861-1954), 18 May, p.4., viewed 09 Apr 2024, http://nla.gov.au/nla.news-article77129759

1870 'Fatal Accident at Cobb and Co.'s Stables.', The Ballarat Courier (Vic.: 1869-1886; 1914-1918), 6 Apr, p.2., viewed 01 Mar 2024, http://nla.gov.au/nla.news-article191566144

1870 'King Cobb.', The Tarrangower Times and Maldon and Newstead Advertiser (Vic.: 1862-1873), 9 Nov, p.2., viewed 28 Feb 2024, http://nla.gov.au/nla.news-article265380921

1870 'Notes from the Journals of Yesterday.', Geelong Advertiser (Vic.: 1859-1929), 10 Sep, p.3., viewed 19 Feb 2024, http://nla.gov.au/nla.news-article150656786

1870 'Power the Bushranger.', The Age (Melbourne, Vic.: 1854-1954), 5 Aug, p.3., viewed 09 May 2024, http://nla.gov.au/nla.news-article189334519

1870 'Sandhurst Police Court.', Bendigo Advertiser (Vic.: 1855-1918), 14 Sep, p.3., viewed 02 Mar 2024, http://nla.gov.au/nla.news-article87914142

1871 'Advertising', Geelong Advertiser (Vic.: 1859-1929), 22 May, p.1., viewed 06 May 2024, http://nla.gov.au/nla.news-article148764121

1871 'News and Notes.', The Ballarat Star (Vic.: 1865-1924), 19 October, p.2., viewed 12 May 2024, http://nla.gov.au/nla.news-article197573515

1872 'Egerton and Gordon.', The Bacchus Marsh Express (Vic.: 1866-1943), 12 Oct, p.3., viewed 25 Feb 2024, http://nla.gov.au/nla.news-article93142244

1872 'Family Notices', The Ballarat Star (Vic.: 1865-1924), 12 Jun, p.3., viewed 25 Feb 2024, http://nla.gov.au/nla.news-article219155617

1872 'Portland Guardian Almanac 1872.', Portland Guardian and Normanby General Advertiser (Vic.: 1842-1843; 1854-1876), 1 Jan, p.1. (Evenings : Supplement to the "Portland Guardian"), viewed 19 Jan 2024, http://nla.gov.au/nla.news-article65426567

1873 'Local and General News.', Alexandra Times (Vic.: 1868-1877), 18 Jan, p.2., viewed 28 Apr 2024, http://nla.gov.au/nla.news-article58213892

1874 'Advertising', Hamilton Spectator (Vic.: 1870-1918), 3 Jan, p.2. (Supplement To The Hamilton Spectator), viewed 20 Jan 2024, http://nla.gov.au/nla.news-article226075474

1875 'Cobb's Box', by R. P. Whitworth. Carlton : Printed by A. J.Curtiz, 1875. https://collection.sl.nsw.gov.au/record/74Vv5mZPJ5m3

1875 'News and Notes.', The Ballarat Star (Vic.: 1865-1924), 17 Feb, p.2., viewed 06 May 2024, http://nla.gov.au/nla.news-article208251762; 21 May, p.2., viewed 12 Apr 2024, http://nla.gov.au/nla.news-article208328888

1876 'The Australian handbook and almanac and shippers' and importers' directory', https://nla.gov.au/nla.obj-2963513330/view?sectionId=nla.obj-2967254489&partId=nla.obj-2963545248#page/n219/mode/1up

1876 'Advertising', Hamilton Spectator (Vic.: 1870-1918), 11 Mar, p.2. (Supplement To The Hamilton Spectator), viewed 20 Jan 2024, http://nla.gov.au/nla.news-article226037553

1876 'Law And Criminal Courts.', South Australian Register (Adelaide, SA: 1839-1900), 13 Dec, p.1. (Supplement To The South Australian Register.), viewed 25 Feb 2024, http://nla.gov.au/nla.news-article43010065

1876 'Tuesday, December 12.', South Australian Chronicle and Weekly Mail (Adelaide, SA: 1868-881), 16 Dec, p.10., viewed 19 Feb 2024, http://nla.gov.au/nla.news-article92254703

1878 'Advertising', Geelong Advertiser (Vic.: 1859-1929), 30 May, p.1., viewed 21 Jan 2024, http://nla.gov.au/nla.news-article149825183

1878 'Advertising', Gippsland Times (Vic.: 1861-1954), 16 Sep, p.2. (Morning.), viewed 02 Mar 2024, http://nla.gov.au/nla.news-article62025234

1878 'Edward Kelly's Letter.', Gippsland Times (Vic.: 1861-1954), 20 Dec, p.3. (Morning.), viewed 01 May 2024, http://nla.gov.au/nla.news-article62026004

1878 'Maffra.', Gippsland Mercury (Sale, Vic.: 1871-1872; 1874-1886; 1888-1894; 1914-1918), 11 Jul, p.4., viewed 24 Feb 2024, http://nla.gov.au/nla.news-article268048849

1878 'Sandhurst—Past And Present.', Illustrated Australian News (Melbourne, Vic.: 1876-1889), 27 Dec, p.218., viewed 06 Feb 2024, http://nla.gov.au/nla.news-article60095912

1879 'Death of a Bushranger', The Kyneton Observer (Vic.: 1856-1900), 19 Jul, p.2., viewed 09 May 2024, http://nla.gov.au/nla.news-article240932636

1879 'Minhamite Shire Council.', Hamilton Spectator (Vic.: 1870-1918), 31 July, p.3., viewed 13 May 2024, http://nla.gov.au/nla.news-article226053554

1879 'News and Notes.', The Ballarat Star (Vic.: 1865-1924), 8 May, p.3., viewed 20 Feb 2024, http://nla.gov.au/nla.news-article200134810

1879 'On the Road to Fernshaw.', Bendigo Advertiser (Vic.: 1855-1918), 3 May, p.1. (Supplement to The Bendigo Advertiser), viewed 21 Feb 2024, http://nla.gov.au/nla.news-article88226110

1880 'Advertising', Hamilton Spectator (Vic.: 1870-1918), 29 Jan, p.4., viewed 20 Jan 2024, http://nla.gov.au/nla.news-article226056470

1880 'Edward Kelly.', The Herald (Melbourne, Vic.: 1861-1954), 24 Jul, p.3., viewed 01 May 2024, http://nla.gov.au/nla.news-article244691586

1880 'Edward Kelly.', The Herald (Melbourne, Vic.: 1861-1954), 1 Nov, p.3., viewed 01 May 2024, http://nla.gov.au/nla.news-article244689180

1880 'Edward Kelly's Trial.', Weekly Times (Melbourne, Vic.: 1869-1954), 25 Sep, p.19., viewed 01 May 2024, http://nla.gov.au/nla.news-article221764231

1880 'Execution of Edward Kelly.', Mercury and Weekly Courier (Vic.: 1878-1903), 13 Nov, p.3., viewed 01 May 2024, http://nla.gov.au/nla.news-article59577644

1880 'Execution of Edward Kelly.', The Mercury (Hobart, Tas. : 1860-1954), 15 Nov, p.3., viewed 01 May 2024, http://nla.gov.au/nla.news-article8990167

1880 'The Encounter at Glenrowan.', The Mercury (Hobart, Tas. : 1860-1954), 1 Jul, p.2., viewed 01 May 2024, http://nla.gov.au/nla.news-article8984975

1880 'Trial of Edward Kelly.', Border Watch (Mount Gambier, SA: 1861-1954), 7 Aug, p.4., viewed 01 May 2024, http://nla.gov.au/nla.news-article77589019

1880 'Trial of Edward Kelly.', Illustrated Australian News (Melbourne, Vic.: 1876-1889), 6 Nov, p.203., viewed 01 May 2024, http://nla.gov.au/nla.news-article60094482

1880 'Trial of Edward Kelly.', The Age (Melbourne, Vic.: 1854-1954), 29 Oct, p.3., viewed 01 May 2024, http://nla.gov.au/nla.news-article202154813

1880-1889 'Niven's guide book and souvenir of Ballarat : the garden city of Victoria', F. W. Niven, https://trove.nla.

gov.au/9?keyword=%27History%20of%20Ballarat%27%20by%20Withers

1880 'Yarrawonga.', Ovens and Murray Advertiser (Beechworth, Vic.: 1855; 1857-1890; 1892-1955), 22 Jun, p.4., viewed 10 May 2024, http://nla.gov.au/nla.news-article201539724

1881 'Advertising', Hamilton Spectator (Vic.: 1870-1918), 6 Oct, p.1. (Supplement To The Hamilton Spectator), viewed 20 Jan 2024, http://nla.gov.au/nla.news-article226058923

1881 'News and Notes.', The Lorgnette (Melbourne, Vic.: 1878-1898), 2 Jun, p.4. (Edition 1), viewed 06 May 2024, http://nla.gov.au/nla.news-article212694872

1882 'Advertising', Hamilton Spectator (Vic.: 1870-1918), 26 Oct, p.1. (Supplement To The Hamilton Spectator), viewed 20 Jan 2024, http://nla.gov.au/nla.news-article225494222; 16 Dec, p.3., viewed 09 Apr 2024, http://nla.gov.au/nla.news-article225495810;

1882 'Advertising', The Argus (Melbourne, Vic.: 1848-1957), 16 Dec, p.1., viewed 28 Apr 2024, http://nla.gov.au/nla.news-article11562553

1882 'Camels for Cobb's Coaches.', Camperdown Chronicle (Vic.: 1875-1954), 22 Apr, p.4., viewed 09 Apr 2024, http://nla.gov.au/nla.news-article26792511

1882 'Fire at Cobb and Co.'s Stables.', Weekly Times (Melbourne, Vic.: 1869-1954), 30 Dec, p.14., viewed 01 Mar 2024, http://nla.gov.au/nla.news-article221748184

1882 'Summer Hill Company.', The Ballarat Star (Vic.: 1865-1924), 30 May, p.4., viewed 25 Feb 2024, http://nla.gov.au/nla.news-article200672623

1883 'Yea.' Seymour Express and Goulburn Valley, Avenel, Graytown, Nagambie, Tallarook and Yea Advertiser (Vic.: 1882 - 1891; 1914-1918) 2 Nov 1883: 2. Web. 28 Apr 2024 http://nla.gov.au/nla.news-article165088624

1883 'A Mail Coach Stuck Up.', Bendigo Advertiser (Vic.: 1855-1918), 24 May, p.2., viewed 01 May 2024, http://nla.gov.au/nla.news-article88516241

1883 'Advertising', Geelong Advertiser (Vic.: 1859-1929), 23 Aug, p.1., viewed 19 Jan 2024, http://nla.gov.au/nla.news-article150385444

1883 'Advertising', Hamilton Spectator (Vic.: 1870-1918), 16 Oct, p.1 (Supplement to the Hamilton Spectator), viewed 20 Jan 2024, http://nla.gov.au/nla.news-article226052143

1883 'Country News.', The Age (Melbourne, Vic.: 1854-1954), 14 Sep, p.7., viewed 19 Apr 2024, http://nla.gov.au/nla.news-article202611519

1883 'Lake Mundi.', Hamilton Spectator (Vic.: 1870-1918), 22 March, p.3., viewed 13 May 2024, http://nla.gov.au/nla.news-article225493065

1883 'Management at Tallarook Station.', Alexandra and Yea Standard, Gobur, Thornton and Acheron Express (Vic.: 1877-1908), 6 Apr, p.2., viewed 28 Apr 2024, http://nla.gov.au/nla.news-article57166265

1883 'The Ovens District Hospital.', Ovens and Murray Advertiser (Beechworth, Vic.: 1855; 1857-1890; 1892-1955), 4 Dec, p.2., viewed 10 May 2024, http://nla.gov.au/nla.news-article198969998

1883 'With Tom Toke, The Australian Bushranger.', The Maffra Spectator (Vic.: 1882-1920), 20 Aug, p.3., viewed 09 May 2024, http://nla.gov.au/nla.news-article66867509

1884 'A Complaint Against Coach[?] Drivers.', The Argus (Melbourne, Vic.: 1848-1957), 11 Nov, p.10., viewed 13 May 2024, http://nla.gov.au/nla.news-article6061130

1884 'Advertising', Hamilton Spectator (Vic.: 1870-1918), 2 Sep, p.1. (Supplement to the Hamilton Spectator), viewed 20 Jan 2024, http://nla.gov.au/nla.news-article226052538

1884 'Casterton.', Hamilton Spectator (Vic.: 1870-1918), 31 May, p.3., viewed 13 May 2024, http://nla.gov.au/nla.news-article226048892

1884 'Melbourne Cup Winners.', The Mercury (Hobart, Tas. : 1860-1954), 6 Dec, p.6., viewed 06 Mar 2024, http://nla.gov.au/nla.news-article9097147

1884 'Sketches Pen with', The Australasian Sketcher with Pen and Pencil (Melbourne, Vic.: 1873-1889), 9 Apr, p.55., viewed 28 Apr 2024, http://nla.gov.au/nla.news-article60620602

1884 'The Advertiser', Euroa Advertiser (Vic.: 1884-1920), 14 Nov, p.2., viewed 07 Feb 2024, http://nla.gov.au/nla.news-article65486112

1884 'The Wentworth Races.', Adelaide Observer (SA: 1843-1904), 29 Mar, p.17., viewed 08 Feb 2024, http://nla.gov.au/nla.news-article160094750

1884 'Western District Railway and Cobb & Co.'s Coach Routes' - The Warrnambool Standard almanac and tourists' guide to Warrnambool & district, p.29, viewed 6 Apr 2024 https://nla.gov.au/nla.obj-2911443924/view?sectionId=nla.obj-2914503432&partId=nla.obj-2911447637#page/n28/mode/1up

1885 'Handbook to the Colony of Victoria' / prepared under the direction of the Victorian Government by Henry Heylyn Hayter, https://nla.gov.au/nla.obj-258085181/view?partId=nla.obj-258106566#page/n11/mode/1up

1885 'Advertising', Geelong Advertiser (Vic.: 1859-1929), 31 Aug, p.1., viewed 21 Feb 2024, http://nla.gov.au/nla.news-article149009568

1885 'Advertising', Hamilton Spectator (Vic.: 1870-1918), 24 Nov, p.1. (Supplement To The Hamilton Spectator), viewed 20 Jan 2024, http://nla.gov.au/nla.news-article225775637

1885 'Cobb and Co.'s', Portland Guardian (Vic.: 1876-1953), 6 Feb, p.1. (Mornings.), viewed 08 Feb 2024, http://nla.gov.au/nla.news-article63344262

1885 Handbook to the colony of Victoria / prepared under the direction of the Vitorian Government by Henry Heylyn Hayter, Melbourne, pp.7&8, https://nla.gov.au/nla.obj-258085181/view?partId=nla.obj-258105136

1885 'Notes and Queries.', Australian Town and Country Journal (Sydney, NSW: 1870 - 1919), 12 Sep, p.19., viewed 02 Aug 2023, http://nla.gov.au/nla.news-article70983698

1885 'Picturesque Victoria.', The Australasian (Melbourne, Vic.: 1864-1946), 23 May, p.2. (The Australasian Supplement), viewed 28 Apr 2024, http://nla.gov.au/nla.news-article138098404

1885 'The Traveller.', Adelaide Observer (SA: 1843-1904), 12 Sep, p.42., viewed 12 Feb 2024, http://nla.gov.au/nla.news-article160743601

1885 'Yarrawonga Rifle Club.', The Yarrawonga Mercury and Mulwala (N.S.W.) News (Vic.: 1882-1892; 1894-1897), 3 Sepr, p.2., viewed 10 May 2024, http://nla.gov.au/nla.news-article273515446

1886 'Advertising', The McIvor Times and Rodney Advertiser (Heathcote, Vic.: 1863-1918), 24 February, p.1., viewed 13 May 2024, http://nla.gov.au/nla.news-article90147076

1886 'Handbook to the colony of Victoria' / prepared under the direction of the Victorian Government by Henry Heylyn Hayter, 1821-1895; Call Number JAFp BIBLIO F10322; Created/Published Melbourne : John Ferres, Govt. Printer, 1885, https://nla.gov.au/nla.obj-403557522/view?partId=nla.obj-403576360#page/n24/mode/1up

1886 'Picturesque atlas of Australasia', edited by Andrew Garran, Sydney : The Picturesque Atlas Publishing Co., [1886?-1888?] https://nla.gov.au/nla.obj-1759110935/view?partId=nla.obj-1759392768#page/n70/mode/1up/search/bushranger

1886 'Advertising', Hamilton Spectator (Vic.: 1870-1918), 7 Dec, p.1. (Supplement to the Hamilton Spectator), viewed 20 Jan 2024, http://nla.gov.au/nla.news-article226157560

1886 'Advertising', The Lilydale Express (Vic.: 1886-1897; 1914-1956), 22 Sep, p.1., viewed 28 Apr 2024, http://nla.gov.au/nla.news-article249368775

1886 'Cobb and Co's Coaches.', Tungamah and Lake Rowan Express and St. James Gazette (Vic.: 1883-1920), 6 May, p.4., viewed 10 May 2024, http://nla.gov.au/nla.news-article270169130

1886 'Family Notices', The Ballarat Star (Vic.: 1865-1924), 14 Sep, p.3., viewed 25 Feb 2024, http://nla.gov.au/nla.news-article210835323

1886 'Lilydale.', North Melbourne Advertiser (Vic.: 1873-1894), 4 Mar, p.2., viewed 28 Apr 2024, http://nla.gov.au/nla.news-article66155579

1886 'Notes And News.', Globe (Sydney, NSW: 1885-1886), 1 Jan, p.3. (Evening), viewed 07 May 2024, http://nla.gov.au/nla.news-article102564408

1886 'South Melbourne Business Enterprise.', Record (Emerald Hill, Vic.: 1881-1954), 13 Dec, p.3., viewed 07 Mar 2024, http://nla.gov.au/nla.news-article108489000

1886 'To Mr Pat Gooley, of Messrs Cobb and Co.', The Yarrawonga Mercury and Mulwala (N.S.W.) News (Vic.: 1882-1892; 1894-1897), 13 May, p.3., viewed 09 Apr 2024, http://nla.gov.au/nla.news-article273512708

1887 'Advertising', Hamilton Spectator (Vic.: 1870-1918), 6 Sep, p.2. (Supplement to the Hamilton Spectator), viewed 20 Jan 2024, http://nla.gov.au/nla.news-article226154645

1887 'Advertising', The Lilydale Express (Vic.: 1886-1897; 1914-1956), 25 Mar, p.1., viewed 28 Apr 2024, http://nla.gov.au/nla.news-article249370571

1887 'Coach Accident on the Queenscliff Road.', Geelong Advertiser (Vic.: 1859-1929), 21 Nov, p.3., viewed 21 Feb 2024, http://nla.gov.au/nla.news-article150735419

1887 'No Title', The Lilydale Express (Vic.: 1886-1897; 1914-1956), 14 Jan, p.2., viewed 28 Apr 2024, http://nla.gov.au/nla.news-article249369920

1888 'Advertising', Hamilton Spectator (Vic.: 1870-1918), 4 Dec, p.2. (Supplement to the Hamiltion Spectator), viewed 20 Jan 2024, http://nla.gov.au/nla.news-article225764334

1888 'Advertising', The Argus (Melbourne, Vic.: 1848-1957), 19 Dec, p.12., viewed 28 Apr 2024, http://nla.gov.au/nla.news-article6913318

1888 'Advertising', The Lilydale Express (Vic.: 1886-1897; 1914-1956), 9 May, p.1., viewed 28 Apr 2024, http://nla.gov.au/nla.news-article249378800

1888 'Lakes Navigation Co., Limited.', Bairnsdale Advertiser and Tambo and Omeo Chronicle (Vic.: 1882-1946), 6 Mar, p.1. (morning), viewed 07 Feb 2024, http://nla.gov.au/nla.news-article84688260

1888 Picturesque atlas of Australasia, edited by Andrew Garran, Sydney : The Picturesque Atlas Publishing Co., [1886, 1887, 1888] https://nla.gov.au/nla.obj-1759109909/view?partId=nla.obj-1759481496#page/n262/mode/1up

1888 'The End of Cobb and Co. in Sandhurst.', Bendigo Advertiser (Vic.: 1855-1918), 8 Sep, p.5., viewed 09 Apr 2024, http://nla.gov.au/nla.news-article88554099

1888 'The End of Cobb and Co. in Sandhurst.', Ovens and Murray Advertiser (Beechworth, Vic.: 1855-1955), 22 Sep, p.4., viewed 25 Feb 2024, http://nla.gov.au/nla.news-article198925962

1889 'Across The Australian Alps.', The Age (Melbourne, Vic.: 1854-1954), 20 Apr, p.13., viewed 08 May 2024, http://nla.gov.au/nla.news-article196986649

1889 'Advertising', Hamilton Spectator (Vic.: 1870-1918), 12 Feb, p.4., viewed 20 Jan 2024, http://nla.gov.au/nla.news-article225759097

1889 'Advertising', The Argus (Melbourne, Vic.: 1848-1957), 16 Feb, p.18., viewed 28 Apr 2024, http://nla.gov.au/nla.news-article6223117

1889 'Coach Accident on the Fernshaw-Road.', The Australasian (Melbourne, Vic.: 1864-1946), 27 Apr, p.34., viewed 21 Feb 2024, http://nla.gov.au/nla.news-article139699522

1889 'Cobb and Co.'s Coaches.', Bairnsdale Advertiser and Tambo and Omeo Chronicle (Vic.: 1882-1946), 2 May, p.2., viewed 07 Feb 2024, http://nla.gov.au/nla.news-article84812671

1889 'His First Snake.', The Australasian Sketcher with Pen and Pencil (Melbourne, Vic.: 1873-1889), 24 Jan, p.3., viewed 21 Feb 2024, http://nla.gov.au/nla.news-article63225362

1889 The Palace Hotel (Bourke Street) guide to Melbourne. Manufacturer (Melbourne : Fergusson & Mitchell)
httpe://viewer.slv.vic.gov.y=IE4357277&file=FL18598840&mode=browser

1890 'A Winter Trip to Omeo', The Nathalia Herald and Picola, Narioka, Kotupna and Moira Advertiser (Vic.: 1884-1918), 17 Jul, p.8., viewed 07 May 2024, http://nla.gov.au/nla.news-article279959417

1890 'Advertising', Hamilton Spectator (Vic.: 1870-1918), 21 Oct, p.1. (Supplement to the Hamilton Spectator), viewed 20 Jan 2024, http://nla.gov.au/nla.news-article225767846

1890 'Advertising', The Ballarat Star (Vic.: 1865-1924), 22 Feb p.4., viewed 07 May 2024, http://nla.gov.au/nla.news-article209580039

1890 'Advertising', The Ballarat Star (Vic.: 1865-1924), 7 Feb, p.1., viewed 20 Feb 2024, http://nla.gov.au/nla.news-article209579367

1890 'Exit King Cobb', Mount Alexander Mail (Vic.: 1854-1917), 27 Nov, p.2., viewed 28 Feb 2024, http://nla.gov.au/nla.news-article199628220

1890 'Exit King Cobb', Mount Alexander Mail (Vic.: 1854-1917), 27 Nov, p.2., viewed 26 Feb 2024, http://nla.gov.au/nla.news-article199628220

1890 'No title', The Ballarat Star (Vic.: 1865-1924), 18 Apr, p.2., viewed 18 Apr 2024, http://nla.gov.au/nla.news-article209582358

1890 'The Phonograph Entertainment.', Bowral Free Press and Berrima District Intelligencer (NSW: 1884-1901), 12 Jul, p.4., viewed 06 Mar 2024, http://nla.gov.au/nla.news-article118282228

1891 'Advertising', Hamilton Spectator (Vic.: 1870-1918), 3 Sep, p.1. (Supplement to the Hamilton Spectator), viewed 09 May 2024, http://nla.gov.au/nla.news-article226079706

1891 'Advertising', The Argus (Melbourne, Vic.: 1848-1957), 28 Mar, p.12., viewed 21 Feb 2024, http://nla.gov.au/nla.news-article8487113

1891 'Entertainment', Nagambie Times (Vic.: 1882-1920), 28 Aug, p.2., viewed 07 Mar 2024, http://nla.gov.au/nla.news-article265361089

1891 'Hamilton Post-Office.', Hamilton Spectator (Vic.: 1870-1918), 22 Sep, p.2. (Supplement to the Hamilton Spectator), viewed 20 Jan 2024, http://nla.gov.au/nla.news-article226082093

1891 'The Omeo Road Again Blocked.', Bairnsdale Advertiser and Tambo and Omeo Chronicle (Vic.: 1882-1946), 17 Sep, p.2., viewed 07 May 2024, http://nla.gov.au/nla.news-article84815945

1892 'Advertising', Hamilton Spectator (Vic.: 1870-1918), 2 Aug, p.1. (Supplement to the Hamilton Spectator), viewed 20 Jan 2024, http://nla.gov.au/nla.news-article226163816

1892 'Odds and Ends.', Northern Star (Lismore, NSW: 1876 - 1954), 16 Jan, p.2., viewed 18 Apr 2024, http://nla.gov.au/nla.news-article71737490

1892 'Walhalla.', The Kerang Times (Vic.: 1889-1901), 12 Jul, p.2., viewed 27 Feb 2024, http://nla.gov.au/nla.news-article221094604

1893 'Advertising', Hamilton Spectator (Vic.: 1870-1918), 8 Aug, p.1. (Supplement to the Hamilton Spectator), viewed 20 Jan 2024, http://nla.gov.au/nla.news-article225176344

1893 'Alleged Larceny From a Livery Stable', Geelong Advertiser (Vic.: 1859-1929), 25 Sep, p.4., viewed 11 Apr 2024, http://nla.gov.au/nla.news-article150750623

1893 'An Accident at Cobb and Co.'s.', National Advocate (Bathurst, NSW: 1889-1954), 23 Mar, p.2., viewed 19 Feb 2024, http://nla.gov.au/nla.news-article156673674

1893 'Castlemaine.', Leader (Melbourne, Vic.: 1862-1918, 1935), 30 Sep, p.32., viewed 28 Feb 2024, http://nla.gov.au/nla.news-article196642404

1893 'Local and General News.', The Ballan Times and Blackwood, Blakeville and Myrniong Standard (Vic.: 1893-1895), 2 Nov, p.3., viewed 12 Apr 2024, http://nla.gov.au/nla.news-article265220194

1893 'Town Talk.', Geelong Advertiser (Vic.: 1859-1929), 19 May, p.2., viewed 12 Apr 2024, http://nla.gov.au/nla.news-article150283030

1894 'Ocean Grove.', Leader (Melbourne, Vic.: 1862-1918, 1935), 22 Dec, p.3. (The Leader Supplement), viewed 15 Feb 2024, http://nla.gov.au/nla.news-article196507091

1894 'Advertising', Coolgardie Miner (WA: 1894-1911), 20 Nov, p.4., viewed 22 Jan 2024, http://nla.gov.au/nla.news-article216257907

1894 'Advertising', Hamilton Spectator (Vic.: 1870-1918), 11 Jan, p.4., viewed 20 Jan 2024, http://nla.gov.au/nla.news-article225785113

1894 'Fire in Malop-Street.', Geelong Advertiser (Vic.: 1859-1929), 31 Jan, p.2., viewed 29 Feb 2024, http://nla.gov.au/nla.news-article150360545

1894 'News And Notes.', The West Australian (Perth, WA: 1879-1954), 26 Sep, p.4., viewed 23 Jan 2024, http://nla.gov.au/nla.news-article3067069

1895 'Advertising', Hamilton Spectator (Vic.: 1870-1918), 5 Jan, p.2. (Supplement to the Hamilton Spectator), viewed 20 Jan 2024, http://nla.gov.au/nla.news-article225865852

1895 'Classified Advertising', The West Australian (Perth, WA: 1879-1954), 11 Sep, p.3., viewed 23 Jan 2024, http://nla.gov.au/nla.news-article4540355

1896 'Advertising', Hamilton Spectator (Vic.: 1870-1918), 24 Oct, p.4., viewed 20 Jan 2024, http://nla.gov.au/nla.news-article225553344

1896 'Cobb and Co.', Weekly Times (Melbourne, Vic.: 1869-1954), 5 Dec, p.9. (Supplement to Weekly Times), viewed 16 Feb 2024, http://nla.gov.au/nla.news-article221123425

1896 'Coolgardie.', Western Mail (Perth, WA: 1885-1954), 2 Oct, p.6., viewed 18 Jan 2024, http://nla.gov.au/nla.news-article33138134

1896 'Harrow.', Hamilton Spectator (Vic.: 1870-1918), 4 Jul, p.3., viewed 21 Feb 2024, http://nla.gov.au/nla.news-article225872891

1896 'Items of News.', Hamilton Spectator (Vic.: 1870-1918), 18 Aug, p.2., viewed 07 May 2024, http://nla.gov.au/nla.news-article225554963

1896 'Local and General.', The Hannan's Herald (Kalgoorlie, WA: 1895-1896), 28 Jul, p.2., viewed 18 Jan 2024, http://nla.gov.au/nla.news-article227993491

1896 'Mounted Rifles.', Portland Guardian (Vic.: 1876-1953), 11 Nov, p.2., viewed 13 May 2024, http://nla.gov.au/nla.news-article63638332

1896 'Omeo Notes.', Upper Murray and Mitta Herald (Vic.: 1885-1955), 27 Aug, p.3., viewed 07 Feb 2024, http://nla.gov.au/nla.news-article268917556

1896 'The Mail Contracts.', Omeo Standard and Mining Gazette (Vic.: 1893-1928), 19 Feb, p.2., viewed 11 Apr 2024, http://nla.gov.au/nla.news-article269739702

1896 'Will of the Late Mr. A. W. Robertson.', The Argus (Melbourne, Vic.: 1848-1957), 15 Oct, p.6., viewed 05 Apr 2024, http://nla.gov.au/nla.news-article9169849

1897 'A Wonderful Coaching Business.', The Western Australian Goldfields Courier (Coolgardie, WA: 1894-1898), 20 Nov, p.12., viewed 24 Jan 2024, http://nla.gov.au/nla.news-article251215036

1897 'Advertising', Hamilton Spectator (Vic.: 1870-1918), 19 Jan, p.4., viewed 20 Jan 2024, http://nla.gov.au/nla.news-article225551672

1897 'Advertising', The Miners' Daily News (Menzies, WA: 1896-1898), 15 Nov, p.3., viewed 18 Jan 2024, http://nla.gov.au/nla.news-article257637667

1897 'Cobb and Co.', Weekly Times (Melbourne, Vic.: 1869-1954), 4 Sep, p.5. (The Weekly Times Special Show Supplement), viewed 16 Apr 2024, http://nla.gov.au/nla.news-article221133626

1897 'The Walhalla Road.', The Narracan Shire Advocate (Vic.: 1889-1923), 29 May, p.3., viewed 27 Feb 2024, http://nla.gov.au/nla.news-article264455833

1898 'Reminiscences of Cobb and Co.', The Riverine Grazier (Hay, NSW: 1873-1954), 14 Jan, p.2., viewed 31 May 2023, http://nla.gov.au/nla.news-article140688564

1898 'Advertising', The Miners' Daily News (Menzies, WA: 1896-1898), 8 Jan, p.3., viewed 23 Jan 2024, http://nla.gov.au/nla.news-article257639183

1899 'A Well-Known Pioneer Mr William Marwick.', The Argonaut (Perth, WA: 1899-1900), 5 Aug, p.3., viewed 23 Jan 2024, http://nla.gov.au/nla.news-article256055186

1899 'Advertising', Hamilton Spectator (Vic.: 1870-1918), 8 Jul, p.4., viewed 20 Jan 2024, http://nla.gov.au/nla.news-article225680407

1899 'Advertising', Kalgoorlie Miner (WA: 1895-1954), 7 Jun, p.1., viewed 23 Jan 2024, http://nla.gov.au/nla.news-article88163726

1899 'Advertising', Norseman Times (WA: 1898-1920), 1 Mar, p.1., viewed 18 Jan 2024, http://nla.gov.au/nla.news-article149772019

1899 'Advertising', The North Coolgardie Herald and Miners Daily News (Menzies, WA: 1899-1904), 7 Jun, p.4., viewed 23 Jan 2024, http://nla.gov.au/nla.news-article259942117

1899 'Court Horn.', The Ballarat Star (Vic.: 1865-1924), 14 Jun p.4., viewed 04 May 2024, http://nla.gov.au/nla.news-article215326259

1899 'Death of Mr John M'Phee.', The Avoca Mail (Vic.: 1863-1900; 1915-1918), 3 Nov, p.2., viewed 25 Feb 2024, http://nla.gov.au/nla.news-article202695184

1900 'Advertising', Geelong Advertiser (Vic.: 1859-1929), 1 Aug, p.1., viewed 20 Feb 2024, http://nla.gov.au/nla.news-article150143107

1900 'Advertising', Hamilton Spectator (Vic.: 1870-1918), 21 Aug, p.1. (Supplement to the Hamilton Spectator), viewed 20 Jan 2024, http://nla.gov.au/nla.news-article225692086; 22 Nov, p.1. (Supplement to the Hamilton Spectator), viewed 20 Jan 2024, http://nla.gov.au/nla.news-article225690771

1900 'Advertising', The Age (Melbourne, Vic.: 1854-1954), 2 Jan, p.3., viewed 08 Feb 2024 http://nla.gov.au/nla.news-article196023159

1900 'Cobb and Co.', Weekly Times (Melbourne, Vic.: 1869-1954), 1 Dec, p.1. (Supplement to the Weekly Times), viewed 01 Mar 2024, http://nla.gov.au/nla.news-article223441045

1900 'Cobb and Co.', Weekly Times (Melbourne, Vic.: 1869-1954), 1 Dec, p.2. (Supplement To The Weekly Times), viewed 16 Feb 2024, http://nla.gov.au/nla.news-article223441045

1900 'Daylesford.', Weekly Times (Melbourne, Vic.: 1869-1954), 1 Dec, p.43., viewed 22 Apr 2024, http://nla.gov.au/nla.news-article223441005

1900 'News and Notes.', The Evening Star (Boulder, WA: 1898-1921), 14 Mar, p.2., viewed 18 Jan 2024, http://nla.gov.au/nla.news-article202831825

1900 'No Title', Hamilton Spectator (Vic.: 1870-1918), 6 Nov, p.2., viewed 16 Feb 2024, http://nla.gov.au/nla.news-article225692030

1900 'Norseman.', Kalgoorlie Miner (WA: 1895-1954), 25 Dec, p.3., viewed 18 Jan 2024, http://nla.gov.au/nla.news-article88497802

1900 'The Poet's Corner', The Western Champion and General Advertiser for the Central-Western Districts (Barcaldine, Qld.: 1892-1922), 20 Nov, p.10., viewed 21 Feb 2024, http://nla.gov.au/nla.news-article76564309

1900 'Walhalla.', The Gippsland Farmers' Journal (Traralgon, Vic.: 1893-1905; 1914-1922), 5 Oct, p.4., viewed 08 Feb 2024, http://nla.gov.au/nla.news-article264385628

1900 'Work at Norseman.', Kalgoorlie Miner (WA: 1895-1954), 7 Feb, p.4., viewed 18 Jan 2024, http://nla.gov.au/nla.news-article88400502

1901 'Advertising', Geelong Advertiser (Vic.: 1859-1929), 3 Apr, p.1., viewed 07 May 2024, http://nla.gov.au/nla.news-article147716101

1901 'Advertising', Hamilton Spectator (Vic.: 1870-1918), 15 Jan, p.2. (Supplement to the Hamilton Spectator), viewed 20 Jan 2024, http://nla.gov.au/nla.news-article226083762

1901 'Death of Mr John Wagner.', Geelong Advertiser (Vic.: 1859-1929), 29 Jan, p.2., viewed 01 Jun 2023, http://nla.gov.au/nla.news-article147712112

1901 'Family Notices', Geelong Advertiser (Vic.: 1859-1929), 15 Nov, p.1., viewed 20 Feb 2024, http://nla.gov.au/nla.news-article150295960

1901 'Norseman.', Kalgoorlie Western Argus (WA: 1896-1916), 15 Jan, p.29., viewed 18 Jan 2024, http://nla.gov.au/nla.news-article32204768

1901 'Norseman.', Western Mail (Perth, WA: 1885-1954), 25 Dec, p.65., viewed 22 Jan 2024, http://nla.gov.au/nla.news-article33217445

1902 'My Life in Many States and in Foreign Lands.', Train, George Francis. Pp. Xxi. 340. D. Appleton: New York. SR 910.4 T768. Available from: The National Library of Australia

1902 'A Ballad for Cobb and Co.', Table Talk (Melbourne, Vic.: 1885 - 1939), 15 May, p.15., viewed 22 Feb 2024, http://nla.gov.au/nla.news-article145706871

1902 'Country News.', The Argus (Melbourne, Vic.: 1848-1957), 14 Jan, p.6., viewed 20 Feb 2024, http://nla.gov.au/nla.news-article9624032

1902 'Norseman Notes.', Kalgoorlie Miner (WA: 1895-1954), 11 Jun, p.6., viewed 22 Jan 2024, http://nla.gov.au/nla.news-article88707145

1902 'Norseman.', Kalgoorlie Miner (WA: 1895-1954), 1 Nov, p.5., viewed 18 Jan 2024, http://nla.gov.au/nla.news-article88762654

1903 'Cobb and Co.', Windsor and Richmond Gazette (NSW: 1888-1965), 10 Jan, p.1., viewed 11 Apr 2024, http://nla.gov.au/nla.news-article86217886

1904 '[?]s in Brief.', Weekly Times (Melbourne, Vic.: 1869-1954), 2 Apr, p.15., viewed 22 Jan 2024, http://nla.gov.au/nla.news-article222791690

1904 'A Day with Cobb & Co.', The Sydney Stock and Station Journal (NSW: 1896 - 1924), 2 Sep, p.12., viewed 12 Apr 2024, http://nla.gov.au/nla.news-article121569499

1904 'Country Sketcher.', The Australasian (Melbourne, Vic.: 1864-1946), 8 Oct, p.50., viewed 12 Apr 2024, http://nla.gov.au/nla.news-article139119929

1904 'Death of Mr. G. F. Train.', The Register (Adelaide, SA: 1901-1929), 21 Jan, p.6., viewed 20 Jun 2023, http://nla.gov.au/nla.news-article55688107

1904 'No Title', The Narracan Shire Advocate (Vic.: 1889-1923), 26 Apr, p.2., viewed 2 Mar 2024, http://nla.gov.au/nla.news-article256343209

1905 'Obituary.', The McIvor Times and Rodney Advertiser (Heathcote, Vic.: 1863-1918), 19 January, p.3., viewed 18 May 2024, http://nla.gov.au/nla.news-article87328913

1905 'Snow in Melbourne.', Mount Alexander Mail (Vic.: 1854-1917), 26 Sep, p.3., viewed 06 Mar 2024, http://nla.gov.au/nla.news-article200711214

1906 'Advertising', The Ballarat Star (Vic.: 1865-1924), 13 Nov, p.1., viewed 19 Feb 2024, http://nla.gov.au/nla.news-article206490938

1906 'Cobb and Co.'s Excursions.', The Ballarat Star (Vic.: 1865-1924), 7 Mar, p.1., viewed 01 Mar 2024, http://nla.gov.au/nla.news-article209228992

1906 'Death of an Old Coach Driver.', The Age (Melbourne, Vic.: 1854-1954), 20 Jan, p.12., viewed 08 Feb 2024, http://nla.gov.au/nla.news-article196324353

1906 'Death of Mr. Archie Grant.', The Narracan Shire Advocate (Vic.: 1889-1923), 23 Jan, p.3., viewed 08 Feb 2024, http://nla.gov.au/nla.news-article256347997

1906 'Leonora-Lawlers Mail.', East Murchison News (WA: 1901-1911), 3 Feb, p.2., viewed 23 Jan 2024, http://nla.gov.au/nla.news-article253577521

1906 'Obituary.', Bendigo Advertiser (Vic.: 1855-1918), 1 Oct, p.5., viewed 27 Feb 2024, http://nla.gov.au/nla.news-article89557754

1906 'Veteran Of The Turf.', The Herald (Melbourne, Vic.: 1861-1954), 19 Oct, p.6., viewed 17 Feb 2024, http://nla.gov.au/nla.

news-article242557665

1906 'Wiluna.', The Geraldton Express (WA: 1906-1928), 12 Mar, p.3., viewed 22 Jan 2024, http://nla.gov.au/nla.news-article210732709

1907 'Advertising', Murchison Advocate (WA: 1898-1912), 18 May, p.3., viewed 24 Jan 2024, http://nla.gov.au/nla.news-article213843185

1907 'Advertising', The Ballarat Star (Vic.: 1865-1924), 24 Jun, p.1., viewed 19 Feb 2024, http://nla.gov.au/nla.news-article211063187

1907 'Messrs Cobb and Co', Morning Bulletin (Rockhampton, Qld.: 1878-1954), 18 Mar, p.4., viewed 18 Apr 2024, http://nla.gov.au/nla.news-article53093071

1907 'News Items.', Murchison Advocate (WA: 1898-1912), 1 Jun, p.2., viewed 24 Jan 2024, http://nla.gov.au/nla.news-article213841962

1908 'Original Poetry.', The Australasian (Melbourne, Vic.: 1864-1946), 25 Jan, p.51., viewed 21 Feb 2024, http://nla.gov.au/nla.news-article139208276

1908 'Advertising', The Ballarat Star (Vic.: 1865-1924), 8 Aug, p.6., viewed 19 Feb 2024, http://nla.gov.au/nla.news-article218555834

1908 'Drag Excursions.', Geelong Advertiser (Vic.: 1859-1929), 4 Sep, p.3., viewed 15 Feb 2024, http://nla.gov.au/nla.news-article148560103

1908 'Fight with a Tiger Snake.', Worker (Brisbane, Qld.: 1890-1955), 14 Mar, p.15., viewed 11 Apr 2024, http://nla.gov.au/nla.news-article70870241

1908 'From Squatter's Boy to Squatter King.', Barrier Miner (Broken Hill, NSW: 1888-1954), 1 Apr, p.3., viewed 24 Jan 2024, http://nla.gov.au/nla.news-article45036758

1910 'Sandstone Topics.', The Sun (Kalgoorlie, WA: 1898-1929), 2 Oct, p.7., viewed 23 Jan 2024, http://nla.gov.au/nla.news-article211139394

1910 'Advertising', The Argus (Melbourne, Vic.: 1848-1957), 2 Feb, p.16., viewed 08 May 2024, http://nla.gov.au/nla.news-article10831519

1911 'In The Days of Cobb & Co.', Advocate (Melbourne, Vic.: 1868-1954), 11 Feb, p.35., viewed 21 Feb 2024, http://nla.gov.au/nla.news-article170923243

1911 'Kilmore Electric Supply Co. Ltd.', Kilmore Free Press (Kilmore, Vic.: 1870-1954), 24 Aug, p.3. (Morning.), viewed 07 Feb 2024, http://nla.gov.au/nla.news-article58277119

1912 'Advertising', Geelong Advertiser (Vic.: 1859-1929), 28 Sep, p.6., viewed 08 May 2024, http://nla.gov.au/nla.news-article150114569

1912 'A Funny Story.', Chronicle (Adelaide, SA: 1895-1954), 8 Jun, p.21., viewed 11 Apr 2024, http://nla.gov.au/nla.news-article88699036

1912 'Coach Fares.', Geelong Advertiser (Vic.: 1859-1929), 1 Jun, p.10., viewed 16 Feb 2024, http://nla.gov.au/nla.news-article148714473

1912 'Fire in a Bus.', Geelong Advertiser (Vic.: 1859-1929), 15 Jan, p.2., viewed 02 Mar 2024, http://nla.gov.au/nla.news-article149234842

1913 'Cobb's and a Legal Puzzle', Geelong Advertiser (Vic.: 1859-1929), 2 April, p.4., viewed 13 May 2024, http://nla.gov.au/nla.news-article150677518

1913 'Livery Stable Wages.', The Ballarat Star (Vic.: 1865-1924), 21 Jun, p.3., viewed 11 Apr 2024, http://nla.gov.au/nla.news-article217967491

1913 'Pioneering in Western Victoria.', Hamilton Spectator (Vic.: 1870-1918), 19 Jun, p.3., viewed 19 Jan 2024, http://nla.gov.au/nla.news-article225031070

1914 'Advertising', Geelong Advertiser (Vic.: 1859-1929), 1 Apr, p.1., viewed 24 Feb 2024, http://nla.gov.au/nla.news-article120211074

1914 'Advertising', The Argus (Melbourne, Vic.: 1848-1957), 17 Jan, p.23., viewed 19 Feb 2024, http://nla.gov.au/nla.news-article7231505

1915 'Daylesford Telephone Exchange.', Daylesford Advocate, Yandoit, Glenlyon and Eganstown Chronicle (Vic.: 1914-1918), 3 Aug, p.1., viewed 16 Feb 2024, http://nla.gov.au/nla.news-article119536934

1915 'Drang Axle Breaks.', Geelong Advertiser (Vic.: 1859-1929), 26 Jan, p.3., viewed 11 Apr 2024, http://nla.gov.au/nla.news-article120930057

1915 'Mr. Charles Watt.', Benalla Standard (Vic.: 1901-1940), 8 Jan, p.3., viewed 16 Apr 2024, http://nla.gov.au/nla.news-article155586237

1916 'Cobb & Co.'s Kindness.', Geelong Advertiser (Vic.: 1859-1929), 7 Nov, p.4., viewed 21 Feb 2024, http://nla.gov.au/nla.news-article130668582

1916 'Personal.', The Wingham Chronicle and Manning River Observer (NSW: 1898-1954), 11 Mar, p.6., viewed 07 May 2024, http://nla.gov.au/nla.news-article166787309

1916 'Sandstone.', Mount Magnet Miner and Lennonville Leader (WA: 1896-1926), 26 Feb, p.2., viewed 23 Jan 2024, http://nla.gov.au/nla.news-article156313863

1917 'Advertising', Geelong Advertiser (Vic.: 1859 - 1929), 19 December, p. 6., viewed 26 May 2024, http://nla.gov.au/nla.news-article119704689

1917 'Classified Advertising', The Argus (Melbourne, Vic.: 1848 - 1957), 3 January, p. 1., viewed 26 May 2024, http://nla.gov.au/nla.news-article1589259

1917 'Cobb & Co.'s Stables On Fire.', Daylesford Advocate, Yandoit, Glenlyon and Eganstown Chronicle (Vic.: 1914-1918), 23 Nov, p.3., viewed 21 Feb 2024, http://nla.gov.au/nla.news-article119559183

1917 'No title', The Riverine Grazier (Hay, NSW: 1873-1954), 4 Sep, p.2., viewed 21 Feb 2024, http://nla.gov.au/nla.news-article140385807

1917 'Outbreak Of Fire', The Ballarat Courier (Vic.: 1869-1886; 1914-1918), 22 Nov p.5. (Daily.), viewed 01 Mar 2024, http://nla.gov.au/nla.news-article73335651

1917 'The Cobb Cable.', Geelong Advertiser (Vic.: 1859-1929), 11 Aug, p.2., viewed 21 Feb 2024, http://nla.gov.au/nla.news-article119723381

1918 'Advertising', Geelong Advertiser (Vic.: 1859 - 1929), 23 March, p. 1., viewed 26 May 2024, http://nla.gov.au/nla.news-article119713935

1918 'How Rabbits came to Victoria.', Daylesford Advocate, Yandoit, Glenlyon and Eganstown Chronicle (Vic.: 1914-1918), 17 Sep, p.2., viewed 08 May 2024, http://nla.gov.au/nla.news-article119561212

1918 'The Old Coaching Days.', Daylesford Advocate, Yandoit, Glenlyon and Eganstown Chronicle (Vic.: 1914-1918), 10 Sep, p.3., viewed 15 Apr 2024, http://nla.gov.au/nla.news-article119561159

1919 'Cobb and Co.'s Changes Hands.', Geelong Advertiser (Vic.: 1859-1929), 12 Dec, p.2., viewed 21 Feb 2024, http://nla.gov.au/nla.news-article165411235

1919 'Country News.', Geelong Advertiser (Vic.: 1859-1929), 16 Dec, p.5., viewed 16 Feb 2024, http://nla.gov.au/nla.news-article165406295

1920 'Advertising', Geelong Advertiser (Vic.: 1859 - 1929), 6 February, p. 1., viewed 26 May 2024, http://nla.gov.au/nla.news-article165419368

1920 'Stories of the Cobb & Co. Coaching Days.', Sunday Times (Sydney, NSW: 1895-1930), 19 Dec, p.18., viewed 14 Oct 2022, http://nla.gov.au/nla.news-article120522761

1920 'Advertising', Geelong Advertiser (Vic.: 1859-1929), 9 Apr, p.1., viewed 10 May 2024, http://nla.gov.au/nla.news-article165420608

1920 'Advertising', Geelong Advertiser (Vic.: 1859-1929), 17 Apr, p.1., viewed 10 May 2024, http://nla.gov.au/nla.news-article165421821

1920 'Culled Verse.', Worker (Brisbane, Qld.: 1890-1955), 5 Feb, p.3., viewed 24 Apr 2024, http://nla.gov.au/nla.news-article71049493

1921 'Classified Advertising', The Argus (Melbourne, Vic.: 1848-1957), 19 Feb, p.5., viewed 25 Feb 2024, http://nla.gov.au/nla.news-article1737210

1921 'Cobb and Co., Ltd.', The Daily Telegraph (Sydney, NSW: 1883-1930), 14 Nov, p.9., viewed 11 Apr 2024, http://nla.gov.au/nla.news-article239708631

1921 'Commercial.', Geelong Advertiser (Vic.: 1859-1929), 12 Mar, p.8., viewed 16 Feb 2024, http://nla.gov.au/nla.news-article165756654

1921 'Geelong.', The Ballarat Star (Vic.: 1865-1924), 23 Feb, p.6., viewed 21 Feb 2024, http://nla.gov.au/nla.news-article212711686

1921 'Geelong.', The Ballarat Star (Vic.: 1865-1924), 23 Feb, p.6., viewed 01 Mar 2024, http://nla.gov.au/nla.news-article212711686

1922 'Cobb and Co.', The Gundagai Independent and Pastoral, Agricultural and Mining Advocate (NSW: 1898-1928), 9 February, p.4., viewed 10 May 2024, http://nla.gov.au/nla.news-article121497241

1922 'Old Coaching Days.', The Argus (Melbourne, Vic.: 1848-1957), 10 Jun, p.7., viewed 06 Aug 2021, http://nla.gov.au/nla

1922 'Classified Advertising', The Argus (Melbourne, Vic.: 1848-1957), 15 Apr, p.2., viewed 19 Feb 2024, http://nla.gov.au/nla.news-article4665779

1922 'Cobb and Co.', Morning Bulletin (Rockhampton, Qld.: 1878-1954), 20 Jun, p.13., viewed 05 May 2024, http://nla.gov.au/nla.news-article54018319

1922 'Cobb and Co.', Portland Guardian (Vic.: 1876-1953), 5 Jun, p.1. (Evening.), viewed 16 Apr 2024, http://nla.gov.au/nla.news-article64026004

1922 'Story of Cobb and Co.', The Argus

(Melbourne, Vic.: 1848-1957), 20 May, p.5., viewed 24 Feb 2024, http://nla.gov.au/nla.news-article4643657

1922 'The Pioneers.', West Gippsland Gazette (Warragul, Vic.: 1898 - 1930), 28 Feb, p.3. (MORNING.), viewed 02 May 2024, http://nla.gov.au/nla.news-article68625607

1923 'Advertising', Geelong Advertiser (Vic.: 1859-1929), 1 Dec, p.1., viewed 15 Feb 2024, http://nla.gov.au/nla.news-article165982983

1924 'Melbourne in 1854', Labor Call (Melbourne, Vic.: 1906-1953), 18 Dec, p.8., viewed 12 Feb 2024, http://nla.gov.au/nla.news-article250083953

1924 'Good-Bye to Cobb & Co.', The Cessnock Eagle and South Maitland Recorder (NSW: 1913-1954), 5 Sep, p.4., viewed 22 Feb 2024, http://nla.gov.au/nla.news-article99376376

1924 'The Last Coach', The Week (Brisbane, Qld.: 1876-1934), 5 Sep, p.16., viewed 09 Apr 2024, http://nla.gov.au/nla.news-article187198700

1925 'Advertising', Geelong Advertiser (Vic.: 1859-1929), 18 Nov, p.2., viewed 15 Feb 2024, http://nla.gov.au/nla.news-article207872976

1925 'Coaching in the Commonwealth', Sunday Times (Perth, WA: 1902-1954), 17 May, p.9., viewed 16 Apr 2024, http://nla.gov.au/nla.news-article58258535

1925 'Early Melbourne', The News (Hobart, Tas.: 1924-1925), 7 Dec, p.6. (Final Edition), viewed 06 Mar 2024, http://nla.gov.au/nla.news-article233583354

1925 'Shadow of Cobb & Co.', The Voice of the North (NSW: 1918-1933), 10 Sep, p.18., viewed 14 Apr 2024, http://nla.gov.au/nla.news-article112244413

1925 'The Last Of Its Kind', The Herald (Melbourne, Vic.: 1861-1954), 4 Apr, p.4., viewed 10 May 2024, http://nla.gov.au/nla.news-article243766454

1926 'Australasian News in a Nutshell', Weekly Times (Melbourne, Vic.: 1869-1954), 6 Feb, p.8., viewed 22 Feb 2024, http://nla.gov.au/nla.news-article223316286

1927 'Cobb and Co. Link Going', The Sun News-Pictorial (Melbourne, Vic.: 1922-1954; 1956), 10 Feb, p.8., viewed 01 Mar 2024, http://nla.gov.au/nla.news-article274897184

1928 '72-Year-Old Hotel Closes Down', The Sun News-Pictorial (Melbourne, Vic.: 1922-1954; 1956), 10 Jan, p.15., viewed 22 Apr 2024, http://nla.gov.au/nla.news-article275339730

1928 'End of Cobb and Co.', The Gundagai Independent (NSW: 1928-1954), 15 Nov, p.2., viewed 18 Apr 2024, http://nla.gov.au/nla.news-article130881439

1928 'End of Cobb and Co.', The Gundagai Independent (NSW: 1928-1954), 15 Nov, p.2., viewed 12 Apr 2024, http://nla.gov.au/nla.news-article130881439

1928 'In the Day's of Cobb & Co.', The Bacchus Marsh Express (Vic.: 1866-1943), 23 Jun, p.3., viewed 02 Mar 2024, http://nla.gov.au/nla.news-article262279089

1928 'Mails by Camel.', Observer (Adelaide, SA: 1905-1931), 23 Jun, p.36., viewed 12 Apr 2024, http://nla.gov.au/nla.news-article164883887

1928 'Obituary', Ovens and Murray Advertiser (Beechworth, Vic.: 1855; 1857-1890; 1892-1955), 3 Oct, p.2., viewed 21 Apr 2024, http://nla.gov.au/nla.news-article268217931

1928 'Tavern Names.', The Argus (Melbourne, Vic.: 1848-1957), 29 Dec, p.8. (The Argus. Saturday Camera Supplement.), viewed 17 Feb 2024, http://nla.gov.au/nla.news-article3977955

1928 'Those Were The Days!', The Herald (Melbourne, Vic.: 1861-1954), 8 May, p.6., viewed 09 May 2024, http://nla.gov.au/nla.news-article243987674

1929 'In the Days of Cobb and Co.', The Argus (Melbourne, Vic.: 1848-1957), 15 May, p.11., viewed 08 Feb 2024, http://nla.gov.au/nla.news-article4006032

1929 'Out Among the People', The Register News-Pictorial (Adelaide, SA: 1929-1931), 29 Jul, p.6., viewed 12 Apr 2024, http://nla.gov.au/nla.news-article53484286

1929 'Talkie Entertainment', The Herald (Melbourne, Vic.: 1861-1954), 12 Jan, p.28., viewed 07 Mar 2024, http://nla.gov.au/nla.news-article244015928

1931 'Cobb and Co.', The Brisbane Courier (Qld.: 1864-1933), 23 Oct, p.10., viewed 18 Apr 2024, http://nla.gov.au/nla.news-article21737029

1933 'Alexandra's Early Days.', Alexandra and Yea Standard and Yarck, Gobur, Thornton and Acheron Express (Vic.: 1908-1949), 6 Oct, p.2., viewed 28 Apr 2024, http://nla.gov.au/nla.news-article64725104

1933 'Cobb & Co.', Glen Innes Examiner (NSW: 1908-1954), 12 Jan, p.6., viewed 01 Mar 2024, http://nla.gov.au/nla.news-article183563707

1933 'The Mail Boys of Other Days.', The Age (Melbourne, Vic.: 1854-1954), 1 Jul, p.6., viewed 07 Feb 2024, http://nla.gov.au/nla.news-article204379254

1934 'A Pioneer Comes to Town', The Argus (Melbourne, Vic.: 1848-1957), 8 Sep, p.9., viewed 05 May 2024, http://nla.gov.au/nla.news-article10975595

1934 'Coaching Days', Kilmore Free Press (Kilmore, Vic.: 1870-1954), 20 Dec, p.4. (Morning), viewed 28 Apr 2024, http://nla.gov.au/nla.news-article58079548

1934 'Old Stables Burnt', The Argus (Melbourne, Vic.: 1848-1957), 22 May, p.8., viewed 01 Mar 2024, http://nla.gov.au/nla.news-article10939113

1934 'The Coach's Story.', The Age (Melbourne, Vic.: 1854-1954), 2 Jun, p.4., viewed 08 Apr 2024, http://nla.gov.au/nla.news-article204825626

1936 'Obituary.', The Age (Melbourne, Vic.: 1854-1954), 5 Feb, p.8., viewed 01 Mar 2024, http://nla.gov.au/nla.news-article205238180

1937 'a [?] Drive', The Australasian (Melbourne, Vic.: 1864-1946), 31 Jul, p.7., viewed 12 Oct 2022, http://nla.gov.au/nla.newsarticle141807670

1937 'Gossip', Smith's Weekly (Sydney, NSW: 1919-1950), 8 May, p.13., viewed 28 Feb 2024, http://nla.gov.au/nla.news-article235900746

1937 'Kerang Pioneer Dead', Weekly Times (Melbourne, Vic.: 1869-1954), 3 Jul, p.7. (First Edition), viewed 07 Feb 2024, http://nla.gov.au/nla.news-article225717872

1938 'Cr. Vines Dies Suddenly', The Sun News-Pictorial (Melbourne, Vic.: 1922-1954; 1956), 16 May, p.34., viewed 21 Feb 2024, http://nla.gov.au/nla.news-article277671491

1938 'Merriwa and District News', The Muswellbrook Chronicle (NSW: 1898 - 1955), 26 Aug, p.6., viewed 22 Feb 2024, http://nla.gov.au/nla.news-article107617171

1941 'Memories and Musings', Advocate (Melbourne, Vic.: 1868-1954), 22 May, p.14., viewed 25 Feb 2024, http://nla.gov.au/nla.news-article172192085

1942 'Black Thursday', Portland Guardian (Vic.: 1876-1953), 5 Feb, p.3. (Evening), viewed 12 Feb 2024, http://nla.gov.au/nla.news-article64378799

1942 'The Church and the People', The Age (Melbourne, Vic.: 1854-1954), 18 Jun, p.3., viewed 15 Apr 2024, http://nla.gov.au/nla.news-article206813531

1944 'Death of Mr. George Wells', Western Grazier (Wilcannia, NSW: 1896-1951), 27 Oct, p.1., viewed 07 Aug 2022, http://nla.gov.au/nla.news-article139554470

1946 'Shades of Cobb and Co.', Standard (Frankston, Vic.: 1939-1949), 16 May, p.1., viewed 14 Apr 2024, http://nla.gov.au/nla.news-article75057590

1947 'First Coach', The Norseman-Esperance News (WA: 1936-1954), 20 Jun, p.2. (Modern Weekly news magazine), viewed 09 Apr 2024, http://nla.gov.au/nla.news-article258588699

1948 'Historic Firm Recalled', Brisbane Telegraph (Qld.: 1948-1954), 30 Nov, p.6. (STUMPS), viewed 18 Apr 2024, http://nla.gov.au/nla.news-article216566865

1948 'The time has come . . .', Gippsland Times (Vic.: 1861-1954), 1 Mar, p.4., viewed 15 Apr 2024, http://nla.gov.au/nla.news-article63284872

1948-1949 'Annual report and balance sheet / Cobb & Co.'s Old Coach Drivers' Association.' Cobb & Co.'s Old Coach Drivers' Association. [Mont Albert, Vic.] : The Association. 1948-1949

1950 'Cobb & Co. Old Drivers', Kilmore Free Press (Kilmore, Vic.: 1870-1954), 2 Nov, p.5., viewed 01 Mar 2024, http://nla.gov.au/nla.news-article58211771

1951 'In the Days of Cobb & Co.', Narromine News and Trangie Advocate (NSW: 1898-1955), 19 Jan, p.2., viewed 13 Apr 2024, http://nla.gov.au/nla.news-article100191539

1953 'Drove Coaches for Cobb & Co.', Examiner (Launceston, Tas.: 1900-1954), 3 Mar, p.7., viewed 09 Apr 2024, http://nla.gov.au/nla.news-article61079564

1953 'Remembers when had Cobb and Co. Stable', The Horsham Times (Vic.: 1882-1954), 14 Oct, p.2., viewed 02 Mar 2024, http://nla.gov.au/nla.news-article72773685

1954 'Stamp A Tribute To Pioneer', Collie Mail (Perth, WA: 1908-1954), 29 Apr, p.14. (Paper format edition), viewed 16 Apr 2024, http://nla.gov.au/nla.news-article258844660

Index

A. Butler 64, 65, 84, 178, 179, 180, 181, 182, 183, 184
Accidents 6, 11, 32, 71, 73, 74, 84, 102, 122, 124, 125, 134, 156, 157, 158, 160, 161, 174, 176, 177

Advertising:
Ayer's Hair Vigor 125
Ayer's Sarsaparilla 135
Bad Legs and Bad Breasts 68
Best Meat Pie 123
Braceless Trousers 85
Cabbage Tree Hats 84
Clarke's World-Famed Blood Mixture 157
French Corsets 135
Geelong Sea Bathing Company Baths 104
John Creed, Carpenter and Undertaker 122
Lux 143
Marriages Celebrated 136
Money to Lend 135
Prepared Liquid Glue 104
Smith's Patent Crinoline Hats 84
Tobacco 30, 104

Agents:
Blake, James J. 84, 178, 179, 180
Brayton, E. J. 104, 184, 191
Britton, J. F. 64, 67, 178
Britton, John F. 178
Burrall, Joseph 84, 179
Butler/Anthony Butler, A. 64, 65, 84, 178, 179, 180, 181, 182, 183, 184
Butler, N. L. 178, 179, 181, 182, 183, 184
Clapp, G. B. 180
Clapp, O. B. 67, 84, 179, 180
Connoll, J. M. 67
Cook and Son 136, 157, 194, 195
Covington, A. B. 177, 178, 179
Cranstoune and Simson 194
Crowley, J. 65
Crowley, John 178, 179
Flahive, W. 194
Foley, E. J. 181
Foley, E. T. 33, 65, 180, 182, 184
Gallass, K. 123, 192
Gardiner, J. 178, 179
Gardiner, John 177
Gordon, C. R. 180
Haycock, George W. 30, 31, 84, 175, 177, 178
Hay, James 67
Heffernan and Crowley 84, 102, 180, 181, 182
Huddart, Parker and Co. 194, 195
Hutchinson, M. L. 194, 195
Jackson, P. W. 67, 157
Jones, Wm. 67
Kearney & Co. 124, 192, 193
Lamber, I. B. 31, 84
Lamont, J. 184
Larkin, P. 194
Lowe, Jas. 190
Mackenzie, W. 194
McMillian, E. D. 122, 123, 191
Miller, C. W. B. 179
Millie, H. T. 67
Mitchell, W. R. 180, 181, 182
Montegani, A. 67
Newton, T. K. 31, 32, 84, 178
Niven and Co. 194, 195
Niven, F. W. 65, 194
Peck, J. M. 157, 179, 180
Pollack, Chas. D. 65, 67, 102, 182, 183
Roberts, C. 193
Rogers, F. J. 31, 84, 103
Shepard, A. D. 181
Stevenson, W. 186
Stewart, Andrew 192
Stodart, J. W. 186
Sweeney, J. F. 65, 84, 179, 180, 181, 182, 183, 184, 185, 186
Teasdale, B. 68, 185, 195
Tillyer, George 122, 190
Tucker, J. 123, 187
Vines, A. 194, 195
Watts, J. 194
White, L. 136, 195

Airey's Inlet 77, 132, 133, 136, 142, 143, 194, 195
Alexandra College for Ladies 45
Allanford 43
American Civil War 71
American Telegraph Line of Coaches 11
Amherst/Daisy Hill 83, 94, 95, 96, 97, 98, 99, 100, 101, 112, 113, 180, 183, 184, 185, 186, 187, 188, 189
Anakie Hills 10
Anderson, Charles 57, 75
Anderson & M'Phee 56, 57
Anderson's Creek 10

Anecdotes:
Ancient money 161
Big coach load of rushers 73
Brilliant meteor 161
Courting by telephone 123
Fight with a tiger snake 136
Fluttering washing 122
Gored by a cow 160
Groom's fortune 104
Horses bolted 73
How rabbits came to Victoria 144
Jockey's ride 31
Kangaroo dogs 30
Larceny from a livery stable 135
Loss of the finger 158
Mail robbery 85
Not safe in a box in his bedroom 161
On the box seat 166
Phonograph entertainment 31
Pig dealers 102
Playing the bugle 136
Plum pudding for the prisoners 156
Poisoning 84
Prolific Goat 157
Puffing of the smoke 156
Returned soldier welcomed 158
Running of the greyhounds 65
Sir Charles Kingsford-Smith 160
Smoky Dawson 160
Splinter in thumb 161
Surgical operation 102
The domestic economy 124
The rotten egg trade 136
Trip to Omeo 134
Under the hat 143
'Up with the Union Jack' 71
Violent assault 103

Anglesea 77, 120, 132, 133, 136, 142, 143, 157, 193, 194, 195
Antimony 10
Ararat 10, 11, 43, 47, 67, 68, 82, 83, 84, 94, 95, 96, 97, 98, 99, 100, 101, 103, 104, 112, 113, 114, 115, 118, 123, 125, 156, 160, 161, 176, 179, 180, 181, 182, 183, 184, 185, 186, 187, 188, 189, 190, 191, 192
Ascot/Coghill's Creek 74, 95, 97, 98, 99, 100, 101, 112, 113, 185, 186, 187, 188, 189
Australian Bone Mill Company 122
Australian Stage Company 54, 55, 65, 68, 94, 95, 96, 97, 98, 99, 100, 103, 156, 160, 182, 183, 184, 185, 186, 187
Australian Wines 135
Avoca 10, 41, 43, 82, 83, 84, 94, 95, 96, 97, 98, 99, 100, 101, 112, 113, 117, 119, 123, 130, 131, 134, 156, 161, 179, 180, 181, 182, 183, 184, 185, 186, 187, 188, 189, 190, 191, 192, 193
Baby Blakes 28
Bacchus Marsh 41, 43, 73, 77, 82, 83, 95, 96, 97, 101, 112, 113, 116, 117, 118, 119, 120, 121, 123, 130, 156, 160, 161, 179, 181, 183, 184, 185, 188, 189, 191, 192, 193
Bairnsdale 43, 100, 104, 119, 120, 121, 124, 125, 131, 134, 135, 192, 193, 194
Ballaarat 64, 65
Ballarat 55, 67, 75
Ballarat Stage Company 55
Barkly/Navarre 47, 96, 97, 98, 99, 100, 185, 186, 187, 188
Barthelomew. I. T. 61
Barwon Heads 74, 77, 130, 131, 132, 133, 134, 135, 136, 142, 143, 157, 159, 193, 194, 195
Bathurst 4
Baw Baw mountains 85
Beechworth 10, 43, 45, 47, 69, 70, 82, 84, 85, 102, 145, 147, 157, 178, 179, 180, 193
Belfast/Port Fairy 10, 43, 68, 83, 84, 94, 95, 96, 97, 98, 99, 100, 101, 102, 104, 112, 113, 114, 115, 116, 117, 118, 119, 120, 121, 122, 124, 130, 131, 142, 157, 160, 161, 181, 182, 183, 184, 185, 186, 187, 188, 189, 190, 191, 192, 193, 195
Bendigo 54, 68, 70
Bendigo Creek 41
Black Forest 26, 43
Blake, Arthur Lincoln 54, 65, 67, 186
Blake, James Joseph 54, 67
Bock, John 61

Booking Offices & Departure Places:
Apsley, Border Inn 190
Apsley, Botterill's Hotel 187
Ararat, Shamrock Hotel 67
Ararat, Tusons's Hotel 125
Avoca, Avoca Hotel 192
Back Creek, Commercial Hotel 102
Bairnsdale, Club Hotel 193
Ballaarat, Bath's Hotel 64, 178, 179
Bull and Mouth, [Ballarat ?] 32, 64, 84, 178
Camperdown, Leura Hotel 188
Castlemaine, Victoria Hotel 84, 179, 180, 181, 184
Dandenong, Bowman's Hotel 183
Deniliquin, Taylor's Royal Hotel 186
Duchess of Kent Hotel 102, 184
Dunolly, Bendigo Hotel 102
Echuca, Iron's Bridge Hotel 186
Echuca, Martin's Commercial Hotel 193
Geelong, Criterion Coach Office, Moorabool-street 179
Geelong, Exchange 184
Geelong, Union Hotel 187
George Hotels 102, 182, 183
George Lester's 184
Hamilton, General Booking Office 122, 187, 190
Heathcote Hotel 119, 120, 124, 192, 193
Inglewood, Tatchell's Royal Hotel 192
Kyneton, Alexander's Temperance Hotel 95, 182
Lamplough, Shamrock Hotel 102
Malcolm's Victoria Hotel 185
Maldon, Kangaroo Hotel 96, 97, 98, 103, 184, 185, 186
Maryborough, M'Ivor Hotel 67, 103, 178, 179, 184
McKinnon's, Commercial Hotel 184
McKinnon's, Shamrock Hotel 184
Melbourne, 23 Bourke-street east 84, 179, 180
Melbourne, Criterion Hotel 11, 31, 33, 64, 84, 178
Melbourne, Criterion Hotel, Collins street 64
Meredith, Royal Hotel 112, 114, 160, 190
Meredith, Scott's Hotel 187
Newtown, Sharp's Hotel 123, 192
Penola, Cawker's Hotel 185
Penola, Royal Oak Hotel 187
Portland, Mac's Hotel 185, 187, 192

Sale, Club Hotel 104, 124, 125, 192
Sandhurst, Foos's Hotel 102
Sandhurst, Shamrock Hotel 84, 178, 179, 180
Scarsdale, O'Farrell's Hotel 123, 192
Smythes, Eldorado Hotel 123, 192
Star Hotel 184
Thurston's Hotel, [Mount Gambier?] 192
Torquay, Palace Hotel 195
Unicorn Hotel 186
United States Hotel 123, 184
Yarrowee 40, 123, 184
Botanic Garden 28
Box Seat 75, 161, 165, 166, 169
Bradley, William Brown 54, 55, 56, 60, 68, 69
Brandy Creek 85, 116
Brayton, W. H. 30, 54
Britton, John Francis 55, 60, 68, 69
Buangor/M'Donald's 97, 98, 99, 100, 101, 104, 112, 156, 185, 186, 187, 188, 189
Bullarook Forest 44
Bulldog 99, 100, 101, 112, 113, 115, 116, 187, 188, 189, 191
Buninyong 10, 43, 44, 83, 88, 116, 123, 132, 134, 180, 191, 194
Bushfires:
  Black Thursday 26
  Mount Macedon 26
Bushrangers:
  Gypsey Smith 145
  Harry Power 145
  Kelly Gang 146
  Morgan (Mad Dog) 145
  The Encounter at Glenrowan 42
  Toke, Armstrong & Chamberlain 146
Camels 145
Cameron and Jones 55
Camp-hill 42
Cannibel Creek 85
Carisbrook 10, 44, 82, 83, 95, 96, 97, 98, 100, 103, 178, 181, 182, 183, 184, 185, 186, 187
Carlsruhe 31, 178
Castlemaine 64, 65, 67
Caufield races 125
Cawker. J./Cawker, John 55, 56, 57, 98, 113, 114, 118, 119, 122, 185, 190, 192
Cawker, T. 57
Centennial International Exhibition 125
Chewton 42
Circus 102
Clapp, Francis Boardman 59, 65, 66, 67, 72, 123
Clapp, Oliver Blake 54, 67
Clunes 10, 43, 44, 46, 74, 83, 94, 95, 96, 97, 98, 99, 100, 101, 102, 104, 112, 113, 114, 156, 160, 180, 182, 183, 184, 185, 186, 187, 188, 189, 190, 191
Cobb and Co. Coach Factory 59
Cobb, Elisha Winslow 11, 123, 174, 176, 177
Cobb, Freeman 54, 57
Cobb's Washington Express 33
Colclough, Chas. 54
Coleraine 76, 94, 96, 97, 98, 99, 100, 101, 112, 113, 114, 115, 116, 117, 118, 119, 120, 121, 130, 131, 132, 157, 183, 185, 187, 188, 189, 190, 192
Connell's Creek 45
Cooper, Oliver 54, 68
Coyle, J. 61
Craig, Walter 54, 68
Cressy/Frenchman's/ Landsborough 44, 74, 83, 84, 94, 97, 98, 99, 100, 101, 112, 113, 114, 115, 116, 117, 118, 119, 120, 123, 142, 156, 159, 161, 185, 186, 187, 188, 189, 190, 191, 192, 193, 195
Creswick 44, 64, 67, 74, 77, 82, 83, 94, 95, 96, 97, 98, 99, 100, 101, 102, 103, 104, 112, 113, 156, 160, 178, 180, 181, 182, 183, 184, 185, 186, 187, 188, 189
Creswick's Creek 67, 82, 83, 94, 95, 160, 178, 180, 181, 182
Cricket 31, 47, 84, 103
Criminal Courts 75
Croaker, Charles 54, 68
Crooke and Watt 77
Crooke, James Elijah 77
Davey, R. 55, 98
Davies, Thomas 30, 54, 64
Daylesford 44
Deep Creek/Jim Crow 94, 95, 96, 97, 98, 99, 100, 101, 103, 112, 156, 161, 183, 185, 186, 187, 188, 189
Deniliquin 56, 60, 69
Diamond Creek 26
Digger's Rest 45
Dingoes 85
Doctor's Gully 45
Droughts 145
Drove for Cobb and Co. 167
Drummond 45
Earth Worms 85
Edward Kelly's Letter 149
Elphinstone 31
Emerald Hill 10
E. Moore and Co. 55
Essendon 31, 82, 84, 178
Eureka Stockade 43
Execution of Edward Kelly 149
Fallen, J. T. 54, 68
F. B. Clapp and Co. 54, 65, 68, 83, 85, 94, 180, 181, 182
Fernald, B. H. 54, 68
Fiery Creek/Raglan 10, 47, 70, 83, 94, 95, 96, 97, 98, 99, 100, 101, 104, 112, 177, 178, 180, 182, 183, 185, 186, 187, 188, 189
Fires 26, 156
Fireworks 26, 135
Flemington 31, 32, 95, 96, 103, 183
Floods 10, 26, 27, 43, 123
Flour Mill/Mount Bolton 114
Forest Creek/Castlemaine 11, 31, 42, 43, 64, 82, 178
Frankston 125, 158
Gallagher, T. 61
Gap 31, 82, 83, 84, 95, 178, 181, 182, 183
Garden Gully Reef 42
Gardiner, Charles Culwell 54
Geelong 64, 65
Gisborne 10, 31, 45, 82, 83, 84, 95, 157, 178, 181, 182, 183
Gnarr Creek Bridge 73
Gold 10, 25, 27, 28, 29, 32, 42, 43, 44, 45, 46, 69, 81, 85, 93, 97, 102, 104, 135, 175
Golden Gully 30, 42
Goldfields 6, 10, 11, 27, 32, 43, 135, 145, 174
Grant, Alexander Allan 59, 61, 69, 75, 76, 102, 131, 132, 194
Grant, Sheehan & Co. 132
Gravel Hill 42
Graytown 45
Hair-pickers 104
Halfey, John 54, 68
Hall, Walter Russell 60, 61, 68
Hamilton 10, 26, 43, 45, 66, 68, 75, 76, 82, 83, 94, 95, 96, 97, 98, 99, 100, 101, 112, 113, 114, 115, 116, 117, 118, 119, 120, 121, 122, 123, 130, 131, 132, 157, 159, 160, 161, 180, 181, 182, 183, 184, 185, 186, 187, 188, 189, 190, 191, 192, 193
Hastings 45, 125
Hawthorne 27, 95
Hay/Lang's Crossing Place 56, 60, 67, 70, 71, 72, 76, 77, 97, 98, 99, 101, 120, 130, 131, 132, 134, 135, 156, 158, 160, 185, 186, 188, 192, 194
Heathcote 10, 114, 117, 119, 120, 122, 124, 168, 192, 193
Heidelberg 27, 96, 184
Hexham 45, 97, 98, 99, 100, 101, 112, 113, 114, 115, 116, 117, 119, 122, 130, 185, 187, 188, 189, 190, 192
Highway Robbery 102
Hit Or Miss 45
Hopkins 10, 43, 83, 84, 167
Horr, James Courtland 55, 76, 98, 104, 185
Horsham 95, 97, 99, 100, 101, 112, 113, 115, 116, 122, 159, 185, 186, 187, 188, 189, 191
Hoyt, Henry 54, 55, 66, 72, 73, 95, 96, 97, 123, 183, 184, 185
Huntley, J. L. 54, 68
Inglewood 45, 69, 94, 95, 96, 97, 98, 99, 100, 101, 102, 103, 112, 113, 114, 117, 122, 160, 168, 181, 182, 183, 184, 185, 186, 187, 188, 189, 192
Ives, Christopher 54, 67
'Jack' Coach 11, 67
Jackson, Pegleg/Peleg Whitford 54
James, William 56, 60
Jenkins, W. 61
J. F. Britton 64, 67, 178
Jim Crow Creek 42
Jones, David 54, 68, 185
Kangaroo Dogs 30
Kaolin 10
Keilor 31, 32, 41, 43, 64, 82, 83, 84, 95, 96, 97, 101, 112, 113, 117, 118, 119, 123, 156, 178, 181, 185, 188, 189, 191, 192
Kelly, Alexander 54, 68
Kilmore 10, 45, 70, 83, 84, 119, 120, 121, 124, 159, 160, 180, 192, 193
Kirk, C. M. 61
Kyneton 10, 11, 31, 45, 46, 47, 69, 77, 82, 83, 84, 95, 96, 97, 100, 101, 112, 157, 178, 179, 180, 181, 182, 183, 184, 185, 187, 188, 189
Lachlan Gold Fields 69
Lake Mundi 121
Lake Wendouree 41, 122
Lamber, John B. 54
Lamplough 46
Landsborough/New Rush 97, 98, 99, 100, 101, 112, 113, 117, 118, 119, 120, 123, 156, 161, 185, 186, 187, 188, 189, 191, 192, 193
Lane, A. 55, 98
Lascelles, T. A. 54, 68
Latrobe Bridge/Longford 46
Leigh 10, 47, 101, 104, 112, 113, 114, 115, 120, 157, 159, 186, 187, 188, 189, 190, 193, 194, 195
Leviathan Coach 102
Lexton 41, 46, 94, 96, 97, 98, 99, 100, 101, 112, 113, 117, 118, 119, 120, 121, 122, 123, 130, 131, 156, 161, 183, 185, 186, 187, 188, 189, 191, 192, 193
Liardet's 11, 174
Liardet's Beach 27
Lilydale 46, 118, 120, 121, 124, 125, 192
Linton 41, 46, 75, 95, 96, 97, 98, 99, 100, 101, 112, 113, 114, 115, 116, 117, 119, 120, 121, 123, 130, 131, 134, 161, 184, 185, 186, 187, 188, 189, 190, 191, 192, 193, 194
Lismore 46
Lockwood 46, 47, 102
Long Gully 42, 47
Lyall, James A. 76
Mail Boys 145
Malcolm, William 54
Maldon 10
Malmesbury 31, 82, 83, 84, 178, 181
Mansfield 46, 102, 118, 119, 124, 131, 146, 148, 194
Maryborough 10
Matlock 46

Matthew Veal and Co. 56, 57
M'Caw, Matthew 54, 68
McCormick, Mr 54
McGowan, George Alexander 59, 60, 76
Meigs & Anderson 55
Meigs, Jasper Bingham 75, 104
Melbourne Cup 31
Meredith 83, 101, 104, 112, 113, 114, 115, 131, 132, 160, 180, 187, 190, 191, 194
Merino 95, 96, 97, 115, 117, 118, 119, 183, 185, 192
Michel and Hughes 54
Mining Exchange 41
M'Master, R. 61
Moe 75, 85, 100, 104, 130, 131, 132, 160, 194
Moonambel/Mountain Creek 41, 46, 96, 97, 98, 99, 100, 101, 112, 113, 117, 119, 123, 130, 131, 156, 184, 185, 186, 187, 188, 189, 192, 193
Moorabool 10, 40, 41, 104, 135, 156, 157, 179, 194, 195
Morwell 124, 160
Mount Alexander 10, 11, 33, 41, 43, 45, 69, 82, 83, 84, 94, 95, 96, 97, 98, 103, 179, 180, 181, 183, 184, 185, 186
Mount Emu Creek 10
Mount Herbert 42
Mowton, George 11, 28, 174, 175, 176
M'Phee & Co. 54, 55, 56, 57, 58, 73, 95
M'Phee, John 55, 73, 74, 98, 99, 104, 112, 156, 186
M'Phillimy, Hugh 54, 68
Native Bear 85
Nugget 29, 42, 43, 167
Ocean Grove 74, 77, 121, 130, 131, 132, 133, 134, 136, 142, 143, 157, 159, 193, 194, 195
Ogilvie, Thomas 54, 68
Opera Season 30
Order-boxes/Mail Boxes 104
Oven's District 10
Peck, John Murray 54, 59, 67
Penshurst 46, 98, 99, 100, 101, 112, 113, 114, 115, 116, 117, 118, 119, 120, 121, 122, 130, 160, 187, 188, 189, 190, 192
Perkins, G. B. 68
Piggoreet 41, 46, 100, 101, 112, 113, 115, 116, 117, 118, 123, 188, 189, 191, 192
Population 29, 43, 45, 46, 47
Portarlington 46, 112, 113, 114, 130, 131, 132, 133, 134, 136, 142, 157, 159, 190, 191, 193, 194, 195
Port Melbourne 11, 66, 174
Port Phillip 11, 64, 68, 70, 83, 84, 94, 95, 96, 97, 98, 102, 103, 114, 117, 119, 120, 122, 130, 168, 176, 180, 181, 182, 183, 184, 185, 186, 192
Postage Rates 124

Postal System 29
Postmaster 76, 85, 136
Post Offices 10, 33, 103
Prahan 160
Princes Bridge 33
Quarry-hill 42
Queenscliff 47
Queensland 168
Raglan 47, 68, 94, 95, 96, 97, 98, 99, 100, 101, 104, 112, 156, 160, 183, 185, 186, 187, 188, 189
Randle, William 54, 68
Reefs:
　Garden Gully Reef 42
　Hiscock's Reef 43
　Hustler's Reef 42
　New Chum 42
　Victoria Reef 42
Ricards, jun., John R. 54, 68
Richardson, W. J. 61
Rich, Levi 54, 67
Richmond 27, 33, 66, 95, 96, 103, 125, 145, 183
Robertson, Alexander William (A. W.) 30, 43, 54, 55, 56, 57, 59, 60, 61, 65, 66, 68, 69, 70, 71, 72, 186
Robertson, Britton and Co. 54, 55, 60, 68, 69, 95, 96, 97, 103, 183, 184, 185
Robertson, Colin 60, 61
Robertson, Wagner and Co. 55, 56, 57, 58, 59, 60, 61, 69, 72, 96, 97, 98, 99, 100, 101, 112, 113, 114, 115, 116, 117, 118, 119, 120, 121, 122, 123, 125, 130, 131, 143, 186, 187, 188, 189, 190, 191, 192
Robinson, J. D. 54, 68
Rogers, Jacob 54, 67
Rokewood 47
Rosalind Park 42, 47
Rosedale 100, 104, 124, 144, 160
Royal Oak Hotel, Penola 187
Royal Princess's Theatre 42
Russell, Charles 77
Rutherford, James 55, 56, 60, 69
Sailor's Gully 30
Sale 32, 43, 46, 47, 69, 70, 72, 98, 99, 100, 104, 119, 120, 121, 124, 125, 135, 157, 158, 160, 161, 176, 177, 186, 192, 193
Sandhurst 64, 65, 67
Sandridge 26, 27, 45, 47
Sandy Creek/Tarnagulla 97
Sayings:
　Deprived of life 156
　'Pad the hoof' 134
Scott & Nugent 56
Serpentine Creek 47, 83, 95, 181, 182, 183
Shady Creek 85, 100, 104, 144
Sharp, Seth 57, 76, 117, 118, 119, 123, 191, 192
Shaw, F. 61
Shaw, F. C. 61
Shaw, H. W. 61
Skarratt, C. C. 54, 68
Snow 27
Soldiers' Hill 73

Stables 41, 67, 72, 73, 104, 156, 157, 158, 159, 160, 161, 193, 194
Stage Coach Regulations 53
St. Arnaud/New Bendigo 10, 41, 46, 95, 96, 97, 98, 99, 100, 101, 104, 112, 113, 116, 117, 118, 119, 121, 130, 131, 134, 161, 183, 185, 186, 187, 188, 189, 191, 192, 193
Stiles, J. J. 55
Stoneman, Thomas 55, 57, 75, 98, 99, 104, 158, 185, 186, 187
Storm 30, 135
Studdert, Gordon Wallace Fitzgerald 61
Surat 59
Swan Hill 11, 64, 68, 70, 83, 84, 94, 95, 96, 97, 98, 102, 103, 114, 117, 119, 120, 122, 130, 168, 176, 180, 181, 182, 183, 184, 185, 186, 192
Swanton, James 54
Tailoring Establishment 29
Talbot/Back Creek 44, 46, 69, 96, 97, 98, 99, 100, 101, 104, 112, 113, 114, 115, 156, 158, 184, 185, 186, 187, 188, 189, 190, 191
Tallarook 47
Tangil 47
Taradale 10, 82, 157, 178
Tarrangower/Maldon 95
Taylor, H. B. 61
Temperature 27
The Coach's Story 30
The Encounter at Glenrowan 146
The End of Cobb and Co. 168
The Fourth of July 28
The Lachlan 69
The Leviathan 104
The Leviathan Store 104
Tompkins, Joel 54, 68
'Tom Thumb' coach 124
Torquay 59, 74, 77, 132, 133, 136, 142, 143, 157, 194, 195
Tozer, Francis 54, 68
Train, George Francis 11, 28, 174, 177
Tullaroop creek 44
Uhl, L. 61
Valley of Bendigo 41
Verse: 30
　A Ballad for Cobb and Co. 30
　Gold! 93
　Good-Bye to Cobb & Co. 30
　Green and Gold 81
　Long Jim of Cobb & Co. 111
　'Old Jack' of Coaching Days 129
　Shadow of Cobb & Co. 165
　The Dream of Gold 30
　To Mr Pat Gooley, of Messrs Cobb and Co. 155
Victoria Coursing Club 65, 69
Victoria Stage Company 54, 65, 67, 83, 94, 180, 181
Vines, A. N. 59
Vines and M'Phee 57, 58, 59, 74, 118, 119, 120, 121, 123, 124, 130, 131, 132, 134, 156, 157, 192, 193, 194
Vines, Arthur Nicholls 186
Vines, Joshua 55
Violent Assault 103
Voilet Town 47
Wagner, John 55, 56, 57, 59, 60, 69, 70
Warren, William 54, 77, 176
Warrnambool 10, 44, 47, 66, 68, 75, 83, 84, 94, 95, 98, 99, 100, 101, 102, 112, 113, 114, 115, 116, 117, 118, 119, 120, 121, 122, 124, 130, 131, 135, 142, 161, 181, 182, 183, 184, 185, 187, 188, 189, 190, 191, 192, 193, 194, 195
Watson and Hewitt 30, 31, 54, 56, 60, 64, 65, 67, 68, 69, 72, 82, 83, 84, 94, 95, 102, 157, 175, 178, 179, 180, 181, 182, 183, 189
Watt, James 77
Weather 6, 26, 27, 28, 32, 47, 65, 124, 134, 135, 166
Western Stage Company 55, 56, 57, 58, 59, 75, 100, 101, 104, 112, 113, 114, 115, 116, 117, 118, 119, 120, 121, 122, 123, 124, 130, 131, 132, 133, 134, 135, 136, 158, 159, 160, 161, 187, 188, 189, 190, 191, 192, 193, 194
Whitney, William Franklin 56
Whorlom, G. 55
Williams, William 54, 68
Wombat Flat 45
Womersley, H. 30, 59, 74, 77, 142, 159, 195
Woodend 31, 68, 69, 82, 83, 95, 96, 97, 157, 178, 181, 182, 183, 184, 185
Woods, William 54, 68
Woodworth, George Loop 54, 67
Yandoit 47, 77, 95, 96, 97, 98, 99, 100, 102, 183, 184, 185, 186, 187, 188
Yarra River 10, 27, 33, 46, 66, 81, 95, 96, 103, 118, 120, 121, 124, 125, 132, 143, 183, 192
Yarrowee Creek 40

www.ingramcontent.com/pod-product-compliance
Lightning Source LLC
Chambersburg PA
CBHW041710290426

44109CB00028B/2836